Frommer's®
Amalfi Coast
with Naples, Capri & Pompeii

4th Edition

WILEY

John Wiley & Sons, Inc.

Published by:
John Wiley & Sons, Inc.
111 River St.
Hoboken, NJ 07030-5774

ISBN 978-1-118-07467-1 (paper); ISBN 978-1-118-22254-6 (ebk); ISBN 978-1-118-23644-4 (ebk); ISBN 978-1-118-24183-7 (ebk)

Design and Layout by Vertigo Design NYC

Editor: Ian Skinnari
Production Editor: M. Faunette Johnston
Cartographer: Andrew Murphy
Photo Editor: Alden Gewirtz, Cherie Cincilla
Cover Photo Editor: Richard Fox
Production by Wiley Indianapolis Composition Services

Front Cover Photo: Cottages in Ravello © Giovanni Tagini/Alamy

Back Cover: *Left:* Mercato di Montesanto, Naples © SIME/eStock Photo; *Middle:* View of Torre Saracena, Sorrento © SIME/eStock Photo; *Right:* A farmer's market in Positano © R. Ian Lloyd/Masterfile

For information on our other products and services or to obtain technical support, please contact our Customer Care Department within the U.S. at 877/762-2974, outside the U.S. at 317/572-3993 or fax 317/572-4002.

Wiley also publishes its books in a variety of electronic formats. Some content that appears in print may not be available in electronic formats.
Manufactured in China

CONTENTS

LIST OF MAPS

ABOUT THE AUTHOR

Nicky Swallow was born in London but has lived in Florence since the early 1980s when she spent several years playing the viola in the opera house there. She started writing about her travel experiences in Florence and Tuscany in the mid '90s and since then has traveled extensively throughout Italy, but she has always had a soft spot for the south, especially Campania. She wrote the Day by Day guide to Naples and the Amalfi Coast for Frommer's in 2010 and writes regularly for magazines and websites about Italy and all things Italian. Downtime is spent with her photographer partner Gianluca Moggi (who shot the photos for this guide) in their olive grove just outside Florence.

HOW TO CONTACT US

In researching this book, we discovered many wonderful places—hotels, restaurants, shops, and more. We're sure you'll find others. Please tell us about them, so we can share the information with your fellow travelers in upcoming editions. If you were disappointed with a recommendation, we'd love to know that, too. Please write to:

Frommer's Amalfi Coast, 4th Edition
Wiley Publishing, Inc. • 111 River St. • Hoboken, NJ 07030-5774
frommersfeedback@wiley.com

ADVISORY & DISCLAIMER

Travel information can change quickly and unexpectedly, and we strongly advise you to confirm important details locally before traveling, including information on visas, health and safety, traffic and transport, accommodations, shopping and eating out. We also encourage you to stay alert while traveling and to remain aware of your surroundings. Avoid civil disturbances, and keep a close eye on cameras, purses, wallets and other valuables.

While we have endeavored to ensure that the information contained within this guide is accurate and up-to-date at the time of publication, we make no representations or warranties with respect to the accuracy or completeness of the contents of this work and specifically disclaim all warranties, including without limitation warranties of fitness for a particular purpose. We accept no responsibility or liability for any inaccuracy or errors or omissions, or for any inconvenience, loss, damage, costs or expenses of any nature whatsoever incurred or suffered by anyone as a result of any advice or information contained in this guide.

The inclusion of a company, organization, or website in this guide as a service provider and/or potential source of further information does not mean that we endorse them or the information they provide. Be aware that information provided through some websites may be unreliable and can change without notice. Neither the publisher or author shall be liable for any damages arising herefrom.

FROMMER'S STAR RATINGS, ICONS & ABBREVIATIONS

Every hotel, restaurant, and attraction listing in this guide has been ranked for quality, value, service, amenities, and special features using a star-rating system. In country, state, and regional guides, we also rate towns and regions to help you narrow down your choices and budget your time accordingly. Hotels and restaurants are rated on a scale of zero (recommended) to three stars (exceptional). Attractions, shopping, nightlife, towns, and regions are rated according to the following scale: zero stars (recommended), one star (highly recommended), two stars (very highly recommended), and three stars (must-see).

In addition to the star-rating system, we also use **seven** feature icons that point you to the great deals, in-the-know advice, and unique experiences that separate travelers from tourists. Throughout the book, look for:

special finds—those places only insiders know about

fun facts—details that make travelers more informed and their trips more fun

kids—best bets for kids and advice for the whole family

special moments—those experiences that memories are made of

overrated—places or experiences not worth your time or money

insider tips—great ways to save time and money

great values—where to get the best deals

The following abbreviations are used for credit cards:

AE American Express	**DISC** Discover	**V** Visa
DC Diners Club	**MC** MasterCard	

TRAVEL RESOURCES AT FROMMERS.COM

Frommer's travel resources don't end with this guide. Frommer's website, www.frommers.com, has travel information on more than 4,000 destinations. We update features regularly, giving you access to the most current trip-planning information and the best airfare, lodging, and car-rental bargains. You can also listen to podcasts, connect with other Frommers.com members through our active-reader forums, share your travel photos, read blogs from guidebook editors and fellow travelers, and much more.

THE BEST OF CAMPANIA & THE AMALFI COAST

ampania—the region that encompasses Naples and the Amalfi Coast—is, for many tourists, terra incognita. A land of myth and legends, it has been coveted since antiquity for the fertility of its countryside and the beauty of its coasts. In this chapter, we'll help you discover the best of Campania by pointing you toward both its major treasures and its lesser-known delights.

THE best TRAVEL EXPERIENCES

o **Walking Through Naples's Historic District:** Maybe it's a bit defiant, given all the negative press about garbage and the Camorra (the Neapolitan equivalent of the Sicilian Mafia), but we find it exhilarating to be able to enjoy Naples's stunning art after it was literally hidden in grime for decades. Its collection of exquisite frescoes, paintings, and sculptures is now available to visitors in its numerous monasteries, palaces, churches, and museums. Kings and noble families have lavished art on the city as nowhere else in Italy (excepting Rome), making Naples a rival to Florence and Venice in terms of the sheer volume of sights to be seen. A key stop for art lovers during the Grand Tour, Naples was later forgotten due to the total abandonment of its monuments. But thanks to sustained efforts over the past 15 years, the city is again experiencing a tourism boom. See chapter 4.

o **Exploring Capri:** The most glamorous of all the Mediterranean islands remains a magical destination in spite of the crowds of tourists that flock to its shores. To get the best of Capri, come early or late in the season and plan to stay overnight. See chapter 8.

o **Arriving in Naples by Boat:** While arriving in Naples by car can be nerve-racking, confusing, and hot, with most landmarks annoyingly out of view, gliding into the Bay, with a sea breeze behind you and the city spread out ahead of you, can be magnificent. The majestic and somewhat ominous presence of Mount Vesuvius looming over the Bay makes it that much more dramatic. You can arrive by regular ferry from one of the islands or even from one of the other harbors in Campania, such as Salerno or Sorrento. We highly recommend arriving in the very early morning or in the evening, when the sun is sinking below the horizon, bathing the city in a magical gold and orange light; you'll instantly understand the motivation behind the old saying, "See Naples and die." See chapter 4.

o **Hiking the Ancient Paths of the Amalfi Coast:** Taking a stroll on one of the Amalfi Coast's footpaths—once the only means of communication between local towns—is the best way to soak up the intensity of this amazing seascape. Whatever your level of fitness, you'll find a stretch of path to suit you. Trails come in all levels of difficulty, from flat stretches (such as the footpath from Amalfi to Atrani) to steep ones (such as the footpath from Ravello to Minori) to even more demanding ones (such as the Sentiero degli Dei and the Via degli Incanti from Positano). The region's main road, the famed Amalfi Coast

PREVIOUS PAGE: **Scenic view off the coast of Capri.**

Arriving in Naples by boat.

Drive, was built in 1840 and made the area more accessible, perhaps too much so. The old trails, on the other hand, are unique, and lead you through an Amalfi Coast that is missed by many tourists. See chapter 7.

o **Exploring the Greek Ruins in Paestum:** The first colony the Greeks established in Italy was Cuma, near Pozzuoli. From there, they spread south to inhabit the rest of the Campanian coast. The heritage they left in the region is immensely rich—rivaled in Italy only by Sicily—and in a state of conservation seen only in Greece itself. This is Magna Grecia, where ancient Greece first spread its influence into Italy, setting the stage for what we now call Western Culture. In these temples and towns, you literally get the chance to walk in the footsteps of Plato and Aristotle's contemporaries. See chapters 5 and 9.

o **Eating the Best Pizza in the World:** Pizza was invented here, in the narrow lanes of Naples's historic district, and for Neapolitans, their pizza is the only "real" one, thick yet soft-crusted and fragrant. Whether you prefer to sample it in a simple pizzeria or at a more elegant restaurant, you'll share the pride Neapolitans feel for their invention, now adopted by the whole planet. The decor in many pizzerie is simple and traditional (sometimes nonexistent), and, in the most authentic places, you'll find only a limited choice of toppings—only two at Da Michele, which is reputed to make the best pizza in Naples. Yet wherever you choose to eat, we guarantee that your pizza will be tasty, satisfying, and distinctive, because in Naples, no two are alike. See chapter 4.

o **Shopping for Christmas Cribs in Naples:** Naples is one of the best cities in Italy to visit in the run-up to Christmas when the traditional art of crib making, a craft that has been carried out in the city by skilled artisans for hundreds of years, makes its annual appearance in the spotlight. Neapolitan presepi (cribs) feature a range of lifelike figurines that are placed in intricately built nativity scenes along with animals, angels, food, and drink. Neapolitan families build their own presepi at home each year, scouring the narrow streets of the SpaccaNapoli for new additions to their scenes. The shops selling presepi

Da Michele makes some of the best pizza in Naples.

are mostly based in and around ancient Via San Gregorio Armeno, just off the SpaccaNapoli, which turns into one big Christmas crib in early December complete with twinkling lights and canned Christmas music. Much of what you see in the shops is mass produced: see p. 119 if you are concerned about buying quality rather than quantity.

o **Wandering Through Ancient Roman Lanes in Pompeii:** Walking among ancient ruins is romantic and sad, and even a little creepy at times. Campania affords you many opportunities to live this unique experience. Of all the sites in the region, Pompeii and Herculaneum are the most justifiably famous: Walking their streets gives you a particularly eerie feeling. At the center of the lanes' mesmeric attraction is the knowledge that their violent destruction and miraculous preservation both happened on one terrible day nearly 2,000 years ago. And somehow it feels as if it is *always* that day here. Imagination easily bridges the gap to the time when these rooms resounded with talk and laughter (or, for more morbid minds, screams and cries of terror). Yet the best sites in the region might be some of the lesser known, such as the magnificent Villa di Poppea, in Oplontis, with its wonderful frescoes; the Villa Arianna and the Villa di San Marco, in Castellammare di Stabia; and the Villa Romana of Minori. See chapters 5, 6, and 7.

o **Attending the Ravello Festival:** There are many excellent summer music festivals held in Italy, but one of the very best takes place in Ravello. The oldest music festival in Italy, it is noteworthy not only for the quality of its top-notch performances from internationally known musicians but also for the breathtaking venues; it's worth trying to get a ticket even if you are not normally a classical music buff. Running from June through November, concerts are held in magical venues such as the gardens of Villa Cimbrone and Villa Rufolo where a stage is constructed on a terrace overlooking the sea; from where the audience sits, the musicians seem suspended in the air. Truly magical. See chapter 7.

THE best RUINS

o **The Temples of Paestum:** The near-complete set of walls and three temples at this site make up the best Greek ruins in existence outside Greece. Indeed, the grandiose Temple of Neptune (whose restoration was completed in 2004) is considered to be the best-preserved Greek temple in the world along with the Theseion in Athens. You should try and time your visit in spring or fall, when the roses are in bloom and the ruins are at their most romantic. The site is also breathtaking at dawn and sunset in any season, when the temples glow golden in the sun. See chapter 9.

o **The Acropolis of Cuma:** The first Greek colony in Italy, Cuma was built on one of the most picturesque promontories in Campania. In the Phlegrean Fields, the inspiration for so many myths (the Cave of the Sybil, Lake Averno and the entrance to the underworld, the Hell-ish Solfatara), Cuma offers a magnificent panorama and atmospheric ruins. See chapter 5.

o **The Anfiteatro Campano of Santa Maria Capua Vetere:** The largest Roman amphitheater after the Colosseum, this splendid ruin offers a glimpse of ancient artistry in spite of the pillaging that occurred here from the 9th century onward. On-site is the Museo dei Gladiatori, a permanent exhibit reconstructing the life of a gladiator; it is housed in a building located on the probable site of Capua's Gladiator School—whose most famous graduate was Spartacus, the slave made famous by the 1960 Stanley Kubrick film. It is located in Santa Maria Capua Vetere, which occupies the grounds of Roman Capua, the city that Cicero considered second only to Rome in the entire ancient world. The area is rich in other noteworthy ruins, such as the splendid Mitreo (Temple to Mithras), and museum collections. See chapter 10.

o **Pompeii & Herculaneum:** Will enough ever be said to describe these extraordinary sites? Even if you already visited them in the past, new findings are reason enough for a return trip. The magnificent Villa dei Papiri in Herculaneum was opened to the public for the first time in 2004; the Terme Suburbane in Pompeii was opened in 2002. The riches of the archaeological area are best complemented by a visit to the Museo Archeologico Nazionale in Naples, to view its massive array of frescoes and mosaics removed from earlier excavations at both sites. See chapter 5.

o **Oplontis:** Also called the Villa of Poppea, these are the ruins of a splendid Roman villa—believed to have belonged to Nero's wife—with magnificent frescoes and decorations. Lesser known than other sites and often bypassed by hurried tourists, this villa is unique, not only for its state of conservation, but also for the fact that so many of the frescoes have been left *in situ* as prescribed by modern archaeological practice, thereby offering the visitor greater insight into domestic Roman life. See chapter 5.

o **Trajan's Arch in Benevento:** This little-known and out-of-the-way find is an outstandingly well-preserved example of an ancient Roman triumphal arch. It took 14 years of restoration work before the arch was opened again to the public in 2001—it is a masterpiece of carving that depicts the deeds of the admired (and fairly benevolent) Roman emperor Trajan. Careful cleaning has eliminated darker areas in the marble, making the reliefs much easier to read. Inside a little Longobard church nearby is a permanent exhibit on the arch, its restoration, and Roman life under Trajan. See chapter 10.

- **Pozzuoli:** The ruins of the ancient Roman town of Puteoli have been difficult to excavate because the busy modern town of Pozzuoli occupies exactly the same area as the ancient version. Splendidly framed by Pozzuoli's bay, you'll find an underground Pompeii—buried not by a volcanic explosion, but as a result of unstable volcanic ground. The main attractions are the Rione Terra, with Roman streets and shops (closed to the public at presstime); the 1st-century Greco-Roman market (Serapeo); and the Roman amphitheater (Anfiteatro Flavio), where musical performances are held in summer. See chapter 5.

- **The Underwater Archeological Park of Baia:** Due to subsiding ground, a large part of the ancient Roman holiday resort of Baia was submerged by the sea. Excavated and transformed into an archaeological park, it can now be visited with scuba equipment or in a glass-bottomed boat. The itinerary leads you through the streets of the ancient town

The underwater archeological park of Baia, in the Phlegrean Fields.

and inside its beautiful villas, now water-filled. See chapter 5.

- **Velia:** Overshadowed by Paestum and just a bit too far from Naples for a day trip, Velia was the site of an important Greek settlement that dates from around 540 B.C. It gave birth to one of antiquity's most important philosophical schools of thought—the Eleatic doctrines of Parmenides and Zeno. Velia is one of the only Greek archaeological sites showing remains not only of an acropolis with its ruined temples, but also of a lower town with some houses. Portions of the walls here date from the 5th and 4th centuries B.C. A stretch of the original Greek pavement climbs toward the town gate, the famous Porta Rosa. A highlight of the Roman period is the thermal baths. See chapter 9.

THE best CHURCHES & CATHEDRALS

- **Casertavecchia Cathedral:** This medieval church is one of the most beautiful extant examples of Arabo-Norman architecture, built with two colors of tufa stone and white marble, and dotted with strange human and animal figures. See chapter 10.

- **Naples's Duomo:** The most splendid of Naples's churches, and home to some superb artwork, the Duomo is three churches in one. The Cappella di San Gennaro is really a church in its own right, with a fantastic treasure on display in the attached museum. Santa Restituta, the original 6th-century church, contains a magnificent 4th-century baptistery decorated with Byzantine mosaics. See chapter 4.

o **Complesso Monumentale di Santa Chiara:** Another star among Naples's many great monuments, this splendid church and monastery complex holds splendid examples of 14th-century sculpture that escaped the tragic bombing of World War II. (Other parts of the massive structure were not so lucky but have since been restored.) The celebrated cloister, decorated with 18th-century majolica tiles depicting a plethora of mythological, pastoral, and whimsical scenes, is one of the most enchanting corners of the city. See chapter 4.

o **San Lorenzo Maggiore:** Originally built in the 6th century, this Neapolitan church is famous for its literary guests: from Boccaccio, who met his darling Fiammetta here, to Francesco Petrarca and others. It houses some splendid Renaissance sculpture and a multilayered archaeological site, where you can descend through layers of buildings all the way down to a paleochristian basilica and the 1st-century Roman market. See chapter 4.

o **Chiesa della Santissima Annunziata:** This church is located in Minuto, one of the medieval hamlets of the township of Scala, which stretches along the cliffs above Ravello and the Amalfi Coast. The church offers not only some of the region's best examples of Romanesque architecture and beautiful 12th-century frescoes, but also a superb panorama. See chapter 7.

o **Duomo di Santa Maria Capua Vetere:** Dating originally from the 5th century, this beautiful paleochristian church has been redecorated in later centuries, but it contains columns and capitals that reach back to Roman times, as well as examples of Renaissance frescoes and carvings. See chapter 10.

o **Sant'Angelo in Formis:** This is one of the most important Romanesque churches in the country, and its interior is entirely decorated with beautiful frescoes. See chapter 10.

o **Santa Sofia:** Dating back to the early Longobard kingdom in Benevento, this small medieval church is famous for its unique star-shaped floor plan and the integration of Longobard and Catholic symbols. See chapter 10.

o **Certosa di San Lorenzo (Carthusian Monastery of San Lorenzo):** Begun in the 14th century, this magnificent monastery—one of the largest in the world—is a baroque masterpiece, chock-full of art and architectural details. Off the beaten path, but only a short distance from Salerno, it should not be missed. See chapter 9.

THE best CASTLES & PALACES

o **Castel dell'Ovo:** A symbol of Naples and the most picturesque icon of the city's waterfront, this castle is its oldest fortification, having been built on the site of the ancient Greek settlement of Megaris which dates back to the 9th century B.C. It is said the poet-magician Virgil buried an egg in its foundations decreeing that disaster would befall the city if the egg should break. See chapter 4.

o **Reggia di Caserta:** The Versailles of Italy, this splendid royal palace was built by the famous architect Vanvitelli for the Bourbon kings in the 18th century. It holds fantastic works of art and the decorations—walls and floors included—are magnificent. The Reggia is also justly famed for its massive Italianate garden, one of the most beautiful in the world. See chapter 10.

o **Castel Nuovo (Maschio Angioi-no):** This 13th-century castle was the residence of Neapolitan kings until the 17th century. Although a fire in the 16th century destroyed its frescoes, including those by Giotto, there is still enough in this majestic fortress to impress visitors. See chapter 4.

o **Palazzo Reale:** Naples's beautiful Royal Palace, with its neo-classical facade and statues of kings, dominates wide-open Piazza del Plebiscito. In its richly decorated interior, you'll find a splendid collection of art, an exquisite 17th-century theater, and a superb library. See chapter 4.

Castel dell'Ovo in Naples.

o **Castel Lauritano:** This ruined castle in Agerola, a town set in the hills above the Amalfi Coast, is wonderfully picturesque and offers extensive views over both the coast and the interior. See chapter 7.

o **Villa Rufolo:** This splendid villa in Ravello has been made famous by its terrace, gardens, and superb vistas which together inspired Wagner to write some of his *Parsifal*. Today, you can listen to concerts of Wagner's work in the same setting. See chapter 7.

o **Villa Cimbrone:** The gardens of the Villa Cimbrone, the second-most famous villa in Ravellos, also have a magnificently panoramic terrace. The villa itself houses a small, exclusive hotel restaurant. See chapter 7.

THE best MUSEUMS

o **Museo Nazionale di Capodimonte:** This picture gallery is one of Italy's finest, holding paintings from the 13th century onward. The catalog looks like a book on art history, complete with all the famous names of Italian art and many members of the Flemish school. Regular special exhibits draw visitors from all over Italy, Europe, and the world. If you want to avoid standing in line for hours, make sure you reserve in advance for these events; they are always hugely popular. See chapter 4.

o **Museo Archeologico Nazionale:** Even if you are only mildly interested in archaeology, you should not miss this unique museum, which holds the largest collection of ancient Roman artifacts in the world. Created in the 17th century, this is where the best finds from Pompeii, Herculaneum, and other local sites are on display. The huge quantity of frescoes, statuary, and precious objects has greatly benefited from a reorganization, which was finished in 2005. See chapter 4.

o **Museo Nazionale della Ceramica Duca di Martina:** Housed in the elegant Villa Floridiana up in Naples's Vomero neighborhood, this rich ceramic collection includes the most important assemblage of Capodimonte porcelain in the world. See chapter 4.

o **Museo Campano:** This museum in Capua has a tall order, as the repository of the history and culture of the whole Campania region. It does a great job, though, with its several collections, covering the whole ancient history of the area, from the Oscans (about 6th c. B.C.) to the Renaissance. It has a magnificent collection of parchment and illuminated manuscripts. See chapter 10.

o **Museo Diocesano:** Salerno's Cathedral Museum is not large, but it houses a number of priceless masterpieces that date from Roman times to the Renaissance and baroque periods. It includes a unique collection of ivory carvings, a fine picture gallery, and a rich collection of illuminated manuscripts. See chapter 9.

o **Museo del Sannio:** Housed in the atmospheric cloister of Santa Sofia in Benevento, this is a small but well-rounded collection of artifacts from local sites. It includes the largest collection of Egyptian art found at one Italian archaeological site, a local temple. See chapter 10.

o **Museo Irpino:** This modern museum displays a collection of artifacts found in the rich archaeological sites in the outlying region of Avellino. The objects date as far back as 4000 B.C., long before the Romans (or even the Greeks) came to the region. See chapter 10.

o **Museo Archeologico dei Campi Flegrei:** Housed in the picturesque Aragonese Castle of Baia, this is another great treasure-trove of Roman and Greek art within Naples's outlying suburbs. See chapter 5.

The Museo Nazionale di Capodimonte in Naples.

THE best SWIMMING & SUNBATHING SPOTS

○ **Vico Equense:** This little-known resort town on the Sorrentine peninsula is blessed with several beaches—most of them small and hidden away inside picturesque coves—such as **Marina di Equa,** dominated by an imposing 17th-century tower. See chapter 6.

○ **Punta del Capo:** This lovely beach under the cliffs near Sorrento has attracted visitors from time immemorial. Nearby, you'll find the ruins of a Roman villa and a small pool of water enclosed by rocks, known as the Bath of Queen Giovanna. See chapter 6.

○ **Bay of Ieranto:** Part of the Marine Preserve of Punta Campanella, this unique fiord is hard to reach, but possesses a unique beauty. When the light is just right at day's end, the clarity of the waters here creates the illusion of boats floating in midair. See chapter 6.

○ **Grotta dello Smeraldo:** Although this grotto in the village of Conca dei Marini on the Amalfi Coast is usually visited by boat, it is also the destination of a scuba procession on Christmas night. The pretty beach can be visited anytime, however. See chapter 7.

○ **Positano:** The most famous resort on the Amalfi Coast, Positano has several picturesque beaches—although they're hardly deserted. Besides the central **Spiaggia Grande** by the marina, you'll find **Fornillo** to the west of town, and **La Porta, Ciumicello, Arienzo,** and **Laurito** to the east. See chapter 7.

○ **Spiaggia di Citara:** This is the most scenic beach on the island of Ischia, near the little town of Forio. Besides the lovely scenery, there are several natural thermal springs. See chapter 8.

○ **Marina di Paestum:** Greek temples are not the only reason to come to Paestum. The sandy beach here extends for miles along the clear blue sea. See chapter 9.

○ **Baia della Calanca:** In beautiful Marina di Camerota, this is one of the nicest beaches in the Cilento, and it is famed for its clear waters. See chapter 9.

○ **Bagni di Tiberio:** This is the best of the rare and tiny beaches of Capri. As the name suggests, it lies near the ruins of one of Emperor Tiberius's notorious pleasure palaces and is accessible by a steep, rocky path or by boat. See chapter 8.

The Bath of Queen Giovanna at Punta del Capo near Sorrento.

Ischia's Parco Termale Giardini Poseidon.

THE best SPAS

- **Parco Termale Giardini Poseidon:** This is our favorite thermal spa. On beautiful Ischia, the Poseidon boasts scenic outdoor thermal pools from which you can enjoy great views and a variety of treatments. See chapter 8.

- **Ischia Thermal Center:** In the small town of Ischia Porto, this is one of the most modern spas on the island, where you can enjoy a variety of state-of-the-art modern services. See chapter 8.

- **Terme della Regina Isabella:** Among the most famous and elegant spas on Ischia, this historical establishment in exclusive Lacco Ameno offers state-of-the-art facilities. See chapter 8.

- **Castellammare di Stabia:** This pleasant seaside resort is blessed with 28 natural thermal springs which you can enjoy at one of the two public spas: the historical one built by the Bourbon kings or the modern establishment on the slopes of Mount Faito. Both offer a wide range of services, from beauty and relaxation treatments to medical ones. See chapter 6.

- **Scrajo Terme:** At the beginning of the Sorrentine peninsula, just outside the pleasant resort town of Vico Equense, you'll find this historic thermal establishment dating back to the 19th century. Guest rooms are available so visitors can "take the waters" in style. See chapter 6.

- **Telese Terme:** Little known to foreign visitors, this charming thermal spa and resort is a short distance west of Benevento and affords luxury and quiet. See chapter 10.

THE best VISTAS

- **Lungomare Trieste di Salerno:** One of Campania's best-kept secrets may be the seaside promenade of laid-back Salerno. A splendid and completely pedestrian walkway lined with palm trees, it offers views encompassing the whole bay from Capri to Punta Licosa in the Cilento. See chapter 9.

- **Deserto:** From the terraces of this Carmelite hermitage near Sant'Agata dei Golfi, you can enjoy a unique, 360-degree panorama encompassing both the Gulf of Naples (with Sorrento and the islands) and the Gulf of Salerno

Agropoli.

(with the Amalfi Coast). On a good day, you can see almost the entire region, from the Cilento—way off to the south of Paestum—to Capo Miseno, to the islands of Ischia and Procida, and to Capri. See chapter 6.

- **Belvedere dello Schiaccone:** This is the best lookout along the whole Amalfi Drive, located immediately west of Positano and accessible from the road; the views are superb. See chapter 7.

- **Lake Fusaro:** In the once picturesque Phlegrean Fields, not far from Pozzuoli, this beautiful lake was chosen by the Bourbon kings as the site for the Casina Reale, a structural jewel designed by the architect Vanvitelli. Today, the Casina Reale still commands picture-perfect royal views. See chapter 5.

- **Monte Cervati:** The highest peak of the Cilento massif, Cervati is famous for its beauty in summer—when it turns purple with lavender fields—and for the magnificent views from its top. See chapter 9.

- **Agropoli:** From the walls of the medieval citadel you can look down on vast stretches of coastline—a view that helped the Saracens hold onto Agropoli as the base for their incursions until the 11th century. See chapter 9.

THE best RESTAURANTS

- **Don Alfonso 1890** (✆081-8780026): This is one of the top Italian gourmet addresses and the best restaurant south of Naples, created and maintained by hosts Lidia and Alfonso Iaccarino. The luxurious restaurant offers superb food using ingredients mainly from the chefs' own organic farm. See chapter 6.

- **Torre del Saracino** (✆081-8028555): A worthy rival to Don Alfonso 1890, this wonderful restaurant is more informal than its neighbor in the hills, but the food is equally memorable and has earned the young owner-chef Gennaro Esposito two Michelin stars. Gennaro's cooking is rooted in local traditions and ingredients, but his creativity and perfect judgment make a meal here a real journey of discovery. The minimalist dining room is elegant yet relaxed and unstuffy, and a lovely terrace overlooks the beach. See chapter 6.

o **Il Mosaico** (©081-994722): Il Mosaico earned two Michelin stars soon after its opening thanks to the creative genius of chef Nino Di Costanzo. His intricately prepared dishes, based on the local cuisine, look every bit as good as they taste, and a meal here is a feast for the eyes as much as for the stomach. Book the chef's table in the kitchen if you want a really memorable experience. See chapter 8.

o **Taverna del Capitano** (©081-8081028): With its huge picture windows and terrace overlooking the charming little beach at Marina di Cantone, this elegant restaurant enjoys the ultimate seaside setting. Fish and seafood are obviously the key players here, and Chef Alfonso Caputo prepares them to simple perfection. After lunch, you can rent a beach bed and umbrella and sleep it all off. See chapter 6.

o **Il San Pietro di Positano** (©089-875455): Il San Pietro offers the fine cuisine of Chef Alois Vanlangenacker—all based on ingredients from the hotel's own farm—and a delightfully romantic setting that is worth a visit all by itself. See chapter 7.

o **George's** (©081-7612474): Located on the roof terrace of the Grand Hotel Parker's, this truly elegant restaurant is happily devoid of stuffiness or ostentation. There's no snobbery here, only the best that money can buy. Chef Baciòt brings together ingredients to create tasty and healthful dishes that marry tradition with nutrition. The service and surroundings are impeccable, and the wine list is among the best in Italy. See chapter 4.

o **Relais Blu Belvedere** (©081-8789552): This restaurant-cum-small-hotel is a hot address on the Sorrento peninsula. The delightful manager-host will introduce you to the flavors of his beloved native peninsula, be it for predinner drinks, which are served with creative nibbles based on local ingredients, or for a perfectly romantic dinner. High above the rocky coast overlooking Capri, the open-air terrace is spectacular. See chapter 6.

o **L'Olivo at the Capri Palace** (©081-9780111): This restaurant, part of the stylish Capri Palace hotel, is a haven of elegance and good taste, from the furnishings and table settings to the impeccable service and superb creative cuisine. See chapter 8.

o **Rossellinis** (©089-818181): A truly elegant, gourmet experience awaits you at this restaurant in the exclusive Palazzo Sasso in Ravello, where the finest local ingredients are transformed into delectable meals by the talented chef. See chapter 7.

THE best LUXURY STAYS

o **Grand Hotel Parker's** (©081-7612474): This is Naples's most romantic luxury hotel, competing with the Grand Hotel Vesuvio for the title of best hotel in town. Housed in a magnificent Liberty-style building, it offers superb service, classy accommodations, and one of the best restaurants in the city. See chapter 4.

o **Grand Hotel Vesuvio** (©081-7640044): This is generally considered to be the best hotel in Naples, offering palatial accommodations and exquisite service. You will be pampered the moment you step through the doors. The turndown service includes fine chocolates, the linens are top class, and the sumptuous breakfast is served in the most panoramic setting you can imagine, with views over the picturesque Castel dell'Ovo. The gourmet rooftop restaurant is another plus. Every detail here is truly first class. See chapter 4.

The Grand Hotel Excelsior Vittoria in Sorrento.

o **San Pietro** (© 800/ 735-2478): A member of the Relais & Châteaux group, this elegant hotel tops our list of favorite places to stay in the whole of Italy. You'll understand why as soon as you step inside. The kind and attentive service, the tastefully colorful furnishing details, the romantic views from the terraces—we love everything about this place. See chapter 7.

o **Grand Hotel Excelsior Vittoria** (©081-8777111): This gorgeous hotel, housed in what once was a palatial private residence overlooking the sea, is the best in Sorrento, The antiques in the guest rooms, the picturesque terraces, and the service make this a wonderful place to stay and it's right in the center of town with its own elevator down to a private beach. See chapter 6.

o **Hotel Santa Caterina** (©089-871012): Amalfi's most luxurious hotel is set in lush gardens and sits on a cliff just out of town, a fabulous place to be pampered away from the crowds. It has a beautiful private beach and lovely swimming pool and a fine restaurant. See chapter 7.

o **Hotel Le Sirenuse** (©089-875066): Competing for the title of best hotel in Positano with the Hotel San Pietro, this gorgeous hotel is housed in a beautiful 18th-century villa overlooking the sea. It offers palatial accommodations and fine service. See chapter 7.

o **Grand Hotel Quisisana** (©081-8370788): The glitziest resort on Capri, this luxury hotel provides its guests with splendid accommodations and exquisite service. The hotel's bar and restaurant are popular spots for visiting socialites, so it's worth stopping by just to enjoy the atmosphere. See chapter 8.

o **Mezzatorre Resort & Spa** (©081-986111): Taking its name from the 15th-century watchtower that houses part of the hotel, the Mezzatorre is the most splendid resort in Ischia. Set on its own secluded promontory near the town of Lacco Ameno and not far from Forio, it pampers its guests in perfect elegance and style. The views from the park and the swimming pool are breathtaking. See chapter 8.

o **Palazzo Sasso** (©089-818181): The most exclusive hotel in the finest resort on the Amalfi Coast, this 12th-century palace was the home of one of the noblest families in town—and you'll be treated accordingly. See chapter 7.

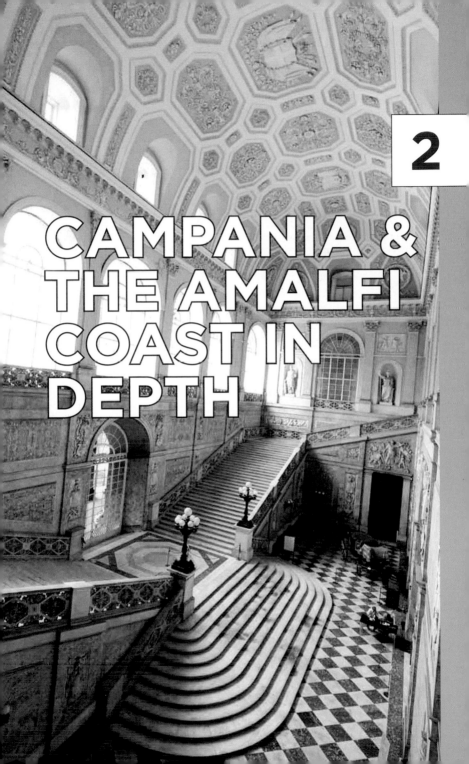

2

CAMPANIA & THE AMALFI COAST IN DEPTH

A land of ancient civilizations, Campania has been inhabited since at least 4000 B.C., as shown by the many excavated necropolises here. A wonderful and fertile land, it attracted many people, who frequently fought for possession of it over the last 3,000 years. Its three main areas each had slightly different historical fates: the plains in the region's northern part and the hinterland of Naples—the Campania Felix of the Romans; the mountainous Sannio dominated by Benevento; and, to the south, the Amalfi Coast and the Cilento.

A LOOK AT THE PAST

This brief survey of Campania's long and complex history is oriented toward the Amalfi Coast, but the rest of Campania is covered as well. Once we hit the Renaissance, the focus shifts primarily to Naples and its surroundings, which became the center of power in the region.

The Greeks

After a short stop on the island of Ischia, Calcidians founded the city of Cuma in 750 B.C., the first Greek city of Magna Grecia—the Greek cities outside the mainland. Cuma became a beacon of Greek civilization in Italy. Greek expansion into the region, though, was contested by the Etruscans (see "The Etruscans," below). In spite of this, the Greeks established other important colonies in the current area of Naples: first Partenope around 680 B.C., then Dicearchia (Pozzuoli) in 531 B.C., and then Neapolis in 470 B.C. In the meantime, Greeks from Sibari founded Posidonia (Paestum) in 600 B.C. and Elea (Velia) in 540 B.C.

Greeks won two major battles in Cuma against the Etruscans, one in 524 B.C. and the other in 474 B.C. Weakened by their fights with the Etruscans, they could not resist the Sannite invasion in the 5th century B.C.

The Etruscans

While the Greeks colonized Campania's coast, the Etruscans colonized the inner plains, the rich agricultural areas around Capua, which they founded in the 9th century B.C., and south all the way down to the hinterland of Paestum. They, too, were weakened by their fights for supremacy in the region against the Greeks, so that when the Sannites began their expansion, Etruscan power in the area came to an end.

PREVIOUS PAGE: **The Palazzo Reale in Naples.** ABOVE: **Etruscan art.**

The Sannites

This mountain people, originally from nearby Abbruzzo, had been expanding south in the Appennines, with an economy based on sheep husbandry. Also a warrior culture, they established a flourishing civilization in Benevento and then moved toward the coast in the 5th century B.C., causing conflict with both Greeks and Etruscans.

Sannite attacks were successful; they took over Capua in 424 B.C. and then took Cuma 3 years later in 421 B.C. Their influence quickly expanded to other cities, such as Neapolis, Pompeii, and Herculaneum, and gave birth to a new civilization, the Oscans (see "The Oscans," below).

The inland Sannites of Beneventum, in the meantime, came into opposition with the Romans who, by the 4th century B.C., had started their expansion southward. This led to the three famous Sannite wars. It took Rome from 343 B.C. to 290 B.C. to overcome the Sannites. The strongly independent Sannites, however, kept creating problems for the Romans. Finally, Beneventum was destroyed and later rebuilt as a Roman colony.

The Lucanians

Another Italic mountain population, the Lucanians came from the nearby region of Basilicata. Slightly less belligerent than their Sannite cousins, they also started a migration toward the coast. They took over Posidonia (Paestum) in 400 B.C., but failed to overcome Elea (Velia). Like the Sannites farther north, they merged with the existing Greek population into the cultural melting pot that became the Oscans.

The Oscans

After their victories over the Greeks and Etruscans, the Sannites in the plains merged culturally with Etruscans and Greeks, giving birth to the Oscan civilization. This original population had strong Sannite roots, blending important cultural elements of the other two civilizations in a way that created a unique individual character with its own language. They made their capital in Capua.

Over time, the Oscans became so distinct from the original Sannites, however, that they actually shifted their support to Rome during its conquest of Campania.

The Romans

The Romans took advantage of the opposition between the Oscans and the Sannites to extend their influence in the region. In exchange for allegiance to the Republic, Rome bestowed Roman citizenship, with the right to vote and decide on public affairs (but with the obligation of military service). Citizen colonies were set up as settlements of Roman farmers after the original people had given allegiance (voluntarily, or by sheer force). This worked better with the Oscans than with the Sannites, who continued to oppose Rome even after they lost the war. The Romans founded Paestum in 273 B.C., Beneventum in 268 B.C., then Salernum and Puteoli (modern Pozzuoli) in 194 B.C. These cities were fortified and linked to Rome by the famous Roman roads, such as the Appian Way, which led to Capua, then Beneventum, and then all the way to Brindisi, on the Ionian Sea on Italy's eastern coast.

In this way, a stern Roman culture was added to the preexisting local mixture. The social war from 91 B.C. to 88 B.C.—and, even more so, the civil war instigated by the dictator Sulla from 82 B.C to 81 B.C.—caused great destruction in Campania, especially to the rebellious Sannio region, which was almost completely wiped out. Peace came again with the advent of Rome's first emperor, Gaius Octavius Augustus.

Under the empire, Campania was completely Romanized, but its agricultural strength was slowly supplanted by the production of Africa and Spain, leading to a strong local recession.

When the empire ended in A.D. 395, the richest plains of Capua and Paestum had been abandoned and were in the throes of a malaria epidemic; the population was forced to found new villages up in the mountains, a situation that would not improve dramatically until the 20th century.

The Byzantine & the Longobards

With the end of the Roman Empire, barbarian invasions began. The Goths from the north invaded the region in 410, while the Vandals from Africa sacked and destroyed Capua in 456; the Byzantines counterattacked against the Goths and finally drove them out in 555; but only a few years later, in 570, the Longobards arrived from the Appennines and took over the interior. The Byzantines struggled to maintain power but eventually lost, keeping only the harbors of Naples, Sorrento, and Amalfi; even Salerno was occupied by the Longobards in 630.

The Longobards' aristocracy oppressed Latin populations, but the yoke was lifted a bit when the Longobards converted to Catholicism thanks to the bishop of Benevento, Barbato; the conversion allowed the monasteries to begin operating again, and their role in preserving classical culture was immense. Later (in the 13th c.), the Abbey of Monte Cassino, in northern Campania, would be, for a time, the home of the greatest philosopher-theologian in Europe, St. Thomas Aquinas.

In the second half of the 8th century, the Longobard prince Arechi II moved his court from Benevento to Salerno, causing increasing tension between the two towns, which resulted in civil war and the splitting of the Longobard realm into two independent principalities in 849. This marked the beginning of the end for the Longobards; in the 10th century, Capua also became an independent principality, after having been destroyed by the Saracens in 841 and refounded on more secure grounds.

In the meantime, Amalfi became independent from the Byzantine Duchy of Naples and started gaining strength and power as a maritime commercial republic, maintaining strong contact with both the Byzantine and the Muslims in the East.

The Saracens

The Arab period in Sicily began in 827. Taking advantage of the Longobards' civil war, the Saracens—Arabs who had started out in the region as mercenaries—took over a few small harbor towns (particularly Agropoli in 882), and started attacking and sacking the other towns along the coast.

Under these repeated assaults, the once-prosperous coastal towns of Campania became deserted, as the people sought refuge in the hills and the countryside. Some of the towns were then reborn, often in more defensive locations and surrounded by heavy fortifications.

The Normans, Swabians & Angevins

Things changed with the arrival of the Normans, who reintroduced the concept of central government and unity in southern Italy. Their first base was Aversa, near Naples, established in 1029, and from there they rapidly expanded their conquest to Capua in 1062, Amalfi in 1073, and Salerno in 1076, where they established their capital until Naples was also annexed to the kingdom in 1139. The Normans then proceeded south and won over Sicily, displacing the Arabs who had ruled the island for 2 centuries.

Salerno became a splendid town and a beacon of culture and learning, thanks to the development of its medical school, the first and most important medical center of the whole Western world. Benevento, on the other hand, became a papal stronghold in the mid–11th century and stayed so, with a couple of brief interludes, until the unification of Italy in 1860.

The Normans introduced feudalism, a repressive social system that discouraged individual economic initiative, and which undermined the very base of the kingdom. When the dynasty became weaker, it passed to the Swebians and then to the Angevins. The feudal chiefs in Sicily revolted and attacked the central monarchy in the famous "Sicilian Vespers" of 1282. Led by Aragonese elements, the Angevins resisted and succeeded in retaining their power in Campania, but the Cilento—right at the border of the reduced kingdom—and the coastal towns suffered immense casualties and depopulation.

In the mid–13th century, the Angevins had established the capital in Naples, which flourished, but the kingdom's interior was abandoned to heavy feudal rule, which smothered commerce and economic activity and led to extreme poverty, which in turn fostered the growth of groups of bandits in the hills who made all road communication unsafe. The legacy of these centuries of stagnation and misrule persists to this day. The situation worsened still when the rule of the kingdom shifted to Spain.

Spanish Rule

Spanish rule was seemingly so backward that even many histories of Naples contain a large blank spot for this 2-centuries-long period. The main events of Spanish rule were revolts against it—in 1547, 1599, 1647, and 1674, to name the major ones. The former kingdom of Naples was ruled by a Spanish viceroy, and the resulting extraction of taxes and the imposition of authoritarian rule were onerous. Philip IV called Naples "a gold mine, which furnished armies for our wars and treasure for their protection." The Spanish did build some great palaces and churches, though it is perhaps symbolic that Naples's Palazzo Reale was built for King Philip III, who never lived here. The great plague also occurred during this period, and wiped out half the population.

The Bourbons

During the tangled period of the War of Spanish succession in the early 18th century, Naples was ruled by Austrians for 27 years. Naples regained its independence in 1734, with Carlo di Borbone. The independence of the kingdom of Naples was at last recognized by Spain and the Papacy. Carlo revitalized the kingdom, improving the roads, draining the marshes in the area of Caserta, and creating new industries—such as the silk manufacturers in San Leucio, the ceramic artistry in Capodimonte, and the cameo and coral industries in Torre del

Greco. The improvements continued during the 10 years of Napoleonic power, when the feudal system was completely dismantled and land was redistributed, creating new administrative and judicial structures. This gave new life to the provinces but, once the Bourbons returned, they were unable to strike a balance with the developing bourgeoisie. The region was thus poised for rebellion when Garibaldi arrived and brought about the unification of Italy in 1861.

A United Italy

Thanks to the brilliant efforts of Camillo Cavour (1810–61) and Giuseppe Garibaldi (1807–82), the kingdom of Italy was proclaimed in 1861. Victor Emmanuel (Vittorio Emanuele) II of the House of Savoy, king of Sardinia, became the head of the new monarchy.

Unfortunately, while the new kingdom was politically good for Campania, it was disastrous for Campania's economy: The northern government imposed heavy taxes, and the centralized administration paid little attention to local differences and needs. This killed the burgeoning industry that had been developing thanks to the Bourbons' paternalism and protection. Despite these setbacks, though, toward the end of the 19th century the coastal area started to develop the agricultural specialties that still exist today.

Fascism & World War II

Fascism achieved little success outside the urban area of Naples and was mostly embraced by prefects and notables in the rest of Campania. The region paid a heavy toll during World War II, when it was heavily bombarded in preparation for the Allied landing on September 8, 1943, when 55,000 Allied troops stormed ashore. Known as the Salerno Invasion, it actually involved landings in a long arc from Sorrento and Amalfi to as far south as the area of Paestum. The Nazis occupied the region and set up a desperate resistance, retreating slowly for long months just north of Caserta along the Garigliano River. This involved one of the war's most notorious battles, the several-months-long siege of Monte Cassino, which left the ancient monastery a heap of rubble. The Nazis destroyed as much as they could during their retreat, sacking and vandalizing everything—even the most important section of the Naples State Archives was burned.

In September 1943, Naples revolted and managed to chase out the occupiers, only days before the Allied forces arrived in the city. Other towns' insurrections resulted in horrible massacres; men and women organized guerrilla groups against the Nazis, hiding out in the mountains and hills and striking mostly at night, while the Allies bombarded their towns and cities. After many hard months of fighting, Campania was finally freed in June 1944.

The Postwar Years

In 1946, Campania became part of the newly established Italian Republic—although Naples had given its preference to the monarchy in the referendum—and reconstruction began. Even though the war had left Italy ravaged, the country succeeded in rebuilding its economy. By the 1960s, as a member of the European Community (founded in Rome in 1957), Italy had become one of the world's leading industrialized nations, prominent in the manufacture of automobiles and office equipment. Campania was slow to recover; the terrible destruction that it suffered, the plague of corruption, plus the rising development

of the Camorra, Campania's Mafia-like organization, hindered the region's development more than others.

The great earthquake (10 on the Mercalli, Cancani, Sieberg scale, or about a 7 on the Richter scale) that hit the region on November 23, 1980, gave it another push back, causing great destruction and economic hardship—over 3,000 people died, especially in the provinces of Avellino and Salerno, at the heart of the quake.

In the 1990s, a new Naples mayor and new regional government began investing more time and money in the restoration of Campania's artistic treasures, the reorganization of old museums, and the creation of new museums throughout the region. Just as important, the new government declared war on corruption and criminality. The millennium celebrations and the Papal Jubilee of 2000 brought about further renovations.

FROM TOP: The 1980 earthquake devastated the Amalfi region; In modern Naples, art isn't confined to the museums.

Results have been spectacular; the center of Naples has been transformed from a depressed state into a sort of open-air museum, with tons of artistic and historical attractions.

At the same time, the escalating war against the Camorra in Naples has attracted much press attention over the past year or so, casting doubt on the city's safety. In our opinion, however, the accounts are sensationalized. Life in the historical part of the city has remained virtually untouched by Camorra violence, and improvements continue to be made, to the extent that Naples's artistic treasures, as well as the attractions of the whole Campania region, become more and more accessible to visitors every day.

ART & ARCHITECTURE IN CAMPANIA

Italian Architecture at a Glance

While each architectural era has its own distinctive features, there are some elements, general floor plans, and terms common to many. Also, some features might appear near the end of one era and continue through several later ones.

From the Romanesque period on, most churches consist either of a single wide **aisle** or a wide central **nave,** flanked by two narrow aisles. The aisles are separated from the nave by a row of **columns** or by square stacks of masonry called **piers,** usually connected by **arches.**

This main nave/aisle assemblage is usually crossed by a perpendicular corridor called a **transept** near the far east end of the church so that the floor plan looks like a **Latin Cross** (shaped like a crucifix). The shorter, east arm of the nave is the holiest area, called the **chancel;** it often houses the stalls of the **choir** and the **altar.** If the far end of the chancel is rounded off, it's called an **apse.** An **ambulatory** is a curving corridor outside the altar and choir area, separating it from the ring of smaller chapels radiating off the chancel and the apse.

Some churches, especially after the Renaissance when mathematical proportion became important, were built on a **Greek Cross plan,** with each axis the same length, like a giant "+" (plus sign). By the baroque period, funky shapes became popular, with churches built in the round or as ellipses.

It's worth pointing out that very few buildings (especially churches) were built in only one particular style. Massive, expensive structures often took centuries to complete, during which time tastes changed and plans were altered.

CLASSICAL: GREEKS & ROMANS (6TH CENTURY B.C. TO 4TH CENTURY A.D.)

The **Greeks** settled Sicily and southern Italy, and left behind some of the best-preserved ancient temples in the world.

The **Romans** made use of certain Greek innovations, particularly architectural ideas. The first to be adopted was post-and-lintel construction (essentially, a weight-bearing frame, like a door). The Romans then added the load-bearing arch. Roman builders were inventive engineers, developing hoisting mechanisms and a specially trained workforce.

Identifiable classical architectural features include these:

o **Classical orders.** These were usually simplified into types of column capitals, with the least ornate used on a building's ground level and the most ornate used on the top: Doric (a plain capital), Ionic (a capital with a scroll), and Corinthian (a capital with flowering acanthus leaves).

o **Brick and concrete.** Although marble is traditionally associated with Roman architecture, Roman engineers could also do wonders with bricks or even prosaic concrete—concrete seating made possible such enormous theaters as Rome's 2.4-hectare (6-acre), 45,000-seat Colosseum.

Most **Greek Temples** in the *Magna Graecia* of southern Italy were built in the 5th-century-B.C. Doric style, including those at **Paestum** south of Naples, and in Sicily at **Segesta** and **Agrigento,** including the remarkably preserved Temple of Concord. **Greek theaters** survive in Sicily at Taormina, Segesta, and Syracuse (which was the largest in the ancient world).

Paestum, southeast of Naples, is home to the remains of three major Doric-style temples.

One of the best places to see **Roman** architecture, of course, is Rome itself, where examples of most major public buildings still exist. These include the sports stadium of the **Colosseum** (1st c. A.D.), which perfectly displays the use of the classical orders; Hadrian's marvel of engineering, the **Pantheon** (1st c. A.D.); the brick public **Baths of Caracalla** (3rd c. A.D.); and the **Basilica of Constantine and Maxentius** in the Roman Forum (4th c. A.D.). By the way, Roman basilicas, which served as law courts, took the form of rectangles supported by arches atop columns along both sides of the interior, with an apse at one or both ends; the form was later adopted by early Christians for their first grand churches.

Three **Roman cities** have been preserved, with their street plans and, in some cases, even buildings remaining intact. These are famous, doomed **Pompeii** and its neighbor **Herculaneum** (both buried by Vesuvius's A.D.-79 eruption), as well as Rome's ancient seaport **Ostia Antica.**

ROMANESQUE (A.D. 800 TO 1300)

The Romanesque took its inspiration and rounded arches from ancient Rome (hence the name). Romanesque architects concentrated on building large churches with wide aisles to accommodate the masses, who came to hear the priests say Mass but mainly to worship at the altars of various saints. To support the weight of all that masonry, walls had to be thick and solid (meaning they could be pierced only by few and rather small windows), resting on huge piers, giving churches a dark, somber, mysterious, and often oppressive feeling.

Identifiable Romanesque features include:

o **Rounded arches.** These load-bearing architectural devices allowed architects to open up wide naves and spaces, channeling all the weight of the stone walls and ceiling across the curve of the arch and down into the ground via the columns or pilasters.

o **Thick walls.**

Inside the ruins of doomed Pompeii.

o **Infrequent and small windows.**

o **Huge piers.**

o **Blind arcades.** A range of arches was carried on piers or columns and attached to a wall. Set into each arch's curve was often a lozenge, a diamond-shaped decoration, sometimes inlaid with colored marbles.

o **Stripes.** Created by alternating layers of white and light-gray stones, this banding was typical of the Pisan-Romanesque style prominent in Pisa and Lucca. The gray got darker as time went on; by the late Romanesque/early Gothic period, the pattern often became a zebra of black and white stripes.

o **Stacked facade arcades.** Another typical Pisan-Romanesque feature was a tall facade created by stacking small, open-air loggias with columns of different styles on top of one another to a height of three to five levels.

Modena's Duomo (12th c.) marks one of the earliest appearances of rounded arches, and its facade is covered with great Romanesque reliefs. **Abbazia di Sant'Antimo** (1118), outside **Montalcino,** is a beautiful example of French Romanesque style. **Milan's Basilica di San Ambrogio** (11th–12th c.) is festooned with the tiered loggias and arcades that became hallmarks of the Lombard Romanesque.

Pisa's Cathedral group (1153–1360s) is typical of the Pisan-Romanesque style, with stacked arcades of mismatched columns in the cathedral's facade (and wrapping around the famous Leaning Tower of Pisa) and blind arcading set with lozenges. **Lucca's Cattedrale di San Martino and San Michele in Foro** (11th–14th c.) are two more prime examples of the style.

GOTHIC (LATE 12TH TO EARLY 15TH CENTURIES)

By the late 12th century, engineering developments freed architecture from the heavy, thick walls of the Romanesque and allowed ceilings to soar, walls to thin, and windows to proliferate.

In place of the dark, somber, relatively unadorned Romanesque interiors that forced the eyes of the faithful toward the altar, where the priest stood droning on in unintelligible Latin, the Gothic interior enticed the churchgoers' gaze upward to high ceilings filled with light. The priests still conducted Mass in Latin, but now peasants could "read" the Gothic comic books of stained-glass windows.

The style began in France and was popular in Italy only in the northern region. From Florence south, most Gothic churches were built by the preaching orders of friars (Franciscans and Dominicans) as cavernous, barnlike structures.

Identifiable features of the French Gothic include:

- **Pointed arches.** The most significant development of the Gothic era was the discovery that pointed arches could carry far more weight than rounded ones.

- **Cross vaults.** Instead of being flat, the square patch of ceiling between four columns arches up to a point in the center, creating four sail shapes, sort of like the underside of a pyramid. The "X" separating these four sails is often re-inforced with ridges called ribbing. As the Gothic progressed, four-sided cross vaults became six-sided, eight-sided, or multisided as architects played with the angles.

- **Tracery.** These lacy spider webs of carved stone grace the pointy ends of windows and sometimes the spans of ceiling vaults.

- **Flying buttresses.** These free-standing exterior pillars connected by graceful, thin arms of stone help channel the weight of the building and its roof out and down into the ground. To help counter the cross forces involved in this engineering sleight of hand, the piers of buttresses were often topped by heavy pinnacles, which took the form of minispires or statues.

- **Stained glass.** Because pointy arches can carry more weight than rounded ones, windows could be larger and more numerous. They were often filled with Bible stories and symbolism written in the colorful patterns of stained glass.

The only truly French-style Gothic church in Italy is **Milan's massive Duomo & Baptistry** (begun ca. 1386), a lacy festival of pinnacles, buttresses, and pointy arches. **Siena's Duomo** (1136–1382), though started in the late Romanesque, has enough Giovanni Pisano sculptures and pointy arches to be considered Gothic. **Florence** has two of those barnlike Gothic churches: **Basilica di Santa Maria Novella** (1279–1357) and **Basilica di Santa Croce** (1294). The decorations inside **Santa Maria Sopra Minerva** (1280–1370), **Rome**'s only Gothic church, are all of a later date, but the architecture itself is all pointy arches and soaring ceilings (though, hemmed in by other buildings, its interior is much darker than most Gothic places).

RENAISSANCE (15TH TO 17TH CENTURIES)

As in painting, Renaissance architectural rules stressed proportion, order, classical inspiration, and mathematical precision to create unified, balanced structures. It was probably an architect, **Filippo Brunelleschi,** in the early 1400s, who first truly grasped the concept of "perspective" and provided artists with ground rules for creating the illusion of three dimensions on a flat surface.

Some identifiable Renaissance features include:

- A sense of proportion
- A reliance on symmetry
- The use of classical orders

One of the first great Renaissance architects was Florence's Filippo Brunelleschi (1377–1476). He often worked in the simple scheme of soft white plaster walls with architectural details and lines in pale gray *pietra serena* stone. Among his masterpieces in **Florence** are the Basilica di Santa Croce's **Pazzi Chapel** (1442–46), decorated with Donatello roundels; the interior of the **Basilica di San Lorenzo** (1425–46); and, most famous, the ingenious **dome** capping **Il Duomo** (1420–46). This last truly exemplifies the Renaissance's debt to the ancients. Brunelleschi traveled to Rome and studied the Pantheon up close to unlock the engineering secrets of its vast dome to build his own.

Urbino architect **Bramante** (1444–1514) was perhaps the most mathematical and classically precise of the early High Renaissance architects, evident in his (much-altered) plans for **Rome's St. Peter's Basilica** (his spiral staircase in the Vatican Museums has survived untouched). Also see his jewel of perfect Renaissance architecture, the textbook **Tempietto** (1502) at San Pietro in Montorio on the slopes of Rome's Gianicolo Hill, where church officials once thought that St. Peter had been crucified (as a plus, the little crypt inside is a riotous rococo grotto).

Renaissance man **Michelangelo** (1475–1564) took up architecture late in life, designing **Florence's Medici Laurentian Library** (1524) and **New Sacristy** (1524–34), which houses the Medici Tombs at Basilica di San Lorenzo. In **Rome,** you can see his facade of the **Palazzo Farnese** (1566) and one of his crowning glories, the soaring **dome of St. Peter's Basilica,** among other structures.

The fourth great High Renaissance architect was **Andrea Palladio** (1508–80), who worked in a much more strictly classical mode of columns, porticoes, pediments, and other ancient temple–inspired features. His masterpieces include **Villa Foscari** and the great **Villa Rotonda,** both in the **Veneto** countryside around Vicenza. His final work is **Vicenza's Olympic Theater** (1580), an attempt to reconstruct a Roman theater stage as described in ancient writings. Other designs include the Venetian church **San Giorgio Maggiore** (1565–1610). He had great influence on architecture abroad as well; his "Palladian" style informed everything from British architecture to Thomas Jefferson's Monticello.

BAROQUE & ROCOCO (17TH TO 18TH CENTURIES)

More than any other movement, the **baroque** aimed toward a seamless meshing of architecture and art. The stuccoes, sculptures, and paintings were all carefully designed to complement each other—and the space itself—to create a unified whole. This whole was both aesthetic and narrative, with the various art forms all working together to tell a single biblical story (or often to subtly relate the deeds of the commissioning patron to great historic or biblical events). Excessively complex and dripping with decorative tidbits, **rococo** is kind of a twisted version of the baroque.

Some identifiable baroque features include:

- **Classical architecture rewritten with curves.** The baroque is similar to Renaissance, but many of the right angles and ruler-straight lines are exchanged for curves of complex geometry and an interplay of concave and convex surfaces. The overall effect is to lighten the appearance of structures and add movement of line and vibrancy to the static look of the classical Renaissance.

○ **Complex decoration.** Unlike the sometimes severe and austere designs of the Renaissance, the baroque was playful. Architects festooned exteriors and encrusted interiors with an excess of decorations intended to liven things up—lots of ornate stucco work, pouty cherubs, airy frescoes, heavy gilding, twisting columns, multicolored marbles, and general frippery.

○ **Multiplying forms.** Why use one column when you can stack a half-dozen partial columns on top of each other, slightly offset, until the effect is like looking at a single column though a fractured kaleidoscope? The baroque loved to pile up its forms and elements to create a rich, busy effect, breaking a pediment curve into segments so that each would protrude farther out than the last, or building up an architectural feature by stacking short sections of concave walls, each one curving to a different arc.

The baroque flourished across Italy. Though relatively sedate, Carlo Maderno's facade and Bernini's sweeping elliptical colonnade for **Rome's St. Peter's Square** make one of Italy's most famous baroque assemblages. One of the quirkiest and most felicitous baroque styles flourished in the churches of the Apulian city **Lecce.** When an earthquake decimated the Sicilian town of **Noto** near Syracuse, it was rebuilt from scratch on a complete baroque city plan; the streets and squares made viewing platforms for the theatrical backdrops of its churches and palaces.

For the rococo—more a decorative than architectural movement—look no further than **Rome's Spanish Steps** (1726), by architect de Sanctis, or the **Trevi Fountain** (1762), by Salvi.

NEOCLASSICAL TO MODERN (18TH TO 21ST CENTURIES)

As a backlash against the excesses of the baroque and rococo, architects began turning to the austere simplicity and grandeur of the classical age and inaugurated the **neoclassical** style by the middle of the 18th century. Their work was inspired by the rediscovery of Pompeii and other ancient sites.

In the late 19th and 20th centuries, Italy's architectural styles went in several directions. The **Industrial Age** of the 19th century brought with it the first genteel shopping malls of glass and steel. The country's take on the early-20th-century Art Nouveau movement was called **Liberty Style.** Mussolini made a spirited attempt to bring back ancient Rome in what can only be called **Fascist architecture.** Since then, Italy has built mostly concrete and glass **skyscrapers,** like the rest of the world, although a few architects in the medium have stood out.

Some identifiable features of each of these movements include:

○ **Neoclassical.** The classical ideals of mathematical proportion and symmetry, first rediscovered during the Renaissance, are the hallmark of every classically styled era. Neoclassicists reinterpreted ancient temples as buildings and as decorative, massive colonnaded porticos.

○ **Liberty Style.** Like Art Nouveau practitioners in other countries, Italian decorators rebelled against the era of mass production by stressing the uniqueness of craft. They created asymmetrical, curvaceous designs based on organic inspiration (plants and flowers), and they used such materials as wrought iron, stained glass, tile, and hand-painted wallpaper.

o **Fascist.** Deco meets Caesar. This period produced monumentally imposing and chillingly stark, white marble structures surrounded by statuary in the classical style.

Of the **neoclassical, Caserta's Royal Palace** (1752–74), outside Naples, was a conscious attempt to create a Versailles for the Bourbon monarchs, while the unbelievably huge (and almost universally derided) **Vittorio Emanuele Monument** (1884–1927) in Rome, which has been compared to a wedding cake or a Victorian typewriter, was Italy's main monument to reaching its *Risorgimento* goal of a unified Italy.

The **Industrial Age** created glass-domed shopping arcades in giant "X" shapes in both **Milan** and **Naples. Liberty** style never produced any surpassingly important buildings, although you can glimpse it occasionally in period storefronts.

Fascist architecture still infests corners of Italy (although most of the right-wing reliefs and the repeated engravings of DVCE—Mussolini's nickname for himself—have long since been chipped out). You can see it at its best in Rome's planned satellite community called **EUR,** which includes a multistory "square Colosseum" so funky that it has been featured in many a film and music video, and in **Rome's Stadio Olimpico** complex.

The **mid–20th century** was dominated by **Pier Luigi Nervi** (1891–1979) and his reinforced concrete buildings, **Florence's Giovanni Berta Stadium** (1932), **Rome's Palazzetto dello Sport stadium** (1960), and **Turin's Exposition Hall** (1949).

Art & Architecture in Depth

Campania's fertile and rich lands have attracted various peoples since prehistoric times, so it's not surprising that the territory bears the marks of many civilizations. Campania boasts Italy's richest trove of monuments from antiquity, with superb Greek ruins and unique Roman remains. You'll also find medieval castles and towns, Longobard, Norman, and Norman-Sicilian (or Arabo-Norman) architecture, and some of the richest collections of Renaissance and baroque monuments in Italy. However, art here didn't die with modern times—Naples continues to be a lively center of artistic life, especially in music and the figurative arts.

PREHISTORY

The islands and mountains of Campania are home to a huge trove of prehistoric art, from the grottoes of Palinuro and Marina di Camerota, to the necropolis of Mirabella Eclano, to the beautiful painted terra cottas of the Grotta delle Felci in Capri, to the rich Grotta di Pertosa near Salerno. Prehistoric Italy is probably the least appreciated aspect of Italian history, but it's fascinating.

THE LEGACY OF THE ETRUSCANS & THE GREEKS ON LOCAL ITALIC ART

The Greeks and the Etruscans started to introduce their artistic styles to Campania in the 9th century B.C. From the ruins of **Cuma**—the first Greek colony in Italy—to the wonderful temples of **Paestum,** to the acropolis of **Velia,** Campania is rich with examples of Greek architecture, and the region's jewelry and metal work bear the mark of Etruscan influence. Etruscan and Greek styles were deeply embedded in the art of the local Italic populations when the Sannites took over the region in the 5th century B.C. The best examples of Italic art are the marvelous statues from the Sanctuary of the Goddess Matuta in **Santa Maria Capua Vetere;** and in particular the superb wall paintings from the tombs of **Cuma, Capua,** and **Paestum,** in the archaeological museums of Naples, Capua, and Paestum.

Sybil's cave in Cuma.

THE ROMANS

With its harbors, fertile plains, and thermal waters, Campania was a key region for the Romans when it came to local artistic development. To the great private homes built along the coasts and on the islands—especially in **Herculaneum, Pompeii, Oplontis,** and **Boscoreale**—Rome added many grand public buildings, such as the amphitheater in **Capua Vetere;** the triumphal arch in **Benevento;** the villas of **Minori, Pozzuoli, Baia;** and the rich collections now in the museums of Naples, Capua, and Salerno.

Trajan's Arch (Arco di Traiano) in Benevento.

THE BYZANTINES, THE NORMANS & THE LONGOBARDS

Most of the early examples of art and architecture of the Middle Ages suffered from extensive damage, particularly by the Longobards. Only with the citizens' conversion to Catholicism and then with the arrival of the Normans did Byzantine art have a rebirth. The cathedrals of **Capua, Salerno,** and **Amalfi** are the richest examples of medieval art in the area, together with the **Basilica of Sant'Angelo in Formis,** the cathedral of **Sant'Agata dei Goti,** and the cathedral of **Casertavecchia,** as well as the Sanctuary of **Montevergine** and the cloister of Sant'Antonio in **Ravello.**

Campania also boasts several examples of magnificent medieval bronze doors, such as the ones in the cathedrals of Amalfi, Atrani, and Salerno. Classic Romanesque and Arab and Sicilian architecture intersect in these cathedrals. So do many of Campania's local cloisters, such as Amalfi's cathedral and the ex-convent of the Capuchins, Ravello's Palazzo Rufolo, and Sorrento's cloister of Saint Francis.

RENAISSANCE & BAROQUE

When the Angevins moved the capital of their kingdom to Naples, the enormous artistic development that was the Renaissance exploded in Campania. Famous artists came here from Tuscany—Lello da Orvieto, Giotto, Tino da Camaino, and Donatello—while local artists emerged on the scene, including Roberto d'Oderisio, Niccolò di Bartolomeo da Foggia, and Colantonio, the teacher of Antonello da Messina. The results are visible in the many churches of Naples and in the Castel Nuovo.

In Salerno, the local painter Antonio Sabatini da Salerno gained renown in the early 16th century. Some of the most powerful examples of Campanian High Renaissance style are in Naples, where many Italian artists were active, including Rossellino, Benedetto and Giuliano da Maiano, Fra Giovanni Giocondo, Fra

Amalfi's St. Andrew's Cathedral.

Giovanni da Verona, Pietro Bernini, Giorgio Vasari, Polidoro da Caravaggio, and Antonio Solaro. The chapels of Monte-Oliveto and the Duomo in Naples are some of the best from this period.

In the 17th century, Caravaggio visited Naples and gave birth to the Neapolitan school of painting, which flourished in the 17th and 18th centuries under such names as Battistello Caracciolo, Andrea Vaccaro, Francesco Guarini, and Luca Giordano. Other Italian artists active in Naples during that period were Artemisia Gentileschi and Domenichino.

As with the rest of Italy, baroque art eventually gained dominance in Naples. The painter Francesco Solimena, together with sculptors Domenico Antonio Vaccaro

A painting by Francesco Paolo Michetti.

(son of Lorenzo) and Giuseppe Sanmartino, were among its most famous practitioners. Among the many area architects, Luigi Vanvitelli, with his work on the Reggia di Caserta, emerged as the preeminent figure. Music by such important artists as G. B. Pergolesi and Domenico Cimarosa was also produced during this period.

CONTEMPORARY ART

The 19th and 20th centuries saw the continuation of Campania's artistic potential, with the School of Posillipo (Anton Pitloo, Salvatore Fergola) and later the Scuola di Resina in the 19th century, the Gruppo Sud, and the Gruppo 1858 in the 20th century. Modern painters such as Domenico Morelli and Francesco Paolo Michetti, along with sculptors such as Francesco Jerace, gained fame in the early 20th century, while one of the more contemporary artists to emerge is the painter Gianni Pisani. While the most famous composers of Italian opera generally hailed from other cities, the region did produce probably the most famous operatic performer of all time: Enrico Caruso, who was born in Naples in 1873.

A TASTE OF CAMPANIA

Food has always been one of life's great pleasures for the Italians. This has been true even from the earliest days: To judge from the lifelike banquet scenes found in Etruscan tombs, the Etruscans loved food and took delight in enjoying it. The Romans became famous for their never-ending banquets and for their love of exotic and even decadent treats, such as flamingo tongues.

Much of Naples's cuisine (spaghetti with clam sauce, or with *ragù* [meat sauce], meatballs, pizzas, fried calamari, and so forth) is already familiar to North Americans because so many Neapolitans moved to the New World and opened restaurants. However, Campanian cuisine has a list of specialties that are much lesser known. **Avellino,** for example, has a number of unique dishes that come from the mountain tradition, such as those flavored with **truffles,** and the delicious cakes made with **chestnuts. Benevento** has a completely different cuisine, reflecting its distinct history—it was part of the church's kingdom from the Renaissance onward—and its strong Sannite heritage. Beneventan cuisine favors meat over fish and includes a large number of specialties made with pork and wild boar. **Salerno** is the homeland of *mozzarella di bufala* and the famous Amalfi lemons.

Dining in Campania

Dining hours tend to be later in Campania than in the United States and the U.K.: Lunch is between 1:30 and 4pm and dinner between 8:30 and 11pm. Restaurants will rarely open before 12:30pm or 7:30pm, and often they'll only be setting up at that time.

Although you are not obliged to eat every course, the typical meal starts with an antipasto, or appetizer followed by a first course (primo) of pasta, or rice. This is then followed by a second course (secondo) of meat or fish, and/or a vegetable side dish or a salad *(contorno)*. Italians will finish a meal with cheese *(formaggio)*, or a piece of fruit *(frutta)*, and, of course, *caffè* (coffee). They'll have dessert *(dolce)* only occasionally, often opting instead for a gelato at a nearby ice-cream parlor.

Note: Ordering a cappuccino after lunch or dinner is a social blunder: Cappuccino is a breakfast or midmorning drink. Also, know that a latte here is a glass of plain milk, not the milk and coffee concoction you are used to. For this, ask for a *caffèlatte*

The Passeggiata

This time-honored tradition takes place nightly in every town in Italy. Shortly after 6pm, men and women, young and old alike and dressed in their best, stroll before dinner in the town center, usually through the main piazza and surrounding streets. Often members of the same sex link arms or kiss each other in greeting. There's no easier way to feel a part of everyday life in Italy than to make the passeggiata part of your evening routine.

Fast-food American style is replaced here by specialized restaurants that serve at the counter: **Spaghetterie** serve a large variety of pasta dishes, and they are usually youth-oriented hangouts; **pizza a metro** and **pizza a taglio** are casual pizza parlors where slices of pizza are sold by weight, with limited or nonexistent seating. A **tavola calda** (literally "hot table") serves ready-made hot foods you can take away or eat at one of the few small tables. A **rosticceria** is the same type of place; you'll see chickens roasting on a spit in the window. **Friggitoria** (frying shops) sell deep-fried vegetables, rice balls *(arancini)*, and deep-fried calzone.

For a quick bite, you can also go to a **bar.** Although bars in Italy do serve alcohol, they function mainly as cafes. *Al banco* is the price you pay standing at the bar counter, while *al tavolo* means you are charged two to four times as much for sitting at a table where you'll be waited on. In bars, you can find local pastries, panino sandwiches on various kinds of rolls, and *tramezzini* (white-bread sandwich triangles with the crusts cut off). The sandwiches run from about 1€ to 3€ and are traditionally put in a press to flatten and toast them.

A **pizzeria** is a restaurant specializing in individual pizzas, usually cooked in wood-burning ovens. They will also sometimes serve pasta dishes, and, typically, the menu includes an array of appetizers as well. A full-fledged restaurant is called an **osteria,** a **trattoria,** or a **ristorante.** Once upon a time, these terms meant something— osterias were basic places where you could get a plate of spaghetti and a glass of wine; trattorie were casual places serving full meals of filling peasant fare; and ristoranti were fancier places, with waiters in bow ties, printed menus, wine lists, and hefty prices. Nowadays, fancy restaurants often call themselves a trattoria to cash in on the associated charm factor; trendy spots use osteria to show they're hip; and simple, inexpensive places sometimes tack on ristorante to ennoble themselves. Many restaurants double as pizzerias, with a regular menu and a separate selection for pizza, sometimes offering a separate casual dining area as well.

The **enoteca** is a marriage of a wine bar and an osteria; you can sit and order from a host of good local and regional wines by the glass while snacking on appetizers or eating from a full menu featuring local specialties. Relaxed and full of ambience, these are great spots for light inexpensive lunches—or simply recharging your batteries.

The *pane e coperto* **(bread and cover charge)** is a 1€ to 4€ cover charge that you must pay at most restaurants for the mere privilege of sitting at a table. To request the bill, say, "Il conto, per favore" (eel *con*-toh, pore fah-*vohr*-ay). A tip of 15% is usually included in the bill these days but, if you're unsure, ask, "È incluso il servizio?" (ay een-*cloo*-soh eel sair-*vee*-tsoh?).

At many restaurants, especially larger ones and in cities, you'll find a *menu turistico* (tourist's menu), sometimes called *menu del giorno* (menu of the day) or *menu à prezzo fisso* (fixed-price menu). This set-price menu usually covers all meal incidentals—cover charge and 15% service charge—along with a first course (*primo*) and second course (*secondo*), and sometimes even a drink, but it almost always offers an abbreviated selection of pretty commonplace dishes. The above menu should not be confused with the *menu dégustazione* (tasting menu) offered by more elegant gourmet restaurants: That's usually the way to go for the best selection of food at the best price. Except in those special restaurants, ordering a la carte will offer you the best chance of a memorable meal. Even better, forego the menu entirely and put yourself in the capable hands of your waiter.

Pasta, Mozzarella & Pizza

The stars of Campanian cuisine are so well known, they have become epicurean symbols of the nation: Italian cuisine as a whole is associated with pasta, pizza, and mozzarella. Yet these three creations were a direct consequence of the fertility and characteristics of Campania, defined by the Romans as "Campania Felix," or the happiest and most perfect of countrysides. To this day, Campania is considered one of the most important and even ideal agricultural provinces around.

Famous for the quality of their **pasta** since the 16th century, the many mills of the Monti Lattari, at the beginning of the Sorrento peninsula, are counted among the best producers of pasta in the world (the ones in Gragnano are particularly renowned). The pasta here is still *trafilata a bronzo* (extruded through bronze forms), a procedure that leaves the pasta slightly porous, allowing for a better penetration of the sauce for tastier results (as opposed to steel forms, which makes the pasta perfectly smooth).

This region created the kinds of pasta that we eat today—penne, fusilli, rigatoni, and so on, each type strictly defined: Spaghetti is thicker than vermicelli, and both are thicker than capellini.

The warm plains of Campania are also home to the rare native buffalo, which is still raised in the provinces of Caserta and Salerno. Campanians have made **mozzarella** with delicious buffalo milk for centuries and look with disdain on what we all know as mozzarella—the similar cheese made with cow's milk—for which they use a different name, *fiordilatte* (literally, "flower of milk"). Indeed, once you've tasted the real **mozzarella di bufala,** with its unique delicate flavor and lighter texture, you'll surely be converted too, and will look down on regular mozzarella as an inferior kind of cheese. It's delicious as is, or try it in the *caprese,* a simple salad of sliced mozzarella, fresh tomatoes, and basil seasoned with extra-virgin olive oil.

Putting together the wheat, the mozzarella, and the third famous produce of this region, the tomato, Neapolitans one day invented **pizza.** The unique local tomatoes—especially those produced on the slopes of Mount Vesuvius—have basically no seeds: Imagine a tomato with no central cavity (no spongy, white stuff, either), but filled just with fruit meat, both flavorful and juicy. These are the *pomodorini* or small tomatoes of Mount Vesuvius. Obviously the result couldn't

Mozzarella.

be anything but a bestseller, and pizza quickly spread from Naples throughout the world.

Be forewarned that many tourists, however, are disappointed by Neapolitan pizza. Here the dough and the tomatoes are the key ingredients—together with the olive oil, of course—and cheese is an option. If you ask for a Neapolitan pizza in Naples, you'll be offered a "marinara:" a thick, puffy crust that is crunchy on the outside and covered with fresh tomatoes, olive oil, and oregano, with no cheese at all. Funny enough, what Romans and the rest of Italy call Neapolitan pizza (pizza Napoletana, with tomatoes, cheese, and anchovies) is referred to here in Naples as "Roman pizza" (à la Romana).

The second-most traditional pizza in Naples is the *margherita*. Named after Margherita di Savoia, queen of Italy, who asked to taste pizza during her residence in the Royal Palace of Naples before the capital was moved to Rome, the pizza bears the colors

Pizza fritta.

of the Italian flag: basil for the green, mozzarella for the white, and red for the tomatoes. The new pizza met with immediate favor, eventually surpassing the popularity of its older counterpart. Pizza evolved with the addition of a large variety of other toppings, but purist pizzerias in Naples (such as Da Michele; p. 92) serve only these two types. In Naples, you can also taste another wonderful type of pizza: ***pizza fritta.*** This wonderful creation is served only in truly old-fashioned places where a double round of pizza dough is filled with ricotta, mozzarella, and ham, and deep-fried in a copper cauldron of scalding olive oil. It arrives as puffy as a ball, but as you poke into it, the pizza flattens out, allowing you to delve into the delicious (though not exactly cholesterol-free) dish.

Antipasti e Contorni

The Italian enthusiasm for food has remained strong in Campania throughout the centuries, seemingly in spite of the region's poverty. In fact, this poverty prompted the development of an important local characteristic when it comes to food: expediency. Ease and quickness, and making something out of almost nothing, were the driving forces behind Campanians coming up with some of the most delicious, yet simplest, concoctions in the history of cuisine. Check out the *antipasti* buffet of any good restaurant, and you'll be certain to find variety, from scrumptious marinated vegetables to seafood dishes such as sautéed clams and mussels, toasted in a pan with garlic and olive oil. Alternatively, go for *polipetti in cassuola* or *affogati* (squid cooked with a savory tomato-and-olive sauce inside a small, terracotta casserole). Among the vegetables, do not miss the typical *zucchine a scapece,* sliced zucchini sautéed in olive oil and seasoned with tangy vinegar and fresh mint dressing (the same preparation is sometimes used for eggplant); or *involtini di melanzane* (a roll of deep-fried eggplant slices, filled with pine nuts and raisins, and warmed up in a tomato sauce) and, when in season, the *friarelli*, a local vegetable that is a cousin to broccoli but much thinner; it's usually served sautéed with garlic and chili pepper, and is traditionally paired with local sausages.

Soups & Primi

One of the most surprising and delicious associations you'll come across here is the delicious *zuppa di fagioli e cozze* (beans and mussels soup), which is common south of Naples and on Capri; another good and unique soup is the *minestra maritata*, a thick concoction of pork meat and a variety of fresh vegetables. The simple comfort food *pasta e patate* (pasta and potatoes smothered with cheese) will surprise you by how tasty it is. At the other end of the spectrum, the elaborated *sartù* (a typical Neapolitan baked dish made with seasoned rice, baby meatballs, sausages, chicken liver, mozzarella, and mushrooms) matches the difficulty of its preparation with the satisfaction of eating it.

Our preferred dish is the local pasta, including *scialatielli* (a fresh, homemade, eggless kind of noodles), served with sautéed seafood (*ai frutti di mare*). Another delicious, but more difficult-to-find pasta, is homemade fusilli. They can be served with all the traditional sauces: *con le vongole* (with clams), *zucchine e gamberi* (shrimp and zucchini), or *al ragù* (a meat sauce, where many kinds of meat can be cooked with tomatoes, including *braciole,* a meat *involtini* with pine nuts and raisins).

Secondi

The cuisine of Naples—shared by most of Campania's coast—focuses on seafood, and some of the best main courses feature fish. The *frittura* (*fritto misto* elsewhere in Italy) of shrimp and calamari is always a great pleasure, and here you will also find other kinds, such as *fragaglie* (very small fish). The local version of *zuppa di pesce* is more difficult to find, but it is a delicious fish stew. Much more common and equally delicious are the *polpi affogati* or *in cassuola,* squid or octopus slowly stewed with tomatoes and parsley. Large fish is served grilled, with a tasty dressing of herbs and olive oil; *all'acqua pazza,* poached in a light broth made of a few tomatoes and herbs; or *alle patate* (baked over a bed of thinly sliced potatoes, and absolutely delicious). You might also find it *al sale,* baked in a salt crust to retain its moisture and flavors. Finally, if you have a taste for lobster, you should not miss out on the rare and expensive local clawless variety—*astice.*

Biscotti di Castellammare.

For the turf, you might try *coniglio all Ischitana* (rabbit with wine and black olives), a very tasty creation typical of Ischia; *brasato,* beef slowly stewed with wine and vegetables; *braciola di maiale,* a pork cutlet rolled and filled with prosciutto, pine nuts, and raisins cooked in a tomato sauce; or the simpler meat *alla pizzaiola,* a beef cutlet sautéed in olive oil and cooked with fresh tomatoes and oregano.

Sweets

If Sicilians are famous for having a sweet tooth, Neapolitans come in a close second, with many delicious specialties on offer. Naples is famous for its *pastiera,* a cake traditionally prepared for Easter but so good that it is now offered year-round in most restaurants. Whole-grain wheat is soaked, boiled, and then used to prepare a delicious creamy filling with ricotta and orange peel in a thick pastry shell.

Another famous dessert is *babà,* a soft, puffy cake soaked in sweet syrup with rum and served with pastry cream. The famous *sfogliatelle* (flaky pastry pockets filled with a sweet ricotta cream) are so good with typical Neapolitan coffee that you shouldn't leave without tasting them; a special kind from Conca dei Marini on the Amalfi Coast is the *sfogliatella Santa Rosa,* filled with pastry cream and *amarene* (candied sour cherries in syrup) instead of ricotta, which was invented in the 14th-century Convento di Santa Rosa.

Each town in Campania, including the smaller villages, has some kind of sweet specialty, such as the *biscotti di Castellammare,* shaped like thick fingers in several flavors, and the several lemon-based pastries from the Sorrento and Amalfi regions: *ravioli al limone* (filled with a lemon-flavored ricotta mixture) from Positano; the *Sospiri* (Sighs)—also called *Zizz'e Nonache* (Nuns' Breasts) depending on which aspect you focus, the taste or the look. The dome-shaped small, pale pastries filled with lemon cream come from Maiori and Minori; and *dolcezze al limone,* the typical lemon pastries of Sorrento, are small puff pastries filled with lemon-flavored cream.

And Some Vino to Wash It All Down

Italy is the largest wine-producing country in the world (more than 1.6 million hectares/4 million acres of soil are cultivated as vineyards). Grapes were cultivated as far back as 800 B.C., probably introduced by the Greeks, and wine has been produced ever since. However, it wasn't until 1965 that laws were enacted to guarantee consistency in winemaking and to defend specific labels. Winemakers must apply for the right to add "D.O.C." (*Denominazione di Origine Controllata*) on their labels, and only consistently good wines from specific areas receive this right. The "D.O.C.G." on a label (the "G" means *garantita*) applies to even better wines from even more strictly defined producing areas. Vintners who are presently limited to marketing their products as unpretentious table wines—*vino da tavola*—often expend great efforts lobbying for an elevated status as a D.O.C.

Of Campania's five provinces, Benevento is the one with the largest number of D.O.C. wines, including the **Aglianico del Taburno, Solopaca, Guardiolo, Sannio, Sant'Agata dei Goti,** and **Taburno,** but Avellino is the only one with three D.O.C.G. wines: the wonderful **Taurasi,** the **Greco di Tufo,** straw-yellow and dry, with a delicate peach-almond flavor; and the **Fiano di Avellino,** a dry and refreshing white wine, which received its D.O.C.G. label only in 1993.

ICE CREAM IN CAMPANIA: A USER'S GUIDE TO gelato

Gelato is the Italian version of ice cream. It is milk or egg white–based, with cream used only for certain flavors, which makes it much easier to digest and in general less caloric, particularly the fruit flavors, which are made with fresh fruit (technically, these are usually water-based, making them sorbetto, or sorbet). Also, the fresh-made gelato contains less sugar than most ice cream, and is cholesterol free.

You can choose to eat your gelato from a cone (cono) or a cup (coppetta); the number of flavors you get depends on the size (two scoops for the small and up to four for the large). Locals often ask for a dollop of whipped cream (panna) on top: Specify if you don't want it: senza panna (sen-zah pan-nah). Here are some important tips to help you spot the best gelato parlors:

- The bar or parlor bears a sign saying PRODUZIONE PROPRIA or PRODUZI-ONE ARTIGIANALE, which means it is made fresh, in small batches, and from fresh, mostly local, ingredients (no large-scale industrial production).

- Avoid overly bright colors—no neon green for pistachio, for instance, or bright yellow for lemon. Natural colors are off-white for banana, pale green for pistachio, white for lemon, and so on.

- The flavors on offer include seasonal fruits, such as peach, apricot, and watermelon in summer, and orange, mandarin, and chocolate in winter.

- They tend to be gelato specialists: Gelato is all they sell, or at least, the section devoted to it is substantial, with a large cold counter well in view.

Another cold treat is granita, a close cousin to slushies. A classic granite is made from frozen lemon juice (made from real lemons, of course) or coffee, but other flavors are sometimes available, such as almond milk, watermelon, or mint. Coffee-flavored granite are usually served with panna. You'll also see street carts selling shaved ice with flavored syrup, which they call granita as well. Though still a refreshing treat, it's not quite the same thing.

Italian wine.

From the volcanic soil of Mount Vesuvius comes the amber-colored *Lacrima Christi* (**Tears of Christ**)**,** and from the area of Pozzuoli, the D.O.C. *Campi Flegrei.* With meat dishes, try the dark mulberry-colored *Gragnano,* in the Sorrento peninsula, which has a faint bouquet of faded violets, and *Penisola Sorrentina.* From the islands come the *Ischia* red and white, and the *Capri.*

The Amalfi Coast also has its share of D.O.C. wines. The *Costa d'Amalfi* includes the *Furore*—white, red, and dry rosé—the red *Tramonti,* and the *Ravello*—white and dry with an idea of gentian, the rosé dry with a delicate violet and raspberry bouquet and with a slightly fuller body, and a red with the most body.

Produced in the Salerno area, the *Castel San Lorenzo* red and rosé are D.O.C., but there is also a *barbera* (fizzy red), a white, and a *moscato* (sweet). Farther south is the *Cilento,* another excellent D.O.C. wine.

From Caserta come the *Falerno,* the D.O.C. *Galluccio,* and the D.O.C. *Asprino d'Aversa,* which is light and slightly fizzy.

Other Drinks

Italians drink other libations as well. The most famous Italian drink is **Campari,** bright red in color and flavored with herbs; it has a quinine bitterness to it. It's customary to serve it with ice cubes and soda as an *aperitivo* before dinner.

Campania also excels at the preparation of *Rosolio,* sweet liquor usually herb or fruit flavored, prepared according to recipes passed down by families for generations. The most famous is *limoncello,* a bright yellow drink made by infusing pure alcohol with the famous lemons from the Amalfi Coast usually served ice cold direct from the deep freeze. Others deserve similar fame, like the rare *nanassino,* made with prickly pears and *finocchietto,* made with wild fennel. Limoncello has become Italy's second-most popular drink (p. 231). It has long been a staple in the lemon-producing region of Capri and Sorrento, and recipes for the sweetly potent concoction have been passed down by families there for generations. About a decade ago, restaurants in Sorrento, Naples, and Rome started making their own versions. Visitors to those restaurants as well as

Limoncello.

the Sorrento peninsula began singing limoncello's praises and requesting bottles to go. Now it's one of the most up-and-coming liqueurs in the world, thanks to heavy advertising promotions.

Beer, once treated as a libation of little interest, is still far inferior to wines produced domestically, but foreign beers, especially those of Ireland and England, are gaining great popularity with Italian youth, especially in Rome. This popularity is mainly because of atmospheric pubs, which now number more than 300 in Rome alone, where young people linger over a pint and a conversation. Most pubs are in the Roman center, and many are licensed by Guinness and its Guinness Italia operations. In a city with 5,000 watering holes, 300 pubs might seem like a drop, but because the clientele is young, the wine industry is trying to devise a plan to keep that drop from becoming a steady stream of Italians who prefer grain to grapes.

CAMPANIAN nightlife

By American and British standards, nightlife in Campania's provincial towns tends to be dull. There isn't a bar culture in southern Italy, and often what's called a pub here is a rather pale imitation. Cultural and social life, though, are always lively, from strolling along the main street or going out for dinner, to having an *aperitivo,* eating handmade gelato, or going to the theater or a movie.

While there are some great nightclubs in Naples, the situation is quite different in the rest of the region. You'll find some good clubs along the Amalfi Coast in summer, but things are quieter in the evening in the country. Your best option will often be a concert. Musical events (both classical and Italian pop) are sometimes staged in even the most remote little towns and villages.

High-proof **grappa** is made from the "mosto," what remains of the grapes after they have been pressed. Many Italians drink this after dinner and some even put it into their coffee. Grappa is an acquired taste—to an untrained foreign palate, it often seems rough and harsh.

WHEN TO GO

April to June and **September to October** are generally the best times to visit Campania; temperatures are usually mild, and the crowds aren't quite so intense. Starting in mid-June, the summer rush begins, especially at the seaside resorts; and from **July to August,** the coast teems with visitors. **Mid-August** is the worst on the coast in terms of crowds: The entire country goes on vacation around the holiday of **Ferragosto,** on August 15; while the cities tend to be deserted—in Naples, Benevento, Avellino, Caserta, and Salerno many restaurants and shops will be closed—the seaside towns and island resorts buzz with activity. By contrast, the region's interior never gets really crowded. From **November to Easter,** most attractions go to shorter winter hours or are closed for renovation, while a number of hotels and restaurants close or take extended vacations. Especially between **November and February,** spa and beach destinations become padlocked ghost towns. Also, it can get much colder than you'd expect (it might even snow).

High season on most airline routes to Naples usually stretches from June to the beginning of September. This is the most expensive and most crowded time to travel. **Shoulder season** is from April to May, early September to October, and December 15 to January 14. **Low season** is from November 1 to December 14 and from January 15 to March 31.

Weather

Campania enjoys four well-defined seasons. Winters are mild, spring and fall are pleasant, and summers are hot. July and August are very hot, especially in low-lying areas. The high temperatures (measured in Italy in degrees Celsius) begin in Naples in May, often lasting until sometime in October. For the most part, the humidity is lower in Campania than, say, in Washington, D.C., so high temperatures don't seem as oppressive. In Naples, temperatures can stay in the 90°F (30°C) range for days, but nights are often comfortably cooler.

Winters are mild by the sea, with temperatures averaging 50°F (10°C), but it gets much colder in the interior and the mountains, which often are subject to rain and snow. Precipitations tend to be rare in summer but increase abruptly in the fall, which tends to be the wetter season. They are somewhat lower in winter and dwindle in spring.

Holidays

Banks, government offices, post offices, and many stores, restaurants, and museums are closed on the following **national holidays:** January 1 (New Year's Day), January 6 (Epiphany), Easter Monday, April 25 (Liberation Day), May 1 (Labor Day), June 2 (Republic Day), August 15 (Ferragosto/Assumption of the Virgin), November 1 (All Saints' Day), December 8 (Feast of the Immaculate Conception), December 25 (Christmas Day), and December 26 (Santo Stefano). Closings are also sometimes observed on **feast days** honoring the patron saint of each town and village, when processions are organized through the historic district and around the town's main chiesa or cathedral. In Naples, September 19 is the Feast of St. Gennaro; in Salerno, September 21 is the Feast of St. Matteo; in Avellino, February 14 is the Feast of St. Modestino; Amalfi celebrates the Feast of St. Andrea on June 27 and November 30.

Campania Calendar of Events

For an exhaustive list of events beyond those listed here, check http://events.frommers.com, where you'll find a searchable, up-to-the-minute roster of what's happening in cities all over the world.

For major events in which tickets should be procured well before your arrival, we prefer using Italy-based services; they are often cheaper and have more comprehensive event offerings (see "Before You Leave Home: Tickets & Seats in Advance," below). You can also check with **Global Edwards & Edwards,** in the United States, at ✆ **800-223-6108.**

JANUARY

Il Presepe nel Presepe (Manger in a Manger), Morcone. This little town near Benevento is a natural background for the reenactment of Jesus' birth. Each January, the villagers here transform their town into a version of Bethlehem, and open their homes to visitors. January 3.

Epiphany celebrations, regionwide. All Roman Catholic holidays are deeply felt in Campania, and festive celebrations for the Epiphany include numerous fairs and processions celebrating the arrival of the Three Kings at Christ's manger. January 6.

Festival Internazionale della Canzone Napoletana ed Italiana (International Festival of Italian and Neapolitan Song), Capua. Gathering performers and lovers of Italian and Neapolitan music for more than 3 decades, this 3-day event is a celebration of Italian folk music, both new and traditional. End of January.

FEBRUARY

Carnival, regionwide. During the period before Lent, float parades and histrionic traditional shows take place in most towns, big and small, throughout the region. Some of the best are in **Capua,** which puts on a grand parade and cabaret and theater performances (call the tourist office at ✆ **0823-321137**), and

in **Montemarano,** where celebrations start on January 17 (call the tourist office at ✆ **0827-63231,** for a schedule of events). **Paestum** schedules great parade and dance shows (call the tourist office at ✆ **0828-811016**). Dates vary, but it's generally held the week before Ash Wednesday.

The Comicon at Castel Sant'Elmo in Naples offers some unique events.

Carnevale Irpino, Avellino. This festival includes traditional representations, such as the famous *Zeza,* a musical farce; parades; and the **Concorso della Zeza,** a large competition for group mummers (masked performers). Contact the **EPT** (✆ **0825-74732** or 0825-74695) for a schedule of the events. The 2 weeks before Ash Wednesday.

Nauticsud, Mostra d'Oltremare, Naples. Spanning both land and water, this boat show displays the latest motor and sailing boats and equipment. Check the website for information at www.nautic sud.info. Mid-March.

Comicon—International Comics Festival, Naples. This international event at Castel Sant'Elmo is a must-see for fans of comic books and animation. Each year the fair is organized around a main theme—such as Japanese comics or mystery—and includes previews and presentations of new productions spanning the spectrum. Contact the organization for a schedule of events (✆ **081-4238127;** www.comicon.it). Late March/early April.

Primavera Sorrentina, Sorrento. The town celebrates the spring and then the summer with an array of events, including various flower fairs, food fairs, and a few musical venues. March through July.

Pasqua (Easter), regionwide. Celebrations include several events: Processions for the benediction of the symbolic palm—usually olive tree branches—take place on the Sunday before Easter Sunday; Stations of the Cross processions (reenacting Jesus' ascent to Golgotha) are staged in almost every church on Holy Friday; finally, Easter Sunday is marked by special religious celebrations. Various dates between end of March and April.

Pasqua a Sorrento (Easter in Sorrento), Sorrento. These Easter celebrations last a whole week; religious processions and concerts are scheduled in the town's cathedral and in the delightful cloister of San Francesco. Other processions take place on the night of Holy Thursday through Holy Friday in the towns surrounding Sorrento: Meta, Piano di Sorrento, and Sant'Agnello. Week before Easter.

Processione dei Misteri (Procession of the Mysteries), Procida. This is one of the most famous traditional religious events in Campania, a procession of plastic scenes from the Passion of Christ sculpted by local craftspeople. Evolving from its original procession in 1627, it is now a glorious show of entire scenes depicting the betrayal of Judas, the Last Supper, and so on, as well as large statues of Christ and the Madonna. Holy Thursday night into Holy Friday morning.

Linea d'Umbra Salerno—Festival Culture Giovani, Salerno. This major international event, in its 16th year in 2011, is dedicated to new talent in Europe and focuses on the passage from adolescence to adulthood—the "shadow line," written about by Joseph Conrad—through film, music, visual and performing arts, and literature. Contact the festival office (✆ **089-662565;** fax 089-662566; www.festivalculturegiovani. it). Varying week in April.

Feast of San Costanzo, Marina Grande, Capri. This day honors St. Costanzo, whose remains, preserved in the local basilica, protected the island from the Saracens' attacks during the Middle Ages. Bishop Costanzo died on the island during his apostolic mission in Capri on his way to Constantinople around A.D. 677. Call the local tourist office for a program, at ✆ **081-8370424.** Third week of May.

Maggio dei Monumenti (Monuments in May), Naples. The *centro storico* (old city center) of Naples comes alive for a whole week with cultural events and special openings of private collections and monuments not normally open to the public. Contact the tourist office for a schedule. Last week of May.

Historic Regatta of the Maritime Republics, Amalfi. Each of Italy's four historical towns—Genova, Pisa, Venice, and Amalfi—alternate turns hosting this annual regatta. Amalfi's last turn was in 2009 and it will come around again in 2013. Contact the tourist office (✆ **089-871107**). First Sunday in June.

Il Trionfo del Tempo e del Disinganno (The Triumph of Time and Enlightenment), provinces of Caserta and Benevento. This festival of medieval, Renaissance, and baroque music is beloved by connoisseurs, who delight not only in the high quality of the performances, but also in the venues: All concerts are held in little-known historical buildings, some of which are not usually open to the general public, and can be visited with a guide just before the concert. Check http://trionfo.altervista.org for a schedule of events. Second half of June through the end of August.

Concerti al Tramonto, Anacapri. Each summer, the Foundation Axel Munthe organizes a series of sunset concerts (classical and jazz) in the Villa San Michele, in a spectacular setting overlooking the island and the sea. Contact Villa San Michele for details (✆ **081-8371401;** www.villasanmichele.eu). June through August.

Leuciana Festival, Caserta. This festival offers a rich program of musical, theatrical, and dance performances in Caserta's Reggia and in the scenic Belvedere di San Leucio. For more information, call ✆ **0823- 237171** or visit www.leuciana.org. June through August.

Music in the Cloister, Amalfi. Organized by the town of Amalfi, this series of concerts, held in the splendid Chiostro del Paradiso at Amalfi's cathedral, is one of our favorite events. Contact the tourist office (✆ **089-871107**) for a program. Usually on Friday at 9pm. Beginning of August to mid-September.

Sagra del Limone (Lemon Fair), Massa Lubrense. Celebrating the fruit that characterizes so much of the local culture and cuisine, this 4-day festival includes walks in the countryside, farm visits, and culinary events. First weekend in July.

Benevento Citta' Spettacolo, Benevento. The ancient Roman theater of Benevento is the venue for a full-fledged summer season of opera and drama. Contact the tourist office (✆ **0824-319911**). July through August.

Neapolis Festival, Naples. Rock might be old-fashioned these days, but this 2-day festival is still hot. It stages the best groups in Italy and the world. Call or check the website for the program (www.neapolis.it). July.

Ischia Film Festival, Ischia. This fast-growing event stages some 100 films from over 20 countries annually. Visit www.ischiafilmfestival.it for more information. One week in July.

Ravello Festival, Ravello. This internationally renowned festival includes classical music, jazz, dance, and the visual arts, with shows by artists of world fame. You must make reservations well in advance. Contact the festival office (✆ **089-858422** or 089-858360; www. ravellofestival.com) for reservations. July through September.

Estate a Minori, Minori. Artists from around the world come to perform with the Amalfi Coast as their backdrop, and the Teatro del Mare inaugurated this year provides an additional stage right on the beach. Contact the local tourist office for the program (✆ /fax **089-877087;** www.proloco.minori.sa.it). July through August.

Festival Ville Vesuviane, Ercolano. Reaching its 25th edition in 2012, this music festival takes the stage in the splendid villas of the Miglio d'Oro—the stretch of some 122 elegant villas built at the foot of Mount Vesuvius during the 18th century by the Bourbon court. Contact the Ente Ville Vesuviane (📞 **081-7322134;** www.villevesuviane. net) for a schedule of events. July.

Festa del Mare, town of Ischia. These spectacular celebrations mark the occasion of the Festival of Sant'Anna. A procession of boats and floats crosses the harbor under the town's illuminated castle. July 26.

Sagra della Sfogliatella di Santa Rosa, Conca dei Marini. This event celebrates the local version of *sfogliatella,* the most famous of Neapolitan pastries, filled with pastry cream and a sour cherry confection. August.

Festival of the Assunta, Positano. In the 9th and 10th centuries A.D., when the Saracens established themselves in nearby Agropoli (see chapter 9), the whole coast was endangered by their repeated incursions and bloody robberies. This festival reenacts the Saracens' attack on Positano and the miraculous intervention of the Madonna who, as legend has it, saved the town. August 14 and August 15.

Surrentum Grandi Eventi, Sorrento. The rich program of this festival centers on dance, theater, and music. The additional draw is the setting: All performances are staged in beautiful Villa Fiorentino. Contact the villa (📞 **081-8782284**) or check their website (www.festival dellospettacolo.it) for a schedule of events. August.

Musica negli Scavi Archeologici, Ercolano. Top-quality concerts are staged in the magic scenery of the ruins of Herculaneum and in the 18th-century Villa Campolieto. Contact the tourist office of Ercolano (📞 **081-7881243**) for a schedule of events. August through September.

Scala Meets New York, Scala. This festival stages internationally renowned artists as well as political and cultural personalities to mark the solidarity of the oldest town on the Amalfi Coast with the most modern city in the world. For more info see the websites of the two organizing associations (www.italiausa.org and www.scalanelmondo.org). August 11 to September 11.

Before You Leave Home: Tickets & Seats in Advance

You absolutely need advance reservations for the Capodimonte Museum in Naples (the one museum in Campania where lines are always several hours long because of the many special exhibits) and for special guided tours of Pompeii, but you might want to make reservations for a number of other attractions and events as well. The best place to make reservations is **Pierreci** (📞 **06-39967700;** www.pierreci.it), the official advance reservation service for a number of museums and events in Campania and in Italy. To get tickets for all kinds of events, the best Italy-based operators are **TicketOne** (📞 **023-92261** [press 9 for an English-speaking operator]; www.ticketone.it); and **Viva**

Ticket (www.vivaticket.it). They have English-language websites where you can make reservations and purchase tickets. U.S.-based companies offering advance tickets for a variety of museums and events in Italy are convenient, but they are usually more expensive and cover only a small selection of monuments and events. The best of these is **Culturalitaly.com** (📞 **800/380-0014;** fax 928/639-0388; www.culturalitaly. com), a Los Angeles–based company that offers seats and reservations for operatic performances in Naples, special guided tours in Pompeii, and even tickets to the famed Festival of Ravello. Most reservations carry a $10 fee, plus the cost of the event.

Incontri Musicali Sorrentini (Sorrentine Musical Encounters), Sorrento. Sorrento offers unending cultural events throughout the year, but during this festival, the peaceful cloister at St. Francis Church comes alive for 3 weeks of classical concerts. Ask the tourist office (✆ 081-8074033; www.sorrentotourism.com) for a schedule of events. August through September.

SEPTEMBER

Settembre al Borgo (September in the Village), Casertavecchia. For 10 days, the ancient *borgo* in this medieval town comes alive with music and other performances focusing on a different theme each year. Contact the Caserta tourist office (✆ 0823-550011), or visit www.casertamusica.com for a schedule of events. End of August to the beginning of September.

Festa di Piedigrotta, Naples. This centuries-old religious and musical festival was successfully revived in 2007 after years of neglect. It was at the 1898 edition of this festival that the world-famous song "O Sole Mio" was presented for the first time, and the festival went strong for decades until it lost its following in the 1980s. It is now back full strength, featuring religious and musical events as well as a children's program and a parade of floats. For more information, visit www.festadipiedigrotta.it. First 2 weeks in September.

Santa Maria della Libera, Capri. Starting from the St. Costanzo in Marina Grande church and crossing the town of Capri, grand processions are staged at this festival, which includes music, fireworks, and market stalls. Contact the tourist office (✆ 081-8370424) for more information. The Sunday closest to September 12.

Ischia Jazz Festival, Ischia. This festival features renowned international jazz musicians. See www.ischiajazz.com for information. Usually first week of September.

OCTOBER

Le lune di Pompei, Pompeii Archeological Area. This is *the* most romantic guided tour of Pompeii's ruins. The tour rotates on seven themes and is scheduled every night for 2 weeks in August and then every weekend night throughout October and November. You can book directly online at www.lelunedipompei.com, or contact the booking office for information (✆ 081-19303885). August through November.

NOVEMBER

Feast of St. Andrew, Amalfi. St. Andrew, the patron of Amalfi and the protector of fishermen, is honored annually by local fishermen, who run with a heavy statue of him on their shoulders from the beach up the cathedral's hundreds of steps, and then present the saint with offerings of fish—both fresh and carved. The town also celebrates with games, folk shows, and magnificent fireworks. The feast is repeated in a mellower form on June 27, the anniversary of the day the saint miraculously saved the town from an attack by Saracen pirates. November 30.

DECEMBER

Sagra della Salsiccia e Ceppone (Sausage and Bonfire Fair), Sorrento. In this celebration of Saint Lucia, locals and visitors cook—and eat—about 91kg (200 lb.) of delicious local sausages barbecued over a huge fire (prepared in the heart of the Santa Lucia neighborhood). The food is accompanied by bottles of excellent local wine. December 13.

Avellino Christmas Concerts, Avellino. For 5 days, the town is alive with music, as local choirs give concerts inside the town's beautiful cathedral. Contact the tourist office (✆ 0825-74732) for a program. Usually December 13 through December 18.

Feast of the Torrone, San Marco dei Cavoti. The typical Christmas candy, the *torrone,* becomes an occasion for celebrations in the little town that has been famous for making its special version—the *croccantino*—since the Middle Ages. You can taste all the variations of the treat along Via del Torrone (Via Roma), and then watch the building of a giant *croccantino* by local masters in the town's main square. Call the tourist office in Benevento (© **0824-319911**) for more information. December 8 and the following weekends until Christmas.

Divers' Procession to Grotta dello Smeraldo, Conca dei Marini. Each December and January, a special pilgrimage embarks to this town's greatest attraction, Grotta dello Smeraldo. Local and guest scuba divers swim from the beach to an underwater manger inside the grotto (see chapter 7). Call the visitor center in Amalfi at © **089-871107** for more information. December 24 and January 6.

Live Manger, Belvedere di San Leucio, Caserta. Come to see this hamlet turn the clock back to the 18th century with historical reenactments, music, and performances during the Christmas period. Contact the Caserta tourist office (© **0823-550011**) for information. December 25 to January 6.

Live Manger, Pietrelcina. This picturesque little town near Benevento hosts a reenactment of Christmas involving the whole town, with events spread over several days. December 27 through December 29.

Sagra della Zeppola (Feast of the Zeppola), Positano. Celebrants at this feast ring in the new year by feasting on *zeppolas,* delicious fried sweet pastries, and by enjoying the Kermesse of dances, music, and fireworks on the beach of Marina Grande. December 31 through January 1.

RESPONSIBLE TRAVEL

Responsible tourism is a key conservation element on the Amalfi Coast and surrounding areas. Nature has done its best to protect itself here, with steep cliffs making construction difficult for developers, but the resulting beauty attracts so many tourists, both local and international, that the entire region is at serious risk. Overbuilding, forest fires, and overuse of water resources are the region's top problems, together with marine pollution: All of these are exacerbated by the enormous tourist pressure. The dawning of conservation and sustainable tourism in recent years has made the local tourist industry well aware of the fragility of the local environment and committed to protect it, together with the Italian government and the numerous local associations working for its preservation. Water and sewage management plans are active in most hotels and restaurants, and a large number of them buy only local produce and services. Shortsighted developers, backed by organized crime, are still very active, though, and constantly try to encroach on protected land, often resorting to arson. We can all make a difference by choosing sustainable resorts and accommodations, and by respecting the local ecosystem.

Naples might hardly be what you picture as an eco-friendly destination, but the rest of the region is actually one of the prime destinations for ecotourism in Italy.

Campania is home to Italy's second-largest national park—the Cilento—and to a large number of parks and nature preserves, including the National Park of Mount Vesuvius, the miniarea of the Valle delle Ferriere in Amalfi, and the marine bioparks of Baia (near Pozzuoli), Procida, Ischia, Punta Campanella (Massa Lubrense), parts of Capri, and of the Cilento coast.

You'll also find a great number of *agriturismi,* working farms that increase their income by turning themselves into small resorts (similar to some ranches in the United States). This movement has been successfully promoted by the

Italian government to reduce acquisition of abandoned farms by developers, and to protect natural areas, and has found a perfect home in Campania, where the countryside often offers dramatic natural attractions and close proximity to the seaside. Also, most of the *agriturismi* have embraced the organic movement, adding increased environmental benefit. Operations are controlled through methods such as surprise inspections, and *agriturismi* are strictly regulated by law to prevent exploitation by corporations and developers: In order to obtain the right to call itself an *agriturismo,* the farm must: (a) offer fewer than 30 beds total; and (b) make most of its profits from the agricultural component of the property—in other words, the property has to remain a farm and not become a glorified hotel.

Staying in an *agriturismo* is a great way to contribute to green tourism in Italy; it can also be quite attractive for the special amenities it offers. For more information, see "Tips on Accommodations," on p. 353.

Throughout this book we recommend services that are committed to sustainable tourism. These hotels may have bathroom fixtures that reduce the amount of wasted water, soap dispensers to reduce the number of empty plastic bottles and unused soap that ends up in the garbage, and energy-saving bulbs. They increasingly rely on energy derived from solar or wind power, and they also invite guests to save water by using towels and bed sheets for more than 1 night. They often have made or are enacting plans for the recycling of gray water, and reduce plastic use by offering fresh, local, and often organic foods rather than industrial prepackaged breakfast goods, and water bottled in recyclable glass bottles.

Several local organizations are good resources: **Associazione Italiana Turismo Responsabile** (www.aitr.org), **Legambiente** (www.legambiente.eu) and its regional section for Campania (www.legambiente.campania.it), **FAI** (Fondo Ambiente Italiano; www.fondoambiente.it), and **WWF Italy** (www.wwf.it). We also recommend a few excellent operators: **Planet Viaggi** (www.planetviaggi.it) organizes enticing eco-tours in Naples and the Cilento, **CTS** (Centro Turismo Studentesco; www.cts.it), and **AMEntelibera** (www.viaggiamentelibera.it).

TOURS
Special-Interest Trips

Our favorite special-interest tour group in the region is the lively Naples-based **Rising Incoming Organizer (RIO),** Via Monte di Dio 9, 80132 Napoli (②081-7644934; www.riorimontitours.com), a family business now in its third generation. It offers a variety of unique, off-the-beaten-path tours that cover all kinds of special interests, from classic art and ceramics—a 12-day tour in Naples, Vietri, the Amalfi Coast, and Cerreto Sannita (near Benevento) that we particularly recommend—to golf, sailing, and culinary adventures, including one featuring Neapolitan pastries.

Another operator we like is the Philadelphia-based **Context Travel** (②800/691-6036 toll-free in the U.S., or 215/392-0303; www.contexttravel.com), offering tours and excursions guided by docents and experts. The list of available walking tours of Naples is impressive; each tour focuses on one area of interest, such as art, archaeology, architecture, history, theology, city ambience, shopping, or cuisine.

San Diego–based **Cultural Italy** (②800/380-0014 or 619/822-1099; www.culturalitaly.com) is also a good source for a variety of tours.

Academic Trips & Language Classes

Our favorite language school in the area is **Sorrento Lingue,** Via S. Francesco 8, 80067 Sorrento (✆ **081-8075599;** www.sorrentolingue.com). It also offers cooking and art classes. Our other favorite is **Centro Italiano,** Vico Santa Maria dell'Aiuto 17, 80134 Napoli (✆ **081-5524331;** www.centroitaliano.it), which also offers excellent seminars on local culture as well as courses on archaeology, ceramics, wine, and yoga.

Both offer high academic value and comparable costs (weekly courses start at about 200€ per person). Another resource is the British-based **LCA** (Language Courses Abroad; www.languagesabroad.co.uk) which organizes language as well as cooking and art classes in the region.

Adventure & Wellness Trips

The Sorrento peninsula and Amalfi Coast are hikers' heavens, while the Cilento simultaneously offers the best to both hikers and bicycle enthusiasts. A great number of agencies, both local and international, offer hiking and biking trips, but you can also hire local guides to organize your own individual trip (see our suggestions in the destination chapters that follow).

Our favorite locally based organization is **Cycling Cilento Adventure** (✆ **328-3652736;** www.cyclingcilentoadventure.com), based in Cilento National Park. It offers a great—both in number and quality—choice of road bike, mountain bike, and hiking tours, all of which allow you to sample the local cuisine and see the best sights.

An excellent agency is **Country Walkers** (✆ **800/464-9255** or 802/244-1387; www.countrywalkers.com); based in Vermont, it organizes great walking tours with highly experienced local guides, from a more laid-back tour of Capri and the Amalfi Coast, to a more taxing hike of the Amalfi Coast.

Another excellent agency is the U.K.-based **Sherpa Expeditions** (✆ **20-8577-2717;** www.sherpa-walking-holidays.co.uk), offering several guided and self-guided walking tours in Campania, both on the Amalfi Coast and in Cilento National Park.

La Dolce Vita Wine Tours (✆ **888/746-0022;** www.dolcetours.com) organizes easier walking tours, including one that covers Capri, Mount Vesuvius, and Pompeii, as well as some of the best vineyards in the region.

Breakaway Adventures (✆ **800/567-6286;** www.breakaway-adventures. com) organizes cycling and walking tours in the Sorrento peninsula and Amalfi Coast as well as in the Cilento.

The region is also a major wellness destination, with the local volcanic activity creating endless natural spa opportunities. The island of Ischia and Castellamare di Stabia are where you'll find the world-renown resorts. We have highlighted the best spas for each destination throughout this book.

Food & Wine Trips

As home to some of the best culinary traditions in Italy, Campania offers a number of food-oriented tours. Our personal favorites are those offered by the **Sorrento Cooking School** (✆ **081-8783255;** www.sorrentocookingschool.com), whose program includes a large variety of choices both in length (from daily excursions to longer tours lasting up to 8 days) and content (from cooking classes and wine tours to gastronomic and cultural explorations).

We also like the Italian cooking school of **Mami Camilla,** Via Cocumella 06, Sant'Agnello di Sorrento (✆ **081-8782067;** www.mamicamilla.com).

Other excellent classes are organized by **Sorrento Lingue** and **Centro Italiano** (see "Academic Trips & Language Classes," above).

Specializing in culinary vacations, **Epiculinary** (✆ **847-9887056;** www. epiculinary.com) hosts a large variety of Italian classes and tours, several of which are in the Sorrento and Amalfi Coast areas.

Chicago-based **International Kitchen** (✆ **800/945-8606;** www.the internationalkitchen.com) is one of the best companies devoted to culinary tours, and its program includes several destinations on the Amalfi Coast, such as the delightful Oasi Olympia Relais in Sant'Agata sui due Golfi, between Sorrento and Positano.

With its "taste your travel" slogan, Italy-based **Pagine di Gusto** (✆ **0461-383120;** www.paginedigusto.com) organizes several discovery tours of Campania, highlighting its art, food, and wines.

Another good resource is **Gourmet Traveler** (www.gourmetravel.com), offering specialized tours of the Amalfi Coast.

As for wine, our favorite tour operator is the Benevento-based **Savour the Sannio** (✆ **0823-953663;** www.savourthesannio.com), operated by Barbara and Federico. They organize delectable tours of the local wineries as well as excellent cooking classes and cultural excursions.

Volunteer & Working Trips

Legambiente (www.legambiente.eu) and its regional section for Campania (www.legambiente.campania.it) and **FAI** (Fondo Ambiente Italiano; www.fondo ambiente.it) regularly organize working vacations during which you volunteer on a specific conservation project, paying only your basic lodging expenses. Another good resource is **Worldwide Opportunities on Organic Farms** (www.wwoof. org), which organizes volunteer work on organic farms.

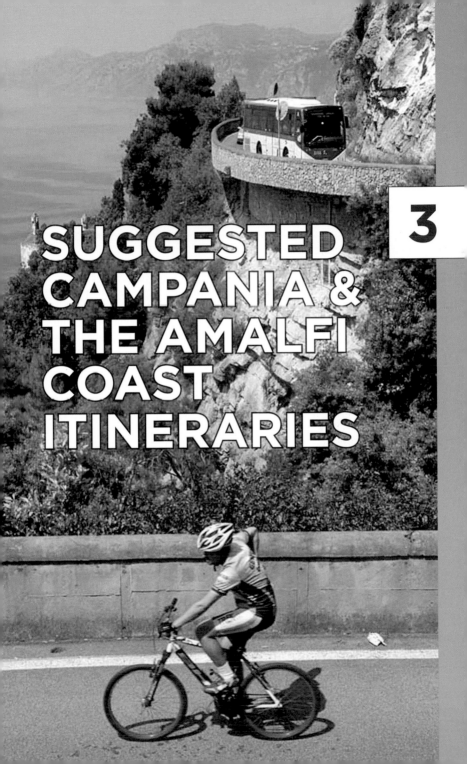

SUGGESTED CAMPANIA & THE AMALFI COAST ITINERARIES

3

ampania's offerings can be explored a number of ways. Public transportation in the region is good, so you can easily move about from one destination to the other by train or bus or even boat. Exploring the countryside, though, will require a car, which you can rent in any city or large town for just the time you need it—with the rocketing car theft rates in Campania (and the parking woes in Naples and the coastal towns), having a car is more of a liability than a asset. Another possibility is renting a car with a driver, an increasingly popular option, particularly for exploring the Sorrento peninsula and the famous Amalfi Drive.

While Naples is usually a port of entry to the region—it is the largest city, and is served by an international airport and harbor—we recommend you keep your exploration of this bustling city for last: Naples can be overwhelming, literally bursting with life and noise, and you'll appreciate it a lot more if you ease yourself slowly into this special cultural universe by starting your visit in smaller towns. Plus, with so much to see in Naples, you might never get to explore the rest of the region. The itineraries below take in all our favorite destinations; you can mix and match them depending on your particular interests and the amount of time you have.

CAMPANIA & THE AMALFI COAST IN 1 WEEK

One week is not long to visit the entire Amalfi Coast region, but you'll certainly be able to get a good idea of its key attractions. Because your time is short, you'll have to pare your exploration to the essentials. You'll miss a lot of the pleasurable lingering, which is so suitable to this region, but you'll have enough time to plunge right into the most phenomenal sights.

You can do a lot of this itinerary by public transportation (including ferries), but you might want to have a car for days 2 and 3, while exploring the region's southern area.

DAYS 1 & 2: Sorrento & the Amalfi Coast

Fly into Naples's Capodichino Airport and get yourself directly to **Sorrento** (there's bus as well as limo service from the airport, or you can rent a car, if you feel more daring). Once there, allow yourself a day of relaxation to recover from jet lag. Wander round the narrow lanes of the old town center, take a swim in the warm sea and, if you are more ambitious, catch a concert in the evening. The best—if you plan in advance to get tickets—are those offered in the cloister of San Francesco (see "Campania Calendar of Events," in chapter 2). On **Day 2,** get an early start and explore the

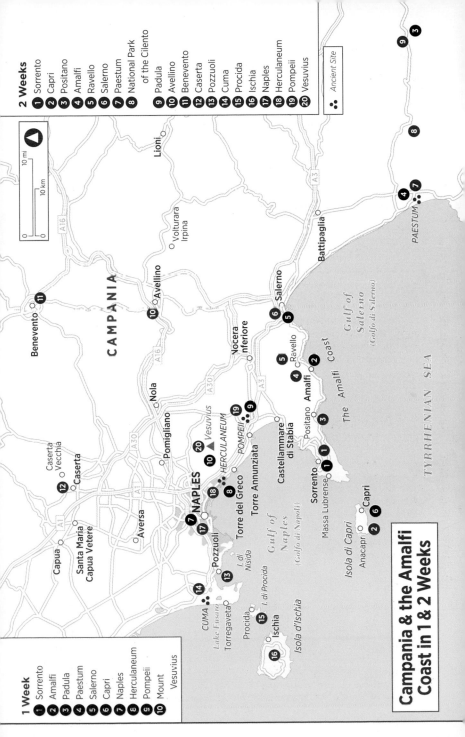

Campania & the Amalfi Coast in 1 & 2 Weeks

1 Week
1. Sorrento
2. Amalfi
3. Padula
4. Paestum
5. Salerno
6. Capri
7. Naples
8. Herculaneum
9. Pompeii
10. Mount Vesuvius

2 Weeks
1. Sorrento
2. Capri
3. Positano
4. Amalfi
5. Ravello
6. Salerno
7. Paestum
8. National Park of the Cilento
9. Padula
10. Avellino
11. Benevento
12. Caserta
13. Pozzuoli
14. Cuma
15. Procida
16. Ischia
17. Naples
18. Herculaneum
19. Pompeii
20. Vesuvius

∴ *Ancient Site*

10 mi

10 km

CAMPANIA

Lioni

Volturara Irpina

Avellino

Benevento

Caserta Vecchia

Caserta

Santa Maria Capua Vetere

Capua

Aversa

Pomigliano

Nola

Battipaglia

Salerno

Nocera Inferiore

Ravello

Amalfi

Positano

The Amalfi Coast

PAESTUM

Gulf of Salerno
(Golfo di Salerno)

TYRRHENIAN SEA

Castellammare di Stabia

Sorrento

Massa Lubrense

Anacapri

Capri

Isola di Capri

Gulf of Naples
(Golfo di Napoli)

Vesuvius

HERCULANEUM

POMPEII

Torre Annunziata

Torre del Greco

NAPLES

Pozzuoli

I. di Nisida

CUMA

Lake Fusaro

Torregaveta

Procida

I. di Procida

Ischia

Isola d'Ischia

53

Sorrento peninsula and **Amalfi Coast.** (Hiring a limo is the best option, as your driver will double as guide.) Hike, swim, and visit the splendid **Amalfi cathedral** (don't miss the interior). You might even have time for some of the smaller towns off the beaten track. Have dinner at one of our favorite restaurants in the area: **Relais Blu, San Pietro, Taverna del Capitano, Ristorante Torre del Saracino,** or **Don Alfonso 1890**—on this stretch of coast, you'll find some of the region's best gourmet haunts, as well as those with the best views. See chapters 6 and 7.

DAY 3: Padula, Paestum & Salerno

In the morning, head to the **Certosa di San Lorenzo** (you can use public transportation, but you'll have to keep a strict timetable; it is best to rent or hire a car) and devote a few hours to this architectural marvel. In the afternoon, drive or take a bus to **Paestum** to visit the stunning temples at sunset—on the way, you'll cross through Cilento National Park. Spend the night in **Salerno** (where you can relinquish your car if you rented one), and have dinner in the **medieval town.** See chapter 9.

DAY 4: Salerno & Capri

After an early stroll through **Salerno,** enjoying its splendid **lungomare,** take a ferry to **Capri,** where you can spend the rest of the day browsing the chic shops and seeing the sights. Stay overnight—this is especially important in summer—to get the full flavor of this mythical island after most of the crowds have gone back to the mainland. See chapters 8 and 9.

DAYS 5 & 6: Naples

The next morning, catch one of the frequent ferry or hydrofoil services to **Naples.** At this point you'll be ready for the big city and its vast artistic riches. Start your visit with the **Maschio Angioino,** not far from the harbor. You might have time for a short visit to both **Palazzo Reale** and the **Museo Nazionale di Capodimonte** before you call it a day. Head down

Salerno.

The Palazzo Reale in Naples.

to the **lungomare** to enjoy the panoramic views of **Borgo Marinari** over a well deserved dinner.

On **Day 6,** have a pizza lunch in one of the nearby historical pizzerie to round out your Old Naples experience. Spend the afternoon at the **Museo Archeologico Nazionale** in preparation for your last day. See chapter 4.

DAY 7: Herculaneum, Pompeii & Mount Vesuvius

For a relaxing, quiet excursion, catch a train on the Circumvesuviana railroad to **Herculaneum;** or go to **Pompeii,** if you like grandiose stretches of excavations. Both sites offer enormous amounts to see—covering both in 1 day is impossible, and we don't recommend trying. Use the other half of your day to climb **Mount Vesuvius,** the burning heart of Campania, and visit one of the ancient Roman villas that lies in its shadow. See chapter 5.

CAMPANIA & THE AMALFI COAST IN 2 WEEKS

Two weeks is an ideal amount of time to explore this culturally and naturally rich region. You'll be able to see some of the best artistic treasures in Italy, but you can also relax and enjoy the sea, coastline, and mountains. We have organized this itinerary so that you can choose whether to rent a car or to use public transportation. If you decide not to rent a car, you can skip the countryside and concentrate on the main destinations, which are all well connected by public transportation. Should you change your mind, you can always hire a car with a driver for a day or two, or rent a car in any big town.

DAY 1: Sorrento

Fly into Naples and take either the bus or a limo service to **Sorrento** (you could rent a car at the airport, but you won't need one until Day 3). Recover from jet lag while relaxing in this splendid resort town: Take in the sights, do some shopping, have a swim. See chapter 6.

DAY 2: Capri

Take a ferry to **Capri,** where you'll spend the night: You'll have a full day to explore this unique island, hike, swim, sunbathe, and shop. See chapter 8.

DAYS 3 & 4: The Sorrento Peninsula & the Amalfi Coast

Take a morning ferry to **Positano,** where you'll visit the town and pick up your car (you can also use public transportation for your exploration, but you'll have to keep a stricter schedule). Spend **Days 3 and 4** taking in **Amalfi, Ravello,** and the lesser-known towns both along the coast and in the interior. See chapters 6 and 7.

DAY 5: Salerno & Paestum

Arrive in **Salerno** in the morning. This town makes a good base for your explorations: Plan to spend 2 nights here.

After a stroll along the **lungomare,** head for the **medieval town** to visit the splendid **cathedral** and have lunch. In the afternoon, arrive in **Paestum,** with its unique temples: Be sure to stay until sunset to enjoy the views. See chapter 9.

DAY 6: Padula & the Cilento

Hire a car to explore the **National Park of the Cilento** and its memorable coast in the morning. Then make your way to the **Certosa di San Lorenzo** for an afternoon visit, crossing through the imposing Cilento massif, with its eerie caves and soaring peaks. You could rely solely on public transportation here, but you'll have to keep to a strict timetable. See chapter 9.

DAYS 7 & 8: Avellino & Benevento

Dedicate **Days 7 and 8** to **Avellino** and **Benevento.** These two towns are each the capital of a sub-region rich in cultural, natural, and artistic

The Park of the Cilento's coastline.

heritage. You could easily dedicate a few days to each; but if you're on a strict schedule, you'll have to satisfy yourself with the highlights. Having a car will allow you to make the most of the area, and you can add a quick tour of the countryside. We recommend that you make time for a visit to the little town of **Sant'Angelo dei Lombardi,** with its castle and famous abbey. Spend Day 8 in **Benevento,** taking in the town's attractions. See chapter 10.

Spiaggia di Citara on Ischia.

DAY 9: Caserta & Surroundings

Leave early in the morning for **Caserta** and start with a visit to the awesome **Reggia** and its gardens. We suggest you also visit the **Cathedral of Casertavecchia** and the **Belvedere di San Leucio,** maybe taking in a concert there if you are visiting during the season and have planned in advance for tickets. See chapter 10.

DAY 10: Pozzuoli, Cuma & the Phlegrean Fields

Arrive in the morning in the splendid Bay of **Pozzuoli,** home to treasures from antiquity and views beloved by Neapolitans. Spend the day visiting the **Parco Archeologico Subacqueo di Baia** and the **Acropolis of Cuma.** (See chapter 5.) In the evening, catch a ferry from Pozzuoli to have dinner on the island of **Procida,** where you can spend the night. See chapter 8.

DAY 11: Ischia

From Pozzuoli (or Procida), catch a ferry to **Ischia.** On the island, hire a local taxi to take you on a tour, or use the excellent public bus system. Then spend a few hours in **Giardini Poseidon**—our favorite outdoor spa on the island—or pick one of the indoor ones we recommend. Then head for the beach: **Spiaggia di Citara** and **Spiaggia dei Maronti** are the best on the island. For dinner, sample the local cuisine and wines. See chapter 8.

DAYS 12 & 13: Naples

In the early morning, catch a ferry to **Naples;** arrive in its famous harbor under the towering shadow of Mount Vesuvius before the sun rises too high, and enjoy the scene in its best light. To see the city, follow **Days 5 and 6** of our "Campania & the Amalfi Coast in 1 Week" itinerary, above.

DAY 14: Herculaneum, Pompeii & Mount Vesuvius

Follow Day 7 of our itinerary for "Campania & the Amalfi Coast in 1 Week."

CAMPANIA & THE AMALFI COAST FOR FAMILIES

If you had any concerns before starting out on this vacation with your kids, they'll melt away as soon as you arrive in this warm and welcoming region. Depending on the attention span and specific interests of your family members, you might have to cut out some artistic attractions, but you'll be more than rewarded with outdoor activities. This itinerary minimizes boring car trips and, instead, relies on ferries—usually more fun for children—to explore the seaside offerings of this region.

DAYS 1 & 2: Ischia

From Naples's Capodichino Airport, take a taxi to Mergellina Harbor where you can catch the ferry to **Ischia.** With lots of water activities and beautiful sandy beaches (instead of the rocky ones on Capri and the Sorrento peninsula), this lesser-known island is more geared to families than its more famous sibling. You'll have your choice of hotels, which are beautiful but less expensive and stuffy than the ones in the region's more glamorous destinations. Pack a picnic lunch and enjoy the views before descending to the beach—**Spiaggia di Citara** and **Spiaggia dei Maronti** are the best on the island. Treat yourself and the kids to some ice cream while strolling along the seaside promenades. See chapter 8.

DAY 3: Capri

Make an early start and catch a ferry to Capri. Spend the rest of the day and night on this mystical island, enjoying its rocky beaches and hiking trails. Climb the **Fenician Staircase** and take a boat tour of the island (much better than waiting in line for the Blue Grotto, if you're there in high season). See chapter 8.

DAY 4: Salerno & Paestum

Catch a ferry to **Salerno** early enough for a leisurely morning: Stroll along the splendid **lungomare** and pay a visit to the noteworthy **cathedral** before having lunch in the **medieval district.** Then catch one of the frequent buses to **Paestum,** where you'll spend the night in one of its seaside hotels. The afternoon is beach time: You can go swimming, if the weather's nice, and then pay a sunset visit to the ancient Greek temples (or save your visit for early the next morning). See chapter 9.

The Fenician Staircase on Capri.

Natural Wonders

1. Vico Equense
2. Punta del Capo
3. Conca dei Marini
4. Furore
5. Capri
6. National Park of the Cilento
7. Paestum
8. Mount Vesuvius
9. Oplontis
10. Boscoreale

For Families

1. Ischia
2. Capri
3. Salerno
4. Paestum
5. Amalfi
6. Naples
7. Herculaneum
8. Pompeii
9. Vesuvius

.. Ancient Site

Campania & the Amalfi Coast for Families and Campania's Natural Wonders

DAY 5: The Amalfi Coast

Hire a car with a driver for a tour of the **Amalfi Coast:** You'll eliminate parking headaches and make the most of your day. You'll want to allot more time to swimming, ice-cream sampling, and hiking than to visiting churches and driving; still, don't miss the splendid **Amalfi cathedral** (see chapter 7). Have the car drop you in Naples for the night.

DAYS 6 & 7: Naples

Follow **Days 5 and 6** of our itinerary for "Campania & the Amalfi Coast in 1 Week," but don't try too hard to pack everything in. Concentrate on the many mighty castles—**Castel Nuovo (the Maschio Angioino), Castel dell'Ovo, Castel Sant'Elmo**—and the church of **San Lorenzo Maggiore,** where you can explore several layers of excavations: Most kids should find this exciting. Also, do not miss a pizza lunch at the historical **Pizzeria di Matteo.** (These are individual pizzas; order one each plus a deep-fried one for the table, to share as an appetizer.) Make sure you take your children on a funicular ride as well, and have dinner in the Vomero area. If you have little ones along, visit the playground in the Villa Comunale on the lungomare. (This was greatly appreciated by our own little guy—so much so that we now have to squeeze in an hour there every day we are in Naples.) There are a couple of sections good for kids in the Certosa di San

Pizzeria di Matteo in Naples.

Martino too; little ones will really enjoy the *presepi* (Christmas cribs) and children and young teens will find the Maritime section interesting, too. See chapter 4.

DAY 8: Herculaneum, Pompeii & Mount Vesuvius

Follow Day 7 of our itinerary for "Campania & the Amalfi Coast in 1 Week." The casts of dead bodies in the museum in **Herculaneum** might be just the thing if your teenagers and preteens are like some we know, but they may disturb younger children. **Pompeii** is a larger and more comprehensive site, but it will be more tiring for younger children. Definitely hire a guide to explore **Mount Vesuvius:** Descending into the crater will thrill older kids, while the nature trails on the north slope of the volcano are fun for all ages. See chapter 5.

CAMPANIA'S NATURAL WONDERS

If you think Campania is all museums, churches, and archaeological areas, you'll miss out on its great natural attractions. This region offers manifold opportunities to combine culture with outdoor activities and superb natural sights. The itinerary below is designed for a week, but you can shorten or lengthen it at your leisure to accommodate your other plans. Driving a car allows the greatest freedom.

DAYS 1 & 2: Vico Equense & the Sorrento Peninsula

Start with one of the lesser-known resorts on the Sorrento peninsula, **Vico Equense,** where you can spend the night and have your first encounter with the sea at **Marina di Equa**—the best beach in town—which is dominated by a powerful 17th-century tower. (If you don't have a car, take the Sorrento-bound bus from Capodichino Airport to Vico Equense.)

Reserve the afternoon for a beautiful hike through the peninsula, taking the moderately challenging footpath from Sorrento toward **Punta Sant'Elia;** this scenic point overlooks the islets of Li Galli in the Bay of Salerno, which have made Positano famous. See chapter 6.

On **Day 2,** continue on to the tip of the peninsula and the beach of **Punta del Capo.** Beloved by the locals, it is located near the ruins of a Roman villa. Nearby, a small pool of water enclosed by rocks is known as the Bath of Queen Giovanna.

In the afternoon, hire a boat from Marina del Cantone to reach the Bay of Ieranto and its marine preserve. You will be rewarded with magical surroundings—when the light is just right toward the end of the day, the boats appear to float in midair. Overnight in Marina del Cantone. See chapter 6.

DAY 3: The Amalfi Coast

Get an early start for your ride along the historic **Amalfi Drive.** Stop for a swim (or have a rowboat take you) into the Grotta dello Smeraldo, in the village of **Conca dei Marini.** Continue with a hike from **Furore** down the ancient footpath to **Marina di Furore,** a deep fiord with a tiny beach at its base. You can then hike the famous Sentiero degli Dei or the Via degli Incanti, and finish your day visiting the natural preserve of Capo d'Orso. From here, walk to the 11th-century monastery and have dinner at the lighthouse. Overnight in Salerno. See chapter 7.

DAY 4: Capri

Take an early morning ferry or hydrofoil to **Capri,** where you'll spend the night. Use the day to explore the island, taking the chairlift up to the top of **Monte Solaro** and descending the famous **Scala Fenicia** into town. End

Amalfi Drive.

Hiking the Vesuvius area.

your day with a swim at the **Bagni di Tiberio,** near the ruins of one of Emperor Tiberius's notorious pleasure palaces. See chapter 8.

DAYS 5 & 6: The Cilento & Paestum

Hop on a ferry early in the morning and rejoin your car in **Salerno.** Head for the **National Park of the Cilento,** starting with the beautiful coast where you can enjoy a variety of watersports, including diving and water-skiing. The best beach is **Baia della Calanca,** in Marina di Camerota. Don't forget the interior, though. Schedule a visit to the **Grottoes of Castelcivita** or **Grottoes of Pertosa** for fantastic spelunking (nothing demanding athleticism or ropes), as well as a hike on **Monte Cervati,** the highest peak of the Cilento massif; another excellent hike is **Monte Alburno.**

Make sure you reserve the afternoon of **Day 6** for **Paestum,** to visit its temples, walk its walls, and swim from one of the best beaches in Italy. See chapter 9.

DAY 7: Mount Vesuvius & Ancient Roman Villas

For your last day, head toward Naples's **Mount Vesuvius** area. Start your visit with **Oplontis** and **Boscoreale**—two excellent sites for exploring ancient Roman ruins—and then take your leave of the region with a hike to the crater of Naples's volcano. What could be more appropriate than ending your trip with a blast? See chapter 5.

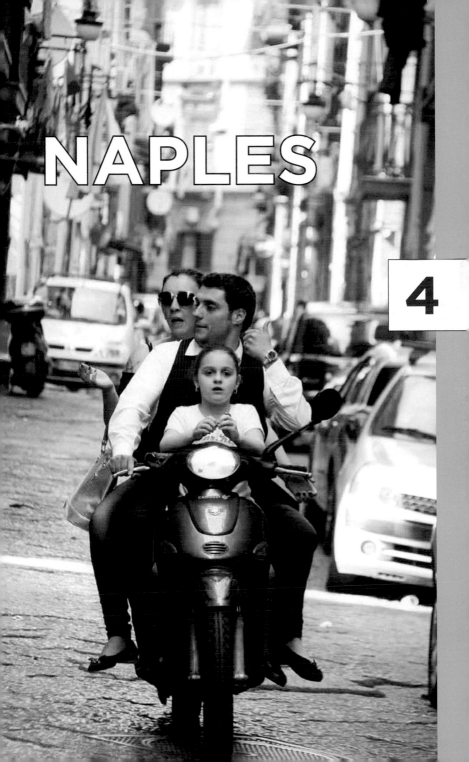

NAPLES

4

Naples is arguably Italy's most vibrant city, and in spite of continuing problems with garbage disposal and crime, it continues to attract visitors for its world-class sights, its natural setting, its food, and its sheer energy. Noisy, chaotic, traffic-clogged, and ,at presstime, dirty, Napoli is also cultured, fascinating, and charming, but if it all becomes too much, you can easily escape to the islands for some calming sea air.

Things to Do The city and its surrounds boast an extraordinary wealth of artistic treasures that span millennia. The remains of the Greek and Roman colonies of Neapolis, the baroque splendor of the **Palazzo Reale,** and the lively contemporary art scene: culture buffs will be kept busy for weeks. Nearby are some of the world's greatest **archaeological sites,** while the magnificent natural beauty of **Vesuvius,** the **Bay of Naples, Capri,** and **Ischia** makes a perfect contrast to the more intellectual attractions.

Shopping In Naples, chic designer stores supply fashionistas with the latest styles, independent boutiques provide something a little more quirky and respected, old-fashioned tailors' shops turn out superbly crafted bespoke suits, shirts, and ties for the city's best-dressed men. Looking for a souvenir to take home? Head to Via San Gregorio Armeno for traditional, intricately crafted Nativity scenes.

Restaurants & Dining The Neapolitans love food and are proud of their culinary traditions. This is home not only to pizza, one of the world's best-loved dishes, but also to Neapolitan ice cream, another universally celebrated culinary export. Restaurants range from elegant temples of creative gourmet cuisine to earthy, back-street *trattorie* where locals tuck into hearty traditional dishes—and don't miss a stand-up snack at one of the chracterful *friggitorie,* which serve deep-fried delicacies sizzling from the pan.

Nightlife & Entertainment The magnificent **Teatro San Carlo** is one of Italy's prime opera houses, while musicals and concerts of traditional Neapolitan music are hosted at **Teatro Bellini.** Naples also has a vibrant **nightlife** scene that encompasses hip, designer-trendy bars serving aperitivi and dinner; grungy student dives with dubious live music acts; and buzzy dance venues that move to the beach in summer.

ESSENTIALS
Getting There

BY PLANE Naples's airport, **Aeroporto Capodichino** (✆ **081-7896259** or 081-7896255; www.gesac.it), is only about 7km (4 miles) from the city center. It is small but well-organized, receiving flights from many Italian and European cities, as well as a few intercontinental flights. See "Getting There"

PREVIOUS PAGE: **Navigating the historic roads and alleys of Naples is best done on foot or by scooter.**

in chapter 11, for more information on airlines that service Capodichino. From the airport, you can easily take a taxi into town (make sure it is an official taxi, white with the Naples municipal logo and a taxi sign on the roof); the flat rate for the 15-minute trip to the station is 15.50€ and to Molo Beverello for ferries to the islands 19€ plus gratuity. Many hotels offer a limousine service, but it is more costly, at about 35€.

If you don't have much luggage to deal with, the convenient Alibus run by the ANM bus company (© 800-639525; www.anm.it) is a viable option (a one-way ticket is 3€). The bus runs to Piazza Municipio in the town center (it stops across from the Teatro Mercadante), with an intermediary stop in Piazza Garibaldi (by the post office at Corso Novara). Buses run every 30 minutes from the airport (Mon–Fri 6:30am–11:39pm; Sat–Sun 6:30am–11:50pm) and from Piazza Municipio (Mon–Fri 6am–11:50pm; Sat–Sun 6am–midnight).

BY TRAIN Naples is on the main southern rail corridor and is served by frequent and fast service from most Italian and European cities and towns. EuroStar trains (marked ES) make very limited stops, InterCity trains (IC) make limited stops, and AltaVelocità (AV) trains are high-speed express trains and are expensive. Regular trains take between 2 and 2½ hours between Rome and Naples, while the AV train takes only 87 minutes, making it by far the best method of transport between the two cities and to destinations farther north. The fare is 44€ one way. The same journey on an Intercity train will cost 22€. Contact **Trenitalia** (© **892021;** www.trenitalia.it) for reservations, fares, and information.

The city has several train stations: **Stazione Centrale** (© 081-5672990 or 892021; www.trenitalia.it), on Piazza Garibaldi, northeast of the city's historical center, is the main railway station for most long-distance trains from all over Italy and Europe. Nearby is the **Stazione Circumvesuviana Napoli-Porta Nolana** (© 800-053939; www.vesuviana.it), on Corso Garibaldi, off Piazza Garibaldi. This is the starting point for commuter lines serving the Vesuvian and coastal area south of Naples, including trains to Sorrento, Pompei, and Ercolano (trains also stop at Napoli Garibaldi, under Naples's Stazione Centrale, which is more convenient by public transportation). The **Stazione Cumana Montesanto** (© 800-053939; www.sepsa.it), in Via Montesanto, off Via Tarsia (west of Via Toledo), receives commuter trains from the Campi Flegrei, including Cuma, Pozzuoli, and Baia. Some long-distance trains also stop at the **Stazione Mergellina** (© 892021), on Piazza Piedigrotta, to the west of Naples's historical center. This station is convenient for transfers to the **ferry** terminal (Terminal Aliscafi). Taxis, subways, and buses connect all these stations with the town center and other destinations nearby (see "Getting Around," later). **Note:** If you are approached by "taxi" drivers—actually gypsy taxis—in the train station, ignore them: They charge outrageous rates and are a source of Naples's bad rap for dishonesty.

BY BOAT Arriving in the Bay of Naples by boat is an unforgettable experience and the best introduction to the city. The major passenger port of central Italy, Naples's **Stazione Marittima** (just off Via Cristoforo Colombo, steps from the Castel Nuovo) receives both cruise ships and regular ferry services from Sicily (Messina, Siracusa Catania, Palermo, and the Aeolian Islands), and Sardinia (Cagliari). Hydrofoil services to Capri, Ischia, Procida, the

Amalfi Coast, and Salerno (all of which are suspended in bad weather) operate from Molo Beverello. Hydrofoil services to Procida and Ischia also operate from Mergellina's **Terminal Aliscafi.** Ferries to and from the gulf islands are served by the new Calata Porta di Massa terminal (just off Via Cristoforo Colombo). See "By Boat," p. 65 for a list of companies. Regularly updated hydrofoil and ferry timetables are published in the excellent local (and free) *Qui Napoli* guide, which you can also access online at www.inaples.it.

BY CAR Car theft—even from guarded parking lots—fierce traffic, and the local passion for speed make driving in Naples a real hassle. Still, arriving or leaving the city by car is not horribly difficult: Major highways connect the city to most other destinations in Italy. From the north, take autostrada A1 MILANO ROMA NAPOLI, whereas from the south take autostrada A3 REGGIO CALABRIA SALERNO NAPOLI. If you are not returning your rental car immediately, you can leave it at your own risk in one of the large and well-posted public parking lots at the city's entrance. The most convenient is the **Parcheggio Brin,** at the Via Brin corner of Via Volta (© **081-7632855;** .30€ per hour or 7.20€ for 24 hr.). Most hotels offer parking which is usually expensive and secure, but driving to your hotel is a challenge best left to those who know the city, with its narrow and labyrinthine streets, pedestrian areas, and confusing one-way systems. Unless you have very precise and up-to-date driving directions or an excellent and recent driving map of Naples (one that marks every street and its driving direction), do not attempt it.

Visitor Information

Naples's Provincial Tourist Office, **EPT,** Piazza dei Martiri 58, by Riviera di Chiaia (© **081-4107211;** www.eptnapoli.info; bus no. 152; Mon–Fri 9am–2pm), maintains tourist booths in the Stazione Centrale (© **081-268779;** Metro: Piazza Garibaldi; Mon–Sat 9am–7pm). They provide basic advice, but **AASCT** (www.inaples.it) has far better information and material. They maintain two excellent tourist information points: **Via San Carlo 9,** off Piazza del Plebiscito (© **081-402394**), and **Piazza del Gesù** (© **081-5512701**), both open Monday to Saturday 9:30am to 6:30pm, Sunday 9:30am to 2pm.

Another excellent resource is the organization **Museo Aperto Napoli** (© **081-5571365;** www.museoapertonapoli.it) although at presstime, this service had been temporarily suspended with no confirmation as to when it will recommence. When active, it runs a cultural center offering free information and guided tours (with a live guide or an audioguide in six languages) of the historical center. It's at Via Pietro Colletta 85 and is typically open daily 10am to 6pm; the center also houses a cafe, bookshop, and small exhibit space selling crafts.

City Layout

A crescent-shaped city resting along the shores of a bay, Naples extends vertically up the steep hills that surround it. Proceeding from west to east, you will find **Posillipo;** then **Mergellina, Chiaia, Santa Lucia;** the **historical center,** with the **Quartieri Spagnoli** along its western side and the **Stazione Marittima** on its southern side; then **Piazza Garibaldi,** with the **Stazione Centrale** and **Stazione Circumvesuviana;** and finally, a number of industrial and poorer neighborhoods.

Above Chiaia and the historical center lies the **Vomero;** farther east is **Capodimonte.** The historical center is the fat part of the crescent, crossed

Piazzetta Nilo's Egyptian statue of the Nile is one of many treasures you'll find in the historic core of Naples.

north-south by three major avenues: **Via Toledo, Via Medina,** and **Via Agostino Depretis.** These are crossed west-east by the continuous **Via Armando Diaz– Via G.Sanfelice–Corso Umberto I** and by the continuous Via Benedetto Croce–Via San Biagio dei Librai, also known as **SpaccaNapoli,** both leading to **Piazza Garibaldi** and the **Stazione Centrale.**

The Neighborhoods in Brief

In this section, we give you a short description of each of Naples's central neighborhoods—including its major monuments—to give you some idea of what each is like and where you might want to stay.

POSILLIPO ★ This residential neighborhood is graced by a number of dramatic villas perched on rocky cliffs over the sea, as well as a few restaurants offering great food and fantastic views.

MERGELLINA ★ Situated well to the west of the historical center, residential Mergellina is served by its own train and hydrofoil stations. It lies near Naples's pleasant marina: The small harbor is lined with restaurants and cafes, where Neapolitans come for dinner by the sea and a romantic promenade.

CHIAIA ★★ Charming and elegant, this neighborhood (which includes the pleasant Villa Comunale public park), is backed by a hillside leading up to Vomero where there are elegant villas and a couple of hotels and restaurants, all of which enjoy dramatic views

The Guglia dell'Addolorata in the Piazza del Gesù.

over the Bay. The shore area along Riviera di Chiaia is famous for its upscale shopping and restaurants around which much of Neapolitan nightlife revolves. The historical center and its monuments are a short ride away on public transportation, but it is also possible to walk.

SANTA LUCIA ★★★ The old fishermen's quarter of Santa Lucia retains some of its original character although the many pavement cafes and restaurants smack of gentrification. The neighborhood is separated from the historical center by steep Monte Echia, which is, in fact, the remains of the rim of a volcanic crater and the site of ancient Paleopolis. It is probably Naples's most famous neighborhood and a favorite with visitors for its waterside location

FROM TOP: The historic center of Naples; Via Partenope.

and splendid views, not to mention its upmarket hotels. **Via Partenope**—the promenade created in the 19th century by filling in part of the harbor—overlooks the Bay and **Castel dell'Ovo** and is lined with elegant hotels and restaurants. **Borgo Marinari,** built in the shadow of the castle, is another popular nighttime spot. Behind the major hotels, you'll find a more authentic neighborhood with grocery shops and cafes frequented by locals.

QUARTIERI SPAGNOLI North of **Piazza del Plebiscito**—the monumental heart of the city—this neighborhood of closely knit narrow streets lies on the western side of **Via Toledo** (called "Via Roma" by Neapolitans). Prior to the 1990s, this area was considered quite dangerous, but the blocks around Via Toledo have experienced an urban renewal, with small hotels and quite a few nice restaurants sprouting up. This budget-friendly area is a perfect base for cost-conscious visitors as it is walking distance from most of Naples's major attractions. The streets farther out, however, still show the original grunginess and are not the best place for your romantic evening stroll.

HISTORICAL CENTER Locally known as the *Decumani,* this is Naples's heart, extending from the **Castel Nuovo** and the **Stazione Marittima** by the sea to the **Museo Archeologico Nazionale** to the north, the **Quartieri Spagnoli** to the west, and **Castel Capuano** to the east. Many of the city's political and administrative offices as well as the University of Naples are here—along with the cascade of small restaurants, bars, and clubs fostered by such institutions. You'll find all of Naples represented here, from the most elegant palaces to pockets of unbelievable grittiness. Many of Naples's major historical and religious attractions are located here, making it a perfect location for visitors. Most of the hotels here are small and housed in historical buildings, but larger and more modern hotels line Via Medina and the parallel Via Agostino Depretis, at the southern edge of this area.

PIAZZA GARIBALDI Across from Naples's main rail station, the Stazione Centrale, this huge square and its surrounding streets are definitely less than glamorous (some of the area, behind the station and away from the main avenues, is positively grungy, with decaying buildings and cheap street vendors lining the narrow lanes, and the nondescript streets by the harbor are dire). It also feels—and *is*—unsafe at night. A number of top-notch hotels catering to businesspeople have opened here, though, and charge a fraction of the price you would pay in Santa Lucia or Chiaia for a similar level of comfort. The neighborhood is very well connected through public transportation to all major tourist destinations both within and outside the city (train station, Metro station, Circumvesuviana rail station—the one to Pompeii and Sorrento—are only steps away). The eastern reaches of the historical center that lie beyond **Castel Capuano** are within walking distance, past a somewhat unsavory belt around the train station (take a taxi after dark). You'll also be near a full range of convenience shopping, from groceries to clothing stores, and a number of good restaurants are in the area. That said, we nevertheless find it too remote.

VOMERO ★ This is the home of the *Napoli bene* (the city's middle and upper classes), and is popular for its fresher air and spectacular views. A quiet, residential neighborhood, Vomero is mostly composed of elegant 19th- and early-20th-century buildings, with good shopping and a few restaurants, plus three famous attractions: the **Castel Sant'Elmo, Certosa SanMartino,** and **Villa Floridiana.**

CAPODIMONTE A middle-class and blue-collar residential neighborhood, this is a good

Heads-Up
Always beware of pickpockets and purse snatchers in Naples; they favor crowded places, such as public transportation and such busy streets as Via Toledo. At night, avoid badly lit and solitary places, because muggings are not unheard of.

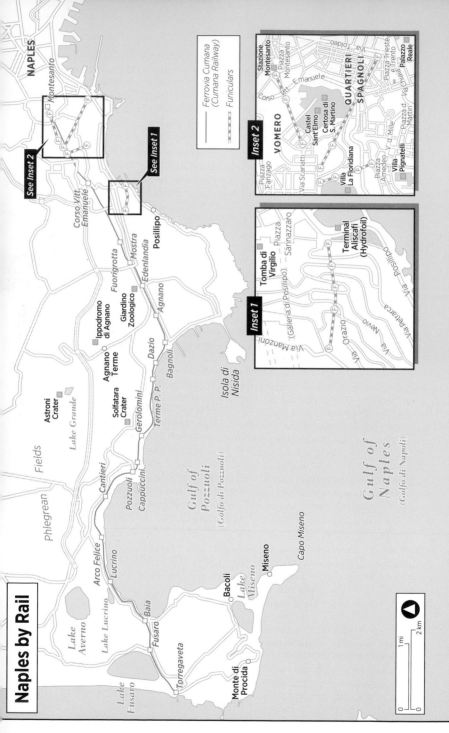

Naples by Rail

— Ferrovia Cumana (Cumana Railway)
▪▪▪ Funiculars

Inset 2

VOMERO

Stazione Montesanto
Piazza Montesanto
Corso Vitt. Emanuele
Castel Sant'Elmo
Certosa di S. Martino
Via Toledo
Piazza Fanzago
Via Scarlatti
Villa La Floridiana
Villa Pignatelli
V. d. Mille
Piazza Amedeo
Piazza d. Martiri
Via Chiaia
Piazza Trieste e Trento
Palazzo Reale

QUARTIERI SPAGNOLI

Inset 1

Tomba di Virgilio
Piazza Sannazzaro
Via Manzoni
(Galleria di Posillipo)
Terminal Aliscafi (Hydrofoil)
Via Orazio
Via Nevio
Via Petrarca
Via Posillipo

NAPLES

Montesanto
Corso Vitt. Emanuele
Fuorigrotta
Mostra
Edenlandia
Agnano
Posillipo

See Inset 2
See Inset 1

Phlegrean Fields

Astroni Crater
Lake Grande
Ippodromo di Agnano
Giardino Zoologico
Agnano Terme
Solfatara Crater
Gerolomini
Dazio
Terme P. P.
Bagnoli
Isola di Nisida

Cantieri
Pozzuoli
Cappuccini
Arco Felice
Lucrino

Gulf of Pozzuoli
(Golfo di Pozzuoli)

Lake Averno
Lake Lucrino
Lake Fusaro

Baia
Fusaro
Torregaveta
Monte di Procida

Bacoli
Lake Miseno
Miseno
Capo Miseno

Gulf of Naples
(Golfo di Napoli)

1 mi
2 km

70

choice in summer, when the air is cooler up in the hills. This is also a good base if you plan to spend a lot of your time in the giant **Museo di Capodimonte** and the wonderful public park that surrounds it. There are plenty of local grocery shops and bars, but only a few hotels and restaurants.

Getting Around

Walking is the best way to explore the historical heart of Naples, which is really quite small. Public transportation works well when you need to travel greater distances and if you want to take in some local color, although at rush hour there might be too much of the latter on the major subway and bus lines. If you have to travel during those hours, take the electric buses that serve the city center and are rarely crowded—or take a taxi.

On Foot Naples is a beautiful city to discover on foot; its attractions are close together and the sea is always in the background. While the free city map offered by the tourist office is perfectly sufficient for your general orientation, we recommend you purchase a more detailed map with a *stradario* (alphabetical list of streets), if you are planning more extensive explorations (see "Fast Facts: Naples," below).

By Public Transportation When you're tired of walking, the best way to get around Naples is its extensive network of public transportation: Buses, trams, subway, and funiculars provide fast transportation to major hubs. **Bus** lines take you everywhere: The R lines (R1, R2, R3, R4) are fast lines with frequent service that stop at major tourist attractions; the electric minibuses (marked E) serve the historic district; C lines serve central Naples, while numbered lines go to the suburbs and are less frequent. All buses operate daily from 5:30am; R lines till midnight, E and some other lines till 11pm. Some lines stop at 8:30pm. A few lines are actually **tramways,** with dedicated tracks, but because of vehicular traffic, these can be as slow as the regular buses. The few *linee notturne* (night lines) start around midnight and run every hour.

Dear to the hearts of Neapolitans is the *funicolare,* a cable railway tunneled through rock to reach the cliffs surrounding the Bay. Three funiculars reach the Vomero: **Montesanto** (at Metro station Montesanto; daily 7am–10pm), **Chiaia** (from Piazza Amedeo; daily 7am–10pm), and **Centrale** (from Via Toledo, off Piazza Trieste e Trento;

Taxi Rates in Naples

The minimum cost of a ride is 4.50€. The meter starts at 3€ on Monday to Saturday from 7am to 10pm; otherwise, the meter starts at 5.50€. It adds .05€ every 65m (213 ft.) or every 10 seconds when waiting or stopped in traffic. Extra charges are .50€ per piece of luggage in the trunk, 1€ for a radio-taxi call (as opposed to you going to a taxi stand), 2.60€ for a ride to the airport, and 3.10€ for a ride from the airport. There are also a number of flat rates, including the following (a card with the complete list is inside each official taxi):

Piazza Municipio to Museo Capodimonte	10.50€
Stazione Centrale to Aliscafi Mergellina	13.50€
Stazione Centrale to Molo Beverello	10.50€
Stazione Centrale to Hotels in Santa Lucia or Chiaia	11.50€

Mon–Tues 6:30am–10pm and Wed–Sun 6:30am–12:30am). **Mergellina** also has a funicular, from Via Mergellina by the harbor up to Via Manzoni (daily 7am–10pm). Also important for negotiating the city are the public elevators and escalators: The *ascensore* (elevator) tucked away in Via Acton, at the corner of Palazzo Reale, ascends to Piazza Plebiscito. On the Vomero, several escalators climb the steepest slopes.

The **Metropolitana** (subway) has two lines, line 1 from Piazza Dante to the Vomero and beyond (daily 6am–11pm) and line 2 from Pozzuoli to Piazza Garibaldi and beyond (daily 5:30am–11pm). At presstime, an extension to line 1 was being constructed with a new station, Università, in Piazza Bovia being inaugurated in March 2011 and another two stations due to open in 2013. You can also use the urban section of the **Cumana** railroad from Montesanto, which is convenient to Mergellina and other coastal locations north of the city center (daily 5am–11pm).

Naples's **Transportation Authority** (℗ **081-5513109;** www.unico campania.it) provides information on all the above and maintains an information booth on Piazza Garibaldi, where you can get an excellent public transportation map. Public transportation tickets are valid on the entire network (see "The Unico Travel Pass," p. 349) and are sold at tobacconists and at some bars and newsstands. A single *biglietto* (ticket) for the city costs 1.20€ and is valid for 90 minutes; a *giornaliero* (day pass) is valid until midnight (the cost is 3.60€ Mon–Sat and 3€ for Sun). The **Artecard** (p. 98) also includes a public transportation pass.

By Taxi Taxis are an excellent, relatively inexpensive way to get around the city. If you've heard that they're dishonest, don't worry; these stories originate with people who have not visited Naples in the past decade or two or who have fallen prey to gypsy cabs. Today, taxis are very reliable and strictly regulated. Official taxis are painted white and marked by the *Comune di Napoli* (Naples municipality). Inside, on the back of the front seat, you'll find a sign listing official flat rates to the seaports, central hotels, and major attractions—although it might be an old sign; refer to "Taxi Rates in Naples," above for current established rates. Also, don't fret if your driver doesn't use the meter—*not* using the meter is legal for all rides that have established flat rates. As elsewhere in Italy, taxis do not cruise but are found at the many taxi stands around town, or, for an extra 1€ surcharge, can be called by phone. Restaurants and hotels will do this for you, but a list of numbers is provided in "Fast Facts: Naples," below. Some of the main taxi stands operating 24 hours are **Piazza Amedeo 8, Piazza Carità** (near Via Cesare Battisti), **Piazza Cavour, Piazza Dante** (by Via Bellini), **Piazza Garibaldi** (by the statue), **Piazza Municipio** (at Via De Pretis), **Teatro San Carlo, Via Santa Lucia** (at corner of Via Nazario Sauro), **Piazza Vanvitelli** (by Via Scarlatti), and **Piazza Vittoria** (by the entrance to Villa Comunale). Other taxi stands close between 2 and 6am or between 11:30pm and 6am.

[Fast FACTS] NAPLES

American Express Every Tours travel agency on Piazza del Municipio 5 (℗ **081-5518564;** bus no. R2 or R3 to Piazza del Municipio) handles American Express business. It's open Monday through Friday from 9:30am to 1pm and 3:30 to 7pm and Saturday 9:30am to 1pm.

Banks Most banks are located in the city center and near the major hotels and have **ATMs** outside their doors. **BNL** (Banca

Nazionale del Lavoro; (℡ **081-7991111**) offers the PLUS network you'll likely need for your ATM card. Its several locations in Naples include Via Toledo 126 and Piazza dei Martiri 23.

Currency Exchange Among the numerous choices in town, the most convenient exchange places are the ones at the airport and around the Stazione Centrale on Piazza Garibaldi (Metro: Piazza Garibaldi). There are four *cambios* (exchanges) on Corso Umberto at nos. 44, 92, 212, and 292 (bus no. R2 to Corso Umberto). Thomas Cook is on Piazza del Municipio (bus no. R2 or R3 to Piazza del Municipio).

Doctors Guardia Medica Specialistica (℡ **081-431111**) is on call 24 hours a day. Consulates maintain a list of English-speaking doctors.

Embassies & Consulates See chapter 11.

Emergencies Call ℡ **113** or **112** for the **police.** For an **ambulance,** call ℡ **118;** for the **fire department** call ℡ **115;** for **first aid** *(pronto soccorso),* call ℡ **118.**

Hospital Ospedale Fatebenefratelli, the central hospital, is at Via Manzoni 220 (℡ **081-5981111**).

Internet Access Centrally located internet points include: Internet Napoli (no phone), Piazza Cavour 146; Internet Plus (no phone), Via F. Morosini 20; Internet Cafè di Napoli (℡ **081-5634836**), Piazza Garibaldi 73.

Laundry & Dry Cleaning Self-service laundromats are on the increase in Naples, but your best bet is a *tintoria* (dry cleaner) or a *lavanderia* (dry cleaner and laundry service). Two good, centrally located businesses are **Lavanderia Speedylava** at Via della Cavallerizza a Chiaia 18 (℡ **081-422405**) and **Lavanderia Suprema** on Via Vannella Gaetani 10 (℡ **081-7643356**)

Mail The **Central Post Office (Ufficio Postale)** is at Piazza Matteotti (℡ **081-4289585;** bus no. R3 to Piazza Matteotti).

Maps You can buy a good map with a *stradario* (street directory) of Naples at any newspaper stand in town (most carry the reliable **Pianta Generale** by N. Vincitorio); if you prefer something smaller, buy the excellent, foldable, credit card–size **Mini-City,** sold at museum shops in town (try the shop at Palazzo Reale).

Newspapers & Magazines Foreign newspapers and magazines are sold at train station kiosks and near the American consulate. Do not miss *QuiNapoli,* the dashing free monthly (bilingual Italian/English) prepared by the city tourist office, which lists all the latest events as well as opening hours of monuments and museums. It's also online at www.inaples.it.

Pharmacies There are several pharmacies open weekday nights and taking turns on weekend nights. A good one is located in the Stazione Centrale (Piazza Garibaldi 11; ℡ **081-440211;** Metro: Piazza Garibaldi).

Police Call ℡ **113** for emergencies or ℡ **112.**

Safety Pickpocketing and car thefts are fairly common throughout Naples. In dark alleys and outside the city center, getting mugged is possible, particularly at night. Steer clear of the area behind the Stazione Centrale at dark, when it gets particularly seedy. The poorest suburbs in the outskirts of Naples to the east and southeast are where crime rates tend to be highest, but these are removed from the major tourist areas.

Smoking Thanks to a 2005 law, smoking is officially banned in public places, bars, restaurants, on public transport, and in taxis. Some restaurants and the odd bar have a separate, closed-off smoking area, but these are few and far between. It must be said that the law is often ignored by smokers.

5707070; www.la570.it); or **Consortaxi** (☏ 081-202020).

Toilets Public bathrooms are basically nonexistent outside museums and major attractions. Your best bet is to use those in bars and cafes; they are reserved for clients, though, so you'll have to buy at least a coffee or a glass of mineral water.

Weather Watch the news, or check out http://meteo.tiscali.it.

WHERE TO STAY
Santa Lucia
VERY EXPENSIVE

Grand Hotel Santa Lucia ★ Next door to the more luxurious Vesuvio (below), this historic hotel offers an old-fashioned atmosphere mixed with elegant decor. The professional service is impeccable, and the public spaces are grand—if a bit dusty and worn in places—and graced by curving staircases, marble floors, and Murano chandeliers. Guest rooms are good size, with wood or carpet floors, period or reproduction furniture, marble bathrooms, and great views over the Castel dell'Ovo and the Bay. Most rooms have balconies to take in the view—they're too small for a table and chairs, though. The buffet breakfast is excellent and the hotel's restaurant is elegant. It must be said that the amenities are not really up to scratch for a hotel of this level and price.

Via Partenope 46 (off Via Santa Lucia by Castel dell'Ovo), 80121 Napoli. www.santalucia.it. ☏ **081-7640666.** Fax 081-7648580. 96 units. 295€–410€ double; from 650€ suite. Extra bed 60€. Children 2 and under stay free in parent's room. Internet specials available. AE, DC, MC, V. Parking 25€. Bus: 152, 140, or C25. **Amenities:** Restaurant; bar; concierge; Internet in lobby (free); room service. *In room:* A/C, TV/VCR/DVD, minibar, Wi-Fi (free).

Grand Hotel Vesuvio ★★ ☺ This elegant hotel may charge steep prices, but it is, in our view, the best in Naples offering exquisite service and accommodations and a sober atmosphere. Even the standard doubles are very roomy (all with large marble bathrooms and Jacuzzi tubs), and come furnished with special details such as linen sheets and extra-firm mattresses. Superior rooms and suites have large balconies from which you can enjoy some of the best views in Naples over Borgo Marinari or Mount Vesuvius. The breakfast buffet—served in a delightful bright room with a view of the harbor—is superb and includes several kinds of freshly squeezed juice, fresh fruit, bacon, and eggs, along with oven-fresh Neapolitan pastries, local cheeses and cold cuts, and a variety of breads. There is a wonderful spa and the hotel's gourmet restaurant, the Caruso Roof Garden has recently undergone refurbishment and is now a splendid place to enjoy both superb food and fabulous views.

Via Partenope 45 (off Via Santa Lucia by Castel dell'Ovo), 80121 Napoli. www.vesuvio.it. ☏ **081-7640044.** Fax 081-7644483. 160 units. 230€–460€ double; from 600€ suite. Rates include buffet breakfast. Children 2 and under stay free in parent's room. Internet specials available. AE, DC, MC, V. Parking 25€. Bus: 152, 140, or C25. **Amenities:** 2 restaurants; bar; babysitting; concierge; fitness center & spa; pool (for a fee); room service; smoke-free rooms. *In room:* A/C, TV/VCR/DVD, minibar, Wi-Fi (3€/30 min.; 10€/8 hr.).

Hotel Excelsior ★★ ☺ In our opinion, this Starwood property has more of a feeling of old-fashioned glamour than its sister hotel, the Vesuvius, and its prices are slightly lower. It shares the same spectacular waterfront location and gorgeous views and also has a splendid roof garden. The bedrooms are all a good size and tastefully decorated and come with all the amenities you would expect for this price including fine linen sheets and marble bathrooms. Front-facing rooms overlook the Castel dell'Ovo while ones on the side have full-on views of Vesuvius; take your pick. The rooftop Terrazza restaurant is a splendid place for a celebratory gourmet meal, and guests can use the spa facilities at the Vesuvius (for a fee).

Via Partenope 48 (off Via Santa Lucia, by Castel dell'Ovo), 80121 Napoli. www.excelsior.it. ℭ **081-7640111.** Fax 081-7649743. 121 units. 200€–400€ double; from 550€ suite. Rates include buffet breakfast. Children 2 and under stay free in parent's room. AE, DC, MC, V. Parking 23€. Bus: 152, 140, or C25. **Amenities:** Restaurant; bar; babysitting; concierge; health club; room service; smoke-free rooms. *In room:* A/C, TV/VCR/DVD, minibar.

Royal Continental ★ This hotel was built by the famous modernist architect Gio Ponti in the 1950s and lies just a few doors away from the two more famous hotels listed above; the front rooms share the wonderful views of the Castel dell'Ovo. It may not have the architectural charm or stately elegance of the older hotels, but the clean lines and modernity of the well-appointed accommodations and the swimming pool on the roof make up for that. Standard rooms are spacious and full of light, and open onto a private balcony, and although they lack the splendid views of the superior rooms, some of them come with nice hardwood flooring. The four executive rooms each have a delightful large private terrace. All rooms have spacious marble bathrooms (some of them with shower only), and a few have Jacuzzi tubs.

Via Partenope 38 (off Via Santa Lucia), 80121 Napoli. www.royalcontinental.it ℭ **081-2452068.** Fax 081-7644616. 400 units. 120€–250€ double; from 200€ junior suite; from 300€ suite. 1 child 2 and under stays free in parent's room. Internet specials available. Parking 20€. Bus: 152, 140, or C25. Dogs accepted. **Amenities:** Restaurant; bar; babysitting; concierge; fitness center; pool; room service. *In room:* A/C, TV, minibar, Wi-Fi (1st 30 min. free; 8.50€/24 hr.).

MODERATE

Hotel Miramare ★ 🦋 Located on the waterfront overlooking the Bay and Vesuvius, this small, elegant hotel offers excellent value and warm service. Originally a private villa built in 1914, it briefly housed the American consulate before opening as a hotel in 1944. The public areas are still decorated in Liberty (Italian Art Nouveau) style, but guest rooms have been renovated, each with its own whimsical assortment of furniture. The attentive family management is reflected in such little touches as cool linen sheets in the summer, and you will be offered an aperitivo in the evening. The rooms overlooking the sea have splendid views, and all those above the mezzanine level are graced by private balconies. We recommend the deluxe rooms, which are oversize, with large balconies, and have bathrooms with tub and shower—others have only a shower. In clement weather, breakfast is served on the roof terrace overlooking the Bay. You'll get special treatment at the restaurants run by the owner's brothers: **La Cantinella** (p. 89), **La Piazzetta, Il Posto Accanto, Rosolino,** and **Putipù.** They all feature Neapolitan cuisine and pizza, and a couple double as nightclubs.

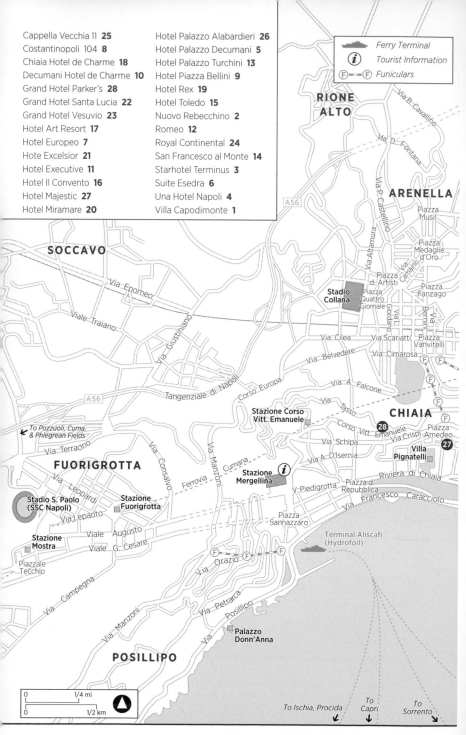

Cappella Vecchia 11 **25**
Costantinopoli 104 **8**
Chiaia Hotel de Charme **18**
Decumani Hotel de Charme **10**
Grand Hotel Parker's **28**
Grand Hotel Santa Lucia **22**
Grand Hotel Vesuvio **23**
Hotel Art Resort **17**
Hotel Europeo **7**
Hote Excelsior **21**
Hotel Executive **11**
Hotel Il Convento **16**
Hotel Majestic **27**
Hotel Miramare **20**

Hotel Palazzo Alabardieri **26**
Hotel Palazzo Decumani **5**
Hotel Palazzo Turchini **13**
Hotel Piazza Bellini **9**
Hotel Rex **19**
Hotel Toledo **15**
Nuovo Rebecchino **2**
Romeo **12**
Royal Continental **24**
San Francesco al Monte **14**
Starhotel Terminus **3**
Suite Esedra **6**
Una Hotel Napoli **4**
Villa Capodimonte **1**

Ferry Terminal
Tourist Information
Funiculars

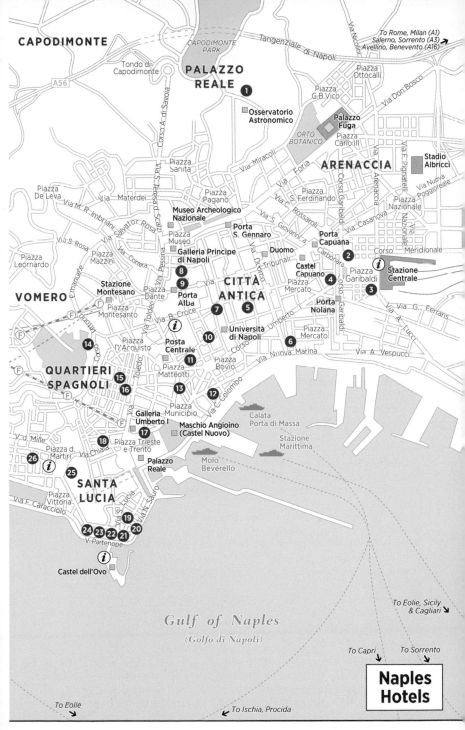

CAPODIMONTE

To Rome, Milan (A1)
Salerno, Sorrento (A3)
Avellino, Benevento (A16)

CAPODIMONTE
PARK

Tondo di
Capodimonte

Piazza
Ottocalli

PALAZZO
REALE ❶

Piazza
G.B. Vico

Osservatorio
Astronomico

Palazzo
Fuga

ORTO
BOTANICO

Piazza
Carlo III

Stadio
Albricci

ARENACCIA

Piazza
Sanità

Piazza
Nazionale

Piazza
De Leva

Piazza
Pagano

Porta
Capuana

Museo Archeologico
Nazionale

Corso Meridionale

Porta
S. Gennaro

❷

Piazza
Museo

Duomo

Stazione
Centrale

Piazza
Leonardo

Galleria Principe
di Napoli

❸

Piazza
Mazzini

❽

Castel
Capuano

Piazza
Garibaldi

CITTÀ
ANTICA

❹

VOMERO

Stazione
Montesano

❾

Piazza
Dante

Porta
Alba

Piazza
Mercato

Piazza
Montesanto

❼

❺

Porta
Nolana

Università
di Napoli

❿

Piazza
Mercato

❻

⓮

Posta
Centrale

Piazza
D'Arquisto

⓫

Piazza
Bovio

QUARTIERI
SPAGNOLI

⓭

Piazza
Matteotti

⓯

⓬

⓰

Piazza
Municipio

Calata
Porta di Massa

Galleria
Umberto I

Maschio Angioino
(Castel Nuovo)

Stazione
Marittima

⓲

Piazza Trieste
e Trento

⓱

V. d. Mille

Piazza d.
Martiri

Palazzo
Reale

Molo
Beverello

㉖

㉕

SANTA
LUCIA

Piazza
Vittoria

㉔㉓㉒㉑⓴⓳

Castel dell'Ovo

V. Partenope

Gulf of Naples

(Golfo di Napoli)

To Eolie, Sicily
& Cagliari

To Capri   To Sorrento

To Eolie

To Ischia, Procida

Naples
Hotels

Via Nazario Sauro 24 (off Via Santa Lucia, by Castel dell'Ovo), 80132 Napoli. www.hotelmira mare.com. ℂ **081-7647589.** Fax 081-7640775. 18 units. 185€–299€ double. Rates include buffet breakfast. Children 5 and under stay free in parent's room. Weekend and Internet specials available. AE, DC, MC, V. Parking 20€ in nearby garage. Bus: 152. **Amenities:** Bar; airport pickup (40€); babysitting; concierge; room service; Wi-Fi (free). *In room:* A/C, TV/VCR (free videos in lobby), minibar, Wi-Fi (free).

INEXPENSIVE

Hotel Rex ☺ 🦴 This hotel is a steal: In a 19th-century palace by the most famous harborside area of Naples, only steps from the top-notch hotels of Via Partenope (see above), it offers spacious accommodations at moderate prices. Word has gotten out about this family-run spot, and it's very popular, especially with groups, so you must reserve well in advance. Guest rooms are simply but carefully decorated; some come with views over the harbor or Mount Vesuvio, and some come with private balconies. Bathrooms are modern and roomy. A simple continental breakfast, served in your room, is included in the rates. Up to two extra beds can be added to a room for the same price.

Via Palepoli 12 (off Via Santa Lucia, by Castel dell'Ovo), 80132 Napoli. www.hotel-rex.it. ℂ **081-7649389.** Fax 081-7649227. 33 units. 150€ double. Rates include continental breakfast. Children 3 and under stay free in parent's room. Internet specials available. AE, DC, MC, V. Parking 20€ in nearby garage. Bus: 152. **Amenities:** Bar; babysitting; concierge. *In room:* A/C, TV, minibar.

Chiaia

EXPENSIVE

Grand Hotel Parker's ★ A landmark building in Liberty (Italian Art Nouveau) style, this glorious villa, which served as Allied headquarters during World War II, still features most of its original architectural details and statuary. The public spaces are splendid and definitely worth a visit, even if you are not staying in the hotel. The spacious guest rooms fronting the Bay share the same spectacular views as the public areas and are decorated with elegant period furniture (different floors are decorated in various styles—Louis XIV, Empire, and so on). Suites are truly elegant duplex apartments on two levels. The back rooms, however, are unremarkable and overlook the garage. The fine spa offers hydrotherapy treatments, all kinds of massages and includes a sauna and Turkish bath. **George's** (p. 88), on the roof, is widely considered to be one of Naples's best restaurants, although for everyday dining, we generally prefer a more down-to-earth atmosphere. The bar has a separate cigar room.

Corso Vittorio Emanuele 135 (up the cliff from Riviera di Chiaia), 80121 Napoli. www.grand hotelparkers.com. ℂ **081-7612474.** 82 units. 300€ double; from 350€ suite. Rates include buffet breakfast. Children 1 and under stay free in parent's room. Internet specials available. AE, DC, MC, V. Parking 20€–30€. Bus: C24 or C27 to Via Tasso-Corso Vittorio Emanuele II. Metro: Piazza Amedeo. **Amenities:** Restaurant; bar; babysitting; concierge; health club; room service; smoke-free rooms; spa. *In room:* A/C, TV/VCR/DVD, fax, minibar.

MODERATE

Hotel Majestic Popular with Italian businesspeople and travelers alike, this hotel is located at the end of the elegant shopping strip in the lower part of Chiaia and offers upscale accommodations. The large guest rooms are decorated with low-key elegance, sporting hardwood floors, streamlined modern furniture, and marble bathrooms. Many of the rooms afford great views of the Bay. **La Giara,** the hotel's restaurant, serves good, creative food.

Largo Vasto a Chiaia 68 (off Riviera di Chiaia), 80121 Napoli. www.majestic.it. ℂ **081-416500.** Fax 081-410145. 112 units. 160€–300€ double; 300€–450€ suite. Rates include buffet breakfast. Children 2 and under stay free in parent's room. Internet specials available. AE, DC, MC, V. Parking 25€. Metro: Piazza Amedeo. **Amenities:** Restaurant; bar; babysitting; concierge; room service. *In room:* A/C, TV/VCR, minibar.

Hotel Palazzo Alabardieri ★ A stylish hotel with a great, central location, the Alabardieri is housed in the ancient cloister of what was once the convent of Santa Caterina a Chiaia. Sleek marble floors in the public areas contrast with the warm hardwood floors in the guest rooms, which are furnished with period furniture and color-coordinated in earth tones and pastel colors. We particularly like the junior suites with their stylish furnishings and designer accents. All units come with good-size marble bathrooms.

Via Alabardieri 38 (off Riviera di Chiaia), 80121 Napoli. www.palazzoalabardieri.it. ℂ **081-415278.** Fax 081-401478. 33 units. 190€–220€ double; 320€ junior suite. Rates include buffet breakfast. Children 2 and under stay free in parent's room. Children ages 3–11 stay in parent's room for 20€ each. Internet specials available. AE, DC, MC, V. Parking 30€. Metro: Piazza Amedeo. **Amenities:** Bar; babysitting; concierge; room service. *In room:* A/C, TV, Internet, minibar.

San Francesco al Monte You cannot beat the atmosphere of this elegant hotel housed in an ex-Franciscan convent, nor the hillside location that overlooks the Riviera di Chiaia; the views are quite spectacular, particularly from the terrace (often booked for wedding receptions) with its restaurant and heart-shaped swimming pool. The tastefully furnished guest rooms (some with just shower) open onto the Bay and occupy the surprisingly roomy ex-monk's cells; they have tiled floors and lots of wood. Some are highlighted with original architectural details, such as an arched doorway or a rounded window. The hotel's restaurant, **Terrazza dei Barbanti,** serves a creative take on local dishes and has matchless views over the Bay.

Corso Vittorio Emanuele 328 (up the cliff from Riviera di Chiaia), 80135 Napoli. www.san francescoalmonte.it. ℂ **081-4239111.** Fax 081-4239471. 45 units. 195€–225€ double; 270€ suite. Rates include buffet breakfast. AE, DC, MC, V. **Parking 25€.** Metro: Piazza Amedeo. **Amenities:** Restaurant; bar; babysitting; pool; room service; smoke-free rooms. *In room:* A/C, TV/ DVD, Internet, minibar.

INEXPENSIVE

Capella Vecchia 11 📠 It turns out there *is* such a thing as a good-value hotel in Chiaia, as we found out when we visited this delightful little B&B situated just off elegant Piazza dei Martiti. Run by a young, super-friendly couple who will help you find your way around the city, it has six bright, comfortable bedrooms with mosaic bathrooms (shower only). You can choose to have breakfast in your room or at a big table in the communal area. This is a great choice if you are driving; there's a big car park almost next door.

Via Santa Maria a Cappella Vecchia 11, 80121 Napoli. www.cappaellavecchia11.it. ℂ **081- 2405117.** Fax 081-2455338. 6 units. 90€–100€ double. Rates include buffet breakfast. AE, MC, V. Parking 18€. **Amenities:** Internet. In room: A/C, TV, Wi-Fi (free), minibar.

Piazza del Plebiscito

EXPENSIVE

Hotel Art Resort Galleria Umberto ★ Smack in the heart of the city and housed on the upper floors of historic Galleria Umberto I (p. 115), this upmarket hotel is steps from many Naples attractions. Access is via a charming hidden entrance inside the gallery and an early-20th-century elevator. The hotel is lavishly decorated in an eclectic style and each of its rooms is dedicated to an artist, from Klee to van Gogh. Rooms with windows overlooking the gallery can be a bit dark, while those facing the street are a bit noisy, but the quality of the furnishings and decor—think four-poster beds, marble floors, and splendid bathrooms—compensates.

Galleria Umberto I 83 (off Via Toledo), 80132 Napoli. www.artresortgalleriaumberto.it. © **081-4976224.** Fax 081-4976281. 16 units. 120€–145€ double; 145€–175€ junior suite. Rates include buffet breakfast. Children 2 and under stay free in parent's room. Internet specials available. AE, DC, MC, V. Parking 25€ in nearby garage. Bus: R2 to Piazza Municipio. **Amenities:** Babysitting; concierge. *In room:* A/C, TV/VCR, minibar, Wi-Fi (free).

Quartieri Spagnoli

MODERATE

Hotel Il Convento ★ ☺ This family-run hotel, housed in a 17th-century former convent, offers pleasant accommodations at moderate prices in the heart of Naples. The pastel-hued guest rooms feature original architectural details such as wooden beams and brick arches and the two top-floor junior suites have delightful private roof gardens. There are also two family rooms with loft bedrooms. All have modern bathrooms. The breakfast buffet includes breads and jams, fruit, cold cuts, and cheese. Guests have access to the sauna facility at the Hotel Executive (see below) and can check their e-mail in the reception area.

Via Speranzella 137/a (2 short blocks west of Via Toledo/Via Roma), 80134 Napoli. www.hotel ilconvento.com. © **081-403977.** Fax 081-400332. 14 units. 83€–110€ double; 125€ junior suite. Rates include buffet breakfast. Children 2 and under stay free in parent's room. Internet and family specials available. AE, DC, MC, V. Parking 15€ in nearby garage. Small pets allowed. Bus: R2 to Piazza Municipio. **Amenities:** Bar; concierge; fitness room & sauna; room service. *In room:* A/C, satellite TV/VCR, minibar.

INEXPENSIVE

Hotel Toledo ️ This small, picturesque hotel is on a narrow side street off Via Toledo. Sharing the same convenient location as the Hotel Il Convento (above), it is less charming than its neighbor, but makes up for it with lower rates and good service. Guest rooms are good size and clean, with adequate if uninspired furnishings, and modern, tiled bathrooms (shower only). The hotel also has excellent amenities for this price level, including a pleasant roof garden and free Internet for guests.

Via Montecalvario 15 (off west side of Via Toledo/Via Roma), 80134 Napoli. www.hoteltoledo. net. ©/fax **081-406800.** 35 units. 65€–100€ double; 120€ suite. Rates include buffet breakfast. Children 2 and under stay free in parent's room. Internet specials available. AE, MC, V. Parking 25€ in nearby garage. Bus: R2 to Piazza Municipio. **Amenities:** Restaurant; bar; fitness room. *In room:* A/C, TV, minibar, Wi-Fi (free).

Citta Antica

VERY EXPENSIVE

Romeo If you like your luxury to come with a good dose of high-tech style, the sleek Romeo is the hotel for you. Situated on the edge of the old city, it is housed in a modern building overlooking the new tourist port, an area which is a bit shady at night but which is at present well on its way into a new development project.

The open plan public spaces on the ground floor are filled with the owner's impressive collection of contemporary art plus some priceless antiques and include a sushi bar and a new games room area with pool table. The super-contemporary bedrooms and slick, glassed-in bathrooms (some shower-only) come with every conceivable gadget including a sheet and pillow menu and Nespresson coffee machines; we highly recommend paying the extra for one at the front of the building where floor-to-ceiling windows look over the Bay of Naples and Vesuvius. We also advise splashing out on a meal at the hotels's 10th-floor gourmet restaurant, Il Commandante. The fabulous new spa offers all sorts of treatments and there's a pool on the roof.

Via Cristoforo Colombo 45, 80132 Naples. www.romeohotel.it. © **081-0175008.** Fax 081-0175999. 83 units. 240€–300€ double. Rates include breakfast. AE, DC, MC, V. Parking 36€ in nearby garage. Metro: Univerista. **Amenities**: 2 restaurants; bar; concierge; fitness center & spa; pool; room service; smoke-free rooms. *In room:* A/C, TV/DVD, minibar, Wi-Fi (free).

EXPENSIVE

Hotel Palazzo Turchini This centrally located hotel offers modern accommodations inside the shell of a 17th-century palace, once part of an orphanage specializing in musical studies. Guest rooms have been redone using state-of-the-art technology to completely soundproof them; all have hardwood floors and are furnished with a stylish mix of modern and period furniture. The marble bathrooms are good size, some with showers and others with Jacuzzi bathtubs. We prefer the executive doubles which are larger and brighter than the "classics," which mostly open onto light shafts and the narrow street. Some executive doubles come with small private terraces, others with lounge areas. There are a few rooms available for those with limited mobility. Breakfast is served on the roof terrace in clement weather.

Via Medina 21, off Piazza Municipio, 80132 Napoli. www.palazzoturchini.it. © **081-5510606.** Fax 081-5521473. 26 units. 260€–300€ double; 340€ suite. Rates include buffet breakfast. Internet specials available. Children 10 and under stay free in parent's room. AE, DC, MC, V. Parking 25€ in nearby garage. Bus: C57, E3, or R3 to Via Medina. **Amenities:** Bar; concierge; room service. *In room:* A/C, TV, minibar, Wi-Fi (free).

MODERATE

Chiaia Hotel de Charme ★ Elder sister to the Decumani Hotel de Charme (see below), this cosy place enjoys an equally good, if a little more upmarket, location on the smart pedestrian-only Via Chiaia. It occupies the first floor of a building with a colourful past that stands on a quiet courtyard: It was once a brothel and the price list is still on display! The reception area, sitting areas, and breakfast room are done out in warm, welcoming colors and the bedrooms are equally inviting. Superior rooms have big bathrooms, some with Jacuzzi tubs (others shower only). Breakfast is excellent and complimentary Neapolitan pastries are laid out in the sitting room in the afternoon.

Via Chiaia 216, 80132 Napoli. www.hotelchiaia.it. © **081-415555.** Fax 081-422344. 33 units. 145€–165€ double. Rates include buffet breakfast. Children under 2 stay free in parent's room. AE, DC, MC, V. Parking 18€ in nearby garage. Bus: R2. **Amenities:** Bar; concierge. *In room:* A/C, TV, minibar, Wi-Fi (free).

Costantinopoli 104 ★ 📱 Located in the heart of the historical center, this charming small hotel is one of our favorites in the city and occupies a 19th-century Italian Art Nouveau palace that once belonged to a marquis. Once inside the tall gates, you will find a luxurious haven of peace and a true refuge from the city's noise and grime. Public spaces have the atmosphere of a palatial private home, from the living room with its fireplace to the private courtyard with palm trees, chaise longues, and a bean-shaped swimming pool. Some guest rooms open onto the terrace where breakfast is served in fair weather, and others have private balconies. All are medium-size and individually decorated with modern furnishings and hardwood floors or hand-painted tiles: the suites have Jacuzzi tubs. Room service shows excellent attention to detail, with homemade liquors and ice cream and a fabulous breakfast.

Via Santa Maria di Costantinopoli 104 (off Piazza Bellini), 80134 Napoli. www.costantinopoli104. com. *©* **081-5571035.** Fax 081-5571051. 19 units. 160€ double; 210€ suite. Rates include buffet breakfast. AE, DC, MC, V. Parking 25€. Metro: Piazza Dante. **Amenities:** Babysitting; concierge; Internet (free); pool; room service; smoke-free rooms. *In room:* A/C, TV, Internet, minibar.

Decumani Hotel de Charme 🛎 The palatial home of the last bishop of the

Bourbon kingdom, Cardinal Sisto Riario Sforza, was recently renovated as an elegant and moderately priced hotel. The good-size rooms (some shower only) are furnished with period furniture and a few antiques, and many feature original architectural details and decorations. The location—just off the SpaccaNapoli—is great if you want to be in the thick of things.

Via San Giovanni Maggiore Pignatelli 15 (off Via Benedetto Croce, btw. Via Santa Chiara and Via Mezzocannone), 80134 Napoli. www.decumani.it. *©* **081-5518188.** Fax 081-5518188. 22 units. 124€–144€ double. MC, V. Rates includes breakfast. Children 3 and under stay free in parent's room. Children 12 and under 12€. Internet specials available. AE, MC, V. Parking 25€ in nearby garage. Metro: Piazza Dante. *In room:* A/C, TV, minibar, Wi-Fi (free).

Hotel Executive ⚓ This comfortable hotel enjoys an excellent location in cen-

tral Naples and offers a lot for its price, making it a good address for both moderately oriented business travelers and tourists. Guest rooms are nicely appointed, with tiled floors, tasteful modern furniture, and good-size, modern bathrooms (shower only). The one available suite is definitely "executive" level, with two balconies as well as a Jacuzzi tub. The hotel also offers a sizeable sauna and a delightful roof garden, where breakfast is served in good weather.

Via del Cerriglio 10 (btw. Via Monteoliveto and Piazza G. Bovio [Corso Umberto]), 80134 Napoli. www.hotelexecutivenapoli.com. *©* **081-5520611.** 19 units. 110€–120€ double; 180€ suite. Rates include buffet breakfast. Internet specials available. Children 2 and under stay free in parent's room. AE, DC, MC, V. Parking 25€. Bus: R2, CS, CD, or C25 to Via San Felice. Small pets accepted. **Amenities:** Bar; concierge; sauna. *In room:* A/C, TV, minibar.

Hotel Palazzo Decumani ★ This elegant, relatively new hotel lies in the heart

of Old Naples, steps from many of the attractions to be found in the historic center. Its restoration successfully complements the original architecture of the palazzo with sophisticated contemporary furnishings. Guest rooms are spacious and bright, with state-of-the-art comforts, including elegant marble bathrooms.

Piazza Giustino Fortunato 8 (btw. Vico San Severino and Via Duomo, off Via San Biagio dei Librai), 80100 Napoli. www.palazzodecumani.com. *©* **081-4201379.** Fax 081-7901540. 28 units. 140€–200€ double; 230€ junior suite. MC, V. Rates include buffet breakfast. Internet and seasonal specials available. Parking 25€. Metro: Piazza Dante. **Amenities:** Bar; smoke-free rooms; Wi-Fi (free). *In room:* A/C, TV, Internet, minibar.

INEXPENSIVE

Hotel Europeo/Europeo Flowers 🏷 It would be difficult to find nicer budget-friendly accommodations in Naples. Close to SpaccaNapoli and all the central sights, this modest hotel (technically two) offers good-size rooms that are adequate and tastefully appointed. The catch? It doesn't have public spaces, and it is on the fourth and fifth floors of a residential building. Yet, if you can do without breakfast and a lounge, the only drawback is that you'll need a small reserve of .10€ coins to operate the elevator. The Europeo Flowers has A/C and the largest rooms, which can accommodate up to four persons.

Via Mezzocannone 109 and 109/c (btw. Corso Umberto and Via San Biagio dei Librai), 80134 Napoli. www.sea-hotels.com. ✆ **081-5517254.** Fax 081-5522212. 17 units. 105€ double; 110€ triple; 114€–130€ quad. Internet specials available. Children 6 and under stay free in parent's room. AE, DC, MC, V. Parking 25€ in nearby garage. Small pets accepted. Metro: Piazza Dante. **Amenities:** Concierge; Wi-Fi (free). *In room:* A/C, TV, minibar (in some).

Hotel Piazza Bellini 🏷 This stylish, contemporary hotel occupies an elegant grey-and-white 16th-century palazzo with a great location right on trendy Piazza Bellini. We like the minimalist yet welcoming rooms with their warm hardwood floors and designer furniture: Some have balconies overlooking the buzzy piazza; four others have big private terraces equipped with sunbeds and showers. The duplex rooms are good for families. Bathrooms (some with shower only) are slick and modern. There are three Internet points in the sitting room, and in summer you can sit out and enjoy breakfast or a drink in the lovely atrium.

Via Costantinioli 101, 80134 Napoli. www.hotelpiazzabellini.com. ✆ **081-451732.** Fax 081-4420107. 48 units. 100€–150€ double. AE, DC, MC, V. Metro: Piazza Dante or Piazza Cavour. **Amenities:** Bar; concierge; Wi-Fi and Internet points (free). *In room:* A/C, TV, minibar, Internet connec-tion (free).

Suite Esedra 🏷 This pleasantly cozy small hotel offers moderately priced rooms in a centrally located aristocratic palace that has been completely restored. Bedrooms, with astronomy motifs, are tastefully furnished, with excellent care to details; some have sweet little balconies. Of the two suites, Venus offers a fantastic private terrace equipped with a small pool. Breakfast is served in a pleasant common room. The drawback? The thundering traffic on nearby Corso Umberto I.

Via Arnaldo Cantani 12 (btw. Via Nuova Marina and Corso Umberto), 80134 Napoli. www.esedra. hotelsinnapoli.com. ✆/fax **081-5537087.** Fax 081-5537087. 17 units. 65€–70€ double. Rates include buffet breakfast. Internet specials available. Children 5 and under stay free in parent's room. AE, DC, MC, V. Parking 15€ in nearby garage. Metro: Piazza Garibaldi or Università. **Amenities:** Bar; concierge; health club. *In room:* A/C, TV, minibar.

Piazza Garibaldi

MODERATE

Starhotel Terminus ☺ A member of the Italian Starhotel group, this hotel offers elegant accommodations with full amenities for both business and leisure travelers as well as excellent service. The spacious guest rooms are stylishly furnished, with warm wood, modern furniture, tasteful carpeting and fabrics, and elegant bathrooms. The "executive" doubles have extras such as trouser presses, a second TV in the bathroom, a cutting-edge CD/DVD system, and a complimentary tea/coffee/hot chocolate tray. The panoramic restaurant and bar on the roof garden have become quite a hit with Neapolitan socialites (see "Naples After Dark," later in this chapter).

Piazza Garibaldi 91 (beside Stazione Centrale), 80142 Napoli. www.starhotels.com/terminus. *©* **081-7793111.** Fax 081-206689. 173 units. 160€–210€ double; 250€ junior suite; 300€ suite. Rates include buffet breakfast. Internet specials available. Children 11 and under stay free in parent's room. AE, DC, MC, V. Free parking in garage. Metro: Garibaldi. Small pets accepted. **Amenities:** Restaurant; bar; babysitting; concierge; fitness room; room service, Wi-Fi (free). *In room:* A/C, TV, minibar, Wi-Fi (5.50€/hour).

Una Hotel Napoli ★ On the opposite end of Piazza Garibaldi to the Terminus (see above), this stylish, contemporary hotel occupies a 19th-century *palazzo.* Located near both the Stazione Centrale and the Circumvesuviana stations, its pleasant public spaces include a panoramic roof terrace with a trendy bar and restaurant. The spacious guest rooms are stylish, with a streamlined modern design and neutral color scheme. The good-size bathrooms are ultramodern.

Piazza Garibaldi 9 (opposite Stazione Centrale), 80142 Napoli. www.unahotels.it. *©* **081-5636901.** Fax 081-5636972. 89 units. 115€–160€ double; 330€ suite. Rates include buffet breakfast. Internet specials available. AE, DC, MC, V. Free parking in garage. Metro: Garibaldi. **Amenities:** Restaurant; bar; concierge; room service. *In room:* A/C, TV, minibar, Wi-Fi (6€/hr.).

INEXPENSIVE

Nuovo Rebecchino *⬧* A few steps from Stazione Centrale and within walking distance of the ancient city, this hotel offers pleasant accommodations at reasonable rates. One of the oldest hotels in Naples, it was restored to its original beauty in 2004. The ample guest rooms have an elegantly classic style, with carpeting and modern features. Bathrooms are good size, and a number of the rooms have Jacuzzi tubs.

Corso Garibaldi 356 (off Piazza Garibaldi and Stazione Centrale to the north), 80142 Napoli. www.nuovorebecchino.it. *©* **081-5535327.** Fax 081-268026. 58 units. 60€–80€ double; 88€ triple; 100€ quad. Rates include buffet breakfast. Children 12 and under stay free in parent's room. AE, DC, MC, V. Parking 20€ in nearby garage. Metro: Garibaldi. **Amenities:** Restaurant; bar; babysitting; concierge; room service. *In room:* A/C, TV, minibar, Wi-Fi (free).

Capodimonte

MODERATE

Villa Capodimonte ★ This 1995 hotel is just steps from the Royal Park of Capodimonte and is surrounded by its own park with splendid views. Family run, it offers personalized and welcoming service, and a variety of public spaces where you can enjoy some downtime. Guest rooms are large and nicely appointed, with classic furniture and wooden floors; each is basically a junior suite opening onto either the garden or a terrace. Many enjoy vistas of Mount Vesuvius and the Gulf.

Via Moiariello 66 (off Via S. Antonio, opposite the south gate of the Park of the Museo Nazionale di Capodimonte), 80131 Napoli. www.villacapodimonte.it. *©* **081-459000.** Fax 081-299344. 57 units. 175€–200€ double; 200€ triple; 250€ quad. Rates include buffet breakfast. Internet specials available. Children 5 and under stay free in parent's room. AE, DC, MC, V. Free parking. Bus: C66 or 24 to Via Ponti Rossi. Small pets accepted. **Amenities:** Restaurant; bar; babysitting; concierge; room service. *In room:* A/C, TV, minibar.

WHERE TO EAT

Neapolitans love to eat and love their traditions: Seafood and pizza dominate the scene (see p. 32 for an introduction to local cuisine and wines) yet many traditional local dishes are vegetarian or meat based. In addition to our suggestions below, consider also some of the **hotel dining** recommended above, and see "Naples After Dark" on p. 120 for *enoteche* (wine bars offering food).

Posillipo

EXPENSIVE

Giuseppone a Mare ★ NEAPOLITAN/SEAFOOD With nearly two hundred years of service behind it, this restaurant is situated right on the seashore and commands a beautiful view of the Bay looking back toward Napoli. The menu is large—two pages are devoted solely to pasta—but the specialties are fish and seafood, which can be cooked to order (priced by the kg). We recommend the delicious *polpi Giuseppone* (squid in a tomato and black olive sauce) and the exceptional fusilli *della Baia* (with swordfish and pumpkin served in a crunchy cheese crust). The space is bright and airy, with an antique majolica floor in lemon hues. Toward the back wall, you can see how the building was literally hewn out of the looming cliff above it. During warm months, you can dine on the terrace outside.

Via Ferdinando Russo 13. ✆ **081-5756002.** www.giuseppone.com. Reservations recommended. Secondi 15€–25€. AE, DC, MC, V. Tues–Sat 10:30am–3:30pm and 8–11:30pm; Sun 10:30am–5:30pm. Only open for dinner in Aug. Bus: C3 to Mergellina (end of line), and then 140.

Rosiello 🎁 NEAPOLITAN/SEAFOOD This elegant restaurant is beloved not only for the quality of its cuisine, but also for the exceptional sea views from its terrace. Locals will line up for an outdoor table from spring to fall, so reserve in advance. You will delight in the excellent dishes such as risotto *alla pescatora* (with seafood) and *scialatielli con melanzane e provola* (fresh pasta with local cheese and eggplant), as well as the perfectly fried calamari and the *pezzogna all'acquapazza* (fish in a light tomato broth).

Via Santo Strato 10. ✆ **081-7691288.** www.ristoranterosiello.it. Reservations recommended. Secondi 10€–25€. AE, DC, MC, V. Thurs–Tues 12:30–4pm and 7.30pm–midnight; May–Sept open daily. Closed 2 weeks each in Jan and Aug. Bus: C3 to Mergellina (end of line), and then 140.

Mergellina

MODERATE

Ciro a Mergellina ★ NEAPOLITAN/PIZZA/SEAFOOD This historic restaurant is a favorite destination for tourists and locals alike, who come for the seafood—sautéed mussels and small clams, pasta dishes, and excellent pizza made with *mozzarella di bufala* (buffalo mozzarella)—and for the excellent service. We also love the seafood salad appetizer, spaghetti *alle vongole* (with baby clams), pasta *all'aragosta* (with lobster), and *spigola fritta* (deep-fried sea bass). The wonderful, homemade ice cream comes in a variety of flavors.

Via Mergellina 18. ✆ **081-681780.** www.ciroamergellina.it. Reservations recommended. Secondi 8€–18€. Tues–Sun 11:30am–11:30pm. AE, DC, MC, V. Bus: 140. Metro: Mergellina. Tram: 1.

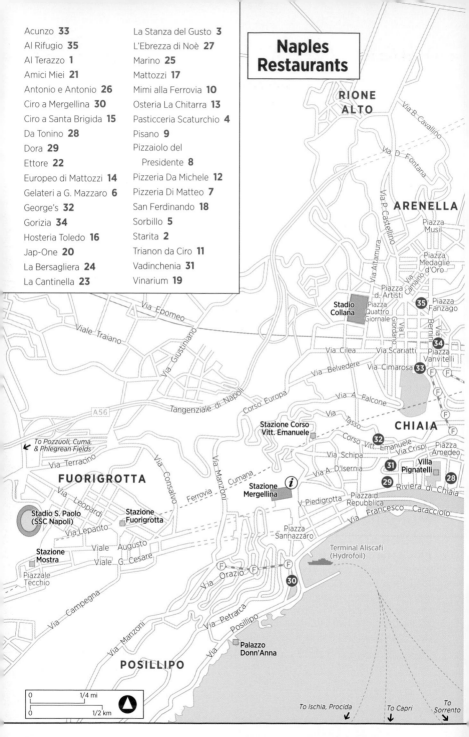

Acunzo **33**
Al Rifugio **35**
Al Terazzo **1**
Amici Miei **21**
Antonio e Antonio **26**
Ciro a Mergellina **30**
Ciro a Santa Brigida **15**
Da Tonino **28**
Dora **29**
Ettore **22**
Europeo di Mattozzi **14**
Gelateri a G. Mazzaro **6**
George's **32**
Gorizia **34**
Hosteria Toledo **16**
Jap-One **20**
La Bersagliera **24**
La Cantinella **23**

La Stanza del Gusto **3**
L'Ebrezza di Noè **27**
Marino **25**
Mattozzi **17**
Mimi alla Ferrovia **10**
Osteria La Chitarra **13**
Pasticceria Scaturchio **4**
Pisano **9**
Pizzaiolo del
  Presidente **8**
Pizzeria Da Michele **12**
Pizzeria Di Matteo **7**
San Ferdinando **18**
Sorbillo **5**
Starita **2**
Trianon da Ciro **11**
Vadinchenia **31**
Vinarium **19**

Naples Restaurants

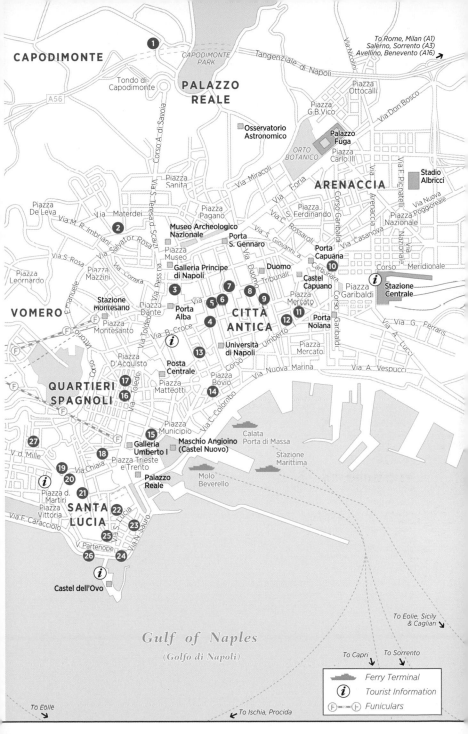

CAPODIMONTE

1

CAPODIMONTE
PARK

PALAZZO
REALE

Tangenziale di Napoli

To Rome, Milan (A1)
Salerno, Sorrento (A3)
Avellino, Benevento (A16)

Tondo di
Capodimonte

Piazza
Ottocalli

Piazza
G.B.Vico

Osservatorio
Astronomico

Palazzo
Fuga

Piazza
Carlo III

Stadio
Albricci

Piazza
De Leva

ORTO
BOTANICO

ARENACCIA

Piazza
Sanita

Piazza
Pagano

Piazza
S. Ferdinando

Piazza
Nazionale

2

Museo Archeologico
Nazionale

Porta
S. Gennaro

Porta
Capuana

Corso   Meridionale

Piazza
Leonardo

Piazza
Mazzini

Piazza
Museo

Galleria Principe
di Napoli

Duomo

10

Stazione
Centrale

VOMERO

Stazione
Montesano

3

Porta
Alba

7

8

Castel
Capuano

Piazza
Garibaldi

Piazza
Montesanto

5 6

CITTÀ
ANTICA

9

11

Porta
Nolana

Via G. Ferraris

Piazza
Dante

4

12

Piazza
D'Acquisto

13

Università
di Napoli

Piazza
Mercato

QUARTIERI
SPAGNOLI

Posta
Centrale

Piazza
Matteotti

Piazza
Bovio

Piazza Nuova Marina

Via A. Vespucci

17

16

14

27

15

Piazza
Municipio

Calata
Porta di Massa

Maschio Angioino
(Castel Nuovo)

Stazione
Marittima

19

18

Galleria
Umberto I

Piazza Trieste
e Trento

20

Palazzo
Reale

Molo
Beverello

21

Piazza d.
Martiri

SANTA
LUCIA

22

25

23

To Eolie, Sicily
& Cagliari

26

24

Castel dell'Ovo

Gulf of Naples

(Golfo di Napoli)

To Capri

To Sorrento

To Eolie

To Ischia, Procida

Ferry Terminal

Tourist Information

Funiculars

Chiaia

EXPENSIVE

Dora ★ NEAPOLITAN/SEAFOOD The prices at this tiny little restaurant may be on the steep side, but it has something of a cult following among both locals and visitors and is well worth a visit if fish and seafood is your thing. Tables are always crammed with diners feasting on the freshest of the day's catch featured in simple local dishes such as spaghetti *alle vongole* (one of the best versions we have ever eaten) and the spectacular linguine *alla Dora* (with prawns, rock lobster, squid, clams and cherry tomatoes), a meal in itself. For a secondo, there is delicious *fritto misto* and perfectly grilled catch of the day.

Via Ferdinando Palasciano 30. ✆ **081-680519.** Reservations essential. Secondi 22€–40€. AE, DC, MC, V. Mon–Sat 1–3:30pm and 7:45pm–midnight (Sept–May open for Sun lunch and closed Mon lunch). Bus 27, 28, or 140.

George's ★★ GOURMET NEAPOLITAN A temple of good taste, located on the top floor of Grand Hotel Parker's, this place has a view second to none. You can watch the sun set on the Gulf as your taste buds are pampered by Chef Baciòt's preparations. He likes to revisit the ancient dishes of Neapolitan tradition, removing a bit of fat and adding a lot of imagination. The menu is seasonal and might include *pizzelle foglia* (eggless homemade leaves of pasta with sautéed garden vegetables), *pezzogna arrosto in guazzetto di tartufi* (local fish in a light sauce with truffles), and *costolette d'agnello con le melanzane* (lamb with eggplants). In addition to its regular menu, George's serves a "de light" menu, in line with the therapies proposed in the hotel's spa and based on the principles of Marc Messegué, the herbal specialist; it's detoxifying yet extremely satisfying. The extensive wine list features only Italian wines, including a large section devoted to Campania.

Corso Vittorio Emanuele 135. ✆ **081-7612474.** www.grandhotelparkers.com. Reservations required. Secondi 22€–30€. AE, DC, MC, V. Daily 12:30–2:30pm and 8–10:30pm. Bus: C24 or C27 to Via Tasso-Corso Vittorio Emanuele II. Metro: Piazza Amedeo.

MODERATE

Amici Miei 🎁 ITALIAN/NEAPOLITAN If you are tired of seafood, this restaurant, located on the hill between Chiaia and the Quartieri Spagnoli, is for you. The menu focuses on meat—as in goose, lamb, pork—as well as on vegetarian choices. We recommend the homemade fusilli *alle melanzane* (with eggplant), the *pappardelle al sugo di agnello* (fresh large noodles with a lamb sauce), and the *costine e salsicce alla brace* (chargrilled lamb ribs and sausages), but anything on the seasonal menu is good. Just try not to fill up on the tasty homemade bread before your meal.

Via Monte di Dio 77. ✆ **081-7646063.** www.ristoranteamicimiei.com. Reservations required. Secondi 12€–13€. AE, DC, MC, V. Tues–Sat 12:30–3:30pm and 7:30–11:30pm; Sun 12:30–3:30pm. Closed July–Aug. Tram: 1 to Piazza dei Martiri.

Jap-One 🎁 SUSHI This trendy sushi bar, hidden away at the end of a winding narrow alley under the cliff of Monte di Dio (taking a cab is the best way to find it), feels more New York than Napoli with its überstylish decor. But thanks to the care and warm personality of owner Roberto Goretti, the atmosphere is friendly and relaxed, with cool jazz in the background and chefs preparing food at the sushi bar in view of the diners. Although the restaurant is Japanese, it has that irrepressible Neapolitan flair, seen in the use of local fish—for example the *maki di astice* (local lobster maki), or the *coccio sashimi* (sashimi of coccio, a local fish), depending on the day's catch.

Via Santa Maria Cappella Vecchia 30/i (off Piazza dei Martiri). © **081-7646667.** Reservations required. Secondi 14€–36€. AE, DC, MC, V. Mon-Sat 8:30–11pm. Tram: 1 to Piazza dei Martiri.

San Ferdinando 🍴 NEAPOLITAN The handwritten menu card at this delightful family-run restaurant changes daily but features superb primi such as *paccheri con calamaretti, caperi e olive nere* (pasta tubes with baby squid, capers, and black olives) or risotto with asparagus and prawns. Start your meal with the deliciously fresh house antipasti and wash it all down with the house falanghina wine, served chilled in bright ceramic jugs. We really like the warm, friendly atmosphere of this place, and judging by the photos on the walls, so do the opera stars from nearby San Carlo.

Via Nardones 117 (off Piazza Triests e Trento). © **081-421964.** www.trattoriasanferdinando.it. Reservations recommended. Secondi 10€–18€. AE, DC, MC, V. Mon-Sat 12:30–3:30pm, Wed-Fri also 7:30–11pm. Bus R2.

INEXPENSIVE

Da Tonino 🍴 NEAPOLITAN One of the few authentic *osterie* left in Naples, Da Tonino has been run by the same family for over a century, and is consistently loved by locals—and an ever-increasing number of tourists. The interior is cramped and rustic and the menu short on choice, but the atmosphere is friendly and lively and the prices are rock-bottom. You can't go wrong with the hearty dishes from the local tradition such as the tasty *ragù* or *seppie in umido* (cuttlefish stewed with tomato). There's also a small but excellent wine list. Prices at dinner are slightly higher than those at lunchtime.

Via Santa Teresa A Chiaia 47. © **081-421533.** Reservations accepted only for large parties. Secondi 5€–9€. MC, V. Daily 1–4pm; Fri-Sat also 8pm–midnight. Metro: Amedeo.

Vadinchenia 🍴 MODERN CAMPANIAN This restaurant, a favorite with local foodies, offers excellent food and professional service in a welcoming setting. The menu is large and varied and includes many unusual and surprisingly delicious offerings, such as the *ricotta farcita* (stuffed ricotta cheese) or deep fried brie with a blueberry compote appetizers, the *fettuccelle ai totani in salsa agro dolce di agrumi* (pasta with squid in an orange and lemon sauce), and the *filetto di maiale al vin santo* (pork filet in a vin santo sauce). The food is well complemented by the moderately priced wine list.

Via Pontano 21 (off Corso Vittorio Emanuele). © **081-660265.** Reservations required. Secondi 7€–15€. AE, DC, MC, V. Mon-Sat 12:30–3pm and 7:30–11:30pm; Sun 12:30–3pm. Closed Aug and Dec 25. Bus: C24 or C27 to Via Tasso-Corso Vittorio Emanuele II. Metro: Piazza Amedeo.

Santa Lucia

EXPENSIVE

La Cantinella ★ NEAPOLITAN/SEAFOOD A well-established address in Naples, this local favorite is always bursting with a chic clientele. The stylish old-fashioned nightclub atmosphere doubles with top-quality, mostly traditional Neapolitan food. Primi such as *pappardelle sotto il cielo di Napoli* (homemade pasta with zucchini, prawns, and green tomatoes) are delicious and we particularly enjoyed the creamy risotto *alla zucca, champagne e provola* (with pumpkin, champagne and provola cheese). For your secondo, the *frittura* (deep-fried seafood) is a winner, but there are also classics such as steak and lobster. Do not skip the delicious homemade desserts such as the superb chocolate soufflé, which requires a bit of a wait. The huge tome of a wine list features wines from all over Italy and beyond. The adjacent piano bar stays open with live music well into the early hours.

Via Cuma 42. *℃* **081-7648684.** www.lacantinella.it. Reservations required. Secondi 19€–30€. AE, DC, MC, V. Mon–Sat 12:30-3 and 7:30pm–11:30. Closed 3 weeks in Aug. Bus: 152, C25, or 140.

La Bersagliera NEAPOLITAN/SEAFOOD The food at the elegant, Belle Epoque Bersagliera may not be the very best in town, but the setting is a total delight and we recommend it for that: With its waterside terrace overlooking the marina and Castel dell'Ovo, it is a perfect place for a lazy lunch in warm weather. The classic starter here is *zuppa di cozze e vongole* (mussel and clam soup) but the pasta with baby octopus, tomato, and olives is also good and you can follow this with an excellent *fritto misto* (deep-fried seafood medley).

Borgo Marinaro 10-11. *℃* **081-7646016.** www.labersagliera.it. Reservations recommended at weekends. Secondi 10€–18€. AE, DC, MC, V. Wed–Mon noon-3:30pm and 7:30pm–midnight. Closed 1 week in Jan. Bus 151.

MODERATE

Antonio e Antonio PIZZA/NEAPOLITAN Located on the beautiful lungo-mare (oceanfront), this restaurant is popular with locals, many of whom come for its youthful atmosphere. The two Antonios who created this restaurant grew up and were trained in two of Naples's most famous, historic restaurants, Zi Teresa and Giuseppone a Mare. The open kitchen zips out 40 types of pizza and all the great Neapolitan classics, including fusilli *di pasta fresca ai pomodorini del Vesuvio* (with super tasty cherry tomatoes from Mount Vesuvius) and *polipetti affogati in cassuola* (squid cooked in an earthware pot with tomatoes and herbs). Appetizers and side dishes are served buffet style. A second location in Chiaia is located on the slopes of the Vomero, at Via Francesco Crispi 89 (*℃* **081-682528**).

Via Partenope 24. *℃* **081-2451987.** www.antonioeantonio.net. Reservations recommended. Secondi 8€–17€; pizza 6€–13€. AE, DC, MC, V. Tues–Sun noon-1am. Bus: 152.

INEXPENSIVE

Ettore *✦* NEAPOLITAN/PIZZA This unpretentious, rustic restaurant has an authentic, neighborhood feel to it. It's so popular with locals, in fact, that we advise you to come early to get a seat; tables spill out onto the sidewalk in summer. The menu is simple but varies often, according to the season. The pizza is really excellent and their specialty is *pagnottiello*—calzone filled with mozzarella, ricotta, and prosciutto.

Via Santa Lucia 56. *℃* **081-7640498.** Reservations recommended. Secondi 6€–20€. AE, DC, MC, V. Mon–Sat 12:30-3:30pm and 7:30pm–midnight. Bus: 152, C25, or 140.

Marino *✦* NEAPOLITAN/PIZZA Situated just a few minutes' walk from some of the city's glitziest hotels, this homey place is a favorite of ours for its modest, old-fashioned atmosphere (complete with garish lighting), delicious pizza, and good, reasonably priced fish dishes. Antipasti of the day (including wonderfully fresh mozzarella) are served from a counter at the front of the restaurant; you can go up with the waiter and show him what you want. Follow this by one of the traditional primi such as spaghetti with mixed seafood or a dish of *polpo alla Luciana* (octopus in a punchy tomato sauce).

Via Santa Lucia 118. ℰ **081-7640280.** Secondi 7€–18€. AE, MC, V. Open Tues–Sun noon–3:30pm and 7:30pm–midnight. Bus 151.

Quartieri Spagnoli

INEXPENSIVE

Hosteria Toledo NEAPOLITAN A picturesque restaurant with a lively atmosphere, the Hosteria Toledo has been serving tasty but inexpensive traditional Neapolitan food to locals and visitors since 1951. We recommend the *ziti al ragù* (pasta with meat and tomato sauce) or *tubettoni con fagioli e cozze* (pasta with beans and mussels) maybe followed by *polipo in guazzetto* (squid in a tomato sauce), or *arrosto di maiale* (pork roast). If you have room left, try one of the luscious desserts, which often include such great classics as *babà* (a sort of brioche with rum) and *pastiera* (a sort of thick, custardy pie).

Vico Giardinetto a Toledo 78. ℰ **081-421257.** www.hosteriatoledo.it. Secondi 8€–15€. AE, DC, MC, V. Tues 12:30–3pm; Wed–Mon 12:30–3pm and 7pm–midnight. Bus: R2 to Piazza Trieste e Trento. Coming from Piazza Trieste e Trento, it's off Via Toledo to the left, across from the Banco di Napoli.

Citta Antica

EXPENSIVE

Europeo di Mattozzi ★★ NEAPOLITAN/PIZZA/SEAFOOD This landmark of Neapolitan dining is one of our favorite places to eat in Naples. The chef/owner creates a welcoming atmosphere and offers a winning interpretation of traditional dishes. Among the primi, you can have a very tasty *zuppa di cannellini e cozze* (bean and mussel soup) or *pasta e patate con provola* (pasta and potatoes with melted local cheese); for a secondo, you could try *ricciola all' acquapazza* (a local fish in a light tomato and herb broth) or *stoccafisso alla pizzaiola* (dried codfish in a tomato, garlic, and oregano sauce). Pizza is also on the menu and is very well prepared, as are the desserts, including hometown favorites such as *babà* and *pastiera*.

Via Marchese Campodisola 4. ℰ **081-5521323.** www.europeomattozzi.it. Reservations required. Secondi 12€–18€. AE, DC, MC, V. Mon–Wed noon–3:30pm; Thurs–Sat noon–3:30pm and 8pm–midnight. Closed 2 weeks in Aug. Bus: R2 or R3 to Piazza Trieste e Trento.

La Stanza del Gusto ★★ CREATIVE NEAPOLITAN Extrovert Chef Mario Avallone's double-face restaurant has become something of a temple to "new" Neapolitan cuisine, and its dual identity means that you can eat either a modest meal for under 20€ or splash out on a gourmet experience. The casual, ground-floor cheese bar offers soups, salads, and the odd hot choice along with a wonderful selection of cheeses and cold cuts. Upstairs, in Stanza del Gusto, the atmosphere is more serious and it is here that the chef's creative flair is on show. The inspired, regularly changing menus are strictly based around locally sourced ingredients that Avallone uses in new ways such as the *capesante e carciofi* (scallops and artichokes) and the *variazione di baccalà* (salt cod prepared in several different modes). If you are prepared to trust the chef, we recommend the 65€ tasting menu *a sopresa* (surprise).

Via Santa Maria di Costantinopoli 100. ℰ **081-401578.** www.lastanzadelgusto.com. Reservations required for the Stanza del Gusto (upstairs restaurant). Secondi (upstairs restaurant) 14€–20€. AE, DC, MC, V. Tues–Sat noon–11:30pm; Sun noon–3pm. Upstairs restaurant Tues–Sat 7–11pm. Closed 3 weeks in Aug. Metro: Piazza Dante.

THE BEST NEAPOLITAN pizza IN THE HISTORIC DISTRICT

Forget all you have ever known about this cheesy treat and open your mind to the experience of pizza in Naples, so different from what we call pizza in the rest of the world. Here is the lowdown on the best pizzerie in Naples, where the decor is minimal, and an individual pizza costs between 3€ and 8€:

Mattozzi, Piazza Carità 2 (© 081-5524322; closed Fri), is one of the oldest pizzerie in Naples, using local ingredients, from the regional flour and the tomatoes of Mount Vesuvius, to the *fiordilatte* from the Lattari Mountains, and the *mozzarella di bufala.*

Pizzeria Da Michele, Via Sersale 1, off Via Forcella (© 081-5539204; www. damichele.net; closed Sun), is where you'll find the best pizza in Naples, according to many locals. In business since 1870, it serves only two varieties: *margherita* or *marinara,* basically with or without cheese. Come early; it is usually packed.

Pizzaiolo del Presidente, Via Tribunali 120 (© 081-210903; closed Sun), was opened in 2000 by Ernesto Cacialli, the former *pizzaiolo* (pizza chef) of Di Matteo (below). He is the one who personally served Bill Clinton in 1994—apparently convincing the president to try his special *margherita* pizza—and has named his pizzeria after that event. Do not miss the *margherita* or the *pizza fritta.*

Pizzeria Di Matteo, Via dei Tribunali 94, at Vico Giganti (© 081-455262; closed Sun), is another historical establishment serving excellent classic pizza and specializing in the to-die-for *pizza fritta,* a delicacy of fluffy thin dough filled with a mix of ham, tomatoes, and local cheese—provola, ricotta, and mozzarella—which you can split as an appetizer or eat on your own. President Clinton ate here during the G7 Summit in 1994.

Sorbillo, Via Tribunali 32 (© 081-446643; closed Sun), provides a more formal setting and an equal quality of pizza.

Open since 1935, it specializes in pizza made exclusively with local high-quality ingredients: the *fiordilatte* from Agerola on the Sorrento peninsula, the local extra-virgin olive oil, and the oregano from Frattamaggiore, which is best savored on the simple marinara.

Starita, Via Materdei 27 (© 081-5441485; closed Mon), is a pleasant, small pizzeria run by one of the best pizzaioli in the city. It is popular for the unique quality of its dough and famous for its *pizza fritta* as well as its *pizza coi fiori di zucca* (with zucchini flowers), which is available only in summer.

Trianon da Ciro, Via Pietro Colletta 42 (© 081-5539426; open daily), is an extremely popular pizzeria, where you'll have to compete for a table with the students of the nearby university and the many local aficionados who come to savor the exceptional *pizza con salsiccia e friarelli* (with sausages and local broccoli greens) and *pizza con pomodorini e mozzarella di bufala* (with Vesuvian tomatoes and buffalo mozzarella).

MODERATE

Ciro a Santa Brigida ★ NEAPOLITAN A traditional restaurant with a formal—but absolutely not stuffy—atmosphere and very professional service, Ciro a Santa Brigida is one of the most famous, and most typical, of all Neapolitan restaurants. Opened in 1932 by the father of the current owners, it is something of a gastronomic institution serving fine food in a warm, traditional atmosphere. Popular with locals for its *fritto* (deep-fried dishes including meat cutlets and seafood), and for side dishes such as hard-to-find traditional vegetables, it also serves good pizza and excellent desserts. Of the traditional Neapolitan specialties on hand, try *rigatoni ricotta e polpettine* (pasta with baby meatballs) and *polpi alla Luciana* (squid cooked in a pocket with tomato and herbs). Counted among the restaurant's famous regular past customers are the writer Pirandello and actors Eduardo de Filippo, Vittorio Gassman, and Totò.

Via Santa Brigida 71 (off Via Toledo). ✆ **081-5524072.** www.ciroasantabrigida.it. Reservations required. Secondi 8€–16€. AE, DC, MC, V. Mon–Sat noon–3:30pm and 7:30pm–midnight. Bus: R2 to Piazza Trieste e Trento.

INEXPENSIVE

Osteria La Chitarra NEAPOLITAN This popular restaurant serves up traditional food prepared with local and strictly seasonal ingredients—which means a menu that varies weekly according to the market finds. We loved the *paccheri lardiati* (homemade noodles with pork tidbits), the authentic lasagna, and the *baccalà con i ceci* (salted cod with chickpeas), as well as the excellent risotto *alla pescatora* (with seafood).

Rampe San Giovanni Maggiore 1bis. ✆ **081-5529103.** www.osterialachitarra.it. Reservations recommended Sat–Sun. Secondi 9€–14€. AE, DC, MC, V. Tues–Sat 12:30–3pm and 7:30–10:30pm. Closed 2 weeks in Aug. Metro: Università.

Pisano ◢ 🎒 NEAPOLITAN/SEAFOOD Hidden behind the Duomo, this pleasant family-run restaurant serves well-prepared dishes from the local culinary tradition. The menu is large and includes both surf and turf. We recommend the *scialatielli ai frutti di mare* (fresh pasta with seafood) and the linguine *al coccio* (with local fish), as well as the *spigola all'acquapazza* (sea bass in a light tomato herbed broth) and the roasted sausages.

Piazzetta Crocelle ai Mannesi 1. ✆ **081-5548325.** Reservations recommended Sat–Sun. Secondi 6€–12€. No credit cards. Mon–Sat noon–3pm and 7:30–10:30pm. Bus: R2 or C57. Closed Aug.

Piazza Garibaldi

MODERATE

Mimì alla Ferrovia ★ 🎒 NEAPOLITAN With its walls hung with the photos of past celebrity diners, this is another of Naples's historical landmark restaurants and has a faithful local following. The traditional menu is fish based (although there is the odd meat choice) and the chef prepares excellent renditions of local favorites, varying according to the season. Depending on the time of year, you'll probably find *scialatielli ai frutti di mare* (eggless homemade pasta with seafood), *polipo alla Luciana* (squid cooked in a pocket with tomato and herbs), *polipo in guazzetto* (squid in a light tomato sauce), and *sartù* (rice with baby meatballs and cheese). Desserts are traditional, too, and include *babà* and *pastiera*.

Via Alfonso d'Aragona 21. ✆ **081-5538525.** Reservations recommended Sat–Sun. Secondi 8€–15€. AE, DC, MC, V. Mon–Sat noon–3pm and 7–11:30pm. Metro: Piazza Garibaldi.

Naples is famous for its desserts, which include such world-famous specialties as *babà, sfogliatelle,* and *pastiera.* To taste these and many others, head to the **Pasticceria Scaturchio** ★★, Piazza San Domenico Maggiore 19 (𝒸 081-5516944). Since its opening in 1903, this historic pastry and coffee shop has been a favorite with the locals who come for a pick-me-up (there's nothing better than a *sfogliatella* as a midmorning or midafternoon snack), or to buy dessert to take to their hosts and family for dinner. Besides the excellent pastries, we recommend that you try a Ministeriale, the chocolate candy that made the shop famous: it's a medallion of dark chocolate with a liqueur cream filling. **Pasticceria Attanasio,** Vico Ferrovia 2 (𝒸 081-285675; www.sfogliatellecalde. com; closed Mon) is another renowned spot to sample *sfogliatella* in Naples.

Caffetteria Pasticceria Gelateria G. Mazzaro ★ (pictured), Palazzo Spinelli, Via Tribunali 359 (𝒸 081-459248; www. pasticceriamazzaro.it; daily 7am–midnight), makes scrumptious pastries and also excellent gelato in many flavors.

Vomero

INEXPENSIVE

Acunzo ★ PIZZA This authentic neighborhood restaurant is often crowded with locals eating pizza with a variety of toppings—the 40-some different choices include pizza *con i fusilli* (with fusilli seasoned with tomatoes, peas, bacon, and mushrooms). Purists may prefer the typical Neapolitan dishes, such as *friarelli* (sautéed broccoli), superb eggplant Parmigiana (Parmesan), and *zuppa di fagioli* (cannellini-bean soup). If you are not planning a visit to Sorrento, try the *gnocchi alla Sorrentina* (potato dumplings with tomato sauce and mozzarella)—it is superb.

Via Domenico Cimarosa 60 (off Via Lorenzo Bernini to the south). 𝒸 **081-5785362.** Reservations recommended for dinner. Secondi 6€–20€. AE, DC, MC, V. Mon–Sat 12:30–4pm and 6:30pm–midnight. Funicular: Vomero. Metro: Vanvitelli.

Al Rifugio ★ 🍴 NEAPOLITAN You shouldn't find many tourists at this local favorite, entered through a wine shop, where heavenly, hearty food is served in a simple, even rustic atmosphere. Good seafood dishes, such as the *zuppa di cozze* (mussels) feature on the menu, but the reason that most people come here is for the steak, a comparative rarity in Naples. You can choose between local, Tuscan,

Irish, and Argentine meat: the best way to eat it is simply grilled. A platter of local cheese and cured meat accompanied by a glass of good red wine is a perfect light meal, and the desserts are homemade and scrumptious. A simple lunch menu is available for 8€ (Mon–Sat).

Via San Gennaro ad Antignano 119 (off Via Gian Lorenzo Bernini to the north). ℂ **081-2292213.** Reservations recommended for dinner. Secondi 8€–18€. AE, DC, MC, V. Wed–Mon 12:30–4pm and 7pm–11:30am; Tues 12:30–4pm. Funicular: Vomero. Metro: Vanvitelli.

Gorizia ★ 🍴 NEAPOLITAN/PIZZA This excellent pizzeria was started in 1916 by the grandfather of the current owners (brothers Salvatore and Antonio). True to local tradition, the two brothers are convinced the secret is in the crust and don't believe pizza needs to be dressed up with fancy toppings to be good. According to them, the crust has to be puffy but not gummy, with a slightly crunchy edge and once you taste the result, you can only agree. There's more to the Gorizia than just pizza. There's a daily menu of a soup and a few pasta and main courses that may include pasta with artichokes, olives, and tomatoes, or *pasta e ceci* (a thick soup made with garbanzo beans). The delicious escarole is stuffed with bread crumbs, olives, pinoli nuts, and raisins. This is a popular place for business lunches, and it helps to have a reservation in the evening.

Via Bernini 31 (off Piazza Vanvitelli). ℂ **081-5782248.** Reservations recommended for dinner. Secondi 6€–18€. AE, DC, MC, V. Daily 12:30–4pm and 7pm–1am. Funicular: Vomero. Metro: Vanvitelli.

Capodimonte

INEXPENSIVE

Al Terrazzo NEAPOLITAN/PIZZA This large, simple neighborhood restaurant has been around since 1945 and is a convenient stop before or after visiting the Museo Capodimonte. It makes excellent pizza—try the *Antica Capri* (with smoked provola and fresh tomatoes)—and has a long menu including specialties such as *scialatielli ai frutti di mare* (eggless fresh pasta with seafood). The restaurant prides itself on its large buffet of *antipasti* and side dishes, offering 50 choices daily. During clement weather, you can dine on the terrace, which is on the second floor and above the traffic and street noise.

Viale Colli Aminei 99 (off Via Capodimonte). ℂ **081-7414400.** Secondi 6€–12€. AE, DC, MC, V. Daily 11am–3:30pm and 6:30–11pm. Bus: R4.

EXPLORING NAPLES

For those willing to see beyond the noise and urban grit, Naples reveals itself as a city of fun, surprise, and wonder that is particularly loved by art lovers and history buffs.

We suggest purchasing an **Artecard** (see "Campania Artecard," below) before starting your exploration of the region. The **City Sightseeing** hop-on-and-off tour is another good idea, particularly if your time is limited (see "Guided Tours," p. 117).

Royal Naples: Palaces & Castles

Castel Capuano ☺ A fortress built by Guglielmo I d'Altavilla in the 12th century and restored in the 13th century by Carlo d'Angió, this castle was transformed into a royal residence by the Aragona dynasty in 1484. In 1540, Don Pedro di Toledo, the viceroy of Naples, decided to change the residence to the

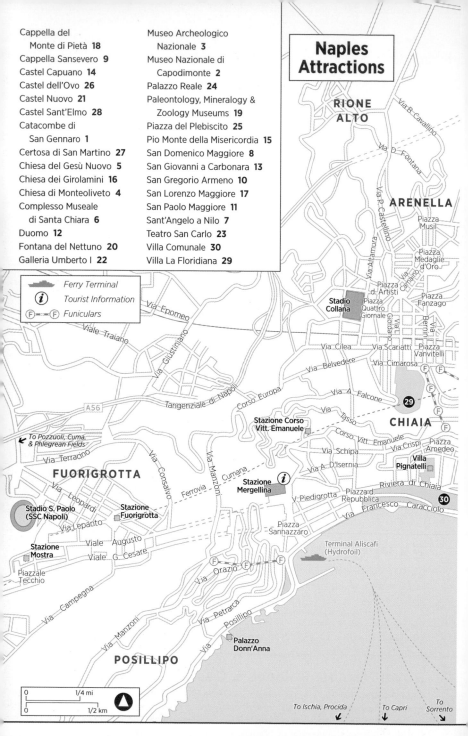

Cappella del
  Monte di Pietà **18**
Cappella Sansevero **9**
Castel Capuano **14**
Castel dell'Ovo **26**
Castel Nuovo **21**
Castel Sant'Elmo **28**
Catacombe di
  San Gennaro **1**
Certosa di San Martino **27**
Chiesa del Gesù Nuovo **5**
Chiesa dei Girolamini **16**
Chiesa di Monteoliveto **4**
Complesso Museale
  di Santa Chiara **6**
Duomo **12**
Fontana del Nettuno **20**
Galleria Umberto I **22**

Museo Archeologico
  Nazionale **3**
Museo Nazionale di
  Capodimonte **2**
Palazzo Reale **24**
Paleontology, Mineralogy &
  Zoology Museums **19**
Piazza del Plebiscito **25**
Pio Monte della Misericordia **15**
San Domenico Maggiore **8**
San Giovanni a Carbonara **13**
San Gregorio Armeno **10**
San Lorenzo Maggiore **17**
San Paolo Maggiore **11**
Sant'Angelo a Nilo **7**
Teatro San Carlo **23**
Villa Comunale **30**
Villa La Floridiana **29**

Naples Attractions

🚢 Ferry Terminal
ⓘ Tourist Information
Ⓕ ---- Ⓕ Funiculars

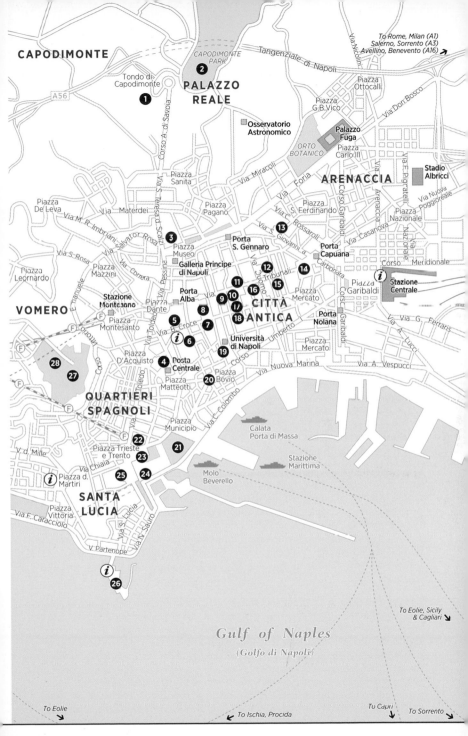

The **Artecard** (📞 **800-600601** or 06-39967650; www.campaniartecard.it) gives you discounted admission to a great number of attractions, free access to public transportation, and discounts to a number of participating businesses. The pass now comes in nine different versions (10€–30€). All grant free admission to the first two or three attractions you visit from the list below and a 50% discount on all the rest, plus a 10% to 25% discount on several other museums and attractions, and free access to all public transportation—including regional trains and special buses—during the validity of the card. A youth card is offered but only to citizens of the European Union and other countries with reciprocity rights. There is also a version that is valid for a year.

The sites that qualify for free or 50% admission (depending on the type of card you choose) are: **Naples**'s Museo Archeologico Nazionale, Museo Nazionale di Capodimonte, Certosa and Museo Di San Martino, Castel Sant'Elmo, Museo Civico di Castelnuovo, Museo Duca di Martina (Villa Floridiana), Museo Pignatelli Cortes, Museo Diocesano, Museo del Tesoro di San Gennaro, MADRE, Palazzo Reale, and Città Della Scienza; **Campi Flegrei**'s Flavian Amphitheatre, Serapeum, archaeological areas of Baia, Museo Archeologico di Baia, Cuma, and Rione Terra; **Mount Vesuvius**'s archaeological areas of Pompeii, Herculaneum, Paestum, Stabia, Velia, Oplontis, and Boscoreale; **Capua**'s Mitreo, Anfiteatro Campano, Museo dei Gladiatori, and Museo Archeologico dell'Antica Capua; **Caserta**'s Belvedere di San Leucio and Reggia; **Cilento**'s Certosa di Padula and Museo del Santuario di Hera Argiva; and **Sorrento**'s Museo.

The list of sites and businesses offering discounts between 10% and 25% is too long to print here, but we have noted them throughout the book. The card is for sale online (see above), as well as at all participating sites and museums, at the Campania Artecard stands at Capodichino Airport and the Napoli Cantrale train station, and some major hotels.

seat of tribunals, a function it has maintained to this day. Less dramatic than the other fortresses in Naples, Castel Capuano takes its name from the nearby gate, Porta Capuana, that once stood at the head of the main road leading to Capua. Inside the courtyard, the medieval structure is visible. You can visit some of the decorated halls and the Cappella Sommaria, with its 16th-century frescoes.

Via Concezio Muzy (off Via dei Tribunali). Free admission. Daily 9am–6pm. Metro: Piazza Garibaldi.

Castel dell'Ovo ★ ☺ Built over the small island of Megaris, where the Greeks first settled in the 9th century B.C., this castle is one of Naples's most famous sites and its solid profile features in many pictures of the Bay. Its name, "Castle of the Egg," refers to the local legend that says that the classic poet Virgil—the author of the *Aeneid* and a reputed magician—placed an egg under the foundations predicting that when it broke, disaster would befall the city. The fortress evolved from the villa of the Roman Lucullus, which was fortified in the Middle Ages and transformed into a castle by Frederick II. Enlarged and strengthened between the 16th and the 18th centuries, it remained a royal residence until the 20th century. Part of the castle now houses the Museum of Ethno-Prehistory, which is open only for special exhibits. The rest of the castle offers the **Sala delle Colonne (Hall of the Columns)** ★ and the **Loggiato** ★—both architectural masterpieces—and great views from two towers, **Torre Maestra** and **Torre Normanna.** The castle occupies only part of the island, which is connected to the shore in front of the Santa Lucia neighborhood by a solid bridge, a popular spot for wedding photos. Around it are the picturesque alleys and fishermen's houses of the **Borgo Marinaro** ★ many of which have been transformed into restaurants.

Borgo Marinari (off Via Partenope). ℂ **081-7954593.** Free admission. Mon–Sat 8am–6pm; Sun 8am–2pm. Bus: 152, C25, 140, or E5 to Via Santa Lucia.

Castel Capuano.

Castel Nuovo, & Museo Civico (aka Maschio Angioino) ★ ☺ An imposing fortress dominating the Bay only steps from the shore, this castle was created by the French architect Pierre d'Angicourt in the 13th century for the new king, Carlo I d'Angió. The first king of the Angevin dynasty, he wanted a more suitable residence than Castel dell'Ovo and Castel Capuano—both used by previous sovereigns. Started in 1279 and finished in 1282, Castel Nuovo was enlarged in the 15th century by Alfonso I d'Aragona, first king of the Aragonese dynasty. The castle has five towers: del Beverello (overlooking the harbor), di San Giorgio,

Castel Nuovo.

di Mezzo, di Guardia, and dell'Oro (note its tufa stone structure)—and a facade (facing inland) graced by the grandiose **Triumphal Arch of Alfonso I of Aragona ★★**, a splendid example of early Renaissance architecture.

Across from the entrance in the courtyard and up a 15th-century staircase is the magnificent **Sala dei Baroni ★★**, an architectural masterpiece. The monumental room is an enormous cube, 27m (89 ft.) wide and 28m (92 ft.) high, with a star-shaped vaulted ceiling originally decorated by Giotto in the 14th century. (His frescoes and most of the sculptures were lost in a fire in 1919). The room is still used for city council meetings today.

The **Museo Civico (Civic Museum) ★** holds a rich collection of artworks from the castle itself and other important monuments in Naples. Part of the museum's exhibit is housed in the lovely **Cappella Palatina ★**, the only surviving part of the Angevin castle. The chapel's facade opens onto the courtyard and is graced with a beautiful 15th-century carved **portal** and a **rose window ★**. Built in 1307, the chapel was completely decorated by Giotto, but only a few fragments remain. Inside you'll see a fine selection of 14th- and 15th-century sculptures, including a **Tabernacle ★★** by Domenico Gagini (a pupil of Donatello and Brunelleschi), depicting a Madonna with Child, and two **Madonna with Child ★** sculptures by Francesco Laurana—one from the portal of this chapel and the second from a nearby church. In the vestibule on the second floor, you'll find a **bronze door ★** with a cannonball hole: It is the original 15th-century door of the castle, which was taken as war booty by the French in 1496 and later returned. In the other rooms, you'll find a collection of 16th- and 17th-century paintings, including works by Luca Giordano and Francesco Solimena. On the third floor is an interesting collection of paintings dating from the 18th to the 20th centuries.

Piazza Municipio. ℂ **081-7952003.** Admission 5€. Mon–Sat 9am–7pm. Ticket booth closes 1 hr. earlier. Bus: R1, R2, R3, R4, E2, E3, C25, C57, 24, or 152.

Castel Sant'Elmo ☺ Dominating Naples from its position on the top of Vomero hill, near the Certosa di San Martino (p. 107), this majestic star-shaped structure, with its six points and several moats, is visible from everywhere in the city. It was originally built by the Angevins in 1329 and called Belforte, then was remade into the present fortress by Viceroy Pedro Toledo in the 16th century. Used as a prison during the Masaniello revolution in 1799, it has recently been restored and now houses special exhibits. You can visit the prisons and the terraces, which offer great views over Naples and the Bay.

Via Tito Angelini 20 (down from Piazza Vanvitelli). ℂ **081-7955877.** Admission 3€; free with admission to the Certosa di San Martino; additional fee for special exhibits. Wed–Mon 8:30am–6:30pm. Ticket booth closes 1 hr. earlier. Closed Jan 1 and Dec 25. Bus: C28, C31 or C36 to Piazza Vanvitelli. Funicular: Centrale to Piazza Fuga or Montesanto to Morghen. Metro: Vanvitelli, and then bus V1 to Piazzale San Martino.

Palazzo Reale ★ This imposing palace was designed by Domenico Fontana and built in 2 years, from 1600 to 1602, for the Spanish king Filippo III. Ironically, he never made it to Naples, and the castle was used by later kings who enlarged it in the 18th century. Luigi Vanvitelli worked on the **facade ★**, closing some of the arches to strengthen the walls and creating niches that were filled in 1888 by Umberto I, king of Italy, with eight statues of Neapolitan kings. Badly damaged by U.S. bombing during World War II, the building has since

The Palazzo Reale.

been completely restored. A guided tour gives you a full appreciation of the sprawling place. The **Royal Apartment** ★ occupies one-half of the palace, and is still furnished with the original furniture plus a number of masterpieces taken from Neapolitan churches that have closed. From the elegant **Cortile d'Onore (Court of Honor)** the magnificent main staircase, a double ramp of white marble, leads to the first floor and the gloriously opulent **Teatrino di Corte,** the private theater of the royal family. Continuing through, you enter the semipublic rooms, including the **Throne Room.** Beyond the corner begins the lavish **Private Appartment,** where the kings lived until 1837, when a fire obliged them to move upstairs. Its rooms open onto the manicured elevated gardens, with beautiful views over the Gulf. With colored marble, tapestries, frescoes, and 19th-century furniture, the rooms are quite splendid, especially the beautifully furnished **Studio del Re (King's Study),** where you can admire a **desk** and two *secretaires* ★ made for Napoleon Bonaparte by Adam Weisweiler. The magnificent **Hall of Hercules** ★, the ballroom, is hung with Neapolitan tapestries and decorated with some beautiful Sèvres vases. The chapel, **Cappella Palatina,** is worth a visit for its carved wooden **doors** ★ dating from the 16th century; its beautiful baroque **marble altar** ★ by Dionisio Lazzari, with inlays of lapis lazuli, agate, amethyst, and gilt; and the splendid 18th-century **Presepio del Banco di Napoli (Nativity Scene of the Bank of Naples)** ★★.

The other half of the palace contains the reception wing: the **Appartamento delle Feste** ★, with elegant rooms dedicated to public celebrations and festivities. It is now, together with the second floor, occupied by the **Biblioteca Nazionale di Vittorio Emanuele III,** the library that was originally established by Charles de Bourbon. The library is one of the finest in Southern Italy housing some two million volumes that include 32,950 manuscripts, 4,563 incunabula, and 1,752 papyrus manuscripts from Herculaneum.

Piazza del Plebiscito 1. ℂ **081-5808111.** www.palazzorealenapoli.it. Admission 4€; courtyard and gardens free. Guided tour by reservation 4€ (2.50€ with Artecard). Thurs–Tues 9am–7pm. Ticket booth closes 1 hr. earlier. Bus: R2 or R3 to Piazza Trieste e Trento.

Villa La Floridiana & Museo Nazionale della Ceramica Duca di Martina

★★ Surrounded by a magnificent park, this museum was once the 18th-century *casale* (country house) of Lucia Migliaccio, duchess of Floridia and second wife of Ferdinand II di Borbone. It now houses the **Museo Nazionale della Ceramica Duca di Martina** ★, a rich collection of ceramics. The core of the museum is made up of the private collection of Duc Placido De Sangro di Martina who, through his travels in Europe, collected precious objects not only in majolica and porcelain, but also glass, ivory, and coral. The collection was then expanded to include objects from other museums in Naples. The star of the show is the *porcellane di* **Capodimonte (Capodimonte porcelain)** ★, the most important collection in the world of this kind, with works from 1743 to 1759 by important artists such as Giuseppe Gricci; and the collection of **Japanese and Chinese porcelain** ★, including precious Ming and Edo dynasty pieces. Decorating the walls are **sketches** by great Neapolitan artists of the 18th century such as Francesco Solimena, Domenico Antonio Vaccaro, and Corrado Giaquinto. Even if you are not interested in ceramics, the villa is well worth a stop both for its architecture and for the splendid views over the whole bay.

One of the many pieces on display at the Museo Nazionale della Ceramica Duca di Martina.

Via Cimarosa 77. ✆ **081-5788418.** Admission 2.50€. Wed–Mon 8:30am–2pm; ticket booth closes 1 hr. earlier. Closed Jan 1 and Dec 25. Bus: C28, C32, or C36. Funicular: Chiaia to Cimarosa. Metro: Vanvitelli.

Great Museums

MADRE (Museo d'Arte Contemporanea Donnaregina) This modern museum has recently opened after a major renovation of the historical **Palazzo Regina,** in the heart of the historical district. The rich collection of the museum comes both from the city's endowment, bestowed in recent decades, and from permanent loans from private collectors. Some of the world's best contemporary artists are represented, including Horn, Kapoor, and Lewitt, as well as a number of Italian artists such as Fabro, Clemente, and Serra. In addition to the permanent collection, the MADRE houses noteworthy temporary exhibits (check with the tourist office for current events). From the Cortile della Caffetteria, also called Cortile Banco dei Pegni, you can now access **Santa Maria di Donnaregina Vecchia,** a beautiful Gothic church that holds a monument to Queen Maria d'Ungheria carved by Tino da Camaino.

Via Settembrini 79 (btw. Via Duomo and Via Carbonara). ✆ **081-19313016.** www.museomadre. it. Admission Wed–Sun 7€; Mon free. Mon, Wed–Saturday 10:30am–7:30pm; Sun 10:30am–11pm. Closed Tues. Bus E1. Metro: Cavour.

Museo Archeologico Nazionale ★★★ ☺ Naples's celebrated Archaeological Museum is home to the greatest collection of ancient art and artifacts in the world, both in terms of the quantity of the pieces on display and their quality. The museum occupies the huge ex-Palazzo degli Studi, a former university, that dates originally from the early 17th century but that was then remodeled specifically to house the immense and precious collection that King Ferdinand I had inherited from his grandmother, Elisabetta Farnese. The Farnese Collection, the core of the museum, was moved here in 1777 and enriched with treasures found during the archaeological excavations of Pompeii, Herculaneum, Stabia, and the rest of the region. For anyone even vaguely interested in ancient art, the museum is jaw-dropping; children will love the Egyptian sections in the basement and teens will be fascinated by the magnificent Farnese Gems and the reconstructions of entire rooms from Pompeii. We should point out that due to organizational problems and ongoing restoration work, rooms and even entire sections may be closed without notice. Sundays and public holidays are the best days to visit if you want to find everything open. To see the whole museum in depth, set aside the best part of a day. If time is limited, concentrate on the Farnese sculpture collection, the mosaics, the Gabinetto Segreto, and the collections of wall paintings and bronzes. We recommend the helpful audioguide.

Start off in the western wing of the first floor (Rooms 30-45, wrapped around three sides of a courtyard) where you will see a mixed bag of ancient sculpture found in the Campania region. The superb **Farnese Collection** of Roman sculpture starts in Room 1, which is dominated by the two massively powerful **Tyrannicides (Tyrant Killers)** ★★ which are 2nd-century-A.D. marble copies of renowned bronzes cast in 477 B.C. by the Greeks Kritios and Nesiotes. At the near end of the long gallery of interconnecting rooms is the magnificent **Ercole Farnese** ★★, a huge

FROM TOP: **A statue at the Museo Archeologico Nazionale; The Alexander mosaic at the Museo Archeologico Nazionale.**

statue of Hercules unearthed at the Baths of Caracalla in Rome in the mid-16th century. It is a signed copy by the Greek sculptor Lisippo of a 4th-century-B.C. bronze and had enormous influence on Renaissance artists. The colossal *Toro Farnese* ★★ stands in Room 16, one of the largest existing sculpture groups from antiquity. Standing over 4m (13 ft.) high, this monumental sculpture is a copy of a Greek original from the 2nd century B.C., representing the torment of the queen of Beotia as she is tied to a bull. Behind the Hercules sculpture, Rooms 9 to 10 house the **Gemme della Collezione Farnese ★★**, a matchless collection of precious objects (over 2,000 pieces), including the unique *tazza farnese* ★★ created in Alexandria in the 2nd century B.C. and carved from a single piece of sardonyx agate into the shape of a drinking cup.

From the first floor, you can also access the **Epigraphic Collection** (inscriptions) ★—the most important epigraphic collection in the world that pertains to ancient Roman and Greek civilizations—and the **Egyptian Collection ★**, holding artifacts from 2700 B.C. up to the Ptolemaic-Roman period of the 2nd and 1st centuries B.C.

On the mezzanine level, besides the reorganized **Numismatic Collection ★**, with over 200,000 coins and medals from antiquity, you'll find the richest **mosaic collection ★★★** in the world, with pieces spanning from the 2nd century B.C. to the 1st century A.D. They come in all shapes and sizes and mainly originate from Pompeii and Herculaneum. On the far wall is the magnificent depiction of *Alexander the Great Defeating Darius of Persia ★★★*, a huge mosaic made up of more than a million *tesserae* (pieces) that covers 20 sq. m (215 sq. ft.); it was found in the Casa del Fauno in Pompei. Also on the mezzanine floor is the *Gabinetto Segreto* (**Secret Room**), a section that was closed to the public for years thanks to the risqué content of is displays. The collection is made up of ancient erotica, mainly found in Pompeii and Herculaneum; some of the images to be seen in the paintings, mosaics, and statuary are remarkably graphic.

More ancient Roman mosaics line the floors of the second level, where you'll find the beautiful **Meridiana Hall ★** and the complete findings from the several Roman towns and villas destroyed by Mount Vesuvius in A.D. 79. The museum's unparalleled collection of ancient Roman **wall paintings ★★★** is on display in rooms 66 to 78 and covers the period from the 1st century B.C. to the 1st century A.D. *Note:* If you have time for only one section of the museum, make it this one: Found in Pompeii, Herculaneum, and the Vesuvian villas and reconstructed here, the works offer an overview of the so-called "Four Styles of Roman Painting" accompanied by clear explanation panels, also in English. Our single favorite room is number 77, with its **landscapes** and a portrait of the girl **Saffo.** Don't miss Rooms 114-117, dedicated to Herculaneum's **Villa dei Papiri ★★**, most significantly the **bronzes.** Look out for the two lean **Athletes** poised for flight, the famous **Drunken Satyr,** the five life-size female bronzes known as the **Dancers** and the celebrated bust of **Seneca,** the Roman philosopher, statesman, and dramatist. Further collections on this floor include precious objects—silver, ivory, pottery, and glass—as well as weaponry and a scale reconstruction of Pompeii. Among the infinite treasures, make sure you seek out the exquisite 1st-century Blue Vase, unearthed in Pompeii, that stands in the center of Room 85.

Piazza Museo 19 (off Via Pessina [Via Toledo]). ℅ **081-4422149.** www.marketplace.it/museo. nazionale. Admission 10€. Audioguide and guided tours 4€ (2.50€ with Artecard) in Italian or English (90 min.). Wed–Mon 9am–7:30pm. Ticket booth closes 90 min. earlier. Closed Jan 1 and Dec 25. Bus R1, R2, or 24 to Via Pessina, or E1 to Via Costantinopoli. Metro: Museo or Cavour.

Museo Nazionale di Capodimonte ★★★ Standing in the middle of a magnificent park that once was a hunting preserve for the Bourbon kings, this museum was created by Carlo III di Borbone in 1743 to house the art collection inherited from his mother, Elisabetta Farnese. The king also founded the Capodimonte workshops in the grounds in 1739. These workshops produced artistic ceramics following a unique technique and style that made them famous around the world. Production slowed down considerably in 1759, when the king left Naples to become king of Spain, but his son Ferdinando kept the factory open until 1805.

The imposing red-and-gray building houses one of Italy's most important art collections, and while the wooded park—still called the *bosco reale* (royal woods) by locals who come here with their families—is a pleasant destination for a stroll, the museum is a prime destination for art lovers.

Together with the important Borghese Collection, Carloo III's inheritance makes up the core of what we see in the museum today, and we advise that if time is limited, you concentrate on these works. Paintings hang according to areas of origin and in chronological order. Rooms 2 to 30 on the second floor make up the Farnese Gallery where the haul of art amassed by several generations of the Farnese family from Parma hangs. Here, the stars of the collections include works by the greatest Italian artists such as **Tiziano, Raffaello, Masaccio, Botticelli, Perugino, Luca Signorelli, Sandro Botticelli, Correggio, Giovanni Bellini, Mantegna, Parmigianino, Guido Reni, Caravaggio**—and by a number of the best artists from the Flemish school, such as **Pieter Bruegel the Elder** and **Van Dyck.** Besides paintings, the gallery also holds sculptures and precious tapestries. Smaller but also worth a visit is the **Borgia Collection ★**, also on the second floor. It contains many precious Renaissance **ivory** and **enamel** pieces.

The **Royal Apartments ★** take up much of the second floor. In the **Porcelain Gallery ★**, you'll find a number of unique pieces, with objects and dinner plates from all the royal palaces of Naples, including *bisquits* (a firing process) of **Sèvres** and **Vienna,** and porcelains of **Meissen** and, of course, the famous **Capodimonte** ceramics created in the local workshops. Nearby is the **De Ciccio Collection** with more porcelain, but also paintings and precious objects. **The Armory** has interesting pieces, but is overshadowed by the famous **Salottino di Porcellana ★★**, a small room completely inlaid with porcelain, made for Maria Amalia in the 18th century for the royal palace of Portici.

A **gallery ★** dedicated to "Painting in Naples from the 13th to the 19th Centuries" occupies the third floor, and provides a unique overview of artists who worked in Naples. It includes works by **Sodoma, Vasari, Tiziano, Caravaggio,** and **Luca Giordano;** here you can also admire the seven beautiful 16th-century **tapestries ★** from the **d'Avalos Collection,** and also the picture collection including work by **Ribera** and **Luca Giordano.** The contemporary art collection extends from the third to the fourth floor, with works by Alberto Burri, Jannis Kounellis, Andy Warhol, and Enzo Cucchi, among others. On the fourth floor you can also find a **Photography Collection** and the **Galleria dell'Ottocento** focusing on painters of the 19th century (Neapolitans, but also other Italians and foreigners).

Note: The special exhibits at this museum are hugely popular; reserve your tickets in advance.

Palazzo Capodimonte, Via Miano 1; also through the park from Via Capodimonte. ⓒ **081-7499111.** www.museodicapodimonte.campaniabeniculturali.it Admission 7.50€; 6.50€ after 2pm. Audioguide (70 min.) 4€ (2.50€ with Artecard). Thurs–Tues 8:30am–7:30pm. Ticket booth closes 1 hr. earlier. Closed Jan 1 and Dec 25. Bus: R4, R24, 137, 160, 161, or 178.

4

NAPLES | Exploring Naples

Religious Naples: Churches & Monasteries

The most religious city in Italy, Naples rivals Rome when it comes to the number and beauty of its churches. It is impossible to list them all so we have chosen the best (which are not necessarily the biggest) to include here.

Cappella del Monte di Pietà 🎭 The sober 16th-century palace of the Monte di Pietà hides one of Naples's art treasures: a perfectly preserved and richly decorated 16th-century chapel. Opening onto the palazzo's courtyard, the chapel is decorated by important artists of the 16th and 17th centuries. On either side of the door are two **sculptures** by Pietro Bernini, father of the famous Lorenzo. Inside the church, the **ceiling** bears a beautiful **fresco** depicting scenes from the life of Jesus by Belisario Corenzio. Farther on, you can visit the adjoining rooms, in particular the **sacristy** ★ at the beginning, and the **Sala delle Cantoniere** ★ at the end, perfectly preserved in 17th-century style, down to the furnishings and floors. *Note:* For a visit, you need to ask the *custode* (keeper), at the Pio Monte di Pietà.

Via Biagio dei Librai 114. ℭ **081-5807111.** Free admission. Sat 9am–7pm; Sun and holidays 9am–2pm. Bus: C57 or R2. Metro: Dante.

Museo Cappella Sansevero ★ ☺ In the 18th century, Prince Raimondo di Sangro of Sansevero remodeled this funerary chapel—built in the 16th century for his family—and lavishly decorated it with sculptures. Among those is one of the most celebrated works in Naples, Giuseppe Sanmartino's *Cristo Velato* **(Veiled Christ)** ★★, created by the Neapolitan sculptor in 1753, and still with the original patina. The challenge of depicting veiled figures in stone seems to have obsessed the prince: Other renowned sculptures here are the *Disinganno,* a technical virtuoso by Queirolo showing a standing figure of a man disentangling himself from a net; and *Pudicizia,* a masterpiece by Corradini showing a veiled naked woman. Prince Raimondo—a student of science, an inventor, and an alchemist—achieved fame as a master of the occult, and the decoration of the chapel has contributed to this reputation. The most striking (and weird) objects here are two actual human bodies conserved in the crypt, whose circulatory systems are perfectly preserved after 2 centuries. The chapel is also used for art exhibits and concerts—call for schedules.

Via Francesco De Sanctis 19 (south of Via dei Tribunali, 1 block east of Via Mezzocannone). ℭ **081-5518470.** www.museosansevero.it. Admission 7€ (6€ with Artcard). Mon and Wed–Sat 10am–6pm; Sun 10am–1:30pm. Last admission 20 min. before closing. Closed May 1 and Easter Monday. Metro: Dante.

Catacombe di San Gennaro (Catacombs of St. Gennaro) ★ ☺ These catacombs, attached to the church of San Gennaro Extra Moenia, are the most important in southern Italy, both for the length of the period they were in continued use—from the emergence of Christianity until the 10th century—and for the well-preserved **fresco cycles** ★ that decorate their corridors and chapels—that date from the 2nd to the 10th centuries. Organized on two levels, its broad corridors and halls distinguish it from the narrower Roman catacombs. Among the most interesting things here is the **Cripta dei Vescovi** ★, a burial chamber used for bishops that is magnificently decorated with mosaics dating from the 5th century. The lower level holds the **Basilica di Sant'Agrippino** *ipogea* ("ipogean," or subterranean) where St. Agrippino, the 3rd-century bishop of Naples, is buried. Also nearby is the **Cubicolo di San Gennaro,** with the tomb of the patron saint of Naples, whose remains were moved here in the 5th century.

One of the frescoes in the Catacombe di San Gennaro.

Via Capodimonte 13. ☏ **081-7443714.** www.catacombedinapoli.it. Admission 8€. By guided tour only. Mon-Sat on the hour 10am–5pm; Sun 10am–1pm. Bus: 24 or R4 to Via Capodimonte, and then down an alley alongside the church Madre del Buon Consiglio.

Certosa e Museo Nazionale di San Martino (Carthusian Monastery and National Museum of St. Martin) ★ Originally built in 1325 and rebuilt in the 17th century, this great monastery complex has been restored to its original beauty. Entering from the courtyard, you first come to the **church ★**, a masterpiece of baroque decoration, from the marble **floor** to the various works of art by artists such as Jusepe de Ribera (various paintings), Giuseppe Sanmartino (sculptures), and Battistello Caracciolo (frescoes). Do not overlook the marble **transenna** of the presbytery, decorated with precious stones (lapis lazuli and agate), and the **Cappella del Tesoro ★**, with a rich altar made of the same materials; beautiful **frescoes** by Luca Giordano—including the *Trionfo di Giuditta*—decorate the ceiling and you will also see a *Deposizione* by Jusepe de Ribera. The peaceful **Chiostro Grande ★★** (the Great Cloister) encloses a smooth lawn; in the corner is the monk's graveyard, topped with creepy marble

Museo Cappella Sansevero.

skulls. The **Quarto del Priore ★★**—the elegant apartment used for the reception of important personalities—contains a number of masterpieces, including a *Madonna col Bambino e San Giovannino* by Pietro Bernini. The monastery also houses the **Museo Nazionale di San Martino,** which has several sections. One of our favorites is the one housing the *presepi* (**Nativity scenes**) ★, off the Chiostro dei Procuratori. Some of these are extraordinarily complex, such as the *presepio* **Cuciniello,** created in 1879 with a collection of 18th-century figures and accessories. Other sections include the **Images and Memories of Naples exhibit ★★**, on the first and second floors, displaying paintings, sculpture, porcelain, and precious objects, and the **Collezione Rotondo ★**, with paintings and bronze sculpures by Neapolitan artists of the 19th century. The Sezione Navale, or Maritime Museum, will appeal to kids who will love the displays of model ships and ship's instruments including the full-size Great Barge that was used by King Charles of Bourbon in the 1700s. In the Gothic **cellars** of the monastery, you will find sections dedicated to sculpture and epigraphy, while on the second floor is the library that houses the **Prints and Drawings Collection,** with over 8,000 pieces.

Largo San Martino 8. ✆ **081-5781769.** Admission 6€. Thurs–Tues 8:30am–7:30pm; ticket booth closes 90 min. earlier. Closed Jan 1 and Dec 25. Metro: Vanvitelli and then bus V1 to Piazzale San Martino. Bus: C28, C31, or C36 to Piazza Vanvitelli. Funicular: Centrale to Piazza Fuga or Montesanto to Morghen.

Chiesa and Quadreria dei Girolamini ★ 👜 Rarely visited, this church and its attached convent hide a fine collection of artwork by some prominent Italian Renaissance artists. The church was built between the end of the 16th century and the beginning of the 17th. Among the masterpieces you'll find inside are in the counterfacade, a **fresco** by Luca Giordano; in the first chapel to the right, *Sant'Alessandro Moribondo* by Pietro da Cortona; in the transept, **frescoes** by Francesco Solimena and **statues** by Pietro Bernini; and over the altar in the sacristy, the painting *San Giovanni Battista,* by Guido Reni.

In the annexed **Casa dei Padri dell'Oratorio** (entrance on Via Duomo 142), you can visit the beautiful **Chiostro Maggiore ★** and the **Quadreria dei Girolamini ★★**, a rich collection of paintings donated to the convent and including notable artists such as Cavalier d'Arpino, Sermoneta, Guido Reni, and Jusepe de Ribera. You can also visit the splendid **library ★**, with its beautiful halls that include the beautiful **Sala Grande.**

Chiesa: Via dei Tribunali. ✆ **081-292316.** Free admission. Mon–Sat 9am–1pm and 4–7pm; Sun 9am–1pm. **Quadreria:** Via Duomo 142. ✆ **081-449139** or 331-4267772. www.girolamini.it. Free admission. Sat 9:30am–1pm and 3–6pm. Other days by appointment only; call ✆ 331-4267772. Bus: R1, R2, R3, or R4. Metro: Dante.

Chiesa del Gesù Nuovo ★ This unusual church was transformed by the Jesuits from 15th century Palazzo San Severino, the one-time residence of the Prince of Salerno, in the late 1700s. Its striking facade, a rare example of *bugnato a punta di diamante* (ashlar work), was preserved from the palazzo's original facade, while a baroque portal was created to encompass the original Renaissance portal. The church's interior is opulent and features stuccoes, frescoes, and marble decorations by some of Naples's best artists from the 16th century to the beginning of the 19th. Among the masterpieces are the impressive **fresco ★** by Francesco Solimena, called the *Expulsion of Eliodorus from the Temple,* and the rich decorations in the left transept, including a beautiful **altar** ★ and **statues** ★ of Jeremiah and David by Cosimo Fanzago. The **oratory** is usually closed, but you can request entry from the *custode* (keeper) of the Liceo at no. 1 of Piazza del Gesù.

On the piazza outside the church, you'll find one of Naples's several baroque spires, the **Guglia dell'Immacolata,** a tall column of statues and reliefs. Typically Neapolitan, this kind of religious monument is modeled after processional objects—part float, part conglomeration of statues and figures—built for religious celebrations from baroque times until the 1950s. This particular spire was created in 1750 by Matteo Bottighero and Francesco Pagano to celebrate one of the major points of the Jesuits' teachings; it depicts Jesuit saints and the story of Mary.

Piazza del Gesù. $\mathscr{C}$ **081-5578111.** Free admission. Mon–Sat 7am–1pm and 2:15–7:30pm; Sun 7am–1:45pm and 4:15–7:30pm. Bus: R1, R2, R3, or R4. Metro: Dante.

Chiesa di Santa Maria di Monteoliveto (aka Sant'Anna dei Lombardi)
★★ The Chiesa di Monteoliveto is not large but, having been one of the favorite churches of the Aragonese royal family, is chock-full of fabulous sculpture. It stands on a pretty square graced by the **Fontana di Monteoliveto,** the most beautiful baroque fountain in Naples that was built for Don Pedro de Aragona in 1699, based on a design by Cosimo Fanzago: It is a grandiose celebration of royal authority, with white marble eagles and lions crowned by the bronze statue of Carlo II d'Asburgo.

In the atrium, behind the church's elegant facade in *piperno* (a unique colorful stone that was carved in underground quarries in the Naples area), is the tomb of the architect Domenico Fontana. Inside the church are three superb Renaissance chapels. The **Cappella Correale** ★ to the right of the entrance has an altar by Benedetto da Maiano topped by a *San Cristoforo* by Francesco Solimena. To the left of the entrance, the **Cappella Piccolomini** ★ is an almost perfect replica of the more famous Chapel of the Cardinal of Portugal in the Florentine church of San Miniato al Monte and is graced by the tomb of Maria d'Aragona by Antonio Rossellino and Benedetto da Maiano. Also to the left lies the **Cappella Tolosa** ★ attributed to Giuliano da Maiano and decorated in the styles of Brunelleschi and della Robbia. To the right of the high altar is an unusual group sculpture, *Mourning the Death of Christ* (1492) by Guido Mazzini; the

Chiesa di Santa Maria di Monteoliveto.

stricken faces of the group are believed to have been modeled on members of the Aragonese court. From here, you can access the old **sacristy** ★ with its vaulted ceilings frescoed by Giorgio Vasari. Its walls, decorated with wood inlays depicting classical panoramas, musical instruments, and other scenes, were created by Giovanni da Verona between 1506 and 1510.

Piazza Monteoliveto 44 (off Via Monteoliveto, 1 block east of Via Toledo/Via Roma). ℂ **081-5513333.** Free admission. Daily 9am–6pm. Bus: R1, R2, R3, or R4. Metro: Dante.

Complesso Museale di Santa Chiara (Museum Complex of St. Clare)

★★ The most famous church in Naples, Santa Chiara was built in 1310 by King Roberto I d'Angió as the burial place of the Angevin dynasty. In the 18th century, it was lavishly decorated by the best artists of the time, but bombings in 1943 destroyed much of the art. A subsequent restoration in 1953 returned it to its original Gothic structure. A large rose window decorates the facade, flanked by a majestic bell tower that dominates the neighborhood (its lower part is 14th c.).

The interior is simple but monumental in size, with 10 chapels opening onto the central nave. It contains many royal tombs, including the grandiose **tomb of Roberto d'Angió** ★, a magnificent example of Tuscan-style Renaissance sculpture that towers over the high altar. It was carved by the Florentine Bernini brothers from 1343 to 1345. From the sacristy you can access the **Coro delle Clarisse (Choir of the Clares)** ★, with its beautiful 14th-century marble portal. The nuns sat in the *coro* during Mass, hidden from public view; only fragments remain, sadly, of Giotto's frescoes that decorated its walls. After your visit to the basilica, walk behind the church and enter the door to the right: It leads to the unique **Chiostro delle Clarisse** ★★, the monastery's main cloister. Strikingly decorated with bright majolica tiles in the mid–18th century, it is considered a masterpiece of Neapolitan art. The spaces adjacent to the cloister house a museum, the **Museo dell'Opera di Santa Chiara,** dedicated to the history of the monastery and housing sculptures and reliefs by local artists, including the beautiful *Crucifiction* and the *Visitation,* both by Tino di Camaino. From here you can visit the excavations of thermal baths from the 1st or 2nd century A.D.

Church: Via Santa Chiara 49 (off Via Benedetto Croce). ℂ **081-7971235.** Free admission. Mon and Wed–Sat 7:30am–1pm and 4:30–8pm. **Cloister & Museum:** Via Benedetto Croce 16. ℂ **081-7971236.** www.monasterodisantachiara.eu. Admission 5€. Mon and Wed–Sat 9:30am–5:30pm; Sun 10am–2:30pm. Bus: R1, R2, R3, or R4. Metro: Dante.

Duomo (Cattedrale di Santa Maria Assunta) ★★★ King

Carlo I d'Angio built Naples's great cathedral, dedicated to San Gennaro, in the 13th century on the site of a 6th-century building that, in turn, stood next to the 4th-century Basilica di Santa Restituta,

The Duomo.

which is now part of the Duomo. Behind the unconvincing, fake Gothic facade, the grandiose interior, built on a Latin cross design supported by 110 ancient granite columns, is lavishly decorated. Among the most precious artwork is the painting *Assunta* by **Perugino,** located on the right side of the transept. Several chapels open from both naves and the transept; the most splendid is the Gothic **Cappella Capece Minutolo** ★★, with its beautiful 13th-century frescoes and mosaic floor. To the right of the presbytery is another Gothic chapel of great beauty, the **Cappella Tocco** ★. On either side of the main altar, stairs lead down to the Renaissance **Succorpo** ★, or Crypt, with intricately carved columns and the elegant marble statue of a kneeling Cardinal Carafa.

From the right nave, the third chapel to the right is the monumental **Cappella di San Gennaro** ★★, dedicated to the patron saint of Naples. Richly decorated with precious marbles, gold leaf, frescoes, and artworks, it is considered by art historians as the highest achievement of Neapolitan baroque. The fresco cycle around the dome, illustrating the life of San Gennaro, is by **Domenichino,** while the oil painting over copper, depicting San Gennaro, is by Jusepe de Ribera—the rich frame of gilded bronze and lapis lazuli is by Onofrio D'Alessio. The famous reliquaries containing the skull and the blood of San Gennaro—which is said to miraculously liquefy each September 19 (Feast Day of San Gennaro) as well as the first Sunday in May and December 16—are inside a safe over the main altar; they are exposed to the public only for 1 week in May, 1 week in September, and on the 16th of December.

From the left nave, the third chapel entrance leads to **Santa Restituta** ★★, which was the city's cathedral until the present building was completed in the 14th century. Built in the 4th century by Emperor Constantine, it is very atmospheric in spite of many changes over the centuries; the facade and atrium were demolished when it was annexed to the Duomo, while the apse was redecorated in baroque style in the 17th century. In addition, the two outermost of its original five naves were closed into chapels to re-inforce the building. We love the sixth chapel on the left, with its luminous 14th-century **mosaic** by Lello da Orvieto and two beautiful 13th-century reliefs. Here you can buy a ticket to the small archaeological area and the **Baptistery of San Giovanni in Fonte** ★★, which should not be missed. Founded in the 4th century, this is the oldest building of its kind in the western world and is decorated with dazzling (although partially damaged) 5th-century mosaics. From the end of the left nave, you can access the small but interesting archaeological area under the Duomo, which reveals a complex of buildings that date from the Greek period through the Romans to the Dark Ages.

Adjacent to the Duomo is the entrance to the **Museo del Tesoro di San Gennaro (Museum of the Treasure of San Gennaro)** ★. The collection here is exceptional both for its quality and quantity: There are so many treasures here that the museum rotates its exhibits annually over a multiple-year cycle. The museum also gives access to the Duomo's **sacristy** ★★, beautifully decorated with **frescoes** by Luca Giordano and paintings by **Domenichino.** In the sacristy, you can also arrange an appointment to visit Santa Restituta and the Cappella Minutolo if you find them closed.

Cathedral: Via Duomo 147. *℃* **081-449065.** Free admission. Mon–Sat 8am–12:30pm and 4:30–7pm; Sun and holidays 8:30am–1pm and 5–7pm. **Excavations:** Mon–Fri 9am–noon and 4:30–7pm; Sat–Sun and holidays 9am–12:30pm. **Museum:** Via Duomo 149. *℃* **081-3442286.** www.museo sangennaro.com. Admission 6€. Daily 9am–6.30pm. Bus: E1 to Via Duomo. Metro: Cavour.

Pio Monte della Misericordia ★★★   One of Naples's most important paintings is housed in this modest, octagonal chapel: Caravaggio's seminal 1607 *Seven Acts of Mercy* ★★★. It was commissioned in 1601 by a charitable institution of seven noblemen whose aim was to alleviate the suffering of the poor and needy in the city through good works, illustrated in this great, dramatic painting that hangs over the high altar. Famous for its *chiaroscuro* (light and dark) effects, it shows the Virgin and Child borne by angels with huge wings; in the background is an earthy street scene set in the SpaccaNapoli, the neighborhood where the chapel is located.

An elevator in the courtyard will take you to the small second-floor picture gallery where there are works by other Neapolitan 17th- and 18th-century masters such as Luca Giordano, Massimo Stanzione, and Giuseppe Ribera. In the third room is the seven-sided table where the original members of the institution met (the confraternity still exists today), while the Sala Coretto opens onto a secret gallery from which the governors could spy into the church below: It looks directly onto Caravaggio's masterpiece.

Via dei Tribunali 253. *℃* **081-446944.** www.piomontedellamisericordia.it. Admission 5€ (4€ with Artecard). Thurs–Tues 9am–2.30pm. Metro: Dante.

San Domenico Maggiore ★   Standing over one of Naples's most beautiful squares—graced by the **Guglia San Domenico,** an intricately carved marble spire erected between 1658 and 1737 in gratitude for the end of that century's plague—this church actually offers its back to the public: Its facade, following an Angevin tradition, is only visible from the inner courtyard. Built by Carlo II d'Angiò between 1283 and 1324, San Domenico Maggiore encloses the older church of **San Michele Arcangelo a Morfisa,** which is still accessible from the transept. Inside both are innumerable works of art, including many **Renaissance monumental tombs** graced by sculptures and carvings, as well as 14th-century **frescoes** and 15th- and 16th-century **paintings.** The main **altar** is a beautiful work of marble inlay from the 16th century.

Piazza San Domenico Maggiore (off Via San Biagio dei Librai). *℃* **081-459188.** Free admission. Daily 8.30am–noon and 3:30–7pm. Metro: Piazza Cavour.

San Giovanni a Carbonara ★ 🏛   Built in 1343 with the annex convent, this church was used by the Angevin dynasty to bury their last family members. It is one of Naples's hidden gems and is likely to stay that way considering that it's rather hard to find. The church stands at the top of a sweeping double stone staircase; at the top of the stairs is the chapel of Santa Monica (closed to the public) with a marble Gothic portal; the entrance to the church is on the left of this portal. Inside are several important works of art, including, over the high altar, the towering **Monumental Tomb of King Ladislao,** a 15th-century masterpiece by several Tuscan artists. Behind the monument is the circular **Cappella Caracciolo del Sole,** with a rare majolica floor and beautiful **frescoes** from the 15th century. To the left of the high altar is another round Caracciolo family chapel, the early-16th-century **Cappella Caracciolo di Vico,** built entirely of marble and graced by a beautifully carved 16th-century altar. At the end of the courtyard, an entrance gives access to yet another chapel: the **Cappella Seripando,** with a *Crucifiction* by Vasari.

Via San Giovanni a Carbonara 5 (5 short blocks east of the Duomo). ℭ **081-295873.** Free admission. Mon–Sat 8am–noon and 4:30–8:30pm; Sun 8am–2pm. Metro: Piazza Cavour.

San Gregorio Armeno Lending its name to the street famous for its manger artists and vendors (see "Shopping for Local Crafts," p. 118), this little visited church has a lavishly decorated baroque interior, a beautiful bell tower, and a peaceful adjoining cloister. Dating from the 8th century, the church's interior was reworked in 1580, with extravagant use of gold leaf and artwork by famous masters of the time: The exceptional **wooden ceiling ★** was carved and painted by Teodoro d'Errico, while the **frescoes ★** in the counterfacade are by Luca Giordano. Don't miss the pretty **cloister ★** of the attached convent (through the entrance outside the church, beyond the bell tower), where the nuns still live and run an infant school; it is beautifully preserved and graced by a marble **fountain** depicting Jesus meeting the good Samaritan.

Via San Gregorio Armeno 44 (btw. Via San Biagio dei librai and Via dei Tribunali, 3 short blocks west of Via Duomo). Free admission. Daily 9:30am–noon. Metro: Piazza Cavour.

San Lorenzo Maggiore.

San Lorenzo Maggiore ★★ ☺ The most beautiful of Naples's medieval churches, San Lorenzo is famous for its literary past—it was here that Giovanni Boccaccio met his Fiammetta in 1334, and the attached convent hosted Francesco Petrarca for a period. Originally a basilica from the 6th century A.D., the church was rebuilt in 1270 by Carlo I d'Angiò and his successor in Gothic style; its facade is baroque as the original was partially destroyed by an earthquake. The interior is airy and holds innumerable works of art, including 13th- and 14th-century **frescoes,** as well as beautiful **altars** and monumental tombs. From the baroque cloister you can visit the Chapter Hall and the refectory of the monastery, built in the 13th century. From the 14th-century cloister, enter the **Greek and**

Roman excavations ★, where you'll see a slice of the city's layers of construction, from the Roman Macellum—the city market dating from the 1st century A.D.—complete with merchant stalls, to a paleochristian basilica, to a medieval building to, finally, the existing buildings. It's a great place to visit with children in tow. The best pieces from the excavations are displayed in the **museum,** which also features a collection of historical ceremonial religious attire and a collection of 18th-century *presepio* (Nativity scene) figures.

Piazza San Gaetano (off Via dei Tribunali, 3 blocks west of Via Duomo). **Church:** ✆ **081-290580.** www.sanlorenzomaggiorenapoli.it. Free admission. Mon–Sat 8am–noon and 5–7pm. **Excavations:** ✆ **081-2110860.** Admission 4€. Mon–Sat 9:30am–5:30pm; Sun and holidays 9:30am–1:30pm. Metro: Piazza Cavour.

San Paolo Maggiore ★ Founded between the 8th and 9th centuries A.D. over a pre-existing Roman Temple of the Dioscuri—two of its columns remain on the facade—San Paolo Maggiore was completely redone in the 16th century. The interior was decorated by many important artists of the 17th and 18th centuries, but the standouts here are the statue *Angelo Custode* by Domenico Antonio Vaccaro to the left of the central nave; the **frescoes** in the sacristy—considered the best work of Francesco Solimena; and the **Cappella Firrao** to the left of the presbytery, one of the most beautiful baroque chapels in Naples.

Via San Paolo (off Via dei Tribunali, opposite Piazza San Gaetano). ✆ **081-454048.** Free admission. Daily 8am–noon and 5–7pm. Metro: Piazza Cavour.

Sant'Angelo a Nilo With its striking red and gray facade, this church was built in 1385 for the Brancaccio family and reworked in the 18th century. It merits a visit for its **Funerary Monument of Cardinal Rinaldo Brancaccio** ★, created in Pisa between 1426 and 1427, and shipped by sea to Naples. It is believed that Donatello carved the bas-relief of the Assumption; it is the great Florentine sculptor's only work in Naples. The two portals to the right of the presbytery, one from the 14th and the other from the 16th century, are also noteworthy.

The Church of Sant'Angelo a Nilo gets its name from the Greek-Roman **Statue of the Egyptian god Nile** that stands in the small square near the church. Originally carved for merchants from Alexandria who worked in the area, the statue was lost for centuries and was recovered in the 1400s. In typical Neapolitan spirit, the statue of the river god, with his babies representing the river tributaries, was interpreted as a representation of motherly Naples, nourishing its children; hence the nickname still in use today among the locals—*cuorp'e Napule* or "body of Naples." The statue's head was a 17th-century addition.

Piazzetta Nilo (off Via Benedetto Croce). Free admission. Mon–Sat 8:30am–1pm and 4:45–7pm; Sun 8:30am–1pm. Bus R2. Metro: Piazza Cavour.

Public Naples

Fontana del Nettuno Naples's most beautiful fountain has a unique history of mobility. Originally built for Viceroy Enrico Guzman, count of Olivares, it stood in front of the Arsenal for 30 years. In 1622, the Duca d'Alba had it moved to the Piazza del Palazzo Reale. In 1637, it was moved again to in front of the Castel dell'Ovo but, a few years later, worried that it was open to attacks from the sea, the city authorities moved it "temporarily" to Piazza delle Corregge. It stayed there until the beginning of the 20th century, when it was moved again to its present—and maybe even permanent—position.

Piazza G. Bovio (off Via Medina). Metro: Universita.

The Fontana del Nettuno,

Galleria Umberto I This gallery is an elegant glass-and-iron covered passage following a Greek cross shape, with each of its four arms opening onto a street on one end and meeting at a rotunda, covered with a cupola, on the other. Built at the end of the 19th century—20 years after its larger Milanese counterpart—this is a splendid Liberty-style (Italian Art Nouveau) construction with obvious Parisian inspiration. Inside, the galleria is lined with elegant shops and cafes.

You'll find a second Liberty-era gallery in town, **Galleria del Principe di Napoli** (off Piazza Cavour to the right; Metro: Piazza Cavour), which is virtually unknown, probably because of its location outside the most touristy area of Via Toledo.

4 entrances: To the right off Via Toledo as you come from Piazza del Plebiscito, Via Giuseppe Verdi, Via Santa Brigida, and Via San Carlo. Bus: R2 or R3 to Piazza Trieste e Trento.

Piazza del Plebiscito ★★ This graceful, wide-open piazza is arguably the most beautiful in Naples. It is defined by the majestic, curving colonnade of **San Francesco di Paola**—an 1817 church built in full neoclassical style and inspired by the Roman Pantheon—and the elegant neoclassical facade of the Royal Palace. In the square are two equestrian statues, one of **Carlo III** by Antonio Canova and one of **Ferdinando I** (only the horse is by Canova). The square is fittingly called the "salotto" (living room) by Neapolitans, as it has been completely closed to traffic and locals use it as a gathering place. Nearby is Piazza Trieste e Trento, with the Fontana del Carciofo, and the start of Via Toledo (Neapolitans call this Via Roma), an extremely popular promenade and shopping street.

Off Piazza Trieste e Trento (btw. Via Chiaia and Via C. Console). Bus: R2 or R3 to Piazza Trieste e Trento.

Teatro San Carlo ★ Built for Carlo Borbone by Antonio Medrano, the Teatro San Carlo is among Europe's most beautiful opera houses and one of the most famous. A neoclassical jewel with an ornate gilded interior, the San Carlo was inaugurated on November 4, 1737. The facade was added in 1812 by Antonio Piccolini, who also rebuilt the interior after it was destroyed by fire in 1816.

The auditorium holds 1,470 seats and is considered to have even better acoustics than Milan's famous La Scala and has a distinguished roster of past conductors that includes Donizetti, Rossini, and even the great Maetrso Giuseppe Verdi. You can appreciate its architecture and magnificent red-and-gold interior by taking the guided tour (in Italian or English). Even better, book a ticket for a performance (see "Naples After Dark," later in this chapter) to see the building in its full glory.

Via San Carlo 93. *C* **081-7972111;** ticket office e-mail biglietteriaeatrosancarlo.it; 081-797233 guided tours reservations. www.teatrosancarlo.it. Guided tours 10€. Ticket office hours: Mon–Sat 10am–7pm; Sun 10am–3:30pm. Bus: R2 or R3 to Via San Carlo.

FROM TOP: **Piazza del Plebiscito.; Teatro San Carlo.**

Villa Comunale ★ ☺ Created in 1780 according to a design by Luigi Vanvitelli, as the private Royal Promenade for King Ferdinando IV Bourbon, this park was later transformed by the king into a public garden. It is graced by statues, fountains—including the beloved **Fontana delle Paperelle** ("fountain of the ducks")—and several elegant buildings such as the **Casina Pompeiana, the Chiosco della Musica,** and the **Stazione Zoologica** housing Europe's oldest **aquarium,** specializing in the study of local marine life. The Villa Comunale also hosts a popular antiques market, usually held on the 3rd and 4th weekends of each month, 8:30am to 1pm; call the tourist office (p. 66) for details. You can find excellent souvenirs as well as more important pieces. If you have young children, we also recommend the merry-go-round and playground located in the southeast corner of the park; it might not be up with the best in the

U.S. but still is very welcome by the younger ones. It's pleasant for parents as well who can sit and look at the seaside promenade.

Park: Piazza Vittoria. Daily 7am–midnight. **Aquarium:** ℂ 081-5833111. Free admission. Tues-Sun 9am–5pm. Bus: C82 or R2.

The Kid Zone

Throughout this book, look for the "kids" icon to indicate that an attraction is kid friendly. The **CitySightseeing** open-top bus tours, the fascinating **Napoli Sotterranea** (see below), and the University of Naples museums (ℂ 081-2537587; www.musei.unina.it), are great for the younger set. The university's **Museo di Paleontologia (Paleonthology Museum),** Largo San Marcellino 10 (ℂ 081-2537516), contains a large fossil collection, with splendid fish fossils from local digs, and even a carnivorous dinosaur. For some cool rocks and minerals from around the globe, the **Museo di Mineralogia (Mineralogy Museum),** Via Mezzocannone 8 (ℂ 081-2535163), has a unique section on Vesuvian minerals as well as a real gold nugget, a diamond from South Africa, meteorites, and beautiful crystals. Animal lovers will enjoy the **Museo di Zoologia (Zoology Museum),** Via Mezzocannone 8 (ℂ 081-2535164). Admission is 2.50€ for one museum (1.50€ kids), 3.50€ for two museums (2€ kids), or 4.50€ for all of them (3€ kids; Mon–Fri 9am–1pm; Mon and Thurs also 3–5pm; bus E1, R2 to Corso Umberto-Mezzocannone or Metro Cavour). See "Family Travel," p. 357 for more tips.

Guided Tours

CitySightseeing Napoli (ℂ 081-5517279; www.napoli.city-sightseeing.it) offers hop-on-hop-off double-decker bus tours of the city. Buses depart from Piazza Municipio/Parco Castello and run with varying frequency to all major attractions. Tickets are valid for 24 hours on all lines and can be purchased onboard for 22€ for adults, 11€ for children ages 6 to 15; and 66€ for a family (two adults and three children 18 and under). You'll get a 10% discount with your Artecard (p. 98).

MAN-Museo Aperto Napoli (ℂ 081-5636062; www.museoaperto napoli.it) is the cultural organization serving Naples's historic district. It is based in a large cultural and information center (Via Pietro Colletta 85, to the right of Castel Capuano, at the eastern edge of the historic district; daily 10am–6pm) where you'll find a knowledgeable and kind multilingual staff, a multimedia center with information on the historic district, exhibits on the area, as well as a cafe offering typical local products, a bookshop, a small space with crafts for sale, and, luckily, bathrooms. The center offers all kinds of services useful to the tourist, from maps and information on the historic district, to umbrellas on loan and excellent guided tours: Choose among four self-guided audio tours or walking tours with a live guide; all tours are offered in six languages. At presstime, the service had been suspended temporarily with no deifinate date for re-opening. Ask at the tourist office for information (p. 66).

Napoli Sotterranea (ℂ 081-296944; www.lanapolisotterranea.it), or "Naples Underground," organizes guided tours of the city's abandoned aqueduct tunnels. The tunnels date back some 5,000 years and feature ancient Greek and Roman remains—in particular a recently excavated Greek theater—as well as more modern sites, such as the galleries used as hideouts during World War II. The tour lasts about 2 hours and meets at Piazza San Gaetano 68, on Via dei Tribunali near the church of San Lorenzo (Metro: Dante). Especially popular

The Best Gelato in Naples

The following list of our favorite gelato is not complete without a mention of **Gelateria G. Mazzaro** (p. 94). For more info on Italian gelato, see p. 38.

* **Chalet da Ciro,** Via Caracciolo, in Mergellina (✆ **081-669928**; closed Wed), is known for its superlative *nocciola* (hazelnut flavor).

* **Fantasia Gelati,** Via Toledo 381 (✆ **081-5511212**), has another branch on Piazza Vanvitelli, in Vomero.

* **Gelateria La Scimmia,** Piazza Carità 4, off Via Toledo (✆ **081-5520272**), prepares its gelato from scratch with fresh fruits. This is the original parlor, more atmospheric than the branch at Piazzetta Nilo, off Via Benedetto Croce.

* **Gelateria Otranto,** Via Scarlatti 78, off Piazza Vanvitelli (✆ **081-5587498**; closed Wed) is our favorite in the Vomero neighborhood.

* **Gran Bar Riviera** (pictured), Riviera di Chiaia 181 (✆ **081-665026**), is popular particularly among the evening crowds.

* **Polo Nord,** Via Pietro Colletta 41 (✆ **081-205431**; closed Sun) is not too touristy, but is also convenient to the Duomo.

* **Bilancione,** Via Posillipo, off Piazza San Luigi, Posillipo (✆ **081-7691923**), has views over the Bay that rival the gelato.

among older children and teens, the tours last around 1 hour and 20 minutes and cost 9.30€ (10% off with Artecard), 6€ for children under 10. Tours in English are scheduled daily, year-round, at 10am, noon, and 2 and 4pm.

For more classic city tours, the agency **Every Tours,** Via Santa Brigida (✆ **081-5518564**) organizes tours of the city as well as day excursions to Vesuvio and other sights. It's open Monday through Friday from 9am to 1:30pm and 3:30 to 7pm and Saturday from 9am to 1pm. Another good agency is **NapoliVision** (✆ **081-5595130;** www.napolivision.it), offering guided tours of Naples, Pompei, and Capri starting at 30€ per person (20% discount with Artecard).

SHOPPING FOR LOCAL CRAFTS

Naples is a great source for Italian designer clothes and accessories, as well as for antiques and crafts. You have to know your stuff, though, because it was here that counterfeit goods were invented back in the 17th or 18th century. We advise you to stay away from fakes altogether, even if the price seems right; you risk heavy fines at Customs on your way home, as most countries are cracking down on such purchases as a way to protect brand identity. You also run the risk of being fined on the spot by the police.

THE presepio

Although the tradition of Nativity scenes—called *presepi* in Italian—dates back to the 13th century, the art form really reached its peak in the 18th and 19th centuries when the aristocracy competed to acquire figurines for their mangers, modeled by the famous sculptors of the time who all participated in this game, creating the terra-cotta parts of the figurines (usually the head and limbs). These were then mounted on mannequins of wire and *stoppa* (fiber) by craftsmen, and richly dressed with precious silk clothes embroidered with gold. Skilled sculptors, goldsmiths, tailors, and scenographers created everything from the figures to the complicated settings—grottoes, buildings, rivers, and ponds—combining their crafts into the first examples of multimedia art. Only the wealthier aristocrats were able to purchase such works of art while the others had to make do with copies produced by Nativity craftsmen.

The *presepio* tradition is still very much alive today, and Neapolitan mangers go beyond typical Nativity representations to depict current social and political events. Among the figures you'll find on sale are such recognizable characters as Princess Diana, Mother Teresa of Calcutta, Versace, and Silvio Berlusconi. **Via San Gregorio Armeno,** near the Duomo, is where most of the traditional workshops are located alternating with shops selling the mass-produced versions. Inevitably, the number of true artisans (who learned their skills from their fathers) is in sharp decline,

but it is worth seeking these craftsmen out and buying from them even though prices will be higher. In the shops along this street, you'll find everything from characters and rocks, to grottoes and miniature street lamps. At the back of the few authentic laboratories, you'll also find figurines carefully crafted in different sizes, from amazingly precise half-inch miniatures to life-size figures and amazingly realistic scenes. While commercial mangers come in a variety of prices, the authentic *presepi* are out of the price range of many customers: A medium-size hand-painted and hand-crafted terra-cotta shepherd can cost as much as 300€.

Opening hours for stores are generally Monday to Saturday from 10:30am to 1pm and from 4 to 7:30pm.

Riviera di Chiaia, Via Calabritto, Via dei Mille, Via Filangeri, Via Poerio, and Piazza dei Martiri in **Chiaia** are where to go for the big-name **Italian fashion** labels, such as Valentino, Versace, Prada, and, of course, Salvatore Ferragamo—a Naples native (the latter four are on and around Piazza dei Martiri). The area is also great for exploring the many smaller boutiques and stores that mostly sell accessories and clothing.

In the vicinity are old-time local favorites, such as **Marinella,** Via Riviera di Chiaia 287 (✆ **081-7644214**), famous for handmade classic and colorful ties; **Aldo Tramontano,** Via Chiaia 149 (✆ **081-414837**), for his handbags; and **Mario Talarico,** Vico Due Porte a Toledo 4/b (✆ **081-401979**), for his handcrafted umbrellas. You'll also find some of the most reputable **antiques** dealers, such as **Bowinkle,** Piazza dei Martiri 24 (✆ **081-7644344**), and **Navarra,** Piazza dei Martiri (✆ **081-7643595**), but also **Maurizio Brandi,** Via Domenico Morelli 9 (✆ **081-7643882**).

Every third Saturday and Sunday of each month from 8am to 2pm (except in Aug), a *fiera antiquaria* (antiques fair) is held in the Villa Comunale di Napoli on Viale Dohrn.

In the **Vomero,** the best shopping is centered on Via Scarlatti.

For more casual shopping and some specialty stores, try strolling the popular **Via Toledo/Via Roma** in the Quartieri Spagnoli/historical center. Here you will find the historical chocolate factory **Gay-Odin,** Via Toledo 214 and Via Toledo 427 (✆ **081/417-843;** www.gay-odin.it). The area is also home to the elegant shops of the **Galleria Umberto I,** such as **Ascione 1855** (✆ **081-421111**) and its **cameo** workshop, where you can observe the delicate process of carving agate and coral, and also purchase unique jewelry.

The best places to shop for traditional crafts are in the historic district. Head for **Via San Gregorio Armeno ★★** if you are looking for a *presepio*. The most reputable workshops are **Gambardella Pastori,** Via San Gregorio Armeno 40 (✆ **081-5517107**); **Giuseppe Ferrigno,** Via San Gregorio Armeno 10 (✆ **081-5523148**); and **Amendola,** Via San Gregorio Armeno 51 (✆ **081-5514899**). Via San Biagio dei Librai is lined with interesting shops selling paper goods and jewelry. Good addresses for antique prints and books are **Libreria Colonnese,** Via San Pietro a Majella 32 (✆ **081-459858**); **Dante e Descartes,** Via Mezzocannone 75 (✆ **081-5515368**); and Colonnese, Via Carlo Poerio 92 (✆ **081-7642627**).

NAPLES AFTER DARK

A warm southern city, Naples is best experienced outdoors, and the Neapolitans make the best of the balmy summer evenings by passing the time on the terraces of the city's many popular cafes. One of our favorites is the elegant **Gran Caffè Gambrinus,** Via Chiaia 1, in Piazza Trento e Trieste (✆ **081-417582**). The oldest cafe in Naples, its original Liberty-style interior was decorated by Antonio Curri in the 1860s. Another very popular spot is **La Caffetteria,** Piazza dei Martiri 25 (✆ **081-7644243**), frequented by a chic, local crowd who come here for evening aperitivi.

Opera

If you have the time, try and catch a performance at **Teatro San Carlo,** Via San Carlo 98/f (✆ **081-7972412** or 081-7972331; fax 081-400902; www.teatrosan carlo.it), a world-class venue with a consistently high-level program. Performances take place Tuesday through Sunday, December through June. Tickets cost between 30€ and 100€; you'll get a 10% discount with an Artecard (p. 98).

Another historic theater we recommend is **Teatro Mercadante,** Piazza Municipio 1 (✆ **081-5513396;** www.teatrostabilenapoli.it), which always has a prestigious program although plays will almost certainly be in Italian. Tickets cost from around 12€ to 30€, depending on the performance; you'll get a 10% discount with an Artecard (p. 98).

Music

Music lovers will find plenty of scope in Naples. At any given time, the city is alive with concerts spanning the classics to the most avant-garde performances. If classical music is your preference, besides the concerts at **Teatro San Carlo** (see above), the **Centro di Musica Antica Pietà dei Turchini,** Via Santa Caterina da Siena 38 (✆ **081-402395;** www.turchini.it), is one of the best venues in town; ticket prices depend on the performance, and you'll get a 25% discount with your Artecard (p. 98). Another great venue is the **Associazione Alessandro Scarlatti,** Piazza dei Martiri 58 (✆ **081-406011;** www.associazionescarlatti. it), which also organizes a successful concert series at Castel Sant'Elmo; tickets prices range from 15€ to 25€, with a 20% discount given to those with an Artecard (p. 98). For immersion in Neapolitan traditional music, the best address in town is the newly re-opened **Teatro Trianon Viviani,** Piazza Vincenzo Calenda 9 (✆ **081-2258285;** www.trianonviviani.it); the concert season usually starts in April, with performances Thursday through Sunday, but check the theater for changes in the programs. Ticket prices depend on seat and performance, but you'll get a 10% discount with the Artecard (p. 98).

Enoteche

Naples is home to a growing number of excellent *enoteche*. The Italians rightly believe that you should never drink on an empty stomach, so aside from a good choice of wines both by the glass and by the bottle, these wine bars usually also serve food that can range from cold snacks featuring local specialities to full-blown meals. We recommend the quiet **Berevino,** Via Sebastiano 62 (✆ **081-0605688,** www.berevino.org; closed Mon), as well as **Barrique,** Piazzetta Ascensione 9 (✆ **081-662721;** closed Mon), where you can sample the best local wines and a large choice of grappa and *rhums* while delighting in scrumptious small dishes from the weekly menu. The elegant and trendy **L'Ebrezza di Noè,** Vico Vetriera 9 (✆ **081-400104;** daily 7:30pm–12:30am), serves a simple menu of cured meats, cheeses, and appetizers to accompany the wide selection of wines from its excellent cellar. It specialises in unusual and lesser-known wines and vintages of great quality; don't be afraid to ask for guidance from the experienced staff. **Vinarium,** Vico Cappella Vecchia 7 (✆ **081-7644247;** Mon–Fri 10:30am–4:30pm, Mon–Sat 7pm–2:30am), is also popular but less upscale and serves a more rounded menu to accompany the large choice of Campania's best D.O.C. wines (see "And Some Vino To Wash It All Down," p. 37) as well as other wines from farther afield. A specially priced selection of wines is introduced each day. **Cantina di Triunfo,** Via Riviera di Chiaia 64 (✆ **081-668101;** Tues–Sat 10am–7:30pm wine store, Mon–Sat 7:30pm–midnight wine bar/restaurant), offers a limited but excellent menu to accompany its large choice of wines. **Enoteca Belledonne,** Vico Belledonne a Chiaia 18 (✆ **081-403162,** www.enotecabelledonne.com; closed Sun) has a large choice of wines and snacks.

Bars, Discos & Clubs

Naples is a port, a cosmopolitan city, and a university town all rolled into one, so its nighttime scene is eclectic and lively. Trendy bars and cafes stay open until at least until 2am every day of the week, while clubs stay open even later—usually until 4 or 5am—but often only from Thursday to Saturday. Bars and cafes usually don't charge covers, but clubs may charge about 14€.

Good places to grab a drink range from **Enoteca Belledonne,** Vico Belledonne a Chiaia 18 (✆ 081-403162; www.enotecabelledonne.com), a relaxed wine bar that has a late-night following to the sleek and exotic **Miami Bar Room,** Via Morghen 68C (✆ 081-2298332). Upmarket **S'move,** Vico dei Sospiri 10A (✆ 081-7645813) is a good place to dance.

For jazz, head up to Vomero and the small but friendly **Around Midnight,** Via Bonito 32A (✆ 333-7005230; www.aroundmidnight.it). **Bourbon Street,** Via Vincenzo Bellini 52 (✆ 338-8253756) is also a good bet every night except Mondays. For live Neapolitan bands, check out **Vibes Cafè,** Via San Giovanni Maggiore Pignatelli 10 (✆ 081-5513984), where you can dance inside or outside on the terrace in summer. Another good place for live music is **Il Re Nudo,** Via Manzoni 126 (✆ 081-7146272), where you can hear anything from jazz to South American groups. **Rising South,** Via San Sebastiano 19 (✆ 335-8790428) and **Kestè,** Largo San Giovanni Maggiore 26 (✆ 081-5513984; www.keste.it) are favored by younger crowds (20s and early 30s).

An elegant nightclub worth checking out is **Chez Moi,** Via del Parco Margherita 13 (✆ 081-407526), in the Riviera di Chiaia. Nearby **La Mela,** Via dei Mille (✆ 081-4010270), is also worth a visit as is **Tongue,** Via Manzoni 202 (✆ 081-7690888) in Posillipo, a club with a good mix of gays and lesbians as well as a straight clientele.

In summer, the hottest clubbing action moves to the beach, and although these waterside nightspots are a bit of a way from the city center (the easiest way is by taxi), the cool factor justifies the effort to get there. In Bagnoli, the **Arenile,** Via Coroglio 14B (✆ 338-8817715; www.arenilereload.com) is open from May to October and is the nearest beach club to the city; it features live music as well as DJ sessions. **Vibes on the Beach,** Via Miseno 52, Capo Miseno (✆ 081-5232828) is a cool, jazzy place open daily June to September, while **Nabilah** at Via Spiaggia Romana 15, Fusaro (✆ 081-8689433; www.nabilah.it) is the chicest of them all and is open Friday to Sunday May to September.

For a gay-men-only spot, head for **Bar B,** Via Giovanni Manna, off Via Duomo (✆ 081-287681), a famous gay sauna—with Turkish and Finnish spas on three levels, and with two bars and five dark rooms—that turns into a disco on Thursday and Saturday nights; music ranges from Latin to techno. For a mixed/gay-male scene, check out **Sputnik Club** at Via Santa Teresa degli Scalzi 154 bis (✆ 081-19813222).

POMPEII, HERCULANEUM & BEYOND

5

Many of the sites identified in ancient mythology are to be found in the volcanic areas that surround Naples, Mount Vesuvius, and the Phlegrean Fields—where bubbling springs and hot mud conjure up images of the underworld. Once considered as highly desirable by the Romans who built opulent villas in these idyllic areas, they have now been engulfed by the sprawl of Naples's suburbs that inevitably come complete with pockets of squalor. Yet the extraordinary natural and archaeological attractions that are to be found within spitting distance of Naples cannot be overlooked.

The area's abundant archaeological remains are a paramount reason to come, and these range from the fascinating ruins of ancient Cumae—the first Greek colony in Italy—to the underwater archaeological park of Baia. In Campi Flegrei is Lake Fusaro; Solfatara has its volcanic hot mud and sulfur springs; the promontory of Capo Miseno affords views of the delightful bay; and Lake Averno is the mythical entrance to the Kingdom of the Dead.

And what would Naples's skyline be without Mount Vesuvius? You'll discover the love-fear relationship Neapolitans have with their volcano when you climb its slopes and taste its marvelous *Lacrima Christi* wine, very aware that the volcano *will* blow its top again one day. The Bay of Naples is home not only to two of the world's most renowned ancient ruins—Pompeii and Herculaneum—but also to lesser-known sites such as the Roman villa of Oplonti (a UNESCO World Heritage Site) and the thermal Baths at Stabiae (see chapter 6).

Mount Vesuvius had been dormant for centuries when the great explosion of A.D. 79 occurred. At the time of the eruption, it seems that nobody knew it was a volcano, and its slopes—sought after for the fertile soil—were heavily inhabited (as they are today). Towns, villages, and estates were covered by lava and ash during the eruption, causing thousands of deaths, devastation of property, and immense economic loss. Pompeii was the first of the lost towns to be excavated—the discovery dates from the 16th century. Recently, modern archaeologists have unveiled many other sites, and these newer sites have not been spoiled by illegal digs over the years.

Herculaneum is striking for the fact that the buildings have been preserved so well. Rarely visited by foreign tourists, the grandiose Roman villa of Oplontis is still decorated with magnificent frescoes, and we also recommend the smaller villas of Boscoreale and Boscotrecase.

All of the destinations we describe in this chapter make an easy day trip from Naples, but if you are not planning to visit the city itself, it is a good idea to stay in the area, which offers less-pricey accommodations than Naples. We give options for Campi Flegrei and Vesuvius–Herculaneum, Pompeii, and nearby Torre del Greco, or, a bit farther down the coast, Castellammare di Stabia (see chapter 6).

PREVIOUS PAGE: **The ruins of Pompeii.**

HERCULANEUM ★★★

9.5km (6 miles) SE of Naples

The volcanic mud that covered Herculaneum during the eruption of Vesuvius in A.D. 79 killed most of the town's estimated 5,000 inhabitants and quickly hardened to a semirock material, protecting the structures underneath but also making archaeological excavations much slower than at other sites. Herculaneum was discovered in 1709, and although excavations started shortly after and proceeded alongside those in Pompeii, the uncovered area here is much smaller than that of the more famous sibling site. Also, unlike at Pompeii, much of the ancient town lies under the modern one, making excavation even more difficult. The findings, however, have been stunning.

Although many questions about Herculaneum remain unanswered, researchers tell us that this town was about a third of the size of Pompeii and had a different urban makeup. A glitzy seaside resort for wealthy Romans, Herculaneum had little commercial and industrial activity although it was a moderately busy harbor. Most of the town was composed of elegant villas—many even more richly decorated than those of Pompeii—and some apartment blocks for poor laborers, while the middle-class of merchants and artisans, which was so present in Pompeii, was almost completely absent here.

Getting There

The easiest way to reach Herculaneum is via the **Circumvesuviana railway** (© 800-053939 toll-free within Italy; www.vesuviana.it), with lines between Naples, Sorrento, and Poggiomarino/Sarno. From Naples, trains stop at **Ercolano Scavi,** and the 20-minute ride costs 1.80€. From Sorrento, the 40-minute ride costs 1.90€ (for more information on fares, see "The Unico Travel Pass," p. 349). Outside the station, you can then get a shuttle bus to the archaeological site or grab a taxi.

You can also take a **taxi** from Naples (the official flat rate for a round-trip to Herculaneum is 70€, and includes a 2-hr. wait at the ruins), or a **car service** from any location. For recommended taxi and car service companies, see "Getting Around," in chapter 11.

If you are based in Naples, another excellent option is to sign up for a guided tour from Naples (p. 117).

We do not recommend driving, as modern Ercolano lies in the poorer outskirts of Naples, with terrible traffic, difficult parking, and questionable safety (you shouldn't leave your car unattended or, at the very least, don't leave anything in it). If you really need to use your car, Ercolano lies along the busy coastal SS 18, which links Naples to Torre del Greco and Pompeii. From autostrada A3, take the ERCOLANO-PORTICI exit and follow the brown signs for the archaeological area, or *scavi.*

Exploring Herculaneum

The archaeological area lies in the heart of the modern town of Ercolano, a rather depressed and not exactly tourist-friendly suburb of Naples. The town is perfectly safe during the day, particularly by the archaeological area, but rather ugly. If you are up for a little exploring, though, you might also want to visit the showroom of a local talented artist, a maker of **cameos,** named **Biagio Piscopo.** He is located at Corso Resina 318 (© 081-7391214), conveniently near the

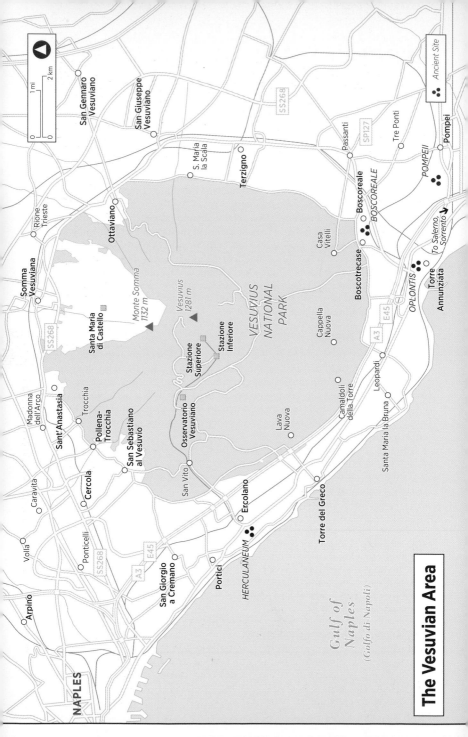

The Vesuvian Area

Herculaneum Archeological Area.

archaeological site. The intricate art of cameo making was first developed in nearby Torre del Greco (see "Cameo Making," below), and the beautiful jewels produced here are exported all over the globe.

The town is struggling to reverse a relatively recent downturn, dating back only about a century. Before—and since—Roman times, Ercolano had been a posh resort for Naples's patricians, who built their summer villas at the foot of Mount Vesuvius, to enjoy the cooler weather. The 122-odd mansions, built during the 18th century by members of the Bourbon court, made up the so-called **Miglio d'Oro,** the Golden Mile. Abandoned after Ercolano became an impoverished suburb of modern Naples, some of the villas have been restored under the supervision of the association **Ente Ville Vesuviane** (ⓒ 081-19244532; www.villevesuviane.net). The Museo Diffuso is a self-guided visit to three villas, the starting point being **Villa Campolieto,** where you pick up the audioguide. The Grand Tour is a longer circuit with five main stops, also starting from Villa Campolieto (ⓒ 081-3625121 reservations; villadelleginestre@villevesuviane. net). In late July/early August, the restored villas are the stage for the **Festival Ville Vesuviane,** featuring concerts—classical, jazz, and pop—and dance.

Herculaneum Archeological Area ★★★

Much smaller and easier to visit than Pompeii, Herculancum may appear at first to also be less impressive. However, once you get down into the town from the entry ramp, you will soon be overtaken by the eerie sensation that, far from being a place of dusty ruins, the town was abandoned only recently rather than nearly 2,000 years ago. This

> ### Stretch Your Euros
>
> If you are planning an extensive visit to the Vesuvian archaeological sites, save on admission prices by purchasing the **Biglietto Unico (Vesuvian area cumulative ticket)** which grants access to all the archaeological sites—Herculaneum, Pompeii, Oplontis, Stabiae, and Boscoreale—for 20€ and is valid for 3 days.

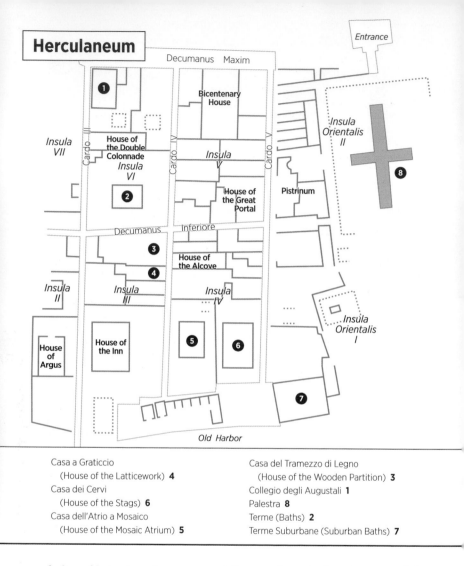

Herculaneum

Entrance

Decumanus Maximus

Bicentenary House

Insula VII

House of the Double Colonnade

Insula VI

Cardo III

Cardo IV

Insula V

Cardo V

Insula Orientalis II

House of the Great Portal

Pistrinum

Decumanus Inferiore

House of the Alcove

Insula II

Insula III

Insula IV

Insula Orientalis I

House of Argus

House of the Inn

House of the Mosaic Atrium

Old Harbor

Casa a Graticcio (House of the Latticework) **4**	Casa del Tramezzo di Legno (House of the Wooden Partition) **3**
Casa dei Cervi (House of the Stags) **6**	Collegio degli Augustali **1**
Casa dell'Atrio a Mosaico (House of the Mosaic Atrium) **5**	Palestra **8**
	Terme (Baths) **2**
	Terme Suburbane (Suburban Baths) **7**

feeling of being in a ghost town partially stems from the fact that many of the houses still have their upper floors: The particular quality of the volcanic mud that enveloped the site allowed for the unusual preservation of wood, from housing structures to room furnishings, allowing archaeologists to learn an incredible amount about daily life and building techniques in Roman times.

The excavated area stretches from the **Decumanus Maximus** (the town's main street) to what was once the shoreline (now a kilometer to the west); the rest of the Roman town remains inaccessible beneath the buildings of modern Ercolano. The archaeological area is a work in progress as ongoing excavations lead to new discoveries such as the boat that was found near the old shoreline in the 1990s, still filled with the corpses of victims caught in frantic postures of escape.

The highlights of your visit should definitely include the **Sede degli Augustali Collegio degli Augustali (Hall of the Augustals)** ★★, with its marble floor and wall paintings; the custodian's room has also been preserved, together with the bed where a man's corpse was found, presumably killed in his sleep. We also recommend a tour of the elegantly decorated **Thermal Baths,** and the **Palestra,** a monumental sports arena used for competition and training. Among the private homes, the most interesting are the **Casa del Tramezzo di Legno (House of the Wooden Partition),** with its perfectly preserved facade, and the **Casa dei Cervi (House of the Stags)** ★★, the most elegant ruin in the excavated area, with terraces that would have overlooked the sea and magnificent decorations. The **Casa a Graticcio (House of the Latticework)** is particularly fascinating because it's one of the very few examples of working-class housing that has survived from antiquity (a fate usually destined for only grand public buildings and the solidly constructed villas of the wealthy); notice the partitions, cheaply made of interwoven cane and plaster. Another interesting house is the **Casa del Mosaico di Nettuno e Anfitrite (House of the Neptune and Anfitritis Mosaic)** ★ with its bright blue mosaic in the rear of the building; the annexed shop still has amphorae stacked on the shelves.

Elegant villas dotted what was the western seashore of Herculaneum, and one of the most famous is the **Villa dei Papiri** ★★, so-called because of the 1,000-odd badly charred papyrus scrolls that were revealed during excavations: They are now preserved in the Biblioteca Nazionale di Vittorio Emanuele III in the Palazzo Reale (see chapter 4). The villa also yielded a treasure-trove of nearly 90 magnificent sculptures, both in bronze and marble; these were Roman copies of Greek originals and are now housed in rooms 114-117 of the Museo Archeologico Nazionale in Naples (see chapter 4). *Note:* Tours of the villa have been suspended since late 2007 for ongoing excavation. No reopening date had been announced at presstime.

The **maritime pavilion** contains the remains of a Roman boat that was found in front of Herculaneum and painstakingly restored, plus other discoveries from the harbor. However, at presstime it was closed to the public.

Corso Resina, Ercolano. ✆ **081-8575347.** www.pompeiisites.org. Admission 11€ or free w/Artecard (p. 98). Nov–Mar daily 8:30am–5pm; Apr–Oct daily 8:30am–7:30pm. Last admission 90 min. earlier. Closed Jan 1, May 1, and Dec 25.

MAV-Museo Archeologico Virtuale ☺ The installation at the new Virtual Archeological Museum—in a larger complex that contains a media library and spaces for special exhibits—has over 30 visual segments recreating various aspects of life in Herculaneum and the other archaeological sites of the Vesuvian area.

Via IV Novembre (the street opposite the main entrance to the Herculaneum Archeological Area), Ercolano. ✆ **081-19806511.** www.museomav.com. Admission 7.50€; 6€ 18 and under w/Artecard. Tues–Sun 9am–5pm.

Where to Stay

You really don't want to spend more time in Ercolano than is necessary; if you want to sleep in the area, we recommend heading for nearby **Torre del Greco,** a modern seaside resort a couple miles south of Ercolano (both towns are about 9.5km/6 miles southeast of Naples), with hotels and restaurants that cater both to tourists and business travelers who are attracted by the seaside and the flourishing craft of cameo making. By public transportation the town is two stops beyond the Ercolano Scavi station on the **Circumvesuviana railway** (📞 **800-053939;** www.vesuviana.it); take either the Sorrento or the Poggiomarino line (see "Getting There," above). **Taxis** also wait outside the train station. By **car,** take the SS 18 toward Torre del Greco and Pompeii, or, from the autostrada A3, take the exit marked TORRE DEL GRECO NORD or TORRE DEL GRECO SUD.

Hotel Holidays   This modern family-run hotel caters mostly to Italian tourists and is a good budget option, offering basic but welcoming accommodations only steps from the beach. Guest rooms are spacious and nicely appointed, with tiled floors, comfortable furnishings, and updated bathrooms (shower only). Only the best rooms—with sea views or private terraces—have air-conditioning and a minibar. The **restaurant** specializes in local cuisine and regional wines, and enjoys great views over the bay.

Via Litoranea 154 (off Via Santa Maria La Bruna), 80059 Torre del Greco. www.holidayshotel. it. 📞 **081-8832170.** Fax 081-8836305. 38 units. 75€–100€ double; 95€–115€ triple; 100€–130€ quad. Rates include breakfast. Children 2 and under stay free in parent's room. Family specials available. AE, DC, MC, V. Free parking. Train: Btw. Circumvesuviana stop Via Monaci and Villa delle Ginestre. **Amenities:** Restaurant; bar. *In room:* A/C (in some), TV, minibar (in some).

Hotel Marad   In a quiet area outside town, this hotel enjoys a great panoramic position on the slope of Vesuvius. It is a relaxing place to take a break from visiting the ruins, with a pleasant garden and a swimming pool. Rooms are quiet and well-appointed, with quality furniture, tiled or carpeted floors, and modern bathrooms. All rooms have a private balcony. Guests have access to a spa and gym nearby.

Via Benedetto Croce 20 (off Via Guglielmo Marconi, north of autostrada A3), 80059 Torre del Greco. www.marad.it. 📞 **081-8492168.** Fax 081-8828716. 74 units. 110€–140€ double. Rates include buffet breakfast. Children 2 and under stay free in parent's room. AE, DC, MC, V. Free parking. Train: Circumvesuviana stop Torre del Greco. **Amenities:** 2 restaurants; bar; babysitting; concierge; pool; room service. *In room:* A/C, TV, minibar, Wi-Fi (free).

Miglio D'Oro Park Hotel ★ ☺   Convenient for visiting the ancient site, this restored villa offers rather grand accommodations with plenty of amenities and takes its name from the fact that it was one of the patrician summer residences of the Miglio d'Oro (see "Exploring Herculaneum," earlier). On the main road that runs parallel to the A3 autostrada, the hotel is often booked for weddings and events. Guest rooms have a contemporary decor and are spacious and full of light, with state-of-the-art details, including Jacuzzi bathtubs. The grounds are beautiful and have a small pond.

Corso Resina 296, 80056 Ercolano. www.migliodoroparkhotel.it. 📞 **081-7399999.** Fax 081-7777049. 53 units. 180€–200€ double; 330€ junior suite; 370€ suite. Rates include buffet breakfast. Children 2 and under stay free in parent's room. AE, DC, MC, V. Free parking. Train: Btw. Circumvesuviana stops Ercolano-Scavi (Piazzale Circumvesuviana, off Via 4 Novembre) and Ercolano-Miglio D'Oro (Via Doglie). **Amenities:** 3 restaurants; bar; concierge; room service. *In room:* A/C, TV, minibar, Wi-Fi (3€/hour).

Sakura ★ ☺   Also on the slopes of Vesuvius, affording cooler air during the summer, this hotel offers accommodations of a similar quality to the more sober Marad, but is farther from the Circumvesuviana train stop. The spacious guest rooms are individually decorated in an Asian theme, with a mix of classic and contemporary furniture, hardwood floors, and state-of-the-art bathrooms with Jacuzzi tubs. The discounted transfers from Naples's rail station and airport are a plus.

Via Enrico De Nicola 28, 80059 Torre del Greco. www.hotelsakura.it. ℰ **081-8493144.** Fax 081-8491122. 80 units. 150€ double; 195€ triple or junior suite; 225€ quad. Rates include buffet breakfast. Children 2 and under stay free in parent's room. Internet specials available. AE, DC, MC, V. Free parking. Train: Circumvesuviana stop Torre del Greco. **Amenities:** Restaurant; 2 bars; airport transfers (10€); concierge; pool; room service; train transfers (7€). *In room:* A/C, TV, minibar.

Where to Eat

We can recommend only one good dining option in Ercolano, Viva Lo Re, located not far from the *scavi*. There are a few places just outside the entrance to the site as well as the snack bars and grocery shops on the town's main drag. Nearby Torre del Greco offers a better dining scene and its restaurants are popular among Italians who come to sample the excellent fresh seafood cuisine and to sample the local D.O.C. wines. The whole stretch of the main seashore road is lined with restaurants large and small, some simple shacks and others more upscale. Lots of others are hidden away on the inner streets. The town also has an array of excellent pizzerie; we recommend **Pizzeria la Bruna** ★, Via Nazionale

---

Cameo Making

Coral jewelry and cameos have a long history in Torre del Greco. Coral-fishing in the area dates from antiquity, when the art of the cameo was first invented. Lost during the Middle Ages, the craft boomed in the 19th century when local artisans took inspiration from the jewelry found during the excavations of Pompeii and Herculaneum. In 1879, the Scuola di Incisione del Corallo (School of Coral Carving) opened, giving further impulse to the development of the industry. Today, the school is called the **Istituto Statale per l'Arte del Corallo e l'Oreficeria** and maintains its own museum, the **Museo del Corallo** ★★, Piazza Palomba (ℰ **081-8811360**), where you can admire a large collection from the 18th century onward. Also in town is the **Museo Liverino del Corallo e dei Cammei** ★★, Via Montedoro 61 (ℰ **081-8811225**), which is owned by one of the historic cameo factories and which displays over 3,000 pieces dating from the 16th century on.

Although the local coral beds are practically exhausted, which is a cause of concern for some (p. 132), cameo making still flourishes today, thanks

to the use of corals and shells from the Pacific Ocean. About 90% of all coral fished around the world makes its way to this little town on the Italian coast, and the jewelry produced here is exported worldwide. Among the many cameo workshops in the area, some of the most reputable congregate around Via Enrico de Nicola. At no. 1 is **Giovanni Apa** (ℰ **081-8811155**); no. 25 is **Antonino del Gatto** (ℰ **081-8814191**); **Baldo Liguoro** (ℰ **081-8812600**) inhabits no. 35; and **Vincenzo Ricevuto** (ℰ **081-8814976**) occupies no. 38.

678 ($\textcircled{C}$ **081-8832431**; Circumvesuviana train to Villa delle Ginestre), which makes delicious Neapolitan pizza and has a private garden.

Chiarina A'Mmare ★★ NEAPOLITAN/SEAFOOD An institution since 1898 and run by the Accardo family for four generation, Chiarina A'Mmare is our favorite in town. It's also very popular with the locals, especially at weekends. Situated right on the harbor with exceptional views, it specializes in fish and seafood, which is brought in hopping fresh from the boats that moor right outside. The seasonal menu always includes traditional specialties; we recommend spaghetti *zucchine e cozze* (with mussels and zucchini), *calamarata* (ring-shaped pasta with calamari), *sauté di frutti di mare* (sautéed mussels and clams), and *pesce all'acquapazza* (fish cooked in a light tomato broth). At presstime, the restaurant was closed for major renovation work; it is due to re-open in January 2012.

Via Calastro 32, Torre del Greco. $\textcircled{C}$ **081-8812067** or 340-4609724. Reservations recommended Sat–Sun. Secondi 8€–22€. AE, DC, MC, V. Thurs–Tues 12:30–3:30pm and 7:30–10:30pm. Closed Dec 20–Jan 5. Train: Circumvesuviana stop Torre del Greco.

Il Poeta Vesuviano ★ 🖋 NEAPOLITAN/SEAFOOD Although there are some meat options at this sober, elegant (and great-value) restaurant not far from the sea, Chef Carmine Mazza's menus are based on fresh, locally caught fish and seafood plus seasonal produce from his kitchen garden, much of it organic. His interpretation of the dishes from local traditions has a modern touch; we loved the *gnocchietti al limone con vongole e calamaretti* (lemon-spiked gnocchi with clams and baby squid), the *filetto di pesce spada* (sword fish steak) served with green beans and local apples drizzled with cinnamon oil, and the *sfogliatella all napolitana rivisitata agli agrumi* (Neapolitan pastry with citrus fruits). Breads, pasta, desserts, and after-dinner petits fours are all homemade and there's a great wine list. The set menus, at 25€ and 35€, are a particularly good value.

Viale Europa 42, Torre del Greco. $\textcircled{C}$ **081-8832673.** Reservations essential for lunch, recommended for dinner. Secondi 10€–12€. AE, MC, V. Tues–Sat 1–2:30pm and 8–11pm; Sun 1–2:30pm. Train: Circumvesuviana stop Leopardi, but better by taxi.

Viva Lo Re ★★ 🎁 NEAPOLITAN/WINE BAR Located about halfway between the scavi and the Miglio d'Oro and a surprising find in down-at-heel

---

Coral: A Costly Souvenir

While exquisite coral jewelry is abundant in Naples and much sought after by collectors, ecologically minded shoppers may wish to steer clear. Because Mediterranean coral reefs are already so depleted, much of the coral crafted in Naples arrives from Thailand, the Philippines, and other Asian-Pacific nations, where there is little to no regulation of coral harvesting and where reefs are disappearing at an alarming rate. The World Wildlife Fund is urging coral designers and manufacturers to pledge not to use red and pink coral, the most at-risk—and also the most precious—varieties, until the industry is more closely regulated. Though we cannot attest to the sustainability of their practices, the most respected firm is the century-old **Basilio Liverino**, Via Montedoro 61 ($\textcircled{C}$ **081-8811225**; www. liverino.it). If you wish to appreciate coral artistry without making a purchase, you can visit their museum (call ahead), displaying the world's best collection of cameos and corals.

Ercolano, this modern osteria with its rustic, exposed brick walls started life as a wine bar and has a selection of some 1,500 labels (including 400 from Campania) to choose from. If you just want something light, there's a great selection of cheeses to accompany a glass of wine, or you order the mixed antipasto plate which has six little "tastes" of different dishes such as eggplant *parmigiano*. For a more substantial meal, choose from the daily menu—written on a blackboard—which includes dishes such as cannelloni *di ricotta e zucchini con frutti di mare* (stuffed with fresh cheese and zucchini with seafood) and saddle of local Irpino lamb. Dessert is a must. Not far from the osteria lies Villa Campolieto with three stylish bedrooms (65€ double including breakfast) under the same ownership.

Corso Resina 261, Ercolano. © 081-7390207. www.vivalore.it. Reservations recommended. Secondi 12€–18€. AE, DC, MC, V. Tues–Sat noon–3:30pm and 7:30–11:30pm; Sun noon–3:30pm. Train: Circumvesuviana stop Ercolano Scavi or Ercolano Miglio l'Oro.

POMPEI ★★★

27km (17 miles) SE of Naples

Pompeii is Italy's most famous archaeological site and with good reason: With an excavated area of 44 hectares (109 acres), it is unique in the world and no other ancient town has been brought to light so completely. Discovered by chance during excavations for a canal in the 16th century, the ruins of the ancient city of Pompeii were not recognized for what they were until further explorations in the 18th century. Formal excavations started only at the end of the 19th century, but continued steadily until most of the ancient town was uncovered and still continue today. Based on calculations of the city walls—only partly excavated—it is believed that Pompeii covered an area of 66 hectares (163 acres). Originally an Etruscan and then a Sannite town, it was colonized by the Romans in 80 B.C. At the time of the eruption, experts estimate the town was home to about 35,000 souls. Note that the ancient site is spelled Pompeii while the modern town is spelled Pompei; it can be confusing!

Getting There

Served by three train stations, Pompeii is easily accessible by public transportation. A few **FS-Trenitalia trains** (© 892021 in Italy; www.trenitalia.it) stop in **Pompei FS rail station** in the center of town, but service is much more frequent on the **Circumvesuviana railway** (© 800-053939; www.vesuviana.it) between Naples, Sorrento, and Poggiomarino/Sarno. On the Sorrento line, get off at **Pompei–Villa dei Misteri,** only a few yards from the Porta Marina entrance to the archaeological area. If you take the Poggiomarino line, get off at **Pompei-Santuario,** in the center of Pompei, only steps from the sanctuary and a couple hundred yards from the Piazza Anfiteatro entrance to the site. The ride from Naples takes 45 minutes and costs 2.40€; from Sorrento it's 30 minutes and 1.90€ (for more information on public transportation fares, see "The Unico Travel Pass," p. 349).

Taking a **taxi** from Naples is a good alternative (the official flat rate for a round-trip to Pompei is 90€, and includes a 2-hr. wait at the ruins), or take a **car service** from any location (see "Getting Around" in chapter 11).

From Naples, you can also sign up for a guided tour (p. 117).

By **car,** take the autostrada A3 and exit at POMPEI OVEST or POMPEI EST. Follow the brown signs for POMPEI SCAVI.

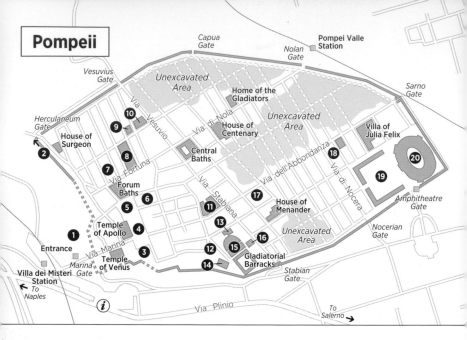

Pompeii

Exploring Pompei

Until quite recently, the modern town of Pompei was very depressed—run-down by cheap sprawl, slums, poverty, and the resultant petty crime. Lately, however, the town has experienced a certain degree of urban renewal, and visitors now can enjoy its other attractions. Dedicated to the Madonna, the **Santuario della Madonna del Rosario,** Piazza Bartolo Longo 1 (✆ **081-8577111;** www.santuario.it; Mon–Sat 7am–7pm; Sun and holidays 6am–8pm), is one of Italy's major religious centers and is a pilgrimage destination for Catholics worldwide. Built in the 19th century, the richly decorated sanctuary is well worth a visit. The attached buildings house a school and the offices of a number of important charities.

Vineyards around Pompei.

The archaeological area is, of course, the main attraction in Pompei. Come prepared, as the site is huge and a visit here is quite demanding in terms of both time and energy. Bring comfortable shoes, a hat, sunscreen, and plenty of water. We also recommend taking a **guided tour** (from 106€ for a family of up to six people that lasts about 2 hr.) or at least purchasing the excellent official guidebook (10€, also published in English), that includes itineraries and photographs, for sale at the bookstore located just beyond the ticket booth. Guidebooks are available in various languages, including English. The **Ufficio Scavi** (© 081-8575347; www.pompeii sites.org) sometimes offers thematic guided tours that are fascinating: Each focuses on one aspect of the town's life. Some are seasonal, as the **Vendemmia (Grape Harvest)**, where you can visit the vineyards that produce an excellent red wine (the Villa dei Misteri label) using 2,000-year-old techniques. You can reserve these as well as guided tours of specific buildings and houses at online at www.arethusa.net.

Excavations of Pompeii (Scavi) ★★★ In Roman times, Pompeii was an important industrial and commercial town, with a complex layered society, that is reflected in the urban structures on view today. Besides elegant villas belonging to the richer citizens, there were blocks of more modest housing, as well as shops, restaurants, hotels, and public buildings. The eruption covered Pompeii with volcanic ash and pumice stone, a much lighter material than what rained down on Herculaneum. This meant that the survivors of the disaster were able to retrieve some of their possessions, leaving less behind than in other locations. It also made it easier for the site to be excavated—and, unfortunately looted—in more recent centuries. In the 19th and early 20th century, precious mosaics and frescoes were carefully detached and placed on display in museums although the contemporary approach is to leave everything *in situ* to depict the town as it would have been at the time.

Surrounded by walls, Pompeii was much closer to the sea than it is now, as the water has receded substantially since the days of the eruption. Civic life revolved around three centers: the **Forum;** the **Triangular Forum** with the **Theater District;** and the complex with the **Amphitheatre** and the **Palestra.** The rest of town was residential and commercial.

Antiquity Online

You can now purchase admission tickets to all the archaeological sites **online** at **www. pompei.napoli.com.** The procedure is simple: You pay by credit card and then print your tickets. *Note:* You need to be certain of the date of your visit: The tickets sold online are valid only for the date you choose and are nonrefundable.

Streets were lined with small shops and taverns, and the walls were covered with red writing advertising the candidates to the local elections. You'll also see black charcoal graffiti, and painted signs for bars and shops. All these are still visible in the area of the so-called **Nuovi Scavi** (still bearing the name that it was given in 1911) to the southeast of town.

The **Forum** is a large, rectangular open space covering over 17,400 sq. m (58,000 sq. ft.) and surrounded by a portico on three sides. On the fourth is the **Temple of Jupiter,** dating from the 2nd century B.C., built over a high foundation. The Forum was decorated with bronze and marble statues of im-

portant citizens, but the niches stand empty because their objects were removed after the tragedy in A.D. 79. On the Forum was the **Macellum,** the covered food market. Opposite the market was the **Basilica,** the largest building in town, which housed the meeting hall and tribunal.

The **Triangular Forum** is another large area that was once surrounded by a portico. In the middle are the ruins of the **Doric Temple** from the 6th century B.C. This was the heart of the **Theater District,** with the beautiful **Teatro Grande ★** from the 2nd century B.C., which could hold an audience of 5,000. Farther on is the **Odeion,** or Small Theater, from the 1st century B.C., used for music and mime shows, which could hold 1,000 spectators. Nearby are the **Temple of Isis ★**, one of the best-conserved temples

FROM TOP: **Pompeii; The Temple of Isis.**

to this goddess to survive from antiquity, and the **Terme Stabiane (Stabian Baths)** ★, one of the town's four **public baths,** with well-preserved mosaic, painting, and marble works.

From the Forum, you can take **Via dell'Abbondanza,** the town's main commercial street, lined with shops of all kinds and leading to the southeast of town, the most recently excavated area. One of the most curious shops is the **Fullonica Stephani (Stephen's Dry-Cleaning);** the shop is on the ground floor and the owner's apartment on the second. Farther on is the **Casa di Loreius Tiburtinus,** with an elegant internal **loggia** ★ bordering a long pool and decorated with small marble statues; at the end is the **Triclinium,** with two beautiful **paintings** ★★. At the end of the road to the right is the complex with the **Palestra,** where sports events were held, with a grandiose swimming pool and surrounded by plane trees (you can see the plaster casts of the stumps). Farther on is the **Amphitheatre,** the oldest Roman amphitheater in the world, built in 80 B.C., with seating for 1,000 people.

Among the other famous private houses here is the elegant **Casa dei Vettii (House of the Vettii),** with its magnificent paintings that belonged to two rich merchants; they had just redecorated after the damages caused by the earthquake in A.D. 62, so all of the paintings were in excellent shape. The magnificent frescoed **Triclinium (Dining Room)** ★★ features figures and *amorini* (cupids) on Pompeiian red-and-black backgrounds. Nearby is the **Casa del Fauno (House of the Faun),** the largest of private homes—it takes up an entire block. The finest decorative pieces of this once-exquisite mansion are now in the Museo Nazionale Archeologico in Naples. Another famous house is the **Casa del Poeta Tragico (House of the Tragic Poet),** with its famous CAVE CANEM (Beware of Dog) mosaic by the entrance; most of its paintings have been removed to the Archaeological Museum in Naples. The gilded cupids that ornately decorated one of the rooms of **Casa degli Amorini Dorati (House of the Gilded Cupids)** ★ (by guided tour only) are in the same museum, but many of the frescoes and marble decorations remain.

On the edge of town, along Via Villa dei Misteri, was Pompeii's fourth thermal establishment, **Terme Suburbane** ★★ (by guided tour only). These privately owned thermal baths were opened to the public in 2002 after lengthy restoration. Much looted over the centuries, they were the newest of the bath establishments in Pompeii and the most unusual. Contrary to traditional Roman custom, the baths are "mixed," for both men and women. The interior holds beautiful **frescoes** and **mosaic** decorations, including some of erotic content: One even shows a homosexual scene between women, uncommon in Roman iconography.

Outside Pompeii's walls the excavations continue along Via dei Sepolcri, a road lined with funerary monuments that leads outside the city walls toward the Porto Ercolano, Pompeii's harbor (about a 1km/half-mile walk). The **Villa dei Misteri (House of the Mysteries)** ★★ is a suburban estate famous for its frescoes that illustrates the three styles of Pompeiian painting. Its most famous one is the large **fresco** on the wall of what was probably a *triclynium* (dining room), depicting several figures participating in a ceremony thought to be related to the cult of Dionysus (Bacchus).

Tip: Guided tours are offered with advance reservation (✆ **081-8575347;** www.arethusa.net). If you are signing up for more than one tour, keep in mind that it might take more than 30 minutes to walk between sites.

Porta Marina, Via Villa dei Misteri, Pompei (secondary entrance at Piazza Anfiteatro, Pompei).

℃ **081-8575347.** www.pompeiisites.org. Admission 11€ or free w/Artecard (p. 98). Nov 1–Mar 31 daily 8:30am–5pm; Apr 1–Oct 31 daily 8:30am–7:30pm. Last admission 90 min. before closing. Closed Jan 1, May 1, and Dec 25.

Virtual Pompei ☺ This exhibit allows you to check out a reconstruction of the ancient town to see how it might have looked before the eruption. In addition to showing 3-D films, demonstrations of ancient Roman craft-making are given by live artists. The presentations are only organized for groups of 20 or more, but individual visitors can join existing groups by reserving in advance.

Via Plinio 105 (91m/300 ft. from the entrance to the archaeological area of Porta Marina), Pompei. ℃/fax **081 5783593.** www.virtualpompei.it. Admission 6€ by reservation only.

Where to Stay

The once sketchy town of Pompei has notably improved, and there are several pleasant hotels located close to the archaeological area. You should still be careful, though, and avoid night strolls along deserted streets.

Hotel Diana ☺ This small family-run hotel is really welcoming, thanks to the efforts of the charming hosts. Guest rooms are well-appointed and pleasantly decorated, with all the expected amenities, although some are a little noisy. Similar to the Iside below, it is slightly less convenient to the ruins yet closer to the town center and right by the FS train station.

Vicolo Sant'Abbondio 12 (off Via Sacra, by the FS train station), 80045 Pompei. www.pompei hotel.com. ℃/fax: **081-8631264.** 22 units. 110€ double; 130€ triple; 150€ quad. Rates include buffet breakfast. Children 2 and under stay free in parent's room. AE, DC, MC, V. Free parking. Pets accepted. **Amenities:** Bar; concierge; room service; smoke-free rooms. *In room:* A/C, Internet, TV.

Hotel Forum ★ ☺ More elegant than the other options reviewed here, this family-run hotel is quite close to both the excavations and the Santuario. Guest rooms are individually decorated, some with tiled floors, others with wood, and good-size bathrooms (some with shower only). Some rooms open onto the garden, and suites have panoramic views over the excavations or Vesuvius and Jacuzzi tubs in their bathrooms. The largest rooms, which can accommodate up to five guests, are good for families.

Via Roma 99, 80045 Pompei. www.hotelforum.it. ℃**081-8501170.** Fax 081-8506132. 36 units. 120€ double; 170€ junior suite. Rates include buffet breakfast. AE, DC, MC, V. Free parking. **Amenities:** Bar; Internet in lobby (free). *In room:* A/C, TV, minibar.

Hotel Iside This good budget hotel offers basic, clean, and quiet accommodations in the center of town, only 180m (600 ft.) from the Piazza Anfiteatro entrance to the *scavi*. Guest rooms are plain but spacious and open either onto a private balcony or onto the hotel's pleasant citrus garden. Some have views over the ruins or Vesuvius. Bathrooms are good-size (some are shower only).

Via Minutella 27, 80045 Pompei. www.hoteliside.it. ℃/fax: **081-8598863.** 18 units. 90€ double. Rate includes buffet breakfast. Children 2 and under stay free in parent's room. AE, DC, MC, V. Free parking. **Amenities:** Bar. *In room:* A/C, TV.

Hotel Villa dei Misteri ☺ This old-fashioned, family-run hotel has the advantage of being right by the main entrance to the excavations. Built in the 1930s, it has a certain charm and is an excellent choice if you don't need a huge range of amenities. Guest rooms are spacious and well-appointed, with modern quality furnishings and tiled floors; some have private balconies. Some overlook the amphora-shaped pool, while others have street views. If you want a room with A/C (for an additional 9€ per night), you must book well in advance. The staff is extremely accommodating, and the pool and restaurant are great pluses, particularly if you have children.

Via Villa dei Misteri 11, 80045 Pompei. www.villadeimisteri.it. © **081-8613593.** Fax 081-8622983. 34 units. 75€ double; 97€ triple. Half- and full-board plans available. Children 2 and under stay free in parent's room. DC, MC, V. Free parking. **Amenities:** Restaurant; bar; pool. *In room:* A/C (in some, 7€ fee), TV (in some), Wi-Fi (2€/hour).

Where to Eat

Most establishments in Pompei are tourist joints catering to large groups of visitors from around the world. The following restaurants have their share of tourist groups but are also favored by locals for their high-quality food.

Il Principe ★★ NEAPOLITAN/ANCIENT ROMAN With a dining room designed to emulate the luxury of ancient Pompeii, this is the best restaurant in the area and a perfect conclusion to a day spent visiting the ruins. Right in the center of town, it serves excellent food in a lively atmosphere with outdoor dining. The talented chef and owner is a real epicurean; the seasonal menu includes a choice of tasty ancient Roman recipes, such as the *lagane al garum* (homemade egg-free pasta with an anchovy-paste sauce). More modern choices include excellent spaghetti *alle vongole* (with baby clams) and delicious maccheroni with zucchini and prawns. The lounge bar with live music is extra reason to come here.

Piazza Bartolo Longo. © **081-8505566.** www.ilprincipe.com. Reservations recommended. Secondi 12€–24€. AE, DC, MC, V. Tues–Sat 12:30–3pm and 8–11pm; Sun 12:30–3pm.

Ristorante President ★ NEAPOLITAN This is the most upscale place to eat in the area, offering gourmet food and great service. In addition to the wine list you'll be offered a water list, a beer list, a cheese list, and a honey and dried-fruit list, as well as the usual dessert menu. The food is seasonal and focuses on seafood, with such appetizers as smoked swordfish or tuna and delicious pasta dishes such as the *scialatielli allo scorfano* (homemade flat pasta with scorpion-fish). The secondi, which come with a vegetable side dish—unusual for Italy, but most welcome—include a large choice of fish masterfully prepared au gratin, baked in a salt crust, or simply baked. We also recommend the tasting menus (call or check the website for a schedule of events), that explore the regional cuisine, from the modern to the ancient Roman (35€–55€ with wine pairings). Desserts are excellent and strictly homemade.

Piazza Schettini 12 (parking at back entrance, Via San Giuseppe 16). © **081-8507245.** www. ristorantepresident.it. Reservations recommended Sat–Sun. Secondi 12€–25€. AE, DC, MC, V. Tues–Sat noon–3pm and 7pm–midnight; Sun noon–3pm (and 7pm–midnight in summer). Closed late Jan for 2 weeks.

OPLONTIS ★

20km (12 miles) SE of Naples

Not far from **Torre Annunziata**—the ugly coastal town famous for its flour mills, its pasta industry and, it must be said, for its crime rate—is one of the more recently excavated archaeological areas on the slopes of Mount Vesuvius. Much remains to be done here, but what has already been uncovered is quite spectacular.

The size of the site is much more manageable than Pompeii or even Herculaneum, making it a good choice for those desiring a brief archaeological visit, and few tourists make it this far.

Getting There

You can easily reach to Oplontis using the **Circumvesuviana railway** (✆ 800-053939 toll-free within Italy; www.vesuviana.it) running between Naples, Sorrento, and Poggiomarino/Sarno; get off at **Torre Annunziata-Oplonti Villa di Poppea** (a few stops after Ercolano Scavi). The 20- or 35-minute ride (depending on the train) from Naples costs 1.80€, from Sorrento 1.90€ for a 30-minute ride (for more information on public transportation fares, see "The Unico Travel Pass," p. 349)

By car, take the autostrada A3 Napoli-Salerno and exit at TORRE ANNUNZIATA SUD, then follow the brown signs for SCAVI DI OPLONTI.

Exploring Oplontis

As of the 1st century B.C., Oplontis was an elegant residential suburb of nearby Pompeii. Indeed, the very name probably derives from the Latin *opulentia* meaning opulence, and the über rich had their countryside villas here. Although it was first discovered in the 18th century, the site was not excavated until the 1960s. Only the ruin of one extraordinary villa is currently open to the public, yet it is well worth a visit.

Villa di Poppea ★★ This is the largest ancient Roman suburban villa ever discovered and has been declared a UNESCO World Heritage Site because of the unique quality of its frescoes. It was certainly a villa belonging to the imperial family, and scientists believe it was the property of the famous Poppea Sabina, the second wife of Emperor Nero: An amphora bearing the name of her freedman and a vase bearing her mark were found on the villa's grounds. The villa was enormous, with a large portico opening onto a garden with a huge pool surrounded by statues, and innumerable rooms, passages, and cubicles, including a kitchen that is still recognizable as such today.

The most outstanding feature is the villa's truly superb decorations: Frescoes, stucco work, and mosaics have been left *in situ,* unlike in Pompeii or Herculaneum where, with the exception of the most recent excavations, they were removed to museums. Most of the interior was lavishly painted and many of the frescoes are still in very good repair, closely recalling the more famous ones in the Villa dei Misteri of Pompeii and in the Museo Archeologico Nazionale of Naples.

The villa also yielded a treasure-trove of high-quality statuary, second only to the findings in the Villa dei Papiri in Herculaneum (see Herculaneum Archeological Area, earlier in this chapter), but, it was found tucked away in a storeroom. In fact, the entire villa was devoid of signs of daily life, leading experts to believe that it was being restored at the moment of the eruption, maybe as a consequence of the preceding earthquake of A.D. 62.

Via Sepolcri 12, Torre Annunziata. ✆ **081-8621755.** www.pompeiisites.org. Admission 5.50€ includes same-day entry to Boscoreale and Stabiae; or free with purchase of Artecard. Nov–Mar daily 8:30am–5pm; Apr–Oct daily 8:30am–7:30pm. Last admission 90 min. earlier. Closed Jan 1, May 1, and Dec 25.

The Villa di Poppea.

BOSCOREALE

31km (19 miles) SE of Naples

In ancient Roman times, this agricultural center for wine, wheat, and olive oil on the slopes of Mount Vesuvius was part of the northern suburbs of Pompeii. Boscoreale today still has farms and vineyards (nearby Boscotrecase is famous for the production of Lacrimae Cristi, the amber-colored D.O.C. Vesuvian wine). Over 30 Roman villas have been found in Boscoreale to date, but only one has been completely excavated.

Getting There

Circumvesuviana trains (⌀ **800-053939;** www.vesuviana.it) run between Naples and Poggiomarino/Sarno, and stop at **Boscoreale.** The 40-minute ride from Naples costs 2.40€. From Sorrento, you need to change at Torre Anninziata; the 40-minute journey costs 1.90€. From the station, take a taxi or switch to the local bus to Villa Regina. By **car,** take the autostrada A3 and exit at TORRE ANNUNZIATA; follow the brown signs for COMUNI VESUVIANI and BOSCOREALE. *Note:* For more information on public transportation fares, see "The Unico Travel Pass," p. 349.

Exploring the Archaeological Area

Excavations in this area started at the end of the 19th century and were mostly performed by local landowners for the sole purpose of plundering valuable art. Once the objects were extracted and the frescoes detached, the villas were buried again. Most of the finds from these early excavations are on display in various museums around the world, including Paris's Louvre and the Metropolitan Museum in New York. Of some 30 villas discovered in the area, one, the **Villa della Pisanella,** yielded a real treasure: over 1,000 gold coins, some jewelry, and a complete set of silverware, including richly decorated cups and pitchers. Most of this treasure is now in the Louvre.

Sweet Stop

If you have a sweet tooth, like us, you'll love the local specialty, the *zandraglia*. Sold at pastry shops in the area, this traditional treat is a large sweet cookie shaped like a butterfly. Dedicated to the pastry, the *Sagra della Zandraglia* is a fair that's held on the second Sunday of July. For the best *zandraglia* (which are only made at this time of year), head for **Vaiano,** near the excavations at Via Cirillo Emanuele 163 (*℃* **081-5374372**).

Modern excavations are on-going, and from them, archaeologists have learned a great deal about ancient Roman life. Farms were typically organized around a rural villa within which were richly decorated apartments for the rare visits of the landlord, and larger quarters for the workmen and slaves.

Adjacent to the antiquarium (below), **Villa Regina** is the only local villa that was completely excavated with the aid of modern technology. Discovered in the 1970s, the villa is modest in size, but reflects the typical structure of Roman rural houses of this kind, with an elegant residential space for the owner and a farm producing wine and grains. The villa is now a kind of living museum: Vineyards have been replanted with historical accuracy, and the ancient *torcularium* (the room for pressing grapes) and the cellar, which had a capacity of 10,000 liters (over 2,600 gal.), have been replicated. ***Note:*** Villa Regina was closed for repairs at presstime. It is due to re-open in early 2012.

Antiquarium Nazionale Uomo e Ambiente nel Territorio Vesuviano ☺

Most of the recent finds from the local sites have been collected in this museum and divided into two sections. The first is dedicated to the running of a Roman farm, with exhibits on the techniques and objects related to agriculture and husbandry; the second focuses on architecture and, specifically, how these farming villas were structured differently than other Roman villas on the coast, which were solely dedicated to leisure.

Via Settetermini 15, Località Villaregina, Boscoreale. *℃* **081-5368796.** www.pompeii sites.org. Admission 5.50€ includes same-day admission to Villa Regina, Oplonti, and Stabiae; or free w/Artecard. Nov–Mar daily 8:30am–5pm; Apr–Oct daily 8:30am–7:30pm. Last admission 90 min. earlier. Closed Jan 1, May 1, and Dec 25.

A statue on display at the Antiquarium Nazionale Uomo e Ambiente nel Territorio Vesuviano.

VESUVIUS

One of the most romantic volcanoes in the world, Vesuvius is also one of the most dangerous; yet, people continue to live on its fertile slopes, in spite of the eruption in 1944, as they have since antiquity.

Named Vesvinum or Vesuvinum after its vineyards, which were famous

TREADING LIGHTLY ON mount vesuvius

Stand at the bottom of the great market-place of Pompeii, and look up at the silent streets . . . over the broken houses with their inmost sanctuaries open to the day, away to Mount Vesuvius, bright and snowy in the peaceful distance; and lose all count of time, and heed of other things, in the strange and melancholy sensation of seeing the Destroyed and the Destroyer making this quiet picture in the sun.

—Charles Dickens, *Pictures from Italy*

A volcano that has struck terror in Campania, the towering, **Mount Vesuvius** looms over the Bay of Naples. On August 24, A.D. 79, Vesuvius blew its top and buried Pompeii, Herculaneum, and Stabiae under a toxic mixture of ash and volcanic mud. (Many of the finds from these archeological sites are on display in Boscoreale at the Antiquarium Nazionale Uomo e Ambiente Territorio Vesuviano.) Vesuvius has erupted periodically ever since: thousands were killed in 1631, and in 1906 it blew the ring off its crater. The last spectacular eruption was on March 31, 1944.

The approach to the top of Vesuvius is dramatic, with the terrain growing increasingly foreboding. Along the way, you'll see villas rising on its slopes, and vineyards: The citizens of Pompeii enjoyed wine from grapes grown here. Today, the grapes produce an amber-colored wine, Lacrimae Christi (Tears of Christ).

It might sound like a dubious invitation, but it's possible to visit the rim of the crater's mouth. As you look down into its smoldering core, you might recall that Spartacus, a century before the eruption that buried Pompeii, hid in the hollow of the crater, which was then covered with vines.

for their excellent wine even millennia ago, the volcano's first known eruption was in A.D. 79. Others followed in 202, 472, 512, 1139, and 1306. A long period of quiet lulled the local inhabitants into a false sense of security which was violently shattered in 1631 when a particularly strong eruption caused widespread destruction. Further eruptions in 1794 (nicely timed for Goethe's visit, when a guide hauled him up through the poisonous smoke to look into the crater), 1871, 1906, and 1944 were less devastating. The most recent signs of activity were in 1999—some puffs of smoke, just to keep everybody on their toes. However, it is widely acknowledged that Vesuvius has lain dormant for long enough; it's now a question of *when* rather than *if* it will blow its top again and experts believe that the next eruption will be similar to that of A.D. 79.

Getting There

The **Circumvesuviana railway** (© 800-053939 toll-free within Italy; www. vesuviana.it) runs from Naples, Sorrento, and Poggiomarino/Sarno to Vesuvius.

From Naples, trains stop the 12-minute ride costs 1.10€ (for more information on public transportation fares, see "The Unico Travel Pass," p. 349). From Sorrento, the journey can take up to an hour and 20 minutes (you have to change) and costs 3.40€. Once at the station, you can then get a **shuttle bus** to Vesuvius or a **taxi** (confirm the price before getting in).

A good alternative is taking a taxi from Naples (flat rate of 90€ includes round-trip transport and 2-hr. wait), or a **car service** from any location (see "Getting Around," in chapter 11).

From Naples, another excellent option is a guided tour (see chapter 4, p. 117).

Note: All transportation gets you only as far as the park entrance at 1,017m (3,337 ft.) in altitude; the trails are not wheelchair accessible.

What to See & Do

The only volcano still active on mainland Europe, Mount Vesuvius is part of the **Parco Nazionale del Vesuvio** (✆081-8653911; www.parconazionaledel vesuvio.it). The car park and entrance to the park are at an altitude of 1,000m (3,281 ft.). Of its nine trails, the most popular is *Gran Cono* (path number 5) which ascends to the **crater ★**. Admission is by guided tour only (8€, free for children 7 and under). Tours are led by a volcanologist and are offered throughout the day (no reservation necessary). The climb traverses hardened lava to the rim, 170m (558 ft.) above the park entrance, and 1,170m (3,839 ft.) above sea level. The trail affords great views of the crater itself and the whole Gulf of Naples. The park is open daily (Nov–Mar 9am–3pm; Apr–May 9am–5pm; June–Aug 9am–6pm; Sept–Oct 9am–5pm). *Note:* The trail to the crater closes in extreme weather.

Below the park entrance, at 608m (1,995 ft.) is the **Observatory** (✆081-6108483; www.ov.ingv.it): Established in 1841 to monitor Mount Vesuvius's activity, it is the oldest and one of the most respected volcanology research centers in the world. You can visit its rich scientific library and **Geological Museum ★**, Via Osservatorio 14 (✆081-6108483), which holds a vast collection of minerals and scientific instruments from the 18th century onward (Mon–Fri 9am–noon; Sat–Sun 10am–noon; Mar–May also open daily 1:30–3pm; closed Jan 1 and 6, Easter and Easter Monday, Aug 1–31, Dec 8, 24–26, and 31; free admission).

THE PHLEGREAN FIELDS ★

18km (11 miles) W of Naples

The peninsula that flanks the Gulf of Naples to the west is a land of hills, craters, lagoons, and tarns. Naples's sprawling suburbs have tarnished its original charm, and the area was officially established as a national park in 1993 to protect it from further development. On the positive side, this has not detracted from the magnificent views over the Gulf of Naples and the islands of Ischia and Procida that make this peninsula one of the most scenic spots in Campania.

Named the "burning fields" during antiquity because of its boiling mud craters, this area was highly prized during Greek and Roman times for its hot springs, its fertile soil, and good harbors, and excavations have brought to light many ruins and archaeological remains. Highlights here are Solfatara, with its lunar landscape and bubbling fumaroles; Pozzuoli, with its amphitheater and temples; Baia with its submerged Roman city; and Cuma, with its Sybilla Cave and Greek ruins.

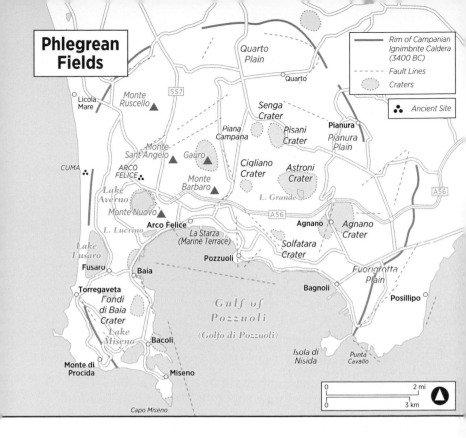

Phlegrean Fields

Rim of Campanian Ignimbrite Caldera (3400 BC)

Fault Lines

Craters

∴ *Ancient Site*

Quarto Plain

Quarto

Licola Mare

Monte Ruscello

SS7

Senga Crater

Pisani Crater

Pianura

Pianura Plain

Piana Campana

Monte Sant'Angelo

Gauro

Cigliano Crater

Astroni Crater

CUMA

ARCO FELICE

Monte Barbaro

L. Grande

A56

Lake Averno

Monte Nuovo

Arco Felice

La Starza (Marine Terrace)

Agnano

Agnano Crater

L. Lucrino

Solfatara Crater

Fuorigrotta Plain

Lake Fusaro

Pozzuoli

Fusaro

Baia

Bagnoli

Posillipo

Torregaveta

Fondi di Baia Crater

Gulf of Pozzuoli

(Golfo di Pozzuoli)

Lake Miseno

Bacoli

Isola di Nisida

Punta Cavallo

Monte di Procida

Miseno

Capo Miseno

0 — 2 mi
0 — 3 km

Pozzuoli ★★

This small, lively town was once the Greek colony of Dicearchia, founded in 530 B.C.; it then became the Roman Puteoli in 194 B.C., an important Roman harbor favored by the Roman emperors over Partenope (Naples), which had maintained closer allegiance to Greece. The town was destroyed by the barbarian Alaric in A.D. 410, but the acropolis, on a tufa-stone promontory pushing into the sea, continued to be inhabited, and modern Pozzuoli slowly developed around it. Because the town is just a few kilometers from Naples, you'd expect it to be downright suburban, but it maintains a life of its own—even though many of its residents commute to Naples for work each day. The town boasts unique monuments from its past as well as sweeping views over the sea and the islands of Ischia and Procida in one direction, and the island of Nisita (linked to the mainland by a causeway) on the other.

ESSENTIALS

VISITOR INFORMATION The **tourist office,** Largo Matteotti 1A, 80078 Napoli (*© **081-5266639*** or 081-5261481; www.infocampiflegrei.it), dispenses information on Pozzuoli, the Phlegrean Fields region, and the province of Naples and its islands.

GETTING THERE Pozzuoli is very well connected by public transportation to Naples and the islands, particularly to Ischia and Procida (see chapter 8). The most scenic way to arrive in Pozzuoli is by **city bus:** No. 152 starts in Piazza Garibaldi near Naples's Stazione Centrale and traverses the whole city, following the shoreline to the center of Pozzuoli—picturesque, but slow. Less scenic but faster is the **Metro** (line 2) or the **Cumana Railroad** (✆ 800-053939), starting from Piazza Montesanto.

GETTING AROUND Taxis (✆ 081-5265800) operate from a stand in Piazza della Repubblica. You can also use the **buses** operated by **Consorzio Trasporti Pubblici** (✆ 800-482644; www.ctpn.it) and **EAV** (✆ 800-053939; www.eavbus.it), with several lines connecting the train and Metro stations to the harbor and other parts of the Phlegrean Fields.

EXPLORING POZZUOLI

The modern town tightly encloses Pozzuoli's ancient monuments. The original Greek Acropolis, **Rione Terra ★**, was the first inhabited area of Pozzuoli. Located near the harbor, it has been progressively subsiding under the sea, so much so that it had to be abandoned in the 1970s. A large, ongoing excavation and restoration campaign, begun in 1993, has uncovered a virtually untouched Roman town—a kind of underground Pompeii. Along the main *Decumano* (the central avenue running east-west) and some minor streets, are shops, *osterie* (taverns), a *pistrinum* (mill), and the *ergastula* (slaves' cells) with some drawings by prisoners still visible on the walls. At presstime, the site was closed to the public with no foreseeable opening date; call the tourist office for updates. Sculptures and other important objects from ancient Pozzuoli are on display in the Museo Archeologico dei Campi Flegrei in Baia (p. 150).

Not far from the harbor, at Via Roma 10, is the entrance to the **Serapeo ★**, the ruins of the ancient town's marketplace. The large structure, built in the 1st century A.D., was lined with porticos where shops and taverns operated. At its center are the remains of a temple, much ruined over the centuries (its alabaster columns, for instance, were used to decorate the Royal Palace in Caserta; see

The Rione Terra.

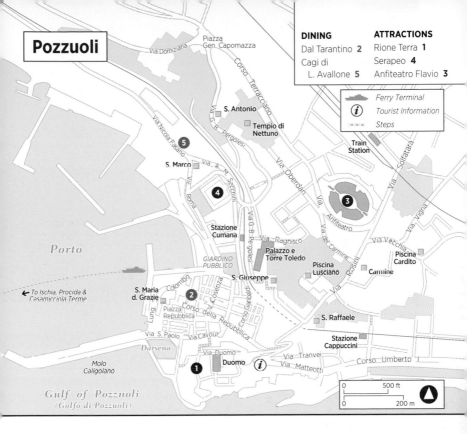

(see chapter 10). Named after the Egyptian god Serapis because of the statue found here during excavations, this ruin has been used to study the geological phenomenon of bradyseism where large tracts of land slowly subside beneath sea level while others rise up; you can see little holes in the marble of the columns where they were submerged in water. A bit farther inland, at Via Terracciano 75, is the **Anfiteatro Neroniano/Flavio ★**. Started by Roman emperor Nero and finished by Emperor Vespasiano, it is in the upper part of town, where the roads to Cuma, Pozzuoli, and Naples converged in Roman times. This was the third-largest amphitheater in the Roman world after the Colosseo and the Anfiteatro Campano in Capua (see chapter 10). Admission for both sites is 4€; the ticket also includes the Museo Archeologico dei Campi Flegrei, Parco Archeologica di Baia, and Scavi di Cuma, and is valid 2 days. (June–Sept Wed–Mon 9am–7pm; Oct–May Wed-Mon 9am–4pm, last admission 3pm; closed Jan 1, May 1, Dec 25). The theater, which could accommodate more than 20,000 spectators, is used today for special musical events; check with the local tourist office for information.

Solfatara ★★

The dormant volcano crater (770m/2,550 ft. in diameter) that is today known as Solfatara was called "Forum Vulcani" by the ancients, who believed it to be the residence of the god Vulcan. Extinct it may be, but the lunar landscape spews sulfurous steam that hisses out of the ground in steaming jets, or fumaroles, that

A visitor to Solfatara takes in its sulfurous steam.

reach a temperature of 160°C (320°F). With the heavy stench of rotten eggs in the air, you can walk around the crater, stand in the clouds of steam, and marvel over the **Bocca Grande,** the largest fumarole. No wonder it was a favorite stop on the Grand Tour (the obligatory educational trip through Europe taken by any aristocrat worth his title in the 19th c.). At the center of the crater is the **Fangaia,** an area of hot mud that gently bubbles away at a temperature of 284°F (140°C); you can understand why the ancient Romans believed this to be the entrance to hell. We highly recommend a visit here for children and adults alike.

GETTING THERE

The park is 10km (6¼ miles) from Naples. The easiest means of travel is the Metro (line 2) to **Pozzuoli-Solfatara** station, which is only about 732m (2,400 ft.) from the entrance to the park. You can walk the distance or catch the local P9 bus from outside the Metro station. City bus no. 152 from Naples to Pozzuoli also stops at Solfatara. You can also walk the 1.6km (1 mile)—a 20-minute trek uphill from Pozzuoli. A taxi from Naples is a flat rate of 40€ one-way to Solfatara.

EXPLORING SOLFATARA

The site is a nature reserve covering an expanse of 33 hectares (81 acres), with large wooded areas where a number of rare birds, plants, and small animals have found refuge. At the **entrance,** Via Solfatara 161 (© **081-5262341;** www.solfatara.it), pick up the nature trail that leads to the points of interest in the park; the whole thing takes about 45 minutes to 1 hour. Highlights are the **Fangaia,** with its huge bubbling mud holes, and the **Bocca Grande,** Solfatara's main crater. Because Solfatara is the epicenter of the Phlegrean Fields' volcanic area, the ancients believed this was the residence of the god Vulcanus. Nearby are the **Stufe** (Italian for stoves): a number of small caves constantly filled by hot steam. During antiquity, they were used as natural saunas. Entry fees are 6€ for adults, 4.50€ for children 4 to 9, and free for children 3 and under; Artecard holders receive a 20% discount. The park is open daily from 8:30am to 1 hour before sunset.

Baia ★★

On the coastal stretch that bounds the Gulf of Pozzuoli to the west, the fishing town of **Baia** maintains something of its picturesque past, with pastel-colored buildings opening onto a small harbor. Ancient Roman Baia was a flourishing seaside resort adjacent to the large harbor Portus Julius. Due to the geological phenomenon of bradyseism, many of the ancient structures have been preserved underwater, creating a unique submerged archaeological area.

GETTING THERE

Baia is well connected to Pozzuoli public transportation (see "Getting Around," p. 348). Or take a taxi, either from Pozzuoli's Metro station (agree on the price beforehand; it should cost around 25€) or from Naples, where taxis offer a flat rate of 85€ for a round-trip to the archaeological area of Baia and Solfatara with a 3-hour wait.

EXPLORING BAIA

The unique attraction here is obviously the **Parco Sommerso di Baia ★**, Harbor of Baia (✆ **081-8688923;** www.baiasommersa.it), the submerged archaeological site. The ruins are only a few feet below the surface, and the visit is an eerie and magical experience, however you choose to go about viewing it. Many of the structures have been excavated and in places roped off and labeled for visitors coming by **guided scuba or snorkeling tour** (not available in winter) or by **boat** equipped with a submerged video camera or clear bottom. Visits by boat are possible only during good weather (mid-Mar to mid-Nov Tues–Sun 9:30am–1:30pm and 3:30–7:30pm); boats depart from the dock in Baia's harbor, and the tours cost 25€ inclusive of admission, insurance, and boat transport. If you want to enjoy the ruins from underwater, a guided scuba tours costs 35€ and a snorkeling tours costs 20€ including boat transport, equipment hire, admission, and insurance. You can book these tours either through the park (at the above number) or with one of the local authorized diving centers: **Centro Sub Campi Flegrei** (✆ **081-8531563;** www.centrosubcampiflegrei.it) or **Centro Subacqueo 'Ulisse'** (✆ **081-3043824** or 338-2918942).

The unsubmerged part of Baia boasts some quite exceptional ruins. The **Parco Monumentale ★**, Via Bellavista (✆ **081-8687592;** free admission; open daily 9am to 1 hr. before sunset; last entrance 1 hr. before closing time) is a huge archaeological area covering 14 hectares (34 acres) of "historical landscape" on which excavations are ongoing and where you can walk among the ruins of imperial residences and elegant villas now shaded by pine trees to a backdrop of fabulous views. The **Parco Archeologico Terme di Baia ★★**, whose main entrance is at Via Sella di Baia 22 (✆ **081-8687592;** admission 4€, includes Anfiteatro Flavio

Parco Archeologico Subacqueo.

and Serapeo in Pozzuoli, Museo Archeologico in Baia, and Scavi di Cuma, and is valid 2 days; Tues–Sun 9am to 1 hr. before sunset, last entrance 1 hr. before closing time; closed Jan 1, May 1, and Dec 25), features the ruins of the Imperial Palace and the **thermal baths.** These were the most celebrated of ancient Roman baths, beloved by the VIPs of ancient Rome both for the therapeutic properties of their waters and for the matchless scenery. Built by Emperor Ottaviano between 27 B.C. and A.D. 14, the baths took advantage of local, natural hot springs and were hydraulically engineered to be fed by gravity only. The shifting ground, however, altered the original construction, and little water reaches the baths today. We recommend starting with the Parco Monumentale and taking the scenic **footpath** ★, which starts from the **Esedra** (the park's main square) and connects with a secondary entrance to the Parco Archeologico (which doesn't offer ticket sales).

Don't miss the **Museo Archeologico dei Campi Flegrei** ★★, Via Castello 39 (𝄞**081-5233797** or 848-800288), a small but perfectly formed museum housed in the scenic **Castello Aragonese** which overlooks the harbor from atop a small promontory. Built in 1442 by Alfonso d'Aragona, the castle is worth a visit in itself, if nothing else for the view. Inside is a superb collection, including chunks of rooms that were carefully excavated from local ancient Roman villas and reconstructed here, such as the **Sacello degli Augustali** ★★ and the famous **Ninfeo di Punta Epitaffio** ★★★ (a ninfeo is an ancient Roman porch enclosed with columns—this one was found underwater) from the excavations of Baia and Miseno, and the **Ninfeo of Emperor Claudius.** Admission is 2.50€, or you can buy a combined ticket for 4€ that includes the entrance to Anfiteatro Flavio and Serapeo in Pozzuoli, Zona Archeologica in Baia, and Scavi di Cuma (valid 2 days). Hours are Tuesday to Sunday from 9am to 1 hour before sunset (museum closed Jan 1, May 1, and Dec 25).

Baia is also a good base for exploring the bay; you can rent a boat from the **Associazione Barcaioli di Baia** (𝄞**081-8701222**), or join an organized boat excursion with the ferry company **Alilauro** (𝄞**081-4972222**; www.alilauro.it). All the above companies are located along the dock in the harbor.

Last but not least, you can enjoy a bit of relaxation ancient-Roman style in the **spa Terme Stufe di Nerone,** Via Stufe di Nerone 45, Bacoli (𝄞**081-8688006**; www.termestufedinerone.it), where there are two operating natural saunas. Hours vary, so call before your visit.

Cuma ★★

Easily overlooked, this special little place is where the ancient Greeks founded Cumae, their first stable colony in the western Mediterranean, giving birth to what would become Magna Grecia. The peninsula today is a trifle more built-up, but enough remains for one to imagine Cuma high atop a promontory, dominating the Phlegrean Fields peninsula, and overlooking what at the time was a green expanse of land interspersed with volcanic lakes and surrounded by the sea on both sides. The city of Cumae proved to be the most important Greek colony on this coast, keeping the Etruscans and later the Romans at bay (see chapter 2 for more history).

GETTING THERE

Although local **EAV** buses are available from Pozzuoli and the nearby **Fusaro** stop of the Cumana train line (𝄞**800-053939**; www.sepsa.it), a **taxi** from Pozzuoli is a more comfortable option (see "Getting Around," p. 348).

EXPLORING CUMA

The entrance to the archaeological area, Parco Archeologico di Cuma (© 081-8543060), is at Via Acropoli 1. The site has several ruins. On the **Acropolis** ★ are two **temples**—one to **Apollo** and the other to **Jupiter**—which served as churches from the Middle Ages; beyond the **fortified walls** is the **Necropolis** and an **amphitheater** dating from the late 2nd century B.C. Nearby is Cuma's most intriguing and atmospheric site, the mysterious **Antro della Sibilla (Sibylla's cave)** ★★. According to legend, this is where the famous oracle received her supplicants. Whatever the truth, the majestic proportions of the long, narrow trapezoidal tunnel and the engineering feat of its construction out of sheer rock are admirable. The terrace outside the cave provides a splendid **view** ★★ over the harbor of Cuma, which is in itself reason enough for a visit. Admission to the park alone is 2.50€ or you can buy a combined ticket for 4€ that includes entry to the Anfiteatro Flavio and the Serapeo in Pozzuoli, the Museo Archeologico and the Zona Archeologica in Baia, and is valid 2 days (daily 9am to 1 hr. before sunset; last admission 1 hr. before closing time; closed Jan 1, May 1, and Dec 25).

As you leave the excavations, notice the imposing arch the local road passes under: Named **Arco Felice** by locals, it dates from the 1st century A.D., when the mountain was cut and a viaduct was built for the passage of the Domitian Road, an immense engineering feat realized under Emperor Domitian. Also nearby is **Lake Averno:** Described by classic poet Virgil in the *Aeneid* as the entrance to the underworld, this volcanic lake is strangely dark and quiet. Its name is ancient Greek for "no birds," and it is believed that volcanic vapors might have kept the animals away. Despite its dark fame, in 37 B.C. Marco Agrippa had it connected via a long channel to the nearby lagoon Lucrino for use as a Roman shipyard. On the eastern shore are the remains of a large **thermal bath complex,** known as Tempio di Apollo.

Sybilla's cave.

The largest of the volcanic lakes is **Lake Fusaro** ★, a short distance farther to the south. It was known to the ancients as Acherusia Palus, or the Infernal Swamp. In 1782, quite indifferent to the ancients beliefs, Ferdinando IV Bourbon had architect Carlo Vanvitelli (son of the famous Luigi) build a hunting and fishing lodge, the **Casina Reale** ★ (Via Fusaro, Bacoli), on a little island in the lake. You can arrange a visit by appointment only (✆ **081-8687080**).

WHERE TO STAY

There are few good-quality hotels in this area; however, staying locally is a good alternative to booking a more-expensive—and logistically less-convenient—hotel in Naples, particularly if you are planning a full day of sightseeing followed by a visit to Ischia or Procida (see chapter 8).

Cala Moresca ★ Set on the cliffs of Capo Miseno, this pleasant and welcoming hotel offers comfortable accommodations and lots of extras, such as an outdoor swimming pool, a playground, a country trail, and outdoor activities such as tennis and squash. A path descends to a large shelf of rock on a secluded cove from which swimmers plunge into the blue sea. Guest rooms are large and bright, with simple modern furnishings, tiled floors, and good-size bathrooms. Most rooms have private balconies overlooking the sea. There are also studios and one-bedroom serviced apartments that rent for a minimum of 3 days during high season and 1 week the rest of the year, for similar rates as the hotel's doubles. The on-site **restaurant** is a great place for a very good and moderately priced meal.

Via Faro, 34, 80070 Bacoli. www.calamoresca.it. ✆ **081-5235595.** Fax 081-5235557. 27 units. 135€–160€ double. Rates include buffet breakfast. Children 2 and under stay free in parent's room. AE, DC, MC, V. Free parking. Closed Dec 24–26. **Amenities:** Restaurant; bar; pool; room service; tennis court. *In room:* A/C, TV, minibar.

Hotel Ristorante il Gabbiano The pluses at this hotel are the courtesy shuttle (to local destinations; otherwise, discounted taxi rates are offered), the good **restaurant,** and the welcoming service. The amiable management does its best to compensate for a not-so-glamorous location in town near busy roads (it also has soundproof windows). The hotel is not by the water but enjoys good sea views from some rooms. All rooms are spacious, full of light, and classically decorated with period furniture. Bathrooms are modern and good-size.

Via Cicerone 21, Baia. www.ilgabbianohotel.com. ✆ **081-8687969.** Fax 081-8040255. 23 units. 170€ double; 185€ triple; 250€ junior suite. Rates include buffet breakfast. Half- and full-board available. Children 3 and under stay free in parent's room; children 4–12 50% discount. AE, DC, MC, V. Free parking. Closed Dec 24–26. **Amenities:** Restaurant; bar; Internet (free); room service. *In room:* A/C, TV, minibar.

Villa Giulia 🎁 The delightful host has tastefully restored this ancient farmhouse, creating a haven of beauty in the mist of unsightly new construction (happily invisible from the premises). The homey B&B offers only five units, ranging in size from studios to huge one-bedroom accommodations, each complete with kitchen and its own patio or garden. The large garden is full of flowers in fair weather, and the good-size pool is another bonus. The week-long cooking classes that focus on pizza and other Neapolitan specialties are fun and well organized.

Via Cuma Licola 178, 80072 Pozzuoli. www.villagiulia.info. ✆ **081-8540163.** Fax 081-8044356. 5 units. 110€–130€ double; 150€ triple. Rates include buffet breakfast. Children 2 and under stay free in parent's room. AE, DC, MC, V. Free parking. **Amenities:** Restaurant; pool. *In room:* TV.

WHERE TO EAT

In addition to the following restaurants, also consider the restaurants in the hotels we list above and the local farms that operate as *agriturismi*: One we like for the quality of the food and the hospitality is **Il Casolare di Tobia,** Contrada Coste Fondi di Baia, Via Pietro Fabris 12–14, 80070 Bacoli (✆ **081-5235193;** www.datobia.it; reservations recommended), which is located in a valley that is actually an extinct crater and serves traditional dishes using organic produce from the garden. **Il Cetrangolo,** Via Faro 64, Capo Miseno (✆ **081-5232688;** www.ilcetrangolo.it) offers excellent food at moderate prices and great views to boot.

Great Gelato Breaks

For the best gelato in the area, head to Via Napoli in Pozzuoli. Among the many bars and *gelaterie* lining the street, our favorites are Anema e Cono, Corso Umberto I 59 (✆ 081-5263254), and Sneezy, Corso Umberto I 165 (✆ 081-5264777).

Expensive

Dal Tarantino ★★ NEAPOLITAN/SEAFOOD Situated on a characterful lane a pigeon's spit from Pozzuoli's bustling port area, this is a good place to enjoy the freshest of local fish and seafood. The three set menus (45€, 50€, and 65€) are good value and make the decisions for you or you can choose a la carte; we recommend the mixed antipasti to start followed by spaghetti *cafoncelli* (with clams, cherry tomatoes, and pecorino cheese) or roast monkfish served on a bed of potatoes. Leave room for dessert; the *torroncino* (nougat) mousse is fantastic.

Via Puteolana 20, Pozzuoli. ✆ **081-5266290.** www.trattoriadaltarantino.it. Reservations recommended Sat–Sun. Secondi 20€–40€. AE, DC, MC, V. Wed–Mon noon–3pm and 8pm–midnight. Closed 1 week in Dec and 1 week in Jan.

Moderate

Arturo al Fusaro ★ 🍴 NEAPOLITAN This excellent restaurant offers traditional local cuisine in a pleasant atmosphere, and at reasonable prices. The specialty is seafood, which is extremely fresh and served up in appetizers, pasta and rice dishes, and main courses. You might want to sample the flawless risotto *ai frutti di mare* (with seafood); vermicelli *cozze e vongole* (with mussels and clams); or one of the catches of the day prepared *all'acqua pazza* (in light herbed broth), grilled with herbs, or baked over a bed of potatoes.

Via Cuma 322, Bacoli. ✆ **081-8543130.** Reservations recommended Sat–Sun. Secondi 7€–14€. AE, DC, MC, V. Daily noon–3pm and 7–10:30pm.

Cagi Di Ludovico Avallone ★ NEAPOLITAN This is a good address in Pozzuoli for meat as well as seafood. All dishes are prepared traditionally, with good local ingredients. We are partial to spaghetti *alle vongole* (with clams), but the fusilli *al ragù* (with Neapolitan meat sauce) is also excellent; for secondo, we recommend the *fettina alla pizzaiola* (beef in a tomato and oregano sauce).

Via Roma 17, Pozzuoli. ✆ **081-5268255.** Reservations recommended Sat–Sun. Secondi 12€–18€. AE, DC, MC, V. Tues–Sat noon–3pm and 7:30–11pm; Sun noon–3pm.

Inexpensive

Abraxas Osteria & Wine Bar NEAPOLITAN Popular with the younger crowd and the Anglo-American community from the nearby NATO base, this trendy restaurant offers good cuisine, pleasant views, and a great garden for outdoor

5

POMPEII, HERCULANEUM & BEYOND

The Phlegrean Fields

dining. It is also active at organizing wine tastings and other special culinary and cultural events. We particularly appreciated the great attention to the wine list, with many little-known but excellent local choices (such as the very good house wine), and to the ever-changing menu, merging creativity with a love for the hearty products of this region. If they are on the menu, do not miss the *crespelle* (thin savory crepes/pancakes with a cheese and walnuts sauce) or the *coniglio in porchetta* (roasted boneless rabbit). The chef also prepares a great grilled steak and, in winter, superb sausage-based dishes, such as the *verza con salsicce e castagne* (savoy cabbage with sausages and chestnuts) and polenta, served grilled with sausages or with sauce.

Via Scalandrone 15, Lucrino. ✆ **081-854-9347.** www.abraxasosteria.it. Reservations recommended Sat–Sun. Secondi 10€–15€. AE, DC, MC, V. Wed–Sat 7:30–11pm; Sun noon–3pm.

Garibaldi NEAPOLITAN/SEAFOOD This seaside restaurant makes for an excellent stop after a visit to the museum or the archaeological area of Baia. It takes advantage of its prime location by specializing in seafood—simply prepared, but using fresh ingredients and traditional recipes. Fusilli *ai frutti di mare* (with seafood) is a perfect way to begin the meal, but you shouldn't miss out on the secondo: excellent *polpo in guazzetto* (squid in a tomato sauce), as well as some of the most flavorful grilled fish in the area.

Via Spiaggia di Bacoli 36, Bacoli. ✆ **081-5234368.** Reservations recommended Sat–Sun. Secondi 8€–16€. AE, DC, MC, V. Tues–Sun noon–3pm and 7–11pm.

Il Tucano PIZZA It's a bit touristy, yes, but excellent pizza and traditional specialties make this restaurant worth a visit. The heir of the historical Trattoria Miramare, which occupied this spot since 1929, Il Tucano makes a real effort to honor the old trattoria's menu and to offer a wide selection of local wines. It also serves up a large variety of pizzas—including the exceptional *quattro formaggi e gamberetti* (four cheese and shrimp). The slices are served "by the foot:" you ask for a length, and they cut it and charge you accordingly.

Via Molo di Baia 40, Baia. ✆ **081-8545046.** Pizza 3€–8€. MC, V. Tues–Sun noon–midnight.

THE LAND OF SIRENS:

SORRENTO & ITS PENINSULA

The unique beauty of Sorrento's coast has inspired many myths. This is where the Sirens are said to have waylaid travelers with their irresistible song, as befell Ulysses in Homer's *Odyssey*.

Today, the pull of the sea and imposing rock-bound coast remain as compelling as in Homer's day, attracting legions of visitors, and it is unlikely that you will feel alone here, especially if you come during the summer months. Sorrento's charms are not tarnished by the crowds, however, as the town is only made merrier by the bustle. If you are seeking a bit of solitude, there are plenty of off-the-beaten-path attractions along this peninsula, which is one of the most beautiful in the Mediterranean.

A rocky point of land jutting 20km (12 miles) into the sea and dominated by the high mountains of the Monti Lattari, the Sorrentine peninsula looks a bit like a finger pointing towards Capri (which is just 5km/3 miles away), dividing the Gulf of Naples from the Gulf of Salerno. Visitors come here to hike rugged paths, discover medieval watchtowers and rural villages, explore ancient ruins, and sample a cuisine rich with locally produced ingredients, including cheeses and cured meats that are unique to this little corner of southern Italy.

The gateway to the Sorrento peninsula is **Castellammare di Stabia,** a modern town and thermal resort built over the ancient Roman settlement of Stabiae. **Sorrento** is the main town of the peninsula and lies about midway along the northern shore that opens onto the Gulf of Naples. Scattered among the surrounding rugged mountains and along nearby cliff sides are many small villages connected by narrow, winding local roads which, thanks to their inaccessibility, are destined to remain delightfully quiet backwaters, undiscovered by mass tourism.

On the southern side of the peninsula lies an authentic, little-explored stretch of coast. Harsh and rocky, it is the geographical continuation of the famous Amalfi Coast which begins at Positano (see chapter 7) and is rich in unexplored surprises in spite of lying just kilometers from one of the Mediterranean's most popular destinations.

CASTELLAMMARE DI STABIA ★

33km (20 miles) SE of Naples

If you have a taste for restful and leisurely sightseeing, then the town of Castellammare di Stabia is the place for you. Opening like a fan onto the Bay of Naples, the town enjoys a beautiful location between beaches and hills. It is blessed with multiple natural springs—28 of them, each with its own therapeutic characteristics—that have made Castellammare a popular resort since antiquity. The Romans called it Stabiae, and it was popular among the VIPs of the day including Cicero who used to spend his vacations here. The eruption of A.D. 79 obliterated the town, and although the settlement was reborn after the disaster, its inhabitants were forced to take refuge in the mountains to escape the incursions of Goths and Longobards.

PREVIOUS PAGE: View of Sorrento from Marina Piccola, the smaller of the town's two harbors.

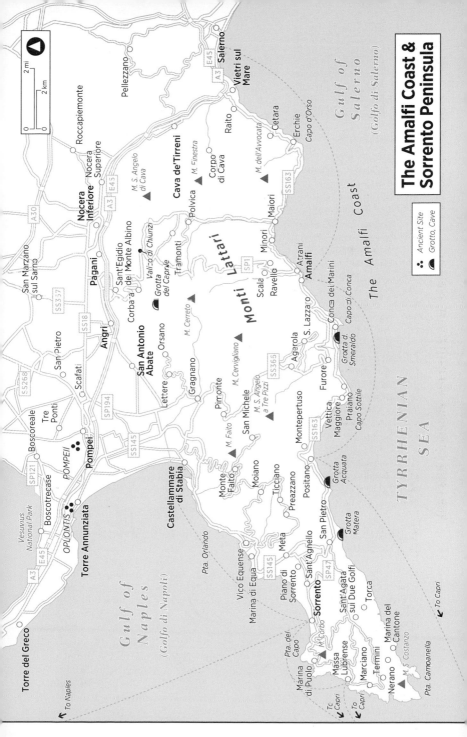

The Amalfi Coast & Sorrento Peninsula

∴ Ancient Site
🕳 Grotto, Cave

Gulf of Salerno
(Golfo di Salerno)

Gulf of Naples
(Golfo di Napoli)

TYRRHENIAN SEA

The Amalfi Coast

In the 9th century, the citizens build Castrum a Mare, the castle that lent the town its modern name. The Angevin dynasty later surrounded the town with walls, enlarged its harbor, and built the Royal Palace for the king's vacations. The Bourbons subsequently created a prosperous shipyard that fueled the development of the town, and today it remains an important shipyard.

Essentials

GETTING THERE & AROUND The **bus** is a good option, with **SITA** (✆089-405145; www.sitabus.it) offering service from Naples, and Sorrento, and **Curreri Viaggi** (✆081-8015420; www.curreriviaggi.it) offering regular departures from Naples's Capodichino Airport as well as from Rome (respectively for 10€ and 16€). A faster option is the **train.** The **Circumvesuviana** (✆800-053939; www.vesuviana.it) railroad from Naples and nearby towns offers frequent service and makes four stops in town; the ride takes 45 minutes from Naples and costs 2.40€ (for more information on public transportation fares, see "The Unico Travel Pass," p. 349). You can also use the **FS** national rail service (✆892021 in Italy; www.trenitalia.it); trains arrive at Castellammare FS station on Piazza Giacomo Matteotti.

From Naples or another seaside location, **ferries** provide the most scenic method of travel to Castellammare: **Metro del Mare** (✆199-600700; www.metrodelmare.net) runs from Pozzuoli, Naples, and Sorrento (service is suspended in winter). In 2011, the service was reduced to a minimum and only ran during July and August, but we were told that a fuller schedule should be resumed by 2012. Other companies offering seasonal service are **Alilauro** (✆081-4972222; www.alilauro.it), **LMP** (✆081-7041911; www.consorziolmp.it), and **NLG** (✆081-5520763; www.navlib.it). By **car,** take autostrada A3 to the exit for CASTELLAMMARE DI STABIA; once on SS 145, follow the CASTELLAMMARE DI STABIA signs directly into town.

Buses and trains are the best way to get around the area; in town, there are local buses, but **taxis** are more convenient. As elsewhere in Italy, drivers wait at taxi stands, at Piazza Matteotti and Piazza Unità d'Italia.

VISITOR INFORMATION The **tourist office,** Piazza Matteotti 34, 80053 Castellammare di Stabia (✆081-8711334), provides comprehensive local information, from spas to archaeology. You'll find a **pharmacy** (✆081-8701077) at Via Plinio il Vecchio 62. The **hospital,** Ospedale San Leonardo (✆081-8729111), is on Viale Europa. Dial ✆118 for an **ambulance** and ✆113 or 112 for the **police.** The **post office,** Piazza Giovanni XXIII 4 (✆081-8711449), is open Monday to Saturday from 8am to 2pm. For your banking needs, **Banco di Napoli** (✆081-8737111) is at Corso Vittorio Emanuele 76.

Exploring the Town

In addition to its excavated ancient Roman villas, **Scavi di Stabia,** Castellammare prides itself on a number of other worthy attractions. In addition to the archaeological area, we highly recommend an excursion up **Monte Faito** ★, the tall mountain (1,100m/3,609 ft. high) looming over the town which offers unrivaled views over the Gulf of Naples. Although you can drive, we'd much rather take the *funivia* **(funicular)** from the center of town (Piazza Stazione Circumvesuviana).

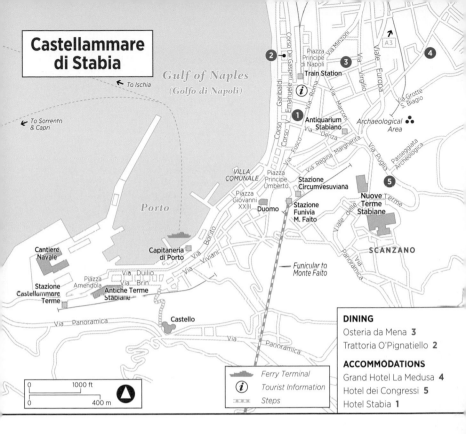

Castellammare di Stabia

Gulf of Naples
(Golfo di Napoli)

← To Ischia

← To Sorrento & Capri

2 Piazza Principe di Napoli
Train Station 3
4

A3

(i)

Antiquarium Stabiano 1
Via Denza

Archaeological Area

Via Grotte S. Biagio

VILLA COMUNALE
Piazza Principe Umberto
Stazione Circumvesuviana

Piazza Giovanni XXIII
Duomo

Stazione Funivia M. Faito

5
Nuove Terme Stabiane

Porto

Cantiere Navale

Capitaneria di Porto

SCANZANO

Stazione Castellammare Terme
Piazza Amendola
Via Duilio
Via Brin
Antiche Terme Stabiane

— *Funicular to Monte Faito*

Castello

Via Panoramica

Via Panoramica

0 ——— 1000 ft
0 ——— 400 m

Ferry Terminal
(i) Tourist Information
Steps

DINING
Osteria da Mena 3
Trattoria O'Pignatiello 2

ACCOMMODATIONS
Grand Hotel La Medusa 4
Hotel dei Congressi 5
Hotel Stabia 1

From April to October, it runs every half-hour, and the round-trip fare is 7€. You can return via funivia, or hike down (it's about an hour for the descent; inquire at the tourist office for more information).

Nuove Terme Stabiane ★, Viale delle Terme 3, on the slopes of Monte Faito (✆ **081-3913111;** www.termedistabia.com), is a state-of-the-art thermal spa near **Villa Quisisana,** the historic royal summer palace. Downtown, **Villa Comunale,** off Piazza Giovanni XXIII, near the Stazione Circumvesuviana (free admission; open from sunrise to sunset), is a public garden that opens onto the Gulf of Naples. Not to be missed is the elegant **Cassa Armonica** (bandstand)— a Liberty masterpiece created by Eugenio Cosenza in 1901. The **castle** above the town is private and cannot be visited, nor can you tour the **Villa Quisiana,** the grand residence of Bourbon royals, which has been recently renovated. For now, the villa is open to the public only for special exhibitions and concerts, although future plans may involve a more permanent opening.

Scavi di Stabia ★ This archaeological area comprises the remains of Stabiae, the ancient Roman resort town that was destroyed in A.D. 79 in the same eruption that devastated its more famous neighbors, Pompeii and Herculaneum. Little of the town itself has been excavated, but some of the elegant *villae di otium* (pleasure residences) were uncovered in the 18th century; much of the art that was found is on display in the National Archaeological Museum of Naples. Further excavations in the 1950s uncovered more artifacts that were left *in situ.*

The Villa di Arianna in Scavi di Stabia.

A superb example of an ancient Roman patrician villa, the **Villa di Arianna** ★, Via Piana di Varano (from town, take Viale Europa and turn left onto SS 366 toward Gragnano, and then immediately left again onto Via Piana di Varano), takes its name from a painting found inside: a beautiful **fresco** depicting the mythological Ariadne as she is discovered sleeping by Dyonisius.

Built in a dramatic location, the villa was designed to take maximum advantage of the views over the sea and Mount Faito. Though partly ransacked in the 18th century after its discovery, it retains many of its decorative elements: Particularly lovely are the frescos in the rooms to the left of the summer *triclinium* (**dining room**)—the one of Ariadne described above and another depicting Ganimede taken by an eagle up to Jupiter. Nearby is a room decorated with diagonal stripes of delicately **painted tiles** although only a few remain; others can be seen in the archaeological museum in Naples. You should also visit **Villa di San Marco** ★, Via Passeggiata Archeologica, a patrician villa that is still impressive in spite of damage suffered in the 1980 earthquake. Built in the 1st century B.C. as the residence of a wealthy family, it was enlarged in the 1st century A.D. and became quite palatial, with porticos, halls, and private thermal baths (in three temperatures: *calidarium, tepidarium,* and *frigidarium*), all decorated with stucco work, paintings, and frescoes.

Within walking distance is the **Grotta di San Biagio (St. Biagio's Grotto),** a tufa-stone quarry used in Roman times for the construction of the villas in Stabiae that was transformed into a paleochristian oratory in the 5th to 6th centuries A.D. The first bishops of Stabiae are buried here, making it one of the oldest known Christian burial sites. It is decorated with well-preserved frescoes and paintings that date from the 5th to 6th centuries and from the 9th to 10th centuries; the three frescoes by the entrance are from the 14th century.

Via Passeggiata Archeologica (follow directions for Varano, also for Grand Hotel La Medusa). ℂ **081-8575347.** www.pompeiisites.org. Admission 5.50€, includes same-day admission to

Boscoreale and Oplonti. Artecard discount available (p. 98); 3-day cumulative ticket (includes Herculaneum, Pompeii, Oplontis, Stabiae, and Boscoreale) 20€. Train: Circumvesuviana to Via Nocera stop, then switch to bus no. 1 rosso. Nov–Mar daily 8:30am–5pm; Apr–Oct daily 8:30am–7:30pm. Last admission 90 min. earlier.

Where to Stay

Castellammare is a good jumping-off point for visits to the archaeological areas of Vesuvius, including Pompeii and Herculaneum, and your money will go further than in crowded Naples, Vico Equense, or glitzy, expensive Sorrento.

Crowne Plaza Stabiae Sorrento Coast ★ ☺ Housed in a refurbished cement factory in Pozzano, just south of town, this seaside hotel is large but charming. Amenities include access to a small private beach—one of the rare stretches of sand in the area—and a spa that is the pride of the hotel, with 12 treatment rooms, two hydro baths, a Jacuzzi, a solarium, a sauna, fitness facilities, and specially tailored health and beauty programs. Guest rooms are light-filled and spacious although only the better rooms enjoy the best sea views. Some open onto a private terrace, and "family rooms" are actually two-bedroom units with separate bathrooms. All bathrooms have tub/shower combinations.

Strada Statale Sorrentina (SS 145, Km 11), Pozzano, 80053 Castellammare di Stabia. www.crowne plazasorrento.com. (*) **081-3946700.** Fax 081-3946770. 150 units. 170€–220€ double; from 400€ suite. Rates include buffet breakfast. Internet specials available. AE, DC, MC, V. Free parking. **Amenities:** Restaurant; bar; concierge; pool; room service; spa. *In room:* A/C, TV, minibar, Wi-Fi (free).

Grand Hotel La Medusa ★★ This luxury hotel has the best setting in town: Occupying a beautifully restored 19th-century villa surrounded by a splendid park and terraced garden, it is simply picture-perfect and oh so romantic. It is convenient to the archaeological area, albeit farther from the center of town and the shore. The hotel features plush public spaces and salons, and elegantly appointed guest rooms, which are decorated with a sophisticated mix of classic and modern furnishings, beautiful tiled floors, and Oriental carpets, as well as fine linens and fabrics. Bathrooms are a good size (some with shower only), and the best rooms have Jacuzzi tubs and views over the Gulf of Naples. We recommend upgrading to a superior or a deluxe room, as the "traditional" ones are a bit dark.

Via Passeggiata Archeologica 5, 80053 Castellammare di Stabia. www.lamedusahotel.com. (*) **081-8791234.** Fax 081-8717009. 52 units. High season 170€–280€ double; 300€ suite. Rates include buffet breakfast. Internet specials available. AE, DC, MC, V. Free parking. **Amenities:** Restaurant; 2 bars; concierge; pool; outdoor tennis courts; room service. *In room:* A/C, TV, minibar.

Hotel dei Congressi ★ ☺ This highly service-oriented establishment is conveniently located across from the Nuove Terme Stabiane and a short distance from the archaeological area. In a more modern building than La Medusa, the hotel offers spacious public spaces, including a large swimming pool and a pleasant terrace garden. Guest rooms are large and bright, each with a private balcony large enough for a table and chairs. The furnishings are tasteful, and rooms have tiled floors and ample modern bathrooms. The best rooms share superb panoramic views with the terraced swimming pool. The triple and quad rooms are a plus for families or small groups.

Viale Puglia 45, 80053 Castellammare di Stabia. www.hoteldeicongressi.it. (*)/fax **081-8722277.** 100 units. 150€–250€ double. Rates include buffet breakfast. Children 2 and under stay free in parent's room. AE, DC, MC, V. Free parking. **Amenities:** Restaurant; bar; concierge; pool; room service. *In room:* A/C, TV, minibar.

Hotel Stabia ★ 🏨 Serving guests since 1876 and offering professional service and fine accommodations, this fetchingly pink hotel is the best of Castellammare's historic establishments. Built in the 19th century along the downtown seaside promenade, the hotel has been carefully restored to preserve its neoclassical style. Both communal spaces and bedrooms have been redecorated, but many of the original furnishings have been incorporated into the design, inspiring a sense of peaceful elegance. Guest rooms are spacious, with tiled floors and neoclassical furnishings; many rooms have their own small balconies or terraces sharing views of Monte Faito or—in the best rooms—of the Gulf of Naples and Ischia. There is a new Beauty Centre offering massages and treatments plus a hammam and fitness suite.

Corso Vittorio Emanuele 101, 80053 Castellammare di Stabia. www.hotelstabia.it. ✆ **081-8722577.** Fax 081-8722105. 94 units. 115€-155€ double. Rates include buffet breakfast. AE, DC, MC, V. Free parking. **Amenities:** Restaurant; bar; room service. *In room:* A/C, TV, Internet, minibar.

Where to Eat

Osteria da Mena ★ 🏨 SORRENTINE This little osteria offers well-prepared local specialties in a relaxed atmosphere. The homemade pasta is very good—if you're lucky you'll find excellent *scialatielli ai frutti di mare* (thick spaghetti with basil and shellfish)—and the *frittura* (deep-fried medley of seafood) is crisp and juicy. Meat often features on the seasonal menu, including excellent *pollo arrosto* (roasted chicken) and tender *arrosto di maiale* (pork roast).

Via Pietro Carrese 32. ✆ **081-8713048.** Reservations recommended. Secondi 10€-18€. No credit cards. Daily noon–3pm and 7:30–11pm.

Trattoria O'Pignatiello ★ 🏨 SORRENTINE/SEAFOOD This authentic local hangout is excellent for simple and traditional food, prepared with local ingredients. Family run, it always offers a well-rounded choice of dishes, though it prides itself on the seafood specialties. As an appetizer, we highly recommend the *insalata di polipo* (octopus salad), and you could follow this with the delicious spaghetti *ai frutti di mare* (spaghetti with seafood). The grilled meats are also an excellent choice. The lunch menu, including a pasta dish and a secondo, is a steal at 12€.

Via Alcide De Gasperi 207. ✆ **081-8715100.** Reservations recommended. Secondi 12€-20€. AE, DC, MC, V. Daily noon–3pm and 7:30–11pm. Closed Dec 24–Jan 6.

VICO EQUENSE ★

42km (26 miles) SE of Naples

Smaller and more laid-back then Sorrento, Vico Equense is visited by far fewer foreign tourists. Built on a tufa-stone platform overlooking the sea, the town's charm and personality make it popular with Italian tourists, who arrive in force, especially in August.

Essentials

GETTING THERE You can easily reach Vico Equense by **train,** via the **Circumvesuviana Railway** (✆ 800-053939; www.vesuviana.it), or by **bus,** via **SITA** (✆ 089-405145; www.sitabus.it) service from Naples, Sorrento, and the Amalfi Coast. **Curreri Viaggi** (✆ 081-8015420; www.curreri viaggi.it) offers service from Naples's Capodichino Airport as well as from Rome (for 10€ and 16€, respectively).

Vico Equense.

If you are coming by **car,** from the autostrada A1, switch to the A3, and take the exit CASTELLAMMARE DI STABIA. Follow the signs for VICO EQUENSE and SORRENTO to SS 145, the coastal road that leads to Vico Equense.

GETTING AROUND Vico is not a large town and everything is pretty much within **walking** distance, including the beaches and mountain trails. You can also call a **taxi** at ✆ 081-8015405, or go to the taxi stand on Piazza Umberto I.

VISITOR INFORMATION The **tourist office** (✆ 081-8015752; fax 081-8799351; www.vicoturismo.it) is at Via San Ciro 16 and maintains an information stand at Piazza Umberto I 19. The **hospital** (✆ 081-8016287) is on Via D. Caccioppoli. You'll find a **pharmacy** (✆ 081-8015525) on Via Roma 18 as well as several **banks,** including a Banco di Napoli (✆ 081-8016681). For first aid or an ambulance, dial ✆ 118. You can call the **police** at ✆ 113 and the **fire department** at ✆ 115. The **post office** (✆ 081-8016811) is at Via San Ciro 57.

Exploring the Town

Excavations in the ancient town of Vico Equense have revealed remains dating from the 6th century B.C., proving the existence of Oscan, Etruscan, and Greek occupants (evidenced by the **Necropolis** of Via Nicotera). Named *Aequa* during Roman times, the town survived the eruption of A.D. 79 and flourished until it was destroyed by the Goths in 553. It was then reestablished as "Vico Equense" by the Angevins in the 12th century. To discover Vico's delightful medieval buildings, start in the main square, **Piazza Umberto I,** take **Via Filangieri,** and turn right onto **Via Monsignor Natale.**

This street is the heart of the medieval town, and its palazzi shelter delightful courtyards, such as the splendid one at no. 3. Continuing on, you can enjoy the great view from **Largo dei Tigli,** and, retracing your steps to Via Vescovado, visit the **Chiesa dell'Annunziata,** Via Vescovada (Sun and holidays 10am–noon, other days open by request only; ✆ **081-8798004**), a 14th-century church partially rebuilt after the 1688 earthquake. In the upper town is the privately owned 13th century **Castello Giusso** (renovated and enlarged in later centuries), and thermal springs that feed the local **spas.**

Scrajo Terme ★ A thermal spa created in the 19th century and built on a cliff overlooking the beach, this is the best place in town to "take the waters." The old-fashioned jewel lies a short distance west of Vico off the main road to Sorrento (the SS 145) and offers a wide range of treatments and therapies (fees start at 24€). The public spaces overlook the shore in a cascade of terraces, and the spa has a delightful ambience. You can swim off the private beach where the sulfur spring flows into the sea, creating a mineral mix with unique healing properties. The charming **restaurant** is housed in a Liberty-style (Italian Art Nouveau) hall, with a bar and attached terrace affording beautiful views over the sea. There are also seven bright and well-furnished guest rooms (150€–220€ double, including breakfast and access to the spa).

Via Luigi Serio 10 (SS 145), Località Scrajo, 80069 Vico Equense. ✆ **081-8015731.** www.scrajo terme.it. AE, DC, MC, V. May 2–Nov 30; booking opening hours vary during the season; booking required.

Staying Active

Vico is a good base from which to explore the area's natural attractions of sea, beaches, and mountains. Across from the Municipio in the center of town, you can take **Via Castello Marina,** the steep old footpath which descends through olive groves and leads to **Vico Marina** where you will find small **beaches** hidden within picturesque coves. One of the nicest is **Marina di Equa,** just west of a defense tower built in the 17th century.

Another great hike—but one that requires you to be moderately fit and is best accomplished with a good trail map (available from the tourist office in town)—is the old footpath to **Positano.** Although the area has been inhabited for thousands of years, the SS 163 (the Amalfi Coast Drive) dates only from 1840; before then, footpaths were the only means of travel and communication on the peninsula. For centuries, residents trekked over mountain paths and commuted by boat to points along the coast. Walking the succession of trails to Positano will require about 3½ hours. Follow the directions for Ticciano until you reach the **bridge over the Milo;** there, on your left, you'll find a dirt road to the pass of **Santa Maria al Castello** (altitude 685m/2,247 ft.). Just before the church, to your left, is the connection to the **Sentiero degli Dei (Footpath of the Gods)** that leads toward Nocelle. Instead of taking this, turn left at the dirt track directly across from the church; this is the trail that leads to Positano. When you reach the fork, the western spur climbs to Monte Comune (altitude 877m/2,877 ft.), with its sweeping views; the eastern branch begins the descent to Positano. Along this trail are several tricky passages around points of rock, so follow your map carefully.

The many *agriturismi* (farmhouses) in the area are great places to have lunch and to experience daily agricultural activities; you can also arrange an overnight stay. One of our favorites is **Coop-Agrituristica La Ginestra,** Via Tessa 2, Santa Maria di Castello (*©* **081-8023211;** www.laginestra.org; 80€ double, including breakfast), a beekeeping farm that makes delicious organic honey. Another *agriturismo* is **Masseria Astapiana Villa Giusso,** Via Camaldoli 51, 80069 Vico Equense (*©*/fax **081-8024392** or 081-403797; www.astapiana.com). A historic patrician farm building, it dates from the 17th century, and many of the original frescoes have been preserved. Surrounded by parkland, it has a museum, offers organized tours and cooking classes, and serves dinner. It also has a few simply appointed rooms and a self-catering apartment for rent (100€–120€ double).

Where to Stay

Hotels in Vico command dramatic views and are cheaper and less crowded than those in Sorrento, making them a good base from which to explore the area. **Scrajo Terme** (p. 164) or the two *agriturismi* mentioned above are particularly good choices for families.

Grand Hotel Angiolieri Situated just outside Vico Equense in the village of Seiano, the elegant Angiolieri offers comfortable accommodations and superb views in a grand villa that was built in the 18th century on the ruins of an ancient Roman patrician residence said to have belonged to Cicero. The restoration added a few questionable details but, on the whole, it works. Guest rooms are not large—(it's definitely worth upgrading from the small standard doubles) but they are attractive, with a mix of contemporary furniture and classic details. Bathrooms are nicely styled with bright mosaic tiles (some with shower or bathtub only). Pricier rooms enjoy sea views; some of these units, and all the suites, have private terraces or balconies. The swimming pool is a plus, and the gourmet restaurant **L'Accanto** serves beautiful food from a breathtaking terrace.

Via Santa Maria Vecchia 2, 80066 Seiano di Vico Equense. www.grandhotelangiolieri.it. *©* **081-8029161.** Fax 081-8028558. 37 units. 229€–349€ double; 399€–459€ suite. Rates include buffet breakfast. Children 2 and under stay free in parent's room. AE, DC, MC, V. **Amenities:** Restaurant; pool. *In room:* A/C, TV, Internet, minibar.

Hotel Aequa This hotel has been serving its guests in the heart of town by the medieval area since the 1940s, and renovations have not compromised its old-fashioned charm. The property is perched on the cliffs overlooking the sea and affords excellent views: We highly recommend an evening aperitivo under the glorious wisteria on the terrace overlooking Vesuvius. Guest rooms are spacious and well-appointed with hardwood floors and classic furnishings; bathrooms are modern and good-size.

Via Filangeri 46, 80069 Vico Equense. www.aequahotel.it. *©* **081-8015331.** Fax 081-8015071. 68 units. 145€ double. Rates include buffet breakfast. Children 2 and under stay free in parent's room. AE, DC, MC, V. Parking 10€. **Amenities:** Restaurant; bar; pool. *In room:* A/C, TV, minibar.

Hotel Capo La Gala In the cliffs among olive groves and lemon-tree terraces overlooking the sea, this hotel enjoys a rare quiet not far from town. Guest rooms are bright and tastefully decorated with streamlined modern furniture and local hand-painted tiles; each has its own private balcony and great views. The outdoor swimming pool is filled from a natural spring of sulfur thermal water (the smell takes some getting used to, but it is oh so good for your skin), or you can use the facilities at the rocky beach on the Tyrrenian Sea. Management might require a minimum stay of 3 nights during the months of July and August.

Via Luigi Serio 8 (1km/½ mile before Vico coming from Castellammare), Scrajo Terme 80069 Vico Equense. www.capolagala.com. ✆ **081-8015758.** Fax 081-8798747. 22 units. 350€–550€ double. Rates include buffet breakfast and rental of beach facilities. Internet specials available. AE, DC, MC, V. Free parking. Closed Nov–Mar. **Amenities:** Restaurant; pool; room service; spa. *In room:* A/C, TV, minibar, Wi-Fi (3€/hour).

Where to Eat

In addition to the following restaurants, good local food is available at the hotels and *agriturismi* above. Great for a picnic, **La Tradizione ★★★**, Via Raffaele Bosco 969, Seiano di Vico Equense (✆**081-8028437;** www.latradizione.com; Tues–Sun 9am–2pm and 4:30–9pm), sells wine, olive oil, delicious bread, and local mozzarella (which can be braided and studded with olives and prosciutto), as well as preserves and crispy *taralli* (local savory cookies). You'll find superb gelato at **Da Gabriele ★★**, Corso Umberto I 5 (✆**081-8798744**).

Da Gigino Pizza a Metro, L'Università della Pizza ★★★ PIZZA At the opposite end of the spectrum from the Torre (above), this casual eatery is a temple to pizza. In the 1950s, Gigino Dell'Amura baked a pizza that was so long a visiting journalist termed it "pizza a metro," or pizza by the meter. Its unique, crispy dough quickly became famous, and today Dell'Amura's five sons maintain the tradition in their cavernous, ever-popular restaurant. A meter (about 3 ft.) of pizza is a good serving for five people, and the price depends on the toppings. Don't be put off by all the tourists: This place not only serves some of the best pizza in the area, but it also offers delicious appetizers, such as *frittelle di alghe* (seaweed fritters), a local specialty.

Via Giovanni Nicotera 15, Vico Equense. ✆ **081-8798426** or 081-8798309. www.pizzametro.it. Reservations not accepted. Pizza from 7€. No credit cards. Daily noon–1am.

Nonna Rosa ★★★ 🛋 MODERN SORRENTINE Occupying a house that dates from the 1600s and tucked away on the road that ascends Monte Faito from the center of town, this restaurant is a well-kept local secret. The countryside elegance of the small dining room provides a comfortable background for the excellent and unusual dishes featured on the seasonal menus. We recommend the *pasta e ceci con le seppioline* (chickpea and pasta soup with baby squid) if it's on the menu, and the slow-roast pork with a sauce made from local *annurche* apples. This is also a good place to sample *baccalà* (salt cod).

Via Privata Bonea 4 (off Via Raffaele Bosco, Pietrapiano), Vico Equense. ✆ **081-8799055.** www. osterianonnarosa.it. Reservations recommended. Secondi 20€; tasting menus 65€ and 75€. AE, DC, MC, V. Tues–Fri 7:30–11pm; Sat–Sun 12:30–3:30pm and 7:30–11pm.

Ristorante Torre del Saracino ★★★ MODERN SORRENTINE This is a special and justly renowned restaurant, where the food is truly extraordinary and the service perfect. Affable host and Chef Gennaro Esposito puts guests at ease in his sleek yet welcoming restaurant overlooking the sea. His seasonal menus are made up of creative versions of the regional cuisine using many locally sourced ingredients. We loved the risotto flavored with local lemons and *burrata* (a type of creamy mozzarella) served with a delicate local broccoli puree and topped with a mixture of raw, marinated red mullet and candied ginger. If you are overwhelmed by the a la carte choices, we recommend the two tasting menus (100€ and 120€), which are the best way to experience the culinary spirit of the chef. Whatever you do, leave room for the unique desserts, such as the *babà al rhum con crema pasticcera e fragoline di bosco* (rum cake with cream and local wild strawberries). Via Torretta 9, Marina d'Equa. ✆ **081-8028555.** www.torredelsaracino.it. Secondi 20€–35€. AE, DC, MC, V. Tues–Sat 12:30–3:30pm and 7:30–11:30pm; Sun 12:30–3:30pm. Closed mid-Feb to mid-Mar.

SORRENTO ★★★

39km (20 miles) SE of Naples

Sorrento has been the preferred destination of kings and emperors for millenia: Emperor Augustus and his successor, Tiberius, were two of its early devotees. In later years, the town became a preferred destination for artists and writers, and a favorite stop on the Grand Tour. These days, the tourism is a little less exclusive, but although the presence of crowds may dull some of its magic at times, Sorrento's charming cobblestone streets, matchless views, seaside setting, and lively cultural scene keep getting our high votes.

Essentials

GETTING THERE Sorrento is connected to most other destinations in the region by the **Circumvesuviana** railway (✆ 800-053939; www.vesuviana.it), and the ride takes about 50 minutes from Naples. **SITA** (✆ 089 405145; www.sitabus.it) offers frequent **bus** service to Sorrento from Naples, Amalfi, Positano, and Salerno. **Curreri Viaggi** (✆ 081-8015420; www.curreri viaggi.it) maintains routes from Naples's Capodichino Airport, as well as from Rome and Naples, with stops in Castellammare di Stabia, Vico Equense, Meta, Piano di Sorrento, and Sant'Agnello. The ride to Sorrento from Naples takes about 1 hour and costs 10€; from Rome it is about 3½ hours and costs 16€ (for more information on fares, see "The Unico Travel Pass," p. 349). **Marozzi** (✆ 080-5790111; www.marozzivt.it) has daily connections from Rome to Sorrento with stops in Naples, Pompeii, Castellammare di Stabia, and Vico Equense.

In summer, ferries and hydrofoils are a pleasant way to travel. **LMP-Linee Marittime Partenopee** (✆ 081-5513236; www.consorziolmp.it), **NLG-Navigazione Libera del Golfo** (✆ 081-8071812; www.navlib.it), and **Linee Lauro** (✆ 081-4972222; www.alilauro.it) make daily runs to and from Naples, Ischia, and Capri. **Caremar** (✆ 199-116655; www.caremar. it) also serves Capri; and **Volaviamare** (✆ 081-4972291; www.volaviamare. it) makes runs from Amalfi and Positano. **Metrò del Mare,** at the Marina Piccola downtown (✆ 199-600700; www.metrodelmare.net), is a summer-only commuter ferry serving the whole coast between Salerno and Bacoli.

Taxis offer a flat rate of 100 to Sorrento from Naples, and **car service** can be arranged in advance with **2golfi,** Via Deserto 30/e, 80064 Sant'Agata sui due Golfi (✆ 339-8307748 or 339-3494479; www.due golficarservice.it). **Curreri Viaggi** (above) offers a **shuttle service** (120€ for four passengers).

By **car,** take the exit for CASTELLAMMARE DI STABIA off autostrada A3, and then follow signs for VICO EQUENSE, META DI SORRENTO, and SORRENTO; these will lead you to route SS 145, the Sorrento peninsula's coastal road.

GETTING AROUND The **Circumvesuviana** railway (see "Getting There," above) is convenient, as are **ferries** to harbors along the coast (see "Getting There," above). Another option is to **rent a boat** (see "Outdoor Activities," p. 171) or join a **tour group** (see "Tours," p. 170).

You will find **taxi** stands at the harbor, on Piazza Tasso (both ✆ **081-8782204**), and in the adjacent village of Sant'Agnello (✆ **081-8781428**).

Car-rental companies in town include **De Martino,** Via Parsano 8 (✆ **081 8782801;** www.autoservizidemartino.com), which also provides car service and rents boats and motor scooters. You can rent a motor scooter at **Penisola Rent,** Corso Italia 259 (✆ **081-8774664;** www.penisolarent.com), which also rents cars; and at **Sorrento Car Service/Rent a Scooter,** Corso Italia 210 (✆ **081-8781386;** www.sorrento.it). For **bicycle rentals,** head to **Reaction Retail,** Viale Nizza 58 (✆ **081-8770613;** www.emporiobici.com).

VISITOR INFORMATION The **AASCT tourist office** (✆ **081-8074033;** fax 081-8773397; www.sorrentotourism.com) is at Via Luigi De Maio 35, off Piazza Tasso. It's open Monday to Friday from 9am to 4:15pm; in summer it's also open on Saturday mornings. Besides a good city map, it carries copies of the excellent free magazine *Surrentum.*

FAST FACTS You'll find a **pharmacy** (✆ **081-8781226**) on Corso Italia 131. The **hospital** (✆ **081-5331111**) is on Corso Italia 1. For an **ambulance,** dial ✆ **118.** You can call the **police** at ✆ **112,** 113, or 081-8075311; and you can reach the **fire department** at ✆ **115.** You will find several **ATMs** in town; one is at the **Deutsche Bank,** Piazza Angelina Lauro 22. The **post office** (✆ **081-8770811**) is at Corso Italia 210; it's open Monday to Friday from 8am to 6pm and Saturday from 8am to 12:30pm. For **Internet access,** go to **Sorrento info,** Via San Cesareo 101 (✆ **081-8074000**).

Exploring the Town

Sorrento has ancient Greek, Etruscan, and Oscan beginnings, and was colonized by the Romans in the 1st century B.C., when it became a valued resort for the affluent. But the town's history is checkered, to say the least; this seaside jewel has been fought over many times. After the fall of the empire, it was taken by the Goths, and then reconquered by the Byzantines in A.D. 552 and remained part of the Byzantine Duchy of Naples until the 10th century. Having been conquered by the Prince of Salerno at the beginning of the 11th century, it succeeded in gaining its independence as a Duchy in 1067, and remained so until conquest by the Normans in 1133; it then passed into the hands of the Angevins. Saracen incursions and rivalry between the nearby towns of Vico Equense and Massa Lubrense made life difficult in Sorrento—and there was worse to come. The town was completely destroyed by Barbary pirates on the nights of June 12 and 13, 1558, but was immediately rebuilt, this time with numerous defensive towers along the surrounding coast and a new set of walls.

We love strolling through the heart of Sorrento, where many of the medieval buildings are still intact. From the west side of **Piazza Tasso,** start off on **Via Pietà;** at no. 14 you'll find **Palazzo Veniero,** with its facade of typical 13th-century decorations that look a little like wood marquetry. At no. 24 is **ex-Palazzo Correale** with its original 14th-century portal and two windows. A few steps away, we recommend a visit to the beautiful 15th-century **Duomo,** the

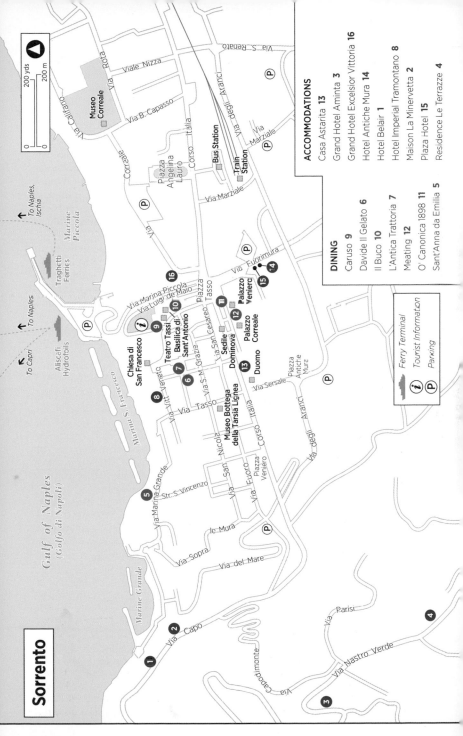

Sorrento

To Naples, Ischia
To Naples
To Capri Aliscafi Hydrofoils
To Naples, Ischia

Gulf of Naples
(Golfo di Napoli)

Marine Grande

Marina S. Francesco

Marine Piccola

Marina Piccola

Traghetti Ferries

Museo Correale

Via Califano
Via B. Capasso
Via Rota
Viale Nizza
Via Correale
Corso Italia
Via degli Aranci
Via S. Renato
Via Marziale
Via Marziale
Bus Station
Train Station
Piazza Angelina Lauro

Via Marina Piccola
Via Luigi de Maio
Chiesa di San Francesco
Teatro Tasso
Basilica di Sant'Antonio
Piazza Tasso
Via San Cesareo
Sedile Dominova
Palazzo Veniero
Palazzo Correale
Duomo
Piazza Antiche Mura
Via Sersale
Via degli Aranci

Via Vitt. Veneto
Via Vitt. Veneto
Via Tasso
Via Tasso
Via S. M. Grazie
Via San Nicola
Museo Bottega della Tarsia Lignea
Piazza Veniero
Corso Italia
Str. S. Vincenzo
Via Marina Grande
Via Capo
Via Capodimonte
le Mura
Via Sopra
Via del Mare
Via Parisi
Via Nastro Verde
Via Fuorimura

0 200 yds
0 200 m

ACCOMMODATIONS
Casa Astarita **13**
Grand Hotel Aminta **3**
Grand Hotel Excelsior Vittoria **16**
Hotel Antiche Mura **14**
Hotel Belair **1**
Hotel Imperial Tramontano **8**
Maison La Minervetta **2**
Plaza Hotel **15**
Residence Le Terrazze **4**

DINING
Caruso **9**
Davide Il Gelato **6**
Il Buco **10**
L'Antica Trattoria **7**
Meating **12**
O' Canonica 1898 **11**
Sant'Anna da Emilia **5**

Ferry Terminal
i Tourist Information
P Parking

Cathedral of San Filippo and San Giacomo, Corso Italia 1 (© 081-8782248; daily 8am–noon and 4–8pm), with its striking Romanesque facade graced by a fresco over the portal. The stubby bell tower, with its majolica clock and four antique columns at the base is particularly interesting; only three of its five levels are original (the two top ones were later additions). Inside the Duomo, you can admire 14th- and 15th-century bas-reliefs and a wooden choir decorated with superb intarsia.

Sorrento is famous for its historical craft of marquetry and wood inlay. We suggest a stop at the **Museo Bottega della Tarsia Lignea ★**, Via San Nicola 28, 2 blocks from Corso Italia (© 081-8771942; admission 8€; daily 10am–1pm and 3–6pm; closed national holidays), where you can admire an intriguing collection of 19th-century marquetry furniture in addition to the beautiful frescoes that decorate the 18th-century **Palazzo Pomaranci Santomasi,** which houses the museum.

Continuing your stroll through medieval Sorrento, you'll come to Piazzetta Padre Reginaldo Giuliani (at the crossroads with Via Cesareo) and the **Sedile Dominova.** With its fading frescoes, this arched, 15th-century building was once an open-air meeting place for the local aristocracy; those are their coats of arms on the walls. Nearby is Sorrento's second-most important church, **Basilica di Sant'Antonino standing** in Piazza Sant'Antonino, off Via Luigi de Maio. Built in the 11th century over a preexisting oratory dedicated to Saint Anthony, it was later redone in the present baroque style, but the interior retains some 15th-century decorations.

Walking back toward the seafront promenade, you will come upon the 18th-century church of **San Francesco,** Piazza Francesco Saverio Gargiulo, off Via San Francesco (daily 8am–1pm and 2–7pm); hidden inside is the charming little 14th-century **Chiostro del Paradiso ★★**, a famous venue for concerts, art shows, and weddings. Contact the tourist center (p. 168) for details. Across from the church is the entrance to **Villa Comunale,** a park with a panoramic terrace and a perfect spot for a quiet rest. From here, you can take the steep ramps of steps descending to **Marina Piccola,** Sorrento's main port. The town's other port, picturesque **Marina Grande,** is Sorrento's original fishing harbor which is today lined with restaurants and bars strung out along the shoreline.

Another interesting attraction is the **Museo Correale di Terranova,** Via Correale 48 (© 081-8781846; admission 7€; Wed–Mon 9:30am–1:30pm except national holidays), once the home of the brothers Alfredo and Pompeo Correale, counts of Terranova—an old aristocratic family of Sorrento—who donated their villa and private collections to the public. The museum gives a unique overview of decorative art from the 16th to the 19th centuries: Stocked with its original furnishings, it houses some excellent Flemish paintings, a collection of Italian and foreign porcelain from reputedly the best 17th- and 18th-century manufacturers, and a number of unusual clocks.

The streets leading to this museum are part of the package: **Via Correale ★★**, starting off Piazza Tasso, is one of the few streets that preserves the flavor of 19th-century Sorrento. We encourage you to continue beyond the museum until you reach the little town of **Sant'Agnello,** with its stately villas built in the past century or two and many elegant hotels.

TOURS

You can rent a car service with a driver (p. 168), but the open-top buses of

Sorrento City Sightseeing, Via degli Aranci 172, 80067 Sorrento (℡ 081-8774707; www.sorrento.city-sightseeing.it), are a good option if your time is limited. Departures are from Piazza De Curtis (stazione Circumvesuviana) for the seven-stop, hop-on-and-off loop through Massa Lubrense, Termini, Sant'Agata sui Due Golfi, and Sorrento. Tickets are valid for 6 hours and cost 12€ for adults, 6€ for children 5 to 15 (free for children 4 and under), and 45€ for a family (two adults and up to three children). The route to Positano has three departures from Sorrento in the morning and three returns from Positano in the afternoon (round-trip 12€ for adults and 6€ for children). These bus tours run between April and October.

Marine Club (℡ 081-8772621; www.marineclub.it) offers two daily minicruises: One takes in Ischia and Procida, and the other the Sorrentine and Amalfi coasts (with a swimming break in Capri), both with 1- or 2-hour stops at each attraction. The cost is 35€ per person, and the round-trip takes a full day.

OUTDOOR ACTIVITIES

Most visitors come to Sorrento for the cultural activities, but those in the know also take advantage of the many opportunities to enjoy the great outdoors. You'll soon realize though that the ruggedness that makes this stretch of coast so beautiful can be a serious obstacle to your physical enjoyment of the shimmering sea:

Renting a boat is a great way to explore Sorrento's coastline.

While rocky points and cliffs are part of the visual charm, swimming from them isn't easy. Most of the major hotels in town have worked this out by building their own floating docks that are equipped with umbrellas and lounge chairs—usually connected by elevator to the top of the cliff and the hotel. The only small stretch of pebbly beach is at **Marina Grande,** but it isn't the perfect swimming spot. For real sand, you need to venture east out of town to the small **Marinella Beach,** or farther away to **Vico Equense** (p. 162).

Nautica Sic Sic, Via Marina Piccola 43 (℡ 081-8072283 or 330-706947; www.nauticasicsic.com; closed Nov–Apr), is a good place to rent boats; they cost from 50€ for an hour, depending on the size and type. Sic Sic also organizes cruises and offers certified diving courses. Another reputable vendor is **Tony's Beach,** Marina Grande (℡ 081-8782170).

A half-hour away by boat (or a longer trip on foot, from a trail starting from the Calata Capo di Sorrento, off Via Capo) **Bagno della Regina Giovanna (Queen Giovanna's Bath)** at **Punta del Capo** ★ is our favorite local swimming spot: A small pool of water enclosed by rocks, it was once the private harbor of an ancient Roman villa—**Villa of Pollio Felice**—the ruins of which you can visit at the top of the cliff. Another pleasant boat ride is the one to the **Grotta delle Sirene (Grotto of the Sirens),** which is east of Marina Piccola and past Sant'Agnello. In the grotto, the constantly changing light causes the water to take on surprising hues—as if by the charm of magical sea creatures.

Hiking is also high on our list, and the great number of trails, most of which are well maintained and marked, offer treks for people of all skill levels. We recommend using a good trail map; the best is *Carta dei Sentieri* published by C.A.I., the Club Alpino Italiano and for sale at libraries and some newsstands in town. It covers the **Monti Lattari, Penisola Sorrentina,** and **Costiera Amalfitana,** and costs 10€. One of the most beautiful hikes is the one to **Punta Sant'Elia ★★★**, starting from Piazza Sant'Agnello in Sant'Agnello; the trail ends at a rocky point across the peninsula overlooking the little islands of Li Galli, along the Amalfi Coast in the Gulf of Salerno. To reach the trail, take Via Bonaventura Gargiulo up to **Trasaella,** at an altitude of 196m (643 ft.), and then continue toward **Colli di Fontanelle** at an altitude of 343m (1,125 ft.). From the center of this village and across Via Belvedere begins the trail to Punta Sant'Elia.

It is also possible to hire a professional guide; we recommend **Giovanni Visetti** (✆ **339-6942911;** www.giovis.com), an expert on this coast and its hinterlands, who organizes guided hikes of varying difficulty and cost.

Where to Stay

This mecca of international tourism offers myriad choices, but be prepared to shell out if you want to be in Sorrento proper. Sant'Agnello, adjacent to Sorrento to the east, is slightly cheaper, and Vico Equense (p. 162) is another valid alternative for visiting the area.

EXPENSIVE

Grand Hotel Excelsior Vittoria ★★★ ☺ Occupying an impressive villa and its estate right in the heart of town, this is a world-class hotel and one of our favorites. Owned by the same family since its opening in 1834, it offers exquisite, personalized service, superb facilities and a charming Belle Epoque atmosphere.

The elegant public spaces and terraces—still with the original 19th-century furnishings—are perfect places to enjoy a drink. The huge, elegant guest rooms are finely decorated and furnished with many antiques along with all modern comforts, and they have splendid marble bathrooms. Most rooms open onto a private balcony or terrace; the best have views over the Gulf of Naples while others overlook the delightful garden. From the hotel, elevators whisk guests down to the private beach-pier off Marina Piccola. In a splendid

---

○ Taking a Cooking Class

If you want to replicate the local cuisine, sign up for a cooking class at the **Sorrento Cooking School,** Viale dei Pini 52 (✆ **081-8783255;** www.sorrentocookingschool. com). Classes last 3 hours and end with lunch or dinner, at which you eat what you prepared (or what the chef prepared, in the worst case), and drink local wine. The price of 60€ per person includes lunch or dinner and you get to take your apron, with its special logo, home.

setting overlooking the gulf, the **Terrazza Bosquet** restaurant offers the most romantic gourmet dining in Sorrento.

Piazza Tasso 34, 80067 Sorrento. www.exvitt.it. © **081-8777111.** Fax 081-8771206. 105 units. 390€–698€ double; from 660€ suite. Rates include buffet breakfast. Internet and family specials available. Children 3 and under stay free in parent's room. AE, DC, MC, V. Free parking. **Amenities:** 2 restaurants; bar; concierge; pool; room service; spa. *In room:* A/C, TV, minibar, Wi-Fi (free).

Parco dei Principi ★★ This retro stylish hotel is located just out of town at Sant'Agnello. Gio Ponti, the celebrated Milanese architect, designed the whole place (including the furniture, fittings, and lighting) in the 1960s and a stay here whisks you back to those heady, glamorous days. The modern building, with its clean, white lines, sits on a cliff top with fabulous views over the Bay of Naples and the '60s stylish blue-and-white color scheme throughout gives the place a nautical feel. Needless to say, the best rooms are the ones with sea views; each room has differently patterned blue-and-white floor tiles. There's a seawater pool, a private beach, a spa, and a lovely garden.

Via Rota 1, Sant'Agnello, 80067 Sorrento. www.hotelparcodeiprincipi.net. © **081-8784644.** Fax 081-8783786. 96 units. 229€–279€ double; 400€–700€ suite. Rates include buffet breakfast. Children 2 and under stay free in parent's room. AE, DC, MC, V. Free parking. **Amenities:** 2 restaurants, bar; pool; private beach; room service; spa. *In room:* A/C, TV, minibar, Wi-Fi (free).

MODERATE

Grand Hotel Aminta ★★ ☺ In a dominant position above Sorrento (3km/2 miles away by free shuttle service), this modern hotel is an excellent choice for anyone wanting respite from the crowds down in town and offers breathtaking views, professional yet friendly service, and good amenities. The airy, welcoming public spaces feature wide arches and marble floors and a sweeping staircase left over from the original '60s decor. Guest rooms are all bright and tastefully decorated with modern furnishings. Some are more spacious, but all have contemporary, scrupulously clean bathrooms; most have balconies with magnificent sea views. For post-sightseeing relaxation there is a large pool. A hundred meters from the main building and accessed via a garden path lies the renovated 18th-century Villa Aminta with 19 additional rooms. The **restaurant** has a magnificent terrace where live music and dancing are often scheduled on summer evenings. If you come to Sorrento off season, the Aminta is one of the few hotels in town that stays open almost year-round; it only closes in January.

Via Nastro Verde 23, 80067 Sorrento. www.aminta.com. © **081-8781821.** Fax 081-8781822. 81 units. 100€–300€ double; 250€–500€ junior suite. Rates include buffet breakfast. Internet specials available. Children 4 and under stay free in parent's room. AE, DC, MC, V. Free parking. **Amenities:** Restaurant; bar; concierge; pool; smoke-free rooms. *In room:* A/C, TV, minibar, Wi-Fi (free).

Hotel Antiche Mura ★ Situated in the heart of town, this lovely hotel is housed in an elegant Art Nouveau–style palazzo built on top of the defensive walls that gives the place its name. Guest rooms are sunny and bright, decorated with Vietri-tile floors and Sorrentine marquetry furniture. "Comfort" rooms are more spacious, and we particularly liked the junior suites, large corner rooms with wraparound windows. All rooms are equipped with state-of-the-art bathrooms with tub and special hydromassage showers. While the indoor public spaces are elegant and comfortable, guests gravitate towards the lovely garden which is bordered by the 16th-century city walls. Here, among the lemon trees, is a pool, lounge chairs, and snack bar serving drinks and light meals from 11am to 4pm.

Via Fuorimura 7 (entrance on Piazza Tasso), 80067 Sorrento. www.hotelantichemura.com. ✆ **081-8073523.** Fax 081-8071323. 46 units. 190€–250€ double; 290€ junior suite; 350€ suite. Rates include buffet breakfast. Internet specials available. Children 2 and under stay free in parent's room. AE, DC, MC, V. Parking 10€. **Amenities:** Bar; concierge; pool; Wi-Fi (free). *In room:* A/C, TV, minibar, Wi-Fi (free).

Hotel Imperial Tramontano ★ ☺ Another of Sorrento's historic hotels (past guests include Lord Byron and Henrik Ibsen), the Tramontano enjoys a dramatic position on a cliff overlooking the sea, a short distance from the center of town. Surrounded by a beautiful garden, the hotel offers the luxury of a patrician abode, with elegant public spaces and top-notch amenities. The spacious guest rooms are furnished with antiques and are bright and welcoming; some have private balconies and sea views. Guests have access to the hotel's private beach via elevator—or a hair-raising series of steps originally built by the Romans. The hotel's **restaurant** is one of the best in the area, and music events are regularly staged on the **terrace.**

Via Vittorio Veneto 1, 80067 Sorrento. www.hoteltramonto.it. ✆ **081-8782588.** Fax 081-8072344. 116 units. 250€–380€ double; from 420€ suite. Rates include buffet breakfast. Family specials available. Children 3 and under stay free in parent's room. AE, MC, V. Free parking. Closed Jan–Feb. **Amenities:** Restaurant; bar; concierge; pool; room service. *In room:* A/C, TV, minibar.

Hotel Belair ★ Suspended between sky and sea, this little hotel's charm and matchless views compensate for its location outside the center of town. Built on the cliff overlooking Marina Grande, the hotel is connected to the shore by a picturesque set of stairs carved into the rock. Each of the guest rooms is different in shape and individually decorated, with a small seaview balcony or terrace. Most rooms are spacious and all are bright and pleasantly decorated, with ceramic floors and quality classic furniture. Bathrooms are good-size and very clean.

Via Capo 29, 80067 Sorrento. www.belair.it. ✆ **081-8071622.** Fax 081-8071467. 49 units. 229€– 340€ double; from 369€ suite. Rates include buffet breakfast. Internet specials available. Children 3 and under stay free in parent's room. AE, DC, MC, V. Free parking. Closed Nov–Mar. **Amenities:** Restaurant; bar; concierge; pool. *In room:* A/C, TV, Internet, minibar.

Maison La Minervetta ★★★ La Minervetta started life in the 1950s as a popular seafood restaurant and is now back in the hands of the original owner's family who have given the place a thorough makeover: The result is a delightful boutique hotel that successfully combines contemporary design with bold Mediterranean colors, and it's one of our favorites. The upside-down building (car park and reception at the top, bedrooms underneath) clings to the cliff side just above Marina Grande and has fabulous views of the Bay of Naples and Vesuvius from public spaces and all the bedrooms. The huge living room has tables piled with magazines and arty books; it leads onto a wide sun terrace where an outstanding breakfast (one of the best we've come across) and drinks are served in warm weather. Far below is another terrace with a small Jacuzzi pool. The bedrooms all have bright fabrics, huge beds, and full on sea views through floor-to-ceiling windows and the modern bathrooms are done out with colorful handmade tiles.

Via Capo 25, 80067 Sorrento. www.laminervetta.com. ℂ **081-8774455.** Fax 081-8784601. 12 units. 320€–420€ double. Rates include buffet breakfast. Internet specials available. Children 2 and under stay free in parent's room. AE, DC, MC, V. Free parking. **Amenities:** Concierge; Jacuzzi pool; Wi-Fi (3€/hour). *In room:* A/C, TV, minibar, Wi-Fi (3€/hour).

Plaza Hotel ★★ The Plaza is better than ever after a "green" overhaul that added natural and renewable materials, thermal insulation, energy and water conserving equipment, and biodegradable cleaning substances. We love their eco-friendly philosophy, but also the central location in town and competent service. Guest rooms are modern and streamlined, with contemporary details. Bright and welcoming, some open onto private balconies. The contemporary bathrooms (some with shower only) are a good size. Guests get discounted access to a nearby beach (10€, including changing room and lounger).

Via Fuorimura 3, 80067 Sorrento. www.plazasorrento.com. ℂ **081-8782831.** Fax 081-8073942. 65 units. 190€–260€ double. Rates include buffet breakfast. Internet specials available. Children 2 and under stay free in parent's room. AE, DC, MC, V. Parking 10€. Closed Jan-Mar. **Amenities:** 2 bars; concierge; pool; room service. *In room:* A/C, TV, minibar, Wi-Fi (free).

Relais Villa Savarese 🛏 The perfect place to enjoy Sorrento as a 19th-century nobleman might have, this B&B/boutique hotel occupies a former patrician villa complete with garden and pool. The location along the road that leads out of Sorrento into adjacent Sant'Agnello is pleasant and quiet. Guest rooms are spacious and well-appointed. Bathrooms are good-size and modern (some with shower only).

Corso M. Crawford 59, 80065 Sant'Agnello. www.relaisvillasavarese.com. ℂ **081-5324920.** Fax 081-8774187. 10 units. 240€–300€ double; 370€ junior suite. Rates include buffet breakfast. Internet specials available. AE, DC, MC, V. Parking 15€. Closed Nov-Mar. **Amenities:** Bar; concierge; Internet; pool. *In room:* A/C, TV, minibar.

INEXPENSIVE

Casa Astarita ★ 🍴 We really like this cozy little B&B which enjoys an excellent central location and is run like a private home by the Astarita sisters. Each of the 7 bright bedrooms is different from the next, but all are stylish and comfortable with tiled bathrooms. Avoid the noisy room at the back of the building; those at the front are quieter. A delicious breakfast complete with homemade cakes is served around a communal table.

Corso Italia 7, 80067 Sorrento. www.casastarita.com. ℂ **081-8774906.** Fax 081-8071146. 7 units. 90€–110€ double. Rates include buffet breakfast. AE, MC, V. Parking 15€. *In room:* A/C, TV, Internet

Residence Le Terrazze ☺ This pleasant hotel in a panoramic position high above Sorrento is convenient to town as well as to the best beaches and attractions. Family-run and immaculately kept, it offers moderately priced miniapartments in various sizes, all with kitchenette—a good solution for families. The whitewashed rooms are plain but bright, with no-frill tiled floors, rattan or pine furniture, and good-size bathrooms with all the essentials. The new swimming pool is a great addition.

Via Nastro Verde 98, 80067 Sorrento. ℂ **081-8780906.** Fax 081-8774187. www.residencele terrazze.it. 16 units. 120€–160€ double; 170€ triple; 200€ quad. Rates include buffet breakfast. Internet specials available. Children 2 and under stay free in parent's room. AE, DC, MC, V. Free parking. Closed Jan 8–Feb. **Amenities:** Concierge; pool. *In room:* A/C, TV, kitchenette.

Where to Eat

While the **Excelsior Victoria** and the **Imperial Tramontano** (both reviewed above) offer the most exclusive—and memorable—dining experiences with superb food served on terraces overlooking the sea, there are many other restaurants along Sorrento's waterfront and in the medieval center that cater to every taste and budget.

EXPENSIVE

Il Buco ★★ CREATIVE SORRENTINE Occupying the wine cellar of an ancient convent near Piazza Sant'Antonino, this restaurant offers a menu of fine, imaginative cuisine that changes daily according to market availability; Only the best of local ingredients make their way to the kitchen. We loved the *mezzanelle con ragù di pesce in bianco* (pasta in a delicate seafood sauce flavored with black olives and wild fennel), and the *agnellodi paese al timo* (tender lamb served with rosemary roasted potatoes and savoy cabbage). The *piatti unici* are one-course meals for two and include a perfect Florentine steak and a superb fish stew. The flower-filled outdoor terrace is delightful in summer.

2d Rampa Marina Piccola 5 (off Piazza Sant'Antonino). ℂ **081-8782354.** www.ilbucoristorante. it. Reservations recommended. Secondi 20€–30€; tasting menus 75€–85€; prix-fixe menu 55€. AE, DC, MC, V. Thurs–Tues 12:15–2:30pm and 7:30–11:30pm. Closed Jan.

L'Antica Trattoria ★ SORRENTINE This picturesque restaurant—that comes complete with master mandolin player—has been serving excellent food for some 80 years. The dining rooms are cozy, but we adore the outdoor terrace, where you can dine under the arbor vines. The chef's sophisticated recipes explore the combination of local produce, seafood, and wines. Fixed-price choices include a four-course menu of local fish and seafood dishes for 46€ and the splendid seven-course Tasting Menu for 80€. Vegetarians and celiacs are also catered to. Dishes vary with the seasons but you will always find delicious homemade ravioli—maybe flavored with local cheese and tomatoes, or with seafood and local citrus fruits—and elegantly presented meat and fish dishes, such as *branzino con scarola, capperi, olive, e slasa di alici* (sea bass with escarole, olives, capers, and anchovy sauce).

Via Padre Reginaldo Giuliani 33. ℂ **081-8071082.** www.lanticatrattoria.com. Reservations recommended. Secondi 20€–40€. AE, MC, V. Tues–Sun noon–3:30pm and 7–11:30pm. Closed 3 weeks in Jan–Feb.

MODERATE

Caruso ★ SORRENTINE A local institution, this upscale restaurant doubles as a museum dedicated to Enrico Caruso, the famous Italian tenor who so loved Sorrento. The excellent menu offers gourmet renditions of traditional recipes. The seasonal cuisine includes such delicious meals as ravioli *all'aragosta* (with lobster), ravioli *con salsa di melanzane* (with an eggplant sauce), lasagna *ai frutti di mare* (with seafood), and risotto *zucchine e gamberi* (with shrimp and zucchini).

Via Sant'Antonino 12. ℂ **081-8073156.** www.ristorantemuseocaruso.com. Reservations recommended. Secondi 16€–32€. AE, DC, MC, V. Daily noon–midnight.

Meating 🍴 ITALIAN/MEAT The perfect place to come when you've had your fill of fish and seafood, new-kid-on-the-block Meating (get it?) styles itself as a steakhouse and is, appropriately enough, housed in an ex-butcher's shop. Steak comes in all shapes and sizes from a vast, chargrilled *bistecca alla fiorentina*

A Gelato to Remember

The absolute best gelato parlor in the whole area—and maybe in the whole country—is **Davide Il gelato** ★★, Via Padre Reginaldo Giuliani 39 (℃ **081-8072092;** closed Wed in winter), producing divine homemade gelato made with typical regional fruits and specialties. Among the 60 flavors (more or less, depending on the day), we favor the sweet and deliciously creamy *noci di Sorrento* (Sorrento walnuts), the rich *cioccolato con canditi* (dark chocolate cream studded with candied oranges), the sinful *rhum babà* (rum-flavored cream with bits of soft cake), and the heavenly *delizia al limone* (a delectable lemon cream). You'll definitely have to return, at least once (or twice, or three times . . .) to sample them all.

(Florentine-style T-bone steak) or *filetto ai funghi porcini* (filet steak with porcini mushrooms), but you can also order a burger, beef carpaccio, duck a l'orange, and *cotolette d'agnello* (grilled lamb chops). There's also a great selection of cheeses and cold cuts, and a wine list featuring around 400 labels.

Via della Pieta 20. ℃ **081-8782891.** Reservations recommended for dinner. Secondi 8€–30€. AE, DC, MC, V Thurs–Tues noon–3pm and 7pm–midnight.

O'Canonico 1898 ★ 🍴 SORRENTINE This historic restaurant on Sorrento's main square has successfully maintained its quality despite its well-trafficked location. Canonico offers professional service and a well-prepared traditional cuisine that incorporates only the freshest ingredients. We recommend the excellent *tagliatelle di pasta fresca con frutti di mare e zucchini* (fresh pasta with seafood and zucchini) and the *pescato del giorno* (fresh-caught fish of the day) in a potato crust. The wine list is extensive.

Piazza Tasso 5. ℃ **081-8783277.** Reservations recommended Sat–Sun. Secondi 16€–30€. AE, DC, MC, V. Daily noon–3:30pm and 7–11:30pm (closed Mon or Tues Nov–Mar).

INEXPENSIVE

Sant'Anna da Emilia ★ ☺ SORRENTINE Our favorite place to eat in Sorrento, this moderately priced trattoria offers informal dining in an ancient boat shed in Marina Grande, complete with an outdoor terrace on a wooden pier. It is mobbed in summer, so be prepared to wait if you want to taste the great homestyle cuisine that varies daily with the market offerings. Simplicity is the key to success here, and we promise you won't taste a better caprese (mozzarella di bufala and tomato salad) or spaghetti *alle cozze* (with mussels). We also recommend the *gnocchi alla Sorrentina* (Sorrento-style potato dumplings) and *fritto misto* (deep-fried calamari and little fish) accompanied by wonderful *patatine fritte* (french fries). Order a jug of the excellent white house wine to go with your meal; it's chilled and refreshing.

Via Marina Grande 62. ℃ **081-8072720.** Reservations not accepted. Secondi 8.50€–14€. No credit cards. Daily noon–3:30pm and 7:30–11:30pm (closed Tues in winter). Closed Nov.

Shopping

Via San Cesareo is Sorrento's main shopping street. Specialty shopping includes the bounty from local farms and groves—lemons and lemon products, walnuts,

D.O.P. olive oil, and Penisola Sorrentina D.O.C. wine (some experts call it "the Beaujolais of Campania")—and the slowly disappearing local crafts: lace and embroideries, and wood intarsia and marquetry furniture.

For fresh ricotta formed in traditional handmade baskets and a sample of local products, head to one of **Apreda**'s two locations: Via Tasso 27 (⌀**081-8782351**) or Via del Mare 20 (⌀**081-8074059**). You can find excellent *limoncello* and other specialties at **Sapori & Colori,** Via San Cesareo 57 (⌀**081-8784278**), and **Luigia Gargiulo,** Corso Italia 48 (⌀**081-8781081**), sells lovely, intricate embroideries. **Gargiulo & Jannuzzi,** Piazza Tasso 1 (⌀**081-8781041**), is right next to Bar Fauno and offers the best wood intarsia; you can visit the workshops for a demonstration of this ancient technique that follows centuries-old patterns. At the weekly **street market,** vendors sell everything from crockery to swimming suits (Tues morning, parking lot on Via San Renato).

Sorrento After Dark

The narrow streets of Sorrento's *centro storico* are alive with cafes, clubs, and restaurants, which become positively crowded during the sweet nights of summer. Locals and visitors alike enjoy the lively terrace of the **Fauno Bar,** Piazza Tasso 13 (⌀**081-8781135;** www.faunobar.it), for an *aperitivo* (aperitif) and people-watching till late into the evening. Other popular venues for pre- and postdinner drinks are, of course, the romantic terraces of the many historic hotels.

Spring and summer are a special time in Sorrento, as music festivals and other musical programs are staged in venues throughout town. Some of the most popular are the concerts at the **Grand Hotel Cocumella,** Via Cocumella 7, Sant'Agnello (⌀**081-8782933;** www.cocumella.com), and those in the **cloister of San Francesco,** Piazza Francesco Saverio Gargiulo. Contact the tourist office (p. 168) for a schedule of events, including those staged at many restaurants and taverns in town.

Be sure to spend an evening enjoying Sorrento's lively cafe and restaurant scene.

For dancing and more lively entertainment for a more mature clientele (40s and up), head to Piazza Tasso and the nightclub **Fauno Notte Club** (✆ 081-8781021; www.faunonotte.it; cover 25€). It also offers a colorful **Tarantella Show,** the frenetic traditional folk dance, between stretches of DJ music (Mar–Oct; daily 9–11pm).

Sorrento Musical is a revue of Neapolitan songs hosted by **Teatro Tasso,** Piazza Sant'Antonino (✆ 081-8075525; www.teatrotasso.com; tickets about 25€ depending on show; 50€ including dinner). Live music (a changing menu of pop, folk, jazz, and so on) can also be heard at **Circolo dei Forestieri,** Via Luigi de Maio 35 (✆ 081-8773263; closed Nov–Feb).

For more leisurely entertainment (a la drinks with some background music), we love the laid-back atmosphere at **Chantecler,** Via Santa Maria della Pietà 38 (✆ 081-8075868; www.chanteclers.com); there's some dancing on weekends, and always some food. Other choices are **Chaplin's Video Pub,** Corso Italia 18 (✆ 081-8072551), and the **English Inn,** Corso Italia 55 (✆ 081-8074357); located across from each other, both stock a good selection of beers and maintain a lively atmosphere—sometimes even too lively on summer weekends. Depending on the season, the crowd can be a mix of nationalities.

BEYOND SORRENTO: MASSA LUBRENSE & SANT'AGATA SUI DUE GOLFI

60km (38 miles) S of Naples

Much less traveled, the tip of the Sorrentine peninsula is also the most authentic. Villages—sometimes little more than handfuls of houses—dot the rocky coast and cliffs, and you'll find peace and quiet even in the middle of the summer season. Such a surprising feat has been accomplished via mundane means: terrible roads and transportation. The train stops in Sorrento, and the main loop road (SS 145) passes through Sant'Agata sui due Golfi, but bypasses Massa Lubrense completely, swerving back toward the coast on the other side of the peninsula to rejoin SS 163, the famous Amalfi Drive. The result is a little-visited, though ruggedly beautiful corner that feels more remote than it is. You can easily visit the whole area in 1 day; yet, once you have arrived, you'll hardly want to leave.

Essentials

GETTING THERE & AROUND Sorrento is the gateway to the rest of the peninsula (see "Getting There," p. 167). Although **SITA's** (✆ 089-405145; www.sitabus.it) **bus** service from Sorrento is frequent and efficient, we feel that, unless you have unlimited time, renting a **scooter** or a **car**—or even better, a **taxi** or **limousine** with a driver—is a lot more functional: You'll be able to see more, have a flexible schedule, and your driver will double as a guide. Distances are short, hence charges remain quite reasonable (consider about 45€ per hour for two people, with discounts for longer periods). You can rent a car from the major operators listed in chapter 11 (p. 347) or from a number of local vendors (p. 168).

Another option is renting a small launch from one of the many boatyards, or hiring one of their captains to guide you; or you may sign up for one of their organized excursions. We recommend Peppe, and his beautiful boat, *La Granseola,* Marina del Cantone (© 081-8081027, c/o Ristorante Le Sirene; mobile 338-9542573; www.lagranseola.com). Other reliable providers are **Coop Marina della Lobra,** Marina della Lobra (© 081-8089380; www.marinalobra.com); **Cooperativa S. Antonio,** Marina del Cantone (© 081-8081638; cooperativasantonio@libero.it); and **Nautica 'O Masticiello,** Marina del Cantone (© 081-8081443, or 339-3142791; www.masticiello.com).

VISITOR INFORMATION Your best source of local information is the small **Proloco tourist office,** Viale Filangeri 11, Massa Lubrense (© 081-5339021). You'll find a **pharmacy** (© 081-8789081) at Via Palma 16, Massa Lubrense. The **hospital** is in Sorrento (p. 168). For an **ambulance,** dial © 118. You can call the **police** at © 113 or 112, and you can reach the **fire department** at © 115. You'll find a **post office** (© 081-8789045) in Massa Lubrense at Via Massa Turro 13 and another in Sant'Agata sui due Golfi at Corso Sant'Agata 32 (© 081-8780162). There is a **Banco di Napoli** (© 081-8089687) at no. 15 on Viale Filangeri in Massa Lubrense, and a **Deutsche Bank** (© 081-8089530) at no. 26.

Exploring the Area

Massa Lubrense was once an important town and a powerful rival to Sorrento for dominance over this coast. Times have changed, and Massa is now just one of the small villages that dot this rocky point. The diminished political importance of this area has not deprived it of its unique beauty, though, and the town and surrounding area are popular with Italians in the know both for its natural assets and sense of being off the beaten track.

Massa Lubrense prides itself on its church, **Santa Maria delle Grazie** (Piazza Vescovado), which was built in 1512 and redone in the 18th century. In the transept and presbytery you'll find some fine remnants of the original **majolica floor ★**, and from the terrace to the right of the church are fine views towards

Enjoy views of Capri from Santa Maria delle Grazie's terrace.

Capri. Below Massa is **Marina della Lobra ★**, a picturesque fishing hamlet with a little harbor—and also one of the peninsula's rare stretches of sand. The sanctuary that stands on the road leading down to the village—**Santa Maria della Lobra**—was built in the 16th century over a Roman temple, probably dedicated to Minerva. Inside you can see the original 17th-century, wood-carved **ceiling** and the 18th-century **majolica floor.**

Back up in Massa, from Santa Maria delle Grazie, follow the sign toward **Annunziata;** the road leads to the old Massa Lubrense, established in the 10th century and destroyed by the Angevins in the 1300s. Here you'll find the church of the **Santissima Annunziata,** the original cathedral of Massa, rebuilt in the 17th century. Nearby are the ruins of the castle—only one tower is standing—which was built in 1389. From the **Belvedere,** weather permitting, you can enjoy a magnificent **panorama ★★** that encompasses Capri and the whole Gulf of Naples.

Farther on toward the tip of the Sorrentine peninsula is the village of **Nerano,** perched atop a cliff at 166m (544 ft.). Below the village is the fishing hamlet of **Marina del Cantone ★** with its lovely beach where locals keep their boats. It's a lively little resort in summer and boasts two Michelin-starred restaurants, quite an achievement for such a small place. Nearby **Termini** is another small town built on a natural terrace overlooking Capri. From Termini, drive down the local road to **Punta Campanella,** on the tip of the Sorrento peninsula, with its famous lighthouse (see "Outdoor Activities," below).

Finally, after a steep climb into the hills, you will reach **Sant'Agata sui Due Golfi ★★**. One of the region's largest villages, it benefits from its matchless position overlooking the two gulfs—of Naples and of Salerno—hence its name. The village is focused around **Santa Maria delle Grazie,** a 17th-century church that boasts a beautiful **altar** of colored marble and semiprecious stones. Follow the signs toward **Deserto ★,** once a Carmelite hermitage and now a Benedictine monastery. Standing at an altitude of 456m (1,496 ft.), it affords a spectacular **circular panorama ★★★** over the Campanian coast from the terrace, and on a clear day, you can see all the way from Ischia to Punta Licosa, south of Paestum. Opening times are unreliable to say the least; if you want to visit, you need to call ahead (© 081-8780199). Entrance is free, but contributions are appreciated. From Sant'Agata, you can also head toward **Torca,** a village only a few minutes away, perched at 352m (1,155 ft.) above sea level. From the village, take in the beautiful view over Li Galli, Positano's small archipelago.

A SPECIAL TOUR

In addition to the recommended tours of the area (p. 170), the **Due Golfi Train Tour ★** (© 081-3505983; www.duegolfitraintour.com) is a gastronomic ride on a small train that will delight children and adult foodies alike. The train departs from the Agip of Sant'Agata sui Due Golfi gas station and loops through Massa Lubrense's scenic hamlets, stopping at local farms for tastings of mozzarella, jams, and other local specialties. Departures are daily at 10am, with an additional ride at 4pm on Tuesday and Thursday from October to April and also at 6:30pm from May to September. The cost is 20€ for adults and 10€ for children.

OUTDOOR ACTIVITIES

You can do some swimming from the **beach** at **Marina del Cantone,** but to really enjoy the sea, **renting a boat** (with or without a skipper) is a must: It allows you to discover small beaches, inlets, and hidden bays otherwise inaccessible

A boat trip to the Bay of Ieranto.

from the high cliffs (see "Getting There & Around," above). The seashore here is a protected marine park, **Area Marina Protetta di Punta Campanella** (©**081-8089877;** www.puntacampanella.org), extending all the way from Punta del Capo, near Sorrento, to Punta Germano, near Positano.

Our favorite excursion is the one to the **Bay of Ieranto ★★★**, a lovely cove with a magical atmosphere. Well-known to the ancient Greeks who named it Hyeros Anthos, meaning "Sacred Flower," this bay was declared a protected area in 1984 and, as a result, it remains an unspoiled haven. Cut into the cliff, the cove of clear water ends in a beach, Marina del Cantone, where a few boats are usually moored. In the afternoon, oblique sunlight creates the odd illusion that the water has disappeared and the boats are suspended in thin air, a phenomenon we love to watch.

Arriving by sea to this lovely cove is a striking and marvelous experience. Rent a boat (with or without a skipper) and allow about a half-day for the excursion. From the beach, hug the coast heading southwest till you see the large Y-shaped promontory called Sedia del Diavolo, meaning "Devil's Chair," a particularly appropriate name when you see it during a flaming sunset. As you pass the first arm of the Y, with the medieval watchtower **Torre di Montalto,** there is a pretty little cove, which is an introduction to the more spectacular bay that awaits you farther along. Once you pass the second arm of the Y, the Bay of Ieranto opens like a fan in front of your bow and is closed to the west by Punta Campanella (below). Beyond starts the Gulf of Naples.

If you are moderately fit, we highly recommend hiking the local **footpaths** for breathtaking views. The area offers 22 marked and maintained hiking trails, for a total length of 110km (68 miles). One of the best hikes is the one to **Punta Campanella ★**, much more impressive than the drive there (see "Exploring the

Area," above). From the village of Termini, take the small sloping street to the right of the central square: This road slowly descends to the hamlet of Cercito, and then continues down the **Vallone della Cala di Mitigliano.** This beautiful valley is filled with olive groves and typical vegetation (called *macchia mediterranea*), including scented *mirto*, a plant that is quite rare nowadays. The trail then crosses a plateau with large boulders and the ruins of **Torre di Namonte,** a medieval watchtower. Past the tower, the trail begins a steep descent toward the sea as the beautiful profile of Capri looms into view. You'll get clear views of Capri, with Monte Tiberio, Monte Solaro, and the Faraglioni, only 5km (3 miles) away. A modern lighthouse guards this dangerous cape and its waters, made treacherous by the many rocks in the Capri Narrows.

On the last part of the trail, you'll actually be treading the ancient **Via Minerva,** the original road that led to the Greek temple dedicated to Athena (called Minerva by the Romans). To be visible to all passing ships, the temple was positioned near the lighthouse. The olive groves in this area go back thousands of years and were originally planted by the Greeks: Believing that olive oil was a gift from Athena, the goddess of wisdom—we tend to agree with that—they brought gifts of olive oil to her temple.

Punta Campanella takes its name from the bell on **Torre Minerva,** the watchtower—dating from 1335 but rebuilt in 1566—that warned of pirate incursions (*campanella* means "small bell"). Near the tower are the remains of a Roman villa. From a cliff to the east of the tower, you can look down into the wild, but sheltered, Bay of Ieranto. The trail goes from 300m (984 ft.) down almost to sea level; count on spending about 45 minutes for the descent and a bit more for the ascent. If you like a challenge, you could take the alternate trail to Punta Campanella: Starting from Termini, you first climb up **Mount San Costanzo,** at 497m (1,630 ft.) above sea level, before descending to the point. It is even more picturesque, but quite a bit longer and a lot more strenuous (allow about 3 hr. for this trail).

Torre Minerva.

Another of our favorite hikes is the trail to the **Bay of Ieranto.** The terrain is quite steep at times and can be moderately challenging. The best time to go is early afternoon to have a chance to experience the water phenomenon we describe above. From Nerano, take the street at the right-hand side of the village, past the last cluster of houses. This street connects to a trail on the slopes of **Monte San Costanzo,** the westernmost peak of the **Monti Lattari.** The trail descends through *macchia mediterranea* and eventually descends the cliffs overlooking the sea, affording spectacular views. Budget a little over an hour each way.

Impressions
And lo! the Siren shores like mists arise. *Sunk were at once the winds; the air above,* *And waves below, at once forgot to move;* *Some demon calm'd the air and smooth'd the deep,* *Hush'd the loud winds, and charm'd the waves to sleep.* *Now every sail we furl, each oar we ply;* *Lash'd by the stroke, the frothy waters fly . . .* —Homer, *The Odyssey,* book XII, lines 97–101, translation Alexander Pope, 1616

One last hike we highly recommend is the one down to **Fiordo di Crapolla** and its beach. From the village of Torca (see "Exploring the Area," above), take Via Pedara, which eventually turns into a dirt path. The trail descends a steep slope among olive groves and old farmhouses, and then among the rocks of a narrow crack in the cliff. As you descend on the western side of the cliff, you will see the ruins of the 12th-century abbey of San Pietro. Once at the bottom, you'll find a small beach; the blue water beyond the cove is broken by many rocks—the very ones, it is said, where the Sirens wrecked the ships of innocent mariners. By the beach, you can also see the ruins of a patrician Roman villa, where the ancient town of Capreolae (today Crapolla) was built. Figure on spending about 30 minutes on the descent.

Where to Stay & Eat

Massa Lubrense and the surrounding area is a highly sought-after dining destination, with a high density of Michelin-starred restaurants. As an old Italian saying goes, "Pancia fatti capanna," or "Tummy, become as large as a hut." However, you shouldn't miss out on simpler fare, such as the delicious bread made by **Antico Panificio Gargiulo,** Via Rivo a Casa 8 (off Via Roma), Massa Lubrense, studded with your choice of salami, local walnuts, olives, or sweet peppers. It is accompanied by your choice of local cheese: *treccia, scamorza,* or the delicious *triavulilli,* and the small *caciocavallo farcito* (pear-shaped cheese studded or filled with sun-dried tomatoes, butter, olives, or ham).

Some of the best purveyors are **Caseificio Cordiale,** Via Campi 30 (off Corso Sant'Agata), Sant'Agata sui Due Golfi (✆ 081-8080888); **Caseificio Savarese,** Via IV Novembre 19/a, Massa Lubrense (✆ 081-8789825); and **Caseificio Valestra,** Via Bozzaotra 13, Monticchio (✆ 081-8780119).

You'll find a good choice of other local products, including olive oil, cured meats, dried fruits, and spirits, at **Da Ferdinando,** Corso Sant'Agata 53, Sant'Agata sui Due Golfi (✆ 081-8780196), or at **Don Alfonso 1890,** Sant'Agata sui Due Golfi (✆ 081-8780026; see below).

VERY EXPENSIVE

Don Alfonso 1890 ★★★ CREATIVE SORRENTINE Reputed to be the best restaurant in southern Italy—with two Michelin stars—Don Alfonso does indeed offer superb food, location, and service. The elegant dining rooms in this historical residence in the heart of town overlook a delightful garden, and the ambience is welcoming and refreshing. The owners, Livia and Alfonso Iaccarino, also started an organic farm, **Azienda Agricola Le Peracciole** on Punta Campanella, which sources their perfect ingredients. Choose one of the two tasting menus: One features more creative dishes, while the other revisits local classics. The seasonal a la carte menu may include *pesce spada ai ceci e al timo* (swordfish with thyme and chickpeas) or *salame di cinghiale affumicato all'alloro* (smoked boar salami with bay leaves). The roasted chicken—free-range, organically fed, and seasoned with fresh herbs—is exquisite. Ask to visit the century-old cellar. *Note:* In summer, a less formal lunch is served by the outdoor pool.

Don Alfonso also has a cooking school. Taking a class here is an extravagant treat, arguably worthwhile only to his most dedicated fans, or to very serious cooks.

Above the restaurant is the **Don Alfonso 1890 Relais,** with garden, outdoor pool, library, bar, private parking, and nine delightfully appointed suites named after fresh herbs (one is actually an apartment). These have hardwood or tiled floors and elegant classic furnishings, including many antiques (400€–450€ junior suite; 550€–650€ suite; all rates include a top-notch breakfast).

Corso Sant'Agata 11, Sant'Agata sui Due Golfi. © **081-8780026.** Fax 081-5330226. www.don alfonso.com. Reservations required. Children 5 and under not allowed at dinner. Secondi 34€–45€; tasting menu 140€–155€. AE, DC, MC, V. Wed–Sun 12:30–2:30pm and 8–10:30pm (June–Sept also Tues 8–10:30pm).

EXPENSIVE

Oasi Olimpia Relais ★★ SORRENTINE This excellent restaurant is in a former aristocratic villa a short distance from the center of Sant'Agata. You can take full advantage of the splendid grounds in summer, when meals are served in the delightful outdoor arbor terrace covered with wisteria. Otherwise, the elegant dining room provides the perfect background for a romantic dinner. The cuisine is traditional and—while not attempting to rival Don Alfonso's haute cuisine (above)—definitely deserves a mention of honor. The seasonal menu is based on local produce and fish, and we are fans of the delicate risotto *agli agrumi di Sorrento* (with local citrus fruits) and the tasteful *calamarata* (medley of pasta and squid with fresh tomatoes). The wine list is short but top-notch. *Note:* Lunch is a less-formal affair with a simpler menu (it is served by the pool in summer).

The year-round **cooking classes** are definitely the best in the area. Prices are reasonable and the program is solid, though some of the cooking programs are "informal" and rather tentatively scheduled, so you'll need to remain flexible (see www.amalficookingschool.com for more information).

The Olimpia also offers 11 elegantly appointed **rooms;** though less formal than at Don Alfonso's (above), they are more airy and bright, with beautiful sea views. Three apartments are also available in nearby cottages. All guests can enjoy the outdoor swimming pool, courtesy van to the hotel's private beach, tennis courts, and Wi-Fi (190€–250€ double, including buffet breakfast).

Via Deserto 26, Sant'Agata sui Due Golfi. © **081-8080560.** www.oasiolimpiarelais.it. Reservations recommended. Secondi 15€–38€. AE, DC, MC, V. Thurs–Tues noon–3pm and 7:30–10:30pm.

Quattro Passi ★ CREATIVE SORRENTINE From the charming garden terrace among lemon trees and bougainvillea to the somewhat more formal dining room with arched doorways and hand-painted ceramic floors, what you experience here is the soul of the Mediterranean: Its colors and touches of exuberance are matched by professional service and excellent food, all of which has earned two Michelin stars. The sophisticated appetizers include the likes of *totano ripieno di provola con cozza gratinata e tortino di patate* (stuffed squid and mussel au gratin with potato torte). Among the *primi* are *pappardelle fave piselli e formaggio* (wide fresh pasta ribbons with peas, fresh fava beans, and cheese shavings); and the secondi include such intriguing choices as *rose di sogliola con capperi pomodorini e patate* (rosettes of sole with capers, cherry tomatoes, and potatoes). For dessert, try the local specialty, *delizie al limone* (puff pastry filled with lemon cream).

Under the restaurant is the **Quattro Passi Relais,** with five large, well-appointed guest rooms opening on the garden (200€ double, including breakfast). If you want to learn to cook Quattro Passi–style, there's a new culinary school too.

Via Amerigo Vespucci 13, Marina del Cantone, Massa Lubrense. © **081-8082800.** Fax 081-8081271. www.ristorantequattropassi.com. Reservations recommended Sat–Sun. Secondi 21€–42€. AE, MC, V. Thurs–Mon 12:30–3:30pm and 7:30–11pm, Tues 12:30–3:30pm; June–Sept daily 12:30–3:30pm and 7:30–11pm. Closed Dec–Feb.

Relais Blu Belvedere ★★ 📱 CREATIVE SORRENTINE This recently opened hotel and restaurant lies on the road to Massa Lubrense, a short distance from Sorrento (the bus stops nearby). What was once a private villa has been transformed into a strikingly stylish hotel. The views from the terrace opening onto the sea are absolutely breathtaking—Capri feels so close you could touch it—and we highly recommend a visit, if only for drinks at sunset. The warm welcome of Chef Antonino Acampora will make your visit even more special: He has worked with some of the greatest—Heinz Beck and Alain Ducasse for instance—and offers a seasonal menu based on the best ingredients this stretch of coast has to offer. You can also choose a la carte: The updated *pezzogna all'acqua pazza* (local fish in a tomato and herb broth) is a delight as is the lamb with local herbs. You can also take cooking classes.

The 13 **guest rooms,** all with magnificent sea views through huge picture windows boast elegant contemporary furnishings, fine linens, state-of-the-art bathrooms, and private gardens and terraces (310€ double; 360€–410€ suite).

Via Roncato 60, Termini, 80061 Massa Lubrense. © **081-8789552.** Fax 081-8789304. www.relaisblu.com. Reservations recommended. Secondi 30€; 8-course tasting menu 75€. AE, DC, MC, V. Daily noon–3:30pm and 7–11:30pm. Closed Nov 5–Mar 20.

Taverna del Capitano ★★★ CREATIVE SORRENTINE Our favorite on the peninsula, this Michelin-starred restaurant is a refuge of Mediterranean simplicity and top-notch food. Situated on the area's best beach, it offers wonderful homemade cuisine, respectful of local produce and seafood. The three seasonal tasting and a la carte menus feature such dishes as *insalata di aragosta con verdure* (lobster and fresh vegetable salad), *zuppa di gamberi e cicorie selvatiche* (shrimp and dandelion soup), or *pesce alla salsa di agrumi* (fish in citrus sauce). The wine list is short but has an excellent selection of regional and national wines.

The Caputo family also offers hospitality in the **Locanda del Capitano.** The 15 **guest rooms** (160€–230€ double, including breakfast) above the restaurant are nicely appointed with a nautical feeling. The best overlook the sea, and all have private terraces.

Piazza delle Sirene 10, Marina del Cantone, 80061 Massa Lubrense. ② **081-8081028.** Fax 081-8081892. www.tavernadelcapitano.it. Reservations recommended Sat–Sun. Secondi 14€–28€; tasting menus 70€–9€. AE, DC, MC, V. Oct–Mar Tues 7:30–10:30pm, Wed–Sun 12:30–3:30pm and 7:30–10:30pm; Apr–Sept daily 12:30–3:30pm and 7:30–10:30pm. Closed 6 weeks Jan–Feb.

MODERATE

Antico Francischiello ★ SORRENTINE A local favorite, this historic restaurant celebrated 100 years of activity in 2009 and is now run by the third generation of Gargiulos. The food is traditional: No attempts at nouvelle cuisine with skimpy portions here—and you'll find all the local specialties prepared with practiced skill. We like the seafood tasting menu because it allows you to try a large variety of dishes: Our favorites are *cozze gratinate* (mussels au gratin), *gnocchetti verdi all'astice* (green potato dumplings with lobster), and *zuppa di pesce* (fish stew). For smaller appetites, the rich buffet of *antipasti* is enough to suffice as a light meal. The renovated dining premises are a perfect setting for a meal, and if you are here by sunset, an *aperitivo* on the terrace is an absolute must.

Across the street, the management's **Hotel Villa Pina,** Via Partenope 40, offers simple, well-appointed rooms that are welcoming and scrupulously clean (100€ double including breakfast).

Via Partenope 27, 80061 Massa Lubrense. ② **081-5339780.** Fax 081-8071813. www.francischiello.com. Reservations recommended Sat–Sun. Secondi 18€–38€. AE, MC, V. Daily noon–3pm and 7–11:30pm (closed Wed in winter).

Conca del Sogno ★ 🍴 SORRENTINE/SEAFOOD This restaurant is a standout not only for the good food but also for its setting atop a rocky beach: The little cove is known locally as "dream cove," which, by the way, is the name of the restaurant. From Marina del Cantone, a few minutes' ride in a motor dinghy will get you to the restaurant, which caters mostly to the owners of the private sailboats and motor yachts anchored in the little bay. Meals are served throughout the day, with a menu based—you guessed it—on seafood, as well as on local cheeses and produce. We highly recommend the tasty *gamberetti di Crapolla saltati con sale e pepe* (local shrimp sautéed with salt and pepper) and the perfect grilled catch of the day. Everything is simple and delicious, including the homemade desserts.

Baia di Recommone, Nerano. ② **081-8081036.** www.concadelsogno.it. Reservations recommended Sat–Sun. Secondi 12€–25€. AE, MC, V. Daily noon–4pm and 8–11pm. Closed Nov–Mar.

Lo Scoglio da Tommaso ★ 🍴 SORRENTINE Opened in 1958 by the De Simone family, this restaurant is now run by the third generation, with young Tommaso in the kitchen. Everything on the menu is made from local ingredients produced by regional farms or caught by local fishermen. We recommend the delectable and simple spaghetti *con le zucchine* (with zucchini), the fancy linguine *all'aragosta* (with local lobster) and, if it is on the menu—and if you don't mind a bit of work—the excellent *zuppa di pesce* (soupy stew with whole fish). We also recommend the homemade desserts.

There are 14 **guest rooms** (109€–140€ double, including breakfast) that are well-appointed and welcoming, all opening onto a private balcony and sea views. The establishment also offers moorings with launch service, beach chairs and umbrellas, and boat rental.

Piazze delle Sirene 15, Località Marina del Cantone, Massa Lubrense. © **081-8081026.** www. hotelloscoglio.com. Reservations recommended. Secondi 15€–28€. AE, DC, MC, V. Daily noon–4pm and 7:30–10:30pm.

Riccardo di Francischiello CREATIVE SORRENTINE Run by Riccardo, the second son of the elder Francischiello (see **Antico Francischiello,** above), this restaurant serves delicious food such as *frutti di mare* (shellfish) ravioli, and *acquapazza* (a light broth flavored with fresh herbs and tomato, and used to poach fish), all prepared according to traditional recipes. We feel the lighter bill and the pleasant dining spaces—decorated with Vietri ceramics and the adjacent covered terrace, both overlooking the sea—compensate for the less-imaginative and more-casual food presentation.

The 32 rooms in the attached **Hotel Bellavista** (140€–180€ double, including breakfast) enjoy a wonderfully scenic position on the cliffs—the sunset views, with Capri in the foreground, are amazing. Amenities include a swimming pool on a garden terrace overlooking the sea, a new spa with an attached gym, and boat and mountain bike rentals. © **081-8789181.** Fax 081-8089341. www.francischiello. it. Reservations recommended Sat–Sun. Secondi 12€–25€. AE, MC, V. Daily noon–3:30pm and 7–11:30pm (closed Tues Oct–Mar).

Via Partenope 26, 80061 Massa Lubrense. © **081-8789181.** Fax 081-8089341. www.francischiello. it. Reservations recommended Sat–Sun. Secondi 12€–25€. AE, MC, V. Daily noon–3:30pm and 7–11:30pm (closed Tues Oct–Mar).

La Torre ★★ 🎁 SORRENTINE In the shadow of an ancient look out tower in the tiny hamlet of Santa Maria Annunziata (just above Massa Lubrense), this family-run restaurant offers superb, rustic food on a pretty terrace. We recommend starting your meal with the house antipasto; we particularly enjoyed the *frittelle di ricotta e fiori di zucca* (deep-fried zucchini flowers stuffed with ricotta). Delicious dishes include the hearty *paccheri cozze e patate* (pasta with mussels and potatoes) or you could try the tasty *alici fritti* (fresh, fried anchovies). Tiramisu is the house specialty; don't miss it! And don't miss the magnificent view of Capri and the Faraglioni from just across the piazzetta.

Piazzetta Annunziata 7, 80061 Massa Lubrense. © **081-8089566.** Reservations recommended Sat–Sun. Secondi 9€–15€. AE, DC, MC, V. Wed–Mon 1–3:30pm and 7:30–11:30pm (also open Tues dinner in summer). Closed Nov.

INEXPENSIVE

Lo Stuzzichino ★★ ☺ 🎁 SORRENTINE This down-to-earth restaurant is a welcome relief to the area's Michelin-starred restaurants: The atmosphere is informal, and children can play by the pleasant outdoor terrace. The seasonal menu is based on the best locally produced ingredients: We loved the *antipasto della casa*, which includes the *fritto misto Napoletano* (Neapolitan deep-fried rice balls, stuffed ravioli, and mozzarella); the *cannelloni alla Sorrentina* (stuffed pasta baked with mozzarella and tomato); as well as the masterfully prepared *scialatielli ai frutti di mare* (traditional fresh pasta with seafood) and the perfect *frittura di calamari e gamberi* (deep-fried medley of squid and shrimp). If it is on the menu, do taste the delicious *torta di ricotta e pere* (torte with sweet ricotta and pears), a family recipe from your host's grandmother.

Via Deserto 1, Sant'Agata sui Due Golfi. © **081-5330010.** www.ristorantelostuzzichino.it. Reservations recommended Sat–Sun. Secondi 9€–20€. AE, MC, V. Thurs–Tues noon–3:30pm and 7:30–11pm (daily July–Aug). Closed 4 weeks Jan–Feb.

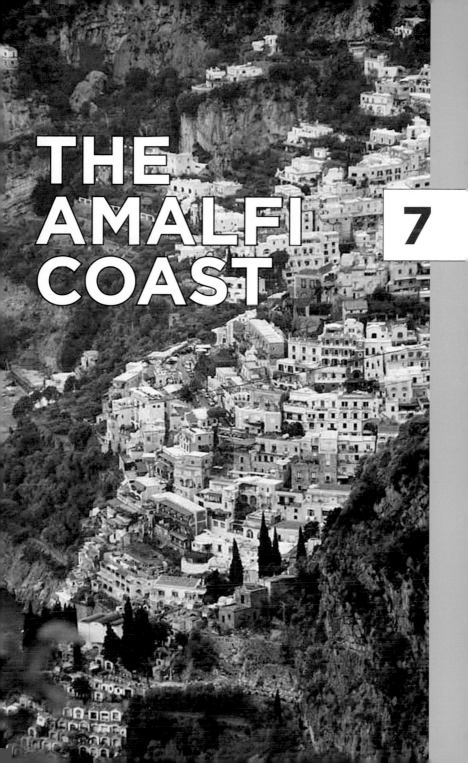

THE
AMALFI
COAST

7

Celebrated by 19th-century tourists as the most beautiful stretch of coast in the world, the beauty of the Amalfi Coast was already well known during antiquity, and its fame has not diminished in modern times. It is a magical landscape of dramatic cliffs overhanging a beautiful sea, interspersed with villages that appear to have grown from the underlying rocks. Here and there, where the mouth of a stream has created a natural harbor, a larger town has developed, as in the case of Amalfi, the queen of the Costiera. Its river valley allowed for the development of paper mills that produced paper for much of Europe during the Middle Ages and well into the Renaissance, while its harbor became the shipyard that fueled Amalfi's mighty political and commercial power.

The Amalfi Coast's unique views and plunging cliffs have inspired the works of many famous artists, writers, and musicians, from Giovanni Boccaccio to Richard Wagner, and its small towns and hamlets have been the refuge of many others, including Henrik Ibsen, Pablo Picasso, Rudolf Nureyev, and, more recently, Gore Vidal.

The most famous destination in Campania—and indeed, one of the most popular in Italy—the Amalfi Coast will enchant you with its dramatic coastline and picturesque villages. From **Vietri sul Mare** to the east—a town famous for its ceramics and majolica—to Piano di Sorrento to the west, the (sometimes harrowing) Amalfi Drive is home to leading resort towns (even though they're not exactly undiscovered): sophisticated **Ravello** (high above the sea), glitzy **Positano** (right on the water), and historic **Amalfi** (also on the sea). We also recommend going off the beaten path to explore lesser-known towns, all with a rich history and impressive views of the coast. East of Amalfi, you will find the fishing harbor of **Cetara;** the coastal villages of **Maiori, Minori,** and **Atrani;** and the inland (and, hence, upward) villages of **Scala** and **Tramonti;** west of Amalfi are the charming seaside villages of **Conca dei Marini, Praiano,** and **Vettica Maggiore** and the mountain villages of **Agerola** and **Furore.**

The Amalfi Coast is one of the most visited seaside destinations in the world, particularly during spring and summer, when each hamlet and village along this coast becomes the stage for art and cultural events, and the sweet evening air is pervaded by the scent of citrus flowers. In winter, everything is much quieter, as many places close down and the sea gets too chilly to swim in. You may have the place all to yourself in these colder months, but you'll miss much of the spirit it shows when in full bloom.

One word about transportation: Public transit is well developed here and is a way to make your vacation in this protected area slightly more ecofriendly.

See p. 157 for a map of the Amalfi Coast.

PREVIOUS PAGE: **Positano.**

POSITANO ★★★

17km (10 miles) W of Amalfi; 51km (101 miles) W of Salerno; 56km (35 miles) SE of Naples

Hugging a semivertical rock formation, Positano is the quintessence of pictur-esque. Once one of the most exclusive retreats in Italy, its unique mix of sea-scapes, colors, art, and cultural life has fascinated famous artists, musicians, and writers from Picasso and Klee to Toscanini, Bernstein, and Steinbeck. This sea-side resort has been thoroughly "discovered" but retains its character and charm in spite of a mass tourist invasion in the summer months, and it remains a de-lightful place to visit, although we do recommend coming off season if possible.

Essentials

GETTING THERE The **bus** is the best and fastest option, with **SITA** (✆ **089 405145;** www.sitabus.it) offering frequent service from Naples, Sorrento, Amalfi, Vietri, and Salerno (for information on fares, see "The Unico Travel Pass," p. 349). For the best views, get a seat on the right side of the bus when you are traveling from Sorrento and the left side from Vietri, Amalfi, and Salerno.

In fair weather, April through September, Positano is also well served by **ferry** and hydrofoils: **Metrò del Mare** (✆ **199 600700;** www.metrodel mare.net) offers regular service to Positano from Naples, Sorrento, Amalfi, Salerno, and other harbors along the coast; fares vary depending on the dis-tance, from 9€ from Amalfi to 16€ from Pozzuoli. The service was limited to July and August in 2011, but should be back to a full schedule in 2012. Amalfi-based **Cooperativa Sant'Andrea** (✆ **089-873190;** www.coopsant andrea.com) offers regular service from Amalfi, Capri, Minori, Salerno, and Sorrento, as well as special cruises and excursions; fares range from 7€ from Amalfi to 35€ from Capri. **Lucibello** (✆ **089-875032;** www.lucibello.it) offers regular service to and from Capri for 17€. **Alicost** (✆ **089/811986;** www.lauroweb.com/alicost.htm) maintains regular *aliscafo* (hydrofoil) and *motonave* (motorboat) service from Capri and Ischia to Positano; fares are 15.50€ from Capri and 21.50€ from Ischia (you must reserve at least 24 hr. in advance).

Travelmar (✆ **081-7041911;** www.travelmar.it) maintains routes to Positano from Salerno, and **LMP** (✆ **081-8071812;** www.consorziolmp. it) offers regular hydrofoil and boat service between Positano, Capri, and Sorrento. Prices range from 10€ to 18€ for both companies.

From Naples or its airport, **taxis** offer a flat rate of 120€ to Positano. **Car services** (see "Getting Around," p. 192) also offer transfers from Naples's Capodichino Airport or train station. Alternatively, **Curreri Viaggi** (✆ **081-8015420;** www.curreriviaggi.it) offers a shuttle service from Capodichino for 150€ for one to three passengers and 12€ for each additional passenger.

If you are traveling by **train** (✆ **892021** in Italy; www.trenitalia.it), the closest station is **Vietri sul Mare,** on the local line between **Naples** (where you'll change trains if you are coming from the north) and **Salerno** (if you are coming from the south).

By car, take autostrada A3 toward NAPOLI-SALERNO to the exit for VIE-TRI SUL MARE. Follow the signs for VIETRI, MAIORI, AMALFI, and POSITANO; they will lead you to the famed SS 163, the coastal road that meanders from Salerno to Positano and a bit beyond. You can also reach SS 163 from

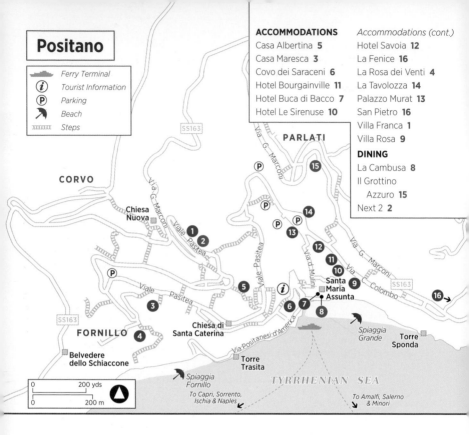

Positano

Legend:
- Ferry Terminal
- (i) Tourist Information
- (P) Parking
- Beach
- Steps

ACCOMMODATIONS
Casa Albertina **5**
Casa Maresca **3**
Covo dei Saraceni **6**
Hotel Bourgainville **11**
Hotel Buca di Bacco **7**
Hotel Le Sirenuse **10**

Accommodations (cont.)
Hotel Savoia **12**
La Fenice **16**
La Rosa dei Venti **4**
La Tavolozza **14**
Palazzo Murat **13**
San Pietro **16**
Villa Franca **1**
Villa Rosa **9**

DINING
La Cambusa **8**
Il Grottino
  Azzurro **15**
Next 2 **2**

Castellammare di Stabia, Piano di Sorrento, Vico Equense, and Sorrento heading east and following signs for POSITANO and AMALFI. **Note:** Because of the solid traffic here in summer, local authorities have occasionally limited car access to SS 163; check with the tourist office and your hotel before making your plans.

GETTING AROUND The simplest and cheapest way to move between villages along this coast is the **bus: SITA** (see "Getting There," above) offers regular service from Positano and its hub in Amalfi. In Positano, the orange town **buses** make the loop of Viale Pasitea, Via Cristoforo Colombo, and Via G. Marconi (SS 163), stopping several times along the way. They run every half-hour, saving your tired knees from some of the town's endless steps. You can purchase the 1.60€ ticket onboard.

Ferries are a convenient alternative to slogging along the local road (see "Getting There," p. 191). You can also hire a **boat,** with or without a skipper, to take you to secluded beaches (see "Beaches & Boating," p. 194). A **boat service** links Marina Grande to Fornillo during the summer, with departures every half-hour (about 5€).

To reach other towns and villages, hiring a **taxi** (© 089-875541) or a **car service** with a chauffeur makes sense, especially if you plan to stay here only a day or two; plus, an experienced local driver can double as a guide. We list specific companies in "Getting Around: by Limousine/Car Service" in chapter 11 (p. 350) as well as in "Getting There" and "Getting Around Sorrento" in chapter 6 (p. 168).

Renting a **car** is an option we don't recommend, especially in summer, but you can do so from major national and international companies (see "Getting Around," p. 348) as well as from **Rent a Car,** Viale Pasitea 74 (✆ **089-812033** or 333-3310224), or one of the companies in Sorrento (see chapter 6). Rent a Car also rents out motor scooters for 60€ per day.

VISITOR INFORMATION The **AAST tourist office** (✆ **089-875067**; www. aziendaturismopositano.it) is at Via del Saracino 4, 84017 Positano. It is open Monday to Saturday 8:30am to 2pm, with additional hours (3:30–8pm) in July and August.

You'll find a **pharmacy** (✆ **089-875863**) on Viale Pasitea. For the closest **hospital,** see "Visitor Information," p. 283; for an **ambulance,** dial ✆ **118.** You can call the **police** at ✆ **113** or 112. The **post office** (✆ **089-875142**) is at Via G. Marconi 320 (SS 163), at the corner with Viale Pasitea; it is open Monday to Saturday 8am to 2pm. You will find several banks with **ATMs,** including **Banco di Napoli,** Piazza dei Mulini 18 (✆ **089-8122367**). The **exchange office** (✆ **089-875864**) is in Piazza dei Mulini. You can get Internet access at **Dimensione Servizi,** Via San Sebastiano 8 (✆ **089-811993**).

The Via Positanesi d'America.

SPECIAL EVENTS Summer Music is an international chamber music festival that takes place in late August/early September every year (2012 marks its 45th anniversary). The **Festival of the Assunta** is a lively event held August 14 and 15, when the violent attack of the Saracens and the Madonna's miraculous intervention are reenacted, accompanied by much noise and fanfare by Positanese of all ages. The histrionics include a fake fire and colorful historic costumes.

Exploring the Town

Positano remains as picturesque as ever in spite of the crowds. It is not a destination for the fainthearted, however, with steep ramps of stairs serving as walkways. The typical pastel-colored houses—cubes with domed roofs and porticoes or loggias overlooking the sea—poke from the overflowing green of gardens and citrus groves. *Tip:* Wearing comfortable shoes without heels is a must here; otherwise, negotiating the steep alleyways and many steps will be an ordeal.

The heart of town is **Marina Grande,** the beach where fishermen used to haul up their boats; a few still do today. At its western end is the pier where ferries arrive and depart. From Marina Grande, **Via Positanesi d'America ★** —a cliff-side pedestrian promenade, stretches along the shore past the cape of **Torre Trasita** to the smaller beach of **Fornillo.** Not far from Marina Grande is the **Collegiata di Santa Maria Assunta ★★**, Piazza Flavio Gioia (**© 089-875480;** daily 8am–noon and 4–7pm), founded in the 13th century and later decorated with a gorgeous majolica dome. Inside, you will find the famous *tavola* of the *Madonna Nera* (Black Madonna), an icon in 13th-century Byzantine style. The church is the focal point of the **Festival of the Assunta** (see "Special Events," above).

In our opinion, however, the best churches of Positano are the lesser-known ones. The small **Chiesa di Nuova,** Via Chiesa Nuova, was restored in the 18th century, and has a striking maijolica **tile floor ★★**, one of the most beautiful in an area known for its colorful tile work. The **Chiesa di Santa Caterina ★★**, Via Pasitea, built for the local Porcelli family, is another small architectural masterpiece in neo-Gothic style, with an elegant bell tower. Just west of Positano on SS 163 is the renowned **Belvedere dello Schiaccone ★★★**, the best lookout on the Amalfi Drive. At 200m (656 ft.) above sea level, it overlooks the archipelago of Li Galli and Capo Sottile over a palm and citrus grove, with the splendid Monte Sant'Angelo a Tre Pizzi in the background.

BEACHES & BOATING

Positano is blessed with four delightful **beaches** besides the central **Spiaggia Grande** by the marina: **Fornillo ★** (linked by boat service from the marina) to the west of town and **La Porta, Ciumicello,** and **Arienzo** to the east. The sand is rather gray and pebbly, but the views are idyllic and the sea is clear and refreshing. You can rent two chairs and an umbrella at the reserved areas for about 25€ per day, or use the free but crowded public beach. Another beach, **Laurito ★**, is

The Belvedere dello Schiaccone.

also a bit out of town, but you can easily reach it with the boat service offered by the restaurants Le Sirene and Da Adolfo (see "Where to Eat," later in this chapter), which both also rent chairs and umbrellas.

For a quieter swim, locals like to take a boat to one of the small coves accessible only by sea. You can **rent a boat** at Spiaggia Grande from **Lucibella** (②089-875032) for between 35€ and 60€ per hour, without skipper, depending on the kind of boat and the duration of the rental. One popular destination is the archipelago of **Li Galli (The Roosters)** ★★, the four small islands visible to the west of Marina Grande. Named Gallo Lungo, Castelluccio, Gallo dei Briganti, and La Rotonda, these are the islands where—according to Homer—the Sirens lived. Indeed, the archipelago is also known as Sirenuse, from the Latin *Sirenusae* (Sirens). According to legend, these creatures attracted mariners with their enchanted songs, causing their ships to run aground on the rocks. In Greek mythology, sirens were represented as birds with human faces and the bodies of fish (hence the name Li Galli, "The Roosters"). Once you skirt past the Sirens and arrive safely on Gallo Lungo, you'll spot a watchtower and the remains of a Roman villa. In more modern times, Rodolf Nureyev spent the last years of his life in a villa on these islands.

HIKING & TREKKING ★★

Hiking the local trails is one of the best ways to enjoy the area's incomparable natural beauty as well as its historic and artistic monuments. Many of these trails start right in the outskirts of the town and most are historic footpaths that were the only land links in the area before the SS 163 was opened in 1840. Still used for bringing animals to pasture, most are well maintained and well marked. If you are a serious hiker, we recommend the map published by the CAI (Club Alpino Italiano), *Monti Lattari Penisola Sorrentina, Costiera Amalfitana: Carta dei sentieri,* sold for 10€ at the best newsstands and bookstores in Ravello, Amalfi, and Tramonti (Positano may have it, but they often run out). The **Comunità Montana Penisola Amalfitana,** Via Municipio, 84010 Tramonti (②089-876354), also has guides and trail information. **Giovanni Visetti** (②339-6942911; www.giovis.com) is an experienced local guide who organizes some of the best treks on the peninsula.

Trails are steep and progress can be hampered by rocks and gravel. To tackle most of the paths you need to be moderately fit and have basic equipment: good shoes, a backpack, a sunhat and a good supply of water (especially in the summer), and a jacket for the rain and cold (all times of year). You also need a head for heights.

One of the more demanding hikes is the path to **Santa Maria di Castello** ★★ (marked no. 33 on the CAI map), with its spectacular natural terrace overlooking Positano. This town straddles the pass between the Sorrento and Positano sides of the peninsula, and it is basically straight up from Positano, through Corvo. You can also cheat and drive yourself to Santa Maria di Castello (the road approaches from Vico Equense, on the Sorrento side of the peninsula, see chapter 6). An easier hike is the ascent 400m (1,312 ft.) to **Montepertuso ★**. This is the first part of a longer **trek ★★** which winds through the citrus terraces between Positano and Amalfi. The going is relatively easy in this direction, but the best views are to be found on the more demanding ascent from Amalfi (see "Outdoor Activities," p. 214). Another scenic trail is the climb to **Nocelle ★★**, at an altitude of 443m (1,453 ft.). In this little paradise, where cars are not allowed, you can have an excellent lunch (or dinner) at **Ristorante Santa Croce** (make reservations in advance by calling ✆**089-811260**). The trail starts from the SS 163, between Arienzo and Laurito, about 3km (1¾ miles) east of Positano. From Montepertuso and Nocelle you can also continue on the **Sentiero degli Dei** (See "Outdoor Activities," p. 214).

Where to Stay

As you would expect of such a world-renowned resort town, you'll find a wide range of accommodations, but rates are high, ridiculously so in high season. In addition to the hotels we review here, see **Pupetto** ★ and **Le Sirene** ★, in "Where to Eat," later in this chapter. If you'd like to stay in the vertical countryside above town, and provided you are adequately fit, we recommend the *agriturismo* **Rifugio degli Dei** ★, Via Arienzo 43 (✆**339-8390809**; ✆/fax 089-811279; www.rifugiodeglidei.it; 80€–100€ doubles), accessed via some 250 stairs and 183m (600 ft.) of footpath; the staff will carry your luggage up from the SS 163.

VERY EXPENSIVE

Hotel Le Sirenuse ★★ This striking red-and-white 18th-century villa with terraces overlooking the bay is a picturesque sight—you may have seen it featured in the film *Only You* with Marisa Tomei and Robert Downey, Jr. Situated directly above the harbor, it was the residence of the Marchesi Sersale family (who still manage the hotel) until 1951, and the public spaces are palatial. Guest rooms are large and bright, with vaulted ceilings, antiques, hand-painted tile floors, and fine fabrics; all have private terraces and luxurious bathrooms. Most have matchless views of the bay. The hotel's swimming pool is perched on a terrace, and a state-of-the-art health club with an attached Aveda spa offers further relaxation. The buffet breakfast here is lavish, and the **restaurant La Sponda** (reservations are required) is highly recommended for meals. Children 6 and under are not accepted in the hotel from May 1 through September 30 (the dates vary slightly each year, so check), or at the restaurant for dinner.

Via Cristoforo Colombo 30, 84017 Positano. www.sirenuse.it. ✆**089-875066**. Fax 089-811798. 59 units. 500€–890€ double; from 1,260€ suite. Rates include buffet breakfast. AE, DC, MC, V. Parking 40€. **Amenities:** Restaurant; 2 bars; concierge; health club; pool; room service; spa. *In room:* A/C, TV, minibar.

San Pietro ★★★ Offering luxurious accommodations and exceptionally professional service in a wonderful location just outside Positano near Laurito Beach, this family-run member of the Relais & Châteaux group is *the* place to stay on the Amalfi Coast. Elegant public areas have French windows opening onto the garden and the sea; spacious guest rooms have antiques, tiled floors, pink-marble bathrooms, and private terraces; some have huge picture windows. The hotel's private beach with its waterside restaurant **Carlino** is accessible by elevator, and there's a splendid panoramic swimming pool, tennis court, and a state-of-the-art fitness center with a wonderful spa. *Note:* The hotel welcomes children age 10 and above only.

The Michelin-rated **Il San Pietro** is unique not only for its exceptional food, but also for its magnificent views, cozy terrace, and lovely garden. Chef Alois Vanlangenacker uses local ingredients—mostly from the hotel's own farm—to create sophisticated yet simple concoctions such as *pollo ruspante in crosta di* *agrumi* (free-range chicken in a citrus crust). The restaurant is closed November through March; reservations are required as well as formal dress for dinner.

Via Laurito 2, 84017 Positano. www.ilsanpietro.it. ☎ **089-875455.** Fax 089-811449. 60 units. 550€–680€ double; from 750€ suite. Rates include breakfast. 3 nights minimum stay in high season (May–Oct 18). AE, DC, MC, V. Free parking. Closed Nov–Mar. **Amenities:** Restaurants; bar; concierge; health club; pool; room service; sauna; spa; tennis court. *In room:* A/C, TV, minibar.

EXPENSIVE

Covo dei Saraceni ★ Named after the fisherman's house that was used as the Saracens's hideout (see "Festival of the Assunta," p. 193), this establishment offers peaceful and alluring accommodations right on the marina but away from the hubbub. Guest rooms are large and bright, with comfortable furnishings, terra-cotta floors, and lovely private balconies or terraces with great views. The seawater swimming pool on the fifth-floor terrace and the restaurant, **Savino,** are added incentives.

Via Regina Giovanna 5, 84017 Positano. www.covodeisaraceni.it. ☎ **089-875400.** Fax 089-875878. 61 units. 296€ double; from 465€ junior suite. Rates include buffet breakfast. Children 2 and under stay free in parent's room. AE, DC, MC, V. Parking 25€. Closed Nov–Mar. **Amenities:** Restaurant; 2 bars; concierge; pool; room service. *In room:* A/C, TV, minibar.

Palazzo Murat ★★ This 18th-century baroque palace near the marina is said to have been built for Gioacchino Murat, Napoleon's brother-in-law who was to become king of Naples, and today it's one of our our favorite places to stay in the town center. The five large (and more expensive) guest rooms in the historical part of the building are decorated with antiques and original furnishings; the ones in the new wings are smaller but still very attractive and have private terraces. All units have good-size bathrooms, and most have ocean views. The rich buffet breakfast is served in the delightful garden under big, white umbrellas when weather permits; in August and September this is the site of chamber music concerts. The hotel's restaurant **Al Palazzo** offers alfresco gourmet dining in a charming setting.

Via dei Mulini 23, 84017 Positano. www.palazzomurat.it. ☎ **089-875177.** 31 units. 200€–450€ double. Rates include buffet breakfast. Children 2 and under stay free in parent's room. AE, DC, MC, V. Parking 25€ nearby. Closed Jan to week before Easter. **Amenities:** Restaurant; concierge; room service. *In room:* A/C, TV, minibar.

Villa Franca 👪 ★ Situated at the top of the town, this delightful family-run hotel overlooking the sea is one of Positano's lesser-known, distinctive hotels. The common areas, with their neoclassical feel, are decorated with reproduction artwork and fine tiles: The motif continues in the elegant, comfortable guest rooms, all of which are decorated in Mediterranean style, with bright, tiled floors and bathrooms. Private balconies overlook the sea. The roof terrace has a swimming pool with a solarium and magnificent, 360-degree views over the town. There are 10 additional rooms in the rather less-inspiring annex (the cheaper "standard" rooms are likely to be here; inquire when you book). The hotel's restaurant serves good food in a romantic setting, and there is a free shuttle bus to the center of Positano.

Via Pasitea 318, 84017 Positano. www.villafrancahotel.it. ☎ **089-875655.** Fax 089-875735. 38 units. 210€–410€ double. Rates include buffet breakfast. Children 2 and under stay free in parent's room. AE, DC, MC, V. Parking 21€. **Amenities:** Restaurant; bar; concierge; health club; pool; room service; spa. *In room:* A/C, TV, minibar.

MODERATE

Casa Albertina ★★ ☺ This small, family-run hotel in the upper part of Positano offers attentive service and great views. The famous Sicilian writer Luigi Pirandello was a regular guest: Maybe he found the beautiful bedrooms as cosy and welcoming as we did. Each is individually decorated, with carefully chosen furniture and a simple, monochromatic theme; French doors open onto private balconies with sea views. In good weather, breakfast is served on the terra-cotta tiled terrace. In the high season, rates include half-board (breakfast and dinner).

Via della Tavolozza 3, 84017 Positano. www.casalbertina.it. ℂ **089-875143.** Fax 089-811540. 20 units. 180€–250€ double. Rates include breakfast. Children 2 and under stay free in parent's room. AE, DC, MC, V. Parking 20€–40€ nearby. **Amenities:** Restaurant; bar; concierge; room service. *In room:* A/C, TV, minibar.

Hotel Buca di Bacco Centrally positioned on the Marina Grande—a great choice if you don't mind a bit of noise—this excellent hotel boasts beautiful rooms that are all large and well furnished. Most have balconies facing the sea, and six superior rooms have full seafront terraces. The less-expensive rooms in the annexed buildings enjoy similar levels of comfort. The hotel's restaurant is extremely popular, as is the less-pricey snack bar.

Via Rampa Teglia 4, 84017 Positano. www.bucadibacco.it. ℂ **089-875699.** 54 units. 245€–450€ double. Rates include buffet breakfast. AE, DC, MC, V. No parking. Closed 2 weeks in winter. **Amenities:** Restaurant; bar; babysitting; concierge; room service; Wi-Fi (free). *In room:* A/C, TV, minibar.

INEXPENSIVE

Hotel Bougainville 🎁 This small, family-run hotel only has 14 rooms but is a good choice if you don't mind sacrificing amenities for location: It lies in the heart of Positano only steps from the beach, and rates are very reasonable. Some of the rear-facing guest rooms open onto flowery private terraces, where you can have breakfast in good weather, while others overlook the town. Try and avoid one of the few standard doubles with miniscule windows. All the rooms have good quality simple, modern furniture, pastel-colored tiled floors and good-size bathrooms (some with shower only).

Via Cristoforo Colombo 25, 84017 Positano. www.bouganville.it. ℂ **089-875047.** Fax 089-811150. 14 units. 125€–180€ double. AE, V. No parking. Closed Nov to mid-Mar. **Amenities:** Bar. *In room:* A/C, TV, minibar, Wi-Fi (3€/hour).

Hotel Savoia ★★ Nestled in the heart of Positano, this quiet, well-run hotel is just steps away from shops and the beach. Guest units are spacious, bright, and comfortably furnished (think good beds and roomy cabinets), with cool tiled floors. Some of the rooms have sea views, while others overlook the village; bathrooms are good-size (some with shower only) and those in the best rooms have sauna showers or Jacuzzi tubs. This place has been run by the D'Aiello family since 1936, and prides itself on courteous service.

Via Cristoforo Colombo 73, 84017 Positano. www.savoiapositano.it. ℂ **089-875003.** Fax 089-811844. 42 units. 120€–190€ double; 240€ suite. Rates include buffet breakfast. AE, DC, MC, V. Parking 25€ nearby. **Amenities:** Bar; babysitting; concierge; room service; Wi-Fi (free). *In room:* A/C, TV, minibar.

STAYING AT A B&B

Given the vertiginously steep prices of hotel rooms in Positano, especially in high season, there has been a huge demand for moderately priced accommodations in recent years; B&Bs and small, guesthouse-style hotels are flourishing. These types of places will mostly have rooms for under 200€ in high season (130€–150€ off season). Our favorites are **La Tavolozza,** Via Cristoforo Colombo 10 (*©* **089-875040**); **Villa Rosa,** Via C. Colombo 127 (*©* **089-811955;** www. villarosapositano.it); **La Rosa dei Venti,** Via Fornillo 40 (*©* **089-875252;** www.larosadeiventi.net); **Casa Maresca,** Via Lepanto 17 (*©* **089-875679;** www.casamaresca.it); **Casa Soriano,** Via Pasitea (*©* **089-875494;** www.casa soriano.it); and **La Fenice,** Via Marconi 4, Chetrara (*©* **089-875513;** www. bbfenice.com).

Where to Eat

The best and most elegant dining in Positano is at the town's top hotels: **Il San Pietro** at the Hotel San Pietro and **La Sponda** at **Le Sirenuse.** Our recommendations for more casual dining options are below.

EXPENSIVE

La Cambusa AMALFITAN/SEAFOOD Baldo and Luigi created this beachfront restaurant in 1970 vowing to serve traditionally prepared fish of the highest quality, and they have stuck to their promise forty years or so on. Only the freshest fish—brought in every morning by local fishermen—is prepared with techniques designed to bring out the natural flavors. Try *paccheri alla pescatrice* (thick pasta tubes with mixed seafood) or our favorite, linguine *agli scampi con pomodorini* (with shrimp and local cherry tomatoes). For the secondo, pick your fish from the display and have it simply grilled or cooked *all'acqua pazza* (with an herb broth).

Piazza Amerigo Vespucci 4, near Spiaggia Grande. *©* **089-875432.** www.lacambusapositano. com. Reservations recommended. Secondi 16€–28€. AE, DC, MC, V. Daily noon–3pm and 7:30–11pm.

MODERATE

Da Adolfo ★ AMALFITAN/SEAFOOD You might like the challenge of reaching this picturesque beach restaurant from the SS 163 via the flight of 450 rugged steps down and then, unfortunately, up again. If not, a free water-shuttle service for the restaurant's guests is available at Marina Grande (daily 10am and 1pm, return 4–7pm; later on Sat nights in July and Aug); you'll recognize the boat by the red fish symbol on the prow. This Positano classic has a laid-back atmosphere, and the menu includes many simple local dishes. The signature dish is mozzarella *alla brace* (grilled on fresh lemon leaves) and a truly special *zuppa di cozze* (mussel stew), but we also recommend the tasty *grigliata di pesce* (medley of fresh grilled seafood). Da Adolfo also offers **beach facilities** with changing rooms, showers, and chair-and-umbrella rentals (12€ for both per day).

Via Spiaggia di Laurito 40. *©* **089-875022.** www.daadolfo.com. Reservations recommended. Secondi 10€–18€. AE, MC, V. Daily 1–4pm. Closed mid Oct to early May.

Donna Rosa ★★ AMALFITAN Situated in the hills above Positano, this elegant restaurant is popular with locals who come to eat homemade pasta and excellent seafood prepared by two sisters and served—in warm weather—on a charming terrace overlooking the sea. The menu surprises with a choice of turf and surf: Our favorites were the excellent *tagliatelle verdi ai frutti di mare* (green tagliatelle with seafood), *tagliatelle con funghi porcini e gamberetti* (tagliatelle with porcini mushrooms and shrimp) and, for a secondo, the lamb cutlets *con rosmarino salvatico* (with wild rosemary)

Via Montepertuso 97. ℂ **089-811806.** www.drpositano.com. Reservations recommended. Secondi 12€–32€. AE, DC, MC, V. Aug Wed–Mon 5–10pm; rest of year Wed–Mon noon–3pm & 5–10pm. Closed Nov–Easter.

Hotel Ristorante Le Sirene ★ AMALFITAN/SEAFOOD This popular restaurant sits right on the beach in Laurito, about 2km (1¼ miles) from the center of Positano. The restaurant's free boat service will pick you up from Marina Grande, a much better option than navigating the several hundred steps down from SS 163. A competitor of Da Adolfo (above), it offers a less casual setting and similarly good food. Naturally, the menu focuses on seafood, such as the *scialatielli allo scoglio* (local fresh pasta with seafood), but also offers such well-prepared local dishes as mozzarella *alla brace* (grilled on fresh lemon leaves). Above the restaurant are eight simply but nicely appointed **guest rooms** (150€–240€ double, including breakfast and lunch or dinner, beach chairs and umbrella; B&B prices on request).

Via Spiaggia di Laurito 24. ℂ **089-875490.** Fax 089-8122877. www.lesirenepositano.it. Secondi 12€–18€. AE, DC, MC, V. Daily noon–4:30pm and 7:30–11pm. Closed Nov–Apr.

Il Ritrovo 🎁 AMALFITAN/PIZZA This pleasant restaurant is located in the village of Montepertuso, high above Positano, and offers a great escape from the crowds, high prices, and summer heat below. There is a cool arbor-covered terrace with magnificent views, and a seasonal menu focused on meat and vegetables from the family farm. Both the *grigliata mista* (grilled meat medley) and the free-range chicken baked with herbs are excellent, as is homemade pasta such as ravioli served with cherry tomatoes, eggplant, and basil or tagliatelle with local *porcini* mushrooms. The SITA bus stop from Positano is nearby, or you can call the restaurant for free pickup. There's live music on Friday and Saturday evenings, and Chef Salvatore also offers well-organized **cooking classes** year-round.

Via Montepertuso 77. ℂ **089-812005.** www.ilritrovo.com. Reservations recommended. Secondi 10€–20€; set-price menu 30€–40€. AE, DC, MC, V. Thurs–Tues noon–3:30pm and 7pm–12:30am; open daily Apr to mid Oct. Closed Jan.

Next 2 ★★ AMALFITAN We really like the classy, contemporary look of this buzzy wine bar and restaurant with its big terrace, and the food is great too. Tanina Vanacore and her son-in-law turn out modern versions of local classics using fresh produce from their own garden. We loved the *fiori di zucchini ripieni di ricotta, mozzarella e basilico* (zucchini flowers stuffed with ricotta, mozzarella, and basil) served with pesto sauce, the *ricciola scottata con le zucchine alla scapece* (local fish with mint and vinegar flavoured zucchini), and the *tagliata di tonno con asparagi* (sliced tuna steak with asparagus). There's a comprehensive wine list, and a wine bar where you can order a plate of cheeses and mixed cold cuts if you want a lighter meal. After dinner, a young crowd moves in for late-night drinks.

Via Pasitea 242. ℂ **089-8123516.** www.next2.it. Reservations recommended in high season. Secondi 16€–25€. AE, DC, MC, V. Daily 7–11pm. Closed Mon off season. Closed Nov–Mar.

Pupetto ★ ☺ AMALFITAN/PIZZA Right on the beach at Fornillo, this historic restaurant cannot be reached by car (an elevator will take you down from the parking lot off SS 163), but is a moderately short walk away from Marina Grande along a seaside path. A 1950s vibe has been preserved, with the colorful and informal dining terrace and down-to-earth menu. The food is good, and your kids can run around on the beach outside (where you can rent umbrellas and chairs). We recommend the excellent spaghetti *alle vongole* (with fresh clams) and the *fritto misto* (deep-fried seafood medley). **Note:** Pizza is served only in the evening. Above the restaurant are 34 large **guest rooms** with basic amenities (170€–220€ double, including breakfast; parking 15€).

Via Fornillo 37, Spiaggia di Fornillo, 84017 Positano. ✆ **089-875087.** Fax 089-811517. www. hotelpupetto.it. 34 units. Secondi 12€–22€; pizza 7€–10€. AE, DC, MC, V. Daily 12:30–3pm and 7:30–10pm. Closed Nov–Mar.

INEXPENSIVE

Il Grottino Azzurro 🎁 AMALFITAN/WINERY This historic wine cellar has been a favorite with visitors and locals for decades. It offers a simple array of well-prepared traditional dishes, centered—for a welcome change—on meat, fresh homemade pasta, and wine. Locals come for delicious cannelloni (tubes of fresh pasta filled with meat and baked with cheese and tomato sauce), Parmigiana (eggplant Parmesan), and succulent roasted chicken. Obviously, you'll find a good number of local and regional vintages to quaff.

Via Guglielmo Marconi 158 (SS 163). ✆ **089-875466.** Reservations recommended. Secondi 10€–16€. MC, V. Thurs–Tues 12.30–3pm and 7:30–11pm (also Wed in summer).

Shopping ★

Positano was once known for its cutting-edge fashion. Those days are long gone and most of what you see in the boutiques these days is decidedly passé, but you can still find attractive summer clothes (linen is a specialty), good beachwear, and gorgeous handmade sandals. The main shopping drag is Via dei Mulini, but you'll find all kinds of small shops and boutiques along the town's steep streets, many of them offering what was once known around the world as "Positano Fashion." You will also find elegant boutiques along Via Pasitea. In the 1960s, the town was home to a number of small tailoring boutiques where garments were made to order. A leftover from those heady days is **Sartoria Maria Lampo,** Viale Pasitea 12 (✆ **089-875021;** www.marialampo.it), one of the remaining original boutiques that's maintained its reputation. Other favorites are **Pepito's,** Viale Pasitea 15 (✆ **089-875446;** www.pepitos-fashion.com); **Nadir,** Viale Pasitea 44 (✆ **089-875975**); **La Bottega di Brunella,** Viale Pasitea 76 (✆ **089-875228**); and **La Tartana,** Via della Tartana (✆ **089-875645**).

The town is also famous for its handmade sandals. Some of the artisan shops will make them for you while you wait. Try **D'Antonio,** Via Trara Genoino 13 (✆ **089-811824**); **Dattilo,** Via Rampa Teglia 19 (✆ **089-811440**); or **Safari,** Via della Taratana 2 (✆ **089-811440;** www.safaripositano.com).

Positano has a number of high-quality antiques shops, such as **Cose Antiche,** Via Cristoforo Colombo 21 (✆ **089-811811;** www.coseantiche positano.it), and **Le Myricae,** Via Cristoforo Colombo 27, with its splendid collection of Art Deco jewelry.

Positano After Dark

During the sweet summer nights, Positano's bars are packed with locals and visitors drinking *aperitivi* and indulging in people-watching. If you are in the mood for luxury, have drinks on the delightful terrace at the hotel **Le Sirenuse** (p. 196); for less-formal entertainment, a perfect spot is **L'Incanto,** Via Marina 4 (✆ **089-811177**), not far from the sea at Spiaggia Grande, and so is popular **Chez Black,** Via del Brigantino 19 (✆ **089-875036**), nearby. Historic **La Buca di Bacco,** Via del Brigantino 35 (✆ **089-811461;** www.bucapositano.it), is right on the beach. It started life as a tavern and nightclub that was the meeting place for the local *dolce vita* back when Positano was an exclusive resort for VIPs; it is still one of the buzziest nightspots in town today. The bar in front is a perfect place for a coffee or a *granita,* while the tavern below has evolved into a pleasant late-night wine bar–cum–art gallery and Internet cafe. At **Conwinum,** Via Rampa Teglia 12 (✆ **089-811687**), a trendy local crowd comes to listen to live jazz on summer weekends and to sip some excellent wines.

Another hot spot is **Caffe Positano,** Viale Pasitea 182 (✆ **089-875082**), a bar with live music on the terrace over the marina (they also make excellent coffee). Popular among locals, **L'Internazionale,** Via Marconi 306, by Chiesa Nuova (✆ **089-875434**), has a good wine selection and yummy pastries. If you have a sweet tooth, you will definitely like **La Zagara,** Via dei Mulini 8 (✆ **089-875964;** www.lazagara.com), where locals come after dinner to enjoy excellent homemade ice cream and *granite* in various flavors—try the melon—in a marvelous garden of citrus trees. Its famous pastry shop serves *torta positanese* (a local cake made with almonds), *delizie al limone* (lemon cream puffs), and *Bavarese* (a pastry filled with wild strawberries and whipped cream).

Music on the Rocks, Via Grotto dell'Incanto 51 (✆ **089-875874;** www.musicontherocks.it), is a two-level dance club including **Le Terrazze,** with food and a piano bar; the disco below, inside a grotto by the beach, has the same owners as Chez Black. The club is open Friday and Saturday nights in May and September, and daily June through August (closed Oct–Apr).

PRAIANO & VETTICA MAGGIORE

6.5km (4 miles) E of Positano; 9km (5 miles) W of Amalfi

Only a short distance from Positano, Praiano offers a more laid-back and less "international" version of the Costiera Amalfitana: You will share your stay mostly with locals and other Italian visitors, as most foreign tourists make a beeline for the more famous destinations.

Essentials

GETTING THERE & AROUND Praiano is the first village you encounter east of Positano and is easily reached from Positano, Amalfi, or Sorrento by **SITA bus, taxi,** or **car service,** or **rental car** or scooter (see "Getting Around," p. 192, 208, and 167). **La Sibilla,** Via Marina di Praia 1, Praiano (✆ **089-874365;** www.lasibilla.org), offers **water taxi** service to and from Marina di Praia from Amalfi, Atrani, Capri, and Positano (about 65€ per hr.); it also offers boat rental, and daily excursions to Capri, the Emerald Grotto (p. 231), and Furore. **Benvenuto Limos,** Via Roma 54, Praiano (✆ **346-6840226;** www.benvenutolimos.com), is the local car service. **Taxi** service is provided by **Umberto Benvenuto,** Via Roma (✆**089-874024**), and **Gennaro Rispoli,** Via G. Capriglione (✆**089-874370**).

VISITOR INFORMATION Praiano's **tourist office** (✆**089-874557;** www.praiano.org) is at Via G. Capriglione.

You'll find a **pharmacy** (✆**089-874846**) on Via Capriglione 142 (SS 163). For the nearest **hospital** see "Visitor Information," p. 283; for an **ambulance,** dial ✆**118.** You can call the **police** at ✆**113** or 112. The **post office** (✆**089-874086**) is on Via Capriglione 80 (SS 163). You'll find an **ATM** by the tourist office; the nearest bank is in Positano.

Exploring the Town

The preferred residence of the Amalfi doges—who loved the beautiful views over Positano, Amalfi, and the Faraglioni of Capri—Praiano is still popular among Italians (and an increasing number of glitz-phobic foreign visitors) for the same reason. The twin villages of Praiano and Vettica Maggiore, to the west, occupy the two faces of the promontory known as Capo Sottile. With a graceful profusion of porticos and domes, the **medieval village** is 120m (394 ft.) above sea level on the slopes of Monte Sant'Angelo. Strolling along the steep streets you'll encounter the church of **San Gennaro**—technically in Vettica Maggiore—crowned by a beautiful oval dome tiled with colored majolica. Its 18th-century majolica floor was re-created in 1966 according to the original design. The **view** from the church square is superb.

OUTDOOR ACTIVITIES

Twin towns, twin harbors: East of town is tiny, picturesque **Marina di Praia ★★**, with its small pebbly beach and clear waters, where you can rent chairs and umbrellas. West of town is the more secluded **Spiaggia della Gavitella ★**, a cove that is only accessible by boat or by footpath. The path starts from the Church of San Gennaro (above), off to the right from Via Masa; it also crosses the SS 163, down across from the tourist office.

From the beach of Marina di Praia, **Via Torremare** is a scenic footpath carved along the cliff. Keep left for the natural grotto housing the nightclub L'Africana (see "Praiana After Dark," below), or head right up to the medieval

---

Myth or Reality: The Truth About the Amalfi Coast Drive

Is the Amalfi Coast Drive as hair-raising as they say? More to the point: "Is driving the best way to enjoy the views?" And the answer is no, not for the driver. One of the world's most famous drives, the stretch of road between Vietri sul Mare and Positano is only 36km (22 miles). While the technical difficulty of the drive is moderate (easier than the road to Hana in Maui, let's say, but more difficult than the Pacific Coast Highway), traffic and the aggressive Neapolitan driving style can turn it into a headache for even the most-experienced driver—and into a complete nightmare if you generally drive on spacious freeways in flat or gentle terrain. Luckily, alternatives—car service, bus, taxi, and ferry—are available and efficient (p. 348). On the other hand, if you want to explore this area in depth within a limited time period, having your own car with driver will provide you with more flexibility.

watchtower **Torre Asciola** (also known as Torre a Mare, or tower by the sea), housing the studio of local artist **Sandulli,** a painter and sculptor. *Note:* The footpath is generally easy but becomes dangerously slippery in bad weather, when the sea has been known to wash people off the path to their possible death below.

From the trail to Spiaggia della Gavitella, a long flight of steps leads to the medieval tower **Torre di Grado.** The walk is particularly romantic at sunset or in the moonlight.

For more serious **hiking,** Praiano is one of the gateways to the Amalfi Coast's most famous trail, the **Sentiero degli Dei (Trail of the Gods)** ★★★.

A ridge trail, it runs high above the sea between Nocella and Bomerano and affords magnificent views of the entire coast. The sentiero is actually a section of the longer **Via degli Incanti,** the **Trail of Charms** ★★, which runs between Amalfi and Positano (see "Outdoor Activities," p. 214). As you walk westward from Praiano, you'll enjoy the best views. The ascent takes you first to Colle Serra and on to San Domenico, where you will start the ridge trail to Nocella and Montepertuso, before heading down to Positano. Moderately difficult and requiring some preparation, it is—as its name suggests—a divine trail.

In Marina di Praia you can also **rent boats** and sign up for excursions with **La Sibilla** ★ (see "Getting Around," above).

FROM TOP: **San Gennaro; The Sentiero degli Dei (Trail of the Gods).**

Where to Stay

EXPENSIVE

Casa Angelina ★★ This super-stylish boutique hotel is housed in a pristine white structure overlooking the sea with spectacular views. The whole place is done out in contemporary minimalist chic: Public areas are well supplied with comfortable white sofas, have warm wood floors, and fabulous views from huge windows. The bright, white-on-white guest rooms have sleek bathrooms supplied with white robes and slippers and private terraces or balconies. All have sea views, and the best have huge private outside spaces. If you don't mind being separated (via the elevator and some 200 steps) from the main hotel and its services, we recommend the four "Eaudesea" suites with kitchenettes that are housed in renovated fisherman's huts just above the Spiaggia della Gavitella. The outdoor pool has Jacuzzi jets, and an elevator takes you halfway down to the private beach below, with umbrellas and chairs reserved for the hotel's guests. You still have to negotiate some 200 steps, however. The top-floor gourmet restaurant, **Un Piano nel Cielo** (p. 206), serves local dishes with a creative twist to a background of magnificent views. Breakfast at Casa Angelina is a sumptuous affair with an enormous buffet that includes local cheeses and savory dishes, homemade cakes, fresh fruit, and squeezed juices, plus made-to-order hot choices.

Via Gennaro Capriglione 147 (SS 163), 84010 Praiano. www.casangelina.com. ☏ **089-8131333.** Fax 089-874266. 39 units. 270€–450€ double; 750€ suite. AE, DC, MC, V. Free parking. **Amenities:** Restaurant; bar; gym; 2 pools; room service; spa. *In room:* A/C, TV, Internet, minibar.

MODERATE

Grand Hotel Tritone ☺ Off the SS 163, a short distance west of Praiano, this family-run hotel offers gorgeous views and quiet accommodations. The old-fashioned elegance creates a welcoming and warm atmosphere. Built over a sheer cliff, with an elevator to the private beach below, it has a terrace garden with a lemon grove. The seawater pool is a great spot, and the hotel even has a picturesque chapel built in a grotto. Guest rooms are well appointed and pleasantly furnished, many with private balconies, sea views, and good-size bathrooms (some with shower only). The 12 suites are gorgeous, each with its own private terrace overlooking the water. The hotel's restaurant, **La Cala delle Lampare,** serves excellent southern Italian dishes.

Via Campo 5 (off SS 163, 2km/1¼ miles) west of Praiano), 84010 Praiano. www.tritone.it. ☏ **089-874333.** 62 units. 210€–240€ double; 280€ triple; from 320€ suite. Rates include buffet breakfast. Children 3 and under stay free in parent's room. AE, DC, MC, V. Free parking. **Amenities:** Restaurant; bar; pool. *In room:* A/C, TV, minibar.

Hotel Onda Verde Perched on a cliff, this friendly hotel occupies several buildings connected by flights of steps. Guest rooms vary in shape and style but are uniform in amenities and service, although some are more conveniently located than others. They are tasteful and well appointed, with modern furniture, tiled floors, and good-size bathrooms (some with shower only); each room has a small, private terrace with a panoramic view. Via more steps, you can descend to the "beach"—a few chairs on the rocks —from which you can swim into the sea.

Via Terramare 3, Marina di Praia, 84010 Praiano. www.ondaverde.it. ☏ **089-874143.** Fax 089-8131049. 25 units. 210€–230€ double; 250€–270€ triple; 280€ quad. Rates include buffet breakfast. Children 2 and under stay free in parent's room. AE, DC, MC, V. Free parking. Closed Nov–Mar. **Amenities:** Restaurant; bar; Wi-Fi (free). *In room:* A/C, TV, minibar.

Hotel Tramonto D'oro ☺ The name of this family-run hotel means "Golden Sunset," and the end-of-day views are indeed superb. Right on the SS 163, it is convenient to the SITA bus, and the warm service and good amenities—including a swimming pool on the terrace, a gym, and free shuttle to the beach—make it a popular choice, often for groups. Guest rooms are spacious and individually decorated, with modern light woods and tiled floors. Bathrooms are good-size (some with shower only). We recommend upgrading to the best rooms, which offer the best sea views and are filled with light. The hotel's **restaurant,** with a panoramic terrace affording spectacular views, serves lip-smacking food (closed Nov–Feb).

Via Gennaro Capriglione 119 (SS 163), 84010 Praiano. www.tramontodoro.it. ℭ **089-874955.** Fax 089-874670. 40 units. 160€–290€ double; 260€–360€ triple; 300€–420€ quad. Rates include buffet breakfast. Children 3 and under stay free in parent's room. AE, DC, MC, V. Free parking. **Amenities:** Restaurant; bar; concierge; gym; pool; sauna. *In room:* A/C, TV, minibar.

INEXPENSIVE

Hotel Margherita ★ ☺ 👔 A high standard of rooms and reasonable prices make this family-run hotel very popular. The swimming pool and panoramic terraces make great spots to lounge, and the beach is only a few minutes' away. Bedrooms are comfortable and well appointed, with tiled floors, traditional painted furniture, and good-size bathrooms (some with shower only). Each opens onto a private balcony: The best have sea views while others look onto the lemon grove. The hotel's **restaurant** prepares excellent local cuisine.

Via Umberto I 70 (off Via Roma [SS 163]), 84010 Praiano. www.hotelmargherita.it. ℭ **089-874628.** 28 units. 110€–150€ double; 160€ triple; 180€ quad. Rates include breakfast. Children 2 and under stay free in parent's room. AE, DC, MC, V. Free parking. **Amenities:** Restaurant; bar; pool; room service; smoke-free rooms. *In room:* A/C, TV, Internet, minibar.

Il Pino This family-run hotel is prized by locals for the sea views from its pleasant terrace, and for the good food in its moderately priced **restaurant,** which offers a menu of enticing local favorites. Above the restaurant, the bright, spacious guest rooms are simply furnished but welcoming with private terraces and sea views, tiled floors, and comfortable-size bathrooms (some with shower only).

Via Gennaro Capriglione 13 (SS 163), 84010 Praiano. www.hotelilpino.it. ℭ /fax **089-874389.** 17 units. 160€ double; 180€ triple; 200€ quad. Rates include breakfast. Children 2 and under stay free in parent's room. AE, DC, MC, V. Free parking. Closed Nov–Mar. **Amenities:** Restaurant; bar. *In room:* A/C, TV.

Where to Eat

In addition to the excellent choices below, we recommend the hotel restaurants of **Il Pino, Margherita,** and **Tramonto d'Oro,** as well as the restaurant **La Cala delle Lampare,** in the Grand Hotel Tritone (see "Where to Stay," above).

EXPENSIVE

Un Piano nel Cielo ★★ CREATIVE AMALFITAN In line with the decor in the rest of the hotel (p. 205), Casa Angelina's gourmet restaurant is a study in sleek, contemporary chic. Situated on the top floor of the building, the views from the indoor dining room through vast picture windows and from the terrace are magnificent. Those views combined with the superb food and slick service make for a memorable dining experience. The seasonal menu is based on traditional, local dishes to which the chef adds a clever, creative twist. We were impressed by monkfish wrapped in bacon on a bed of baby broad beans, *paccheri* with mixed seafood served with broccoli purée, and local tuna filet prepared with an orange lacquer. Leave room for dessert; we recommend the warm chocolate soufflé and the pistachio mousse. The wine list is a huge, comprehensive volume with bottles from all over Italy and beyond, but we advise sampling one of the excellent local wines; the knowledgeable sommelier will help you choose.

Via Gennaro Capriglione 147 (SS 163). ☎ **089-8131333.** www.unpianonelcielo.it. Reservations recommended. Secondi 20€–36€. AE, DC, MC, V. Daily 1–3pm and 7:30–10:30pm. Closed Nov–Easter

INEXPENSIVE

La Brace ★★ AMALFITAN/PIZZA In the perfect location to enjoy the beautiful scenery, this is our favorite restaurant in Praiano. The food is excellent and moderately priced, and the hosts are delightful. The seasonal menu includes many simple home-cooked dishes, based on the market offering of seafood, meat, and veggies. The homemade pastas are to die for—try the fusilli *con provola, melanzane, e basilico* (with provola cheese, sautéed eggplant, and fresh basil)—and so is the tasty grilled fish. The desserts are strictly homemade and deliciously traditional. The pizza—only served in the evenings—is also superb.

Via Gennaro Capriglione 146 (SS 163). ☎ **089-874226.** Reservations recommended. Secondi 9€–20€; pizza 5€–10€. AE, DC, MC, V. Thurs–Tues 12:30–3pm and 7:30–11:30pm (also Wed Apr–Sept).

A *liutai* at work at Bottega Scala.

Shopping

Do you have a musician in the family? You might not have thought of purchasing a musical instrument while on your vacation, but once you've visited this artisans' workshop, you might change your mind. At **Bottega Scala** ★★, Via Umberto I 68A (☎ **089-874894;** www.liuteria scala.com), the *liutai* (stringed instruments makers) Pasquale and Leonardo Scala create instruments using traditional techniques. They specialize in classical guitars but also make reproductions of early stringed instruments that date from medieval and baroque times and their famous clients include Pino Daniele.

Praiano after Dark

For a good evening out and a historic pilgrimage, we suggest a visit to **L'Africana** ★★, off SS 163 in Vettica Maggiore; take the elevator down to the seashore (☎ **339-2025267**). This popular nightclub was a mythical hangout during the *anni ruggenti* (roaring years)

of the 1960s, when it was the destination of choice of VIPs and their trendy friends. Set in a grotto right above the lapping sea, it re-opened in July 2011 after a three-year "rest" and is experiencing something of a revival. Don't be surprised if fishermen pull their nets up from the sea just beyond the edge of the dance floor; their fresh catch is what's on tomorrow's menus in town. The club is open Tuesday to Sunday from 9pm (closed Oct–Apr).

AMALFI

34km (21 miles) W of Salerno; 61km (38 miles) SE of Naples

Once a glorious Maritime Republic, Amalfi today is a busy tourist resort with a picturesque old center and a magnificent setting against the steep slopes of the Valle dei Mulini. Its bustling seafront and lively piazza give the place more energy than most of the other towns on the coast, and its central location makes it a popular base for exploring the area.

Beaches There are two narrow, often-crowded **beaches** on either side of the harbor, but for something more substantial, head east to nearby **Atrani.** To the west of the town there is a series of quieter coves and small beaches where the clear water is perfect for swimming.

Things to Do With its lively central **piazza** and atmospheric old streets, Amalfi is perfect for aimless wandering. Sights include the Arabo-Norman style **Duomo,** the small **Museo Civico,** and the **Museo della Carta** documenting the town's papermaking history. Shoppers should ignore the touristy goods in the stores lining the main drag and head for the artisan papermakers' shops for handmade **Amalfi Paper.**

Eating & Drinking The town is set among terraced lemon groves where the famous **Limoni di Amalfi** are cultivated and used in dishes such as *risotto al limone, granita di limone,* sugary-sweet *delizie al limone,* and the ubiquitous *limoncello.* Fish and seafood dominate menus here and the town's restaurants that range from elegant, Michelin-stared **La Caravella** to simple beachside trattorie.

Nature The best way to explore the ins and outs of this stretch of coast is by **hiring a boat.** For the more energetic, there are several excellent **hikes;** one of the easiest passes along the **Valle dei Mulini.** A more substantial hike is the bewitching **Via degli Incanti** which links Amalfi to Positano.

Essentials

GETTING THERE The **bus** is an easy option, with **SITA** (*℘* **089-405145;** www. sitabus.it) offering frequent service from Naples, Sorrento, Positano, Vietri, and Salerno (for more information on fares, see "The Unico Travel Pass," p. 349). For the best views, remember to sit on the right side of the bus when traveling from Sorrento and the left side from Vietri and Salerno. Amalfi is the largest harbor in the area after Salerno and is well served by **ferries** and hydrofoils. The **Metrò del Mare** (*℘* **199-600700;** www.metrodelmare. net) offers a regular service from Naples, Sorrento, Positano, Salerno, and other harbors along the coast. Fares vary depending on the distance, from 9€ from Positano to 18€ from Pozzuoli. In 2011, the schedule was reduced to a minimum service for July and August, but we are told that a fuller

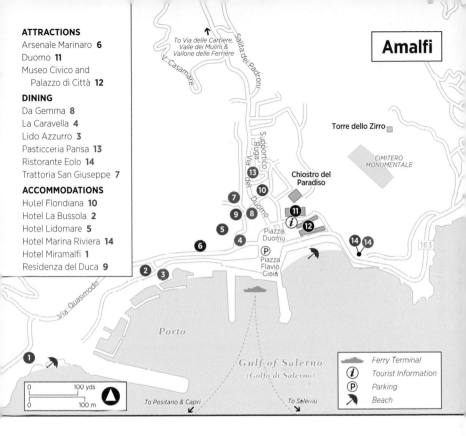

ATTRACTIONS
Arsenale Marinaro **6**
Duomo **11**
Museo Civico and
  Palazzo di Città **12**

DINING
Da Gemma **8**
La Caravella **4**
Lido Azzurro **3**
Pasticceria Pansa **13**
Ristorante Eolo **14**
Trattoria San Giuseppe **7**

ACCOMMODATIONS
Hotel Floridiana **10**
Hotel La Bussola **2**
Hotel Lidomare **5**
Hotel Marina Riviera **14**
Hotel Miramalfi **1**
Residenza del Duca **9**

Amalfi

To Via delle Cartiere,
Valle dei Mulini &
Vallone delle Ferriere

Torre dello Zirro

CIMITERO
MONUMENTALE

Chiostro del
Paradiso

Piazza
Duomo

Piazza
Flavio
Gioia

163

Porto

Gulf of Salerno
(Golfo di Salerno)

To Positano & Capri

To Salerno

0 — 100 yds
0 — 100 m

Ferry Terminal
Tourist Information
Parking
Beach

service will be restored in 2012. Amalfi-based **Cooperativa Sant'Andrea** (© **089-873190;** www.coopsantandrea.it) offers regular service from Capri, Minori, Positano, Salerno, and Sorrento, as well as special cruises and excursions; fares vary with the distance, from 6€ to about 16€.

    LMP (© **081-8071812;** www.consorziolmp.it) maintains *aliscafo* (hydrofoil) and *motonave* (ferry) services between Amalfi and Capri. **Travelmar** (© **081-7041911;** www.travelmar.it) makes runs between Salerno, Amalfi, Minori, Maiori, and Positano during the summer. Fares are 10€ to 18€ for both companies.

    From the Naples Capodichino Airport, **taxis** offer a flat rate of 130€ to Amalfi. **Car services** (see "Getting Around," below) also offer transfers from Naples's airport or train station. Alternatively, private company **Curreri Viaggi** (© **081-8015420;** www.curreriviaggi.it) offers a shuttle service from the airport for 150€ for one to three passengers and 12€ for each additional passenger.

    By **train** (© **892021** in Italy; www.trenitalia.it), the closest station is **Vietri sul Mare,** on the local line between **Naples** (where you'll change trains, if you are coming from the north) and **Salerno** (if you are coming from the south). Faster, though, is to get off in Salerno and take a SITA bus or a taxi directly to Amalfi.

By car, take the autostrada A3 toward NAPOLI-SALERNO to the exit for VIETRI SUL MARE, then follow the signs for VIETRI, AMALFI; they will lead you to the famed SS 163 that hugs the Amalfi Coast. You can also reach SS 163 from Castellammare di Stabia, Piana di Sorrento, Vico Equense, and Sorrento, heading east and following signs for POSITANO and AMALFI— scenic but longer. *Note:* Because of the solid traffic here in summer, local authorities occasionally limit car access to the SS 163; check with the tourist office and your hotel before making plans.

GETTING AROUND The boat companies mentioned above offer transfers to nearby harbors. The **SITA terminal** on Piazza Flavio Gioia (✆ 089 405145) is the hub for all the local **bus lines.** Adjacent to the terminal is the **taxi stand** (✆ 089-872239).

VISITOR INFORMATION The **tourist office** (✆ 089-871107; www.amalfi touristoffice.it) is in Palazzo di Città, Corso delle Repubbliche Marinare 19, 84011 Amalfi. It is open Monday through Friday 9am to 1pm and 2 to 6pm, Sat 9am to noon. In winter, it is only open in the mornings.

You'll find a **pharmacy** at Piazza dei Dogi (✆ 089-871063). The closest **hospital** is in Salerno (see "Visitor Information," p. 283); for an **ambulance,** dial ✆ 118. The **police** can be reached at ✆ 113 or 112. The **post office** (✆ 089-8304811) is at Via delle Repubbliche Marinare, next to the tourist office, and is open Monday to Saturday 8am to 2pm. Next door, you will find a Deutsche Bank **ATM. Amalfi Servizi Express,** Piazza dei Dogi 8 (✆ 089-873447; www.amalfiservizi.it), has Internet access.

SPECIAL EVENTS On the first Sunday of June, the **Historic Regatta of the Maritime Republics** is held, hosted in turn by each of the four historical towns—Genova, Pisa, Venice, and Amalfi. Amalfi's turn was in 2009 and will come again in 2013. Civic pride and thousand-year-old rivalries are at stake, and the boat races are run with pomp, athleticism, and great seriousness. The spectacular, colorful event is accompanied by parades and musical performances.

Exploring the Town

Set among terraces of lemon groves and olive trees that slope down to the sea, and built up the sides of a deep ravine, Amalfi is a jewel of a small town, full of momentos of its glorious past. Its central square, **Piazza Flavio Gioia,** lies just outside the old town walls and opens onto the harbor: It commemorates the inventor of the compass, or at least the man who perfected it for marine use. Indeed, Amalfi's mariners were the first in Europe to use the properties of magnetism for navigation, starting back in the 12th century; they provided material for the first nautical charts of the Middle Ages.

The medieval heart of Amalfi, characterized by covered porticos and narrow streets, stretches

---

🎁 Amalfi by the Book

Amalfi is best known to English readers from John Webster's masterpiece, *The Duchess of Malfi* (1623). This bloody tale of love, lust, and murder captures the scandalous side of Renaissance court life; what's more, it may actually be true. The original source is the **Novelle** of the Dominican priest Matteo Bandello (1485–1561), who served several courts and no doubt knew whereof he spoke.

Piazza Flavio Gioia.

from **Piazza Duomo** along **Via Genova** and **Via Capuano.** To get a flavor of the place, stroll under the Supportico Sant'Andrea Apostolo till you reach Largo Filippo Augustariccio. There, a characteristic Arab-style trilobate arch leads into another covered passage, Campo de Cinnamellis, the seat, in medieval times, of Amalfi's spice market.

Be sure to visit the **Convento di San Francesco**—now the Hotel Luna Convento (p. 215)—where you can see the well-preserved 13th-century cloister and attached church. Its 16th-century watchtower overlooks the bay to the east of town and is an annex of the hotel.

Arsenale Marinaro It was here, at the Republic of Amalfi's shipyard, that the vessels which maintained power over the Mediterranean in the Middle Ages were constructed. Established in the 11th century, the shipyard was restored in the 13th century and in its heyday it produced galleys up to 40m (131 ft.) long. Only half of the building remains today —the other half, which reached into the sea, was destroyed by a series of storms in the 14th century. No matter; you can still see the building's beautiful architecture, with its pointed arches and cross vaults resting on stone pillars. Between the Arsenale and the Porta della Marina is a tile panel depicting Amalfi's commercial empire in the Middle Ages; it was created by the artist Renato Rossi in the 1950s.

Via Matteo Camera (off Piazza Flavio Gioia). Free admission. Easter–Sept 9am–8pm.

Duomo ★★ This superb example of Arabo-Norman architecture dates to the 9th century, when the Republic of Amalfi was just rising to power. The majestic facade is decorated with a mosaic of gold leaf and majolica; the magnificent **bronze doors ★★** were made in Constantinple in the 11th century, and the lovely Romanesque bell tower was finished in 1276. The Duomo was enlarged between the 16th and 18th centuries, when it was also given a baroque interior; the steep, imposing external staircase leading to the beautiful atrium in black-

and-white marble also dates from this time. Restoration in 1929 removed the baroque excesses and restored the interior to something near its 13th-century state.

From the left-hand end of the porch, you enter the breathtakingly beautiful **Chiostro del Paradiso ★★★**, dating from 1266. The cloister, in Arab-Sicilian style, is decorated with interlaced arches over double columns and was originally built as the cemetery for the city's religious and political elite. The site now holds a small museum with ancient Roman and medieval artifacts. Among the best pieces are the **Roman sarcophagus of Ottavio Rufo ★**, richly carved with bas-reliefs, and two other sarcophagi. From the cloister, you enter the **Cappella del Crocifisso,** the original cathedral of Amalfi dating from the 10th century, where other artworks are preserved. July through September, concerts are held in the cloister on Friday nights (see "Amalfi After Dark," later in this chapter).

From the right nave of the Cappella, you can climb down to the **Crypt,** the repository for the remains of the apostle St. Andrew, the protector saint of Amalfi. It

The Chiostro del Paradiso in the Duomo.

was built in the 13th c., when the remains of the saint were brought back from the 4th Crusade; it was redecorated in 1719. Over the main altar is the beautiful bronze **Statue of Sant'Andrea** by Michelangelo Naccherino.

Piazza del Duomo, 84011 Amalfi. **Duomo:** ✆ **089-871059.** Free admission. Nov–Feb daily 10am–5pm; Mar–Oct 9am–9pm. **Museum and cloister:** ✆ **089-871324.** Free admission.

Museo Civico & Palazzo di Città The Palazzo di Città is Amalfi's Town Hall. On its southern wall hangs a famous **Pannello in ceramica ★**, a majolica panel relating key moments in Amalfi's history. Created in the 1970s by artist Diodoro Cossa, it is made of two large colored tiles, which you can read from left to right. In the Town Hall, the **museum** is interesting mostly for local history buffs. It contains, however, one very important piece: the *Tabula Amalphitana,* the original maritime code written around the end of the 11th or beginning of the 12th centuries to regulate maritime traffic in the Mediterranean (this was enforced till at least the 16th century). The original code was lost, but many copies were made at the time, one of which ended up in Austria. This was acquired by the Italian government in 1929 and donated to the town of Amalfi. Also interesting are the original pastel drawings for the Duomo's mosaics by Domenico Morelli.

Piazza Municipio. ✆ **089-8736211.** www.comune.amalfi.sa.it. Free admission. Mon–Fri 8am–1pm.

Museo della Carta (Museum of Paper) This museum is the perfect place to learn more about the history of the local paper industry. Housed in one of the abandoned paper mills, the museum has a wonderful collection of original tools

AMALFI & THE INDUSTRY OF papermaking

Amalfi is believed to be the first place in Europe to make paper in the form that we know it today. The process was discovered by the Arabs and perfected in the town of El-Marubig, where the original name *bambagina* referred to the special kind of paper that was to become known as *paper of Amalfi*. This was made from recycled cotton, linen, and hemp cloths. The process was then exported to Amalfi through the close commercial relationship the republic had with the Arab world. Considered less durable than parchment, paper was still forbidden in 1250 for public use, but the industry developed rapidly and Amalfi sold its paper far and wide throughout the Middle Ages and the Renaissance. Paper continued to be made by hand until the 18th century, when machines were finally introduced; at that time there were 16 paper mills in the area, 10 of which are still active today. The cloths (or rags) were reduced to a poultice in large vats and then strained in forms marked with the symbol of the paper mill. The paper was then pressed between layers of woolen felt to extract excess water, air dried, and finally "ironed." It may have been considered inferior to parchment or vellum, but this paper was of high quality: The oldest sheets still in existence date from the 13th and 14th centuries. The *bambagina* of Amalfi is still highly prized; the Vatican, for example, uses Amalfi paper for its correspondence.

If you wish to visit one of the working mills, **Cartiera Amatruda,** Via delle Cartiere 100 (© **089-871315;** www. amatruda.it), is still run by the original family, who welcomes visitors and will give you a tour of their facilities. **Antonio Cavaliere** (pictured), Via del Giudice 2 (© **089-871954**), one of the descendants of the ancient master papermakers, is another, smaller option. Antonio's specialty is paper made with real dried flowers as filigree, ideal for very special letters.

Both shops produce paper of an almost forgotten quality, made completely by hand, which is sold to the most exclusive paper shops in Italy, Europe, and the U.S. The water for this craft still comes from the covered river that crosses town and was the key resource in the development of Amalfi's paper industry. Both workshops are open regular business hours.

and machines and also maintains a library with over 3,000 texts on the origins of paper. There is also a gift shop.

Palazzo Pagliara, Via delle Cartiere 24. © **089-8304561.** www.museodellacarta.it. Admission 4€. Nov–Mar Tues–Sun 10am–3pm; Apr–Nov daily 10am–6:30pm.

BUS TOURS

City Sightseeing Sorrento, Via degli Aranci 172, 80067 Sorrento (℃ 081-8774707; www.sorrento.city-sightseeing.it), has partnered with SITA to offer tours on open-deck buses on two different routes: one along the coast to Minori and Maiori and one inland to Ravello. Buses depart hourly from Piazza Flavio Gioia in Amalfi (one ride 3€; day pass, valid for four rides on the Amalfi-Maiori line and one round-trip on the Ravello-Amalfi line, 10€).

OUTDOOR ACTIVITIES

Amalfi used to have large **beaches,** but sea erosion and landslides have reduced the beach to two narrow strips on either side of the harbor. Most hotels on the waterfront have small private beaches carved out of the cliffs. For a larger stretch of sand, take the footpath to Atrani, an easy 15-minute stroll eastward.

From the harbor at **Marina Grande** you can rent **boats**—with or without skipper—to explore the nooks and crannies of the coast. **Cooperativa Sant'Andrea** (℃ 089-873190; www.coopsantandrea.it) offers regular service to the beaches of Duoglio and Santa Croce, only a few minutes' away from Molo Pennello; boats leave every 30 minutes between 9am and 5pm. It also serves **Grotta dello Smeraldo ★★** in Conca dei Marini (p. 230), leaving every hour between 9:30am and 3:30pm (10€ round-trip).

Amalfi is a great starting point for a number of beautiful **hikes.** The most popular is the pleasant and easy walk along **Valle dei Mulini (Valley of the Mills) ★,** which is the valley of the Torrente Canneto, Amalfi's small river. This valley has been declared a World Heritage Site by UNESCO, precisely because of its unique environment. Head up Via Genova from Piazza del Duomo where the street turns into a picturesque trail that leads to the area known as the **Mulino Rovinato (Ruined Mill),** about 1 hour away. The namesake flour mills were put out of business by the development of the pasta industry farther north, where the conditions were more favorable. In contrast, the paper mills continued to prosper, and some are still active today. Continuing up, you'll reach the more demanding trail through the **Vallone delle Ferriere ★★**. The going is good but quite steep as you near the ancient *ferriere* (iron mills), with their imposing walls partly hidden by growth. Already extant in the Middle Ages, they were active until the 19th century. Those in good shape can climb even farther up to the waterfalls; the ascent is short but steep. Allow 6 hours for the round-trip on the 12km (7.5-mile) trail.

Less demanding but still highly rewarding is the famous *Via degli Incanti* **(Trail of Charms) ★★** that connects Amalfi to Positano. The trail is indeed bewitching, wending through the cultivated terraces and citrus groves of the Amalfi countryside. The hike is moderate, with some taxing passages, but, due to its length, most people choose to do only a section of it, or do the whole trip over several days. The best views are heading west, though the footing will be a bit more hazardous. From the Valle dei Mulini above, take the trail to the left, climbing through the outskirts of town to Pogerola. Continuing up and left, you'll reach San Lazzaro. From here, the path procedes to Bomerano, where you'll join the section of the trek called the **Sentiero degli Dei ★★★**. You'll then continue to Montepertuso, before descending to Positano.

Where to Stay

VERY EXPENSIVE

Hotel Santa Caterina ★★★ This is the most luxurious hotel in Amalfi (and indeed one of the best of the coast), offering top-notch, family-run service and a superb cliff-side location. Guests have access to a private beach, which you can reach by elevator or a winding garden path; the pleasant swimming pool is filled with seawater and is set in luscious gardens. Guest rooms are spread throughout the main building and three annexes. All are large and elegant, with antique furnishings, ceramic tiles from Vietri, and luxurious bathrooms (some with shower only). Each opens to a private balcony or terrace with views over the sea. Some of the suites are absolutely fantastic—we loved the luxurious Follia Amalfitana and Casa dell'Arancio in particular; they are independent bungalows immersed in a citrus grove, with a private garden and a small pool. At the **Ristorante Santa Caterina ★★** (p. 217) you can sample sophisticated local dishes while the **Ristorante a Mare ★**, laid out on a terrace above the beach, offers more casual dining (open during the summer months only).

Via Nazionale 9, 84011 Amalfi. www.hotelsantacaterina.it. ℂ **089-871012.** Fax 089-871351. 49 units. 420€–790€ double; from 930€ suite. Rates include buffet breakfast. AE, DC, MC, V. Parking 15€. **Amenities.** 2 restaurants; bar; concierge; gym; pool; room service; spa. *In room:* A/C, TV, Internet, minibar.

EXPENSIVE

Hotel Luna Convento ★★ Transformed into a hotel in 1822, the Luna Convento occupies the ancient monastery, complete with beautiful original cloister and church, founded by Saint Francis in 1222, and Amalfi's watchtower dating from 1564. Situated on the promontory that protects Amalfi's harbor and only 273m (896 ft.) from the town's center, this family-run place counts Henrik Ibsen (who wrote *A Doll's House* here in 1879) among its famous guests. The space remains as artistically inspiring as ever: The hotel is surrounded by a garden, with sun terraces and a large seawater swimming pool carved out of the cliff. There is also a private, rather rocky beach and a highly praised gourmet restaurant, where you have to make reservations long in advance. The watchtower houses a disco and piano bar, as well as another restaurant with fantastic views. Guest rooms vary in size and decor, but all are bright and spacious, with sweeping vistas, and spacious tiled bathrooms: We advise paying the extra for a private terrace.

Via Pantaleone Comite 33, 84011 Amalfi. www.lunahotel.it. ℂ **089-871002.** Fax 089-871333. 48 units. 250€–340€ double; from 440€ suite. Rates include buffet breakfast. Children 2 and under stay free in parent's room. AE, DC, MC, V. Parking 18€. **Amenities:** 2 restaurants; bar; babysitting; concierge; outdoor pool; room service. *In room:* A/C, TV, hair dryer, minibar.

Hotel Marina Riviera ★ ☺ With a great location above Amalfi's easternmost bay, this hotel has both views and proximity to the harbor and historic district. Guest rooms are not large, but are bright and pleasant, with Vietri tiled floors and simple furnishings. All enjoy sea views, and better rooms open onto private balconies or terraces. Bathrooms are a good size (some with shower only). The hotel's restaurant is **Eolo** (p. 218).

Via Pantaleone Comite 19, 84011 Amalfi. www.marinariviera.it. ℂ **089-871104.** Fax 089-871024. 34 units. 260€–340€ double; 400€ junior suite; from 500€ suite. Rates include buffet breakfast. AE, DC, MC, V. Parking 15€. Closed Nov–Mar. **Amenities:** Restaurant; bar; babysitting; concierge. *In room:* A/C, TV, Internet, minibar.

Hotel Miramalfi On a rocky point west of town, this family-run hotel offers attractive rooms and views in every direction. It has its own private beach, as well as a pool (accessible by elevator) and a cookery school. There is also a free shuttle-bus service into town. Guest rooms are welcoming, modern in style, and have good-size bathrooms (most with shower only); all have balconies and views overlooking the sea, but the best are the front-facing ones with large terraces. Lunch is served in a new restaurant set just above the beach.

Via Salvatore Quasimodo 3, 84011 Amalfi. www.miramalfi.it. © **089-871588.** Fax 089-871287. 49 units. 270€–330€ double; 500€ suite. Rates include breakfast. Internet specials available. Children 2 and under stay free in parent's room. AE, DC, MC, V. Parking 15€. **Amenities:** Restaurant; bar; concierge; pool; room service; Wi-Fi (free). *In room:* A/C, TV, minibar.

MODERATE

Hotel La Bussola ★ We like this welcoming hotel right on the beach by the harbor, with its clean lines and decor, and eco-friendly policies. A great example of industrial architecture, La Bussola occupies the former Pastificio Bergamasco, a historic pasta-making factory. A short walk away from the medieval town, it offers pleasant accommodations and kind, professional service. Guest rooms are bright and comfortable, with colorful tiled floors, and modern bathrooms (some with shower only). Most rooms open onto private balconies, with the better ones enjoying full ocean views. Standards do not have A/C, and only some have balconies and minibars; it is worth paying the extra 10€ to upgrade to a "class A" room or above. The **restaurant** ★ is excellent and focuses on seafood.

Lungomare dei Cavalieri 16, 84011 Amalfi. www.labussolahotel.it. © **089-871533.** Fax 089-871369. 64 units. 120€–250€ double. Rates include buffet breakfast. Children 2 and under stay free in parent's room. AE, DC, MC, V. Parking 10€. **Amenities:** Restaurant; bar; Wi-Fi (2€/30 min.). *In room:* A/C (in most), TV, minibar (in most).

Residenza del Duca 🏠 We highly recommend this tiny welcoming hotel housed in a lovingly restored 16th-century *palazzo* in the medieval part of town. Each guest room opens onto its own balcony or small terrace, with views either over the sea or of the medieval district, and has its own character, with wooden beams, replicas of the original ceramic tiles, original architectural details, and period furniture. Families might consider renting one of two self-catering apartments detached from the hotel.

Via Duca Mastalo II 3, Amalfi. www.residencedelduca.it. ©/fax **089-8736365.** Fax 089-8736550. 5 units. 120€–160€ double. Rates include buffet breakfast. Children 2 and under stay free in parent's room. AE, MC, V. Parking 16€–20€. *In room:* A/C, TV, hair dryer, minibar.

INEXPENSIVE

Hotel Floridiana 🗝 Only steps from the Duomo and not far from the harbor, this hotel occupies an elegant palazzo dating back to the 12th century: The central location combined with value for money makes it an attractive option. Guest rooms are a good size (particularly the "superior") and welcoming, nicely done with Vietri ceramic tiles and a mix of modern and classic furnishings. Bathrooms are a good size (most with shower only). Breakfast is served in a vaulted hall decorated with original frescoes. The hotel is on a side street only accessible on foot. Its garage is nearby, though, and your luggage can be collected at no extra expense.

Via Brancia 1, 84011 Amalfi. www.hotelfloridiana.it. © **089-8736373.** Fax 089-873907. 36 units. 140€–170€ double; 170€ suite. Rates include buffet breakfast. Children 2 and under stay free in parent's room. AE, DC, MC, V. Free parking. **Amenities:** Restaurant; bar. *In room:* A/C, TV, minibar, Wi-Fi.

Hotel Lidomare ✦ This small family-run hotel in a 13th-century building is a good budget choice, offering friendly service in the heart of the *centro storico*, just steps from the Duomo and not far from the beach. Guest rooms are pleasant, with bright tiled floors and a mix of modern furniture and antiques. The small bathrooms (some with shower only) are perfectly kept. A room upgrade will get you more space, sea views, and a Jacuzzi tub.

Largo Duchi Piccolomini 9 (off Piazza Duomo), 84011 Amalfi. www.lidomare.it. ✆ **089-871332.** Fax 089-871394. 15 units. 145€ double; 165€ triple; 190€ quad. Rates include breakfast. Children 2 and under stay free in parent's room. AE, MC, V. Parking 15€. *In room:* A/C, TV, minibar, Wi-Fi (3€/hour).

Where to Eat

In addition to those below, we recommend **La Bussola** ★ (p. 216). For desserts and other sweets, do not miss the historic **Pasticceria Pansa** ★★, Piazza Duomo 40 (✆ **089-871065;** www.pasticceriapansa.it; closed Tues).

EXPENSIVE

La Caravella ★★★ MODERN AMALFITAN Do not expect sea views in this temple of cuisine, where guests are not to be distracted by such frivolities as a sunset. A successful advocate of the marriage between classic and modern culinary traditions, Chef Antonio Dipino offers a seasonal menu with both elaborate and simple dishes prepared only with the freshest local ingredients; his skill earned him the first Michelin star to be awarded in southern Italy. Great attention is paid to service and setting, and you'll be surrounded by sober elegance in the dining hall of this 12th-century palazzo. Go with the tasting menu, or order a la carte: The seaweed fritters are excellent, followed by *tubetti di Gragnano al ragù di zuppa di pesce* (short pasta in a seafood sauce) and a superb *pezzogna* (fresh local fish). Those who prefer meat may favor *ziti di Torre Annunziata ripieni di carne alla Genovese* (pasta tubes filled with beef). The desserts and the wine list are on par with the rest of the menu. To celebrate its 50th year, La Caravella also opened an art gallery and wine bar near the restaurant.

Via Matteo Camera 12. ✆ **089-871029.** www.ristorantelacaravella.it. Reservations required. Secondi 25€–35€; tasting menu 90€. AE, DC, MC, V. Wed–Mon noon–2pm and 7:30–11pm. Closed Nov and Jan.

Ristorante Santa Caterina ★★ CREATIVE AMALFITAN This wonderful restaurant has gained international praise and is now competing with the best restaurants on this stretch of coast. Located in the beautiful Hotel Santa Caterina, it enjoys a glorious setting that well matches the gourmet food: We recommend the delicate *ravioli di zucchine al limone con formaggio fresco di bufala* (zucchini and buffalo ricotta ravioli) as well as the buckwheat tagliatelle with shrimp and eggplant. The excellent meat selection includes great steaks and filet mignon.

Via Nazionale 9. ✆ **089-871012.** Fax 089-871351. www.hotelsantacaterina.it. Reservations required. Secondi 28€–38€. AE, DC, MC, V. Daily 1–3pm and 7:30–10:30pm.

MODERATE

Da Gemma AMALFITAN This upscale yet relaxed restaurant has been serving customers for over a century and has racked up sheaves of reviews attesting to its quality. One of the most famous specialties is *paccheri con gamberetti* (thick pasta tubes with shrimp). *Zuppa di pesce* (fish stew), which comes in a two-person portion, is another winner. Don't forget to try the typical Amalfian side dish known as *ciambotta* (a mix of sautéed potatoes, peppers, and eggplant). Half portions are available for children.

Via Frà Gerardo Sasso 11. ℂ **089-871345.** www.trattoriadagemma.com. Reservations required. Secondi 16€–26€. AE, DC, MC, V. Daily 12:30–2:45pm and 7:30–11pm (closed Wed Nov to mid April). Closed 6 weeks starting in Jan.

Ristorante Eolo ★ CREATIVE AMALFITAN The welcoming dining room and romantic terrace of the hotel **Marina Riviera**'s (p. 218) restaurant is the perfect setting for the gourmet meal that awaits you. The accent is on seafood, and the seasonal menu offers innovative dishes based on the local culinary traditions. Portions are small, but the food is delicious. We recommend the *seppie ripiene* (stuffed cuttlefish) as well as the *cannelloni di mare* (homemade pasta filled with seafood).

Via Pantaleone Comite 3. ℂ **089-871241.** www.eoloamalfi.it. Reservations recommended. Secondi 28€–35€ AE, DC, MC, V. Wed–Mon 12:30–3pm and 7:30–10:30pm. Summer Wed–Mon 7:30–11pm. Closed Nov–Mar.

INEXPENSIVE

'a Paranza ★★ AMALFITAN This simple trattoria is our favorite restaurant in the area. Popular for its well-prepared seafood and moderate prices, it is hidden away off the main street of Atrani—the village adjacent to Amalfi to the east—and does not have sea views or an outside terrace, but the wonderful food makes up for this. The traditional cuisine focuses on the best local ingredients. We recommend starting off with the house antipasti (almost a meal in itself) but other standouts include delicious *scialatielli alla paranza* (homemade pasta with small fish), *polipetti in cassuola* (baby octopus stewed in a terra-cotta pot), or *scampi al limone* (prawns in lemon sauce). Do not miss the homemade desserts such as the pear and ricotta tart. The wine list is short but includes excellent local labels.

Via Dragone 1–2, Atrani. ℂ **089-871840.** www.ristoranteparanza.com. Reservations recommended. Secondi 12€–23€. AE, DC, MC, V. Wed–Mon 12:30–3pm and 7:30–11:30pm (also Tues in summer). Closed 2 weeks in Dec.

Lido Azzurro ★ AMALFITAN This simple restaurant has a prime spot on the town's seaside promenade and great views from its terrace. The menu includes many kinds of pasta with seafood—*tubetti zucchine, vongole e cozze* (short pasta with clams, mussels, and zucchini) is good. We recommend the catch of the day either baked in a potato crust, or *all'acquapazza* (in a light tomato broth).

Lungomare dei Cavalieri. ℂ **089-871384.** Reservations recommended Sat–Sun. Secondi 15€–22€. AE, DC, MC, V. Tues–Sun 12:30–3pm and 7:30–10:30pm. Closed mid-Jan to mid-Mar.

Trattoria San Giuseppe 📬 AMALFITAN/PIZZA Hidden away in the medieval part of town, this simple, down-to-earth place is a real local hangout. It's a great alternative to upscale dining, and the traditional meals include a variety of solid pasta dishes. For our money, the excellent pizza (served only in the evenings) is the best in town.

Salita Ruggiero II 4. ℂ **089-872640.** Reservations recommended Sat–Sun. Secondi 8€–19€; pizza 6€–9€. MC, V. Fri–Wed noon–2:30pm and 7:30–10:30pm.

christmas **ON THE AMALFI COAST**

Christmas *(Natale)*, when twinkling lights and decorations make even the smallest hamlets atmospheric, is always a special time in Italy. *Natale* on the Amalfi Coast is unique in its own way; the already picturesque villages and towns become truly magical with Christmas illumination, and you will find elaborate *presepi* (Nativity scenes, or creches) everywhere. However, besides the more traditional location inside churches—such as the 10th-century church of **Santa Maria** **Maggiore,** whose very fine *presepi* dates from its redecoration in the 18th century (Largo S. Maria Maggiore, Amalfi)—*presepi* are placed in fountains and in grottos. Perhaps the most important of these is the one inside **Grotta dello Smeraldo,** in Conca dei Marini (see "Conca dei Marini," p. 230), which stages a procession on December 24, and again on January 6 (Epiphany). Call the visitor center in Amalfi at ✆ **089-871107** for more information.

Amalfi After Dark

Summer is entertainment time in Amalfi, and musical events are held throughout town. Among the most striking are the piano and vocal concerts held in the **Chiostro del Paradiso** (Piazza del Duomo, off the Duomo's atrium) July through September on Friday evenings.

The town's other key entertainment is visiting one of its many pleasant cafes to sip an *aperitivo* or enjoy a gelato. On Piazza Duomo, try **Bar Francese,** Piazza Duomo 20 (✆ **089-871049**), with its elegant seating and excellent pastries. Overlooking the sea is **Gran Caffè di Amalfi,** Corso Repubbliche Marinare (✆ **089-871047;** www.bargrancaffeamalfi.it), a standout for an *aperitivo.* **Gelateria Porto Salvo,** Piazza Duomo 22 (✆ **089-871636;** closed Jan–Mar), is one of the best *gelaterie* on this coast—try the *mandorla candita* (candied almond) flavor. **Pasticceria Pansa,** Piazza Duomo 40 (✆ **089-871065;** closed Tues), has been creating delicious sweets since 1830; try their *torta caprese* or sticky, lemon-flavoured *delizia al limone.*

RAVELLO

6km (3¾ miles) NE of Amalfi; 29km (18 miles) W of Salerno; 66km (41 miles) SE of Naples

Situated high up in the mountains, Ravello is like a terrace over the sea, overlooking the villages of Minori and Maiori. Long a refuge for VIPs (including Gore Vidal, who only recently sold his villa here), it is worlds away from the clamor down on the coast, and its traffic-free status gives the town an air of classy tranquility. Once the day trippers leave, it reverts to being a sleepy, hilltop village and is a charming place to spend a couple of nights.

Essentials

GETTING THERE The **bus** is the best option, with **SITA** (✆ **089-405145;** www.sitabus.it) offering frequent service from Amalfi (see "Getting Around," p. 210).

Taxi service from Naples's Capodichino Airport costs a fixed 135€. **Curreri Viaggi** (✆ **081-8015420;** www.curreriviaggi.it) offers a shuttle

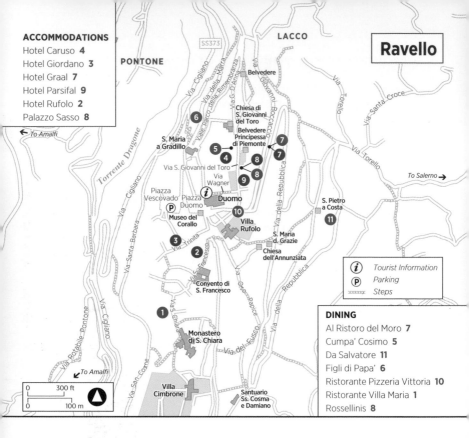

PONTONE

LACCO

Belvedere

Ravello

SS373

Chiesa di
S. Giovanni
del Toro

← To Amalfi

Belvedere
Principessa
di Piemonte

S. Maria
a Gradillo

Via S. Giovanni del Toro

Via
Wagner

To Salerno →

Piazza
Vescovado Piazza
Duomo

Duomo

ⓘ

S. Pietro
a Costa

Ⓟ

Museo del
Corallo

Villa
Rufolo

S. Maria
d. Grazie

Chiesa
dell'Annunziata

Convento di
S. Francesco

Monastero
di S. Chiara

← To Amalfi

ⓘ	Tourist Information
Ⓟ	Parking
⋯⋯	Steps

Villa
Cimbrone

Santuario
Ss. Cosma
e Damiano

0   300 ft
0   100 m

from the airport for 150€ for one to three passengers and 12€ for each additional passenger.

By **train** (𝒞 **892021** in Italy; www.trenitalia.it), the closest station is **Vietri sul Mare,** on the local line between **Naples** (where you'll change trains if you are coming from the north) and **Salerno** (if you are coming from the south). Your best bet is to alight in Salerno and take a SITA bus or a taxi directly to Ravello.

In summer, another option is taking a ferry. The nearest harbors are Salerno and Amalfi; transfer to Ravello from there (see "Getting There," p. 282 and 208).

By **car,** take autostrada A3 to NAPOLI-SALERNO to the exit VIETRI SUL MARE; then follow signs for VIETRI, AMALFI to the SS 163. Follow signs for RAVELLO up the narrow curvy road. *Note:* Because of summer traffic, car access to SS 163 is occasionally limited; contact the tourist office before setting out.

GETTING AROUND The town is largely **pedestrian,** with steep, narrow lanes and many flights of stairs. All cars must stop at the large public parking lot not far from the Duomo. **Taxis** are available at stands on Piazza Duomo, Gradillo, San Giovanni del Toro, and Castiglione, or by calling 𝒞 **089-858000** or 331-5033399.

VISITOR INFORMATION The **AAST tourist office,** Via Roma 18, 84010 Ravello (✆ **089-857096;** www.ravellotime.it), is open June to October daily 9am to 7pm; from November to May it closes at 6pm.

You'll find a **pharmacy** (✆ **089-9840023**) on Via Piazza Duomo. The closest **hospital** is in Salerno (see "Visitor Information," p. 283). For an **ambulance,** dial ✆ **118.** Call the **police** at ✆ **113** or 112. The **post office,** Via Boccaccio 15, off Piazza Vescovado (✆ **089-8586611**), is open Monday to Saturday 8am to 2pm. You'll find **Banca Monte Paschi di Siena** at Piazza Duomo 6 (✆ **089-857120**), and **Banca della Campania** at Via Roma 15 (✆ **089-857872**)—both with **ATMs.**

SPECIAL EVENTS The internationally famous **Festival di Ravello** (✆ **089-858422;** www.ravellofestival.com) focuses on classical music, but it is also an occasion for other events, including jazz, dance, and the visual arts. You need to book seats well in advance as it is very popular, not only for the big names it attracts, but also for the magnificent settings: Performances are held in stunning venues such as Piazza Duomo, Villa Rufolo, and Villa Cimbrone, and in the controversial new auditorium designed by Brasilian architect Oscar Niemeyer. The festival is organized into several series, including the **Festival Musicale Wagneriano**—classical music concerts held in July in the garden of **Villa Rufolo ★**—and the unique **Concerti dell'Aurora,** a group of concerts held at dawn (usually starting at 4am), to welcome the day in music. The festival runs July through September; prices depend on the event, and though some events have free admission, tickets for others can cost anywhere from 15€ to 130€.

Music continues before and after the festival with concerts and events scheduled March through October. You can find information on these other events by contacting **Fondazione Ravello** (✆ **089-858360;** www.fondazioneravello.it), or the **Ravello Concert Society** (✆ **089-858149;** www.ravelloarts.org).

Exploring the Town

According to local legend, Ravello was founded in the 5th to 6th centuries A.D. by Roman patricians fleeing barbarians who were ransacking Rome. The small town flourished in the Middle Ages, when it became part of the Republic of Amalfi and became the residence of choice of some of the wealthiest merchant families of the republic, who built magnificent palaces (several of which have been transformed into hotels) and decorated the churches with precious works of art.

The beautiful, 12th century Romanesque church of **Santa Maria a Gradillo ★** is the first architecturally noteworthy site you will see upon entering Ravello. It has a lovely, plain interior and an Arabo-Norman style bell tower. The heart of town is **Piazza del Vescovado,** a terrace overlooking the valley of the Dragone, and the adjacent **Piazza del Duomo ★★**. Climb up steep, stepped Via Richard Wagner (behind the tourist office) to reach **Via San Giovanni del Toro ★★**, which is lined with some of Ravello's grandest medieval palaces including the 11th-century **Casa Tolla,** today housing the **Municipio** (the town hall). Crossing the **Belvedere Principessa di Piemonte,** where there are fabulous views down the coast, you pass **Palazzo Gonfalone** (today Hotel Palumbo), **Palazzo Sasso** (housing the eponymous hotel), and **Palazzo d'Afflitto** (now the Hotel Caruso Belvedere). The latter stands on a small piazza opposite the church of San Giovanni del Toro which, unfortunately, at presstime was closed for long-term restoration. Further on is **Piazza Fontana,** with its 13th-century **Convent of Sant'Augostino,** today transformed into the Hotel Parsifal.

Chiesa di San Giovanni del Toro ★★ This 12th-century church, restored in 1715 after earthquake damage and again in the 1990s, is one of the most beautiful religious buildings in Ravello. The slender bell tower in Arab-Sicilian style rises beside a facade graced by a triple portal. A steep staircase descends on the right, allowing a view of the three high apses, each crowned by a dome and decorated with intertwined arcs. The interior is decorated with 13th- and 14th-century frescoes, mosaics, majolica, stucco work, and bas-reliefs. Particularly beautiful is the 12th-century **pergamo ★** by Alfano da Termoli, as well as the 14th-century frescoes in the crypt's apse. The church is usually closed, but you can request a visit at Via San Giovanni del Toro 50.

Piazzetta San Giovanni del Toro 3. Closed for restoration; enquire at tourist office.

Duomo ★★★ Dedicated to San Pantaleone, the patron saint of Ravello, this cathedral is a beautiful example of Romanesque architecture and is one of our favorite churches in the area. It was founded in 1086 by Orso Papiro, first bishop of Ravello, and rebuilt in the 12th and 17th centuries. The beautiful facade, graced by three marble portals, was reworked in the 16th century and is famous for its **bronze doors ★★** which were designed by Barisano da Trani in 1179 and cast in Constantinople. To the right is the 13th-century **bell tower,** showing Arab and Byzantine influences. The Duomo's interior is divided into three naves, each with its own apse; in the central nave to the right is the beautiful **Ambone dell'Epistola ★★★**, a pulpit dating from 1130, decorated with precious mosaics representing Jonah being gobbled up by the whale. Facing it is the richly carved and decorated **Pergamo ★★★** from 1272, a splendid work of art by Niccolò di Bartolomeo da Foggia. To the left of the main altar is the **Cappella di San Pantaleone,** built in 1643 for the relic of San Pantaleone. The saint was beheaded in Nicomedia on July 27, 305. On the anniversary of his death, his

Chiesa di San Giovanni del Toro.

blood (contained in a vessel) miraculously liquefies. When the vessel is cracked, the second miracle occurs: No blood leaks out. Beneath the church, the crypt houses a small museum where you can admire the elegant 13th-century **Bust of Sichelgaita della Marra** ★★ (or Sigilgaida Rufolo), sculpted by Bartolomeo da Foggia, as well as several precious relic holders, including the **Bust of Santa Barbara** ★ in silver.

Piazza del Vescovado. © **089-858311,** or 089-857122 for the museum. Duomo: Free admission. Daily 9am–noon and 5:30–7pm. **Museum:** Admission 2€. Summer daily 9am–7pm; winter daily 9am–6pm. Guided tours available.

Museo del Corallo Created in 1986, this small museum has a wonderful collection of precious objects made of coral, including cameos, totaling over 600 pieces. Located on the premises of the workshop **Camo,** which specializes in this traditional art (see "Cameo Making," p. 131), the collection stretches from ancient Roman pieces all the way to the 19th century. Particularly beautiful are the 16th-century **Crucifix** on a crystal cross and a **Madonna** from 1532. Be sure to note the 3rd-century-A.D. Roman amphora with a coral formation inside it and a beautiful set of 14 cherub heads from the 18th to 19th centuries.

Piazza Duomo 9, © **089-857461.** www.museodelcorallo.com. Free admission. Mon–Sat 9:30am noon and 3–5:30pm.

Villa Cimbrone ★ The body of this grand villa dates from the 14th and 15th centuries but it was largely rebuilt in 1904 by its new owner, the eccentric Englishman Lord Grimthorpe (who also designed London's Big Ben). In the 1920s, the villa became a popular hangout for the literary Bloomsbury set, and Greta Garbo hid here in 1937 with her lover, the conductor Leopold Stokowsky. Although today the villa is occupied by a luxury hotel and only accessible to hotel guests (unless you choose to eat in the restaurant), its **glorious grounds ★★★** are open to all. This grandiose garden, suspended high over the azure sea below, is one of the most beautiful in Italy and was also created by Lord Grimthorpe in 1905. Among the garden's many magical spots, the high point (both literally and figuratively) is the **Belvedere Cimbrone ★★★** which has dizzying views over the Bay of Salerno from between the neoclassical statues that grace the stone balustrade. Note that the villa is located some way from the center of town and can only be accessed by foot up a rather steep hill.

Via Santa Chiara 26. © **089-857459,** for reservations. Fax 089-857777. www.villacimbrone.it. Admission 6€ adults, 4€ children. Daily 9am–sunset; last admission 30 min. earlier.

Villa Rufolo ★★ In the center of town, to the right of the Duomo, this beautiful villa was built between 1270 and 1280 for the prominent Rufolo family, then passed on to the Gonfalone e Muscettola family in the 15th century. It was bought in 1851 by the Scotsman Francis Devile Reid, who partially restructured it. A public building since 1975, the villa and its beautiful **gardens ★**—perched a spectacular 340m (1,115 ft.) above sea level—can be visited. The original architecture shows much Arab influence, especially in the detail of intertwined arches, which recurs in the **Entrance Hall** and in the beautiful courtyard. The three-story main building at the end of a tree-lined alley opens to a marvelous **Inner Court.** Across from the entrance is the famous **Terrace ★**, which was renamed Terrazza Wagner in memory of the German composer who wrote the Klingsor Garden scene in the second act of *Parsifal* here. Today, the garden is the setting for the Concerti Wagneriani, part of the Ravello Festival.

Piazza Duomo. ✆ **089-857621.** www.villarufolo.it. Admission 5€. Summer daily 9am–8pm; winter daily 9am–sunset; last admission 15 min. earlier.

Outdoor Activities

What Ravello lacks in beaches, it compensates for in trails. The two **walks** we suggest below are quite easy, allowing you to return by bus or taxi, but the ambitious might undertake a complete loop of the two.

The **Monastero di San Nicola** makes for a pleasant and easy hike. From the center of Ravello, take the road to Chiunzi for 1km (.5 mile) toward the hamlet of Sambuco, 320m (1,050 ft.) above sea level (you can also get to this point by car). Descending from here a few steps to your right, you can reach the trail that climbs to the Monastery of Saint Nicholas at an altitude of 486m (1,594 ft.). Plan on about 2 hours for the 9km (5.8-mile) hike. It is then possible to descend to Minori—or to Maiori if you prefer—in about a half-hour. Hiking the reverse route (starting from Minori or Maiori) is more demanding, but you can do it by taking the small road that connects Maiori with Minori and passes behind the Collegiata to reach the path that climbs gently toward the monastery. The trail becomes progressively steeper and more scenic until you reach the top. Figure on spending about 1 hour for the ascent from Maiori or Minori to the monastery.

Another scenic hike in the area is the one to Minori. From the center of Ravello, take another footpath—a charming mix of steps and hidden alleys—which descends all the way to Minori and the sea. Start from the alley to the left of Villa Rufolo, marked by a small fountain, at an altitude of 350m (1,148 ft.). You will pass by the small 13th-century Annunziata church and by San Pietro church before reaching the hamlet of **Torello,** with its Addolorata Church and graceful bell tower in Arab-Sicilian style. The picturesque trail continues through olive trees down to **Minori.** The hike down takes a half-hour; double that for the ascent.

Where to Stay

For a luxury address in town, provided you don't mind the 10-minute climb on foot from the closest car drop off (a porter will carry your luggage), **Villa Cimbrone ★★** (see "Villa Cimbrone," above) has 19 elegantly appointed guest rooms (410€–660€ double, from 780€ suite; all rates include breakfast). For more modest accommodations, we recommend the few rooms offered by **Da Salvatore** and by **Palazzo della Marra** (see "Where to Eat," below).

VERY EXPENSIVE

Hotel Caruso ★★ ☺ Housed in the the splendid 11th-century Palazzo D'Afflitto, this hotel offers top-notch services and facilities and a unique and exclusive experience. Guest rooms are palatial yet welcoming, with baldaquin beds, heavenly linens, and large bathrooms. Most have sea views and open to private balconies, terraces, or small gardens. The hotel's facilities are crowned by a breathtaking outdoor infinity pool; we also recommend asking for a guided tour of the magnificent gardens. Guests enjoy access to two golf courses and a tennis court, though you do have to pay a fee. PlayStations, toys, and kids' bathrobes and slippers are available upon request.

Piazza San Giovanni del Toro 2, 84010 Ravello. www.hotelcaruso.com. ✆ **089-858801.** Fax 089-858806. 48 units. 760€–925€ double; from 1,200€ suite. Rates include American buffet breakfast. Children 12 and under stay free in parent's room. AE, DC, MC, V. Parking 20€. Closed Nov–Mar. **Amenities:** 2 restaurants; 2 bars; babysitting; concierge; gym; pool; room service; spa. *In room:* A/C, TV/DVD, minibar, Wi-Fi (free).

EXPENSIVE

Palazzo Sasso ★★★ Housed in a 12th-century patrician palace, this opulent hotel enjoys a splendid location between plunging cliffs and steep mountainside. One of the best hotels in the world, it is *the* place to stay in Ravello. Guest rooms are luxuriously appointed with real antiques and handmade Vietri ceramic floors. Some afford gorgeous views—the best are from room nos. 1, 201, 204, and 301, and suite no. 304. Some of the suites are as big as a good-size apartment, and even the lower-priced rooms are spacious (though a few have no view). Bathrooms are done up in marble, with large tubs. A free shuttle takes guests down to Sasso by the Sea (open May–Sept), the hotel's beach club where there is a small outdoor pool, and a waterside terrace with lounge chairs and umbrellas. For more formal dining, book a table at the Michelin-rated **Rossellinis** (p. 226) in the main hotel.

Via San Giovanni del Toro 28, 84010 Ravello. www.palazzosasso.com. ℂ **089-818181.** Fax 089-858900. 44 units. 350€–710€ double; from 990€ suite. Rates include buffet breakfast. Children 2 and under stay free in parent's room. AE, DC, MC, V. Parking 34€. Closed mid-Oct to Mar. **Amenities:** Restaurant; bar; concierge; gym; Jacuzzi; pool; room service; spa. *In room:* A/C, TV, Internet, minibar.

MODERATE

Hotel Rufolo ★ This family-run hotel is located in the heart of town overlooking the gardens of Villa Rufolo. Housed in a modern building decorated in a traditional style, it offers comfortable accommodations and friendly service. The views from the terrace gardens, the restaurant terrace, and the sun decks are superb. Guest rooms are spacious and attractive, with tiled Vietri floors and classic furnishings. Bathrooms are a good size and well maintained (some with shower only). Better rooms open onto private balconies and enjoy gorgeous views, while others overlook the town or garden. The hotel's restaurant, **Sigilgaida** ★, serves tasty cuisine prepared with produce from the hotel's organic gardens and select local ingredients (closed Jan–Feb).

Via San Francesco 1, 84010 Ravello. www.hotelrufolo.it. ℂ **089-857133.** Fax 089-857935. 30 units. 290€–350€ double; 550€ junior suite. Rates include buffet breakfast. Children 2 and under stay free in parent's room. AE, DC, MC, V. Free parking. **Amenities:** Restaurant; bar; babysitting; concierge; gym; pool; spa. *In room:* A/C, TV, minibar.

INEXPENSIVE

Hotel Giordano Not far from Villa Rufolo, guest rooms at this newly renovated, family-run hotel are on average a bit smaller than at the Rufolo, but there are some exceptions—the largest are good options for families and have private small terraces. The large swimming pool in the garden is very pleasant, and free use of the hotel's garage near Ravello's main square is included (porters collect your luggage). Guests enjoy access to the splendid gardens of **Villa Eva** and special rates for meals at **Villa Maria** ★ (see "Where to Eat," p. 226).

Via Trinita 14, 84010 Ravello. www.giordanohotel.it. ℂ **089-857170.** Fax 089-857071. 30 units. 185€–300€ double; 355€ triple; 410€ quad; 450€ junior suite. Rates include breakfast. Children 2 and under stay free in parent's room. AE, DC, MC, V. Free parking **Amenities:** Bar; concierge; pool. *In room:* A/C, TV, minibar.

Hotel Graal 🍃 This small hotel offers great accommodations in a scenic location, is moderately priced for such a fashionable part of town, and practices sustainable hospitality, including water and energy saving, and waste management. Public areas are a bit faded, but guest rooms are bright and modern, with good-size bathrooms (some with showers only) and balconies with sea views. The hotel's restaurant, **Al Ristoro del Moro** ★ (p. 226), offers a nice setting, well-prepared food, and uses excellent ingredients, but hotel guests who choose half- or full-board eat in a separate dining room.

Via della Repubblica 8, 84010 Ravello. www.hotelgraal.it. ⓒ **089-857222.** Fax 089-857551. 42 units. 80€–220€ double; 250€–300€ junior suite. Rates include breakfast. Children 2 and under stay free in parent's room. AE, DC, MC, V. Parking 11€. **Amenities:** Restaurant; bar; babysitting; concierge; Wi-Fi (free). *In room:* A/C, TV, minibar.

Hotel Parsifal 📖 In the northern part of town, this former 13th-century convent is a good budget option, with charming architectural details throughout. Guest rooms vary in size and shape—some with nice views over the sea; all are pleasantly done with bright Vietri tiled floors, whitewashed walls, and good-size bathrooms (some with shower only). The hotel's **restaurant** ★ is very good.

Via Gioacchino D'Anna 5, 84010 Ravello. www.hotelparsifal.com. ⓒ **089-857144.** 17 units. 135€–210€ double. Rates include buffet breakfast. Children 2 and under stay free in parent's room. AE, DC, MC, V. Parking 15€. **Amenities:** Restaurant; bar; concierge; Wi-Fi (free). *In room:* A/C (in some), TV, minibar.

Where to Eat

In addition to the restaurants below, we recommend the **Parsifal** ★ in the hotel of the same name, the **Sigilgaida** ★ in the Hotel Rufolo, and, for a special experience, the restaurant at **Villa Cimbrone** ★★ (p. 223).

EXPENSIVE

Rossellinis ★★★ CREATIVE AMALFITAN Elegance and impeccable service are the background for a sophisticated menu and perfect dining experience at this highly praised gourmet destination that boasts two Michelin stars. Talented chef Pino Lavarra creates delicious meals from local ingredients best showcased in his tasting menu. Dishes might include delectable *ravioli di totano gigante ripieni di granchio e zucchine* (squid ravioli filled with crab meat and zucchini) or *merluzzo in crosta d'olive di Gaeta* (Mediterranean cod encrusted with local olives).

Via San Giovanni del Toro 28 (in the Palazzo Sasso, p. 226). ⓒ **089-818181.** Fax 089-858900. www.palazzosasso.com. Reservations required. Secondi 28€–32€; tasting menu 120€. AE, DC, MC, V. Daily 7:30-11pm. Closed Nov–Mar.

MODERATE

Al Ristoro del Moro ★ AMALFITAN On the premises of the Hotel Graal (above), the terrace at this popular restaurant affords superb views but is open only in warm weather (usually Apr or May until Sept or Oct). The menu is well-balanced between excellent seafood dishes and a good selection of meat options. We like the *scialatielli ai frutti di mare* (homemade pasta with seafood) and the ravioli, as well as the tasty *tagliata* (steak). Save room for dessert.

Via della Repubblica 8. ⓒ **089-857901.** www.alristorodelmoro.it. Reservations recommended. Secondi 12€–22€. AE, DC, MC, V. Daily 12:30-3pm and 7:30-10pm. Closed Nov–Mar.

Ristorante Villa Maria ★ In the hotel of the same name, this restaurant features a delightful arbor terrace with breathtaking views. Enjoy delicious variations of original family recipes prepared with ingredients from the hotel's own organic gardens: We recommend the shrimp and asparagus risotto followed by sea bass in *acqua pazza* (an herby-tomato broth) or the *grigliata mista* (grilled fish or meats). The restaurant offers cooking classes, too.

Via Santa Chiara 2. ✆ **089-857255.** Fax 089-857071. www.villamaria.it. Reservations recommended. Secondi 16€–25€. AE, DC, MC, V. Daily 12:30–3pm and 7:30–10pm. Closed Dec 24 and 25.

INEXPENSIVE

Cumpà Cosimo ☺ AMALFITAN/PIZZA Once a simple wine bar, this place has blossomed into a popular restaurant favored by both locals and visitors. Family run since it opened in 1929—the second generation is still at the helm—it serves generous portions of homemade traditional dishes. The seasonal menu always includes mouthwatering homemade pasta —we love the cannelloni (pasta tubes filled with meat or fish and baked with sauce)—and succulent *secondi*—you might find *zuppa di pesce* (fish stew) and a fine *fritto misto* (deep-fried medley of seafood), or roasted lamb with herbs. Pizza is served in the evening. The staff is particularly accommodating to the needs of little ones and allows half-portions.

Via Roma 44. ✆ **089-857156,** Reservations recommended. Secondi 11€–18€; pizza 6€–10€. AE, DC, MC, V. Daily 12:30–3pm and 7:30–11pm. Closed Mon Nov–Feb.

Da Salvatore ★ AMALFITAN This simple restaurant offers local cuisine in a striking setting—the views are superb both from the dining room and the garden terrace, which is open for alfresco dining in warm weather. The style and atmosphere are relaxed, with simple tables and chairs. In addition to the scrumptious homemade breads, savor fish or meat from among the traditional dishes, which include *gnoccoloni al pomodoro e basilico* (potato dumplings with fresh tomatoes and basil), grilled fish, and roasted veal. The restaurant has six **guest rooms** for rent (98€ double including breakfast).

Via della Repubblica 2. ✆ **089-857227.** www.salvatoreravello.com. Reservations recommended. Secondi 12€–25€. AE, DC, MC, V. Tues–Sun 12:30–3pm and 7:30–10:30pm (also Mon Apr–Oct).

Figli di Papà 🎁 In the historic 13th-century Palazzo della Marra, this pleasant restaurant serves hearty cuisine with a creative twist. We recommend the *crespolini* (thin pancakes filled with seafood or meat in a creamy sauce) and the *grigliata* (medley of grilled meat or fish). The tourist menu for 15€ is an excellent deal. The management also maintains four simply furnished **guest rooms** (90€ double) on a B&B basis (Via della Marra 3; www.palazzodellamarra.com).

Via della Marra 7, 84010 Ravello. ✆ **089-858302.** www.ristorantefiglidipapa.it. Reservations recommended. Secondi 10€–15€. AE, DC, MC, V. Daily 12:30–3pm and 7:30–10pm.

Ristorante Pizzeria Vittoria 🎁 AMALFITAN/PIZZA This family-run place is a good choice for a moderately priced meal: The dining room is welcoming and the service is prompt. The wood-oven pizza is top-notch, and the menu includes many tasty choices such as spaghetti *alle vongole* (with clams), risotto *al limone e gamberi con bottarga di muggine* (with lemon and shrimp sprinkled with mullet roe), and the excellent *tagliata di tonno con aceto balsamico* (sliced, seared tuna steak with balsamic vinegar).

Via dei Rufolo 3. ✆ **089-857947.** www.ristorantepizzeriavittoria.it. Reservations recommended Sat–Sun. Secondi 15€–18€; pizza 6€–9€. AE, DC, MC, V. Wed–Mon 12:30–3pm and 7:30–11pm (also Tues Apr–Oct).

Ravello After Dark

Ravello's nightlife isn't exactly riveting: Most locals spend their evenings sipping an *aperitivo*—or nibbling on sweets—at one of the town's cafes. Things heat up in the summer when the activity can take on a theatrical air as people-watching reaches its prime. At the **Bar Calce,** Via Roma 2, next to the Duomo (© **089-857152**), people gather for the excellent pastries and homemade ice cream during the day and *aperitivi* in the evening.

Side Trips: Scala & Tramonti

Little known by most tourists, the environs of Ravello offer dramatic mountain and sea views as well as unspoiled rural retreats.

Scala, only 2.5km (1½ miles) from Ravello, was once a fortified town protecting the Amalfi Maritime Republic. Its two castles—one guarding inland approaches, the other overlooking the sea—were connected by walls that enclosed the town completely, but are now in ruins. The 12th-century **Duomo,** Piazza Municipio 5 (© **089-857397;** daily 8am–1pm and 6–7pm), contains a **crypt ★** with a 14th-century **funerary monument ★★** for Marinella Rufolo, erected by her husband Antonio Coppola. Of the smaller surrounding hamlets, each a small replica of Scala's defensive structure, **Minuto** is our pick: Only 1km (a half-mile) south of Scala, its

FROM TOP: The funerary monument for Marinella Rufolo inside the Duomo's crypt; The view of Ravello from Scala.

interesting **Chiesa della Santissima Annunziata** ★★ was probably Scala's original cathedral. Built between the 11th and 12th centuries, it's one of the best examples of Romanesque architecture on the whole Amalfi Coast (and the view alone is worth a stop). Be sure to visit the **crypt,** where you will find **12th-century frescoes** ★★, including a Christ Pantocraor that accurately represents Byzantine style. *Note:* The church is open only for Mass on Sunday (9:30–10:30am), but can be visited upon request (ask at the parish house on Via Ficuciello).

About 10km (6 miles) farther inland from Scala, is **Tramonti,** a fertile agricultural area *intra montes,* or "between the mountains" which comprises 13 historic *casali* (farms), each graced by its own small church. This area is famous today for its D.O.C. wine and for **concierto,** a bittersweet digestive liquor concocted in the 17th century by the nuns of the local convent using nine different mountain herbs and spices. The convent, **Regio Conservatorio dei Santi Giuseppe e Teresa,** Località Pucara, is open to visitors, and still makes the drink—which makes an excellent souvenir. We also recommend the drive to **Valico di Chiunzi,** the high pass in the mountains once guarded by a powerful castle, now reduced to a single tower. At an altitude of 656m (2,152 ft.), it affords a spectacular **panorama** ★★★ of the plain of Pompeii and Mount Vesuvius.

If you'd like to explore the area on horseback, sign up for a pleasant **horse ride and guided excursion** in the countryside at one of the horse farms in Scala; the best is **La Piccola California,** Via Sento (℃ **089-858042**). Alternatively, the best **hike** in the area is from **Campidoglio di Scala**—one of the bourgs connected to Scala, at an altitude of 470m (1,542 ft.). The first part is a ridge trail, extremely scenic and not very arduous. You can make the walk more challenging by descending all the way to Amalfi. Along the way you will find, on your left, the ruins of the 12th-century church of Sant'Eustachio. The trail continues through a natural rock formation in the form of an amphitheater, showing the ruins of ancient fortifications, called Castello. About halfway through the descent, you will reach the waterfalls at the top of the Vallone delle Ferriere of Amalfi (see "Outdoor Activities," p. 214). If you want, you can then walk down along the Vallone and reach Amalfi through the Valle dei Mulini. Figure on spending about 2 hours to get to the waterfall and an additional 2 hours to get to Amalfi.

WHERE TO STAY & EAT

To have a full experience of the countryside here, we recommend staying in an *agriturismo;* we like **Azienda Agrituristica Le Chiancolelle,** Via Valico di Chiunzi, Località Campinola, 84010 Tramonti (℃ **089-876339;** 5 units), and **Azienda Agrituristica Mare e Monti,** Via Trugnano 3, Località Campinola, 84010 Tramonti (℃ **089-876665;** www.agriturismomaremonti.it; 2 units). The area also boasts several excellent restaurants.

Da Lorenzo ★★ 🎁 AMALFITAN We love this countryside restaurant, with its great outdoor dining area overlooking the valley, Ravello, and the sea. The cuisine is simple and traditional, with homemade dishes based on fish in summer and meat in winter. The bread is made in a wood-burning oven that also turns out excellent pizza in the evening. Some of our favorite dishes are *scialatielli ai frutti di mare* (fresh pasta with shellfish), *pappardelle con il coccio* (wide noodles with fish), *grigliata di gamberoni* (perfectly grilled large shrimp), *scamorza alla brace* (grilled local cheese), and a selection of cured meats.

Via Frà G. Sasso, Santa Maria, Scala. ℰ **089-858290.** www.trattoriadalorenzo.com. Reservations recommended. Secondi 15€–25€. AE, DC, MC, V. Winter Sat–Sun noon–2:30pm and 7:30–10:30pm; summer daily noon–2:30pm and 7:30–10:30pm; July and Aug open until midnight.

Da Nino 🍴AMALFITAN/PIZZA Affectionately called "Ninuccio" (little Nino) by the locals, this trattoria offers a warm welcome and delicious specialties, made in large part with ingredients from the owners' farm. For an appetizer, taste the superb salamis and *sottoli* (vegetables preserved in olive oil) with homemade bread and local mozzarella. Follow this with a secondo of pasta or the whole-wheat pizza—the one with veggies *(con le verdure)* is particularly tasty.
Via Pucara 39, Tramonti. **089-855407.** Reservations recommended Sat–Sun. Secondi 8€–15€. No credit cards. Wed–Mon noon–3.30pm and 7:30–11 pm (also Tues in summer).

La Violetta 🍴 AMALFITAN The views are gorgeous and the food is divine at this simple, honest restaurant. The hearty menu includes lots of salamis produced on the farm here, as well as homemade pasta and gnocchi. The risotto *ai chiodini* (with local wild mushrooms) bursts with flavor, and the grilled meats are superb. A good local red wine is also served.
Via Valico di Chiunzi, Tramonti. ℰ **089-876384.** Reservations recommended Sat–Sun. Secondi 5€–12€. No credit cards. Thurs–Tues 12:30–3pm and 7:30–midnight (also Wed in Aug).

OFF THE BEATEN PATH

While the three pearls of the Amalfi Coast—Positano, Ravello, and Amalfi—are the undisputed stars of the area, lesser-known and often more-authentic towns can be found along the coast and farther inland. Those on the coast can also provide a good base as an alternative to the more crowded communities, provided you don't require loads of amenities.

Conca dei Marini

5km (3 miles) W of Amalfi

Little more than a hamlet, Conca is rarely visited, in spite of being right on the main road between Positano and Amalfi; most visitors usually limit themselves to the **Emerald Grotto** (see "Exploring the Town," below).

ESSENTIALS

GETTING THERE & AROUND Conca is on SS 163 between Positano and Amalfi. Take a **SITA bus** from Amalfi or Positano or a **taxi** or a **car** (see "Visitor Information," p. 210 and 191).

VISITOR INFORMATION You can get **tourist information** at the municipal office: Casa Comunale (ℰ**089-831301**).
　　　　The closest **pharmacy** and **bank** are in Amalfi, the nearest **hospital** in Salerno (p. 283). For an **ambulance,** dial ℰ **118.** You can call the **police** at ℰ **113** or 112. The **post office** (ℰ**089-831286**) is on Piazza Olmo 3, off SS 163.

EXPLORING THE TOWN

Rambling Conca is built on a hillside overlooking a picturesque cove and a tiny beach, **Marina di Conca,** where a few boats are moored. This quiet hamlet was once an important commercial stronghold for the Amalfi Republic: Its small

limoncello & OTHER *ROSOLI*

The typical liqueur of the Costeria, *limoncello* is the most famous of the *rosoli*—sweet liqueurs made locally from fruits and herbs. The most unusual are *finocchietto* (wild fennel), *lauro* (bay leaf), *mirto* (myrtle), *nocello* (walnut), *nanassino* (prickly pear), the exotic *mandarino* (mandarin), and *fragolino* (wild strawberry).

Limoncello is probably the most versatile *rosolio*. You will find local versions—and endless claims of paternity—from Vico Equense on the Sorrento peninsula all the way to Vietri and beyond, to the islands of Ischia, Capri, and Procida. The liqueur's actual origin is probably the area of Maiori, Amalfi, and Vietri—although Sorrento has good foundations for its claim.

Almost every family In Campania has its own recipe, passed on for centuries. True *limoncello* is made from *sfusatu di Amalfi*, a particular lemon that has obtained D.O.P. recognition (the stamp of controlled origin for produce, similar to D.O.C. for wine). The Amalfi lemon is large, long, and light in color, with a sweet and very flavorful aroma and taste, almost no seeds, and a very thick skin.

Limoncello is sold in pretty, hard-to-resist bottles. If you plan to buy a few bottles as gifts, don't forget to give the recipient tips on how to drink it. Always served very cold (often straight from the deep freeze where the alcoholic content keeps it just liquid), the drink can be sipped as a digestive after a meal. It also makes an excellent lemon-flavored long drink—dilute with tonic water or seltzer. Some like it as a cocktail with a small quantity of champagne or prosecco. To make *granite*, dilute the *limoncello* with simple syrup and freeze it, stirring occasionally.

You can buy these liqueurs from various specialty stores, the most reputed of which is **Limunciel,** Corso Vittorio Emanuele 9, Minori (✆ **089-877393**). This shop was also among the first to commercialize the local *rosolio,* which it makes in small batches according to a generations-old recipe. Another excellent shop is **Profumi della Costiera,** Via Trinita 37, Ravello (✆ **089-858167;** www.profumidellacostiera.it).

harbor had boat building and commercial facilities that made it richer than neighboring Amalfi until raiders destroyed the town in 1543. The view from the Church of **San Pancrazio** (Salita San Pancrazio) is splendid, and the 14th-century **Convento di Santa Rosa** (where nuns invented the famous *sfogliatella* of the same name, see "Sfogliatella di Santa Rosa," below), off Via Roma (above SS 163), makes for a pleasant excursion. In summer, the convent's church, Santa Maria di Grado, hosts chamber music concerts held by the **Ravello Concert Society** (✆ **089-858149;** www.ravelloarts.org).

Discovered in 1932, the **Grotta dello Smeraldo (Emerald Grotto)** ★★ is a beautiful underwater grotto that shines with a unique blue-green light when

The Grotta dello Smeraldo (Emerald Grotto).

the sun is high and the sea calm. Less famous than Capri's Blue Grotto, it is still impressive, at 30m (98 ft.) long by 60m (197 ft.) wide, with stalactites, stalagmites, and an underwater ceramic manger that was submerged in 1956. It is accessible by boat from the tiny beach, by swimming, on foot down a long series of steps from SS 163, or via the elevator by the Conca Azzurra hotel and the SITA bus stop (Positano-Amalfi line) on SS 163. Excursions are also offered from Amalfi and Praiano. The grotto is open daily, weather permitting, November to February from 9am to 4pm and March to October from 9am to 7pm. Admission is 6€ and includes the rowboat ride from the beach or elevator (**Note:** You're not expected to tip the oarman unless he goes especially out of his way to accommodate you.).

WHERE TO STAY & EAT

Hotel Il Belvedere This beautiful hotel occupies a 19th-century cliff-side villa only minutes from the Emerald Grotto. Public spaces include a pretty seawater pool overlooking a rocky private beach. The bright, large guest rooms are comfortably furnished with period furniture or reproductions, and have colorful tile floors. Bathrooms are also nicely tiled, with modern fixtures. Each room has a small terrace (large enough for a table and chairs) with an ocean view.

Sfogliatella di Santa Rosa

In the 17th century, the nuns at **Convento di Santa Rosa** replaced the traditional ricotta-cheese filling of a Neapolitan *sfogliatella* pastry with a delicate pastry cream and a spoonful of *amarene*—candied sour cherries in syrup—a change that met with immediate success. Today you can taste this delicious creation in local pastry shops such as **Pasticceria Pansa** in Amalfi (p. 217) and in Conca dei Marini in August during the festival dedicated to it, **Sagra della Sfogliatella di Santa Rosa.**

Via Smeraldo 19 (off the SS 163), 84010 Conca dei Marini. www.belvederehotel.it. ☎ **089-831282.**
Fax 089-831439. 36 units. 220€–240€ double. Rates include buffet breakfast. AE, DC, MC, V.
Free parking. Closed Nov–Mar. **Amenities:** Restaurant; bar; pool, Wi-Fi (free). *In room:* A/C, TV,
minbar.

La Tonnarella ★★ AMALFITAN On the beach at Marina di Conca, this is
one of the best restaurants in the area. Opened in the '50s in what was then a
boat shed, it is now best reached from the sea (call for a pickup from the nearest harbor). The menu focuses on hopping-fresh seafood which is taken straight
from the fishing boat to the kitchen, and prepared simply but perfectly. The
chef is justly proud of his *scialatielli ai frutti di mare* (fresh pasta with seafood
and tomatoes), which we suggest followed by a traditional dish of *totani alle patate* (squid and potatoes), or a delicious *pezzogna alla'acquapazza* (fish in herbed
broth). The vegetarian *grigliate* (grilled plate) is excellent.

Via Marina 1, Borgo Marinaro, Conca dei Marini. ☎ **089-831939.** www.ristorantelatonnarella.it.
Reservations required. Secondi 15€–30€. AE, DC, MC, V. Tues–Sat 12:30–3pm and 7:30–11pm;
Sun–Mon 12:30–3pm. Closed Nov–Mar.

Furore

10.6km (6½ miles) W of Amalfi

On the cliff above Conca dei Marini and the SS 163, this rural community
was virtually unknown to the public until recently, when its wine obtained the
D.O.C. label.

ESSENTIALS

GETTING THERE & AROUND In addition to hopping on the **SITA bus** from
Amalfi, you can come by **taxi** or **car** from Amalfi or Positano (see "Getting
Around," p. 210 and 191). If you are **driving,** take the sharp turn off SS 163
on SS 366 at Conca dei Marini (btw. Positano and Amalfi).

VISITOR INFORMATION Visitors can obtain **tourist information** at the municipal office, Via Mola 39 (☎ **089-874100**).

The **pharmacy** (☎ **089-831109**) is at Via Mola 35. The nearest **hospital** is in Salerno (see "Visitor Information," p. 283). For an **ambulance,**
dial ☎ **118.** You can call the **police** at ☎ **113** or 112. You'll find the **post
office** (☎ **089-874129**) at Via Mola 33. For **banks,** head to Agerola and
Amalfi.

EXPLORING THE TOWN

Furore is more a sparsely built rural area than a proper village, and little would
justify a visit here if it weren't for the local wine and good food. A visit to the
local winery, Marisa Cuomo's **Cantine Gran Furor,** Via Lama 14 (☎ **089-
830348,** www.marisacuomo.com), is a relaxed business, and the award-winning
wine is great. **Hikers** will enjoy the scenic **Sentiero della Volpe Pescatrice
(Fishing Fox Trail)** ★ (about 45 min.) that leads from Contrada Sant'Elia down
to **Marina di Furore** the small beach at the bottom of the narrow gully—a fiord,
really—where the local fishermen keep their boats. The long, steep trail was
the regular village path that cut down the rocky walls of the fiord created by the
brook that still flows at the bottom (*furore* means rage and refers to the way the
sea rises in the fiord during storms). You can also reach the cove by boat, from
one of the harbors nearby.

WHERE TO STAY & EAT

Antica Hostaria di Bacco ★★ Surrounded by vineyards and views, this historic address is now a foodie destination. Founded in 1930 and expertly run by the third generation of Ferraiolis, it also offers comfortable accommodations and kind service. The menu is a delightful journey through superb renditions of local recipes long forgotten elsewhere on the coast. Do try the *ferrazzuoli alla nannarella* (a type of fresh pasta handmade using a small iron tool and seasoned with a mix of grape tomatoes, smoked sword fish, raisins, red pepper, and arugula) and the *frittura* (deep-fried seafood). The simple guest rooms are bright, with Wi-Fi and private terraces (100€ double).

Via G.B. Lama 9, 84010 Furore. ✆ 089-830360. Fax 089-830352. www.baccofurore.it. Reservations required. Secondi 12€–20€. AE, DC, MC, V. Sat-Thurs 12:30-3pm and 7:30-11pm (also Fri June–Sept).

Furore Inn Resort ★★ This luxury spa-hotel is a striking whitewashed structure with dramatic sea views that are pleasantly equaled by the elegant interior. The panoramic rooms all feature Vietri tiled floors and classic furnishings; the best open onto private terraces, but all are equipped with an elegant tiled bathroom (some with shower only). The pool is great, and the spa offers a wide range of beauty treatments and massages. Of the two restaurants, **La Volpe Pescatrice** is renowned for its creative Amalfitan fare and the beautiful views from its terrace, while the **Italian Touch** offers modern Italian cuisine in a more formal atmosphere. They both offer tasting menus: 60€ and 70€ at La Volpe, and 75€ and 90€ at the Touch.

Via dell'Amore 1, Contrada Sant'Elia, 84010 Furore. ✆ 089-8304711. Fax 089-8304777. www.furoreinn.it. 22 units. 380€–490€ double; from 600€ suite. AE, DC, MC, V. Free parking. Closed Nov–Mar. **Amenities:** 2 restaurants; bar; concierge; pool; room service; spa; outdoor tennis court. *In room:* A/C, TV, minibar.

Agerola ★

14.5km (9 miles) W of Amalfi

A sparse rural area on a high plateau in the Monti Lattari range, Agerola is famous for its beauty and its cows' and sheep's milk for which the mountains were named (*latte* means milk). The region's best cheese comes from Agerola's farms—indeed, some of the most excellent cheese in the country is made here. Completely bypassed by most, this rural area offers visitors beauty and autenthicity.

ESSENTIALS

GETTING THERE & AROUND In addition to the **SITA bus** from Amalfi, you can come by **taxi** or **car** from Amalfi or Positano (see "Getting Around," p. 210 and 191). If you are **driving,** take the sharp turn off SS 163 on SS 366 at Conca dei Marini, and continue about 4km (2½ miles) farther up the cliff past Furore.

VISITOR INFORMATION The **Proloco tourist office** (✆ 089-8791064) is on Viale della Vittoria.

A **pharmacy** (✆ 081-8791085) is at Via Armando Diaz 14. The closest **hospital** is in Salerno (see "Visitor Information," p. 283). For an **ambulance,** dial ✆ 118. You can call the **police** at ✆ 113 or 112. You'll find **post offices** at Via Roma 1 (✆ 081-8731573) and at Via Ponte 1 (✆ 081-8731266). There's a **bank,** Banca Intesa, at Via Roma 16 (✆ 081-8740511).

EXPLORING THE TOWN

A collection of farming hamlets, Agerola has its administrative center in **Pianillo.** The most scenic of Agerola's bourgs is **San Lazzaro** where, past the church to the left, you will find the **Punta,** a natural terrace offering dramatic **views ★★** over the sea. Via the road to the right of the church, more awesome panoramas open from the terrace by the former **Castle Avitabile** (Colonia Montana), and from the ruins of **Castel Lauritano ★★★.** The whole area offers unending **hiking** opportunities, including the demanding but extremely scenic 5-hour hike to the **Vallone delle Ferriere** waterfall, starting from San Lazzaro.

Visit a cheese shop to sample *fiordilatte, caciocavallo,* and *scamorze.* Among the best are **Caseificio Agrisole,** Via Case Sparse 81 (✆ **081-8731022**); **Caseificio Belfiore di Cioffi,** Via Belvedere 35 (✆ **081-8791338**); and **La Montanina,** Piazza Avitabile Gennaro 3 (✆ **081-8025272**).

WHERE TO STAY & EAT

Don't expect luxury, but a few local hotels offer simple, adequate accommodations, such as **Albergo Ristorante Risorgimento,** Via Antonio Coppola 32, Località San Lazzaro, 84051 Agerola (✆/fax **081-8025072**; www.hotel risorgimento.it; 90€ double), a welcoming historic hotel (established 1878) with an attached restaurant serving good pizza and a number of local specialties. Better still is a meal at one of the local *agriturismi:* The best are **Il Castagno,** Via Radicosa 39 (✆ **081-8025164**); **Mare e Monti,** Via Santa Lucia 24–26 (✆ **081-8025226** or 340-7394470); and **Zi' Carmine,** Via Fontana 59 (✆ **081-8025032**). Call ahead for reservations at all three.

Minori

3km (2 miles) E of Amalfi

This tiny harbor at the mouth of a small stream—the Reginna Minor—enjoys the largest beaches on the Costiera after Maiori (p. 237) and hides a few little-known art treasures.

ESSENTIALS

GETTING THERE & AROUND Minori is on the SS 163, between Amalfi and Vietri, west of Maiori. In addition to the **bus** from Amalfi, you can take a **taxi** or **car** from Amalfi or Positano (see "Getting Around," p. 210 and 191). The town is small enough to explore **on foot,** but you can get a **taxi** at the harbor (or call ✆ 089-877435). To explore by sea, you can **rent motorboats and sailboats** at **Noleggio,** Via Marte 3 (✆ **089-852149** or 335-5443010; www.amalficharter.it).

VISITOR INFORMATION The **tourist office** (✆ **089-877087**; www.proloco. minori.sa.it) is on Piazza Cantilena.

The **pharmacy** (✆ **089-877200**) is on Corso Vittorio Emanuele, but the closest **hospital** is in Salerno (see "Visitor Information," p. 283). For an **ambulance,** dial ✆ 118. For the **police,** call ✆ 113 or 112. The **post office** (✆ **089-877087**) is on Via Pergola. Several banks have **ATMs,** including **Banco di Napoli,** Corso Vittoria Emanuele 29 (✆ **089-877150**).

SPECIAL EVENTS A number of festivals and events take place in summer. The much-acclaimed **summer music festival** enlivens the town's cultural scene, and the Associazione Musical Costiera Amalfitana hosts the annual **Jazz on**

the Coast (✆ 338-4076618; www.
jazzonthecoast.it) festival in July. Contact the tourist office for a full schedule of events.

EXPLORING THE TOWN

Minori is a quiet, picturesque little town
with a beautiful sandy beach, gloriously
nestled between blue seas and citrus groves.
With its small harbor on a beautiful cove,
however, the village was once the arsenal
for the medieval Republic of Amalfi. A few
steps from the beach is the **Basilica of
Santa Trofimena.** Dating from the 11th
century, the cathedral was completely rebuilt in the 19th century; its original crypt
(restored in the 17th c.) houses the remains
of Saint Trofimena, Amalfi's protector saint.
A wonderful 12th-century **Campanile ★**
, the sole remnant of the church of Santa
Annunziata, sits high on the hill among the
lemon groves overlooking the town. You can
climb up to admire its original inlay decorations and the fine view; take the road to the
left of the Basilica and follow the signs—
and steps—up to "Campanile Annunziata."

Minori's Campanile.

Following the canal along the road from the beach, you will come to **Villa
Romana,** aka **Villa Marittima ★**, Via Santa Lucia (✆ 089-852893; Mon–Sat
9am to 1 hr. before sunset), a patrician villa dating from the 1st century A.D. It
was discovered in 1932 but was not excavated until the 1950s. The villa was
built on two floors around a vast courtyard graced by a pool and surrounded by
a portico. One side of the portico opens onto the beautiful ninfeo, a hall richly
decorated with frescoes and stucco work. Also of architectural interest are the
perfectly preserved thermal baths. The **Antiquarium** contains a collection of
artifacts and frescoes from this and nearby excavations.

WHERE TO STAY

Hoel Santa Lucia ☺ This modern hotel offers comfortable accommodations on
the outskirts west of town. Guest rooms are appointed with no-nonsense furnishings, good-size bathrooms (shower only), and private balconies (in some). Good
options for families, quads rent for a reasonable 165€. Guests enjoy special rates
at the nearby beach. The hotel's **restaurant** is good and moderately priced.

Via Nazionale 44, 84010 Minori. www.hotelsantalucia.it. ✆ **089-853636.** Fax 089-877142. 35
units. 124€ double. Rates include buffet breakfast. Children 2 and under stay free in parent's
room. AE, DC, MC, V. Parking 18€. Closed Nov–Mar. **Amenities:** Restaurant; bar; room service;
smoke-free rooms. *In room:* A/C, TV, minibar, Wi-Fi (3€/hour).

Hotel Villa Romana ★ In our opinion, the welcoming Villa Romana is the
best hotel in town and offers spacious and pleasantly furnished guest rooms, with
whitewashed walls, woodwork, and tiled floors. Bathrooms are modern and a good

size (some with shower only). The swimming pool with solarium is a bonus.
Corso Vittorio Emanuele 90, 84010 Minori. www.hotelvillaromana.it. ℂ **089-877237.** 50 units.
165€ double. Rates include buffet breakfast. Children 2 and under stay free in parent's room.
AE, DC, MC, V. Free parking. **Amenities:** Restaurant; bar; pool; room service. *In room:* A/C, TV,
minibar.

WHERE TO EAT

Minori is a little culinary heaven that is proud of its specialties, both savory
and sweet. In the former category are *sarchiapone* (squash filled with ground
meat and ricotta and cooked in a tomato sauce) and *'ndunderi* (fresh homemade
dumplings made of spelt flour and fresh cheese, served with olive oil, cheese,
local herbs, and often chopped walnuts). The latter category is best represented
by the mouth-watering *sospiri,* or *Zizz'e monache;* the first name translates as
"sighs," and the second as "nuns' breasts"—the sacred and profane names for
the delicious dome-shaped pastries filled with lemon cream. You can taste *sospiri*
and additional wonderful pastries at **Pasticceria De Riso,** Piazza Cantilena 1
(ℂ**089-877396;** www.deriso.it), one of the best pastry shops in Italy.

Il Giardiniello ★ AMALFITAN/PIZZA Good food and a cozy atmosphere
mark this restaurant that is especially charming in nice weather, when you can
dine in the lemon grove. The menu focuses on seafood—try the splendid *lagan-
elle alla marinara* (fresh eggless pasta with squid, shrimp, arugula, and cherry
tomatoes), a rich *riso al nero di seppia* (rice with squid ink), or the satisfying *alici
impanate con la provola* (fresh anchovies deep-fried with cheese). In the evening,
pizzas are offered—and very good ones at that.
Corso Vittorio Emanuele 17. ℂ **089-877050.** www.ristorantegiardiniello.com. Reservations
recommended. Secondi 14€–22€; pizza 5€–11€. AE, DC, MC, V. Thurs–Tues noon–3pm and
7–11:30pm (also Wed June–Sept).

La Botte 🍴 AMALFITAN/PIZZA In a former church near the Villa Romana's
archaeological site, the rustic decor of this popular restaurant makes a picturesque setting for a hearty meal, and the arbor terrace is delightful in summer.
The cuisine ranges from the classic *scialatielli ai frutti di mare* (fresh homemade
pasta with shellfish) to such adventurous choices as ravioli *con aragosta e crema
d'asparagi* (ravioli with lobster and cream of asparagus). Chef Mastro Pantaleone
makes his own pasta, such as the delightful pumpkin ravioli, which is served with
provola cheese, tomatoes, and porcini mushrooms. In the evening, the menu includes a whopping 36 kinds of pizza.
Via S. M. Vetrano 15. ℂ **089-877893.** Reservations recommended Sat–Sun. Secondi 7€–18€.
DC, MC, V. Wed–Mon 12:30–3pm and 7:30–11pm (also Tues in summer). Closed 3 weeks in Jan.

Maiori ★
6km (4 miles) E of Amalfi on SS 163

Maiori opens onto one of the largest—and, consequently most developed—
beaches of the whole Costiera. The area is popular among Italians as a seaside
resort, but few foreign tourists come this way. While it might lack the unique
charm of Positano and Ravello, Maiori enjoys the same beautiful sea and its own
distinctive character.

ESSENTIALS

GETTING THERE & AROUND Maiori is on SS 163 between Amalfi and Vietri, a short distance east of Minori. In addition to the **bus** from Amalfi, you can grab a **taxi** or a **car** from Amalfi or Positano (see "Getting Around," p. 219 and 191). The town is walkable, but you can find a **taxi** (✆ 089-8541608) on the Lungomare Amendola.

VISITOR INFORMATION Azienda Autonoma di Soggiorno e Turismo (✆ 089-877452; www.aziendaturismo-maiori.it) provides tourist information at Corso Reginna 73.

You'll find **pharmacies** at Via Santa Tecla (✆ 089-877063) and Corso Reginna (✆ 089-877052). The nearest **hospital** is in Salerno (see "Visitor Information," p. 283). For an **ambulance**, dial ✆ 118. You can call the **police** at ✆ 113 or 112. The **post office** (✆ 089-877095) is at Via Orti. Banks with **ATMs** include **Banco di Napoli** (✆ 089-854162) on Lungomare Amendola, and **Monte dei Paschi** (✆ 089-851675) at Via Nuova Provinciale Chiunzi 19.

EXPLORING THE TOWN

In the Middle Ages, Maiori was an important town, surrounded by walls and defended by towers and castles, with elegant palaces and buildings along the covered-over Reginna Maior river. Like Amalfi, the river ran under the main street, but a disastrous flood in 1954 took out the road, collapsing all the adjacent buildings and destroying the medieval town. It was rebuilt with nondescript modern edifices, but if you venture out of the town center, you'll discover some narrow medieval streets spared by the flood. Dominating the village from atop 108 steps is a memento of Maiori's glorious past, the **Collegiata di Santa Maria a Mare,** Corso Reginna (✆ 089-877090). Built in the 12th century, this church is graced by a large majolica cupola, a richly carved wooden ceiling dating from the 16th century, and, in the crypt, the original majolica floor from the same period. Adjacent to the church, the **Museo d'Arte Sacra Don Clemente Confalone** houses valuable art from the church's past.

The wide **seaside promenade** is a pleasant place to enjoy excellent views all the way to the diminutive rocky harbor to the west of town. The **beach** below gets rather crowded in summer and is the usual Italian affair, with establishments renting out chairs, umbrellas, and **boats**—motor or rowboats—with which you can explore the coast. You can also rent boats at the harbor. One easy **boat excursion** ★★ is to follow the beach east past the Norman Tower. In the cliff below is a grotto, whose dubious attraction is a sulfur-smelling mineral spring; but farther on is a secluded crescent of beach and, beyond that, the partially underwater entrance to **Grotta Pannone.**

An area to explore on foot is the promontory of **Capo d'Orso** ★★, east of town. Covering 500 hectares (1,235 acres), with an average altitude of 70m (230 ft.), the protected natural area extends all the way to Torrente Bonea and is perhaps the most scenic stretch of the whole Amalfi Coast. The underlying limestone promontory has been eroded by the sea, and stones poke through the blanket of *macchia mediterranea,* creating a unique dolomitic landscape. A scenic trail ★ leads from SS 163 to the **lighthouse** and the entrance to the preserve. Right on the SS 163/Via Diego Tajani is the **Abbazia di Santa Maria de Olearia** ★; you can call the Town Hall in Maiori to arrange a visit: (✆ 089-814209). Locally known as the Catacombe di Badia, this extraordinary place

The Abbazia di Santa Maria de Olearia.

was completely carved out of the solid cliff face. Begun in the 10th century as a shrine to Santa Maria de Olearia, it was soon surrounded by a few cliff dwellings, which were then transformed into a monastery in the 11th century. The main chapel has a vaulted ceiling and an apse, both decorated with 11th-century fresco work; underneath is the crypt, where well-preserved frescoes depict the Virgin Mary and two saints.

WHERE TO STAY

Hotel San Francesco This well-designed modern hotel is in a quiet location a short distance from the sea, near the harbor and the center of town, and is surrounded by a garden. Guest rooms are spacious and pleasantly furnished with hardwood, wrought iron, tiled floors, and private balconies affording superior views. Bathrooms are modern, but not large, and the hotel is scrupulously clean. Guests enjoy beach rights on the hotel's beach, and the formal **restaurant** has a pleasant garden and serves local cuisine, with an emphasis on seafood.

Via Santa Tecla 54, 84010 Maiori. www.hotel-sanfrancesco.it. ⓒ/fax **089-877070.** 44 units. 170€–200€ double. Rates include buffet breakfast. Children 2 and under stay free in parent's room. AE, DC, MC, V. Free parking. Pets accepted. **Amenities:** Restaurant; bar; room service. *In room:* A/C, TV, minibar.

Reginna Palace Hotel ★ This desirable hotel is the perfect base for a leisurely vacation. Management favors week-long bookings, but shorter stays are accommodated depending on availability. An elegant property right in the heart of Maiori, it is surrounded by a luxurious garden. The noteworthy swimming pool is filled with seawater. Guest rooms are spacious and furnished in contemporary style with fine fabrics and artistically tiled floors and bathrooms. A number of the rooms have ocean views, and some have private balconies. Guests enjoy access to the hotel's beach (15€–21€ per day for an umbrella and chair, depending on the season), only 46m (150 ft.) away; and the elegant on-site **restaurant** has a lovely outdoor terrace for dining on warm summer nights.

Via Cristoforo Colombo 1, 84010 Maiori. www.hotelreginna.it. ✆**089-877183.** Fax 089-851200. 65 units. 150€ double. Rates include buffet breakfast. Children 2 and under stay free in parent's room. Internet specials available. Minimum 2-week stay around Aug 15. AE, DC, MC, V. Parking 18€. Closed Nov–Mar. **Amenities:** Restaurant; 2 bars; pool; room service. *In room:* A/C, TV, minibar.

WHERE TO EAT

Maiori has lots of good restaurants, starting with those in the hotels we recommend above.

Faro di Capo d'Orso ★★ MODERN AMALFITAN In an elegant glassed-in dining room, with spectacular views over Capri and Ravello, this restaurant offers haute cuisine and an elegant atmosphere. The chef loves the bounty of his region and takes the utmost care in combining ingredients. The menu changes with the seasons, the market, and his inspiration, with lots of raw or rare fresh seafood. Among the innovative offerings you might find are *totanetti di paranza farciti di gamberetti bianchi* (local squid stuffed with white shrimp), or *linguine con ragù di calamaretti, pomodorini, prezzemolo e ricci di mare* (pasta with squid, cherry tomatoes, and sea urchins). The desserts are equally elaborate, and the wine list includes the very best of the local vineyards. In the hot summer months "light lunch," a daily menu of cold dishes (salads, *insalata caprese,* and so on) is served on the terrace.

Via Diego Tajani 48 (Strada Statale Amalfitana Km 44). ✆**089-877022.** www.ilfarodicapodorso. it. Reservations recommended. Secondi 20€–30€; tasting menus 65€ and 130€. AE, DC, MC, V. Wed–Mon 12:30–3pm and 7:30–11pm. Closed 2 weeks in Jan.

Torre Normanna ★ CREATIVE AMALFITAN Founded in 1992 by the three Proto brothers, this restaurant has recently moved and changed its name, and there are now four Proto brothers working here. It is currently housed in a 13th-century tower, but luckily, the delicious food has remained the same, and it is still a moderate, reliable choice. A large variety of *antipasti* is complemented by tasty and rich homemade pasta, such as *tortelli con crostacei e porcini* (large ravioli with shellfish and porcini mushrooms) and *quadroni di carne con burro e salvia* (meat ravioli in sage and butter). The menu includes excellent meat options, so when it comes to the secondo you might try the lamb or rabbit for a change of pace from the Costiera's omnipresent fish.

Via Diego Taini 4. ✆**089-851418.** www.torrenormanna.net. Reservations recommended. Secondi 20€–45€. AE, DC, MC, V. Daily 12:30–3pm and 7:30–11pm (closed Mon Nov–Mar). Closed 3 weeks in Nov and 3 weeks in Jan.

Mammato 🗣 AMALFITAN Set on the seafront, this relaxed, no-frills restaurant is popular among locals who come to eat seafood prepared according to the region's traditional recipes. Among the noteworthy classics are *scialatielli ai frutti di mare* (homemade pasta with basil and seafood), and *frittura* (deep-fried calamari and small fish).

Lungomare Amendola. ✆**089-877036.** www.ristorantemammato.it. Reservations recommended. Secondi 7€–18€. AE, DC, MC, V. Wed–Mon noon–3:30pm and 6:30pm–midnight (also Tues in summer). Closed 2 weeks in Nov.

Cetara ★

6km (3¾ miles) W of Vietri; 15km (9⅓miles) E of Amalfi on SS 163

Off the beaten path for most foreign tourists, Cetara is a picturesque village with a still-active—if controversial—fishing tradition. It is a great place for relaxing on the beach or for a meal by the sea.

ESSENTIALS

GETTING THERE & AROUND In addition to the **SITA bus** from Salerno and Amalfi, you can come by **taxi** or **car** (see "Getting Around," p. 282 and 208). If you are **driving,** take SS 163 past Vietri; Cetara is the next town. The town is small and you'll be able to travel **on foot.**

VISITOR INFORMATION The **Proloco tourist office** (✆089-261593; www. prolococetara.it) is at Corso Garibaldi 15.

You'll find a **pharmacy** (✆089-261082) at Corso Umberto 43. The closest **hospital** is in Salerno (see "Visitor Information," p. 283). For an **ambulance,** dial ✆118. To reach the **police,** call ✆113 or 112. The **post office** (✆089-261065) is at Corso Federici, and a **bank** (✆089-261313) with an **ATM** is at Corso Garibaldi 11.

EXPLORING THE TOWN

An important fishing port since Roman times—Cetara actually derives its name from the Latin *cetaria* (tuna fishery)—this still is the main fishing port in the area and very authentic. The town's *tonnare* (tuna-fishing facilities) were big complexes built mostly over the sea: the Tuna were trapped in huge netting channels out at sea and brought to underwater cages. From there, the fish were pushed into a seawater pool, where they were processed. Today, most catches happen at sea, with massive trawlers and often with the help of planes that scour the Mediterranean for the red tuna.

This is definitely an industry, not a sport, and we don't endorse unsustainable practices, no matter how traditional. Recent research shows that the tuna collected are actually young tuna that have not yet reached full maturity, which in turn contributes to the depletion of the species. Yet locals proudly defend their traditional fleet, the only one left in the Tyrrenian Sea, as well as their traditional cuisine.

Locals celebrate in July with the **Sagra del Tonno (Tuna Festival),** when preserved tuna and other local delicacies are sold in town; the festival also features music and other scheduled events. Contact the **Proloco tourist office** (p. 241) for more information.

The rest of the year, the key attraction is the **San Pietro** church, with its bright majolica cupola and 13th-century bell tower. We recommend a stroll around the back streets of the village, rarely visited by tourists.

The best beach in the area is **Marina di Erchie,** technically in Maiori. It's past the next village, only 2km (1¼ miles) west of Cetara. If you don't want to venture that far, check out the small beaches by Cetara's harbor.

WHERE TO STAY

Hotel Cetus ★ ✦ ☺ In a spectacularly panoramic cliffside location just outside town, this is a great hotel (and the only one in town). Guest rooms are larger than average, comfortable, and bright, with scenic views and colorful tiled floors and bathrooms. The Cetus is particularly welcoming to children; it has its own sandy cove with umbrellas and chairs for its guests, along with a playground. Of the on-site restaurants—both upscale—**Il Gabbiano** offers excellent, traditional food; and Falalella serves up gourmet international cuisine.

Corso Umberto I 1, 84010 Cetara. www.hotelcetus.com. ℂ/fax **089-261388.** 43 units. High season 260€ double; 320€ suite. Rates include breakfast. Children 2 and under stay free in parent's room. AE, MC, V. Free parking. **Amenities:** Restaurant; bar; babysitting; concierge; room service. *In room:* A/C, TV, hair dryer, minibar.

WHERE TO EAT

Cetara's secret has spread from nearby Salerno to the rest of Italy, and gourmets come to partake of the local cuisine based on the freshest seafood just brought in from the harbor. Anchovies are the specialty here—be they roasted, grilled, deep-fried, or dressed with local herbs. You can buy fresh fish and preserved anchovies at **Pescheria Battista Delfino,** Via Umberto I 78 (ℂ **089-261069**), or at **Pescheria San Pietro,** Via Umberto I 72 (ℂ **089-261147**).

Acquapazza ★ AMALFITAN This small and trendy trattoria just up the hill from the harbor is a good place to sample local fish and experience high cuisine without spending a fortune. It prepares a wonderful array of *antipasti,* including *tortino di melanzane e alici* (fresh anchovy and eggplant flan), marinated tuna, and *carpaccio di pesce* (raw fish in a citrus sauce), and a number of tasty pasta dishes, such as *tubetti al ragù di pesce* (short pasta with a seafood and tomato sauce). For a secondo, you can pick your fish from the daily catch display and have it prepared as you choose; fish is charged by weight.

Corso Garibaldi 38. ℂ **089-261606.** www.acquapazza.it. Reservations recommended Sat–Sun. Secondi 20€–30€. AE, DC, MC, V. Tues–Sun 12:30–3pm and 7:30–11pm. Closed Nov.

Ristorante Pizzeria Al Convento ★ ☺ AMALFITAN/PIZZA The perfect place to satisfy the whole family, this welcoming restaurant offers delicious local specialties as well as tasty *pizza al metro* (pizza by the yard) in the tradition of Vico Equense (p. 162); **Note:** The pizza is excellent but is served only at dinnertime. The frescoed dining hall is a great setting for a meal, but so is the outdoor arbor terrace. The menu is centered on seafood, and particularly on anchovies, the local fish. Try the classic spaghetti *alla colatura di alici* (seasoned with anchovies), and the *totani e patate* (calamari with potatoes). **Cooking classes** are offered, which start at the market and guide you all the way through to the presentation of the finished meal.

Piazza S. Francesco 15. ℂ **089-261039.** www.alconvento.net. Reservations recommended. Secondi 12€–18€; tasting menu 30€. AE, DC, MC, V. Thurs–Tues 12:30–4pm and 7pm–2am (open daily May 15–Sept 30).

San Pietro ★ AMALFITAN This elegant yet pleasantly down-to-earth and reasonably priced restaurant has a small dining room and a few tables under an arbor, where you can enjoy a most satisfying meal. In addition to the perfectly prepared dishes that uphold the local tradition—such as vermicelli *con colatura di alici* (with anchovy essence) and fried anchovies—we recommend the innovative dishes that might include *riso con sconcigli* (rice with fresh seafood and seaweed) or *pezzogna allo sfusato di Amalfi* (fish with local lemon sauce).

Piazza San Francesco 2. ℂ **089-261091.** www.sanpietroristorante.it. Reservations recommended. Secondi 15€–30€. AE, DC, MC, V. Wed–Mon noon–3pm and 7–10:30pm (open daily in summer). Closed 2 weeks in Jan–Feb.

Vietri sul Mare ★★

5km (3 miles) W of Salerno on SS 163

The gateway to the Amalfi Coast, Vietri is a small working town with a well-established traditional craft industry. Vietri's main street, with its famous ceramic shops, gets a lot of tourist attention; but it usually makes for a hit-and-run shopping excursion, which leaves the area otherwise undisturbed. Vietri is also well worth a visit for its scenic seashore.

ESSENTIALS

GETTING THERE & AROUND In addition to the **SITA bus** from Salerno and Amalfi, you can use a **taxi** or a **car** (see "Getting Around," p. 282 and 208). If you are **driving,** take SS 163 north, and Vietri is the first town. Once there, you'll be able to get around **on foot.**

VISITOR INFORMATION The **Proloco tourist office** (✆089-211285) is in the Municipal Building on Piazza Matteotti.

You'll find a **pharmacy** (✆089-210181) at Corso Umberto 12. The closest **hospital** is in Salerno (see "Visitor Information," p. 283). For an **ambulance,** dial ✆118. You can reach the **police** at ✆113 or 112. The **post office** (✆089-211897) is at Via Giuseppe Mazzini 38. **Banks** with **ATMs** include the **Banco di Napoli,** Via Giuseppe Mazzini 30 (✆089-763154).

EXPLORING THE TOWN

The heart of town is Via Madonna degli Angeli, closed to car traffic and lined with shops selling local ceramics (p. 244). No visit is complete without a stop at the **Duomo ★**, the church dedicated to **San Giovanni Battista,** with its cupola adorned with painted majolica. Inside, in addition to some excellent 17th-century ceramics, is the impressive carved and gilded 18th-century ceiling and artwork that includes a 16th-century polyptych of the Virgin Mary and an 11th-century crucifix.

The most famous of the ceramic shops is **Ceramica Artistica Solimene Vincenzo ★**, Via Madonna degli Angeli 7 (✆089-210243; www.solimene.com), one of Vietri's historic workshops. Besides visiting the showroom and buying contemporary ceramics, admire the building itself—a beautiful example of organic architecture from the 1930s by Paolo Soleri, who went on to work in the U.S. with Frank Lloyd Wright.

From Piazza Matteotti in the center of town, descend Via Costabile about 1km (a half-mile) to arrive at the beach of **Marina di Vietri ★**, dominated by a watchtower that was transformed into a villa; across its surrounding park is a small, more secluded beach, but it becomes crowded and dirty at the height of summer.

SHOPPING

Famous for their quality and vivid colors, the local ceramics make for a perfect souvenir for yourself or a gift for someone at home. The town feels like an open-air showroom, with walls along the main streets lined with beautiful tableware, ceramics of all kinds, and shelves burgeoning with variously shaped bowls and vases. After an initial pass-through, you'll begin to see stylistic differences and be able to spot individual artists, each characterized by a proprietary pattern and

Vietri sul Mare's Duomo and its painted majolica.

color palette. Most artists sell directly from their premises in town, or in the nearby suburb of Molina, due north past the train station along Via Enrico De Marinis. In town, some of the showrooms belong to individual artists, while other boutiques sell pieces from a variety of artists. Some of them specialize by technique, depending whether the terra cotta is thrown or pressed (the latter uses a mold).

Recommended studios include **Ceramiche Artistiche Pinto,** Corso Umberto I 27 (✆089-210271); **Vietritaly,** Corso Umberto I 45 (✆089-211122;** www.vietritaly.it); **Solimene Ceramica,** Via Case Sparse, Fontana Vecchia (✆089-210188;** www.solimeneceramica.com); **Tortora & Giordano,** Via Travertino 17 (✆089-211894); and **Antonio D'Acunto,** Via Enrico De Marinis 33, Molina Di Vietri Sul Mare (✆089-211143). For pressed terra cotta we also recommend **Cotto Artistico Vietrese,** Via Travertino 17 (✆089-211894); **Alfonso Fasano,** Via E. De Marinis 45, Molina Di Vietri Sul Mare (✆089-211598); and **Giuseppe Landi,** Via Chellavanna 51, Molina Di Vietri Sul Mare (✆089-211819), whereas for thrown terra cotta, try **Il Vasaio Vietrese Di Apicella Benvenuto,** Via D. Taiani 110 (✆089-761152). We are very fond of the little goats that are the trademark of **D'Amore,** Via De Marinis 64; they have been imitated by many, so look for his signature on each piece. Most shops will ship your purchases home for you, but ask before buying.

Raito: An Excursion to the Interior

Along the road that heads out of town and inland, we discovered **Raito ★,** a picturesque little village of whitewashed houses and gardens that enjoy excellent views of the bay. The highlights here are the 16th-century church **Madonna delle Grazie ★,** with a chapel decorated by Luca Giordano, and the historic **Villa Guariglia ★,** surrounded by a park. In the scenic Torretta Belvedere is the **Museo della Ceramica,** Via Nuova Raito (✆089-211835; free admission;

Tues–Sun 8am–7pm; closes earlier in winter). Created in 1981, the museum's collection retraces the history of the local ceramic production and includes a number of masterworks from religious art and everyday items to the "German period," with works created or inspired by the wave of foreign (mainly German) artists who came to Vietri between 1929 and 1947. On most evenings during the summer season, Villa Guariglia is the enchanting setting for classical music **concerts;** call the tourist information office in Vietri (p. 243) for information on the program. To reach Raito, take SP 75 off SS 163; it's about 2km (1¼ miles) west of Vietri. Only 1km (a half-mile) farther on is the little hamlet of **Albori,** with its 16th-century church, **Santa Margherita ad Albori,** and prime sea views.

The Villa Guariglia.

WHERE TO STAY & EAT

Hotel Raito ★ This luxurious, modern resort hotel enjoys a superior position high on the cliffs in the village of Raito, west of Vietri. Guest rooms are spacious and comfortable, with modern, stylish furnishings; most offer breathtaking views and balconies. The newly added Seiren wing offers exclusive decor and service, including free Wi-Fi and daily fruit and spumante. All units have good-size (and new) bathrooms. Guests can ride the free hotel shuttle down to the private beach or just take it easy and enjoy the pools and the spa. The hotel's **restaurants** serve a range of traditional and international cuisine.

Via Nuova Raito 9, Frazione Raito, 84010 Vietri sul Mare. www.hotelraito.it. ✆ **089-7634111.** Fax 089-7634801. 75 units. 220€–280€ double; from 490€ suite. Rates include buffet breakfast. Internet specials available. AE, DC, MC, V. Free parking. **Amenities:** 3 restaurants; bar; babysitting; concierge; pool (for a fee); room service; spa (for a fee). *In room:* A/C, TV, Internet, minibar.

THE JEWELS OF THE GULF OF NAPLES:

THE ISLANDS OF CAPRI, ISCHIA & PROCIDA

M uch of the splendor of this part of Italy lies in the islands that define the Gulf of Naples. Ischia and Procida are the organic extension of Capo Miseno beyond the Phlegrean Fields, and Capri is the natural continuation of Punta Campanella at the tip of the Sorrentine peninsula. Each with its own character, these three islands have enjoyed completely different fortunes as far as tourism is concerned. Capri, the most well known (not to mention the most glamorous), has been a lively resort since antiquity, famous for the debauches of Emperor Tiberius. Ischia, also known to the ancient world, was noted for its spas, and has traditionally remained a place for relaxation. Procida was and still is a low-key fisherman's haunt, where locals continue to make their living from the sea and foreign tourists are comparatively rare.

Of the three, Capri is the most sought after, and the fame of its sights, such as the fabled Blue Grotto, attracts droves of tourists each year. But in spite of huge crowds, it remains a must-see.

Because of their proximity to the mainland, each of these islands makes an easy day trip. Even Ischia, the largest of the three, can be enjoyed in a day: You can arrive early in the morning, check in at one of the spas—we love the ones with scenic outdoor facilities—and leave after a gourmet dinner. Of course, visitors who choose to stay the night will find the islands at their most romantic: Once the last ferryboat full of day-trippers leaves and darkness begins to fall, you begin to get a sense of what these jewels were like before the onset of mass tourism.

ISCHIA: ISOLA VERDE & THE ISLAND OF ETERNAL YOUTH ★★★

42km (26 miles) NW of Naples; 20km (13 miles) W of Pozzuoli

When the Greeks arrived on this coast in the 8th century B.C., they first landed in Ischia, seeing the island as a perfect base from which to dominate the mainland. Yet they quickly changed their minds and moved to nearby Cuma, by modern Pozzuoli (see chapter 5), and it was under the Romans that this volcanic island became famous for its thermal waters with their curative properties. In the Middle Ages, Ischia frequently came under attack from North African Saracens and was further troubled by regular volcanic activity resulting in devastating lava flows. At various times during the ensuing centuries, the island was controlled

PREVIOUS PAGE: **Ischia Ponte.**

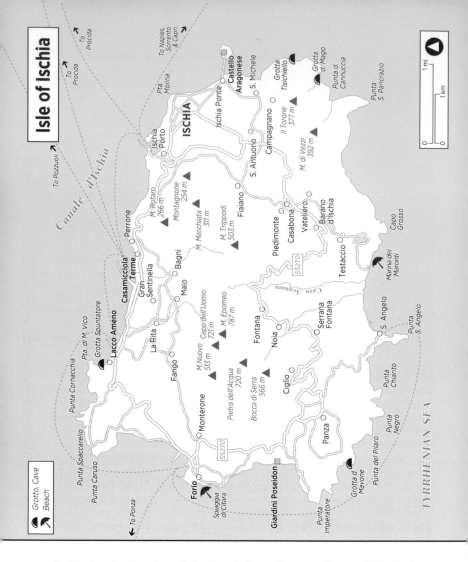

Isle of Ischia

Grotto, Cave
Beach

To Pozzuoli

Canale d'Ischia

To Ponza

Legend and map labels:

To Procida
To Procida
To Naples, Sorrento & Capri

Pta. Molina
Castello Aragonese
Ischia Ponte
S. Michele
Grotta del Mago
Punta d. Carruccia
Punta S. Pancrazio

Ischia Porto
ISCHIA
Campagnano
Grotta Tischiello
Il Torone 377 m

Perrone
M. Rotaro 266 m
Montagnone 254 m
S. Antuono
M. di Vezzi 392 m

Casamicciola Terme
Gran Sentinella
M. Maschiata 311 m
Fiaiano
Piedimonte
Vateliero
Barano d'Ischia
Capo Grosso

Bagni
M. Trippodi 503 m
Casabona

Maio
Cava Acquara
Testaccio
Marina dei Maronti

Lacco Ameno
Grotta Spuntatore
Pta. di M. Vico

La Rita
Capo dell'Uomo 721 m
M. Epomeo 787 m
Fontana
Serrana Fontana
S. Angelo
Punta S. Angelo

Fango
M.Nuovo 513 m
Nola

Monterone
Pietra dell'Acqua 720 m
Bocca di Serra 566 m
Ciglio
Panza
Punta Chiarito

Punta Spaccarello
Punta Caruso
Punta Cornacchia

Forio
Spiaggia di Citara
Giardini Poseidon
Punta Imperatore
Grotta d. Mavone
Punta del Pilaro
Punta Negro

SS270

To Naples, Sorrento & Capri

TYRRHENIAN SEA

1 mi
1 km

248

by Naples, the French, and the British, but still managed to establish the basis of the thriving spa industry that we see today. The first thermal establishment opened in Casamicciola Terme in 1604, and by the 19th century, the thermal waters of Ischia made a compulsory stopover on any Grand Tour itinerary. To this day, savvy travelers flock to the island's thermal baths and hotels for fabulous spa vacations. Monte Epomeo, a 788m-high (2,585-ft.) dormant volcano has enough life in it to feed the mineral hot springs and therapeutic muds that are used by the more than 150 spas on the island. Yet the atmosphere still remains quieter than on Capri, partly because of Ischia's larger size, but also because its large beaches are an attraction for families who help keep things low-key, preserving its calm and bucolic character.

Essentials

GETTING THERE Ischia's three main harbors—Ischia Porto (the largest), Forio, and Casamicciola—are very well connected to the mainland, with most ferries leaving from Pozzuoli and Naples's two harbors of Mergellina Terminal Aliscafi and Stazione Marittima. Both ferry and hydrofoil *(aliscafi)* services are frequent in summer but slow down during the winter, when some of the hydrofoil lines are suspended because of rough seas. **Medmar** (℗ 081-3334411; www.medmargroup.it), **Caremar** (℗ 199-116655 within Italy; www.caremar.it), and **SNAV** (℗ 081-4285555; www.snav.it) offer regular service from Napoli, Pozzuoli, and Procida to Ischia Porto and Casamicciola. **Alilauro** (℗ 081-4972222; www.alilauro.it) runs hydrofoils from Naples (Mergellina and Molo Beverello) to Ischia Porto and to Forio; **NLG-Navigazione Libera del Golfo** (℗ 081-5520763; www.navlib.it) operates from Salerno to Ischia; **Alicost** (℗ 089-234892; www.lauroweb.com/alicost.htm) offers connections from Salerno, Capri, Amalfi, and Positano to Ischia Porto. *Note:* During high season, car access to the island is restricted and the number of car slots is limited; if you are planning to bring your car, check with the transport company and make your reservations well in advance.

GETTING AROUND Ischia is quite large and hilly, and you will need some form of transportation. Public transportation is good, with a well-organized **bus** system with EAV (℗ 800-0539309 toll-free within Italy). One line circles the island toward the right (*circolare destra* marked CD), and one toward the left (*circolare sinistra,* marked CS), plus a number of other lines crisscross the island among its major destinations. Tickets cost 1.30€ and are valid for 90 minutes (a daily pass costs 4.20€ and a 2-day pass costs 6.50€; they are on sale at bars, tobacconists, and news kiosks). You can get a printout of the bus schedule from the tourist office (see "Visitor Information," below).

Ischia.

More expensive, **taxis** wait at stands strategically located around the island, including Piazza degli Eroi (✆ 081-992550) and Piazzetta San Girolamo (✆ 081-993720) in **Ischia Porto;** Piazza Bagni (✆ 081-900881) in Casamicciola; and Piazza Girardi in Lacco Ameno (✆ 081-995113).

Some of the taxis are picturesque three-wheelers—*motorette*—but they are rapidly disappearing. A 10€ minimum charge applies in the small town of Ischia (it's pretty much a flat rate), while drivers use the meter for trips outside town.

You can **rent motor scooters, bicycles,** and **cars** on the island from a number of agencies, including **Autonoleggio In Scooter** in Forio (✆ 081-998513 or 320-4218039; www.autonoleggioinscooter.it) and **Island Center,** Via V. Di Meglio 161 in Barano (✆ 081-902525).

For **boat** rentals, contact **Futurnautica,** Via Porto 86 (✆ 081-993699), or **Nautica Effe,** Via Iasolino 110 (✆ 081-993185), in Ischia town.

VISITOR INFORMATION The **AACST tourist office** (✆ 081-5074231; www.infoischiaprocida.it) is at Via Sogliuzzo 72, Ischia Porto, where you'll find free maps of the island as well as information and brochures. In addition, the **Proloco** (✆ 081-4972293; www.prolocoischia.it) maintains an information booth at Piazza Antica Reggia 11, Ischia Porto, and organizes guided tours.

You'll find **pharmacies** in each of the main villages on the island, including in Ischia, at Via Alfredo De Luca 117 (✆ 081-3331275) and Via Michele Mazzella 143 (✆ 081-985089); in Lacco Ameno, at Corso Rizzoli 77 (✆ 081-900224); and in Casamicciola Terme at Piazza Marina 1 (✆ 081-994060). The **hospital** (✆ 081-5079111) is in Lacco Ameno, on Via Fundera, and the **medical center** (✆ 081-998989) is on Via Cava delle Pezze, Forio. For an **ambulance,** dial ✆ 118. You can call the **police** at ✆ 113 or 112. The main **post office** (✆ 081-992180; Mon–Sat 8am–2pm) is at Via Sogliuzzo, on the corner of Via Pontano. You will find several banks with **ATMs,** including a **Banco di Napoli** (✆ 081-993480), at Via Iasolino 26, Ischia Porto.

SPECIAL EVENTS In May, the island hosts **Ipomea,** an international exposition of rare temperate-zone plants that is held on the exclusive grounds of the **Parco Termale del Negombo** (✆ 081-986152; www.negombo.it).

The **Festival of Sant'Anna** on July 26 is celebrated with fireworks and torchlit boats by the Aragonese Castle. The festival originated from the adoration of Saint Ann, the mother of Mary, who is believed to protect pregnant women. Originally, locals would sail to the small bay of Cartaromana with candles on their bows to honor the saint. Slowly, this tradition developed into the spectacular **Festa del Mare,** in which a procession of boats and floats crosses the water, and the castle and harbor are illuminated. If you are in the area around this time, be sure not to miss this memorable sight.

Summer is also the height of the musical season at **La Mortella** (✆ 081-986220; www.lamortella.it), the seat of the William Walton Foundation. Besides the concerts, the foundation also hosts a yearly music and opera workshop. An additional musical event is the **Ischia Jazz**

Festival (www.ischiajazz.eu or www.circuitojazz.it), which usually takes place over 5 days in the beginning of September.

The Ischia Film Festival (www.ischiafilmfestival.it) is a fast-growing event that takes place in early July each year, based in the Castello Aragonese.

Exploring the Island

Ischia is the largest of Campania's islands, covering about 46 sq. km (18 sq. miles). Its velvety slopes, green with pine woods and vineyards, have earned it the nickname **Isola Verde (Green Isle),** while its fame as a healthy retreat has earned it another nickname, **Island of Eternal Youth,** for its peaceful atmosphere and its spas. These are fueled by the widespread volcanic activity still present on the island, although its volcano, Mount Epomeo, has long been dormant. Hot springs, mineral-water springs, and steam and hot-mud holes dot the island's slopes.

Once separate, **Ischia Porto** and **Ischia Ponte ★★** have now merged into one; together they make up the largest town on the island, lying on its northeastern corner. The two are linked by the pleasant promenade of Via Roma and Corso Vittoria Colonna (known locally as "Il Corso") stretching about 2km (1¼ miles). The majority of activity is concentrated in **Ischia Porto,** around its naturally round harbor which is, in fact, an extinct volcano crater. The town was founded in the 18th century by the Bourbons who fell in love with a villa-cum-spa built by a doctor, Francesco Buonocore, and decided to establish their residence there. They transformed the villa overlooking the lake into a small palace—what happened to the doctor is unknown; maybe he graciously donated his home to their majesties—the **Casina Reale Borbonica,** which today houses a military spa (closed to the public). They also cut a channel into the outer shore of the lake, transforming it into the present-day large harbor. Inaugurated in 1854, it has been the island's major port ever since. Today, Ischia Porto is a typically bustling and attractive Mediterranean port town with a yacht-filled marina, a busy commercial port, and plenty of restaurants and bars strung out along the water's edge.

Ischia Ponte is more attractive and retains something of the atmosphere of a sleepy fishing village. It is dominated by the vast bulk of the **Castello Aragonese ★★** which looms over the town from atop a rocky islet that is linked to the main island by a causeway-like bridge (or "ponte"). This islet, with its small natural harbor, is the site of the original Greek settlement which was fortified in the 5th century B.C. Alfonso of Aragon re-inforced the fortifications in the mid–15th century and added the bridge. We recommend a visit to the **castle ★★** (Piazzale Aragonese, Ischia Ponte; ✆ **081-992834;** www.castellodischia.it; 10€ adults, 6€ youth 9–19; free for children 8 and under; winter 10am–4:30pm, summer 9am–7:30pm) for the spectacular views from its terraces and ramparts; you can take the elevator to the top or walk up, but it's a steep climb. The last eruption of Mount Epomeo, in 1301, destroyed most of the village that had grown around the small natural harbor. The population resettled, but closer to the castle and bridge.

A short distance (6.5km/4 miles) from Ischia town, along the coast to the west, lies the small village of **Casamicciola Terme ★**, with its scenic harbor and **marina** (although, being right on the main road, its charm is compromised somewhat by the traffic), and **Villa Ibsen,** where the famous Norwegian writer wrote *Peer Gynt*. Founded in the 16th century to take advantage of the area's

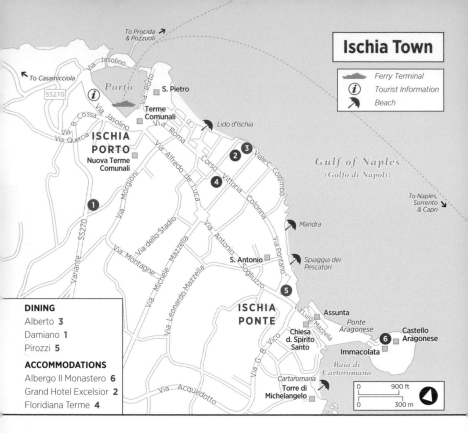

To Procida ↗
& Pozzuoli

To Casamicciola ←

Porto

SS270

i

Via Jasolino

Via Porto

S. Pietro

Terme Comunali

Lido d'Ischia

Via B. Cossa

Via Jasolino

Via Quercia

Via

ISCHIA PORTO

Nuova Terme Comunali

Via Roma

Via Alfredo de Luca

Corso Vittoria Colonna

Viale C. Colombo

❷ **❸**

❹

Gulf of Naples
(Golfo di Napoli)

To Naples, Sorrento & Capri ↘

❶

Via Morgioni

Via dello Stadio

Via Michele Mazzella

Via Leonardo Mazzella

Via Antonio

Via Sogliuzzo

Mandra

S. Antonio

Spiaggia dei Pescatori

Via Montagne

Variante

SS270

Via Pontano

❺

ISCHIA PONTE

Via Luigi Mazzella

Assunta

Ponte Aragonese

Chiesa d. Spirito Santo

Immacolata

Castello Aragonese

❻

Via G. B. Vico

Via Acquedotto

Baia di Cartoromana

Cartaromana
Torre di Michelangelo

Legend	
Ferry Terminal	
i Tourist Information	
↗ Beach	

DINING
Alberto **3**
Damiano **1**
Pirozzi **5**

ACCOMMODATIONS
Albergo Il Monastero **6**
Grand Hotel Excelsior **2**
Floridiana Terme **4**

0   900 ft
0   300 m

thermo-mineral springs, Casamicciola Terme is where the first "modern" spa was opened on the island in 1604. Tragedy struck, however, in 1883 when the village was virtually destroyed by a violent earthquake. It was immediately rebuilt, but closer to the shore, in its current position by the marina. The remains of the original town can be seen a little way inland in the hamlet of **Bagni,** with the island's oldest spas opening onto its main square, and in the village of **Majo,** farther up the slope.

Adjacent to Casamicciola, 8km (5 miles) west of Ischia Porto, is the picturesque **Lacco Ameno ★★**, famous for the mushroom-shaped rock that stands in the shallow water a few yards from the sandy shore. The ancient Greeks established their first settlement on this coast, although daunted by the frequent—at that time—earthquakes and eruptions, they never developed a colony. An unassuming fishing harbor until the 1950s, it was then shaken out of its torpor by Italian publisher Angelo Rizzoli. He built his villa on the promontory of Monte Vico, overlooking the village to the west, and decided to invest in the area and transform it into an exclusive resort. His plan was successful and the promontory has become the most exclusive spa destination in Italy, offering many luxurious hotels and villas. **Villa Arbusto,** Angelo Rizzoli's own summer home, is today a museum—**Museo Civico Archeologico di Pithecusae ★** (*©* **081-900356;** admission 3€; Tues–Sun 9:30am–1pm and 4–8pm)—displaying the findings of local archaeological excavation. It is worth a visit, if only to admire the famous **Coppa di Nestore** or Nestor's Cup. Dating from 725 B.C., this drinking vessel bears one of the oldest known Greek inscriptions, which, appropriately, celebrates the wine of Ischia. Nearby is an important Catholic pilgrimage site, the **Sanctuary of Santa Restituta** (𝒞 **081-980161;** daily 10am–1pm and 4–7pm), with its attached **archaeological excavations** and **museum.** The original church was created in the 4th or 5th century A.D. by adapting an ancient Roman water cistern, and later restructured.

On the west side of the Monte Vico promontory are the lovely **gardens of Villa La Mortella** ★★, Via F. Calise 39, 80075 Forio (𝒞 **081-986220;** www.lamortella.it). Covering 2 hectares (5 acres), the gardens were created by the famous British landscape gardener Russell Page for Susana Walton, the Argentinean wife of composer Sir William Walton, who collected many rare botanical species. Admission is 12€ for adults, 10€ for children 8 to 16 and adults over 60, 6€ for children 5 to 7, and free for children 4 and under (Apr 1–Nov 15 Tues, Thurs, and Sat–Sun 9am–7pm; ticket booth closes 30 min. earlier).

On the western coast of the island, 13km (8 miles) west of Ischia Porto, is the lively town of **Forio,** with its wealth of bars and beaches. Popular among Naples residents, it is usually bypassed by foreign tourists. A favorite retreat of writers and musicians for centuries, Forio is known for its plethora of fine restaurants and its particularly delicious locally produced wine. The attractive town center is dominated by **Il Torrione,** a solid, late-15th-century watchtower that was one of 12 such constructions built to ward off frequent Saracen attacks. It is occasionally opened for special exhibitions. **La Colombaia,** Via F. Calise 130, 80075 Forio (𝒞 **081-3332147;** www.fondazionelacolombaia.it), is the historic villa of Italian film director Luchino Visconti; it houses a film school and a small **museum** (Mon–Sat 9:30am–12:30pm and 3:30–6:30pm). Our favorite church on Ischia, the

The gardens of Villa La Mortella.

tiny, whitewashed **Madonna del Soccorso** ★★ stands in a spectacular position on a headland jutting out to sea just to the west of the town. Inside, you will find model ships offered to the Madonna by sailors who have survived shipwrecks.

The southern half of Ischia is more agricultural, with only one town on the southern shore: the tiny fishing harbor of **Sant'Angelo** ★★, 11km (7 miles) south of Ischia Porto. Shaded by a tall promontory jutting into the sea and connected to the shore by a sandy isthmus (10m/328 ft. long) that is closed to vehicles, it is one of Ischia's most picturesque sights. Far from the hype of the high-priced spa resorts, it is quite exclusive and secluded. The other villages on this part of the island are nestled on the steep slopes of the mountain, overlooking the sea. **Serrara Fontana** ★★ (9.5km/6 miles southwest of Ischia Porto) is a tiny hamlet centered on a lookout terrace affording spectacular views.

OUTDOOR ACTIVITIES

Ischia's shoreline alternates between rugged cliffs and stretches of sand, to the delight of sunbathers and swimmers. The island's beautiful **beaches** are all the more special because they are a commodity almost completely lacking in the Bay of Naples and the Amalfi Coast. The town of Ischia has a beach—or rather several small ones, the best being the **Spiaggia dei Pescatori,** where local fishermen beach their boats, a short distance west of the Aragonese Castle. You can do way better, though. The island's most beautiful beach is **Spiaggia dei Maronti** ★★★, stretching for about 2km (1¼ miles) east of the village of

> ### Flower Power
>
> Ischia's unusual volcanic characteristics have produced more than spa-perfect conditions. The fertile soil and unique subtropical climate have been so favorable to flowering plants and shrubs that you can find on the island 50% of the entire European patrimony of flower species, a number of them indigenous to Ischia.

Spiaggia dei Pescatori.

Parco Termale Castiglione.

Sant'Angelo, straight down the cliff from **Barano d'Ischia** (4km/2½ miles south of Ischia Porto), but be warned; like others on the island, these long, scenic stretches of sand are very crowded in the summer. The **Spiaggia di Cartaromana ★★**, down from the village of San Michele on the east coast of the island, is on a slightly more secluded cove. North of Forio is the **Spiaggia di San Francesco ★**, overlooked by the promontory of Monte Vico, while south of Forio is the **Spiaggia di Citara ★★**, which used to be the island's largest and most beautiful sandy beach. Though much diminished by erosion, it is still very pleasant and is popular for the hot mineral springs that flow out to sea at its south ern edge; these springs are the same ones that are used by the spa Giardini Poseidon (see "Spas & Thermo-Mineral Treatments," below). We also highly recommend **renting a boat** from one of the harbors and visiting the many coves that are accessible only by sea.

If you are not into swimming or relaxation, you can leave the shoreline and explore the island's hinterland which is dotted with **vineyards** producing excellent D.O.C. wines. You could combine wine tasting with some interesting **hikes** up the slopes of Mount Epomeo. We recommend you get hold of a copy of the small brochure from the tourist office in Ischia, titled *Lizard Trails,* which has descriptions and maps of the island's best trails.

SPAS & THERMO-MINERAL TREATMENTS

What attracts most visitors to Ischia are the island's many **spas,** which offer an endless variety of **thermo-mineral health and beauty treatments.** With over 56 different mineral springs scattered across the island's slopes and beaches, Ischia is spa-paradise with a natural resource that has been harnessed by over 150 spa operators.

A number of the island's modern facilities operate as day parks and are perfect for a one-off visit. If you want to stay longer, many hotels have their own spas and will offer package stays including meals and basic spa services, such as the use of the thermo-mineral pools. Even if you are not particularly interested in spa treatments, the outdoor spa parks are a unique and relaxing experience. **Note:** Many establishments specialize in medical treatments, in which even beauty care and stress relief are tackled from a scientific rather than a pampering

The D.O.C. Wines of Ischia

Ischia's vineyards produce wines that have been increasingly appreciated by connoisseurs; three even earned the D.O.C. label—a government recognition reserved only for those superior wines from specific areas that answer to severe requirements of consistently good quality and characteristics. The winning wines are the red Monte Epomeo, the Ischia (red and white), and the white Biancolella. Wine enthusiasts around the world have to thank the Greeks for this bounty, for it was they who recognized the local potential and planted the varieties of grape still used today to produce the area's wines.

viewpoint. In any case, remember to pack an old swimsuit, possibly dark colored, as the high mineral content of some waters will stain the fabric, or leave a sulfurous smell that is almost impossible to remove.

Located between Ischia Porto and Casamicciola, **Parco Termale Castiglione ★★** (℮ 081-982551; www.termecastiglione.it) is a state-of-the-art facility offering thermo-mineral waters and mud treatments in a mix of indoor and open-air facilities. The scenic outdoor pools range in temperature from 82° to 104°F (28°–40°C). On the promontory of Monte Vico near Lacco Ameno, you'll find **Parco Termale Negombo ★★** (℮ 081-986152; www.negombo. it) nestled in the island's most picturesque cove, **Lido di San Montano.** Here you can enjoy magnificent gardens, a secluded beach, and elegant thermal pools. South of Forio, on the pretty Bay of Citara, is **Parco Termale Giardini Poseidon ★★★**, Via Giovanni Mazzella Citara, Forio d'Ischia (℮ 081-9087111; www. giardiniposeidon.it), an open-air facility with 22 pools (both relaxing and curative), a large private beach, and several restaurants. Finally, to the east of Sant'Angelo, you'll find the **Parco Termale Giardini Aphrodite-Apollon** (℮ 081-999219; www.hotelmiramare.it), an indoor-outdoor facility with lovely grounds and pools that is part of the Park Hotel Miramare (see "Where to Stay," below).

For a more traditional spa experience, we recommend the state-of-the-art **Ischia Thermal Center ★★**, Via delle Terme 15, Ischia (℮ 081-984376; www.ischiathermalcenter.it), which offers a wide range of health and beauty treatments. We also recommend the four historical spas of **Casamicciola Terme**—Terme Manzi, Belliazzi, Elisabetta, and Lucibello—that open onto the famous **Piazza Bagni** in the hamlet of Bagni. For an even more exclusive experience, head to the **Terme della Regina Isabella ★★** (see "Where to Stay," below), a five-star hotel and thermal resort in **Lacco Ameno** and one of the most elegant spas on the island.

Where to Stay
VERY EXPENSIVE
Hotel Regina Isabella ★★ ☺ Set in a beautiful location, with views over the village and harbor, this historic, highly prestigious hotel offers fine

accommodations, a Michelin-starred restaurant, a state-of-the-art thermal spa (p. 255), and a private beach set in a small cove. The public spaces are palatial, with many original furnishings, and the extra amenities will make your stay idyllic. The large guest rooms are decorated with a mix of contemporary and antique, with hand-painted ceramic floors and luxurious bathrooms, and many have private balconies, opening onto views of the sea or the gardens. The hotel's private cove is equipped with floating chairs, suitable for lounging.

Piazza Santa Restituta 1, 80076 Lacco Ameno d'Ischia. www.reginaisabella.it. ℂ **081-994322.** Fax. 081-900190. 126 units 460€–660€ double; from 980€ suite. Rates include buffet breakfast. Children 2 and under stay free in parent's room. Internet specials available. AE, DC, MC, V. Free parking. Closed Nov–Mar, but open 1 week over the New Year. **Amenities:** 2 restaurants; 2 bars; babysitting; children's programs during school holidays; concierge; pool; room service; spa; tennis courts; Wi-Fi (5€/hour). *In room:* A/C, TV, minibar.

Mezzatorre Resort & Spa ★★ Situated near Lacco Ameno, this is arguably the best hotel on the island. Set atop its own rocky point looking straight down to the sea and surrounded by a 3-hectare (7-acre) wooded park, the hotel is built around a 15th-century watchtower that now houses some of the more requested guest rooms (directly connected to the spa by elevator). All guest rooms are spacious and individually decorated in a tasteful mix of Mediterranean and contemporary style, with geometric-design tiled floors, quality furnishings, and warm-colored fabrics. All are equipped with state-of-the-art bathrooms, some with Jacuzzi tubs. Many rooms enjoy private terraces or gardens, and a number of them have splendid sea views. The saltwater pool on a cliff-side terrace is fantastic, and guests can walk down a footpath to the rocky beach.

Via Mezzatorre, 80075 Forio d'Ischia. www.mezzatorre.it. ℂ **081-986111.** Fax 081-986015. www. mezzatorre.it. 60 units. 440€–580€ double; from 720€ suite. Rates include buffet breakfast. Children 1 and under stay free in parent's room. AE, DC, MC, V. Free parking. Closed Nov–Apr. **Amenities:** 2 restaurants; bar; babysitting; concierge; health club; pool; room service; spa; outdoor tennis courts. *In room:* A/C, TV, minibar.

EXPENSIVE

Grand Hotel Excelsior ★ With a perfect location that is convenient to both Ischia Ponte and Ischia Porto, this hotel offers top-notch service and amenities, such as its own private beach. Posh public spaces—a pool with a view, elegant lounges, a spa with a beauty center—are complemented by beautiful, spacious guest rooms. Furnished with great taste and attention to detail, they have wrought-iron bedsteads, hand-painted tile floors, and designer-tiled bathrooms; each room has a private patio-terrace. It is definitely worth paying extra for a room with a view.

Via E. Gianturco 19, 80077 Ischia. www.excelsiorischia.it. ℂ **081-991522.** Fax 081-984100. 76 units. 160€–230€ double; from 380€ suite. Rates include buffet breakfast Children 1 and under stay free in parent's room. AE, DC, MC, V. Closed mid-Oct to mid-Apr. **Amenities:** Restaurant; bar; concierge; health club; pool; room service; spa; *In room:* A/C, TV, minibar.

Park Hotel Miramare Old-fashioned in style but not in spirit, this hotel is in the small village of Sant'Angelo. Opened in 1923 and run by the same family ever since, its real strength is the attached spa, **Aphrodite-Apollon ★**, which includes 12 different pools, extensive treatments and fitness programs, and a private beach. A portion of it is reserved only for nudists, one of the only such beach areas on the island. Guest rooms are bright and comfortable, furnished in an old-fashioned seaside style, with wicker and wrought-iron furniture plus antiques and quality reproductions. Bathrooms are modern (some with shower only), and all the rooms open onto private balconies or terraces overlooking the sea. The hotel also has a few rooms in two separate houses near the spa and beach; guests there have access to the hotel's facilities (192€ double).

Via Comandante Magdalena 29, 80070 Sant'Angelo d'Ischia. www.hotelmiramare.it. © 081-999219. Fax 081-999325. 50 units. 250€–420€ double; from 660€ suite. Rates include buffet breakfast. AE, DC, MC, V. Closed mid–Nov to early Apr. **Amenities:** 2 restaurants; bar; babysitting; children's program; concierge; spa; Wi-Fi (free). *In room:* A/C, TV, hair dryer, minibar.

MODERATE

Floridiana Terme 🏨 This centrally located yet quiet hotel is in the pedestrian area near the harbor in Ischia Porto. Housed in an elegant villa surrounded by greenery, it is only a short walk from the sea. Guest rooms are large, bright, and nicely appointed, with quality furnishings, colorful tiled floors, and good-size bathrooms. All the rooms open onto their own private balcony or terrace, and some have sea views. ***Note:*** The hotel only offers half-board, which means that breakfast and dinner are included in your nightly rate.

Corso Vittoria Colonna 153, 80070 Ischia. www.hotelfloridianaischia.com. © **081-991014.** Fax 081-981014. 64 units. 260€ double. Rates include buffet breakfast and dinner. Children 1 and under stay free in parent's room. AE, DC, MC, V. Closed Nov–Mar. **Amenities:** Restaurant; bar; babysitting; concierge; health club; pool; room service; spa. *In room:* A/C, TV, minibar.

Hotel Casa Celestino 🏖 We like this unassuming hotel that is built vertically, hugging the cliff above the pedestrian promenade in Sant'Angelo and overlooking the pretty harbor. Guest rooms are large and bright, decorated in modern Mediterranean style, with simple furnishings, colorful ceramic-tiled floors, and coordinated fabrics in bold, tasteful colors. Guests appreciate the tiled bathrooms and private terraces (complete with table and chairs), as well as the superb sea views.

Via Chiaia di Rose, 80070 Sant'Angelo d'Ischia. www.casacelestino.it. © **081-999213.** Fax 081-999805. 20 units. 230€ double; 280€ suite. Rates include buffet breakfast. Children 2 and under stay free in parent's room. AE, DC, MC, V. Closed Nov–Mar. **Amenities:** Restaurant; bar; Internet; room service; access to spa. *In room:* A/C, TV, minibar.

INEXPENSIVE

Albergo Il Monastero ★ 🏨 Housed in a former monastery inside Ischia's Aragonese Castle (p. 251), this is the island's most spectacularly situated hotel and offers a unique atmosphere, a warm reception, and superb views. Guest rooms are spacious—especially considering they were monks' cells—and are decorated with stylish sobriety, from the whitewashed walls and tiled floors to the solid dark wood or wicker furniture. The bathrooms are small but fully tiled, with a tasteful design (some are downright tiny, with space for only showerheads and a drain in the tile below). A few rooms boast small but delightful private terraces, while others open onto a common terrace. The restaurant, with tables on a scenic terrace in warm weather, serves excellent local specialties. ***Note:*** The hotel is only accessible by foot.

Castello Aragonese. www.albergomonastero.it. © **081-992435.** Fax 081-991849. 20 units. 120€–160€ double. AE, DC, MC, V. Closed Nov–Mar. **Amenities:** Restaurant; concierge. *In room:* A/C.

Where to Eat

Ischia offers a lively dining scene, especially in the neighborhood of **Ischia Ponte** with its many restaurants and bars, and the exclusive **Via Porto**—called Rive Droite by the locals—lined with elegant nightclubs and restaurants. However, several of the best restaurants are in Forio.

EXPENSIVE

Melograno ★★ CREATIVE ISCHITAN/SEAFOOD We love this restaurant, tucked away from the main streets of Forio. Elegant and welcoming, it offers delightful outdoor dining in a pleasant garden, and truly interesting and delicious cuisine that has received a Michelin star. Three tasting menus are available, and an a la carte menu—centered on seafood—changes with the market and the whims of the talented chef, Libera Iovine. On our last visit we enjoyed *mezzi paccheri al ragù bianco di scoglio* (local pasta with a seafood sauce) and the *crostacei al vapore con salsa di agrumi* (steamed crustaceans with a tangy citrus sauce). Don't miss the local cheese selection and the creatively delicious desserts.

Via G. Mazzella 110, Forio. © **081-998450.** www.ilmelogranoischia.it. Reservations recommended. Secondi 22€–35€; prix-fixe menus 55€, 60€, and 75€. AE, DC, MC, V. Nov–Jan Tues–Wed 7.30–11pm, Thurs–Sun noon–3:30pm and 7:30–11pm; Mar–Sept Mon noon–3:30pm, Tues–Sun noon–3:30pm and 7:30–11pm; Oct Tues–Sun noon–3:30pm and 7:30–11pm. Closed Jan 7–Mar 15.

Mosaico ★★★ CREATIVE ISCHITAN Chef Nino di Costanzo's trail-blazing, highly creative food has earned him two Michelin stars in quick succession, and dinner at his restaurant in the Hotel Manzi Terme is a really special treat. Seasonal menus feature a succession of beautifully balanced fish and meat dishes, some delicately flavored with unusual spices and aromas, that use locally sourced ingredients. The presentation is original and exquisite; service is impeccable. We recommend one of the tasting menus, and you should try and book the "chef's table" in the kitchen and watch the chef at work; it's a fascinating experience.

Piazza Bagni 4, Casamicciola Terme. © **081-994722.** www.manziterme.it. Reservations required. Secondi 27€–40€; menu 95€–130€. AE, DC, MC, V. Wed–Mon 8–10pm. Closed Nov to early Apr.

Umberto a Mare ★★ CAMPANIAN/SEAFOOD This historic restaurant has been drawing diners for decades and is one of our favorites. The beautiful terrace—which affords a matchless panorama and is so romantic at sunset—combines with the gourmet cuisine for a perfect dinner. The menu changes daily according to market availability with a strong focus on seafood. From the copious choices of *antipasti* we loved the *insalatina di mare* (seafood salad) and the *tartare di palamito al profumo d'arancia* (tartar of local fish with citrus). We recommend you follow it with the delicious *pennette all'aragosta e agli asparagi* (short penne with lobster and asparagus) or with the catch of the day, either classically prepared on the grill or *all'acqua pazza* (in a light herb broth).

Via Soccorso 2, Forio. © **081-997171.** www.umbertoamare.it. Reservations recommended. Secondi 25€–36€; prix-fixe menus 60€ and 70€. AE, DC, MC, V. Daily 12:30–3pm and 7–11:30pm. Closed Nov 5–Dec 28 and Jan 7 to late Mar.

MODERATE

Alberto ★ ISCHITANO/SEAFOOD This traditional restaurant, with a veranda right on the beach promenade between the harbor and the Aragonese Castle (p. 251), is an excellent spot for sampling this coast's freshest seafood. The a la carte menu is small and focuses on local specialties as interpreted by the chef, and there are two tasting menus. We highly recommend the *marinata mista* appetizer, a medley of fish marinated in a tangy and delicate citrus sauce, to be followed by the superb linguine *alle vongole* (with clams) and the delicious *pesce all'Alberto* (oven-baked fish with potatoes, olives, and capers). The wine list offers an ample choice of local wines.

Via Cristoforo Colombo, Ischia Porto. ☎ **081-981259.** www.albertoischia.it. Reservations recommended. Secondi 16€–30€; tasting menus 50€ and 60€. AE, DC, MC, V. Daily 12:30–3pm and 7:45–11pm. Closed Nov–Mar except 1 week over the New Year.

Damiano ★ ISCHITANO/SEAFOOD A favorite among locals and visitors who love to come for a romantic dinner, this restaurant is in the outskirts of town, on the steep slope of the mountain. It offers equally tantalizing views and food, with a menu centered on seafood. The dishes change with the market, but we recommend the linguine *con le cozze* (with mussels) and the superb grilled catch of the day. Do absolutely leave room for the fantastic homemade desserts.

Via delle Vigne 30 (in the upper part of town), Ischia Porto. ☎ **081-983032.** Reservations recommended. Secondi 15€–28€. DC, MC, V. Daily 8–11pm. Easter–Oct daily 8pm–midnight.

Trattoria da Peppina ★ 🎁 ISCHITANO/PIZZA Popular among locals in the off season, this restaurant is a great choice for traditional Ischitan food, with a menu featuring local vegetable and meat dishes. We recommend starting with the tasty *bruschette* (slice of grilled peasant bread) seasoned with a choice of beans, smoked sausage, and mushrooms, followed by ravioloni *in salsa di noce* (in walnut sauce). The *grigliata di carne alla brace* (mix of grilled meats) is superb, as is the *coniglio all'Ischitana* (rabbit cooked with tomatoes and herbs in a terracotta casserole).

Via Montecorvo 42, Forio. ☎ **081-998312.** www.trattoriadapeppina.it. Reservations recommended. Secondi 11€–20€; pizza 6€–9€ AE, DC, MC, V. Mar–May and Oct–Dec Thurs–Tues 7pm–midnight; June and Sept daily 7pm–midnight; July–Aug Mon–Sat 7pm–midnight, Sun noon–3:30pm and 7pm–midnight.

INEXPENSIVE

Pirozzi ★ ☺ ISCHITAN/PIZZA/SEAFOOD Conveniently located on the main promenade to the Aragonese Castle (p. 251), this pleasant restaurant offers a nice veranda with sea views and no-nonsense local cuisine at moderate prices. The excellent pizza, offered only in the evening, is popular with children (but is so good you might want it too). Among the more elaborate offerings on the menu, the risotto *alla pescatora* (with seafood) and the tasty grilled fish are top-notch.

Via Seminario 51, Ischia Ponte. ☎ **081-983217.** Reservations recommended for dinner. Secondi 7€–14€; pizza 3€–10€. AE, DC, MC, V. Daily noon–3pm and 7pm–midnight.

Trattoria il Focolare ★ 🎁 CAMPANIAN This famous, family-run country restaurant offers a welcome break from the fare at other restaurants along this coast, with a focus on the turf rather than the surf. The hearty seasonal menu offers masterfully prepared dishes from the local tradition, such as the excellent *tagliata* (steak) or the *tagliatelle al ragu di cinghiale* (steak with wild boar ragout). This is *the* place to sample the local specialty of *coniglio all'Ischitana* (rabbit stewed with garlic and tomatoes), but you need to reserve it in advance. The desserts are also good, including Neapolitan favorites such as *pastiera* (pie filled with ricotta and orange peels).

Via Cretajo al Crocefisso 3, Barano d'Ischia. © **081-902944.** www.trattoriailfocolare.it. Reservations recommended. Secondi 8€–25€. AE, MC, V. Daily 7:30–11:30pm; Fri–Sun 12:30–3pm and 7:30–11:30pm. Closed Wed Nov–May.

Zelluso ★ 👜 😊 ISCHITAN PIZZA/SEAFOOD Hidden away from the marina on a back street, this is a good place to partake of some local culture. Popular with locals and tourists alike, it is often crowded, and you'll have to factor in a wait, even if you made reservations. The pizza, offered only in the evening, is one of the best you'll ever have and is a great favorite among children. Of the traditional seafood offerings, we recommend the well-prepared *sautee di cozze* (sautéed mussels) followed by the linguine *alle vongole* (with clams), and *fritto misto* (medley of deep-fried squid and small fish).

Via Parodi 41, Casamicciola Terme. © **081-994423.** Reservations recommended for dinner. Secondi 10€–15€. AE, DC, MC, V. Daily noon–2.30pm and 7–11pm

Ischia After Dark

The sweet Ischitan nights are best spent outdoors, enjoying a bit of people-watching from the terraces of the many cafes strategically located on the most picturesque seaside promenades and panoramic outlooks. The elegant cafes around the harbor in Ischia are perfect for *aperitivo,* but we also like the unassuming **Da Lilly,** a shack on the rocks, with a simple terrace overlooking the **Spiaggia dei Pescatori** (p. 254) in Ischia Ponte. **La Floreana** (© 081-999570), at the belvedere of Serrara Fontana, is perfect for a sunset *aperitivo* (there is also a simple restaurant). Another great place for a sundowner (plus dinner if you like) is the laid-back **La Tavernetta del Pirata** (© 081-999251), which overlooks the little harbor at Sant'Angelo. Other pleasant cafes line the seaside promenade of Forio and Lacco Ameno; we enjoy **Bar Franco,** Via Roma 94, Lacco Ameno (© 081-980880), where you can sit at the pleasant outdoor terrace facing the beach or simply sample their excellent ice cream. We are rather partial to ice cream and highly recommend those made at **De Maio,** Piazza Antica Reggia 9, Ischia Porto (© 081-991870), the best ice-cream parlor on the island; claiming 80 years of experience, the shop makes wonderful creamy flavors. A few doors away is **Da Ciccio,** Via Porto 1, Ischia Porto (no phone), which makes more creative flavors by adding in nuts, chocolate bits, and so on.

We recommend the **concerts** of classical music and jazz organized by the William Walton Foundation in the lovely gardens of **Villa La Mortella,** Via F. Calise no. 35, 80075 Forio Isola d'Ischia (© 081-986220; www.lamortella.it). The season runs from April to November; concert tickets include admission to the garden and cost 20€ for adults, 15€ for children 13 to 18, and 10€ for children 6 to 12. If you are lucky enough to be on the island for the **Ischia Jazz Festival** (www.ischiajazz.eu) in September, make advance reservations for the scheduled concerts, which usually include some famous international names.

ROMANTIC & UNSPOILED PROCIDA ★★

32km (20 miles) NW of Naples; 12km (8 miles) W of Pozzuoli; 7.8km (5 miles) W of Ischia

The smallest island in the Bay of Naples is also the most densely populated but it is by far the most genuine of the three. Low-key—except for July and August when the population doubles thanks to an influx of Italian holidaymakers—and charming, Procida is largely overlooked by international tourism but is popular with a sailing crowd, whose yachts line the gleaming new marina, and local daytrippers who often come over just for lunch or dinner. The landscape is dotted with pretty houses in pastel hues set in flower-filled gardens and citrus groves, and the coastline is fringed by lovely beaches. A handful of small hotels provide a pleasant choice of lodgings for a few days and there are some excellent restaurants. Above all, you won't find yourself battling with the crowds—and high prices—that blight Capri.

Essentials

GETTING THERE & AROUND Procida is easily reached from Pozzuoli and Naples: **Medmar** (✆ 081-3334411; www.medmargroup.it), **Caremar** (✆ 199-116655; www.caremar.it), and **SNAV** (✆ 081-4285555 or 081-4285500; www.snav.it) offer ferry and hydrofoil service from Napoli, Pozzuoli, and Ischia.

Given Procida's diminutive size (see "Exploring Procida," below), the best way to see the island is definitely **on foot,** or by **bicycle** (which you can rent at most hotels)—although cars are plentiful, and traffic jams are a regular occurrence, especially in summer. You can also take one of the four **public bus** lines run by **SEPSA** (✆ 081-5429965). All of the buses start from Marina Grande; tickets are 1€ per ride. **Taxi stands** are at each of the three marinas and at the ferry terminal; or you can call one for pickup (✆ 081-8968785).

VISITOR INFORMATION The main **AACST tourist office** responsible for Procida is actually on Ischia (✆ 081-5074211; www.infoischiaprocida.it); see p. 250, under Ischia. However, there is a small **Proloco** tourist office on Procida at Via Marina Grande near the ferry dock (✆ 081-8101968). It is open May to September, Monday to Saturday from 9am to 1pm and 3 to 7pm; the rest of the year it's only open mornings. The travel agency **Graziella,** Via Roma 117 (✆ 081-8969594; www.isoladiprocida.it), is another good resource for help with hotel reservations and boat rentals.

You'll find a **pharmacy** (✆ 081-8968101) on Piazza dei Martiri 1, Madonna delle Grazie. There is a small **hospital** on Procida at Via Vittorio Emanuelle, near Chiaiolella (✆ 081-8100510); the **First Aid** medical center (✆ 081-8969058) is at Via Vittorio Emanuele 191; to call an **ambulance** dial ✆ 118. The **police** can be reached at ✆ 113 or 112. For the main **post office** (✆ 081-8967001; Mon–Sat 8am–2pm) visit Via Liberta. Banks with **ATMs** include the **Banco di Napoli** (✆ 081-8967180) at Via Vittorio Emanuele 158.

Exploring Procida

The island is basically one sprawling village, parts of it more densely populated than others, interspersed with citrus groves and gardens and the occasional vineyard. The traffic system is based on a principal, one-way road running roughly northeast-southwest with a network of narrow lanes serving the more remote locations. We recommend **hiring a scooter** to get around the island; it's far the best (and quickest) way and is quite safe. You can rent one from **General Rentals** (✆ 081-8101132) in Marina Grande. The distance from Marina Grande—where the ferry terminal is—on the northeastern tip of the island to Marina di

FROM TOP: The Terra Murata; Marina di Chiaiolella.

Chiaiolella, all the way to the opposite end, is only about 3km (1¾ miles).

Marina Grande, or Marina di Sancio Cattolico, is the major harbor of the island, and the location of the ferry terminal. A few steps away, along the main street, **Via Principe Umberto,** is **Piazza dei Martiri,** the village's main square. From here you can climb to the **Terra Murata,** the highest point of the island, fortified by 16th-century walls. This is where Procida's rulers had their residences, and where you can enjoy some of the most magnificent views of the island and its surroundings. As you climb, you will find a **belvedere ★** affording good views of the Marina della Corricella; farther up beyond the Piazza d'Armi, you enter the **medieval citadel** of **Terra Casata ★★** and its belvedere, with a magnificent view over the Gulf of Naples. On the square is the church of **San Michele Archangelo.** Originally dating from the 11th century (but later rebuilt), it is balanced over a sheer rock face above the sea and has a beautiful coffered ceiling that includes a fresco of the Archangel Michael by Luca Giordano.

From Piazza dei Martiri, it is a short walk down to **Marina della Corricella ★★,** a picturesque and charming fishing village originally established in the 17th century with colorful houses and narrow streets that line the small port.

If you continue toward the southwestern tip of the island, you should not miss the detour to the left for **Punta Pizzaco ★★★,** from where you can enjoy one of the best views on the whole island.

Farther on, you'll finally reach **Marina di Chiaiolella ★★** at the southwestern tip of the island. This crescent-shaped harbor was once the crater of a volcano and now is a pleasant marina, lined with little restaurants and bars. The harbor is dominated by the tiny, half-moon shaped island of **Vivara,** today a wildlife reserve run by the World Wildlife Federation and home to some 150 species of birds plus a type of rat that walks on its back legs. It is connected to Procida by the 362m (1,188-ft.) bridge, but both bridge and the island were closed to visitors at presstime with no opening date in sight.

We also highly recommend signing up for a **boat excursion** ★★ around the island. You can rent a boat, with or without a skipper, from any of the three harbors on the island: Marina Grande, Marina della Corricella, and Marina di Chiaiolella. You'll spend about 25€ for a 2-hour trip with a boat and skipper.

Where to Stay

In addition to the hotels reviewed below, we also recommend staying at **Crescenzo** (see "Where to Eat," below).

Hotel Celeste This pleasant, family-run hotel near the Marina di Chiaiolella is a traditional structure where guest rooms open onto the outdoors. Some have private terraces, but others open onto the veranda, the inner courtyard, or the terrace/garden. All are simply furnished with tiled floors and small outdoor spaces with a table and chairs. The service from Signora Concetta and her family is warm and welcoming. The view from the terraces and the solarium is lovely. *Note:* In August, all guests must pay an additional 20€ half-board fee, which entitles you to lunch or dinner. Continental breakfast is included in all rates, and pets are welcome.

Via Rivoli 6, 80079 Procida. www.hotelceleste.it. ☎ **081-8967488.** Fax 081-8967670. 34 units. 120€ double; 160€ triple; 190€ quad. Rates include buffet breakfast. In Aug half-board (20€/person) mandatory. AE, DC, MC, V. Closed Oct–Mar. **Amenities:** Restaurant; bar; bike rental. *In room:* A/C, TV, minibar (in some).

La Casa sul Mare 🛏 Housed in a typical 18th-century building at the foot of Terra Murata (the historic *borgo* or village of Procida), this small hotel offers high-quality accommodations with beautiful views over the Marina della Corricella. The elegant guest rooms are furnished with taste, with beautiful tiled floors, wrought-iron bed frames, and good-size bathrooms. Each opens onto its own private terrace with a beautiful view over the sea; you can order breakfast here in good weather.

Salita Castello 13. www.lacasasulmare.it. ☎/fax **081-8968799.** 10 units. 170€ double. Rate includes buffet breakfast. Children 1 and under stay free in parent's room. AE, DC, MC, V. **Amenities:** Bar; bike rental; concierge; Internet. *In room:* A/C, TV, minibar.

Where to Eat

Caracalè ISCHITANO This picturesque restaurant sits on the quayside at Corricella and offers traditional cuisine and a lively atmosphere. The food is well prepared and gratifying and includes many local specialties, most focusing on seafood, but vegetarian and meat choices are also available. Try the risotto *ai frutti di mare* (with seafood) and the catch of the day, *all'acqua pazza.*

Via Marina Corricella 62. ☎ **081 8969192.** Reservations recommended. Secondi 10€–13€. AE, DC, MC, V. Wed–Mon noon–3pm and 7–11pm; daily in Aug. Closed Nov 15–Dec 15 and Jan 15–Feb 15.

La Conchiglia ★ ☺ ISCHITANO This romantic restaurant stands right on Chiaia beach; it's a wonderful place for a long, lazy summer lunch. You can ask to be picked up by boat at Corricella or climb down (and up again) a long ramp of steps from the road. Menus are based on what the fishermen bring in: We particularly like the linguine *all'aragosta* (with local lobster) and the *spiedini di mazzancolle* (prawn skewers), but the grilled catch of the day is always good, too.

Via Pizzaco, Discesa Chiaia. ✆ **081-8967602.** Reservations recommended. Secondi 12€–23€. AE, DC, MC, V. Apr and mid-Sept to Oct daily 12:30–3pm; May-to mid Sept daily 12:30–3pm and 7:30–11pm. Closed Nov–Mar.

La Gorgonia ★ ISCHITANO/SEAFOOD Housed in a pink-washed building on Corricella's charming quayside, La Gorgonia serves delicious, unpretentious island food. You can start your meal with *bruschetta con polipetti* (toasted bread topped with baby octopus) and marinated anchovies before tucking into a plate of highly prized spaghetti *ai ricci* (with sea urchins) and a superb *fritto misto* (deep-fried seafood medley).

Via Marina di Corricella 50. ✆ **081-8101060.** Reservations recommended in high season. Secondi 10€–20€. MC, V. Tues–Sun noon–4pm and 8–11pm; daily July–Aug. Closed Nov–Feb.

Lo Scarabeo ★ ISCHITANO This excellent restaurant in the heart of town offers a pleasant atmosphere, particularly if the weather is good enough to sit out under the delightful lemon arbor. The menu is seasonal and changes with market offerings, but leans towards seafood. We recommend the spaghetti *alle vongole* (with clams) followed by *totani ripieni* (stuffed squid), should they be available when you visit, and, of course, the refreshing *insalata di limoni,* a Procida specialty where chunks of local lemons are mixed with fresh mint and chili, then dressed with olive oil.

Via Salette 10. ✆ **081-8969918.** Reservations recommended. Secondi 10€–18€. AE, DC, MC, V. Dec–Easter Sat-Sun 1–3pm and 7:30–11pm; after Easter–Oct Tues–Sun 1pm and 7:30–11pm. Closed Nov–Dec 20.

CAPRI, THE FARAGLIONI & THE BLUE GROTTO ★★★

33km (21 miles) SW of Naples

Lying a few kilometers off the tip of the Sorrentine Peninsula, Capri is a rugged, mountainous island jutting dramatically from the sea. This chic playground for millionaires was the haunt of eccentrics and intellectuals in its past, and in spite of the daily tourist invasion, it continues to beguile with its spectacular scenery, impossibly azure sea, and air of glamour.

Beaches Capri is not strong on beaches. Its coastline is made up of soaring cliffs, rocky coves, and the odd small stretch of sand, all surrounded by the bluest, clearest water imaginable. The sea is tantalisingly close, but often difficult to reach, and most of the accessible "beaches" are run by paying beach clubs.

Things to Do The network of footpaths covering the island is a delight. The best view is from **Monte Solaro;** take the chairlift up and walk down. Culture vultures can visit **Villa Jovis,** the remains of Emperor Tiberio's pleasure palace, Axel Munthe's **Villa San Michele,** and the charming **church of San Michele** in Anacapri, with its beautiful tiled floor.

Eating & Drinking The local cuisine, featuring fresh fish and seafood, rabbit, and seasonal vegetables, doesn't disappoint, and one of the most universally known of all Italian dishes, the ubiquitous *insalata caprese* (mozzarella and tomato salad) comes from here. Other specialities are ravioli *capresi* (stuffed with local cheese and marjoram) and the rich *torta caprese,* a chocolate and almond torte.

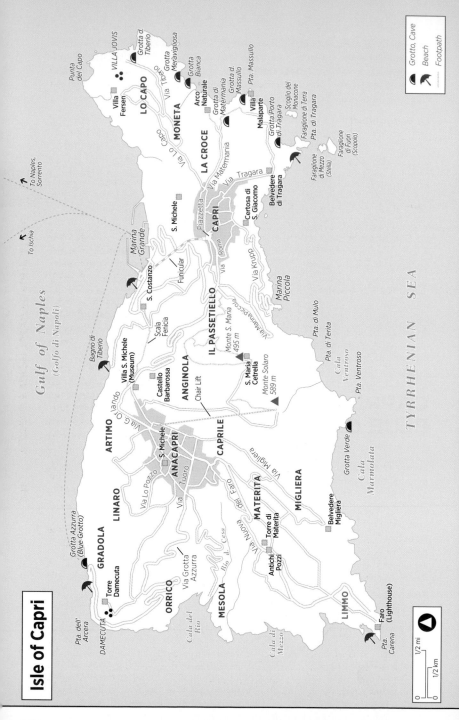

Isle of Capri

Shopping Capri is heaven for fashionistas with all the big-name designers represented along Via Vittorio Emanuele and Via Camerelle. Good gifts include soft cashmere garments made on the island and local Carthusia perfumes. Anacapri is less glitzy, and here you will find artisan shoemakers and some interesting gift shops and independent boutiques.

Essentials

GETTING THERE Just as all roads lead to Rome, ferries (*aliscafo* [hydrofoil] or *motonave* [motorboat]) leave for Capri from almost every harbor in Campania. Prices range from 11€ to 17€ (by regular ferry) or 115€ to 19€ (by hydrofoil) depending on the season and distance. **Caremar** (✆ 199-116655 within Italy; www.caremar.it) runs ferries to Capri from Naples and from Sorrento. **NLG-Navigazione Libera del Golfo** (✆ 081-5520763; www.navlib.it) runs to Capri from Naples, Sorrento, and Castellammare di Stabia. **Alicost** (✆ 089/234-892; www.lauroweb.com/alicost.htm) and **Alilauro** (✆ 081-4972222; www.alilauro.it) connect Capri to Salerno, Positano, Amalfi, and Ischia. **SNAV** (✆ 081-4285555; www.snav.it) runs hydrofoils and catamarans to Capri from Mergellina and Naples (Molo Beverello). **Travelmar** (✆ 081-7041911; www.travelmar.it) maintains regular service from Salerno. **LMP** (✆ 081-5513236; www.consorziolmp.it) has regular hydrofoil and boat service from Positano and Sorrento. **Volaviamare** (✆ 081-4972211; www.volaviamare.it) has fast boats between Naples, Sorrento, Amalfi, Positano, Salerno, Ischia, and Capri. During the summer, **Metrò del Mare** (✆ 199-600700; www.metrodelmare.com) makes daily runs to Capri; Amalfi-based **Cooperativa Sant'Andrea** (✆ 089-873190; www.coopsantandrea.it) offers scheduled service from Amalfi, Capri, Minori, Salerno, and Sorrento; Positano-based **Lucibello** (✆ 089-875032; www.lucibello.it) makes runs to and from Capri. **Blue Cruises** (✆ 081-4972222; www.blucruises.it) and **Capitan Morgan** (✆ 081-985080; www.capitanmorgan.it) offer minicruises to Capri from Ischia. Not cheap but convenient, **Taxi del Mare** (✆ 081-8773600; www.taxidelmare.it) plies the waters within the Naples and Salerno bays (about 600€ from Naples to Capri). From the harbor, you can take a **taxi** or the **funicular** up to town (see "Getting Around," below). *Note:* You'll do best to hire a **porter** (*facchino*) for the climb from the ferry landing to your hotel; it is well worth the 6€ to 8€ per piece of luggage (depending on size). The service is perfectly trustworthy, so just leave your luggage and head to your hotel. If you like, you can save money by lugging your bags to the funicular or taxi and up into town, where the porters charge a little less per piece to the hotels not accessible by car.

GETTING AROUND Capri gets its name from the ancient Greek *kapriae*, meaning "island of the wild goats." Indeed, only goats can tread these steep slopes and cliffs with ease. Today modern roads—including a short stretch of "highway"—allow for easy transfers, but the price to pay is traffic and congestion, especially in summer. One way of helping to ease the situation is to use the efficient local public transport network rather than taxis, and we suggest this whenever possible. *A word of advice:* Even when travelling by bus or the *funicolare* (funicular), wear comfortable shoes: there's always lots of walking involved on Capri. The *funicolare,* run by **SIPPIC** (✆ 081-8370420), is the picturesque means of transportation between the harbor of Marina Grande—where the ferry and hydrofoil landings are—and the town of Capri, where it arrives in the heart of town, off Piazza Umberto I. Funiculars leave about every 15 minutes for the 5-minute ride, and you need to purchase tickets in advance at the ticket booth by the ferry landing. **Taxis** wait by the harbors and at

South Winds

A visit to Capri is a perfect occasion to read Scottish writer Norman Douglas's witty novel *South Wind* (1917), part homage to the island and part satire on its eclectic (and even mad) inhabitants.

the main **stands:** Piazza Martiri d'Ungheria, in **Capri** (✆ 081-8370543), and Piazza Vittoria, in **Anacapri** (✆ 081-8371175). The minimum rate is 8€, and there are flat rates for a few destinations: 15€ between the harbor at Marina Grande and Capri town; 15€ between Capri and Anacapri; 20€ between the harbor at Marina Grande and Anacapri. There are supplements for baggage (2€ per piece), and nighttime services. The well-run public **bus** system is great, but in high season, a ride in one of these diminutive vehicles can feel like being in a sardine can and guarantees a hair-raising ride along the narrow cliff roads that crisscross the island. **ATC** (part of SIPPIC, above) offers service between Marina Grande, Capri, Marina Piccola, and Anacapri, while **Staiano Autotrasporti** (✆ 081-8372422; www.staianogroup.it) offers service between Anacapri, Faro (Lighthouse), and Grotta Azzurra. Tickets cost 1.40€ for either the bus or funicular. You can also get a 60-minute ticket for 2.20€, valid for one funicular run and unlimited bus runs during the time limit, or a day pass for 6.90€, valid for two funicular rides and unlimited bus service. You can also rent scooters: The most environmentally friendly is **Rent an Electric Scooter,** Via Roma 68 (✆ 081-8375863), but there are others, such as **Antonio Alfano,** with two locations: Via Marina Grande 280 (✆ 081-8377941) and Piazza Barile 26, Anacapri (✆ 081-8373888). Boat rental, with or without a skipper, is readily available at the **Marina Grande beach** from **Banana Sport** (✆ 081-8375188) and **Leomar** (✆ 081-8377181); at **Marina Piccola** from **Rent a Boat** (✆ 081-8370355); and from **Sercomar,** Via Cristoforo Colombo 64, Capri (✆ 081-8378781).

VISITOR INFORMATION The **AACST** (✆ 081-8375308 or 081-8370424; fax 081-8370918; www.capritourism.com) is at Piazzetta Italo Cerio 11.

You'll find several **pharmacies,** including one at Via Roma 45 (✆ 081-8370485). The **hospital** (✆ 081-8381205) is at Via Provinciale Anacapri 5; to call an **ambulance** dial ✆ 118. You can call the **police** at ✆ 113 or 112. The main **post office** (✆ 081-9785211; Mon–Sat 8am–2pm) is at Via Roma 50. Several banks have **ATMs,** such as **Banco di Napoli,** Via Vittorio Emanuele 37, Capri (✆ 081-8374311), as well as its other locations at Via G. Orlandi 150, Anacapri (✆ 081-8382169) and Via Cristoforo Colombo 78, Marina Grande (✆ 081-8374526).

GUIDED TOURS Capri Time Tours (www.capritime.com), founded by American ex-pat Rebecca Brooks, offers a variety of tours and classes, both on Capri and the mainland. Two companies offer regularly scheduled cruises: **Gruppo Motoscafisti** (✆ 081-8377714; www.motoscafisticapri.com) and **Laser Capri** (✆ 081/8375208), both departing from Marina Grande. We recommend the cruise around the island, which costs 13€ and 10€, respectively. They also offer a Blue Grotto cruise for 11€ and 10€—which does not include admission or rowboat fees (p. 271)—among other choices.

Exploring the Island

Tourists usually pass through **Marina Grande,** the largest harbor on the island, on their way from the ferry to town and pay little attention to the unassuming hamlet. It's worth taking time, however, to pop into the island's oldest church, **San Costanzo ★**. Dating back to the 5th century, it was enlarged in the 14th century, when its orientation was turned 90 degrees so that the original apse can still be discerned in the right nave. A bit farther to the west are the ruins of the **Palazzo a Mare,** one of several ancient Roman palaces scattered around the island.

Up the steep slope (most people take the funicular railway) is **Capri Town ★★★**, the heart of the island. With its narrow streets hiding shops, a wide variety of restaurants and clubs, and some of the islands most exclusive hotels, this is Capri's most picturesque destination. Social life radiates from the famous **Piazzetta** (Piazza Umberto I), a favorite spot for seeing and being seen. We highly recommend a walk through the narrow streets of the old town. Start from the Piazzetta, graced by the 14th-century **Palazzo Cerio,** the best medieval building remaining on the island. It houses the **Museo Ignazio Cerio** (✆ 081-8376681; admission 3€), which has exhibits depicting the island's natural history. Take Via Vittorio Emanuele, the town's main street, past the famous **Grand Hotel Quisisana** (p. 273), which was built in the 19th century as a sanatorium. Make a right on Via Ignazio Cerio, which leads to the **Certosa di San Giacomo ★** (✆ 081-8376218; free admission; Tues–Sun 9am–2pm), a religious complex—built in the 14th century and later enlarged—that

includes a church, a cloister, and a garden with a belvedere affording great views. Nearby are the **Giardini di Augusto ★**, the terraced public gardens that offer more magnificent vistas.

From the Capri Town, a walk of about 2.4km (1½ miles) ending with a steep climb will bring you to the ruins of **Villa Jovis ★★** (Viale Amedeo Maiuri) on the northeastern tip of the island. Admission is 2€ and it is open daily 9am until sunset (the ticket booth closes an hour earlier). This is the best preserved of the 12 villas built on the island by various Roman emperors. Augustus laid claim to a few of them, but the depraved Tiberius had one built for each of the most important gods of the Roman pantheon. Villa Jovis is dedicated to Jupiter and here, as in his other abodes on the island, Tiberius pursued his illicit pleasures away from the prying eyes of the Roman Senate. A massive complex, it covered over 5,853 sq. m (63,001 sq. ft.): Its architectural marvels include the **Loggia Imperiale,** a covered promenade on the edge of the cliff which ends in the Salto di Tiberio, a 330m-high (1,083-ft.) precipice from where, it's

The Giardini di Augusto.

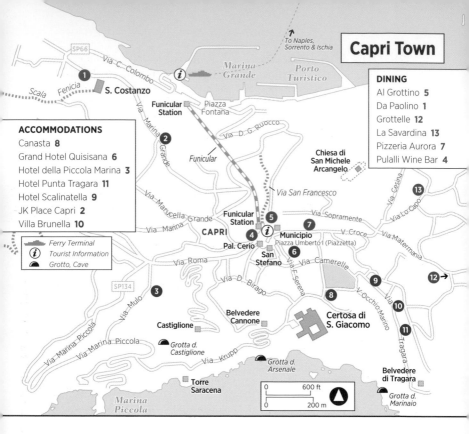

Capri Town

↑
To Naples,
Sorrento & Ischia

DINING
Al Grottino **5**
Da Paolino **1**
Grottelle **12**
La Savardina **13**
Pizzeria Aurora **7**
Pulalli Wine Bar **4**

ACCOMMODATIONS
Canasta **8**
Grand Hotel Quisisana **6**
Hotel della Piccola Marina **3**
Hotel Punta Tragara **11**
Hotel Scalinatella **9**
JK Place Capri **2**
Villa Brunella **10**

Ferry Terminal
ℹ Tourist Information
Grotto, Cave

said, Tiberius used to hurl anyone who angered him. The views from the villa are, to put it mildly, fit for an emperor of even the most jaded tastes.

From Capri town, you can also walk (or take a bus or taxi) to the small harbor of **Marina Piccola ★★** on the southern shore. This is especially popular for its vantage point, from which you can admire the famous **Faraglioni ★★★**, three rock stacks that jut out of the sea a short distance from the coast, one of the most iconic of Capri's many famous views. The outermost rock is home to a particular type of bright blue lizard that is found nowhere else on the planet.

Linked to Capri town through the famous **Scala Fenicia** (see "Staying Active," below), is the village of **Anacapri ★★**, perched on the higher part of the island among hills and vineyards. The **Church of San Michele** (admission 2€; Apr–Oct daily 9am–7pm, Nov–Mar 10am–2pm; closed the first 2 weeks of Dec) is worth a visit for its beautiful 18th-century **majolica floor ★★** which illustrates Adam and Eve's expulsion from the Garden of Eden accompanied by a veritable Noah's Ark of bizarre animals. A short distance from the town to the east is **Villa San Michele ★** (☎**081-8371401;** www.sanmichele.eu), the home of Swedish doctor and writer Axel Munthe who built this house in the 19th century on the ruins of one of Tiberius's villas. The gardens are also well worth the visit just to enjoy the matchless views from the terrace (admission 6€; Jan–Feb 9am–3:30pm, Mar 9am–4:30pm, Apr 9am–5pm, May–Sept 9am–6pm, Oct 9am–5pm, Nov–Dec 9am–3:30pm).

We highly recommend the excursion from Anacapri that takes you up to the top of **Monte Solaro ★★★**, Capri's highest peak that rises to an altitude of 589m (1,932 ft.). The **Seggiovia Monte Solaro** (✆ **081-8371428**) is a chairlift that departs from Via Caposcuro; the ride to the top only takes 12 minutes, but the matchless views from the top that, on a clear day, take in Vesuvius and the gulfs of Naples and Salerno. Tickets cost 7€ one-way, 9€ round-trip, free for children 8 and under; hours of operation are March through October 9:30am to 4.30pm.

Northwest of Anacapri (a 50-min. walk or a short bus or taxi ride away) is the island's most celebrated attraction, the **Grotta Azzurra (Blue Grotto) ★★**. The magical colors of the water and walls of this huge grotto are indeed extraordinary, and writers have rhapsodized about it at length since its so-called discovery by foreign tourists in the 19th century. In fact, the grotto has been charted since antiquity: On its southwestern corner, the Galleria dei Pilastri displays the remains of a small, ancient Roman dock. The grotto is part of what appears to be a vast system of caverns that is only partially explored. Unfortunately, you'll have no chance to explore on your own, especially if you come at the height of the season. During this period, motorboats line up outside the grotto, waiting for the small rowboats—the only vessels allowed inside—to squeeze a few passengers at a time under the grotto's narrow opening (because of rising sea levels the aperture now extends only about .9m/3 ft. above sea level, and you'll have to lie back in the boat). Because of the long lines, you'll be allowed inside the grotto only for a few minutes. Kids will love the adventure, which conjures up visions of secret expeditions, but adults might find the whole experience wearisome

The grotto is open daily 9am to 1 hour before sunset; admission is 4€, plus 7.50€ for the rowboat fee. Rowboats depart from the beach at the bottom of the footpath (the trail head is on the main road by the bus stop). The alternative is

The Monte Solaro chairlift.

The Grotta Azzurra.

to sign up for a cruise (23.50€ per person) from Marina Grande (see "Guided Tours," above), but we do not particularly recommend this option, as you'll have to factor in even longer waits and negotiate the switch from the large motorboat to the rowboat—in the open sea, this can be quite tricky, particularly when the waters are not perfectly calm. (It is also the least eco-friendly option.). **Note:** the grotto is subject to closure during bad weather.

Staying Active

Capri's crystalline waters offer great swimming, which you can easily do from one of the small but picturesque local **beaches.** Most are organized by paying beach clubs (*stabilimenti balneari*), which will provide you with a changing cabin, towels, and two deck chairs for about 35€ per day (more if you want sunbeds); they are usually open mid-March to mid-November, 9am to sunset. **Bagni di Tiberio ★** is a nice, sandy beach on the north side of the island, near the ru-

ins of a Roman villa. The beach is only about 1km (a half-mile) from Marina Grande, but getting there involves a steep and rocky descent that can be arduous on the return leg. We recommend going by boat instead—you can get passage there and back for 6€ from Marina Grande.

You'll find two more pleasant beaches in Marina Piccola, on the southern side of the island. To the east of the village is **Marina di Pennaulo,** and to the west is **Marina di Mulo;** both were a

> ### Impressions
>
> *Know'st thou the land where the pale citrons grow,*
> *The golden fruits in darker foliage glow?*
> *Soft blows the wind that breathes from that blue sky!*
> *Still stands the myrtle and the laurel high!*
> *Know'st thou it well that land, beloved Friend?*
> *Thither with thee, O, thither would I wend!*
> —Johann Wolfgang von Goethe, *Mignon Song* (trans. Samuel Taylor Coleridge), c. 1760

favorite haunt of the 1950s and 1960s jet set. The only **other beaches** on the island are a small one by the Blue Grotto (Via Grotta Azzurra), one by the Faro (lighthouse), and one by the Faraglioni (Via Tragara).

We also recommend a **boat tour of the island ★★★**. You can hire a private boat, with or without a skipper, from both Marina Grande and Marina Piccola (see "Getting Around," p. 267), or sign up for a tour.

Even if you are only moderately fit, do not miss the opportunity to **hike** Capri's cliffs and soak in the beauty of its trails—a great escape from the swarming crowds. Before setting out, stop at the tourist office (see "Visitor Information," earlier), which has a map of the paths. One of the easiest treks is the short trail from **Capri to Marina Piccola ★**. From Via Roma in town, turn left onto Via Mulo; a series of steps and a dirt path will lead you down to the harbor through cultivated fields and gardens.

A more demanding hike is the *Scala Fenicia* **(Fenician Staircase) ★★**, which descends—or climbs, for the most intrepid— from **Anacapri to Capri.** Built by the Greeks in the 8th century B.C., it was the only access to the sea or to the village of Anacapri until 1877, when the current road was built. The steep path—basically a long staircase with 881 steps—rewards the daring with superb views. Another hike we recommend is the descent from **Mount Solaro ★★** (p. 271), on a clearly marked dirt path (after taking the chairlift to the top).

Where to Stay

As a rule of thumb, accommodations in Anacapri tend to be cheaper than those in glitzier Capri town. However, if you want to enjoy the nightlife, you'll end up taking cabs from between the two, which can diminish your overall savings.

VERY EXPENSIVE

Grand Hotel Quisisana ★★★ This luxury hotel offers splendid accommodations and top-notch service. More traditional than the island's other top hotel, the stylish Capri Palace, in Anacapri, it is right in the heart of the action, yet well insulated from the hubbub. Built in the 19th century as an exclusive sanatorium (the name *qui si sana* means "here we heal"), it quickly changed into a hotel catering to those in need of pampering. Guest rooms are big and bright, opening onto wide arcades, and decorated with stylish period furniture. The large bathrooms are outfitted in marble or with designer tiles. Most of the rooms overlook the garden and pool—a few have views of the town—but only the more expensive suites claim the superb views you can otherwise enjoy from the hotel terraces. Even if you don't stay here, come for a drink at one of the elegant bars on the premises. We also recommend the hotel's restaurants, particularly the elegant **Quisi ★★**, perfect for a gourmet candlelight dinner (tasting menu 110€; secondi 36€ –42€; daily 7:30–11pm).

8

THE ISLANDS OF CAPRI, ISCHIA & PROCIDA

Capri

Via Camerelle 2, 80073 Capri. www.quisisana.com. ✆ **081-8370788.** Fax 081-8376080. 148 units. 350€–600€ double; from 850€ suite. Rates include buffet breakfast. Children 3 and under stay free in parent's room. AE, DC, MC, V. Closed Nov–Easter. **Amenities:** 3 restaurants; 3 bars; babysitting; concierge; health club; pool; room service; spa; outdoor tennis courts. *In room:* A/C, TV, minibar.

EXPENSIVE

Hotel Punta Tragara ★★ Standing high on a cliff with spectacular views over the famous Faraglioni, this hotel is in a quiet location slightly removed from the tourist madness of Capri town. Originally a luxurious private villa, it was designed by one of the greatest architects of the 20th century, Le Corbusier. Guest rooms have large windows and open onto private terraces, balconies, or small patios. They feature elegant modern furnishings, spacious bathrooms (some with shower only), and a restful ambience. The **restaurant** is worth a detour, even if you're not a guest.

Via Tragara 57, 80073 Capri. www.hoteltragara.com. ✆ **081-8370844.** Fax 081-8377790. 45 units. 500€–850€ double; from 920€ suite. Rates include buffet breakfast. Children 2 and under stay free in parent's room. Internet specials available. AE, DC, MC, V. Closed Nov–Easter. **Amenities:** Restaurant; bar; concierge; gym; pool; room service; spa. *In room:* A/C, TV, minibar.

Hotel Scalinatella ★ Like the Punta Tragara (above), this sophisticated hotel enjoys a unique setting overlooking Capri's Faraglioni (p. 270) and offers a pleasant atmosphere and luxury accommodations. Guest rooms are spacious and bright, with pretty tiled floors, high-quality furnishings, and comfortable bathrooms (some with shower only). Most rooms open onto private terraces; the more expensive rooms and the junior suites enjoy views over the sea.

Via Tragara 8, 80073 Capri. www.scalinatella.com. ✆ **081-8370633.** Fax 081-8378291. 45 units. 430€–560€ double; 700€ junior suite. Rates include buffet breakfast. Children 2 and under stay free in parent's room. AE, DC, MC, V. Closed Nov–Mar. **Amenities:** Restaurant; concierge; gym; pool; room service; outdoor tennis court. *In room:* A/C, TV, minibar.

JK Place Capri ★★ Great attention to detail, elegance, and beautiful views make this discreetly luxurious boutique hotel a winner, in spite of its less-than-desirable location on the main road from the harbor up to Capri and Anacapri. The cream-and-blue guest rooms are spacious and welcoming, decorated with a perfect mix of stylish elegance and comfort. The best have sea views and are filled with sunlight. Bathrooms are large (some with shower only). The hotel's **kitchen** serves excellent meals on the terrace or in the bar lounge.

Via Marina Grande 225 (up from the harbor), 80073 Capri. www.jkcapri.com. ✆ **081-8384001.** Fax 081-8376150. 22 units. 700€–900€ double; from 1,000€ suite. Rates include buffet breakfast. Internet specials available. AE, DC, MC, V. Closed Nov–Mar. **Amenities:** Restaurant service; bar; concierge; gym; pool; room service; spa. *In room:* A/C, TV, Internet, minibar.

MODERATE

Hotel della Piccola Marina ★ Set in a pleasant, shady garden five minutes' walk from the Piazzetta, this modern hotel is also located only steps from the bus stops and taxi stands. It is also only ten minutes' walk down a steep footpath from Marina Piccola. The cool, airy bedrooms have a stylish, contemporary feel and all but a handful have private terraces or balconies overlooking the gardens and pool. Bathrooms (some with shower only) are done out with smart blue-and-white tiles; some are even big enough to accommodate two showers. Buffet breakfast is served on a pretty arbor terrace, and the poolside bar serves light lunches and snacks (noon–6pm) and drinks.

Via Mulo 14–16, 80073 Capri. www.hoteldellapiccolamarina.it. ✆**081-8379642.** Fax 081-8378483. 40 units. 230€–300€ double; 400€ suite. Rates include breakfast. Children under 2 stay free in parent's room. AE, DC, MC, V. Closed end Oct to Easter. **Amenities:** Bar; concierge; pool; room service; Wi-Fi (free). *In room:* A/C, TV, minibar, Wi-Fi (free).

Villa Brunella 🛗 We particularly like the Brunella, set in a panoramic position and a private villa until 1963, when it was transformed into its current incarnation as a pleasant family-run hotel. Guest rooms have a welcoming atmosphere and each double has its own flowered terrace or balcony with a sea view. Bathrooms are modest in size but come with modern fixtures and designer tiles. Guests have access to the beach club at Marina Piccola. The hotel's restaurant **Terrazza Brunella ★** offers excellent food in a lovely setting and elegant service.

Via Tragara 24, 80073 Capri. www.villabrunella.it. ✆ **081-8370122.** Fax 081-8370430. www.villa brunella.it. 20 units. 270€–370€ double; 460€ junior suite. Rates include buffet breakfast. AE, DC, MC, V. Closed Nov-Apr. **Amenities:** Restaurant; bar; pool; room service. *In room:* A/C, TV, minibar.

INEXPENSIVE

Canasta This small, recently renovated budget hotel is not too far from the center of Capri town. Guest rooms are not huge, but are nice and clean in their simplicity, with colorful tiled floors, wrought-iron beds, and whitewashed walls. Bathrooms are adequate, modern, and scrupulously clean. The pool is larger than the Carmencita's (below).

Via Campo di Teste 6, 80073 Capri. www.hotel-canasta.com. ✆ **081-8370561.** Fax 081-8376675. 16 units. 170€–250€ double. Rates include buffet breakfast. Children 2 and under stay free in parent's room. AE, DC, MC, V. Closed 1 week for Christmas and Jan to mid-Mar. **Amenities:** Pool. *In room:* A/C, TV, minibar.

Hotel Carmencita This small hotel is a good budget choice in an expensive destination. Located in the modern part of Anacapri, it opens onto a private garden with a pool and offers comfortable and quiet accommodations at moderate rates. Guest rooms are spacious and nicely furnished—a bit dated but clean—with tiled floors and private balconies. The swimming pool is small but is a bonus in this price category.

Viale T. De Tommaso 4, 80071 Capri. www.carmencitacapri.com. ✆ **081-8371360.** Fax 081-8373009. 20 units. 129€–175€ double; 170€–220€ triple. Children 2 and under stay free in parent's room. AE, DC, MC, V. Closed Nov-Mar. **Amenities:** Bar; babysitting; concierge; Internet; pool. *In room:* A/C, TV.

Where to Eat

In addition to the restaurants we recommend in this section, **Quisi ★★**, in the **Grand Hotel Quisisana** (above), is special enough for a very romantic or celebratory occasion. Some of our favorite hotels above also offer remarkable—and less pricey—dining experiences, particularly **Punta Tragara, Villa Brunella ★**, and **Luna.**

EXPENSIVE

L'Olivo ★★ CREATIVE CAPRESE The double Michelin-starred restaurant of the Capri Palace Hotel, is the perfect address for a truly exclusive experience. Stylish and pricey, it combines aesthetics (hand-blown glasses, silver cutlery, luxurious fabrics, and details), perfect service, and gourmet haute cuisine. German Chef Oliver Glowig has now moved on to pastures new, but L'Olivo is still considered to be among the best places to eat on the island, and Glowig's successor, Andrea Migliaccio, bases his light, innovative cuisine on regional and Mediterranean specialties. The menu is seasonal and best exemplified by the tasting menus.

Via Capodimonte 2, Anacapri. ℂ **081-9780111.** www.capri-palace.com. Reservations recommended. Secondi 35€–46€; tasting menus 150€ and 190€. AE, DC, MC, V. Daily noon–3pm and 7–10pm. Closed Nov–Mar.

MODERATE

Al Grottino ★ CAPRESE/NEAPOLITAN Serving seafood and other Neapolitan dishes since 1937, this restaurant was a preferred hangout for VIPs in the 1950s. The food is still good, and you can choose from a variety of traditional Neapolitan comfort food, such as *frittura* (medley of deep-fried seafood) and *mozzarella in carrozza* (deep-fried mozzarella)—prepared in several different ways. We recommend the *sciaratelli* (local handmade pasta) with shrimp and zucchini flowers and the excellent *zuppa di cozze* (mussel soup) and ravioli *alla caprese* (with fresh mozzarella and marjoram), both *caprese* specialties.

Via Longano 27, Capri. ℂ **081-8370584.** Reservations required for dinner. Secondi 13€–25€. AE, MC, V. Daily noon–3pm and 7pm–midnight. Closed Nov–Mar.

Da Paolino ★★ CAPRESE Popular among locals, this restaurant serves deliciously simple food under a splendid lemon arbor terrace. The menu is traditional and down-to-earth, with a great array of grilled Mediterranean vegetables seasoned with the best local olive oil, and the freshest seafood. In addition to the great buffet of *antipasti*, we highly recommend the *sauté di cozze e vongole* (shellfish), and the *calamarata* (ring-shaped pasta with calamari).

Via Palazzo a Mare 11, Marina Grande. ℂ **081-8376102.** www.paolinocapri.com. Reservations required for dinner. Secondi 18€–32€. AE, DC, MC, V. Daily 7pm–midnight. Closed Nov–Mar.

Il Riccio ★ CAPRESE Born from the proverbial ashes of the historic Add'o Riccio, this contemporary re-invention of the beach restaurant is part of the Capri Palace Hotel. The stylish club strikes the perfect balance between casual and chic with a fabulous location steps from the Blue Grotto, and a terrace overlooking the sea. The menu focuses on seafood and traditional dishes: From the classic *caprese* salad to the *linguine all'astice* (with spiny lobster), everything is well prepared with only the freshest ingredients. For an extravagant treat, order the giant platter of *frutti di mare* (mixed seafood) to share with a friend. The secluded solarium carved in the rocks is available for private parties.

Via Gradola 4, Anacapri. ℂ **081-8371380.** www.ristoranteilriccio.com. Reservations recommended. Secondi 18€–25€. AE, DC, MC, V. Daily 12:30–3.30pm and 8–11pm. Closed Nov–Mar.

La Savardina ★★ CAPRESE This historic address continues to lure both locals and visitors for its excellent traditional food, hospitable service, and delightful lemon and orange arbor terrace. We love it for the variety of its menu, including many vegetarian and meat-based dishes in addition to the typical seafood favorites. We recommend you start with a simple antipasto of grilled vegetables and local cured meat, followed by the very well-prepared ravioli *alla caprese* (filled with mozzarella), or with the linguine seasoned with capers, cherry tomatoes, and fresh herbs. For a secondo, the *coniglio* (rabbit) is excellent, or try the excellent fish *all'acqua pazza* (in a light herb broth). The *torta caprese* (traditional chocolate and nut torte) is delicious.

Via I o Capo 8, Capri. ℂ **081-8376300.** www.caprilasavardina.com. Reservations recommended. Secondi 12€–18€. AE, DC, MC, V. Mar–Apr and Sept–Oct Wed–Mon 12:30–3.30pm and 6.30–11pm; May–Aug daily 12:30–3:30pm and 6:30–11pm. Closed Nov–Easter.

Pizzeria Aurora ★ CAPRESE/PIZZA For a trendy see-and-be-seen kind of place, you can't go wrong with this establishment—and the food is good too. Choose from a menu including modern renditions of traditional dishes, such as the excellent pasta with zucchini flowers and Parmesan, or the simple spaghetti *al pomodoro* (with cherry tomatoes). Thin and crispy pizza is served in the evening.

Via Fuorlovado 18, Capri. ℂ **081-8370181.** www.auroracapri.com. Reservations recommended. Secondi 18€–25€. AE, DC, MC, V. Daily 12:30–3pm and 7:30 11pm. Closed Jan–Mar.

Pulalli Wine Bar 🍴 You wouldn't think that there could be a culinary "discovery" to be had in the world-renowned Piazzetta, but this attractive wine bar and restaurant, with its delightful little terrace offering a bird's eye view of the famed square, is just that. There's no obvious sign on the street; climb the steep steps that lead up from the right of the newsstand under the clock tower. The menu features the ubiquitous fish and seafood, but plenty more besides: We loved the tasty *pennette 'aumm aumm'* (small pasta tubes with eggplant, tomato, mozzarella and Parmesan) and the *risotto al limone* (lemon-flavored risotto) that is served in a half lemon. For a secondo, go for one of the grilled meats (the filet steak is tender and delicious) accompanied by *polpettine di melanzane* (deep-fired eggplant croquettes), a Pulalli speciality.

Piazza Umberto 1 4, Capri. ℂ **081-8374108.** Reservations recommended. Secondi 10€–25€. AE, DC, MC, V. Wed–Mon noon–3pm and 7pm–midnight. Closed Nov until just before Easter.

INEXPENSIVE

Grottelle 🍴 CAPRESE This small, off-the-beaten-track restaurant has a panoramic terrace just above the Arco Naturale and is a great place for sampling the local cuisine. The menu is centered on traditional Caprisian cuisine, and we highly recommend the *zuppa di fagioli* (bean soup) as well as the simple but delectable spaghetti *con pomodoro e basilica* (with fresh tomatoes and basil), followed by the perfect *frittura di paranza* (deep-fried seafood). The homemade desserts are very good.

Via Arco Naturale 13, Capri. ℂ **081-8375719.** Fax 081-8389234. Reservations required for dinner. Secondi 15€–30€. AE, DC, MC, V. Fri–Wed noon–3pm and 7–11pm. Closed Nov–Mar.

La Rondinella 🍴 CAPRESE/PIZZA This relaxed family-run restaurant is a good choice for a quiet, reasonably priced meal. In the evening, it prepares many varieties of brick-oven pizza. The menu is traditional and includes delicious ravioli *alla caprese* (mozzarella, fresh tomatoes, and marjoram); *pezzogna all'acqua pazza* (local fish in a light tomato sauce); and *frittura* (deep-fried seafood medley), which they prepare particularly well. In the evenings, there is a wide variety of pizza baked in a wood oven. For dessert, local specialties such as *torta caprese* (chocolate and almond cake) are excellent.

Via G. Orlandi 245, Anacapri. ✆ **081-8371223.** Reservations required for dinner. Secondi 11€–16€; pizza 6€–10€. AE, DC, MC, V. Fri–Wed noon–3pm and 7–11pm. Closed Nov–Mar.

Shopping for Local Crafts

Dedicated shoppers will lose themselves in Capri's little shops. Many of the island's visitors return just to buy more of the locally made goods, especially the sandals and the jewelry. One of the most famous shopping stops is

Carthusia.

Carthusia ★★, a perfume maker that counts many stars among its customers. Its **laboratory/store,** Viale Matteotti 2d (✆ 081-8370368; daily 9:30am–6pm; www.carthusia.it), has been concocting unique perfumes from local herbs and flowers since 1948. There are three outlets on the island: Via Camerelle 10, Capri Town (✆ 081-8370529); Via Federico Serena, Capri Town (✆ 081-8375335); and Via Axel Munthe 26, Anacapri (✆ 081-8373668).

Stylish sandals (handmade, of course) can be found at **Amedeo Canfora** ★, Via Camerelle 3, Capri (✆ 081-8370487; www.canfora.com), and at Antonio Viva's **L'Arte del Sandalo Caprese** ★, Via Giuseppe Orlandi 75, Anacapri (✆ 081-8373583; www.sandalocaprese.it). Finally, the island has an old jewelry-making tradition. You can admire—and purchase—fine examples at **La Perla Gioielli,** Piazza Umberto I 21 (✆ 081-8370641).

Capri After Dark

Sweet summer nights are lively in Capri, and the nights are long. The island of VIPs will not let you down, so prepare yourself for a trendy scene, with beautiful people dressing up and convening at the famous **Piazzetta** at nightfall. Fashionistas, take note: To compete with the local beauties, you'll have to learn how to walk on the steep cobblestone streets of Capri in your stilettos! Nightlife here centers on the see-and-be-seen at the elegant and trendy bars and restaurants. The **piano bars** in the **Grand Hotel Quisiana** and in the **Capri Palace** are the most exclusive venues, with prices to match; the newly opened **Rendez Vous,** in the **Grand Hotel Quisiana** (p. 273), is more affordable. For a more relaxed scene, **Anema E Core,** Via Sella Orta 39/a, Capri (✆ 081-8376461; www.anemaecore.com), is a lively nightclub with live music; and the **Wine Bar,** Vico San Tommaso 1 (✆ 081-8370732), in the historic restaurant **La Capannina,** is a cozy place to have a drink and listen to some music.

SALERNO
WITH PAESTUM, PADULA & THE CILENTO

The largest town in Campania after Naples, Salerno is the southern gateway to the Amalfi Coast (see chapter 7), and among our favorite off-the-beaten track destinations. Largely undiscovered by tourism, its wealth of artistic and historical offerings makes it well worth a visit. The city prides itself on having one of Italy's most beautiful seafront promenades and a delightful medieval center—full of small shops and restaurants—with a superb 11th-century Duomo.

Salerno is also the departure point for the Cilento, one of Italy's best-kept secrets and an area that is virtually unknown to foreign tourists. Covering a large section of the southern part of Campania, the Parco Nazionale del Cilento—the second-largest park in Italy—contains many exciting natural attractions, including two huge caves, a beautiful hilly, unexplored interior, small fishing towns, and seaside resorts with fine sand beaches. The Cilento was where the ancient Greeks built some of their most important colonies, whose grandeur is still visible in the unique ruins of **Paestum,** home to the best-conserved Greek temple after the Theseion in Athens. The beautiful coastline of the area is popular with Italians at the height of summer, and, it must be said, has been rather spoiled by sprawling development. Most foreign tourists make a beeline for the temples at Paestum and move on, thereby completely missing out on the Cilento's wild, uncharted interior, the scenic shores, and last but not least, the wonderful cuisine.

SALERNO ★★★

55km (34 miles) SE of Naples

With 150,000 inhabitants, Salerno is a lively, industrial, modern town situated at the eastern edge of the Amalfi Coast, with an atmospheric medieval center and what is arguably the most beautiful *lungomare* (seafront promenade) on this coast. It's made all the more enjoyable by the lack of crowds. The most important port of Campania after Naples, Salerno became the first capital of the Southern Kingdom. An Etruscan settlement founded around the 6th century B.C., it was absorbed into Magna Grecia, the conglomerate of Greek colonies in southern Italy, during the 5th century B.C. and became the Roman colony of Salernum in 194 B.C. Salerno became an independent principality under the Longobards in the 9th century and its growth continued in medieval and Renaissance times, when it was established as an important cultural center thanks to its renowned medical schools. The principality was subsequently ruled by Normans, Swabians, Angevins, and, finally, the Bourbons, but its political and cultural importance declined when Naples became the capital of the new kingdom and Salerno sank back into the quiet life of a smallish provincial town.

"Modern" Salerno enjoyed a brief flash of glory in 1944 when, after Allied troops landed just to the south and forced the Germans to withdraw, the city became the seat of the Italian government for 4 months. Today it is a lively, gritty yet

PREVIOUS PAGE: **Agropoli.**

Salerno

200 yds
200 m

Castello di Arechi

Ferries to Capri, Amalfi & Positano

Ferry Terminal
i Tourist Information
P Parking

enlightened city with an important port, a world away from its troubled neighbor Naples. At presstime, a new Maritime Terminal, designed by world-renowned architect Zaha Hadid that will include shops and restaurants, was well on the way to completion, proof that Salerno is moving with the times.

Essentials

GETTING THERE The closest international and intercontinental airport to Salerno is **Naples**'s Capodichino (p. 64).

Salerno lies on the main north-south rail corridor and is well served by **train,** with frequent service from a number of Italian and European cities to its train station *(stazione)* on Piazza Vittorio Veneto. Trains leave Naples every 10 to 30 minutes for the 35-minute ride to Salerno; the fare is about 6€. Contact **Trenitalia** (✆ 892021 in Italy; www.trenitalia.it) for more fares and information.

Slower but far more scenic, the **ferry** is our favorite means of transportation on this coast, especially in the summer, when roads tend to be crowded. Salerno is a major sea terminal, and ferries arrive here from other ports in the Mediterranean (see "Getting There," in chapter 11). Local ferries connect Salerno to nearby harbors: **Alicost** (✆ 089/234-892; www.alicost. it) and **Alilauro** (✆ 081-4972238; www.alilauro.it) with Capri, Amalfi, Positano, and Ischia; **Travelmar** (✆ 081-7041911; www.travelmar.it) with Positano, Amalfi, Minori, and Maiori; and **Cooperativa Sant'Andrea** (✆ 089-873190; www.coopsantandrea.it) with Amalfi, Capri, Minori, and Sorrento. Operating only in the summer (Apr–Sept), **Metro del Mare** (✆ 199-600700; www.metrodelmare.net) offers commuter-style connections with all the harbors along this stretch of coast, from Pozzuoli south, including Naples, Sorrento, Positano, Amalfi, and the Cilento; purchase of a **Terra&Mare ticket** entitles you to the boat transfer plus ground transportation for the 45 minutes before and 45 minutes after the ferry link. In 2011, the schedule was reduced to a single trip each day for July and August; we are told that by 2012 the full service will be resumed.

Salerno is also well connected by **SITA** (✆ 089-405145; www.sitabus.it), which runs a regular **bus service** between the city and Naples, as well as to the various towns of the Amalfi Coast and the Sorrento peninsula. **CSTP** (✆ 089-252228 or 800-016659 toll-free within Italy; www.cstp. it) services Salerno, Pompeii, Paestum, and the Cilento. The **bus terminal** is in Piazza della Concordia, near the train station. See "The Unico Travel Pass," p. 349, for fare information.

You can also reach Salerno by **car.** Off the autostrada A3, take the exit marked SALERNO, and follow signs for the city center. Once there, follow signs for the **Jolly Hotel** and the **public parking,** where you'll need to leave your car, as the town center is pedestrian only.

GETTING AROUND Although large compared to the compact towns of the Amalfi Coast, Salerno has a compact town center, extending along its waterfront, which can be explored **on foot.** The town's historic district is a pedestrian-only area; it stretches from the train station, on **Piazza Vittorio Veneto,** to Piazza Amendola, at the western edge of the medieval center. **Taxis** are your best bet for destinations outside the historic district; taxis wait at stands near points of major interest, including **Piazza Vittorio Veneto** in front of the railway station; **Piazza Amendola;** and **Piazza XXIV Maggio;** or call **Radiotaxi** directly at ✆ **089-757575.** The city has a good **public bus** system run by **CSTP** (see "Getting There," above); the bus hub is Piazza Vittorio Veneto, across from the rail station. **Bus, train,** and **ferries** (see "Getting There," above) are also an excellent way to reach other destinations near Salerno.

You can also **rent a car** at the Pontecagnano airport from **Hertz or Maggiore;** more companies have agencies downtown.

VISITOR INFORMATION The **AACST tourist office** (✆ 089-224744; www. aziendaturismo.sa.it) is at Via Roma 258. The tourist office for the whole province, including the Cilento, is the **EPT,** Via Velia 15, 84100 Salerno (✆ **089-230401;** www.eptsalerno.it). Another office is on Piazza Vittorio Veneto, at the train station (✆ **089-614259;** www.turismoinsalerno.it), which is open Monday to Saturday from 9am to 2pm and 3 to 8pm (until 7pm in winter).

You'll find several pharmacies in town, including one at Corso Vittorio Emanuele 223 (✆ **089-231439**), not far from the train station, and one at Via Mercanti 62 (✆ **089-225142**), in the medieval district. The **hospital, San Giovanni di Dio e Ruggiero d'Aragona** (✆ 089-671111), is on Via San Leonardo. For an **ambulance,** dial ✆ **118.** Dial ✆ **113** or 112 for the police, ✆ **115** for the fire department, and ✆ **116** for Automobile Club of Italy (ACI) road assistance. You will find several **banks** and **ATMs** in Salerno along Corso Vittorio Emanuele, not far from the train station; **Banca Nazionale del Lavoro** is in the train station. The main **post office**—in a majestic building—is at Corso Garibaldi 203 (Mon–Sat 8am–2pm).

SPECIAL EVENTS The **Salerno Film Festival Linea d'ombra (Shadow Line)** ★ is a major international event, dedicated to new talents in Europe and focusing on the passage from adolescence to adulthood—the "shadow line" of maturation, a term coined by Joseph Conrad and taken as the festival's motto. The festival (✆ **089-662565;** fax 089-662566; www. festivalculturegiovani.it) is an annual, weeklong event that takes place in April. Besides films, it includes a number of interesting musical events. During the **Ravello Music Festival,** concerts are also held in the monastery of Santa Maria della Mercede in Salerno; contact the festival office for a schedule of events (p. 44). In advance of your visit, you can check out what's going on in Salerno at www.salernocity.com (Italian only).

Exploring Salerno

During World War II, Salerno was designated the capital of Allied Italy, and much of the town was destroyed by severe bombing. Only the medieval center and part of the 19th-century waterfront were miraculously spared. The reconstruction and expansion that followed, especially to the southeast and northeast of the seafront, gave the town a more modern look. However, in the 1990s, a renovation campaign brought the old sections of Salerno back to their original splendor, particularly its seafront promenade.

Lined with palm trees and opening onto the seascape of the Costiera Amalfitana and Cilentana, **Lungomare Trieste** ★★ is the most beautiful seafront promenade in the whole region. At the western end, you'll find the **Villa Comunale** (Piazza Amendola), a pleasant and orderly public garden, adjacent to the **Teatro Verdi** ★ (Piazza Luciani; ✆ **089-662141;** www.teatroverdi salerno.it; daily 8am–2pm and 4–8pm). This historic theater was inaugurated on

Lungomare Trieste.

April 15, 1872, with a performance of Verdi's *Rigoletto*. A recent face-lift has brought the beautiful baroque and neoclassical decorations back to life, including the magnificent hall, with its frescoed ceiling by Domenico Morelli. The theater hosts many important concerts and performances (see "Salerno After Dark," later). The town is dominated by the **Castello di Arechi,** Via Benedetto Croce (© **089-2854533;** www.ilcastellodiarechi.it; free admission; Tues-Sun 9am–2pm and 4pm–sunset); originally built by the Byzantines, probably over older fortifications, the castle took on its current mantle under Spanish rule in the 16th century. It now hosts special events, but it's worth a visit just for its view. It can be reached by car, taxi, or on foot—a steep 40-minute climb along a pedestrian ramp.

The medieval heart of Salerno—where most of the town's attractions are concentrated—is a picturesque place for a stroll. From Piazza Amendola you can take the exclusive shopping street **Via di Porta Catena** and follow it to charming **Piazza Sedile del Campo,** the medieval market square, graced by the beautiful little **Fontana dei Delfini (Fountain of the Dolphins)** ★ and the **Palazzo dei Genovesi** (at no. 3)—today a school—with its grand **portal** ★. Off the piazza, in Via Roteprandi, you'll find the church of **Sant'Andrea de Lama,** one of the oldest medieval buildings in Salerno—note its pretty 12th-century bell tower—and, a few steps farther, the even older church of **Sant'Alfonso,** dating from the 10th century. Inside, admire some recently restored frescoes dating from the Longobard era. Return to **Piazza Sedile del Campo** to access **Via dei Mercanti** ★, Salerno's major shopping street, which dates from medieval times. This is where you'll find some of the best boutiques and most elegant stores in town. Off to the left is the **Vicolo dei Sartori** with the **Palazzo Fruscione** ★, notable for its medieval decorations, including a pretty loggia and intertwined arches. Not far off, on Vicolo Adalberga, is the ancient **Palatine San Pietro a Corte** church ★. Its 11th-century frescoes have survived, and excavations of its layered strata have revealed the structure of an ancient Roman thermal bathhouse. Farther along Via dei Mercanti is the 10th-century **Chiesa del Crocifisso** ★★, Piazza Matteotti 1 (© **089-233716;** daily 9am–noon and 4–7pm), famous for its beautiful 13th-century **frescoes** in the main and right

The Fontana dei Delfini (Fountain of the Dolphins).

apses of the crypt. One depicts the Crucifixion and the other three saints; this fresco is reproduced in mosaics over the main altar of the church.

Scuola Medica Salernitana (Salerno Medical School) was one of the first medical schools in the Western world: Scholars believe it was the medical school that operated in the Greek colony of Velia in the 6th century A.D. and developed in later centuries to attract scholars from all over Europe. Today what is left is a small **museum,** Via dei Mercanti (© **089-2576126**); Mon–Sat 9am–1pm and 4–7pm, Sun 9am–1pm), inside the former St. Gregorio church that contains documents and a collection of medical instruments, and the school's **botanical garden, Giardino della Minerva ★**, Via Ferrante Sanseverino 1 (© **089-252423;** www.giardinodellaminerva.it), originally created in the 14th century by one of the school's masters, Matteo Silvatico, in the terraced garden of his house. His **Giardino dei Semplici (Garden of Simples)** is considered the first botanic garden in the Western world. The name refers to the few key plants from which most basic remedies were obtained. The garden is open Tuesday through Sunday from 10am to 1pm and 5pm to sunset; admission is 2€.

Chiesa di San Giorgio ★ Built in 1647 over an 8th-century church, this is the most beautiful baroque church in Salerno. An atrium with a carved portal stands in front of the imposing facade, and the interior is typically baroque, with ornate gilded stucco and numerous frescoes and paintings. The fresco cycle depicting the *Passion of Christ* in the cantoria, as well as the *Crucifixion* and *San Benedetto* in the transept, are all by Angelo Solimena. *San Michele* (over the fourth altar to the right) and the frescoes of the large chapel are by Franceso Solimena, and other paintings are by Andrea da Salerno. A beautiful carved wooden pulpit is supported by four lions.

Via Duomo 19. © **089-228918.** Free admission. Daily 9:30am–12:30pm.

Duomo/Cattedrale di San Matteo ★★★ One of Italy's loveliest medieval churches, the Duomo was built in 1076 and consecrated in 1085 to house the relics of Saint Matthew the Evangelist. You enter the church through the **Sala San Lazzaro,** which is believed to have been the Main Hall of the **Scuola Medica Salernitana (Salerno Medical School).** A 17th-century staircase leads to the 11th-century Romanesque portal known as **Porta dei Leoni,** with its finely carved architrave; it leads to the church's elegant **atrium ★**. This is surrounded by a portico decorated with stone and tufa inlay and is dominated by a splendid Romanesque **bell tower ★★** (you'll get a better view of the bell tower from Via Roberto Il Giscardo, to the right of the Duomo). From here you can admire the facade of the Duomo, with its beautifully carved **central portal,** closed by two **bronze doors ★★**, which were cast in Constantinople in 1099. In spite of serious damage caused by the 1688 earthquake and of 18th-century over-restoration, the Duomo's interior still holds an amazing quantity of impressive artwork, starting with the two magnificent **ambones ★★★**, or pulpits, in the central nave. The smaller is from the 12th century, while the larger dates from the 1400s and is composed of 12 red-and-gray granite columns blossoming with birds, figures, and vegetation. On the ambone's facade, note the remarkable mosaic showing a sinner with a snake biting him in the breast, and an

Salerno's Duomo.

eagle digging his talons into the unfortunate sinner's head. The monumental **candleholder ★** in front of the ambone is also impressive. Adjacent to the ambones is the choir, whose sides and floor are embedded with mosaics from the 12th century. The **Cappella delle Crociate (Chapel of the Crusades) ★★**, in the right apse, is where the Crusaders had their weapons blessed before sailing for the Holy Land. Fine 13th-century mosaics and later frescoes cover the walls and ceiling. Conserved under the altar are the remains of Pope Gregorio VII, who died in exile in Salerno in 1085.

Piazza Alfano I. *C* **089-231387.** Free admission. Daily 7:30am–noon and 4–7pm.

Museo Diocesano ★★ Adjacent to the Duomo is the museum, which contains a large art collection dating from Roman times. One of the most impressive rooms in our opinion is the one that holds the ivory collection, including some extraordinarily intricate carvings. The best is a 12th-century *paliotto* **(altar front) ★★★**, composed of 54 carved scenes by different artists. Note that four frames are missing; one is in the Louvre in Paris, one in Berlin, one in Budapest, and the last in the Met in New York. In the other rooms are several other important pieces, including paintings and bas-reliefs from the 16th century, and paintings by such artists as Andrea Vaccaro, Luca Giordano, Jusepe de Ribera, and Francesco Solimena. The museum also has a collection of illuminated manuscripts from the 13th and 14th centuries.

Largo Plebiscito 12. *C* **089-239126.** Free admission. Mon–Fri 9am–1pm.

Where to Stay

Salerno is yet to be discovered by international tourism and its hotels do not have the amenities and services of many of the more glamorous destinations to the north. However, if you can do without satellite TV and Jacuzzi tubs in the room, the hotels offer good value for money.

Hotel Olimpico ★ ☺ Lying about 10km (6 miles) south of the city center, this four-star hotel is set in a tropical garden with pool right on the beach, so it is a good choice if you are traveling with kids. A regular free shuttle service will run you into town or take you to the boat docks for the islands and other coastal destinations. Bedrooms, with cool tiled floors, are bright and sunny: Most have private balconies either overlooking the beach or the garden. Deluxe rooms have huge bathrooms with Jacuzzi tubs and big private terraces furnished with sunbeds.

Via Lago Trasimeno, Pontecagnano, 84098 Salerno. www.hotelolimpico.it. 𝄢 **089-203004.** Fax 089-203458. 50 units. 69€–229€ double. Internet specials available. Rates include breakfast. AE, DC, MC, V. Free parking. **Amenities:** Restaurant; bar; concierge; pool; Wi-Fi (free). *In room:* A/C, TV, Wi-Fi (free), minibar.

Hotel Montestella This family-run hotel enjoys a very central location in the pedestrian area between the train station and the medieval center. The good-size guest rooms come with comfortable, modern furnishings and medium-size bathrooms (some with shower only) with new fixtures.

Corso Vittorio Emanuele 156, 84122 Salerno. www.hotelmontestella.it. 𝄢 **089-225122.** Fax 089-229167. 46 units. 94€ double. Rate includes breakfast. Children 2 and under stay free in parent's room. AE, DC, MC, V. No parking. **Amenities:** Bar; room service. *In room:* A/C, TV, minibar.

Hotel Plaza This hotel is in a large neoclassical building across from the railway station. Inside, it has been completely modernized. The guest rooms are not large; but they are certainly adequate, with simple furnishings, carpeting, and either tubs or showers in the bathrooms.

Piazza Vittorio Veneto 42, 84123 Salerno. 𝄢 **089-224477.** Fax 089-237311. www.plazasalerno.it. 42 units. 90€ double. Rate includes buffet breakfast. Children 2 and under stay free in parent's room. AE, DC, MC, V. Parking 15€. **Amenities:** Bar. *In room:* A/C, TV, minibar.

Villa Avenia ★ ☺ This B&B has a very special location in the historic district, inside one of the villas surrounded by terraced gardens that extend from the medieval town up to the Castello di Arechi (p. 284). It pretty much feels like being in a private home, which, in fact, you are. The lack of amenities and the simple accommodations are largely compensated for by the silence and the garden—a small oasis with a diminutive animal farm (with a Tibetan goat, a donkey, and a few chickens) that will delight younger children.

Via Porta di Ronca 5, 84100 Salerno. www.villaavenia.com. 𝄢/fax **089-252281** or 340-3611813. 6 units. 90€ double. Rates include breakfast. No credit cards. Parking in nearby garage 12€. **Amenities:** Bar; cafeteria; Wi-Fi (free). *In room:* A/C, TV, Wi-Fi (free).

Where to Eat

In addition to the restaurants listed below, you'll find plenty of snack bars and *pizzerie* in the old town catering to local university students and the mariners from the nearby port. A local favorite is the historic **Antica Pizzeria Vicolo della Neve,** Vicolo della Neve 24 (𝄢 **089-225705;** www.vicolodellaneve.it; closed Wed).

Al Cenacolo SALERNITAN After a recent, contemporary makeover, this restaurant situated opposite the Duomo is once again making a name for itself. New chef Gianni Mellone brings together the best flavors of the region—fresh herbs and vegetables, seafood, local meats, and cheeses—sometimes in new combinations. The menu changes regularly, but you might find *millefoglie di verdure grigliate con scamorza e pomodorino glassato* (millefeuille of grilled vegetables with local cheese and glazed cherry tomato), *paccheri con vongole, calamaretti spillo, carciofi croccanti e bottarga di tonno* (local pasta with clams, baby squid, crispy artichoke hearts, and tuna roe) and, for meat eaters, saddle of lamb in a hazelnut crust with artichokes. The four set menus at 30€ to 35€ are great value and, most unusually, there is no cover or service charge. The breads and the pastas are all homemade, the wines and cheeses superb.

Piazza Alfano I 4. ✆ **089-9952769.** www.ristorantealcenacolo.it. Reservations recommended. Secondi 15€–16€. AE, DC, MC, V. Tues–Sat 7:30–11:30pm; Sun 1–4:30pm and 7:30–11:30pm. Closed 3 weeks in Aug.

Hosteria Il Brigante ★ 🏠 🍴 SALERNITAN We love this rustic osteria, which is a temple to the traditional local cuisine and offers great value. The seasonal menu focuses on pasta: Specialties include spaghetti *alici, pinoli, uva passa e pomodorini* (seasoned with anchovies, pine nuts, raisins, and cherry tomatoes) and the *sangiovannara* (pasta with eggplant and mozzarella). Among the meat and fish dishes, we recommend the *maiale ubriaco* (roast pork "drunk" with red wine) or the calamari *e fiori di zucca* (with zucchini flowers). Finish off with a homemade fruit sorbet.

Via Fratelli Linguiti 4 (behind the Duomo). ✆ **089-9438729.** Reservations recommended. Secondi 6.50€. No credit cards. Tues–Sun 12:30–3pm and 8:30–11pm. Closed 2 weeks in Aug.

Il Ristoro degli Angeli CREATIVE SALERNITAN/SEAFOOD An off-the-beaten track location and a simple-yet-elegant minimalist interior provide the backdrop for young chef Marco De Luca's superb food and we highly recommend a meal here. His seasonal menus are imaginative and accomplished: Top-notch ingredients from the family's organic farm and from local suppliers go into unusual choices such as pork with aromatic salt, chestnut honey, pomegranate, and spinach. De Luca is passionate about rice, so we recommend you try whatever risotto is on the menu; we loved the one made with goat's cheese and local Aglianico wine. Leave room for excellent desserts such as the divine *torta caprese* made with blackberries. Prices here are very reasonable, especially at lunchtimes.

Via Francesco Conforti 16. ✆ **089-2960329.** Reservations recommended. Secondi 14€–20€. AE, DC, MC, V. Mon–Sat 1–3pm and 8–11pm; Sun 1–3pm only with advance reservation.

Ristorante del Golfo SALERNITAN/SEAFOOD This is a charming old-fashioned restaurant overlooking the harbor, offering interesting views from its dining rooms and terraces. The menu presents modern interpretations of traditional dishes. We recommend the nice risotto *ai frutti di mare* (with seafood) or the unusual *ciencioni* (homemade pasta squares in a stew of chickpeas and salted cod), followed by the perfectly prepared grilled catch of the day.

Via Porto 57. ✆ **089-231581.** www.ilristorantedelgolfo.it. Reservations recommended. Secondi 20€–40€. AE, DC, MC, V. Mon, Tues, Thurs–Sat 12:30–3:30pm and 7:30pm–midnight; Sun 12:30–3:30pm.

Trattoria del Padreterno SEAFOOD In the historic district's prettiest square, this restaurant's menu changes daily with the offerings of the local fish market. We recommend classics such as the *cozze gratinate* (mussels au gratin), the *polpi alla Luciana* (stewed octopus), and the splendid spaghetti *cozze, limone, e basilico* (with mussels, lemon, and fresh basil).

Piazza Gioia 12. © **089-239305.** Reservations recommended. Secondi 16€–22€. AE, DC, MC, V. Wed–Mon 1–3pm and 8pm–midnight.

Salerno After Dark

As a university town and a major harbor, Salerno has a lively nightlife and cultural scene, with a large number of clubs, discos, and cafes. Among the places to hang out, we recommend the **Bogart Café,** Via Vernieri 85 (© **089-2960356**), which turns into a disco on weekends. **Dolce Vita,** Via del Navigatori, Pontecagnano (© **348-1451089**), is a big, very popular dance venue on the seafront just south of Salerno with restaurants, bars, and multiple dance floors that features big name DJs; it's open from May until October. **Non ho Sonno** ("I'm not sleepy!") is its wintertime counterpart, located just across the same street. It is open from November until April. For more information on the nightlife scene in Salerno, visit www.discosalerno.it.

For more upscale nightlife, heading the top of the list is **Teatro Verdi,** Largo Luciani (© **089-662141;** www.teatroverdisalerno.it; daily 8am–2pm and 4–8pm), which, true to its namesake, is the venue for Italian opera, but also presents classic or contemporary plays, as well as concerts and dance performances.

THE RUINS OF PAESTUM ★

35km (22 miles) S of Salerno; 100km (62 miles) SE of Naples

Lying just a short distance south of Salerno, the celebrated ruins of Paestum more than fulfill expectations and are enormously evocative. The three majestic Greek temples (which are remarkably well-preserved) sit on a grassy plain that really gives off the sense of an ancient, vanished city, enclosed in its still standing boundary walls. The temples are a magical sight, especially at sunset, and in spring and fall when Paestum's famous roses—praised since antiquity—are in bloom. The archaeological area can be reached as a day trip from all of the destinations covered in this guide; plan on spending a minimum of two hours exploring the temples and an hour for the museum, but count on a whole day for a more in-depth visit.

Essentials

GETTING THERE Paestum is well connected by public transportation, with several **trains** stopping at its two train stations: **Capaccio-Roccadaspide** and **Paestum,** only 5 minutes from each other. The former is in the village of Capaccio Scalo from where there a rather irregular bus service to the ruins while the latter lies about 1 km (half a mile) or a 10-minute walk from the archaeological area. It is a 30-minute trip from Salerno and a 90-minute trip from Naples. Contact **Trenitalia** (© **892021** in Italy; www.trenitalia.it) for fares and information.

Paestum is well connected to Salerno by bus, too. **CSTP** (© **089-252228** or 800-016659 toll-free within Italy; www.cstp.it) has regular

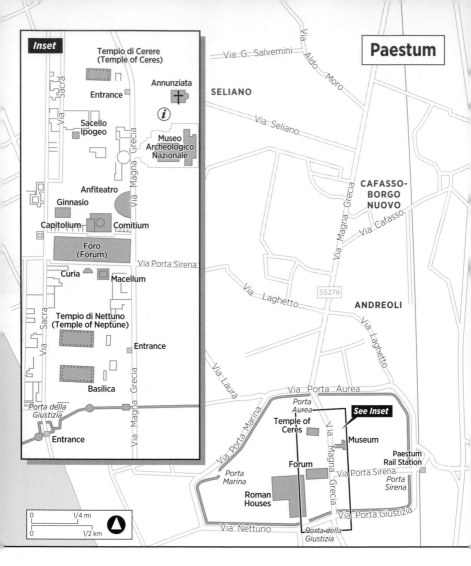

service to Paestum from Napoli and Salerno (both line 34), with both lines continuing on to Agropoli and Acciaroli, in the Cilento. **SITA** (© 089-405145; www.sitabus.it) makes runs from Salerno to Capaccio Scalo; and **Autolinee Giuliano Bus** (© 0974-836185; www.giulianobus.com) has several lines between Naples, Salerno, and the Cilento, making stops in Paestum and Capaccio Scalo (lines 3, 4, 5, 6, 7, and 10).

By **car,** take autostrada A3, exit at BATTIPAGLIA onto SS 18, and follow the brown signs for Paestum.

GETTING AROUND The temples are easily accessible **on foot.** Via Porta Sirena leads from Paestum train station to Via Magna Grecia, which cuts through the middle of the archaeological site. Should you want to explore farther afield, you can rent a **car** from **Autorental,** Via Magna Grecia

(© 199-240909; www.autorental.it); or from **Leonardo D'Onofrio,** Via Cesare Pavese 27 (©0828-721107), which also offers **taxi/car service** with a driver.

VISITOR INFORMATION AACST, Via Magna Grecia 887, 84063 Paestum (©0828-811016; fax 0828-722322; www.infopaestum.it), maintains an information point at Via Magna Grecia 151, by the Archeological Museum, not far from the main entrance to the temples (daily 9am–1pm and 2–4pm).

You'll find a pharmacy on Via Licinella **0828-722653** and several in Capaccio Scalo, including one on Via Magna Grecia 316 (©0828-725382). The closest hospital is in Salerno (see "Visitor Information," p. 283). For an **ambulance,** dial © 118. Dial © 113 or 112 for the police, © 115 for the fire department, and © 116 for ACI road assistance. The **post office** (©0828-811029) is on Via Licinella; and there is one in Capaccio Scalo, at Via C. Dalla Chiesa (©0828-725246). A **bank** (©0828-811141) is at Via Licinella 1.

SPECIAL EVENTS The occasional **Paestum Balloon Festival** is a great opportunity to take some pictures of the balloons taking off from the Greek temples and soaring into the sky. For those fortunate enough to secure a flight, the view on a clear day stretches from the Appenines to Capri and beyond. The event is usually scheduled in the fall; visit **www.mongolfiere. it** for information.

Exploring the Ruins

The Greeks established the colony of Poseidonia—the name Paestum is Roman—in the 7th century B.C., around the same time that the nearby Sanctuary of Hera Argiva (p. 294) was built. The town flourished for almost 3 centuries but its fortunes dramatically declined after it was overtaken by the Lucanians, a local mountain people, in the 4th century B.C. Only when the Romans established the colony of Paestum in 273 B.C. did the city revive, quickly growing wealthy from its agricultural and commercial activity. The city lost its supremacy during the Middle Ages, when the inhabitants were forced into the hills by repeated Saracen attacks and the spread of malaria (caused by the fertile plain's transformation into marshland). The Normans arrived in the 11th century, plundering the temples and other buildings for their statuary. The ruins remained known but undisturbed for centuries until the state road was built in the 18th century and the first archaeological studies were performed.

Note: The archaeological area is not huge, but the two temples dedicated to Hera are some way from the one dedicated to Athena, and you should be prepared to walk; wear comfortable shoes, and carry water and a hat, particularly if it's hot.

Archaeological Area of Paestum ★★★ The enclosed site contains the three temples (all built facing east) and a number of other ruins that were part of the sacred area at the center of the ancient Greek town. The **Tempio di Hera** (or Temple to Hera, commonly known as the **Basilica**) ★★★ is the oldest of the three structures and was built in 550 B.C. in Doric-Archaic style. The 50 columns of its monumental portico are still standing and show the pot-bellied profile typical of archaic temples, but the roof and the pediment collapsed long ago. In front is a partially ruined sacrificial altar and, on its side, the square *bothros*—the sacrificial well where the remains were thrown. Based on the rich trove of findings in the immediate area, experts now believe that the temple and surrounding structures were actually part of a huge complex dedicated to Hera, the goddess of fertility and maternity (who is also honored in the Sanctuary of Hera Argiva, p. 294). Indeed, several other smaller religious buildings, all dedicated to Hera, have been discovered nearby. The complex is to the south of the archaeological area, near the secondary entrance.

To the right of the basilica is the **Tempio di Nettuno** ★★★ or Temple of Neptune, possibly dedicated to Poseidon or, according to a more recent theory, to Apollo or Zeus. This grandiose building, dating from around 450 B.C., is lined in travertine stone and glows a magical gold color when hit by the sun's rays. It is considered the best example of a Doric temple in the world, with its perfect proportions and a number of architectural tricks—the columns at the corners have an elliptical section instead of round, and the horizontal lines are slightly convex instead of perfectly straight—giving it slender elegance and power at the same time. It is also the best preserved of Paestum's temples: only the roof and the internal walls are missing. At the temple's front are two sacrificial altars; the smaller was added by the Romans in the 3rd century B.C.

Paestum.

The Statue of Zeus in the National Archaeological Museum of Paestum.

The third temple, the **Tempio di Cerere (Temple of Ceres) ★★**, stands near the main entrance to the archaeological area. The smallest of the three, it was built at the end of the 6th century B.C., probably in honor of the Goddess Athena. Transformed into a church in medieval times, inside its portico are three Christian tombs. Between here and the Basilica is the **Roman Forum.** The forum was the hub of any Roman city and this one was enclosed on four sides by a covered colonnade with taverns and shops of which little remains today. Nearby, at the edge of Via Magna Grecia, is the **Roman Amphitheatre.** The **Via Sacra (Sacred Street)** runs arrow straight through the length of the site, connecting all three temples, its Roman pavement laid over the original Greek road. When it was built, the road continued for about 12km (7½ miles), to connect the Greek town of Poseidonia with the Sanctuary of Hera.

Main entrance Via Magna Grecia 917; secondary entrance Porta della Giustizia (Justice Gate, off Via Nettuno; for ticket holders only). © **0828-721113.** www.infopaestum.it. Admission 6€; free with purchase of the Artecard. Daily 9am–sunset (last admission 60 min. earlier).

National Archaeological Museum of Paestum ★★ This museum archives the finds from the excavations: From Paestum, the 6th-century-B.C. **Statue of Zeus ★★** is well worth seeing as is the rich collection of 6th-century-B.C. **vases ★★** with red or black figures. Among the finds from the nearby necropolis, the most interesting are the exquisite, celebrated Greek frescoes from the **Tomb of the Diver ★★** that date from the 5th century B.C. Also very interesting are the paintings and objects found in the **Lucanian Tombs,** dating from the 6th to the 3rd centuries B.C. One entire area of the museum is dedicated to the architectural remains from the Sanctuary of Hera Argiva (below), including the complete **frieze ★** of metopes and triglyphs; a number of the metopes are unfinished, which helps shed light on the carving techniques.

Via Magna Grecia 918 (across from the entrance to the temples). © **0828-811023.** Admission 4€; free with purchase of the Artecard. Daily 9am–6:45pm (last admission 45 min. earlier). Closed the 1st and 3rd Mon each month.

Sanctuary of Hera Argiva (Heraion) Lying near the mouth of the river Sele, a protected natural area, these ruins are the remains of what must have been a glorious religious complex. The Heraion (sanctuary to the goddess Hera) was one of the most famous temples of antiquity, described by many ancient writings on Magna Grecia (the conglomerate of Greek colonies in the Mediterranean). Sought by archaeologists since the 18th century, it was discovered by two young archaeologists—Paola Zancani Montuoro and Umberto Zanotti Bianco—in the 20th century. Ruins include the foundation of the main temple, together with parts of the smaller *thesaurus* (treasury), and a portico with outlying buildings. All the decorations—metopes and votive statuettes—are conserved in the National Archaeological Museum of Paestum (above). A short distance away from the ruins, in a restored farmhouse, is the **Museo Narrante del Santuario di Hera Argiva** ★. It houses an excellent multimedia installation describing the discovery of the ruins and the function of the sanctuary. The cult of Hera (Juno, in Latin), which was very powerful in antiquity, did not disappear with the advent of Christianity but was actually absorbed into Christians' devotion to the Virgin Mary. In the nearby 11th-century sanctuary of the **Madonna del Granato** (road to Capaccio Vecchia; Aug 15 only), the Madonna holds a pomegranate, the symbol for Hera/Juno.

Ruins: Near the mouth of the river Sele, about 1.5km (1 mile) inland from the sea and 11km (6¾ miles) north of Paestum. **Museum:** Masseria Procuriali, Via Barizzo, Foce Sele Capaccio (about 2km/1¼ miles from the ruins and 9km/5½ miles from Paestum). Ⓒ **0828-861440.** Free admission. Ruins daily 9am–7pm (July–Sept until 10pm). Museum Tues–Sun 9am–4pm.

Staying Active

Usually bypassed by harried tourists, ancient Paestum's defensive **walls** offer the opportunity for a unique walk where the going is relatively easy and the views are great. Once completely surrounding the town and originally built by the Greeks, they were restored by the Lucanians and then the Romans and today they are some of the best-preserved sets of ancient walls left standing. Five meters (18 ft.) thick on average, with several towers, they mark a pentagonal perimeter of 4,750m (15,584 ft.), with four main gates at each of the cardinal directions. In 1828, when the Bourbon government built the Via delle Calabriae—today's Via Magna Grecia—they caused the almost complete destruction of the northern gate (Porta Aurea) and part of the southern walls. The western side is the best preserved. At the monumental western gate, **Porta Marina** ★, you can climb the walls and walk on the patrol paths, enjoying the great views over coast and ruins.

Though famous for its archaeological area, Paestum is also a great seaside destination. **Marina di Paestum** ★ is the place to bask in the sun, with miles of sandy **beaches;** the warm sea is great for swimming, too.

Where to Stay

In addition to the following hotels, we also recommend staying at **Le Trabe** (p. 296).

Il Granaio dei Casabella ★ ☺ This hotel enjoys an unbeatable location right next to Paestum's archaeological area. It is a charming property, occupying what was originally a *granaio* (granary). Tastefully restored, it offers simply decorated guest rooms that are spacious and welcoming (although some are a bit dark), with tiled floors and rustic wooden furniture. Bathrooms are functional and modern (some with shower only). The **restaurant** ★ (p. 296) is excellent.

Via Tavernelle 84 (off Via Magna Grecia), 84063 Paestum. www.ilgranaiodeicasabella.com. ✆ **0828-721014.** Fax 0828-811893. 14 units. 120€ double; 170€ family room (sleeps 4). Rates include breakfast. AE, DC, MC, V. Free parking. Closed Nov–Feb. **Amenities:** Restaurant; bar. *In room:* A/C, TV.

Mandetta ☺ Charmingly old fashioned, this budget hotel is right on the beach and only 550m (1,800 ft.) from the archaeological area. In addition to the hotel, the family-run property includes a few cabins (with kitchen and small private patio garden), and an RV park. Guest rooms are not large but are functional, simply decorated, and have tiled floors. The hotel has a private beach and facilities, including activities for kids (for a fee). The family-run **restaurant ★** offers a solid traditional menu that makes it popular among locals.

Via Torre di Mare 2, 84063 Paestum. www.mandetta.it. ✆ **0828-811118.** Fax 0828-721328. 20 units. 115€ double. Rate includes breakfast. AE, DC, MC, V. Free parking. **Amenities:** Restaurant; bar. *In room:* A/C, TV.

Savoy Beach Hotel ☺ Near the beach and a short distance away from the archaeological area, this modern hotel offers more amenities than the Granaio (below) and somewhat more upscale accommodations. Guest rooms are a good size and comfortable, with classic furnishings and modern bathrooms (some with shower only). Some have carpeting, others wood floors, and others yet are tiled; more expensive units open onto private balconies. Don't expect sea views, as the hotel is surrounded by a garden, with a large swimming pool; the beach is 183m (600 ft.) down the road, and guests have access to the hotel's private facilities there. For a fee, guest can use the health center, including a heated indoor pool, a fitness room, and spa. The restaurant, **Tre Olivi ★**, is gourmet.

Via Poseidonia 41, 84063 Paestum. www.hotelsavoybeach.it. ✆ **0828-720100.** Fax 0828-720807. 24 units. 198€–220€ double; from 240€ suite. Rates include buffet breakfast. AE, DC, MC, V. Free parking. **Amenities:** Restaurant; bar; pool; room service; outdoor tennis. *In room:* A/C, TV, Internet, minibar.

Tenuta Seliano This pleasant *agriturismo* is a good choice if you want to stay in the countryside. Set in a 19th-century hamlet, the picturesque buildings have been turned into lodgings with large, comfortable guest rooms with country-style elegance and good taste. A well-groomed garden with a swimming pool and some 91 hectares (225 acres) of land complete the property, part of which is dedicated to raising buffaloes (for mozzarella, of course). The cuisine prepared by Signora Bellelli—who also offers cooking classes—completes the service. You can choose to have all your meals at the farm, or only breakfast.

Via Seliano, Borgo Antico (Capaccio Scalo), 84063 Paestum. www.agriturismoseliano.it. ✆ **0828-723634.** Fax 0828-724544. 14 units. 120€ double. Rate includes breakfast. AE, DC, MC, V. Free parking. Closed Nov–Dec 27 and Jan 7–Feb. **Amenities:** Pool. *In room:* A/C, TV.

Where to Eat

We highly recommend a visit to the **Tenuta Vannulo ★★**, Via Galileo Galilei, Contrada Vannulo, Capaccio Scalo (✆**0828-727894;** www.vannulo.it), a buffalo farm producing magnificent mozzarella and other buffalo products. We confess, we really came here just to taste the **gelato ★★★**, which is famed to be among the best in Italy, and discovered a gourmet paradise. Antonio Palmieri's farm is certified organic, and he justly takes great pride in his operation: You can visit the premises, meet the buffalo, and taste the products, including the best mozzarella you can dream of. The Tenuta also has a few **guest rooms** where you can spend the night.

In addition to the restaurants below, we recommend **Tre Olivi,** in the Savoy Beach Hotel (above).

Il Granaio dei Casabella ★ SALERNITAN Across from the walls of ancient Paestum, this countryside restaurant inside the hotel of the same name (p. 294), offers refined dining and a delightful veranda overlooking an internal garden. We loved the delicious *granatine di lardo ai frutti di mare* (shellfish fritters); gnocchi *con zucca e gamberi in zimino* (with shrimp, pumpkin, and a spinach-and-herb sauce), and risotto *carciofi e aragosta* (with lobster and artichokes). For something simpler, try the grilled fish.

Via Tavernelle 84 (off Via Magna Grecia), Paestum. ✆ **0828-721014.** www.ilgranaiodeicasabella. com. Reservations recommended. Secondi 10€–18€. AE, DC, MC, V. Daily 12:30–3pm and 7:30–11pm. Closed Tues Sept–Mar.

Le Trabe ★★ SALERNITAN This beautiful and stylish restaurant is housed inside an old hydro-electrical plant in a lovely setting of gardens and streams. The menu is seasonal and changes often, with dishes reminiscent of the local multicultural tradition (Greek, Roman, French, and so on). You may find *taccozzette gamberi e porcini mantecati al provolone* (homemade pasta with shrimp and porcini mushrooms baked with provolone cheese) or *filetto di cernia all'uva* (grouper filet with grapes), or an excellent ragout. The restaurant also has a few rooms (90€ double, including breakfast) to rent for the night.

Via Capo di Fiume 4, Capaccio Scalo. ✆ **0828-724165.** www.letrabe.it. Reservations recommended. Secondi 15€–24€. AE, DC, MC, V. Tues–Fri 8.30–10:30pm; Sat 12:30–3pm and 8:30–10:30pm; Sun 12:30–3pm.

Nonna Sceppa ★★ SALERNITAN This popular restaurant is considered to be one of the best in the region. The menu changes seasonally but always includes well-prepared traditional dishes. Everything is homemade, from the bread and delicious pasta to the delectable mozzarella and the desserts. The summer menu focuses on seafood and may include *rombo al forno con patate* (turbot baked on a bed of potatoes), while the winter menu highlights meat dishes, such as the traditional *tiano di carne* (ragout of sausages, pork ribs, and pork rind). We highly recommend the spaghetti *con l' aragosta* (with spiny lobster) and the classic and masterfully grilled catch of the day. The outdoor terrace is a pleasant bonus during fair weather.

Via Laura 45, Capaccio Scalo. ✆ **0828-851064.** www.nonnasceppa.com. Reservations recommended. Secondi 12€–25€. AE, DC, MC, V. Oct–May Fri–Wed 12:30–3pm and 7:30–10pm; June–Sept daily 12:30–3pm and 7:30–10pm. Closed 3 weeks in Oct.

Ristorante Nettuno ★ SALERNITAN This picturesque and upscale restaurant is in one of ancient Paestum's preserved gate towers, itself part of a 19th-century farmhouse. It opens onto a charming garden that is highly sought after for weddings. Appropriate to the surroundings, the cuisine is traditional but sophisticated, and the menu includes both meat and fish choices. You'll find *crespoline* (savory crepe stuffed with mozzarella and ham), and excellent pasta dishes, as well as a variety of secondi.

Via Nettuno 2 (by the secondary entrance to the archaeological area), Paestum. ✆ **0828-811028.** www.ristorantenettuno.com. Reservations recommended. Secondi 12€–20€. AE, DC, MC, V. Daily noon–3:30pm. Closed 3 weeks Nov and 7 Jan–7 Feb.

PADULA & CERTOSA DI SAN LORENZO ★★★

98km (59 miles) SE of Salerno

Little known to foreign tourists, the Carthusian Monastery of St. Lorenzo—one of the largest in the world—is prized for its architectural splendor and rich collection of artistic treasures. Off the beaten path in Salerno's hinterlands, this grandiose 16th-century monastery nestles in the slopes of the hill near the little town of Padula. It is an easy day trip from Salerno, Naples, or Paestum.

Essentials

GETTING THERE & AROUND Trenitalia (© 892021 in Italy; www.trenitalia.it) offers direct connections from Naples and Salerno to Battipaglia, where you will need to switch to a shuttle bus (which runs on schedule with the trains) to Padula and the monastery. You can also take a **bus** directly from Salerno: **Lamanna** (© 0975-520426) and **Curcio Viaggi** (© 089-254080; www.curcioviaggi.it) both make runs to Padula from Piazza della Concordia near the train station. Curcio Viaggi also offers direct connection to Padula from Firenze and Siena. From Naples, **Autolinee SLA** (© 0973-21016; www.slasrl.it) offers direct service to Padula; **Simet** (© 0983-520315; www.simetspa.it) has a daily bus that leaves Piazza Garibaldi (across from Stazione Centrale) at 10am. By **car,** take the exit marked PADULA-BUONA-BITACOLO off the A3 to SS 19, and follow the signs for PADULA.

Padula is small and can be visited **on foot;** the monastery is at the base of the hill on the edge of town.

VISITOR INFORMATION The local tourist office is **Associazione Pro Loco Padula,** Via Italo Balbo 45, Padula (© 0975-778611; www.proloco padula.com).

You'll find a **pharmacy** (© 0975-74587) on Via Nazionale in Padula. The nearest **hospital** (© 0975-312111) is in the town of Marsicovetere, a few miles east. For an **ambulance,** dial © 118. Dial © 113 or 112 for the **police,** © 115 for the **fire department,** and © 116 for **ACI road assistance.** You will find a **bank** with an ATM, **Banco di Napoli** (© 0975-778593), on Piazza Umberto I 15.

Exploring Padula & the Monastery

Padula is a small hill town, with interesting churches and *palazzi* lining its historic streets. The big attraction here is the Carthusian Monastery.

Certosa di San Lorenzo ★★ Established in 1306, this monastery was enlarged over the centuries, reaching the height of its fame during the Renaissance, when it was one of the richest monasteries in Italy. The huge complex of buildings and courtyards covers an area of 51,500 sq. m (554,341 sq. ft.) and boasts 320 halls, 52 staircases, 100 fireplaces, 13 courtyards, and 41 fountains. Abandoned in 1866, the Certosa was only recently reopened to the public after extensive restorations, including repair after the earthquake of 1980. It is now the setting for important cultural events and international exhibits, not the least of which is the Ravello Music Festival (p. 44), which schedules a number of concerts on the grounds every year.

The Certosa di San Lorenzo.

Many of the original medieval structures were redecorated in baroque style, making it one of the most important baroque works of art in Italy. The first **cloister ★★**, near the entrance to the monastery, dates from 1561 and is graced by an elegant portico and fountain. The richly decorated church boasts two magnificent wooden **choirs ★★★** inlaid with intarsia artwork; one, created for the monks, dates from 1503, while the other, designed by Giovanni del Gallo in 1507, was meant for the lay brothers. Near the church is the original cemetery from 1552, now a **cloister.** The later, larger cemetery is in the splendid 17th-century **main cloister ★★★**. Along the two levels of porticos decorated with beautiful carvings are the monks' secluded **"cells"**—miniapartments of three to four rooms with private porticos, small gardens, and even a workshop/studio for some. Note the small opening for delivering food and the aperture that allowed in light, both by the entrance to the cell. You can climb to the upper floor via a beautiful **staircase** in an octagonal tower, where you'll see the **Monk's Promenade ★** around the cloister and the **Apartments of the Prior ★★**.

The **library** and **reception halls** of the monastery house an **archaeological museum,** which holds a collection of ancient artifacts from the nearby necropolis.

Viale Certosa 1. ✆ **0975-77745.** www.magnifico.beniculturali.it/certosa.html. Admission 4€; free with purchase of the Artecard. Daily 9am–8pm. Last admission 1 hr. earlier. Closed Jan 1, Aug 15, and Dec 25.

Where to Stay & Eat

The monastery is an easy excursion from Salerno or nearby towns, but few visitors stay the night. We highly recommend stopping for a meal, though: The popular **Taverna Il Lupo ★★**, Via Municipio (✆ **0975-778376;** www.taverna illupo.it; secondi 7€–12€; closed Sun dinner and all day Mon), is a rustic and welcoming trattoria serving traditional local cuisine. If you do want to stay for the night, the best hotels in town are the atmospheric **Villa Cosilinum,** Corso Garibaldi, Località Sant'Eligio, 84034 Padula (✆ **0975-778615;** www.villa cosilinum.it; 100€ double, including buffet breakfast) and **Grand Hotel Certosa,** Viale Certosa 41, 84034 Padula (✆ **0975-77046;** www.certosa.it; 95€ double, including breakfast), each with elegant guest rooms and good **restaurants.**

THE NATIONAL PARK OF THE CILENTO

110km (68 miles) S of Naples

The Cilento is Campania's loneliest wilderness, well off the beaten track and one of the least inhabited areas in Italy. The population is concentrated along the beautiful coast, while the remote hinterland is crossed by only a few roads. Established as a national park in 1991, this is the second-largest national park in Italy, offering a variety of land- and seascapes, from the mountains of the Alburni (home to some of the most interesting caves in the world) and Monte Cervati (the highest mountain in Campania), to the splendid promontory of Cape Palinuro, so justly praised by Virgil. The Cilento is also rich in archaeological and architectural mementoes of the various civilizations that have inhabited the area since prehistoric times.

Essentials

GETTING THERE For such a remote area, the Cilento is well connected by public transportation, with its major towns connected by train, its major harbors by ferry, and its smaller villages by bus. During the summer, **Metrò del Mare** (✆ **199-600700;** www.metrodelmare.net) offers a **boat service** that connects Agropoli, Acciaroli, Palinuro, and Camerota with Pozzuoli, Naples, Sorrento, Positano, Amalfi, and Salerno. In 2011, the schedule was reduced to a once-a-day service in July and August, but we're told that by 2012, a fuller service should resume.

Direct **trains** link Naples and Salerno to Agropoli/Castellabate, Pisciotta/Palinuro, and Vallo della Lucania. Contact **Trenitalia** (✆ **892021** in Italy; www.trenitalia.it) for fares and information.

Each of the towns and villages in the park are also served by **bus** from Naples, Pompeii, Salerno, and Paestum: **CSTP,** Piazza Matteo Luciani 33, Salerno (✆ **089-252228** or 800-016659 toll-free within Italy; www.cstp.it), runs several lines from Napoli, Pompeii, Paestum, and Salerno to Vallo della Lucania, Agropoli, Santa Maria di Castellabate, Acciaroli, and Pollica. **Curcio Viaggi** (✆ **089-254080;** www.curcioviaggi.it) offers lines from Rome and Salerno to Sicignano degli Alburni, Scario, and Polla. **SCAT** (✆ **0974-838415**) connects Salerno and Paestum with Agropoli, Santa Maria di Castellabate, and villages along the coast in between. **Lamanna** (✆ **0975-520426**) offers service from Salerno to Polla. **Autolinee Giuliano Bus** (✆ **0974-836185;** www.giulianobus.com) covers Naples and Salerno to Roccadaspide, Agropoli, Vallo della Lucania, and Pioppi. Finally, **SITA** (✆ **089-405145;** www.sitabus.it) has lines from Salerno to Pertosa and Polla.

By **car,** take autostrada A3 to the exit marked SERRE, turning onto SS 19 toward Serre. Turn right on SS 488 following signs for ROCCA D'ASPIDE into the park.

GETTING AROUND In spite of good public transportation inside the park, only a **car** will provide the necessary flexibility for extensive exploration of the interior, particularly in the off season, when connections are less frequent and ferry service is suspended. In addition to the major **car-rental** companies (p. 347), you can rent a car through **Alba Rent Car,** Via Alcide de Gasperi, Agropoli (✆ **0974-828099**); and **Smec,** Peppino Manente Comunale 35, Castellabate (✆ **0974-961565**). For a **taxi** in the Castellabate area, call ✆ **339-4820303.**

VISITOR INFORMATION The park's **Visitor Center** (✆ **0974-719911;** www.cilentoediano.it) is on Piazza Santa Caterina 8, 84078 **Vallo della Lucania,** the gateway to the park.

You'll find **pharmacies** in each of the major towns and villages in the area, including at Via Roma 6 (✆**0974-4974**), in Vallo della Lucania, and at Corso Garibaldi 43 (✆**0974-823054**), in Agropoli. The **hospital** (✆**0974-827511**) is on Contrada Marrota in Agropoli. For an **ambulance,** dial ✆**118.** Dial ✆**113** or 112 for the **police,** ✆**115** in case of **fire,** and ✆**116** for **ACI road assistance.** You'll find **banks** with ATMs in all major towns and villages in the park.

GUIDED TOURS **CitySightseeing** (www.napoli.city-sightseeing.it) offers a series of park tours exclusively for **Artecard** (p. 98) holders. Departures are from Pestum, Agropoli, and a number of other towns in the park, including Acciaroli, and Palinuro. The cost is between 5€ and 10€ depending on the itinerary.

Exploring the Park

The park was declared part of the Biosphere Preservation program of UNESCO in 1997 for its pristine natural environment, rich in rare plant species, such as the *primula di Palinuro*—a rare dune flower that has been adopted as the symbol of the park—and the wild orchid of San Giovanni a Piro, a Mediterranean orchid (*orchidee spontanee*). The park covers almost 180,000 hectares (444,790 acres), and encompasses two mountain masses—the Alburni to the north and Monte Cervati to the south—and several small towns and villages. Vallo della Lucania, the seat of the park information office, is a good base for discovering the interior and enjoying hiking opportunities.

ARCHAEOLOGICAL SITES

Beyond a belt of uninteresting modern development, Agropoli's well-preserved **medieval citadel ★** (about 49km/30 miles south of Salerno) crowns a promontory dominated by a **castle ★**, today partially ruined and overlooking the harbor and the small fishing harbor below. On a clear day, you can see all the way to Punta Campanella and Capri from the castle's walls. We also recommend a stroll along the **seafront promenade ★**.

Teggiano ★ (100km/62 miles south of Salerno and 14km/8¾ miles north of Padula) also makes for a pleasant excursion. The **Cathedral of Santa Maria Maggiore** has beautiful sculpture, particularly the 13th-century ambone and the 14th-century tomb of Enrico Sanseverino. More art is in the **Museo Dioccsano** (**℗ 0975-79930;** free admission; Tues–Sun 10am–1pm and 3–6pm), in the 13th-century church of San Pietro. The imposing **castle ★★** dates back to Norman times; owned by the Macchiaroli family, it is not open to the public. Other villages worth the detour are **Castellabate** (20km/13 miles south of Paestum), with its picturesque 12th-century castle, and **Acciaroli** (80km/50 miles south of Salerno) and the adjacent medieval hamlet of **Pioppi.**

The **archaeological excavations of Velia ★**, 90km (56 miles) south of Salerno (**℗ 0974-971409;** daily 9am–sunset; admission 2€, free with purchase of the Artecard), are near the coastline, on the outskirts of Marina di Ascea. These ruins are lesser known than those at Paestum; they are the remains of the Greek colony of **Elea,** created around 540 B.C. as the seat of the famed Eleatic school of philosophy. Elea had grown into such a beacon of Greek culture by Roman times that even after it fell under the rule of the empire it was allowed the privilege of maintaining Greek as its official language. That is when its name was changed to Velia. The **lower town** features portions of the walls from the 5th and 4th centuries B.C., as well as, around the south gate, houses originally from the same period but modified in Roman times. Also of note are the Roman thermal baths, with beautiful mosaics in the *Frigidarium.* From there you can climb to the famous **Porta Rosa ★★**, on a stretch of the original Greek pavement. In the **Acropolis** (the upper town), you'll find ruins of a theater, an Ionic temple that was partially covered by a Norman castle, and a sanctuary to Poseidon. The northern sections of the city walls are still well preserved.

Agropoli's medieval citadel.

The Grotte dell'Angelo.

NATURAL ATTRACTIONS

The best attractions in the park are its **grottoes**. Most superb are the **Grotte dell'Angelo** ★★★ in Pertosa (✆ 0975-397037; www.grottedellangelo.sa.it; Mar-Oct daily 9am–7pm, Nov-Feb daily 10am–4pm; three guided tours 10€, 13€, and 16€, free with purchase of the Artecard). Created by the stream that still flows there, the grottoes have parts still underwater. A visit here starts with a ride on a raft across the first cave. The corridors extend for over 3km (2 miles), but the actual walk depends on the length of the tour you choose: the Inferno (60 min.), the Purgatorio (75 min.), or the Paradiso (90 min.). Each subsequent hall contains marvelous formations of shapely stalactites and stalagmites, and some pure crystal formations. The grotto's inhabitants built pile dwellings during the Neolithic period, and more traditional dwellings during the Bronze and early Iron ages. The caves were kept in use during Lucanian and ancient Roman times, and during the Christian era, when they were consecrated in the name of Saint Michael, the 11th-century archangel. Experienced spelunkers can book a tour to less accessible parts of the grottoes, including the active subterranean stream. To reach the grottoes, follow the signs for PERTOSA on SS 19; the parking area is a short distance off the road to the left. **Note:** Thursday and Friday, when school is in session, access to the grottoes is reserved for classes; they open to the public at 2pm.

An interesting complement to a visit to the grottoes is the recently opened **MIdA,** Piazza de Marco, Pertosa (✆ 0975-397220; www.fondazionemida.it), a museum dedicated to the local ecosystem with a multimedia exhibit on spelunking (admission 2€, free with purchase of the Artecard; Tues–Sun 10am–1pm, Nov–Mar also 3–6pm and Apr–Oct also 3–7pm).

Ernest Hemingway

The fishing harbor of Acciaroli was the preferred hideaway of Ernest Hemingway, who stayed here several times. Built on a promontory, the village is dominated by a square defense **tower** overlooking the harbor and the pretty 12th-century **church of the Annunziata.** The story goes that Hemingway got the idea for *The Old Man and the Sea* after befriending a local fisherman.

The **Grotte di Castelcivita ★★** (℡ 0828-7772397; www.grottedi
castelcivita.com; admission 10€, 20% discount with purchase of the Artecard)
is an astounding succession of large galleries and natural halls extending for over
5km (3 miles) under the Alburni mountains. Inhabited from Paleolithic times to
the Bronze Age, the grottoes are composed of a central section of galleries and
halls. Lateral chambers that depart from the main core have been only partially
explored. Some halls have beautiful stalactite and stalagmite formations, others,
such as the so-called *Tempio* (Temple), have multicolored formations. Remember
to bring a jacket: It's chilly even in summer. The grottoes are accessible by guided
tour only, with visits starting every 90 minutes (Mar 16–Sept 30 10:30am–6pm;
Oct 1–Mar 15 10:30am–3pm). To reach the grottoes, follow SS 488 toward the
small town of Controne; the grottoes are a few miles down the road.

OUTDOOR ACTIVITIES

The best of the many **hiking trails** in the park ascend Monte Cervati
(1,898m/6,227 ft.), and Monte Alburno (1,742m/5,715 ft.). **Monte
Alburno ★★** is nicknamed Mount Panorama for the sweeping views you can
enjoy from the top. Climb up one of two trails from **Sicignano degli Alburni,** a
town off SS 19 not far from Serre. The first trail climbs directly up to the western
peak; the second leads to a fork at 1,400m (4,593 ft.), where one branch heads
east and the other west. Allow at least 4 hours for either climb. The region's highest mountain is **Monte Cervati ★★.** Cervati is a dramatic sight, especially in
the summer, when its extensive lavender fields are in bloom. You can make the
ascent via two different trails, both starting from the town of **Sanza,** on SS 517.
Allow about 6 hours for either.

   Beaches at the leading resorts are pretty crowded in the high summer during the Italian holiday season (mid-July through Aug). Loudspeakers with music
and activities for kids turn what was once an idyllic setting into a noisy affair. So,
if you are after a secluded beach, you'll have to rent a boat or come off season.
Palinuro ★ is a fishing and resort harbor set among olive groves in a picturesque
bay protected by a promontory, famous for its grottoes in the cliffs. The most
beautiful of them, the **Grotta Azzurra ★★,** is far less mobbed than its more
famous cousin in Capri, yet its water takes on magical colors, especially around
noon and sunset. You'll find boats with or without crew for rent in the harbor; we
recommend **Cooperativa dei Pescatori. Santa Maria di Castellabate ★**
is blessed with two beautiful beaches: The one to the north—the largest—has
unusually fine sand, while the smaller one to the south enjoys the proximity of a
shady pine grove. The whole stretch of coast here, around **Punta Licosa,** is a bi-
ological protected area and marine park, which offers some interesting **snorkeling** and **scuba diving. Cilento Sub,** Via Roma 3, Santa Maria di Castellabate
(℡ 0974-961628; www.ascilentosub.com), provides guides and equipment and
organizes excursions to the Cilento national underwater park. The little fishing
harbor and seaside town of **Marina di Camerota** is beloved by locals for its less-
developed coastline and variety of sandy or rocky beaches—such as **Baia della
Calanca ★**—as well as its coves, grottoes, towers, and great scuba diving.

Where to Stay

International tourism is new to this area, and accommodations, with the exception of Palazzo Belmonte (see below) are quite basic. We tend to prefer the quality of service—and food—at an eco-friendly *agriturismo.*

In a panoramic position in Palinuro is the **Agriturismo Sant'Agata,** Via Sant'Agata Nord (✆**0974-931716;** www.agriturismosantagata.it), offering excellent cuisine, **cooking classes ★**, and simple but tasteful guest rooms. Another address serving excellent food and wine is **Il Vecchio Casale,** Contrada Vigna, 84070 Vatolla di Perdifumo (✆**0974-845235;** fax 0974-821296; www.il vecchiocasale.it), inland of Castellabate: The elegant farmhouse dates from the 18th century and has a pleasant swimming pool. **Principe di Vallescura,** Via Marina Campagna, Località Vallescura, near Pollica (✆**0974-973087;** www.principedivallescura.com), affords beautiful sea views and beach access; and **I Fornari,** Località Fornari 2, 84076 Stella Cilento (✆**0974-909204** or 3383621071; www.agriturismoifornari.it), offers upscale accommodations in an atmospheric 18th-century mill and has great amenities, including a pool.

EXPENSIVE

Albergo Santa Caterina The best hotel in Palinuro, the welcoming Santa Caterina is located right in the heart of town. Housed in an elegant building, it offers pleasant public spaces and nicely appointed pastel-colored guest rooms, decorated with hand-painted Vietri tiles. The rooms are not huge, but comfortable and pleasantly decorated; most open onto private balconies and small terraces. Bathrooms are a bit on the small side but are well kept (most with shower only). The hotel offers a shuttle to the beach plus a beach umbrella and chairs for 10€ per day.

Via Indipendenza 53, 84064 Palinuro. ✆**0974-931019.** Fax 0974-938325. www.albergosanta caterina.com. 20 units. 110€ double. AE, DC, MC, V. Free parking. Closed New Year's Eve and Day. **Amenities:** Restaurant; bar; concierge. *In room:* A/C, TV, minibar.

Hotel Antichi Feudi This hotel, housed in a recently restored baronial palazzo in Teggiano's medieval district, offers an excellent price-quality ratio. Guest rooms are large and tastefully, if a bit sparsely, decorated, some with original tiled floors. Bathrooms are modern and a good size (some with shower only). The **restaurant** is formal, and the food is good.

Via S. Francesco 2, 84039 Teggiano. ✆**0975-587329.** Fax 0975-587421. www.antichifeudi.com. 12 units. 45€ double; 70€ suite. AE, DC, MC, V. Free parking. **Amenities:** Restaurant; bar; concierge. *In room:* A/C, TV, minibar.

La Colombaia This small family-run hotel is in a charming hillside villa surrounded by olive groves. It offers quiet and well-appointed accommodations, tastefully furnished with period furniture and tiled floors, and all with sea views; bathrooms are small but well kept (most with shower only). *Note:* A 2-day minimum stay is required.

Via La Vecchia 2, Piano delle Pere, 84043 Agropoli. ✆/fax **0974-821800.** www.lacolombaia hotel.it. 10 units. 50€ double; 70€ suite; 140€ family room for 4. Rates include breakfast. MC, V. Free parking. Closed Nov–Feb. **Amenities:** Restaurant; bar; pool. *In room:* A/C, TV, minibar, Wi-Fi (free).

Palazzo Belmonte ★★★ The best hotel in the area, this was once a private noble residence, and indeed, the present owner, Principe Angelo di Belmonte still lives on the property. The huge palazzo (which dates from the 17th c.) stands in a beautiful garden on the seashore on the edge of Santa Maria di Castellabate, surrounded by a high wall. It has been converted into elegant guest suites and self-catering apartments that are large and airy, their original architectural features—such as vaulted ceilings—untouched. All are beautifully furnished with antiques and modern pieces; some have private terraces. You can choose your view or either the flower-filled courtyard or the gardens and sea: About half the rooms are housed in two modern annexes in the grounds. For swimming, there's a lovely pool or a private beach a few minutes' walk away. The restaurant is well worth a visit.

Via Flavio Gioia 22, 84072 Santa Maria di Castellabate. www.palazzobelmonte.com. ☎ **0974-960211.** 50 units. 273€–427€ double; 458€–745€ suite. Prices of apts. on request. AE, DC, MC, V. Free parking. Closed Nov–Apr. **Amenities:** Restaurant; bar; concierge; pool; private beach; Wi-Fi (in the main palazzo; 5€/hour). *In room:* A/C.

Where to Eat

In addition to the following dining opportunities, we suggest eating at the restaurants of the *agriturismi* mentioned in "Where to Stay," above.

MODERATE

Da Carmine CILENTAN/SEAFOOD Right on the beach near Castellabate, this restaurant prides itself on its "Mediterranean diet:" All dishes on the menu are low cholesterol, cooked with excellent local olive oil, and include plenty of fresh seasonal vegetables. Of the many seafood dishes, we recommend the spaghetti *alle vongole* (with clams) and the grilled catch of the day. The establishment also has a few tastefully appointed **guest rooms,** most of them with sea views (100€ double with breakfast; 180€ double with half-board, required in Aug).

Via Ogliastro Marina, Ogliastro Marina, 84060 Castellabate. ☎ **0974-963023.** www.albergodacarmine.it. Reservations recommended Sat–Sun. Secondi 10€–20€. AE, DC, MC, V. Daily 12:30–3pm and 7:30–10:30pm. Closed Nov–Feb.

Il Ceppo ★ CILENTAN/SEAFOOD This local favorite has been a reliable choice for decades. The pleasant atmosphere and friendly professional service matches the quality of the food. The menu focuses on traditional dishes, such as the delicious *tagliolini con gamberi, fiori di zucca e vongole* (fresh pasta with clams, shrimp, and zucchini flowers) and the excellent catch of the day cooked in a salt crust until perfectly moist and savory. Attached to the restaurant is a small modern hotel offering 20 well-furnished, comfortable rooms, a pretty garden, and a shuttle to the beach (90€–100€ double; 115€–130€ triple; prices include breakfast and free parking).

Via Madonna del Carmine 31, 84043 Agropoli. ☎ **0974-843036.** www.hotelristoranteilceppo. com. Reservations recommended Sat–Sun. Secondi 10€–21€. AE, DC, MC, V. Wed–Mon 12:30–3pm and 7:30–10:30pm (also Tues in Aug). Closed 10 days in Nov.

INEXPENSIVE

Angiolina ◈ CILENTAN This historic trattoria is a local institution for its authentic food and moderately priced yet generous portions. Try the house specialty, spaghetti *con le alici* (with local anchovies), followed by the daily catch *all'acquapazza* (cooked in herbed broth) or the splendid *frittura* (fried seafood platter).

Via Passariello 2, Pisciotta. ☎ **0974-973188.** www.ristoranteangiolina.it. Reservations recommended Sat–Sun. Secondi 8€–15€. AE, DC, MC, V. Daily 12:30–2:30pm and 7:30–11pm. Closed mid-Oct to Easter.

La Cantina del Marchese CILENTAN In the heart of Marina di Camerota, this rustic, family-run restaurant, where the waiters dress in traditional costume, specializes in the hearty local cuisine with many ingredients, such as the excellent cured meats, being produced in-house. We recommend the *lagane e ceci* (homemade pasta with chickpeas) and the perfect *tagliatelle* (fettuccine), followed by the succulent *capretto al forno* (roasted baby goat) and grilled meats. Definitely leave room for the delicious homemade desserts.

Via del Marchese 13, Marina di Camerota. ✆ **0974-932570.** www.lacantinadelmarchese.com. Reservations recommended Sat–Sun. Secondi 7€–10€. AE, DC, MC, V. June–Sept daily 5pm–1am; Sun also 12:30–3pm. Oct–May Fri–Sun 5pm–1am; Sun also 12:30–3pm. Closed Nov–Feb except for Christmas and New Year holidays.

La Chioccia d'Oro ★ CILENTAN This is the place to come for a warm welcome, an enticing menu, and a hearty traditional meal. For a perfect, down-to-earth dining experience, we highly recommend the wonderful homemade pasta, such as the rich lasagna or the *fusilli al ragù* (with meat sauce). The *grigliata* (medley of grilled meat) makes a splendid secondo, or you could try one of the local specialties of mushrooms or the tasty *coniglio farcito* (stuffed rabbit). The homemade desserts are good, as is the house wine.

Via Biblio di Novi Velia, Vallo della Lucania. ✆ **0974-70004.** www.chiocciadoro.com. Reservations recommended. Secondi 8€–16€. MC, V. Sat–Thurs 12:30–3pm and 7:30–10pm. Closed 1 week in Feb and 1 week in Sept.

La Taverna del Pescatore CILENTAN/SEAFOOD This popular tavern, with its delightful terrace, is where locals come for great seafood. The menu includes traditional dishes as well as some more innovative choices, but all are prepared with the freshest of local seasonal ingredients. If it's on offer, we highly recommend the splendid *zuppa di pesce* (fish stew); rich with local fresh seafood, it is a meal on its own. The risotto *con crema di carciofi e scampi* (with artichokes and prawns) is also delicious. For *a secondo,* we like the simply grilled catch of the day but you could go for something a little different such as the *totani* (a type of squid) stuffed with provola cheese and bitter greens.

Via Lamia 31, 84062 Castellabate. ✆ **0974-968293.** Reservations recommended. Secondi 11€–18€. MC, V. Apr–June and Sept–Oct Tues–Sun noon–3pm and 7:30–11pm; July–Aug Tues–Sun 7:30–11pm. Closed Nov–Mar.

La Veranda 🦐 CILENTAN/SEAFOOD This is the perfect place to have a great seafood meal without spending a fortune. A short distance from the harbor and the medieval citadel, this convivial restaurant offers a seasonal menu featuring traditional dishes. We loved the *scialatielli ai frutti di mare* (homemade local pasta with seafood) as well as the *ravioloni di ricotta al pesto di rucola* (cheese ravioli with arugula pesto), followed by the perfectly grilled daily catch or the excellent *gamberoni al Fiano* (jumbo shrimp stewed in local Fiano wine).

Via Piave 38, Agropoli. ✆ **0974-822272.** Reservations recommended Sat–Sun. Secondi 8€–16€. AE, DC, MC, V. Sept–June Tues–Sun 1–3pm and 8–10pm; July–Aug Tues–Sun 8–10pm. Closed 1 week at Christmas and 2 weeks in July.

CAMPANIA'S WELL-KEPT SECRETS:
CASERTA, BENEVENTO & AVELLINO

10

nternational tourism is only starting to come to this area of Campania, which is little-known even among Italians and yet there is so much to discover: simple authentic villages, such as the hill towns of Irpinia near Avellino, a handful of very choice artistic treasures such as the Royal Palace in Caserta (known as the Reggia), the Cathedral of Capua, the Roman amphitheater in Santa Maria Capua Vetere, and Benevento's Roman arch and some remote and unexplored countryside.

These attractions probably owe their semiforgotten state to their distance from the main train lines and highways. In spite of being within easy distance of the major tourist meccas of Naples and the Amalfi Coast, they are often sidestepped. But for anyone interested in genuine, off-the-beaten-track destinations, the quiet, little-visited towns and villages in this area are well worth a detour.

CASERTA

17km (11 miles) NW of Naples

The busy town of Caserta, only a few miles north of Naples, is an agroindustrial center serving its fertile environs. It had its moment of glory in the 18th century, when the new Bourbon king decided to move his capital here from Naples, and Caserta suddenly appeared on international maps. The **palace** he built was designed to rival Versailles. The king also gave new breath to the local economy, creating a small silk industry in nearby **San Leucio.**

Essentials

GETTING THERE Caserta is easily reached by train from Naples. Trains leave Napoli Stazione Centrale every 10 to 20 minutes for the 30-minute trip to Caserta. Contact **Trenitalia** (✆ 892021 in Italy; www.trenitalia.it) for fares and information. Trains arrive at Caserta's **railway station** in Piazza Giuseppe Garibaldi, only a few steps from the Reggia, on the other side of Piazza Carlo III. Caserta is also served by **Metro Campania Nord-Est** (✆ 800-053939 toll-free in Italy; www.metrocampanianordest.it) from Naples.

By car, from either Rome or Naples, take autostrada A1 to the exit marked CASERTA NORD, and follow the signs for CASERTA CENTRO. Coming into town, you will see signs for SAN LEUCIO, CASERTA VECCHIA, and REGGIA. The Reggia (Royal Palace) is in the center of town; from the Royal Palace head northeast and follow the signs reading CASERTAVECCHIA; the medieval town is about 10km (6 miles) up the hill. Head northwest from Piazza Vanvitelli, following the signs for SAN LEUCIO to reach the Belvedere.

GETTING AROUND Public transportation connects all the major sights. You can use the bus to reach Casertavecchia: Bus no.110 leaves from Piazza Garibaldi

FACING PAGE: Casertavecchia.

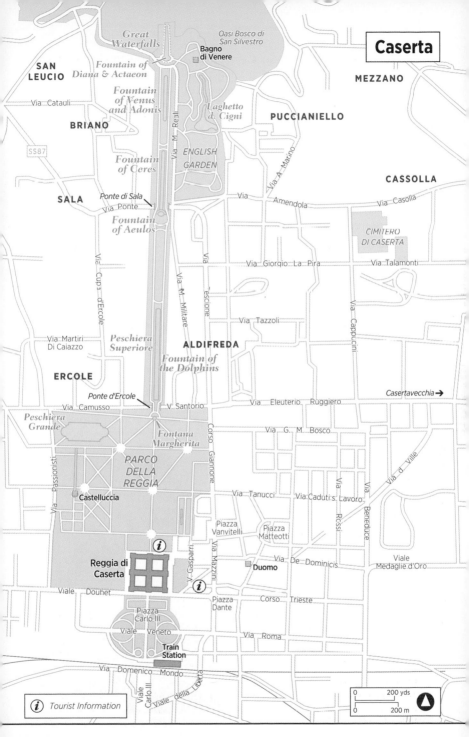

Caserta

SAN LEUCIO

Great Waterfalls

Oasi Bosco di San Silvestro

Bagno di Venere

MEZZANO

Fountain of Diana & Actaeon

Via Catauli

Fountain of Venus and Adonis

BRIANO

SS87

Laghetto d. Cigni

PUCCIANIELLO

ENGLISH GARDEN

Via A. Marino

CASSOLLA

Fountain of Ceres

Via Amendola

Via Casolla

SALA

Ponte di Sala
Via Ponte

Fountain of Aeulos

Via M. Reali

CIMITERO DI CASERTA

Via Giorgio La Pira

Via Talamonti

Via Cupa d'Ercole

Via M. Militare

Via Tescione

Via Tazzoli

Via Cappucini

Via Martiri Di Caiazzo

Peschiera Superiore

ALDIFREDA

Fountain of the Dolphins

ERCOLE

Ponte d'Ercole
Via Camusso

V. Santorio

Via Eleuterio Ruggiero

Casertavecchia →

Peschiera Grande

Fontana Margherita

Via G. M. Bosco

PARCO DELLA REGGIA

Corso Giannone

Via Caduti s. Lavoro

Via d. Ville

Via Benedice

Castelluccia

Via Tanucci

Via Rossi

Via Passionisti

(i)

Piazza Vanvitelli

Piazza Matteotti

Reggia di Caserta

Via De Dominicis

Viale Medaglie d'Oro

V. Gasparri

Via Mazzini

Duomo

(i)

Viale Douhet

Piazza Dante

Corso Trieste

Piazza Carlo III

Viale Veneto

Via Roma

Train Station

Via Domenico Mondo

Viale Carlo III

Viale della Libertà

(i) *Tourist Information*

0	200 yds
0	200 m

309

in front of Caserta train station, across from the palace. **Taxis** wait at the stand on Piazza Garibaldi across from the train station (✆ 0823-322400).

VISITOR INFORMATION The tourist information office for the province, **ETP,** Palazzo Reale, 81100 Caserta (✆ 0823-550011; fax 0823-326300), maintains an information booth at Corso Trieste 9, at the corner with Piazza Dante and Via Douhet (✆ 0823-321137; www.eptcaserta.it). It's open Monday to Saturday 9am to 7pm.

You'll find a **pharmacy,** Corso Trieste 47 (✆ 0823-326147), not far from the entrance to the Reggia. The *ospedale civile* (**hospital;** ✆ 0823-231111**) is nearby, at Via Tescione Gennaro 1; dial ✆ 118 or 0823-321000 for an **ambulance.** You can call the **police** at ✆ 113 or 112, and the **fire department** at ✆ 115. The **post office** is on Via del Redentore 27, off Via Giuseppe Mazzini, and is open Monday to Saturday from 8am to 2pm.

SPECIAL EVENTS Between the last Monday of August and September 15, **Casertavecchia** hosts a well-established music and art festival, **Settembre al Borgo** (www.casertamusica.com), and the *borgo* comes alive with concerts, theater, and dance.

Exploring the Area

Caserta was badly damaged by World War II bombing, and the modern town is not particularly interesting. It does, however, have several truly splendid attractions. In addition to those highlighted below, we recommend a visit to the 15th-century **Complex of Sant'Agostino ★**, which includes a convent, church, and cloister, as well as several museums. There is a Museum of Contemporary Art, a Museum of Traditions, and the newly created **Le Muse ★**. Taking inspiration from Madame Tussaud's wax museum in London, this museum offers a unique insight into local history, presenting the main protagonists in authentic costumes and settings. *Note:* Young children might be disturbed by the lifelike wax figures. You'll find the complex on Largo San Sebastiano, off Via Mazzini (✆ 0823-273843; admission 7€ adults, 5€ children; summer Wed–Mon 9:30am–7:30pm, winter 10am–6pm).

THE REGGIA (ROYAL PALACE) ★★★

One of the most magnificent royal palaces in the world, the Reggia is a masterpiece of harmonious architecture and decorative arts. (If you experience déjà vu during your visit, it may be because the Reggia was used as a location for *Star Wars: Episode I—The Phantom Menace*). When King Carlo III Bourbon decided to leave Naples, which he considered to be too open to attacks from the sea, he asked his architect Luigi Vanvitelli to build him a palace that would rival the courts of Paris, London, and Madrid. Vanvitelli

The Complex of Sant'Agostino.

The Reggia.

dedicated the last 20 years of his life to the construction, for which he used the best materials and workmanship available in the country. The Reggia was finished a year after the architect's death in 1774, but its interior was not fully completed until 1847. The grandiose palace measures over 45,000 sq. m (484,376 sq. ft.), and is divided into four wings, each surrounding a separate courtyard.

Official **guided tours,** led by art historians and lasting about 90 minutes, are offered on weekends and holidays in winter and daily in summer (*℃* **0823-448084;** www.arethusa.net; admission 5.80€, reservations required). On weekend nights, June through October, **Percorsi di Luce nella Reggia (Paths of Light in the Reggia)** ★ (*℃* **0823-462078;** www.percorsidiluce.it) helps visitors discover the palace, its famous gardens, and the kings who inhabited it. These tours are also led by art historians and accompanied by light effects, 18th-century music, short performances, and multimedia presentations. Started in 2003, these events are scheduled only a year at a time and cancellation is always possible due to lack of funds. Make reservations well in advance (18€ adults; free for children 5 and under).

The **horse-carriage tour** of the gardens is relatively short, but very romantic (round-trip 10€ per person). Don't expect it to take you all the way to the top, as the climb is too steep for the horses; the carriages U-turn by the Fountain of Eolus.

Note: A visit to the palace (and even more so the park) involves extensive walking. A shuttle bus is provided between the palace and the entrance to the English Gardens; pay and sign up for the bus at the ticket booth. The palace is wheelchair accessible through a private elevator in back of the ticket booth, and golf carts are available for visits to the gardens; call in advance.

You will find a **cafeteria** inside the Reggia, at the end of the main gallery just before the exit to the gardens; it is open during all visiting hours. In summer, you'll find a temporary snack bar at the entrance to the English Gardens.

Royal Palace & Gardens (Reggia di Caserta) ★★★ A visit to the Reggia di Caserta starts in the very scenic main gallery, where the view stretches all the way to the end of the park and to its majestic waterfall. You then climb the splendid main **staircase** ★★ to a magnificent octagonal vestibule, decorated with precious marble in various colors. The scale of it is almost stupefying: There are 116 stairs, flanked by niches containing sculptures that allude to the grandeur of the kingdom. We love the two sculpted lions by Pietro Solari and Paolo Persico, which are among the most familiar symbols of the Reggia.

The **Palatine Chapel** ★ opens onto the vestibule. Like everything else at the Reggia, it has imposing dimensions (37m/121 ft. long). Inside, over the entrance, you will see the royal box from which the king and queen observed services, while on the main altar you can see the wood model of the ciborium that was never built. Some of the 13 columns defining the gallery still show the damage from the 1943 bombings. Also opening onto the vestibule, to the left of the main staircase, are the **Royal Apartments** ★★. The decorations in the *appartamento nuovo* ("new" apartment) date from the early 19th century, with stuccoes, bas-reliefs, and frescoes. Of the several halls, we like the **Sala di Marte** ★, celebrating military virtues through nine bas-reliefs by Valerio Villareale and a large ceiling fresco by Antonio Galliano depicting mythological scenes from Virgil's *Iliad*. Nearby is the **Throne Room,** which was inaugurated in 1845; it dazzles with gild stucco and 46 medallions depicting all the kings of Naples, from the Norman Roger I to Ferdinand II.

The visit continues through the so-called *appartamento vecchio* ("old" apartment), inaugurated by Ferdinando IV and his wife Maria Carolina of Austria, in 1780. Beautifully furnished and decorated with frescoes, these were the private rooms of the queen and king. First come the "conversation rooms," decorated according to seasonal themes by Antonio Dominici (*Primavera* and *Autunno,* or spring and fall) and Fedele Fischetti (*Estate* and *Inverno*—summer and winter). Spring and summer make up the receiving room and sitting room, respectively, while fall is the dining room, and winter is the smoking room. After these come the bedroom, the king's study, and the queen's parlor. Our favorite furnishings here are the magnificent **Murano glass chandeliers** ★★ and the **carved chairs and sofas** ★, masterpieces of neoclassical Italian furniture by Nicola and Pietro Di Fiore. The **paintings** are by **Jakob Philipp Hackert** ★, a court painter who was kept very busy by the Bourbons. Goethe called him an "inveterate hard worker," who not only painted prolifically but also gave drawing lessons to the royal children and delivered lectures. We particularly like his scenes of the kingdom's harbors in the receiving room, as well as the depictions of royal sites in the king's study. Finally, you'll come to the three rooms of the **library**—notice the frescoes in the third room by Friederich Heinrich Függer, said to contain hidden Masonic meanings, a subject which deeply interested the queen—and to an oval hall which contains the magnificent *presepio reale* (**royal Nativity scene**) ★★.

Through a side door from the octagonal vestibule near the main staircase, you can access the permanent exhibit **Terrae Motus** ★, composed of over 70 pieces by Italian and foreign contemporary artists—there is even a piece by Andy Warhol and one by Keith Haring—in reaction to the terrible earthquake that shook Campania in 1980.

At the end of the main gallery on the ground floor is access to the Reggia's magnificent **gardens** ★★★. Covering about 120 hectares (297 acres), the grounds are not only enormous, but simply the most celebrated Italian gardens in the world. The park stretches from the palace to the nearby hills along a central path 3.2km (2 miles) long, graced by a number of fountains, pools, and gardens. A majestic waterfall created by architect Luigi Vanvitelli cascades from the hills at the end of the park. To fulfill the needs of the palace, he designed an aqueduct to carry water all the way from Monte Taburno, 40km (25 miles) away. The waterfall was the point of arrival of the aqueduct—which he named Caroline Aqueduct after the queen. Today, the water for the fountains is recirculated thanks to pumps, while the aqueduct feeds the town's supply.

Among the fountains depicting mythical events, the most spectacular is the **Fountain of Eolus ★★**, a large construction of grottoes and figures representing the palace of the wind god. Above it and up the hill is a system of **three fountains ★** feeding into each other, Fountain of Ceres, Fountain of Venus and Adonis, and Fountain of Diana and Atteon. This last is the highest, and we recommend climbing up to it for the superb **view ★**. To the right of this last fountain is the entrance to the **English Garden,** created for Queen Maria Carolina di Borbone by Carlo Vanvitelli (the son of Luigi) and English botanist and landscape artist Andrea Graefer. Covering over 30 hectares (74 acres), it is a perfect romantic realization, with a lake, a spring, and a small temple, all decorated with ancient Roman statues taken from the ruins of Pompeii. The queen also indulged her infatuation with the Masons here, and the garden is full of hidden symbols and esoteric references. It is accessible only by guided tour.

Viale Douhet. (✆ **0823-448084** or 0823-277111. www.arethusa.net or www.reggiadicaserta. beniculturali.it. Admission 12€ apts and gardens. Audioguides 7€, or 10€ for 2. Bus shuttle to English Garden 1€. Apts: Wed–Mon 8:30am–7:30pm; last admission 30 min. earlier. Gardens: Wed–Mon 8:30am–sunset; last admission 2 hr. earlier.

CASERTAVECCHIA ★★

Overlooking modern Caserta, this medieval *borgo* is one of the best preserved in Italy. It is the original town of Caserta, abandoned when King Carlo III Bourbon built his palace in the valley below and enrolled a large part of the local population to its service. Dominated by a castle that is now in ruins, the village is built around the **cathedral ★★**, Piazza Vescovado (✆ **0823-371318;** free admission; daily 9am–1pm and 3:30–6pm, till 7:30pm in summer), a fine example of Arabo-Norman architectural style. Dedicated to St. Michael, it was built by the Normans in the 12th century using paleochristian elements as well as material from a nearby temple to Jupiter. The church is built of tufa stone—like the rest of the town—with delicate highlights in white marble: the three portals, the window frames, the decorative columns, and a number of zoomorphic sculptures. The dome is covered by a beautiful *tiburio*—roofed tower—where the Arab influence is readily visible. The octagonal structure has geometric designs in alternate yellow and gray tufa stone, with an ornate intertwining of arches supported by little white columns. Inside you can admire the altar encrusted in mosaic, and the baptismal font from the 4th century. The handsome facade is completed by a 13th-century bell tower, under which passes the main street of the town; it is topped by an octagonal roof and decorated in similar fashion to the cathedral.

Behind the Duomo, on the main street, is the **Chiesetta dell'Annunziata** (daily 9am–1pm and 3:30–6pm; until 7:30pm in summer), a Gothic church built at the end of the 13th century; the portico was added in the 18th century, but

The Casino Reale di Belvedere.

behind it you can admire the original facade with the beautiful marble portal. Farther on is the 11th-century **Norman Castle;** most of its original structure—a central core with six towers—is in ruins, but the powerful main tower remains. Do take the time to stroll through the *borgo's* narrow medieval streets, admiring their original paving and the well-preserved medieval decorative details of the buildings and stone archways. Not surprisingly, the town is a favorite dinner destination for locals, who come to enjoy the food, the view, and the atmosphere, especially during warm weather and on weekends.

SAN LEUCIO ★★

This hill to the northwest of the Royal Palace is where King Ferdinando IV had his hunting preserve, and where he created a self-sufficient colony as a societal experiment. To make the colony economically independent, the king established a silkworm farm and a weaving factory. Following principles that are quite radical even by today's standards (see "The Radical Philosophy of Gaetano Filangeri," below), Ferdinando and his liberal minister Bernardo Tanucci endowed the colony with completely innovative laws and organization. Education was obligatory and free from the age of 6 up, and only those skilled in their jobs were allowed to marry and have children. There was no distinction between sexes, and every manufacturer had to contribute a portion of its gains to the common fund for people who were unable to work due to poor health or old age. The factory became famous for its precious fabrics, exporting its products far and wide. Today it operates privately, under the Stabilimento Serico De Negri, in which expert artisans keep the tradition alive by weaving damasks, brocades, and other fine fabrics.

Opening onto **Piazza della Seta,** the original colony is very scenic, with ordered rows of houses offering beautiful views over the Reggia and the surroundings. The small **church** pre-dates the hamlet and is probably of Longobard origin. The road that leads toward the left from below the steps of the original silk factory on Piazza della Seta climbs to the **Hunting Lodge** of the Aquaviva princes, the original owners of the estate; nearby is the **Vaccheria,** the stables where Ferdinand established the colony's first weaving activity before he built the village.

Casino Reale di Belvedere ★★ This small palace is set in a delightful park connected to the Reggia's gardens. The **Royal Apartments ★★** are richly frescoed with **allegoric scenes** painted by Fedele Fischetti; those in the queen's bathroom are by Jakob Philipp Hackert. The view from the **Belvedere ★★** is superb. The **Museo della Seta** has original weaving machinery that is still in working order—you can ask to see one in action—and displays examples of the wonderful original fabrics that were crafted.

Piazza della Seta (off Strada Statale) SS 87. **✆0823-273151.** www.realbelvedere.it. Admission 6€. Wed–Mon winter 9:30am–6pm, summer 9:30am–6:30pm. Closed Jan 1, Easter, Aug 15, and Dec 24–25.

Where to Stay

Hotel Caserta Antica ☺ Set on a hillside bordering the old *borgo* of Casertavecchia (about a 15-min. walk), this hotel offers a pleasant countryside location and good amenities, including a generous swimming pool—a real bonus in summer. Although the bedrooms are simple, they are quite adequate and have good-size bathrooms (shower only) and private balconies.

Via Tiglio 41, Casertavecchia, 81100 Caserta. www.hotelcaserta-antica.it. **✆0823-371158.** 25 units. 85€ double; 100€ triple; 140€ quad. Rates include breakfast. Children 1 and under stay free in parent's room. AE, DC, MC, V. Free parking. **Amenities:** Restaurant; bar; concierge; pool; Wi-Fi (free). *In room:* A/C, TV, Wi-Fi (free).

Hotel dei Cavalieri ★ A welcome, contemporary addition to the city's accommodations scene, this hotel is just down the road from the Reggia. Guest rooms are not large but have clean, modern lines and the tiled bathrooms are state-of-

THE RADICAL PHILOSOPHY OF gaetano filangeri

Gaetano Filangeri, the mind behind the inventive Bourbon king Ferdinando IV, was an important 18th-century Neapolitan jurist and philosopher. Born near Naples in 1752 as prince of Arianello, Filangeri was an encyclopedist and a reformer; his work was central to the birth of a liberal movement in southern Italy.

Filangeri's key tenet was his strong belief in public education, which he believed to be the foundation for a happy, healthy, satisfied society. Among his other ideas, he believed that honesty was the primary social virtue, and that merit should be the only distinction among individuals.

Little known to most, his ideas were influential to the elaboration of the U.S. Constitution: Benjamin Franklin was in frequent correspondence with Filangeri during the American Revolution. Having obtained several copies of Filangeri's main work—the six-volume *The Science of Legislation*—he incorporated some of the suggested principles into the U.S. Constitution.

Filangeri's work was cut short by his early death in 1788, and the sixth volume is only an outline. However, the preceding volumes have been translated into English, French, German, and Spanish.

the art (most with shower only). There is a pleasant restaurant and bar.

Piazza Vanvitelli 12, 81100 Caserta. www.deicavalieri caserta.com. ✆ **0823-355520.** Fax 0823-355859. 90 units. 180€ double. Rate includes buffet breakfast. Children 2 and under stay free in parent's room. AE, DC, MC, V. Parking 10€ in nearby garage. **Amenities:** Restaurant; bar; concierge; room service; smoke-free rooms; Wi-Fi (free). *In room:* A/C, TV, Internet, minibar, Wi-Fi (free).

Hotel Europa ★ ☺ Only a few steps from the Reggia and the railway station, this hotel offers modern and functional accommodations and good amenities. The large guest rooms have just been remodeled with stylish contemporary furniture and are welcoming and comfortable.

Via Roma 19, 81100 Caserta. www.hoteleuropacaserta.com. ✆ **0823-325400.** 57 units. 130€ double; 160€ suite. Rates include buffet breakfast. Children 2 and under stay free in parent's room. AE, DC, MC, V. Limited free parking. Closed Dec 31–Jan 1. **Amenities:** Bar; concierge; gym; Internet. *In room:* A/C, TV, Internet, minibar.

Hotel Jolly Caserta This large, comfortable hotel inhabits a stately building near Caserta's train station and overlooks the Regia. When we visited, the traditional decor was undergoing a transformation and bedrooms on three of the five floors had been updated in cool, contemporary style with blond wood floors, sleek modern furniture and super-modern bathrooms (some with shower only). Work on the remaining two floors was still in progress at presstime, and the public areas are to follow. The formal **restaurant** is recommended for its well-prepared Italian cuisine.

Viale Vittorio Veneto 9, 81100 Caserta. www.jollyhotelcaserta.it. ✆ **0823-325222.** 107 units. 90€ double. Rate includes buffet breakfast. AE, DC, MC, V. Free parking. **Amenities:** Restaurant; bar; concierge. *In room:* A/C, TV, minibar.

Where to Eat

Alla Tana del Lupo CASERTAN/PIZZA Popular with the younger set, this atmospheric restaurant a short distance from the medieval *borgo* of Casertavecchia offers solid traditional cuisine, kind service, and respect for the environment (low-consumption electrical bulbs and careful waste recycling). The menu offers an ample choice of both surf and turf, true to the Casertan tradition. We recommend the roasted lamb and the fusilli *ai porcini, provola, e noci* (with porcini mushrooms, smoked local provolone, and walnuts). The pizza is excellent, too.

Via Lupara 1, Casertavecchia. ✆ **0823-371333.** www.allatanadellupo.it. Reservations recommended for dinner. Secondi 8€–14€. Pizza 4€–10€. AE, DC, MC, V. Daily 12:30–3pm and 7–10:30pm.

Antica Hostaria Massa ★ ☺ CASERTAN/PIZZA This historic restaurant bustles at lunchtime when locals come to enjoy the good food and the pleasant atmosphere (which includes a small arbor patio in summer). The menu ranges from surf to turf and includes a superb pizza and several reinterpretations of traditional dishes. We recommend pasta *alle cozze e vongole* (with mussels and clams), the mouth-watering local sausages, and the splendid *agnello Lauticada* (roasted lamb). There are two tasting menus for 29€ and 34€ and a kids' menu for 15€ (for your little gourmand).

Via Mazzini 55, Caserta. ✆ **0823-456527.** www.ristorantemassa.it. Reservations recommended. Secondi 10€–35€. AE, DC, MC, V. Mon–Sat 12:30–3pm and 7:30–11:30pm–10:30pm; Sun 12:30–3pm. Closed 10 days in Aug.

Antica Locanda ★ CAMPANIAN/CASERTAN This atmospheric restaurant on San Leucio's picturesque main piazza is an outpost of local culinary tradition, offering reliable local dishes as well as a number of regional favorites. The menu includes both seafood and meat dishes, and the house specialty is the risotto, such as the excellent *porcini e provola* (porcini mushrooms and local smoked provolone). We also recommend the excellent *scialatielli ai frutti di mare* (homemade eggless pasta with seafood) and the grilled suckling pig.

Piazza della Seta 8, San Leucio. © **0823-305444.** Reservations recommended Sat–Sun. Secondi 10€–16€. AE, DC, MC, V. Tues–Sat 12:30–3pm and 7–10:30pm; Sun 12:30–5pm.

Cca' sta' O Masto ★ 🏠☺ CASERTAN/PIZZA This simple, authentic restaurant is a real local hideout, popular for its pizza and delicious local country dishes. Seafood is served only on Fridays when it is worth coming to for the perfect *frittura* (deep-fried calamari and shrimp). The rest of the week, we recommend the simple *antipasti*—a choice of local cheese and cured meats—and the splendid *gnocchi al coccio* (potato dumplings cooked in a terra-cotta dish), as well as the fabulous grilled steak. The 10€ children's menu is appreciated.

Via Sant'Agostino 10, Caserta. © **0823-320042.** Reservations recommended Sat–Sun. Secondi 6€–12€. AE, DC, MC, V. Tues–Sun 12.30–3pm and 7:30–11pm. Closed 2 weeks in Aug.

Da Teresa CASERTAN/PIZZA This large restaurant enjoys a prime location in the medieval *borgo* of Casertavecchia, with a beautiful terrace and a garden offering great views over Caserta and—on clear days—all the way to the sea. There's also a picturesque inner courtyard. In addition to good-quality pizza, the extensive menu offers local specialties, such as *misto alla brace* (charbroiled platter of local vegetables, meats, and sausages). The daily *menu del ghiottone* (gourmet menu) offers choices such as *cinghiale alla brace* (charbroiled wild boar) while the four prix-fixe menus each include a primo, a secondo, a *contorno* (side dish), and a dessert.

Via Torre 6, Casertavecchia. © **0823-371270.** www.ristorantedatheresa.it. Reservations recommended for dinner. Secondi 6€–16€; prix-fixe menus 15€–25€. AE, DC, MC, V. Thurs–Tues 11:30am–3pm and 7pm–midnight.

Le Colonne ★ CONTEMPORARY CASERTAN Directly across from the Reggia, the key word to describe this popular address in Caserta's dining scene is *elegance,* both in terms of the decor and the presentation of the food. The menu showcases the chef's creative take on traditional dishes prepared with the best organic local ingredients. The house specialty is buffalo, from its meat—perhaps filled with ricotta and served with a traditional vegetable stew—to the famed mozzarella, stuffed with peppers and herbs.

Viale G. Douhet (Via Appia) 7, Caserta. © **0823-467494.** www.lecolonnemarziale.it. Reservations recommended. Secondi 18€–25€. AE, DC, MC, V. Wed–Mon 12:30–3pm. Closed 2 weeks in Aug.

SANTA MARIA CAPUA VETERE & CAPUA ★★

The immediate surroundings of Caserta boast a few worthwhile archaeological and historic destinations that are unspoiled by international tourism: the ruins of ancient Roman Capua (in the town of **Santa Maria Capua Vetere**) and its fluvial harbor Casilinium (in the town of **Capua**), Capua's **cathedral,** as well as the **Basilica di Sant'Angelo in Formis,** with its magnificent 11th-century frescoes. All of these attractions make easy day trips from Caserta.

Santa Maria Capua Vetere & Its Amphitheater ★★

6.5km (4 miles) W of Caserta; 24km (15 miles) NW of Naples

Now a suburb of modern Caserta, the small town of Santa Maria Capua Vetere is what remains of glorious Capua, the ancient Roman city that, in its heyday, was second only to Rome. Its imposing monuments are proof of the prosperity it enjoyed in ancient times.

ESSENTIALS

GETTING THERE Trenitalia (© 892021 in Italy; www.trenitalia.it) serves Santa Maria Capua Vetere's **train** station with routes from Rome, Caserta, and Naples. The station is also a stop on the **Metro Campania Nord-Est** line (© 800-053939 toll-free in Italy; www.metrocampanianordest.it) from Naples and Caserta. From Caserta you can also take a **taxi** (see "Getting Around," p. 348). By **car,** exit autostrada A1 at CASERTA NORD and take SS 7 (Via Appia). From Caserta and the Royal Palace, take Viale Douhet west; when it turns into SS 7, follow signs for SANTA MARIA CAPUA VETERE. Two parking lots are off the main road on the left, one behind Piazza San Pietro and another off Via F. Pezzella, which you can access from Corso Garibaldi.

GETTING AROUND Santa Maria Capua Vetere is small enough to explore **on foot;** its most important attractions are along the ancient Appian Way, which is called Corso Aldo Moro.

VISITOR INFORMATION The **Pro Loco office** is in the municipal office, Via Albana, Inst. Lucarelli (© 0823-813213; Mon–Fri 9am–1pm).

Farmacia Salsano (© 0823-798583) is the most convenient pharmacy, at Piazza San Francesco 6, not far from the amphitheater. The **hospital, San Giuseppe e Melorio** (© 0823-891111), is on Via Melorio. For an **ambulance,** dial © 118. You can call the **police** at © 113 or at 112. The **post office,** Piazza Resistenza 1 (© 0823-818411), is open Monday to Saturday from 8am to 2pm. You'll find several **banks** with ATMs, including one on Corso Aldo Moro.

EXPLORING THE TOWN

As you walk around town, keep an eye out for archaeological remains that have been incorporated into more modern buildings over the centuries: pieces of column, sculpted busts of gods and goddesses, and capitals. The western entrance to town on the ancient Via Appia was marked ARCO DI ADRIANO **(Hadrian's Arch),** a majestic triumphal monument that was actually

The remains of Hadrian's Arch.

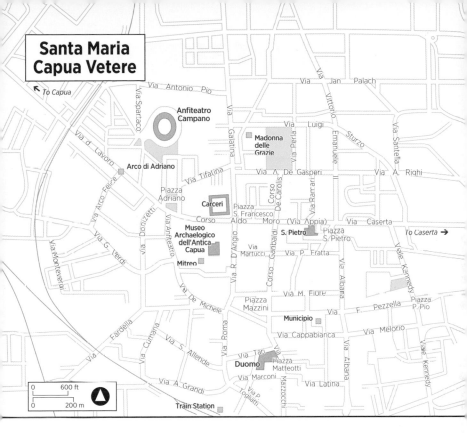

Santa Maria
Capua Vetere

↖ To Capua

Anfiteatro
Campano

Arco di Adriano

Via Antonio Pio

Via Spartaco

Via d. Lavoro

Via Arco Felice

Via G. Verdi

Via Monteverdi

Via Donizetti

Via Anfiteatro

Piazza
Adriano

Carceri

Museo
Archaelogico
dell'Antica
Capua

Mitreo

Via De Michele

Fardella

Via Cumana

Via S. Allende

Via A. Grandi

Via Tifatina

Corso   Aldo   Moro (Via Appia)

Via R. D'Angio

Corso Garibaldi

Via
Martucci

Piazza
Mazzini

Municipio

Via Roma

Via Tari

Via Marconi

Via P. Togliatti

Piazza
S. Francesco

Via P. Fratta

Via M. Fiore

Via Cappabianca

Duomo

Via
Galatina

Madonna
delle
Grazie

Corso
De Carolis

Via Perla

Via A. De Gasperi

S. Pietro

Piazza
S. Pietro

Via Latina

Via Albana

Via Jan Palach

Via Vittorio

Via Luigi

Via Emanuele

Sturzo

Via A. Righi

Via Caserta

To Caserta →

Via Ramari

Piazza
Matteotti

Via Mazzocchi

Via Santella

Viale Kennedy

F. Pezzella

Via Melorio

Via Albana

Piazza
P. Pio

Viale Kennedy

0   600 ft
0   200 m

Train Station

composed of three arches. Today the marble finish has disappeared and only one arch remains—the southern one—although you can see the three brick pillars that supported the central arch. Farther along, at Corso 210, are the remains of a Roman house, **Casa di Confuleio Sabbio** (discovered by chance during construction in 1955), which dates from the 1st century B.C. It was the home of a freedman, a merchant specializing in the production of *sagum:* the heavy woolen cape worn by soldiers and—in a less-refined version—by slaves and paupers. At the corner of Corso and Via Galatina is the large building that was a prison until only a few decades ago; beneath it are the remains of a **criptoportico,** an ancient Roman covered promenade that is believed to have been part of the *Capitolium,* an ancient Roman temple.

Anfiteatro Campano ★★ Second in size only to the Colosseum in Rome, this Roman amphitheater was probably built around A.D. 3, enlarged in 119 by Emperor Hadrian, and further embellished by Emperor Antoninus Pius. It remains majestic in spite of having been used—like so many Roman buildings in Italy—as a quarry for quality marble and construction materials over the centuries. It was also picked apart in the 9th century onwards during searches for bronze and lead (the building's large stone components were broken apart to get at the heavy metal clamps that held them together). Some of its columns and stones were even used to rebuild the town and the Duomo (see below).

Anfiteatro Campano.

The Museo dei Gladiatori.

Judging from what remains, though, the amphitheater must have been quite a sight back in those days. Four stories tall, it was completely covered in travertine stone, with marble busts of gods serving as keystones for each of the 240 arches on the lower floors, and full-length statues under the arches of the second and third floors. You can still see the carved keystones over the main entrance (busts of Ceres and Juno). The giant arena has a maximum length of about 170m (558 ft.) and can seat over 60,000 people. The corridors below the arena are relatively well conserved and still show traces of stuccoes and frescoes. This is where the gladiators waited between combats, and where all the scene props were kept. The bestiary—home of the fighting animals—was also here. You can see the remains of a paleochristian altar and paintings inside one of the small rooms here, which was transformed into a Christian oratory in the 9th century.

The garden in front of the amphitheater has been turned into an open-air museum where you can admire many of the fragments of the original decorations of the amphitheater as well as from other buildings in town. Among the objects on display is a beautiful 2nd-century **mosaic** ★ depicting Nereides and Tritons.

A permanent exhibit dedicated to gladiatorial fights is housed in the **Museo dei Gladiatori (Gladiators' Museum)** ★, also in the garden. On display are four complete suits of gladiator armor, and a model reconstruction of the amphitheater. You can also watch a good animation of a gladiator fight. Spartacus, the slave made famous by the 1960 Stanley Kubrick film, was a graduate of the gladiator school located near this amphitheater.

Piazza Ottobre (off Piazza Adriano). ℂ **0823-798864.** Admission 2.50€ includes Museo Archeologico dell'Antica Capua and Mitreo. Tues–Sun 9am–5:30pm.

Duomo ★★ Dedicated to Santa Maria Maggiore, the core of this church was built in A.D. 432 by Capua's bishop Saint Simmaco over the town's catacombs by the Grotto of Saint Prisco; Arechi II added the two external naves in A.D. 787.

When it was restored in 1666, the apse was completely rebuilt. The interior is quite suggestive, with five naves supported by columns topped with Corinthian capitals taken from the nearby amphitheater and Roman temples. It is richly decorated with Renaissance artwork, including a carved **cyborium** ★ located in the chapel at the end of the right-hand nave, and a **wooden choir** ★ in the apse. Our favorite chapels are the ones opening off the left-hand nave—gated **Cappella del Conforto** ★★, with a beautiful altar in colored marble inlay, and **Cappella della Morte** ★, featuring more notable inlay work at the end of the nave.

Via Sirtori 3 (off Piazza Matteotti). © **0823-846640.** Free admission. Daily 9am–12:30pm and 4:30–6pm.

Museo Archeologico dell'Antica Capua In the Torre di Sant'Erasmo—a tower originating before the Longobards—this museum displays a large collection of local archaeological findings ranging from the 10th century B.C. to the 1st century A.D. Behind the museum is the **Mitreo** ★, Vicolo Mitreo (explorable by guided tour only, which is included in price of admission; sign up at the ticket booth of the Anfiteatro Campano), one of the few existing temples dedicated to the god Mithras (worshipped by a Persian cult that diffused in Rome during the 1st c. A.D.). Discovered accidentally in 1922, the very well-preserved temple was built between the 2nd and 3rd centuries A.D. Its vaulted ceiling is decorated with a large fresco of Mithras sacrificing a white bull. Above the stalls are remains of frescoes depicting the seven stages of initiation into the cult of Mithras.

Via Roberto D'Angiò 48 (off Corso Aldo Moro [Via Appia]). © **0823-844206.** Admission 2.50€ includes access to Anfiteatro Campano and Mitreo. Tues–Sun 9am–6pm.

Capua & Its Churches ★

11km (6½ miles) W of Caserta; 28km (17 miles) NW of Naples

A short distance from Caserta, Capua is a sleepy village on a picturesque bend in the Volturno River. Built as a defensive outpost for the bridge and harbor on the river, it still has most of its fortifications intact. The original village was the Roman harbor of Casilinium, which served the nearby town of Capua and guarded the important bridge built by the Romans over the river for the Appian Way (perfectly operational until 1943, when it was bombed by U.S. forces). When ancient Capua was destroyed by the Saracens in A.D. 840, its inhabitants fled here, salvaging all they could from their old town—including its name. Repeatedly besieged by various powers until the unification of Italy in 1860, it was the seat of a bishopric and played an important religious role, which is still visible in its many churches.

ESSENTIALS

GETTING THERE Capua's train station has **Trenitalia** (© **892021** in Italy; www.trenitalia.it) train service from Caserta and Naples. From Caserta, you can also take a **taxi** (see "Getting Around," p. 348). **By car,** take autostrada A1 to the exit marked CAPUA, which leads to Via Appia. From Caserta, take Viale Douhet past the Reggia and follow it west out of town; follow signs for CAPUA as the road becomes Via Appia and passes through Santa Maria Capua Vetere. The town is to your left after you cross the bridge over the Volturno River. You will find a parking lot off Via Appia at Piazza Umberto I, near the town center.

GETTING AROUND Capua is small and can easily be explored **on foot.** A stroll along Corso Appio (the original Via Appia), the historic district's main street, will take you past most of the town's attractions. You can grab a **taxi** at the stand by the train station (or call one at ℂ **333-6157756** or 360-390297).

VISITOR INFORMATION The Pro Loco **tourist office** (ℂ**0823-962729**) is opposite the municipal building, Piazza dei Giudici 6. Hours are Monday to Saturday 9am to 1pm and 4 to 6pm; Sunday 9am to 1pm.

You'll find a **pharmacy** (ℂ**0823-961224**) at Via Duomo 32. The nearest **hospitals** are in Caserta and Santa Maria Capua Vetere (see "Visitor Information," p. 310 and 318). For **medical aid,** dial ℂ **118.** You can call the **police** at ℂ **113** or 112. The **post office,** Via Pier Delle Vigne 3 (ℂ**0823-620511**), is open Monday to Saturday from 8am to 2pm.

SPECIAL EVENTS During Carnival, Capua is the setting for an important festival that features a grand procession, farcical theatre performances (often on theme of political satire) and cabaret shows among its events. A regular fixture is the famous character **Pulcinella,** whom Capuans claim as one of their own. (Check with the tourist office in Caserta for a schedule of events.)

EXPLORING THE TOWN

Surrounded by walls and castles, Capua maintains the feeling of an ancient town. Its western gate is by the bridge, and the 15th-century eastern gate—Porta Napoli—is near the ruins of the 11th-century Norman **Castello delle Pietre,** on Via Andreozzi, which still has one of its four original crenellated towers. The facades of many buildings are decorated with Roman artifacts, such as the **bas-relief** at Via Pier delle Vigne 26 (off Corso Appio); at no. 34 on the same street is a picturesque Renaissance house with an arched courtyard designed by Guido da Maiano, and a few interesting churches. Particularly noteworthy are the six marble **busts** ★ gracing 16th-century **Palazzo del Municipio** on Piazza dei Giudici, off Corso Appio; they depict Jupiter, Neptune, Mercury, Juno, Ceres, and Mars and were taken from the Anfiteatro Campano of Santa Maria Capua Vetere.

Cattedrale di Santo Stefano e Sant'Agata ★ Caserta's Duomo (cathedral) was severely damaged by bombing in 1943, but a massive restoration project faithfully re-created it according to the original plan. The church dated from A.D. 856, with additions from 1120. The 11th-century

Cattedrale di Santo Stefano e Sant'Agata.

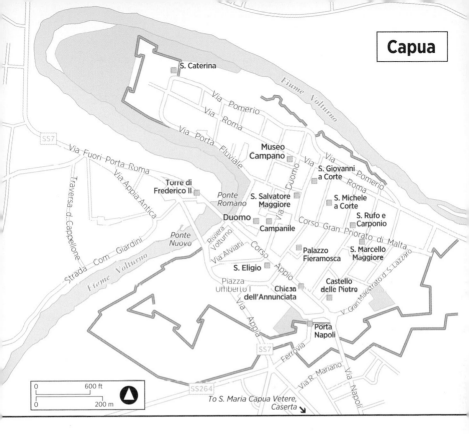

atrium, built with columns and Corinthian capitals from the 3rd century A.D., and the Duomo's 9th-century bell tower, supported at its base by four ancient Corinthian columns, are original. Among the medieval sculptures decorating the bell tower, you can admire three Roman bas-reliefs from the amphitheater in Santa Maria Capua Vetere (see Anfiteatro Campano, earlier in this chapter).

Inside the church, a large range of artwork dates from the 12th century to the present. We love the splendid, lavishly decorated 13th-century **ceremonial candleholder** and the two columns supported by carved lions on the modern pulpit—all that remain of the original 13th-century **ambo.** Other parts of the original ambo, including some mosaics, were used to decorate the small chapel in the **crypt** under the presbytery. In the **Cappella del Sacramento,** at the end of the right-hand-side nave, is a beautiful **altar** made of marble and precious stones, while in the presbytery behind the altar, you'll find the *Assunta* painted by Francesco Solimena. We also recommend a visit to the **Museo Diocesano** (© 0823-961081; admission 3€; daily 9:30am–1pm and 3:30–7pm), housing the church's **treasure** inside the **Cappella del Corpo di Cristo,** adjacent to the cathedral. Among the objects on exhibit is a collection of Islamic carved crystal dating from the 11th and 12th centuries.

Piazza Landolfo (off Via Duomo). © **0823-961081.** Free admission. Daily 8–11am and 5:30–7:30pm.

Museo Campano ★ In the Palazzo Antignano (graced by an unusual 15th-c. **portal** ★ in Catalán-Moorish style, at no. 76 of Via Roma), the museum, established in 1874, is dedicated to the art, religion, and history of Campania. Its wealth of holdings is divided into two sections: Archaeological finds are on the first floor, while medieval displays, including the parchment collection and the picture gallery are on the second.

The archaeology section includes Oscan (the Osci were the local Italic population), Etruscan, and Roman artifacts from a number of sites in the area. Among the Etruscan-Oscan pottery, we liked the beautiful black dishes decorated with fish and dating from the 4th century B.C. The most poignant artifacts, however, are **Le Madri (The Mothers)** ★★, in rooms five through nine. This is a whole group of statues and architectural structures with Oscan inscriptions that were found in a field near Santa Maria Capua Vetere. They pertain to an Oscan sanctuary that was active between the 6th and 1st centuries B.C. and was dedicated to the Italic goddess of fertility and maternity, Matuta. Several of these figures, carved in tufa stone, show mothers offering their children to view and (probably) thanking the goddess for the gift of maternity. The **Roman mosaic** on the second floor in room number 10 was found in the temple of Diana Tifatina, near Sant'Angelo in Formis (see "Sant'Angelo in Formis," below).

Among the holdings in the medieval section, the most famous is the collection of **Federician Sculptures** ★ in room no. 26. Among this group of marble sculptures from the castle built by Federico II in 1239 in Capua are a few portraits of Federico himself. One of the greatest of medieval rulers, he was crowned king of Sicily at the age of 4 and became Holy Roman Emperor in 1220. He participated in the Sixth Crusade, and crowned himself king of Jerusalem in 1229. Called **Stupor Mundi** ("wonder of the world") by his contemporaries, he was also much distrusted by the papacy and was excommunicated twice.

Via Roma 68 (off Via Duomo). ✆ **0823-961402.** Free admission. Tues–Sat 9am–1:30pm; Sun 9am–1pm.

Sant'Angelo in Formis ★★

Isolated on the slopes of Mount Tifata on the outskirts of Capua, this medieval church is among the most fascinating in Italy.

ESSENTIALS

GETTING THERE You can easily reach the village by **buses** that depart from in front of Capua's train station. It is also a stop on the **Metro Campania Nord-Est** line (✆ **800-053939** toll-free in Italy; www.metrocampania nordest.it) from Naples, Caserta, and Santa Maria Capua Vetere. **By car** from Capua, take Via Roma out of town following signs for S. ANGELO IN FORMIS.

VISITOR INFORMATION The nearest **hospitals** are in Caserta and Santa Maria Capua Vetere (see "Visitor Information," p. 310 and 318). For **first aid,** dial ✆ **118.** You can call the **police** at ✆ **113** or 112.

EXPLORING THE ROMANESQUE BASILICA

Enjoying an ideal position high up the mountain overlooking Capua and with a **view** ★ that, on clear days, stretches all the way to Ischia, this basilica was built over the ruins of the **Temple of Diana Tifatina,** the most important pre-Christian sanctuary in this region. Turned into a church sometime before the 10th century, it was then bequeathed to the nearby monastery of Montecassino. Its abbot,

The Temple of Diana Tifatina.

Desiderio of Montecassino, decided to establish the sanctuary as an important religious site, and had the basilica completely rebuilt in 1073. Note how the lateral arches in the portico in front of the church are pointed arches typical of Islamic architecture. Under the portico you will see the first series of frescoes, with a wonderful **Saint Michael ★** from the 11th century, and others from the 12th and 13th centuries. Inside, the basilica is divided into three naves by 14 columns topped with beautiful antique Corinthian capitals. The greatest attraction is really the **frescoes ★★** that were painted by local art students. Along the sides of the central nave is the cycle depicting scenes from the Old and New Testaments, and on the inner facade is the *Last Judgment.* Little remains of the 11th-century mosaic floor—you'll see some at the end of the right nave—and parts of the marble floor are original to the temple of Diana (dated by an inscription from 74 B.C.).

Piazza della Basilica di Sant'Angelo, Formis. ℂ **0823-960492.** Free admission. Summer Mon-Sat 9:30am-noon and 3-7pm, Sun 10am-4pm; winter Mon-Sat 9:30am-12:30pm and 3-6pm, Sun 10am-4pm. Holidays 10am-4pm.

BEWITCHING BENEVENTO

51km (31 miles) E of Caserta; 86km (53 miles) NE of Naples

With its heritage of mysterious witchcraft and Roman art, this pretty hilltop town hides some wonderful artistic treasures, including the best-preserved ancient Roman arch in existence and an intriguing Longobard star-shaped church.

Essentials

GETTING THERE Benevento is well connected by **train,** with frequent services from Naples, Caserta, Avellino, and Rome. Contact **Trenitalia** (ℂ **892021** in Italy; www.trenitalia.it) for fares and information. Trains arrive at Benevento's **stazione** located in Piazza Colonna 2, to the north of town. Benevento is also served by the **Metro Campania Nord-Est** line (ℂ **800-053939** toll-free in Italy; www.metrocampanianordest.it) from Naples.

Marozzi (ℂ **080-5790111;** www.marozzivt.it) offers a regular **bus** service to and from Rome; use **ETAC** (ℂ **0824-28321;** www.etacsrl.it) to and from Salerno, or **AIR Autoservizi Irpini** (ℂ **0825-2041;** www.airspa.it) to and from Avellino.

By **car,** take the autostrada A16 to the exit signed BENEVENTO and continue on the short stretch of highway to the town.

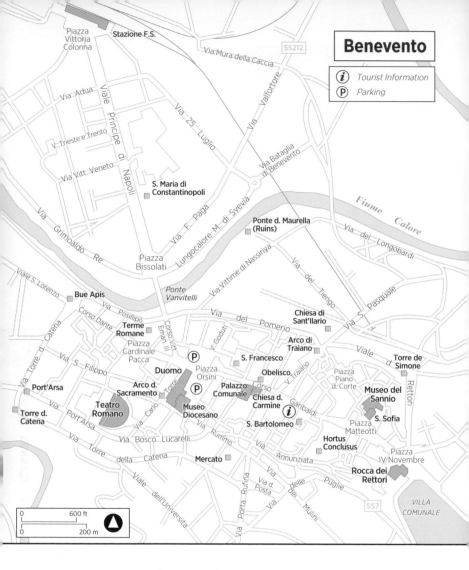

GETTING AROUND The center of Benevento is relatively small and accessible **on foot;** however, it extends uphill, so you might want to use public transportation as well. The town's **bus** system maintains a number of lines that crisscross the area; most leave from the hub across from the train station. Lines 1 and 7 both pass by Trajan's Arch, going up to the Rocca dei Priori in the heart of the historic district. You'll need to buy bus tickets at a tobacconist or a newsstand before boarding; tickets cost .65€ and are valid for 90 minutes. **Taxis** wait at the **stand** on Piazza Colonna, across from the railway station (or call ℰ**0824-50341**).

You can rent a car in town with **Cardillo,** Via dei Mulini 91 (ℰ**0824-52249;** www.avisautonoleggio.it).

VISITOR INFORMATION The excellent local **tourist office** is at Via Nicola Sala 31, 82100 Benevento (✆ **0824-319911;** www.eptbenevento.it).

You'll find a **pharmacy** (✆ **0824-21590**) in Piazza Orsini 13. The hospital is **Ospedale Fatebenefratelli,** Viale Principe di Napoli 14–16 (✆ **0824-771111**). For an **ambulance,** dial ✆ **118,** or call the **Croce Rossa Italiana** (✆ **0824-315000**). You can call the **police** at ✆ **112** or 113. There is a **post office** (✆ **0824-24074;** Mon–Sat 8am–2pm) in Piazza Colonna Vittoria, by the railway station.

Exploring the Town

Built on a hill at the heart of a hilly green valley, Benevento is a very pleasant town. Only fragments of the defensive walls that once completely enclosed the town are still visible today, together with the fortress—**Rocca dei Rettori,** at Piazza IV Novembre—in the highest part of town. Built by the pope in 1321 over the preexisting Longobard and ancient Roman defensive structures, the fortress was recently restored and houses the provincial government; parts of it can be visited when special exhibits are hosted by **ARCOS** (the Museum of Contemporary Art of Sannio). The **Villa Comunale ★** is a delightful public garden, designed in the late 19th century and graced by elegant Liberty-style fixtures such as lamps and benches.

Arco di Traiano (Trajan's Arch) ★★★ One of Campania's finest monuments, this Roman triumphal arch is in remarkable condition considering that it is nearly 2,000 years old. A lengthy restoration—mainly a careful cleaning that took 14 years—was completed in 2001 and the arch is now visible in all its ancient glory. Built between A.D. 114 and 117 by the Romans to honor Emperor Trajan, it stood at the head of the Via Traiana, what was then a new—and shorter—route that led from Benevento to Brindisi, the harbor that was Rome's gateway to the eastern Mediterranean. The carved reliefs celebrate the deeds of Trajan, an illuminated leader who enlarged and strengthened the empire while implementing

Arco di Traiano (Trajan's Arch)

a generous social policy and carrying out numerous public works. During the Middle Ages, the superb arch was enclosed in the city walls and used as the main gate into town (hence the local name for the arch: Port'Aurea), which contributed to its conservation. The nearby church, **Sant'Ilario a Port'Aurea** ★, Via San Pasquale, off the Arco di Traiano (free admission; daily 10am–1pm, in winter also 3–6pm, fall–spring 4–7pm, summer 5–8pm), a Longobard church from the 10th century, houses a permanent exhibit on the arch and on life in Rome under Emperor Trajan.

Via Traiano (off Corso Garibaldi).

Duomo ★ The first version of this church goes back to the 7th century A.D., when it had only a central nave. Consecrated in A.D. 780 during Longobard domination, two naves were added in the 9th century and two others in the 12th century. The structure was then restored and redecorated in the 18th century, at which point it became known as one of the most beautiful Romanesque churches in Italy. However, the U.S. bombing in 1943 destroyed almost the entire ancient church, saving only the bell tower and the elegant Romanesque facade, a 13th-century Pisan-style marvel of striped marble and rich carvings. The richly carved jambs of the central portal date from the 12th century; they once bracketed 13th-century sculpted bronze doors which were considered rivals of the famous ones of Florence's baptistery. They were blown to pieces by the bombing, and what was saved was painstakingly restored; you can now see the 72 frames that composed the doors displayed inside the church. The top 43 are decorated with scenes from the life of Christ, from the Annunciation to the Ascension, while the bottom 29 depict local religious personalities. The **Museo Diocesano**—housed partly in the crypt and partly in the adjacent Palazzo Arcivescovile, Piazza Orsini 27 (✆ **0824-42825**) holds remains from the destroyed Duomo, including what was left of the extremely rich treasure. *Note:* At presstime, the Duomo was closed for restorations and no date was given for the reopening.

Piazza Duomo. Free admission. Daily 9am–12:30pm and 5–7pm.

Benevento History 101

A powerful Sannite town inhabited since the 7th century B.C., the original community was soundly defeated by the Romans in 275 B.C., after fierce opposition. The Roman Empire established a colony and changed the town's name from the original Malies, or Maloenton—which in Latin sounded like a bad omen—to Beneventum. Taken by the Goths at the decline of the Western Roman Empire, it was rescued by the Byzantines, who then relinquished it in turn to the Longobards. Finally, Benevento was absorbed into the state of the Church of Rome in the 16th century and remained relatively peaceful until it was almost completely destroyed by the earthquake of 1688. The city's archbishop—who, in later years, was to become Pope Benedetto XIII—rebuilt the city and supported its cultural and spiritual development. The reborn Benevento enjoyed a new period of prosperity until World War II, when the town was heavily bombarded by the United States in 1943—65% of it, including important monuments, was destroyed, and 2,000 people were killed. The town has since recovered and become a lively and pleasant provincial town with an interesting hinterland.

Museo del Sannio ★ In the former monastery of Santa Sofia (below), this museum holds a picture gallery and a good collection of archaeological and medieval artifacts. Among the most interesting items on display is the collection of Egyptian art coming from the local temple of Isis (built by the notoriously cruel Emperor Domitian in A.D. 88). It was decorated both with statues imported from Egypt and others produced locally in the Egyptian style—including a portrait of Domitian in Egyptian attire. The picture gallery has a collection spanning the 15th to the 20th centuries, including major names such as Francesco Solimena (*Madonna col Bambino e i Santi*) and Carlo Maratta (*Sacra Famiglia*). Part of the collection is displayed in the elegant **cloister** ★, an interesting architectural merger of Moorish arches and Romanesque columns, carved with strange, fantastic, or everyday scenes, such as boar hunts and pilgrimages.

The museum's historical section (documents and signatures of famous historical figures) is in the scenic Rocca dei Rettori (access with the same ticket) on Piazza IV Novembre.

Piazza Santa Sofia. ✆ **0824-21818** or 0824-28831. Admission 4€. Tues–Sun 9am–7pm.

Santa Sofia ★ This medieval church is one of our favorites in Campania. Its unique design singles it out as an architectural marvel and shows the intermingling of Longobard and Christian cultures. Begun in 762 by the Longobard Arechi II when he became Duke of Benevento, the church's star-shaped structure is a central hexagon, covered by a dome, and supported by six powerful columns; around this are eight square pillars and two columns topped by Corinthian capitals. The pillars are aligned with the surrounding walls, which are part circle and part star, creating a strange perspective. In the apse are fragments of a great cycle of frescoes from the 8th century, representing, among other things, scenes of the life of Saint Zaccaria; the surrounding walls are decorated with representations of nature and symbols derived from the Longobard religion. The bell tower stands alone, isolated from the church; it was redone in 1703. Attached to the church is the monastery, now housing the **Museo del Sannio** (above). It was actually a Benedictine convent founded in conjunction with the church. It became one of the most powerful monasteries in Italy during the 12th century, famous for its type of writing, "scriptorium Beneventanum." *Note:* The church was undergoing restoration at presstime, with no date announced for the reopening.

Piazza Matteotti. ✆ **0824-21206.** Free admission. Daily 10am–noon and 4:30–7pm.

Teatro Romano ★ This is one of the largest well-conserved Roman theaters in Italy. Theater performances, including drama, comedy, and poetry as well as music, were very important to Roman culture and a matter of everyday life. Theaters (the classic hemicycle) were ubiquitous, to the extent that even little towns often had more than one. But while grandiose ruins remain of the great amphitheaters dedicated to contests and spectacles—such as Rome's Colosseum and the Anfiteatro Campano in Santa Maria Capua Vetere—most ancient Roman theaters have been integrated into later constructions. This makes Benevento's Roman theater an important exception. Built in the 2nd century A.D., it had a diameter of 90m (295 ft.) and could contain up to 20,000 spectators. Most of the original structure is still visible, and only the third floor was completely lost. The path that leads from the ticket booth to the theater takes you past assorted sculptures, capitals, and massive hunks of marble that once graced the structure. A portion of the second level also still stands, with corridors leading to the mostly

The Teatro Romano.

intact seating area, still used during the summer for opera performances and classical dramas (contact the tourist office for a schedule of events).

Via Port'Arsa. ☎ **0824-47213.** Admission 2€. Daily 9am to 1 hr. before sunset.

Where to Stay
MODERATE

Grand Hotel Italiano ★ Offering lodging since 1920, this family-run hotel has been updated many times but retains its old-fashioned hospitality. It is not far from the train station, in a pleasant residential part of town with lots of shops; the town center is a 15-minute walk or a quick bus ride away. The large guest rooms are comfortable and modern, all with good-size bathrooms. In summer, the hotel offers discounted access to a nearby swimming pool and gym. The **restaurant** ★ on the premises is very good and quite popular among locals.

Viale Principe di Napoli 137, 82100 Benevento. www.hotel-italiano.com. ☎ **0824-24923.** Fax 0824-21758. 71 units. 100€ double; 170€ suite. Rate includes buffet breakfast. Children 2 and under stay free in parent's room. AE, DC, MC, V. Limited free parking. **Amenities:** Restaurant; bar; concierge; Internet. *In room:* A/C, TV, minibar.

Strega—the Brew of Benevento

Appropriately named "witch," this local **liqueur** might well enchant you with its unique bittersweet taste. Concocted in the 17th century from a secret mixture of 17 herbs and spices, it is served as a digestive or to "correct" your espresso (adding a bit of alcohol to it); it is a good complement to fruit salads and ice cream, too. The liqueur also comes in a **cream** variety (similar to Baileys). It is also used for a proprietary candy—*caramella Strega*—an individually wrapped **hard candy** with a soft, creamy Strega-flavored center. All those goodies make excellent souvenirs and are for sale at local shops (see "Stocking up on Souvenirs," p. 332).

THE witches OF BENEVENTO

Legend has it that Benevento is a land of witches and has been for thousands of years. The origins of the legend lie with the Egyptian cult of Isis—goddess of magic and mystery among other things—which found fertile ground in Benevento during the Roman era. The cult remained an important force here even after the cult was replaced by Christianity in other parts of Italy. When the Longobards from Central Europe took the town in A.D. 571, they imported their own religion, a nature cult based on the adoration of the god Wothan and his sacred walnut tree. They elected an old walnut near the **Ponte Leproso** as the town's sacred tree. (The Ponte Leproso was a bridge built by the Romans over the Sabato River at the Via Appia's entrance to Benevento; the bridge is still in use today, and you can see it by taking a short walk west of the Teatro Romano.) Around this walnut tree—known as the Noce di Benevento—the Longobards held their nocturnal open-air rituals which, combined with knowledge of the cult of Isis and the vivid imagination of the locals, gave rise to the witchcraft legend.

The Longobards were converted to the Catholic religion by Saint Barbato, the town's bishop, in the 7th century A.D., and the bishop had the tree cut down. The dances stopped; yet, some say, the witches remained, and can still be seen dancing by the site on certain nights.

Hotel Villa Traiano Aspiring to be the most elegant in Benevento, this small hotel enjoys an excellent location near Trajan's Arch. In a neoclassical villa it affords charming public spaces. Guest rooms are good-size, elegant, and pleasant, with hardwood floors and reproduction furniture; most of the marble bathrooms are fairly spacious (some with shower only). The atmospheric **wine bar** in the cellar is a recent and welcome addition.

Viale dei Rettori 9, 82100 Benevento. www.hotelvillatraiano.it. © **0824-326241.** Fax 0824-326196. 19 units. 120€–160€ double. Rates include buffet breakfast. AE, DC, MC, V. Parking 15€. **Amenities:** Restaurant; 2 bars; concierge; room service. In room: A/C, TV, hair dryer, Internet, minibar.

President Hotel Right in the center of town, this hotel caters mostly to a business clientele, with a number of single rooms (75€). Accommodations are comfortable and classically styled, with hardwood floors and simple but tasteful furniture.

Via Perasso 1, 82100 Benevento. www.hotelpresidentbenevento.it. © **0824-316716.** Fax 0824-316764. 69 units. 110€ double; from 150€ suite. Rates include buffet breakfast. Children 2 and under stay free in parent's room. AE, DC, MC, V. Free parking. **Amenities:** Bar; concierge; Wi-Fi (free). In room: A/C, TV (in some), minibar, Wi-Fi (free).

Where to Eat

Benevento may be small, but dining is taken seriously at the many restaurants in town. Locals also are fond of dining excursions to the nearby villages (p. 333).

MODERATE

Gino e Pina ★ PIZZA/SANNITE A favorite with locals of all ages, this excellent restaurant and *enoteca* (wine bar) serves well-prepared traditional dishes along with D.O.C. wines. Among the seafood, meat, and truly excellent pizza, standouts are *cavatelli con vongole e zucchini* (a short rolled pasta with clams

Among the local specialties we absolutely love is *torrone*. Made in both hard and softer, chewy versions, this wonderful delicacy is a crumbly nougat made of egg whites, honey, and nuts—usually hazelnuts and almonds. A favorite in Roman times—historian Tito Livio mentions it in his writings—it only became popular in Europe in the 17th century, when the Beneventan candy makers created today's traditional varieties, which are covered with dark chocolate or with a special icing flavored with lemon, orange, or coffee. Among the best confectioners in town are **Alberico Ambrosino,** Corso Garibaldi 111; (✆ **0824-28546**); **Umberto Russo,** Via Gaetano Rumno 17 (✆ **0824-24472**); and the **Fabbriche Riunite Torrone di Benevento,** Viale Principe di Napoli 113 (✆ **0824-21624**), a consortium of local torrone producers. You will also find *torrone Strega,* and delicious *caramelle*—small hard candies with a soft center of "cream of Strega" (the Strega version of Baileys liqueur; see box, "Strega—The Brew of Benevento," above).

and zucchini) and the delicious *agnello al forno* (roasted lamb). The restaurant doubles as a cultural center, with a **tourist agency,** a **shop** selling local products, and a **lounge bar.**

Viale dell'Università 2. ✆ **0824-24947**. www.ginoepina.it. Reservations recommended. Secondi 8€–22€; pizza 3.90€–7€. AE, DC, MC, V. Mon–Sat 12:30–3pm and 7:30pm–midnight; Sun 12:30–3pm. July–Aug closed Sun. Closed 2 weeks in Aug.

Locanda delle Streghe ★ BENEVENTAN Another popular restaurant, the atmospheric Locanda of the Witches prides itself on being a stronghold of local culinary tradition. Indeed, the menu includes time-honored dishes that are difficult to find elsewhere. We recommend, of course, the *zuppa delle streghe* (witch stew), a savory, thick soup made from a number of herbs and vegetables, with hot red pepper and cheese, but also the homemade *cavatelli alle erbe* (pasta with wild herbs), and the splendid *pollo alla diavola* (spicy grilled chicken).

Via Manciotti 11. ✆ **0824-29873**. www.locandadellestreghe.it. Reservations recommended. Secondi 9€–16€. AE, DC, MC, V. Wed–Mon 12:30–3pm and 7:30–11pm. Closed 10 days in Aug.

INEXPENSIVE

Nunzia ★ BENEVENTAN This local institution is a family-run restaurant that is so welcoming it almost feels like the home of a Beneventan host. You'll also spend very little, so it's not surprising that this place is very popular among locals. The highlights are the *primi* and the soups, which might include tasty spaghetti *e piselli* (with peas), as well as meats, such as lamb and pork roast. It's worth coming on a Friday to try the house specialty, *baccalá con capperi e olive* (salt cod in an olive-and-caper sauce). In summer, other fish and seafood dishes such as *paccheri* (pasta) with monkfish sauce and grilled sword fish are added to the menu.

Via Annunziata 152. ✆ **0824-29431**. Reservations recommended for dinner. Secondi 6€–12€. AE, DC, MC, V. Mon–Sat 1–3pm and 8–11pm. Closed 2 weeks in Aug.

Ristorante Pizzeria Traiano ★ BENEVENTAN/PIZZA Excellent local cuisine and great pizza (available only in the evening) make this a popular place. Open the almost unnoticeable entrance door, and you'll find yourself in a crammed little restaurant with two small dining rooms, usually filled with people happily downing large dishes of food. In summer, tables are laid on the terrace, which looks straight onto the arch. This place is particularly famous for its variety of *antipasti* that comes either as appetizers or as side dishes—try *involtini di melanzane* (eggplant rolls) if they're available. The restaurant is also famous for its homemade desserts. Both *antipasti* and desserts are on display near the entrance. Pasta dishes—such as spaghetti *alle cozze e vongole* (with mussels and clams)—are also excellent.

Via Manciotti 48. *C* **0824-25013.** Reservations recommended for dinner. Secondi 6€–11€, MC, V. Wed–Mon noon–2:30pm and 7:30–11pm.

Taverna Paradiso ★ BENEVENTAN This is one of our favorite places in the area, not least for its atmospheric setting in a historic tavern that was, for a long time, a wine bar. The varied menu caters to most possible tastes and needs, from celiac to vegetarian to children. The dishes are simple, all based on the local tradition and using local ingredients. We recommend sampling the cured meats and cheese as appetizer, and then trying the *paccheri con pomodorini e caciocavallo* (fresh pasta with cherry tomatoes and local cheese), and a succulent *maiale farcito* (pork roasted stuffed with arucola and cheese). The *baccalà* (salt cod) is also good; try the *polpette* (deep-fried cod and potato croquettes)

Via Mario La Vipera 33. *C* **0824-42914.** www.taverna-paradiso.com. Reservations recommended for dinner. Secondi 8€–16€. AE, MC, V. Wed–Mon noon 3pm and 7:30pm–11pm. Closed first 2 weeks in Aug.

Farther Afield Around Benevento: Discovering Sannio

The hilly area around Benevento is known as the **Sannio** and is famous for the production of some of Italy's best D.O.C. (*Denominazione di Origine Controllata*) wines. Apart from being a perfect destination for wine lovers, anyone interested in history, thermal spas, and genuine country cooking will also find lots to do. Local culture is very much alive here with each town claiming a very individual identity. The Sannio is way off the tourist radar and if you spend the night in a hotel in the area, you are likely to be the only foreign tourist.

Although most of the villages are served by **SITA bus service** (*C* **089-405145;** www.sitabus.it), a **car** is the best way to explore the hills around Benevento (see p. 348, for car-rental companies, and p. 326, for an agency in Benevento).

The D.O.C. Wines of the Sannio

Benevento is the capital of the Sannio region, which is well-known for its wines, claiming an unusually high number of D.O.C. vintages. Among the stars are Aglianico del Taburno, Solopaca, Guardiolo, Sannio, Sant'Agata dei Goti, and Taburno. Another famous name is the refreshing Falanghina, a white wine with an aromatic bouquet and a dry flavor.

VALLE CAUDINA ★

Dominated by the Monte Taburno, this valley extends southwest of Benevento. Take SS 7 (Via Appia) out of Benevento, going toward Capua, and you'll reach the village of **Montesarchio ★**. Ignore the modern area and proceed to the picturesque historic district with its imposing 15th-century **fortress.** For a good meal in the

Sant'Agata dei Goti.

historic district, head to **Ristorante 'O Pignatiello** ★, Via Variante (📞 0824-833276; www.opigniatiello.it). Another noteworthy restaurant is **Barry** ★ (which stands for "bar-ristorante") in the elegant **Cristina Park Hotel,** Via Benevento 102, 82016 Montesarchio (📞 0824-835888; fax 0824-834903; www.cristinaparkhotel.it; 98€ double).

The national park of **Monte Taburno** (1,394m/4,573-ft.; www.parco taburno.it), just outside of town, is a good place for **hiking** ★. The easiest way to reach the trail head is by car, taking the scenic local road marked VITULANO at the eastern edge of Montesarchio; it skirts the fortress and climbs to Piano Caudio (14km/8¾ miles from Montesarchio). Here you bear left at the fork in the road, following the signs for **Rifugio-Albergo Taburno,** a bar/restaurant/hotel at an altitude of 1,050m (3,445 ft.) where the trail starts. From the *rifugio,* the climb is fairly easy and you will reach the top in about an hour; the **panorama** ★★ on a clear day is splendid. Incidentally, this mountain is the origin of the aqueduct that feeds the fountains of Caserta's Royal Palace (p. 312).

Continuing on road SS 7 and then turning on the local road, SP 125, you'll reach the pretty mountain town of **Airola,** dominated by its scenic castle. Its 16th-century church—**Chiesa dell'Annunziata**—is worth a visit, with a beautiful facade that is the handiwork of Luigi Vanvitelli, the same architect who designed the Royal Palace in Caserta and the artwork inside this church.

Farther along, you'll reach **Sant'Agata dei Goti** ★★, a scenic medieval town built on a high tufa-stone cliff. Despite having been severely damaged by the earthquake of 1980, the unique town is still very picturesque, built along an unusual semicircular urban plan. It is famous for its many churches: The most attractive is the **Duomo** (originally from the 10th c.), which retains some of its beautiful mosaic floor and, in the crypt, the original frescoes. Other noteworthy churches are the 13th-century **Chiesa dell'Annunziata** and 11th-century **Chiesa di San Menna.** Sant'Agata is also a reputed destination for wine lovers and foodies. The local vineyard **Mustilli** ★★, Via dei Fiori 20, 82019 Sant'Agata dei Goti (📞 0823-717433; www.mustilli.com), is renowned for its excellent Falanghina and several reds well worth tasting, as well as some outstanding grappa; we definitely recommend a visit to the cellar excavated from the tufa stone (call ahead for reservation). Mustilli also operates as *agriturismo* from the 18th-century **Palazzo Rainone,** the family's home in the historic center of Sant'Agata: The **restaurant ★★** serves superb meals prepared with the products of the farm—homemade pasta *(ravioloni, cavatelli, pacche)* with seasonal sauces, such as wild mushroom in the fall and wild asparagus in the spring, and also *agnello* (lamb) and *arista di maiale* (pork roast). Guests sleep in six elegantly appointed rooms (90€ double; rates include buffet breakfast). Round off your gastronomic tour with the excellent ice cream at **Bar Gelateria Normanno,** Via Roma 65 (*℃* **0823-953042;** www.gelaterianormanno.it); among the many special flavors are *bacio normanno* (chocolate hazelnut) and *spumone all'Annurca* (a sherbet shake made with the renowned local apple variety).

VALLE TELESINA ★★

Spreading northwest from Benevento along route SS 372, this valley is well known by wine lovers destined for **Solopaca,** the village that gave its name to the best of the region's D.O.C. wines. This is a charming valley of green hills dotted with hilltop villages. One of the most attractive is **Torrecuso ★**, with its medieval *borgo* crowned by a castle and great views from its cliff-top location. This is also the location of a reputed vineyard, **La Rivolta,** Contrada Rivolta (*℃* **0824-872921;** www.fattorialarivolta.it), the producer of an excellent Aglianico del Taburno: Terre di Rivolta. The charming 19th-century country residence **Le Vigne ★** (*℃* **0824-872682;** www.levignetorrecuso.it) has elegantly appointed guest rooms a short distance from the vineyard.

Farther along is the popular **Telese Terme ★**, a green and pleasant little town, famous for its sulfuric springs—good for the skin and beneficial to ear ailments as well as respiratory illness—that appeared after an earthquake in 1349. The largest spa is **Terme di Telese ★** (*℃* **0824-976888;** www.termeditelese. it), located in a beautiful park where pavilions and pools have been built over the natural springs, offering baths, mud applications, and a number of other therapies. We also recommend the smaller and more romantic **Aquapetra Resort & Spa ★★**, Strada Statale Telesina 1 (*℃* **0824-941878;** fax 0824-901557; www.aquapetra.com; 250€–350€ double). The best hotel in town is

Valle Telesina.

the elegant 19th-century **Grand Hotel Telese ★**, Via Cerreto 1, 82037 Telese (✆**0824-940500**; fax 0824-940504; www.grandhotel telese.it; 170€ double; 230€ suite; rates include buffet breakfast), near the Terme di Telese but offering its own small spa. Within walking distance of town are two other attractions: About 1km (a half-mile) to the southeast is the pretty **Telese Lake ★**, and a few miles to the west are the ruins of **Telesia ★**, a Sannite and

then Roman town. For a typical Sannite meal and good local wine, head to the **Locanda della Pacchiana,** Viale Minieri 32 (✆**0824-976093**).

North of Telese, **Guardia Sanframondi** has a panoramic medieval castle that protected the surrounding *borgo*. The two churches **Chiesa dell'Annunziata** and **San Sebastiano** are worth a visit for the art that decorates them. Farther north is **Cerreto Sannita ★★**, a harmonious ensemble of late-baroque buildings. The village was rebuilt at the end of the 17th century, after an earthquake completely destroyed it in 1688. Many of its churches are worth a visit, including the **Cathedral, San Martino** and **San Gennaro.** The town is also renowned for its Capodimonte porcelain; local artists in Cerreto and in the nearby village of **San Lorenzello** continue the tradition today. You can admire the local craft at the **Mostra Permanente della Ceramica Antica e Moderna,** Piazza L. Sodo, off Corso Umberto I (✆**0824-861337**), and the **Museo Civico e della Ceramica,** Corso Umberto I, inside the church of San Gennaro and the Convent of Sant'Antonio (✆**0824-815211**). To purchase some of the craftwork, head for **Keramos,** Via Nicotera 84 (✆**0824-861463**), one of the best showrooms in town. Last but not least, Cerreto is popular with locals for its restaurants: We recommend **Il Pozzo dei Desideri ★**, Via Michele Ungaro 122, behind San Martino church (✆**0824-816050;** closed Wed and first 2 weeks in July). It serves delicious homemade pasta, such as pappardelle *ai funghi porcini* (pasta with porcini mushrooms) and a splendid *costata alla griglia* (grilled steak drizzled with local olive oil). Juicy steaks and succulent pasta dishes attract locals from throughout the area to the **Agri Hotel's La Vecchia Quercia ★**, Via Cerquelle (✆**0824-861263;** www.vecchiaquercia.com closed Tues), on the hill overlooking the village, a short distance out of town.

We recommend pushing farther north to the picturesque village of **Cusano Mutri ★★**, with its stone houses and well-preserved Norman castle. Also worth a visit are the two churches: **Chiesa dei Santi Pietro e Paolo** and **San Giovanni.**

VAL FORTORE

Most of the visitors who pass through this valley, which spans north of Benevento along the SS 212, make a pilgrimage to **Pietrelcina** (about 12km/7½ miles from Benevento), the home village of Padre Pio (a monk and a controversial figure, who died in 1968 and was canonized in 2002 by Pope John Paul II). The excursion is well worth it, if only for the ride alone, as the meandering road takes you through scenic green mountains. Should you need another reason to visit, we suggest sampling the cuisine at the impressive local **Boda de Ciondro ★**, Via Tratturo (**©0824-997601;** www.bodadeciondro.it; Tues–Sat 6:30–11pm, Sun and holidays noon–4pm, closed 1 week in July).

Farther north is **San Marco dei Cavoti ★**, the destination of a different kind of pilgrim, one who comes to savor the delicious local specialty: *torroncini*. Made in small batches by local confectioners, these bite-size nougat candies are made with honey and nuts and often dipped in dark chocolate. While you can find *torroncini* in Benevento, only here can you sample a staggering variety. The best are the *baci* (kisses) from **Premiata Fabbrica Cavalier Innocenzo Borrillo,** Via Roma 66 (**©0824-984060**), although his descendants are worthy competitors: **Anna Maria Borrillo,** Via Martiri di Bologna 18 (**©0824-984939**), and **Dolciaria Borrillo,** Contrada Catapano 22 (**©0824-995099**). The runner-up is **Antonina Petrillo,** Vico San Vincenzo 2 (**©0824-969266**), in Montefalcone di Val Fortore, a picturesque village nearby.

ON THE WAY TO AVELLINO ★

More than the scenic surroundings and local history, the real draw here is two **restaurants** that are among the best in the region. Both are very close to Benevento and make great dining excursions. In **Beltiglio,** a hilltop village near the small town of Ceppaloni, about 10km (6 miles) southwest of Benevento, **La Rete ★★**, Via Masseriola (**©0824-46574;** www.ristorantelarete.com; Thurs–Mon 12:30–2:30pm and 8–10:30pm) offers authentic cuisine featuring the best and freshest local ingredients. The succulent appetizers include excellent local cheese, cured meats, and *bruschette* (grilled rustic bread with a variety of toppings), and the meal continues with the superb fusilli *porcini e salsiccia* (with porcini mushrooms and sausages), the unique *gnocchi al tartufo su salsa di parmigiano* (potato dumplings with truffle and Parmesan sauce), or a delicious vegetarian lasagna (with ricotta, basil, and fresh tomatoes). For a secondo, do not miss the grilled boar and lamb. **Children** will enjoy the outdoor **playground.**

The long-established **Antica Trattoria Pascalucci ★★**, Via Ianassi 17, Localitá Piano Cappelle, San Nicola Manfredi (**©0824-778400;** reservations recommended; secondi 12€–22€; daily 12:30–3pm and 8–11pm, closed Dec 24–25) is off the SS 7 (Via Appia) about 4km (2½ miles) southeast of Benevento. The large menu includes tasty local peasant cuisine and seafood recipes from the Naples coast. Start with the *antipasti* for a taste of local cured meats and delicious *sottoli* (vegetables prepared and kept in olive oil). Continue with *tubetti alle cozze* (short pasta with mussels) or fusilli *ai funghi porcini* (with porcini mushrooms). You can then attack the secondo, choosing between perfectly grilled meats and daily catch *al forno in umido* (baked with tomatoes).

AVELLINO & THE HILL TOWNS OF IRPINIA

Surprisingly close to the northeastern outskirts of Naples, Irpinia is a mountainous region of medieval villages amid rolling hills. It is renowned among connoisseurs for its food and wine, considered the best in Campania and among the best in Italy. The capital of the region is **Avellino,** a town that was largely destroyed by earthquakes and was rebuilt with uninteresting modern buildings. The real attraction is the wilderness beyond, with its remote villages and authentic traditions.

Avellino

35km (22 miles) S of Benevento; 54km (34 miles) E of Naples

The capital of Irpinia, Avellino started as a Roman town—Abellinum—which was abandoned in early medieval times because it was too difficult to defend (p. 341). The population moved uphill to a Longobard fortified village (about 3km/2 miles to the west), with a strategic position controlling the road between Benevento and Salerno. The town is uninspiring nowadays, victim of the numerous earthquakes that have hit the area. The last, but certainly not the least, was the 1980 quake that left little standing and whose terrible economic repercussions are still being felt today.

GETTING THERE Avellino is easily reached by **train** from Benevento, Naples, and Salerno. Contact **Trenitalia** (✆ **892021** in Italy; www.trenitalia.it) for fares and information. Trains arrive at Avellino's train **station,** on Via Francesco Tedesco.

If you are arriving by **car,** take the AVELLINO exit off autostrada A16. You'll find a covered garage (✆ **0825-23574**) on Via Terminio 20.

GETTING AROUND You can easily get around Avellino **on foot.** A number of **bus** lines (**SITA;** ✆ **089-405145;** www.sitabus.it) leave from Avellino to serve most villages in the area. In addition to major **car-rental** companies (see "Getting Around," p. 348), **Win Rent,** Corso Umberto I 89 (✆ **0825-756237**), is a good local agency.

VISITOR INFORMATION The local **EPT** tourist office is at Via Due Principati 32A (✆ 0825-74732) and is open Monday through Friday 8:30am to 1:30pm.

You'll find a **pharmacy** (✆ 0825-35097) in Corso Vittorio Emanuele II. You will find a number of banks and **ATMs** along Corso Vittorio Emanuele II such as the **Banca della Campania,** Corso Vittorio Emanuele II 172 (✆ 0825-6511). The new **hospital, San Giuseppe Moscati,** is at Contrada Amoretta (✆ **0825-203111**). For an **ambulance,** dial ✆ **118.** You can call the **police** at ✆ **113** or 112. The **post office** (✆ 0825-781209) is at Via Francesco De Sanctis 3, off Corso Europa.

SPECIAL EVENTS Avellino is famous for its **Carnevale Irpino,** the festival organized for the celebration of Carnival which includes traditional performances, the most famous of which is **Zeza.** Taking its name from the wife of Pulcinella, this musical farce narrates the adventures of the family when their daughter Porzia decides to get married to Don Zenobio. Contact the **EPT** (see "Visitor Information," above) for a schedule of events.

EXPLORING THE TOWN

What remains of the historic district of Avellino is to be found around **Corso Umberto I,** which crosses the medieval town and heads to the **Castello,** a castle that was destroyed not by earthquakes, but during the Spanish wars at the beginning of the 18th century.

Duomo, aka Cattedrale dell'Assunta ★ This 12th-century church was redone and added to in following centuries. The elegant facade is neoclassical, as are the decorations inside. The cathedral holds many masterpieces, including a beautiful **tabernacle** by Giovanni da Nola that you can admire in the chapel to the right of the main one. Also take note of the 16th-century carved **choir** at the back of the church, in the apse. Under the Duomo, you'll find the Cripta

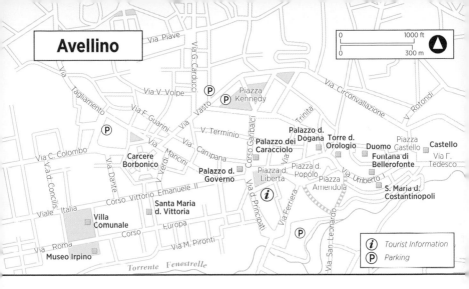

dell'Addolorata, or Church of Santa Maria dei Sette Dolori. It was created in the 17th century by adding a nave to the original Romanesque crypt and is decorated with **frescoes** and with Roman and medieval capitals. From the presbytery, you can access the courtyard, where you can see remains of the original Longobard church and the partially restored Romanesque bell tower, decorated with Roman marble inscriptions from Abellinum.

Piazza Duomo. Free admission. Daily 9–11am and 5–7pm.

Museo Irpino ★★ Across from the public park of Villa Comunale, this modern museum houses an important collection of fascinating artifacts dating as far back as 4000 B.C. The extensive archaeological collection is in the main building, together with the grandiose 18th-century artistic *presepio* and a rich collection of **porcelain** from the late 18th to the early 19th century. The **picture gallery,** with an ensemble of 17th-, 18th-, and 19th-century Neapolitan masters, has been moved to the **Carcere Borbonico** (Piazza d'Armi, off Via Mancini, same hours as the museum), an interesting hexagonal building that once housed the prisons of the Bourbon kings. In rooms two and three are the artifacts excavated from the Aeneolithic necropolis of Madonna delle Grazie (near Mirabella Eclano), including the reconstruction of a complete tomb of a tribal chief, buried with his dog. (By the way, "Aeneolithic" means the transitional period between the Neolithic and the Bronze ages; we looked it up.) A number of findings document life in the old Abellinum, including a great **mosaic ★** from the 1st century (in the entrance hall), ceramics, fragments of frescoes, and the funerary collection from the 2nd-century **tomb of a young woman ★**, all in rooms eight and nine. A new hall displays the recent findings from the Sanctuary of the Goddess Mefite, a cult going back to the 6th century B.C. that persisted through the Roman era. These were found in a site near the Passo di Mirabella.

Corso Europa. **✆ 0825-790501.** Free admission. Mon–Fri 8am–2pm.

WHERE TO STAY

Hotel De La Ville ★ With its central location, luxury service, and elegant romantic vibe, this glitzy modern hotel wins the prize for best in town. Comfortable guest rooms are large and well-appointed, and bathrooms are good size. Public spaces are spacious and furnished with elegance—down to a garden complete with swimming pool (heart shaped, no less). The hotel's restaurant, **Il Cavallino,** is excellent, serving traditional and historical Neapolitan and Irpinian dishes.

Via Palatucci 20, 83100 Avellino. www.hdv.av.it. *©* **0825-780911.** 69 units. 230€ double; from 420€ suite. Rates include buffet breakfast. Children 2 and under stay free in parent's room. AE, DC, MC, V. Parking 10€. **Amenities:** Restaurant; bar; concierge; pool; room service. *In room:* A/C, TV, Internet, minibar.

WHERE TO EAT

Antica Trattoria Martella ★★ IRPINIAN This historical restaurant is prized by locals for its difficult-to-find specialties, and the elegant yet unstuffy setting. The vaulted ceilings, wooden chairs with straw seats, white tablecloths, and attentive service create an old-fashioned atmosphere, which is perfect for experiencing the seasonal local menu. If it's on the menu, try the unusual *fusilli affumicati con ricotta e pancetta* (lightly smoked homemade pasta with ricotta and pork belly) or the tagliatelle *al tartufo nero,* seasoned with the famous local black truffles. We also recommend the *coniglio ripieno con patate* (stuffed rabbit with potatoes).

Via Chiesa Conservatorio 10. *©* **0825-32123.** www.ristorantemartella.it. Reservations recommended. Secondi 8€–12€. AE, DC, MC, V. Tues–Sat 1–3pm and 8–11pm; Sun 1–3pm. Closed Dec 24–26, Jan 1, and 1 week in Aug.

La Maschera ★★ ☺ MODERN IRPINIAN This is our favorite restaurant in town; it has an elegant setting with a charming outdoor terrace and an interesting, varied menu. You can choose among several tasting menus, including a vegetarian and even a children's menu, and the daily menu is based on market offerings. The cuisine is a modern interpretation of the local traditions, offering lighter versions of many favorite dishes. We recommend the *zuppa di cipolla di Montoro* (local onion soup), ravioli *di ricotta con punte d'asparagi di montagna* (with cheese and mountain asparagus), *pollo ruspante alle noci* (free-range chicken with walnuts), and *coniglio ripieno* (stuffed rabbit).

Rampa San Modestino 1. Reservations recommended. Secondi 11€–16€. AE, DC, MC, V. Mon–Sat 1–3pm and 8–11pm; Sun 1–3pm. Closed 10 days July–Aug.

Santuario di Montevergine ★★

Very close to Avellino, this sanctuary with an annexed monastery (*©* **0825-72924;** www.santuariodimontevergine.it) is famous for its art and for the splendid view that takes in the entire valley down to Mount Vesuvius and the Gulf of Naples. On a sunny day, the panorama is impressive enough to justify your whole trip to Campania; in really bad weather, we wouldn't even attempt the drive up.

The summit of Montevergine rises to a height of 1,493m (4,898 ft); almost at the top at 1,270m or 4,167 ft. lies the sanctuary, a popular pilgrimage destination attracting over a million people every year, especially between May and September.

Founded by Guglielmo da Vercelli in 1119, for his order of the Verginiani—June 25 is Saint Patron Day celebrating San Guglielmo—the sanctuary has a hostel, the monastery, a museum and gallery, and **two churches.** The smaller, original church was probably consecrated in 1124; the huge new basilica, finished in 1961, is nestled into the older one at a right angle, over the original church's left nave.

Avellino & Irpinia

CASERTA, BENEVENTO & AVELLINO

In the presbytery of the **New Church,** rich in marble decorations, you can admire the so-called *Throne of the Madonna,* the great 13th-century painting of the **Madonna di Montevergine ★**. On each side of the new presbytery, small doors lead to the **Old Church.** Built in the 12th century, the Old Church was completely redecorated in the 17th century but still shows its Gothic structure. In the presbytery, you will see the splendid 17th-century **main altar ★**, a masterpiece of intarsia in marble and precious stones. In the apse is a beautiful carved choir from the 16th century. At the end of the right nave is the Gothic **Cappella del Sacramento,** holding a magnificent 13th-century **baldaquin ★** in mosaic, and the ornate 15th-century marble **cyborium ★**. The church is rich in funerary monuments with amazing stone inlay work, such as the grandiose **Monument to Caterina Filangeri** from the 15th century, located at the end of the right nave to the left, before the Cappella del Sacramento. The Gothic portal of the original church is also very beautiful, and warmer than the rather austere modern style of the new construction.

We also recommend a visit to the **museum,** which houses a small but interesting collection, including a beautiful *sedia abbaziale* (abbey's throne) dating from the 13th century. Male visitors also have access to the monastery itself, including the portions that date back to the 17th century. On nice days, we recommend the short 1.5km (.9-mile) **hike** to the mountain summit.

To reach the monastery from Avellino (21km/13 miles away), take SS 7 bis and then switch to SS 374 following signs for MERCOGLIANO; here you take the winding mountain road to MONTEVERGINE. Continuing up the road past the monastery, you'll reach, after 1.5km (.9 mile), the trail head to the mountaintop. The short walk takes only about 15 minutes, and from the summit, you can enjoy an even better panorama than from the sanctuary.

En Route to Mirabella Eclano ★★

Heading northeast from Avellino on the SS 7 (Via Appia), or the A16 autostrada, you will eventually reach Benevento, passing many historic villages and towns along the way. Down the hill from Avellino, about 3.5km (2 miles) to the east, is **Atripalda,** where, beyond the belt of modern construction, you can visit the **Collegiata di Sant'Ippolisto.** This church is particularly famous for its **crypt ★★**, which was part of the **Specus Martyrum,** the catacombs that hold the graves of Saint Ippolisto and the other martyrs of Abellinum, killed by the notoriously cruel emperor Domitian. It is decorated with a beautiful fresco of a Christ Pantocrator from the 14th century. Nearby are the ruins of **Abellinum ★** itself, much damaged by the liberal use of the stones as building material throughout the centuries. **Valleverde-Zi Pasqualina ★★**, Via Pianodardine 112, off SS 7 (✆ **0825-626115;** www.ziapasqualina.it; reservations recommended; closed Sun and holidays), in the outskirts of Atripalda is a homey, welcoming trattoria-cum-enoteca that serves hearty portions of excellent local fare. The *antipasto della casa* is a medley of cheese, cured meats, and other local specialties; the homemade fusilli and ravioli are superb; and the *pollo alla cacciatora* (chicken stew) is a flavorful marvel. We also recommend a stop at **Mastroberardino ★★**, Via Manfredi 80, 83042 Atripalda (✆ **0825-614111;** www.mastroberardino. com), a historic vineyard—it's 130 years old—that turns out some of the best traditional wines in the region. The Taurasi is superb, and the vineyard also manages and produces the Villa dei Misteri wine in Pompei (p. 135). The frescoed cellars, where the wines are aged, are also a gallery for fine Italian paintings.

Call ahead for reservations for tours or tastings. (See their website for a list of news and scheduled events.)

A short distance east of Atripalda, following directions for Sorbo Serpico, you'll find another great vineyard, **Feudi di San Gregorio,** Localitá Cerza Grossa (*(C)* **0825-986611;** www.marenna.it), and its excellent restaurant **Marennà** ★★ (*(C)* **0825-986666;** Wed-Sat 12:30–3pm and 7:30–10:30pm, Sun 12:30–3pm, closed first week in Sept; reservations required), offering creative cuisine inspired by the local tradition and, of course, a great choice of wines.

Prata di Principato Ultra is a village about 11km (6½ miles) north of Avellino. The draw here is a visit to the **Basilica dell'Annunziata** ★★ (*(C)* **0825-961019**). The historic church was built by the Longobards over paleochristian catacombs and a 6th-century basilica. From the modern little church, you will access an elliptical **apse,** carved of tufa stone, probably dating from the 7th century, decorated with a fresco of *Madonna and Saints* dating to the 8th century. At the end of a courtyard to the left of the church is the entrance to the grotto, a Christian catacomb from the 3rd and 4th centuries that is decorated with frescoes, altars, and sarcophagi.

About 10km (6 miles) farther north, switch to the SS 90 toward Passo di Mirabella, a scenic road on the mountain slopes leading to an important archaeological area; the most important findings are conserved in the **Museo Irpino** (p. 339) in Avellino. A short distance before Passo di Mirabella are the ruins of **Aeclanum** ★★ (*(C)* **0825-449175**), a Sannite/Roman town that was an important stop along the Via Appia. Destroyed in 662 during the wars against the Longobards, the town was rebuilt—and named Quintodecimo—but was destroyed again in the 11th century during the war between the Byzantines and Saracens. In the archaeological area, you can still see many remains of the Roman town, including segments of the walls, the theater, and the market square, as well as ruins of houses and shops. About 3.5km (2 miles) to the southwest, following signs for TAURASI, you'll come to the **Eneolithical Necropolis of Madonna delle Grazie** ★, with its tombs excavated in the tufa stone and dating back to 2000 B.C.

The lively little town of **Mirabella Eclano** is the heir of Aeclanum, and memories of the past decorate its streets, as marble carvings and inscriptions from Roman and medieval times were built into the walls of the houses. **Santa Maria Maggiore,** in the main square of the old town, features the 12th-century *Crucifix* ★★, a Romanesque masterpiece by a Campanian artist. A good spot for a meal or an overnight in Mirabella is **Radici Resort** ★★, Localitá Piano Pantano (*(C)* **0825-431293;** fax 0825-431964; www.radiciresort.com), in the vineyard property of the Mastroberardino family (p. 341). This is where they make their excellent Taurasi and Fiano di Avellino Radici, D.O.C.G., or Vino a Denominazione di Origine Controllata e Garantita, similar to the D.O.C stamp of approval but the rules on D.O.C.G. eligibility are even more stringent (see box, "The D.O.C. Wines of Ischia," p. 256 for more on D.O.C. requirements). The property includes six spacious guest rooms, a 9-hole golf course, a swimming pool, and the wonderful upscale **Morabianca restaurant.**

Montemarano & Sant'angelo dei Lombardi

South along the original route of the Roman Via Appia lies the heart of Irpinia. Traveling here is a feast for the senses: You'll find art, history, and the region's best cuisine. The medieval town of **Montemarano** ★★ is dominated by its well-preserved **castle,** and the **Chiesa dell'Assunta** is graced by a nicely carved 16th-century portal. Inside the church is a delicately carved 15th-century **folding chair,** decorated with images of the *Sacra Famiglia* by Andrea Vaccaro; the seat was used by the bishop until recent times. This ancient little town is also famous for its **Carnival** celebrations: Festivities start on January 17—the feast of Sant'Antonio Abate—and continue until Mardi Gras. For days, groups of dancers and musicians guided by a Pulcinella tour the little town asking for offerings, and as the Carnival ripens, more events take place, including ritual **tarantella** dances. Rarely seen these days, this famously frenzied dance is still performed according to tradition and not as a tourist show. Among the lighter-weight events are farcical performances and the traditional parade of the Pulcinella, where all the town's characters participate. Contact the tourist office in Avellino for a schedule of events. There are a number of great restaurants in town. At **Gastronomo** ★★, Via Nazionale 39 (©**0827-67009;** Mon–Tues and Thurs–Sat noon–3pm and 7:30–11pm; Sun noon–3pm), simplicity, a welcoming atmosphere, and excellent food and wine combine to make this place a local favorite. The pizza is very good, but we also like the *antipasto della casa,* a sampler of local cheese and cured meats. The homemade ravioli is delicious, and the lamb stew is superb.

Farther east is the delightful medieval town of **Sant'Angelo dei Lombardi** ★★, overlooking the surrounding valley from the top of its hill. Founded by the Longobards, the town is rich in historic monuments, most of which can still be enjoyed despite the severe damage caused by the 1980 earthquake. These include the scenic **Norman Castle** and the 11th-century **cathedral,** housing several funerary monuments such as the beautiful 17th-century **Sepolcro Cecere** found at the beginning of the right nave. About 6.5km (4 miles) out of town to the southwest, in Contrada San Guglielmo, is the **Abbazia di San Guglielmo al Goleto** ★★ (©**0827-24432;** www.goleto.it; call for visits), justly considered one of the most scenic attractions of southern Italy. Founded around 1133 by the same San Guglielmo who founded Montevergine (p. 340), this is the monastery where the saint died in 1142. Originally a double monastery (for men and women), it was very influential until the end of the 14th century. The women's section was suppressed in 1505, while the men's half was annexed to the Monastery of Montevergine, and finally closed in 1807. The body of Saint Guglielmo was then moved to Montevergine, and the monastery was completely abandoned. The religious order, though, decided to save it from ruin, and—thanks to much restoration—it became the seat of a small religious community in 1989. The monastery is huge and surrounded by powerful walls that can be seen from a considerable distance. Originating as a double monastery, it is organized around two cloisters, while the two churches were built one over the other. The facade of both, the top one Gothic (from the 13th c.), and the bottom one Romanesque (from the 12th c.), can be viewed from the left-hand cloister. Also in this cloister are the ruins of the 18th-century church. Stone steps lead to the top church, a wonderful artistic masterpiece with harmonious proportions and elegant decoration. Around the second cloister is the abbey itself, with the massive defensive tower built in the 12th century with stones from a Roman mausoleum. The abbey is open daily (8am–1pm and 6–8pm). You can eat nearby in the memorable **Ristorante Il Porcellino** ★, Via Campoluongo (©**0827-23694**), where the local homemade cuisine is based on pastas and a variety of grilled meats. In winter, there are wonderful soups. It's closed on Mondays.

Avellino & Irpinia

PLANNING YOUR TRIP

TO CAMPANIA & THE AMALFI COAST

taly is an easy country to tour, and Campania is a tourist- and family-friendly destination, whatever your traveling style and needs. The bulk of your planning will be focused on prioritizing which destinations you'll visit and which you'll leave for your next Campanian vacation. Remember: The laid-back *dolce vita* reigns here and you don't want to put too much on your plate—unless it's the local food.

This relaxed culture has the unfortunate (for tourists) side effect that in certain seaside destinations—in particular Capri and the Amalfi and Cilento coasts—many low-end hotels and restaurants close for the entire winter (usually Nov–Mar), with the occasional exception for the Christmas and New Year's holidays. This is a mixed blessing; you'll enjoy this splendid coast without the summer crowds, but your choices will be reduced.

GETTING THERE
By Plane

Campania is served by Naples's **Capodichino Airport** (✆ 081-7896111 or toll-free from within Italy 848-888777; www.gesac.it); its international airport code is **NAP.** All attractions in the region are a short distance away.

Only a few international airlines fly directly to Naples so you may also decide to enjoy the wider choice offered by Rome's Fiumicino-Leonardo da Vinci airport (international airport code **FCO**). You'll then have to transfer to the train (see "By Train," below).

In addition to several low-cost companies, a few major airlines offer international flights to Naples from their European hubs: Alitalia, Air France, Aer Lingus, Austrian Airlines, British Airways, Iberia, and Lufthansa. The only intercontinental nonstop flights to Naples are those offered by **Meridiana** from New York (Meridiana recently purchased Eurofly from Alitalia). From elsewhere in North America and from Australia and New Zealand, you will have to take a connecting flight (Rome is only 50 min. away, Milan about 90 min., and most European hubs about 2 hr.).

FROM THE AIRPORT About 7km (4 miles) from Naples's city center, the airport is only 20 minutes away from the downtown area and the harbor. The easiest way to get to your destination is by taking a **taxi** directly to your hotel: The flat rate for Naples is 19€ plus gratuities, 100€ for Sorrento, 120€ for Positano, 130€ for Amalfi, and 135€ for Ravello. Most hotels and resorts along the coast offer airport pickup: For a limousine booked through your hotel, you'll pay about 30€ for Naples, 90€ for Sorrento, and 115€ for Amalfi. You might get better rates contacting a car service directly (see "By Car," in "Getting Around," later in this chapter).

If you don't have a lot of luggage, the **Alibus shuttle bus** (✆ 081-5513109; www.unicocampania.it) to Naples is a cheaper alternative at 3€. With departures every 20 minutes, it stops on Corso Garibaldi near Napoli

OPPOSITE: **Lungomare Trieste.**

Centrale train station, and in Piazza Municipio at the heart of the historic district. Shuttle bus service to other nearby towns (Sorrento and Castellammare di Stabia, for instance) is also available.

By Train

Italy enjoys an excellent railway system, and trains often are the most convenient way to get from one destination to another. Naples is on Italy's main southern corridor, making it easily accessible from other Italian and European towns. The national railroad company **FS-Trenitalia** (© 892021 from anywhere in Italy, 39-06-68475475 from abroad; www.trenitalia.it) offers local trains as well as the faster, more expensive AltaVelocità, EuroStar, and InterCity trains (designated AV, ES, and IC on train schedules, respectively), which make limited stops. AV trains—Italy's fastest—travel at speeds of up to 300kmph (186 mph). The new AV train takes only 87 minutes between Rome and Naples, and 5 hours and 35 minutes from Milan, making it by far the best way to move between these cities; regular trains take about 2½ and 9 hours respectively for the same connections.

Fares for these fast trains are not cheap, but there are specials if you book online and in advance directly on the **Trenitalia** website (www.trenitalia.it). Children ages 5 to 11 receive a discount of 50%, and children ages 4 and younger travel free with their parents. Seniors and youths ages 25 and under can purchase discount cards. Advance seat reservations, which are obligatory on all AV, ES, and IC trains, are highly recommended for other trains during peak season and on weekends and holidays.

If you plan to travel extensively in Europe by train, it may be cheaper to purchase a **Eurail Pass,** a prepaid train pass for sale at all major rail stations and online (www.eurail.com). You can choose among several possible combinations, including an Italy-only pass granting 3 to 10 unlimited travel days within a 2-month period. Adult rates vary from between 153€ to 346€, depending on time and class. You will need to pay an extra fee for compulsory seat reservations on the faster trains and sleepers, but you'll be entitled to reductions on certain bus and ferry lines of up to 20%. If you prefer to discuss your options with a travel agent, contact **Rail Europe** (© 877/272-RAIL [7245]; www.raileurope.com) or your own travel agent, but they'll charge a commission. Savings are available for youths ages 25 and younger and for groups.

By Boat

Italy is well served by international ferries and is a regular stop on most cruise-ship lines. Two of its major ports are Naples and Salerno, both in Campania. Naples is the main port of central Italy, receiving daily ships and ferries from international destinations. Salerno is only slightly smaller.

Arriving in Naples by ship is a magnificent experience. You'll land at **Stazione Marittima,** only steps from the Maschio Angioino, in the heart of the historic district, the *città antica*. Salerno's harbor is also only a short distance from the historic district.

A number of cruise-ship companies sail to Naples, especially in the good season, from spring well into fall. One of our favorites is **MSC Cruises** (www.msccruises.com), both for the quality of ships and cruises and for the company's commitment to sustainable tourism and minimal ecological impact. Another favorite, both for the quality of its ships and service and its commitment to the protection of the environment, is **Costa Cruises** (www.costacruise.com). Other reliable companies offering cruises to Campania are **Regent Seven Seas Cruises** (www.rssc.com), **Norwegian Cruise Line** (www.ncl.eu), and **Oceania Cruises** (www.oceaniacruises.com).

The major ferry companies offering regular service to Naples are **Tirrenia** (📞 **892123** or 02-26302803; www.tirrenia.it), with boats to Sardinia (Cagliari) and Sicily (Palermo); **Siremar** (📞 **199-118866;** www.siremar.it), with ships to the Aeolian Islands and Sicily (Milazzo); **TTTLines** (📞 **800-915365**; www. TTTLines.it), with ships to Sicily (Catania); **Medmar** (📞 **081-3334411;** www.medmargroup.it), with boats to Ischia and Procida; and **SNAV** (📞 **081-4285555;** www.snav.it), with boats to Sicily, Sardinia, and the Aeolian and Pontine islands. Major companies operating from Salerno are **Grimaldi Lines** (📞 **081-496444;** www.grimaldi-ferries.com), with regular service to Spain (Valencia), Malta (La Valletta), Tunisia (Tunis), and Sicily (Palermo); and **Caronte & Tourist** (📞 **800-627414** toll-free within Italy, or 089-2582528; www.carontetourist.it), with boats to Sicily (Catania and Messina).

Of course, you could also cruise to another of the Italian harbors and then get to Campania by other means. Major navigation companies serving other Italian ports are **Blue Star Ferries** (www.bluestarferries.gr) and **Superfast Ferries** (www.superfast.com), from Greece; **Marmara Lines** (www.direct ferries.it), from Turkey; **Grandi Navi Veloci** (www.gnv.it), from Spain; and **Virtu Ferries** (www.virtuferries.com), from Malta.

By Car

To drive a car in Italy, you will need an **International Driving Permit (IDP)** which is an official translation of your license. Apply in the United States at any **American Automobile Association (AAA)** branch; or contact **AAA's national headquarters** (📞 **800/222-4357** or 407/444-4300; www.aaa.com). Canadians can get the address of the nearest **Canadian Automobile Association** by calling 📞 **613/247-0117,** or by visiting www.caa.ca. Remember that an international permit is valid only if physically accompanied by your home country–issued driver's license and only if signed on the back.

Most car-rental companies require a minimum age of 23 or 25, but a few will accept a minimum age of 21 for their cheaper models. Most rental companies will not rent a car to drivers 76 and older. Insurance on all vehicles is compulsory and can be purchased at any reputable rental firm. You will also need a valid credit card (not a prepaid or debit card) for a standard model and two credit cards for a deluxe model; cash payments will not be accepted.

Car rental in Italy is more expensive then in the United States. Your best bet is to check for specials on companies' websites. Prices vary with car size and special offers, but a compact car will generally rent for between 60€ and 100€ per day.

All of the major international rental companies operate in Italy: **Avis** (📞 **800/331-1212;** www.avis.com), **Budget** (📞 **800/472-3325;** www.budget. com), **Hertz** (📞 **800/654-3131;** www.hertz.com), and **National** in the U.S. (📞 **800/227-7368;** www.nationalcar.com). National is associated with Italy's primary rental company, **Maggiore** (📞 **199-151120** toll-free in Italy; www.maggiore. it). A newer, reputable, and sometimes cheaper company is **Sixt** (📞 **888/749-8227** in the United States; 199-100666 in Italy; www.sixt.it, or www.sixtusa.com for U.S. citizens). If you need a long-term rental, **Auto Europe** (📞 **800/223-5555;** www.autoeurope.com), **Europe by Car** (📞 **800/223-1516,** or 212/581-

3040 in New York; www.europeby car.com), and **Kemwel Holiday Auto** (© **877/820-0668**; www. kemwel.com), might offer better rates. It is worth asking when you book if your American Automobile Association (AAA) or AARP membership will give you a discount. Renting online usually will get you the best prices, but it is worth checking with the local rental office for a better deal. Package discounts are sometimes available when you book your car together with your flight.

Cars in Italy have manual shift, but you can request a car with automatic shift; they usually rent at a premium.

If you are driving to Italy from abroad, you will have to pass the Alps. There are three tunnels (Mont Blanc and Fréjus from France and Grand St. Bernard from Switzerland, all leading to the A5 highway to Turin and Milan) and a few passes (the main one is the Brenner from Austria, leading to the A22 highway to Bologna). Traffic at the border can be delayed by bad weather or at times of mass exodus (such as the beginning and end of school vacations).

Limited-access express highways in Italy are called autostrada and numbered from A1 on. They sometimes are also marked with the European number, starting with the letter E. North of Naples, autostrade are toll roads; they are quality roads with modern gas stations at sensible intervals. Tariffs depend on the size of your vehicle and the type of road; regular cars pay .061€ per kilometer on flat roads, and .072€ per kilometer on mountains, to which you need to add a small surcharge and rounding. To give you an example, Rome-Salerno will cost you a minimum of 14.60€. The official website, www.autostrade.it, offers a tool to calculate your costs and organize your trip, but, for the moment, it is in Italian only.

The Autostrada del Sole A1 from Milan to Naples is the highway to Campania. From Naples, the A3 leads to Salerno. Driving from Milan to Naples will take you about 9 hours on average, and about 10 to Sorrento. But be forewarned, driving in Campania is notoriously dangerous; see "By Car," in the "Getting Around" section below for a few useful tips.

Public Transportation Strikes

You might have heard it before—even the U.S. travel advisory for Italy warns of it— strikes occur in Italy and can hamper public transportation. However, they are a relatively rare occurrence, and planned walkouts are often canceled at the last minute because the parties reach an agreement. Should it actually happen, minimum service is guaranteed and alternate transportation is always made available. The bottom line is that strikes are no reason to forgo public transportation in favor of driving.

GETTING AROUND
By Train

With easy connections between the region's major towns and the Vesuvian attractions of Herculaneum and Pompeii, the train is an excellent way to get around. Local trains are cheap and frequent and you don't need advance reservation: You can buy your ticket at the automatic machines inside the station and hop on the train. An added advantage is that the rail station is usually in the center of town, within walking distance from the major attractions and well connected by public transportation and taxis.

The national railway system, **FS-Trenitalia** (*©* 892021 from anywhere in Italy; www.trenitalia.it), serves the area together with local lines: **Alifana** (*©* 800-053939; www.alifana.it) covers Benevento and surrounding areas; **Circumvesuviana** (*©* 800-053939; www.vesuviana.it) connects Naples with the Vesuvian area including Ercolano, Pompei, Castellammare di Stabia, and Sorrento; and **Metronapoli** (*©* 800-568866; www.metro.na.it) connects Naples with Pozzuoli and the Phlegrean Fields.

National and regional lines serve most major tourist destinations, sometimes in parallel, with the result that even relatively small towns have two stations, one for the national railroad and one for the local line. You will find all the options in the section "Getting There" in each destination chapter in this book.

By Bus

Local bus companies operate throughout Campania, and are a handy resource particularly in hilly and mountainous areas where rail service isn't available. We recommend using the bus, for example, in the Amalfi Coast, where the frequent service offers a good alternative to driving. **SITA** (see below) schedules numerous

The Unico Travel Pass

Traffic might be bad in the region, but paying for public transportation just became a lot easier. With one ticket for the specific area you are visiting, you can board all forms of transportation, from trains and the Metro to buses and ferries. The "**Unico**" is offered in several denominations (usually 45 min., 90 min., 24 hr., and 3 days) and is for sale at stations as well as tobacconists and newsstands near transportation hubs.

Naples's Unico is the most complicated because you can choose between several *zone* (zones), with a U1 covering the historic district, Pozzuoli, and the island of Procida; U2 extending to Ercolano, Baia, and Ischia; U3 to Pompei; U4 Capua and Vicco Equense; and U5 encompassing Naples to Sorrento, the Amalfi Coast, and Salerno. U1 costs 1.60€ for the 90-minute version and 4.80€ for the 24-hour pass (3.20€ on Sun); U5 costs 4€ for the 90-minute version and 12€ for the 24-hour pass (6.30€ on Sun).

The **Unico Campania 3T** covers the whole region, including the Alibus shuttle from Naples's Capodichino Air-

port to the city center, plus public trains, buses, and funiculars on the mainland, Ischia, and Procida. To give you an idea, it includes the Circumvesuviana train to Pompei or Sorrento, the funicular and bus in Naples, as well as the SITA buses on the Amalfi Coast, the FS train to Benevento, and the local bus there. The pass is valid for 3 days, from the first stamp to midnight of the third day, and costs 20€.

The **Unico Costiera** covers all the towns along the Sorrento and Amalfi coasts, from Meta di Sorrento to Salerno. The best deals are the 24-hour pass and the 3-day pass (respectively 7.20€ and 18€), which also include one ride on the City Sightseeing tour buses between Amalfi and Ravello or Amalfi and Maiori. The Unico is also available in 45-minute and 90-minute increments, respectively 2.40€ and 3.60€. Any of the passes will allow you unlimited rides on SITA buses and the Circumvesuviana trains connecting Meta with Sorrento and stations in between.

For more information, visit www.unicocampania.it.

runs between Salerno, Naples, and Sorrento, with extra lines between Amalfi, Positano, and Sorrento, as well as secondary lines from Amalfi and Sorrento to minor destinations along the Costiera. These provide not only convenient but also cheap transport, as you can buy a single pass valid on public transportation for the whole Costiera (see "The Unico Travel Pass," above).

The leading bus operators in the region are **SITA** (℗089-053939; www. sitabus.it), serving the Sorrento peninsula and the Amalfi Coast; **SEPSA** (081-5525125; www.sepsa.it), serving Pozzuoli, Baia, Cuma, and Miseno, as well as Procida and Ischia; **CTP** (℗800-482644; www.ctpn.it), serving Naples and linking it with neighboring towns; **AIR** (℗0825-204250; www.air-spa.it), connecting the Avellino area with Naples; and **CSTP** (℗800-016659 or 089-487001; www.cstp.it), with buses in Salerno, Paestum, and the Cilento.

For more information, see "Getting There" in the destination chapters throughout this book.

By Ferry

Ferries are a great way to get around this region's coastal destinations and, obviously, crucial to reaching its islands. They are a fantastic option particularly during the summer, when the narrow coastal roads become overly congested. Several companies connect the region's top destinations. Hydrofoil service is the fastest, but is suspended in winter and operates only between selected harbors—chiefly Naples, Capri, Ischia, Sorrento, Positano, Amalfi, and Salerno. Other options include large ferries with transport of vehicles, and smaller motorboats, which can reach smaller harbors. All companies charge similar rates for similar service. The only relevant difference is the time schedule.

Naples's two harbors—Stazione Marittima, downtown, and Terminal Aliscafi, in Mergellina—along with **Salerno**'s are the region's main hubs, followed by **Amalfi, Sorrento,** and **Pozzuoli.** All offer multiple daily connections to the islands (**Capri, Ischia,** and **Procida**) and the smaller towns of the Amalfi Coast, including **Positano.**

Companies offering local service are **Alilauro** (℗081-4972222; www.alilauro.it), with hydrofoils to Ischia and Positano; **Caremar** (℗199-116655; www.caremar.it), with ferries and hydrofoils to Ischia, Capri, and Procida; **LMP** (℗081-7041913; www.consorziolmp.it), with hydrofoils to Sorrento; **Medmar** (℗081-3334411; www.medmargroup.it), with ferries to Ischia; **Metrò del Mare** (℗199-600700; www.metrodelmare.net), with commuter-style service between Bacoli and Salerno, with intermediary stops in Pozzuoli, Naples, Vico Equense, Sorrento, Positano, and Amalfi, and summer service to the islands; **NLG** (℗081-5520763; www.navlib.it), with hydrofoils to Capri; **SNAV** (℗081-4285555; www.snav.it), with hydrofoils to Ischia, Capri, and Procida; and **Volaviamare** (℗081-4972211; www.volaviamare.it), with fast boats between Naples, Sorrento, Amalfi, Positano, Salerno, Ischia, and Capri.

Companies offering minicruises and excursions are also great resources for moving around the region: We recommend **Blue Cruises** (℗081-4972222; www.blucruises.it) and **Capitan Morgan** (℗081-4972238; www.capitanmorgan.it).

By Limousine/Car Service & Taxi

A good alternative to renting a car is using a **taxi** or a **car service**—make sure they use cars and minivans with air-conditioning (very important in summer), as well as trained, English-speaking drivers. Official taxis are at the airport and the train station. They are white and have a taxi sign on the roof, a city logo, and a card clearly detailing the official rates inside. The Municipality of Naples has established flat rates for major tourist destinations in the region. These rates are cheaper than if the meter was used, and you have to ask for them before departure. A round-trip to Herculaneum, with a 2-hour wait (during which you visit the ruins), is 70€; Pompeii and a 2-hour wait is 90€; a round-trip tour of the Amalfi Coast (Positano, Ravello, Amalfi, and Sorrento), for an entire day, is 220€; a round-trip to Mount Vesuvius, with a 2-hour wait, is 90€; round-trip to Baia (Scavi Archeologici) and Solfatara, with a 3-hour wait, is 85€; a tour of Naples is 70€.

The best companies are **Radio Taxi Napoli** (📞081-444444, 081-5555555, or 081-5564444; www.consorziotaxinapoli.it), **Cooperativa Partenopea** (📞081-5515151 or 081-5560202; www.radiotaxilapartenope.it), **Radio Taxi La 570** (📞081-5707070; www.la570.it), and **Consortaxi** (📞081-202020). Taxis operate from the airport or various taxi stands at major destinations in and around the city. You can just go to one of these stands and grab a taxi, but book in advance for longer excursions.

Car services tend to be based on the Sorrento peninsula and Amalfi Coast. They are often cheaper than taxis, and drivers also act as guides. Car services we recommend are **Sorrento Limo** (www.sorrentolimo.com), **Cuomo Limousine** (www.carsorrento.it), and **Paolo Bellantonio** (www.bellantoniolimoservice.com), all based in Sorrento; **Benvenuto Limos & Tours** (www.benvenutolimos.com), based in Praiano; and **Avellino Car Service** (www.amedeoavellino.com), based in Vico Equense. We also like two private drivers: **Francesco Marrapese** (www.francescomarrapese.com) and **Angelo** (www.angelodriver.com).

Recommended providers in Naples are **ANA Limousine Service,** Piazza Garibaldi 73 (📞081-282000), and **Italy Limousine** (📞081-8080457 or 338-9681866; www.italylimousine.it). Check individual chapters for more options.

By Car

Distances within Campania on the autostrada (limited-access, toll-express highways) are short: Naples to Salerno is about 30 minutes, and Salerno to Avellino only 20 minutes. Local routes tend to be much more congested, especially in the summer. Driving from Sorrento to Amalfi in the off season will take you less than an hour, but, with summer traffic, a 2-hour ride is more like it. Renting a motorcycle is a good way to get around as well.

Before renting a car or a motorcycle, though, know that Neapolitans have a well-earned reputation for aggressive and daring driving. You need to be a skilled and alert driver if you want to navigate Italian roads, which feature super-high speeds on the autostrade, super-narrow streets in the cities and towns, and one of the highest fatality rates in Europe. The situation gets worse in Naples and surrounding areas, where roads have guardrails only when the road is on a cliff and breaking speed limits is a local sport. Motor scooters are extremely prevalent and their drivers often do not obey traffic laws, so be mindful of them as they zoom and swerve between cars.

Also, driving is not cheap: In addition to high tolls on the autostrada, gasoline prices and parking fees are steep.

If you are planning to visit only major destinations in the region, you'll be better off using public transportation or hiring a car with a driver. However, driving will allow you to see much more of the countryside at your own pace, and it makes sense if you have the time to go exploring off the beaten path.

The two primary Italian car-rental companies are **Maggiore** (www.maggiore.it) and **Travelcar** (www.travelcar.it), but all major international car-rental companies operate here. In addition, you'll also find a number of local companies that rent cars (with or without driver) as well as scooters or motorcycles. We list them for each destination in the "Getting Around" section in each chapter.

RULES OF THE ROAD In Italy, driving is on the right-hand side of the road. Unless otherwise marked, **speed limits** are 50kmph (31 mph) in urban areas, 90kmph to 110kmph (56–68 mph) in suburban areas, and 110kmph to 130kmph (68–81 mph) on limited-access highways. Speed limits for trailers, or towed vehicles, are lower: 70 kmph (43 mph) outside urban areas and 80 kmph (50 mph) on autostrada (100 kmph/62 mph for auto-caravans, or mobile homes). Automatic speed controls are installed on most roads, and you may be ticketed for driving faster than the posted limit.

It is mandatory to have your **headlights** on at all times outside urban areas and to use **seat belts** (front and rear) and age-appropriate **car seats** for children. High-beam headlights are sometimes used to signal to fellow drivers: If you are in the left passing lane and a driver flashes you from behind, you need to move out of the way. If an oncoming car signals you, it means that some danger is ahead, so slow down. If cars ahead of you put on their hazard lights, slow down: The traffic is completely stopped ahead. Horns cannot be used in urban areas except in an emergency.

Only motorcycles and scooters with engines above 150 cubic centimeters can use the autostrade. **Helmet use** is mandatory on all roads.

Drinking and driving is severely punished and there are fines for talking on your mobile phone while driving and for illegal parking.

FINDING YOUR WAY Road signs are posted with one sign about 1.6km (1 mile) before an exit, and then another right at the exit. Destination signs are blue for local roads and green for the toll highway. Destinations of cultural interest (such as monuments and archaeological areas) are posted on brown signs. Often, only the major town on a local road is marked, while smaller towns and villages on the way will not be posted. See "Maps" under "Fast Facts," at the end of this chapter, for information on buying some reliable maps.

GASOLINE Gas stations are distributed along local roads at sensible intervals however, large stretches of countryside are without stations. Pumps are generally open Monday to Saturday from 7 or 8am to 1pm and 3 or 4pm to 7 or 8pm (some have a self-service pump accessible after hours). On toll highways gas stations are positioned every 32 or 48km (20 or 30 miles) and are open 24 hours daily. Most cars take *benzina senza piombo* (unleaded fuel) or diesel (*diesel* or *gasolio*). Among diesel cars, only the newest models take the ecofuel labeled *blu diesel* (blue diesel) Be prepared for sticker shock every time you fill up—even in a medium-size car—as fuel is priced throughout the country at around 1.6€ per liter (diesel is a little cheaper, selling around 1.5€ per liter); a gallon equals about 3.8 liters. Make sure the pump registers zero before an attendant starts filling your tank: A common scam involves filling your tank before resetting the meter (so that you also pay the charges run up by the previous motorist), and it is still performed by some dishonest attendants.

BREAKDOWNS & ASSISTANCE Roadside aid in Italy is excellent. For 24-hour **emergency assistance,** contact the national department of motor vehicles, **Automobile Club d'Italia** (② 803-116 toll-free within Italy; www. aci.it).

PARKING Parking is always limited, particularly during the high season and near major attractions. Parking lots and areas are indicated with a square sign bearing a large white **P** on a blue background.

Parking spots are marked on the pavement with painted lines of various colors depending on the type of parking: Yellow is for reserved parking (deliveries, drivers with disabilities, taxis, and so on); white is free parking (very limited—you won't find many of those on the Costiera); blue is paid parking. Rates vary as they are established by each municipality: Check the sign at the beginning and end of the stretch of parking spots and the sign on the automatic parking machines (usually located at a more or less reasonable distance from your parking spot; look for a gray/white box on a post or on a wall). Machines usually accept only coins, so come prepared (prices usually range 1€–3€ per hour). The timer shows the current time, and as you insert money, it will show you what time you are paid through. When you're done, press the green button, collect the receipt, and place it on your dashboard in a visible spot. Do not even think about skipping this, particularly in tourist areas—authorities are very vigilant.

The alternative is a private parking lot. These are usually located near the historic district (or attractions) in most towns. They are often underground, and attendants will park your car for you. Expect to pay 20€ to 50€ per day, depending on the location.

TIPS ON ACCOMMODATIONS

Most hotels on the Amalfi Coast are structured to take advantage of the mild climate by maximizing outdoor enjoyment, with guest rooms opening onto patios, balconies, terraces, and gardens. Carpeting is the exception, while a tiled floor—often with local, hand-decorated tiles—is the rule. Some of the local cultural idiosyncrasies (such as lack of amenities and small bathrooms) can be less charming; they become more and more apparent as you go down in the level and price of accommodations.

In general, hotels tend to have fewer amenities, particularly in urban areas, than their same-level counterparts in the U.S. and Britain. Swimming pools are a rare luxury in town, though outdoor summer-only pools are more common in seaside and some mountain resort destinations. Fitness clubs, gyms, and especially spas (which can vary from a sauna and a couple of massage rooms to state-of-the-art facilities) are becoming more widespread in general, even in some moderately priced hotels. In-room dining is offered only in the most expensive hotels and rarely on a 24-hour basis. Moderate hotels may not have a restaurant at all, just a breakfast service which they may even cater from the nearby bar. Only the cheapest accommodations don't have TVs, but more expensive hotels may offer satellite TV (necessary for programs in English). Air-conditioning is becoming more widespread, but the climate is so nearly perfect—warm and breezy—that you will rarely need it.

Also, because buildings are old—sometimes centuries old—elevators tend to be small and rarely fully accessible to the mobility challenged: Steps tend to be ubiquitous. Rooms also tend to be smaller than, say, in the U.S. or Britain, but the biggest difference is in the bathrooms, which are often tiny, rarely featuring a bathtub (shower only), with fixtures that look old-fashioned even if they are in perfect working order.

So, if you are planning to spend a lot of time in your room—having drinks with friends and romantic dinners—and in the hotel, lounging in the public areas, the spa, the swimming pool, and the hotel's restaurants and bars, you should consider only the most luxurious hotels. Only there will you find the level of amenities you are seeking. If instead you want to spend most of your time exploring your destination, using your hotel as a sleeping base, then you should definitely consider moderate hotels, because, while their extra amenities are basic, you'll get spacious—sometimes even luxurious—rooms with modern bathrooms.

If all you really want is a good bed, then you can consider inexpensive hotels, where the room's decor will be simpler but accommodations will always include all the basic amenities (comfortable and scrupulously clean bed and bathroom, telephone, and local TV).

Hotels with restaurants often offer a meal plan to go with the room. You can usually choose among B&B service (breakfast only), half-board (breakfast and either lunch or dinner), and full board (breakfast, lunch, and dinner). Some smaller establishments make a meal plan mandatory during the month of August, when many of these same hotels may enforce a minimum-stay requirement of 3 or 7 days.

Most hotels in the region are private—often family-run—properties, yet you will also find a few hotels run by some major chains: In addition to **Best Western** (www.bestwestern.com), **Hilton** (www.hilton.com), **Holiday Inn** (www.holiday-inn.com), and **Starwood Hotels**—including Sheraton, Four Points, Le Meridien, Westin, St. Regis, and Luxury Collection—(www.starwood-hotels.com), you'll find the Italian chain **NH/Jolly Hotels** (www.nh-hotels.it), catering to business as well as family travelers. You'll also find the French chain **Sofitel** (www.sofitel.com), which offers somewhat simpler accommodations and caters mostly to families, and the European **Accor Hotels** (www.accorhotels.com) with its moderately priced Novotel and its more elegant Mercure hotels.

Because most hotels in the area are private—including some of the most famous luxury hotels such as the San Pietro in Positano—you'll do much better researching online with an Italy-based search engine such as **Venere Net** (www.venere.com). Other sites to check out are **Italyhotels** (www.italyhotelink.com), **ITWG.com** (www.italyhotels.com), **Welcome to Italy** (www.wel.it), **Europa Hotels** (www.europa-hotels.com), and **Italy Hotels** (www.hotels-in-italy.com).

Also, always check the hotel's website directly, as these often list the same rates as some supposed discount agencies, but without the extra fee, or even unique online deals.

Remember: It's always a good idea to **get a confirmation number,** record the name of the representative with whom you spoke, and **make a printout** of any online booking transaction.

Agriturismo (Farm Stays)

Another option—a favorite with Italians—is an *agriturismo*: staying on a working farm or former farm somewhere in the countryside (see "Responsible Travel," p. 47). Your lodging usually includes breakfast and at least one other meal (your choice of dinner or lunch), prepared with ingredients produced on the farm or by nearby local farms. Among the rapidly multiplying online agencies, the best are **Agriturist.it** (www.agriturist.it) and **Agriturismo.it** (www.agriturismo.it). Accommodations range from the downright posh and palatial (for example, on famous wine-producing estates) to simple but clean country-inn style. They often offer swimming pools and outdoor activities. Beware that some *agriturismi* offer only basic accommodations: Rates are usually proportional to what is provided.

Renting a Villa

The appeal of renting a villa is obvious, and some of them are truly luxurious. The number of properties for rent in Campania is on the increase although you will find the best choice in the popular tourist areas such as Sorrento and the Amalfi Coast.

Many good agencies specialize in stays on the Amalfi Coast. We like the **Right Vacation Rental** (www.therightvacationrental.com), offering apartment, farmhouse, and cottage stays of 1 week or more; it is a subsidiary of **Idyll Untours** (© 888-868-6871; www.untours.com) and donates part of its profits to provide low-interest loans to underprivileged entrepreneurs around the world. Others we like for their portfolio and commitment are **Doorways LTD** (© 800/261-4460 or 610/520-0806; www.villavacations.com), **Rent Villas** (© 800/726-6702 or 805/641-1650; www.rentvillas.com), **Europe at Cost** (© 800/322-3876; www.europeatcost.com), the **Parker Company, Ltd.** (© 800/280-2811 or 781/596-8282; www.theparkercompany.com), **Villas and Apartments Abroad, Ltd.** (© 212/213-6435; www.ideal-villas.com), and **Villas International** (© 800/221-2260 or 415/499-9490; www.villasintl.com), all U.S. based.

In the U.K., contact **Cottages to Castles** (© 1622-775-217; www.cottagestocastles.com). There's also an Australia-based **Cottages & Castles** (© 03-9889-3350; www.cottagesandcastles.com.au).

Bed & Breakfasts

Bed and breakfasts (B&Bs) are becoming increasingly common in the region and provide a good alternative to hotels. The best Web portals are **www.bedandbreakfast.it**, with the largest portfolio, followed by **www.bbitalia.it**. We also recommend the Naples-based agency **Rent a Bed-Napoli e Campania,** Vico San Carlo alle Mortelle 14, 80132 Napoli (© 081-417721; mobile 392-3174864; www.rentabed.it). In each destination chapter throughout this book we recommend local options.

[FastFACTS] CAMPANIA & THE AMALFI COAST

Area Codes 081 for the province of Naples (including Sorrento, Pozzuoli, Ischia, and Capri); **082** for the provinces of Caserta, Benevento, and Avellino; **089** for the province of Salerno (including the Amalfi Coast); and **097** for the Cilento. To call to and from this region, see "Telephones," later.

Automobile Organizations Two organizations operate in Italy and offer memberships: **Automobile Club d'Italia (ACI;** © **803-116** toll-free within Italy; www.aci. it) provides road assistance throughout the country. Their offices also help with car insurance, registration, and other regulation-related issues. **Touring Club Italiano** (www.touringclub.com) publishes maps and guides and maintains useful databases of services for car travelers.

Business Hours General business hours are Monday through Friday 8:30am to 1pm and 2:30 to 5:30pm. Banks are generally open Monday through Friday 8:30am to 1:30pm and 2:30 to 4pm. Some banks and businesses are also open on Saturday mornings. Shops are usually open Monday through Saturday from 8 or 9am to 1pm and 4:30 to 7:30 or 8pm, with one extra half-day closing per week at the shop's discretion. *Note:* A growing number of shops in tourist areas stay open during the lunch break and on Sunday.

Car Rental See "Getting Around," earlier in this chapter.

Cellphones See "Mobile Phones," below.

Customs Rules governing what tourists can bring in duty-free are detailed at www. agenziadogane.it (click on "Traveler's customs card"). If you are carrying currency in excess of a value of 10,000€, you will need to fill out a Customs declaration.

While there is no special limit on how much you can take out of Italy, certain items are restricted, in particular art objects: You'll need special permits for the export of objects more than 50 years old. *Note:* Italy adheres to CITES (Convention on International Trade in Endangered Species of Wild Fauna and Flora), which means the purchase and export of protected species is prohibited. So is the purchase and export of copies of fashion items (think Vuitton or Chanel and the like) and other copyrighted material. The fines are steep; do not break the law!

For information on what you're allowed to take home, contact one of the following agencies:

U.S. Citizens: U.S. Customs & Border Protection, 1300 Pennsylvania Ave., NW, Washington, DC 20229 (✆ **877/227-8667;** www.cbp.gov).

Canadian Citizens: Canada Border Services Agency, Ottawa, ON, K1A 0L8, Canada (✆ **800/461-9999** in Canada, or 204/983-3500; www.cbsa-asfc.gc.ca).

U.K. Citizens: HM Customs & Excise Crownhill Court, Tailyour Road, Plymouth, PL6 5BZ (✆ **0845-010-9000,** from outside the U.K.; www.hmce.gov.uk).

Australian Citizens: Australian Customs Service, Customs House, 5 Constitution Ave., Canberra City, ACT 2601 (✆ **1300-363-263;** www.customs.gov.au).

New Zealand Citizens: New Zealand Customs, The Customhouse, 17–21 Whitmore St., Box 2218, Wellington 6140 or 0800-428-786; www.customs.govt.nz).

Disabled Travelers Laws in Campania and in Italy have compelled train stations, airports, hotels, and most restaurants to follow a stricter set of regulations for **wheelchair accessibility** to restrooms, ticket counters, and the like. Museums and other attractions have conformed to the regulations, which mimic many of those presently in effect in the United States. Always call ahead to check on accessibility in hotels, restaurants, and sights you want to visit.

Local resources include **Accessible Italy** (www.accessibleitaly.com), a nonprofit association based in San Marino (the ministate in central Italy), which offers specialized tours and assistance for organizing your own vacation, including rental of equipment and lists of accessible accommodations and other services.

Drinking Laws There's no minimum drinking age in Italy. Alcohol is sold day and night throughout the year, and the only limitations are the operating hours of bars and shops (see "Business Hours," above). The law is extremely tough though on drunken behavior, and disturbance of the *quiete pubblica* (public peace) will be punished with stiff fines and jail time. Littering (including potential littering such as drinking from your beer bottle while sitting on an ancient wall) is also severely penalized. Drinking and driving can result in jail time as well as loss of your driving permit.

Driving Rules See "Getting Around," earlier in this chapter.

Electricity The electricity in Italy is an alternating current (AC), varying from 42 to 50 cycles. The voltage is 220. It's recommended that any visitor carrying electrical appliances obtain a transformer (laptop computers usually have one built in their cord; check on the back for allowed voltages). Italian plugs have prongs that are round, not flat; therefore, an adapter plug is also needed. You can purchase both transformer and adapter in any local hardware store.

Embassies & Consulates Embassies are located in Rome, but you'll find most consulates in Naples: The **U.S. Consulate** is at Piazza della Repubblica 2 (✆ **081-5838111;** fax 081-7611869; http://naples.usconsulate.gov); the **Canadian Consulate** is at Via Carducci 29 (✆ **081-401338;** fax 081-406161; www.canada.it); the **U.K. Consulate** is at Via dei Mille 40 (✆ 081-4238911; fax 081-422434; www.britain.it).

Emergencies ✆ **113** or 112 for the police; ✆ **118** for an ambulance; and ✆ **115** for a fire. For road emergencies dial ✆ **803-116.**

Etiquette & Social Customs Volumes have been written on Italian etiquette, as there are rules on everything. Yet, Italians are pretty forgiving of foreigners; and, if you are observant and mold your behavior to theirs, you'll stay away from most blunders.

Appropriate Attire: Italians tend to dress more formally than Americans, particularly in urban settings. Shorts and tank tops are reserved for the beach. Women tend to dress more conservatively, particularly if they are alone. The Catholic Church has strict dress codes for both women and men: No showing of shoulders or legs above the knee in a *chiesa* or on sacred ground.

Courtesy: Get up for anybody who's hampered by packages or children, for the elderly, and for women; and open doors for them especially if you are a man. Offer your seat to the elderly and to pregnant women, or anybody carrying a small child. Don't cut in line: Italians might not queue in an orderly manner like the English, but they respect the order of arrival at an establishment, from the ice-cream counter to the post office. Always acknowledge people when entering and exiting a place, such as a shop, with "Buongiorno" and "Grazie."

Gestures & Contact: Italians do gesticulate a lot, but pointing at someone with your index finger is considered rude. Shake hands with your right hand, and hugging and kissing on the cheek among friends is common.

Eating & Drinking: It is customary for two parties to "argue" over the dinner bill, and you are expected to offer to pay, even if you won't be allowed. If you have been taken out for a meal, then it is good manners to return the invitation. If that is impossible, a small gift (flowers, for example) sent to their home (if it was a private party) or a thank-you note (if it was a business meal) will do the trick. If you are invited to someone's home, never go empty-handed: Flowers, pastries, chocolates, a bottle of wine, or a small gift for the children is the right way to go.

Photography: It is forbidden to take photographs of military, police, or transport (including subway and airport) facilities.

Family Travel The whole country, especially Southern Italy, is completely welcoming to children. Italians love kids and take theirs with them wherever they go. However, don't expect special amenities: There will be no playroom, no babysitting program, and no kiddy area with small tables and crayons. Children in Italy partake in their parents' lives. Kids sleep in the same room or suite—though most hoteliers will add a cot to your room for your child, and most have special rooms or suites designed for families with children, but you need to book in advance. Throughout the region, private attractions offer discounts to all children, while in state-run museums, only E.U. citizens ages 17 and under are admitted free.

Campania is particularly suited for a vacation with children: The ancient sites and castles stimulate children's imagination while the many beaches and resorts are a perfect place for them to vent their energy (though you might want to avoid the rocky Sorrento peninsula and Capri, where sandy beaches are rare, and favor Ischia and the Cilento, which have the best sandy stretches in the region).

The key to a successful family vacation in Italy lies in some smart planning: Involve your children in both the research and the decision-making process; schedule your visits alternating "adult" attractions with those in which your kids will be interested; and plan to make lots of gelato (ice cream) and pizza breaks.

Throughout this book we indicate accommodations, restaurants, and attractions that are particularly kid friendly, with a kids icon. In chapter 3 we also mapped out an itinerary especially for families.

Gasoline (Petrol) Gasoline sells on average for 1.60€ per liter and diesel for about 1.50€ per liter, with small variations depending on the location. Taxes are already included in the printed price. One U.S. gallon equals 3.8 liters or .85 imperial gallons.

Health There are no particular health concerns in Campania. It is always, however, a good idea to protect yourself from mosquito bites, as an increasing number of diseases previously contained within the tropical areas of the world have started spreading. The World Health Organization recommends hepatitis A and B vaccines for travelers to any country in the world, including Europe and Italy, and to keep up-to-date with boosters for your childhood vaccinations.

During the past couple of years, Naples and its suburbs have been struggling with a garbage collection crisis due to the enmeshment of the local Camorra (a Mafia-like secret society) with the local contractors. As a result, refuse cyclically accumulates in many areas. As a form of protest, residents resorted to burning the piles of garbage, creating toxic fumes, which are particularly dangerous in summer. The authorities have largely tackled the problem, but, should it reoccur during your visit, avoid the fumes as they can aggravate respiratory problems.

Availability of Health Care: You'll find English-speaking doctors in most hospitals and pharmacies. Medical staff is generally well trained. The largest hospitals in the region are in Naples, but reputable hospitals, excellent private clinics, and smaller facilities exist in more remote places. We have listed the best hospital or local medical facility under "Fast Facts" for each destination in each chapter.

For travel abroad, you may have to pay all medical costs upfront and be reimbursed later. Medicare and Medicaid do not provide coverage for medical costs outside the U.S. Before leaving home, find out what medical services your health insurance covers. To protect yourself, consider buying medical travel insurance (see "Insurance," below).

U.K. nationals will need a **European Health Insurance Card (EHIC)** to receive free or reduced-cost health benefits during a visit to a European Economic Area (EEA) country (European Union countries plus Iceland, Liechtenstein, and Norway) or Switzerland. The European Health Insurance Card replaces the E111 form, which is no longer valid. For advice, ask at your local post office or see www.dh.gov.uk/travellers.

Over-the-counter medicines are widely available in Campania, and prescriptions are easily filled in any pharmacy. Names of products will be different, so make sure you know the active ingredient of your brand and that your doctor writes the prescription clearly. Most likely you will find a pharmacist who will be able to assist you in finding an English-speaking doctor. If you are bringing **prescription medications** with you, pack them in your carry-on luggage, and carry them in their original containers, with pharmacy labels—otherwise they won't make it through security.

Contact the **International Association for Medical Assistance to Travelers (IAMAT;** ✆ **716-754-4883,** or 416-652-0137 in Canada; www.iamat.org) for tips on travel and health concerns in the countries you're visiting, and for lists of local, English-speaking doctors. The United States's **Centers for Disease Control and Prevention (**✆ **800/232 4636;** www.cdc.gov) provides up-to-date information on health hazards by region or country and offers tips on food safety. **Travel Health Online** (www.tripprep.com), sponsored by a consortium of travel medicine practitioners, may also offer helpful advice on traveling abroad. You can find listings of reliable medical clinics overseas at the **International Society of Travel Medicine** (www.istm.org).

Dietary Red Flags You should always exercise caution when eating seafood, especially in summer when improperly refrigerated seafood spoils faster. Also, be cautious of street food. Water in Campania's cities and towns is potable. The quality varies in some areas of Naples, but hotels, restaurants, and bars all have their own water-purification systems. If you're still concerned, order bottled water.

Sun Exposure: Do not underestimate the sun when you visit archaeological areas such as Pompeii and Herculaneum in the summer, as heat stroke is not impossible. Always use sunscreen and a hat and carry an adequate water supply.

Insurance Buying insurance is a personal decision. We find that trip-cancellation policies are a good idea, particularly if you are investing a lot of money in your trip and you have made plans way in advance.

For information on traveler's insurance, trip-cancellation insurance, and medical insurance while traveling please visit www.frommers.com/planning.

Internet & Wi-Fi An increasing number of hotels and resorts in the region are becoming "hotspots" that offer free high-speed Wi-Fi access or charge a small fee for usage. If you are planning to carry your laptop, check www.jiwire.com and their Wi-Fi Finder, the world's largest directory of public wireless hotspots.

For dial-up access, most medium- and upper-range hotels in the region offer dataports in the room unless they offer Wi-Fi.

Note: Italy uses 220V electricity and round-pronged plugs: See "Electricity," above. Always bring a connection kit of the right power and phone adapters, a spare phone cord, and a spare Ethernet network cable—or find out whether your hotel supplies them to guests. Most phone plugs in hotels and private homes throughout Italy have been upgraded to the standard phone jack used on computers, but some of the old ones with three round prongs are still in use. You can easily buy an adaptor at any local hardware store if your hotel doesn't have one for you.

If you are not planning to bring your laptop, a number of hotels in the area offer Internet access for their clients, usually free of charge, or they'll know how to direct you to the closest paying Internet point in town: You'll find one everywhere but the most remote location. For a directory of cybercafes in the region check www.cyber captive.com and www.cybercafe.com.

Legal Aid If you are pulled over for a driving offense, you'll have the choice to settle the fine right there on the roadside (you will be given a copy of the fine and an official receipt) or pay it at the post office (you will be given a form to fill out). If you are taken to the police station, you can ask for a translator to be sure you understand the situation. If you are actually arrested, the consulate of your country is the place to turn for legal aid, although offices can't interfere in the Italian legal process. They can, however, inform you of your rights and provide you with a list of professional attorneys. If you're arrested for a drug offense, the consulate will notify a lawyer about your case.

LGBT Travelers Since 1861, Campania and Italy have had liberal legislation regarding homosexuality. Ischia and Capri have long been gay meccas, and you'll find a somewhat active gay life in Naples. Still, open displays of same-sex affection are sometimes frowned upon in the highly Catholic country (despite the fact that people in Campania are very physical, and men and women alike embrace when saying hello and goodbye).

ARCI Gay (www.arcigay.it) is the country's leading gay organization, with branches throughout Campania. Naples's section is Circolo Antinoo, Vico San Geronimo 17, Naples (✆ **081-5528815** daily 4:20–8pm). Another major organization is **Gay. it** (www.gay.it), which maintains a search engine (http://guida.gay.it) for gay-friendly bars, restaurants, and the like, and a specialized tour operator **Gayfriendlyitaly.com** (www.gayfriendlyitaly.com).

Gay publications include *Pride,* a free national monthly, available at most gay venues; and *Babilonia,* which is available at most large newsstands.

Mail On the whole, Italian mail works well. Check with www.poste.it for any specific question. Postcards (not in regular letter envelopes) are the slowest: Your family and friends back home might receive your postcards after your return. You are better off slipping your postcard in an envelope and sending it letter rate or higher. International and internal mail is now all sent at the *Posta Prioritaria* rate. Your letter will take 3 to 8 days depending on the destination. Postcards and letters weighing up to 20 grams cost .75€ for Europe; 1.60€ for Africa, Asia, and the Americas; and 2€ for Oceania. You can buy stamps at all post offices and at *tabacchi* (tobacconist) stores.

Maps Tourist offices are the best places to find user-friendly local maps, usually available for free. If you are driving, the best maps are available from Touring Club of Italy (www.touring.it); buy directly from their website, at bookstores abroad, or from most bookstores and newsstands in Italy. Michelin maps are good but generally less detailed. Hiking and trail maps are available from local bookstores.

Mobile Phones If you have a dual-band or triband GSM phone, it will work in Italy and all over Europe. The bandwidth used in Europe for GSM phones is 900–1800 hertz. Just call your wireless operator and ask for "international roaming" to be activated on your account. Unfortunately, charges can be high—anywhere from $1 to $5 per minute.

You can enjoy much cheaper rates by renting or buying an Italian SIM card. You might need to have your phone unlocked by your provider at home so that it will function with any SIM card and network. You can buy an Italian prepaid SIM card, called *scheda pre-pagata,* in mobile phone shops, which exist in most towns throughout Italy. Major networks that have excellent local coverage in the region are Telecom Italia (TIM), Vodafone, Wind, and H3G. The SIM is encoded with the phone number that will be yours for the time of your stay. The *scheda pre-pagata* costs 25€, 50€, 80€, 100€, or 150€.

The other option is to rent a phone with the bandwidth used in Europe and a local SIM card. A number of companies offer mobile phones for rent, and you may also be able to add a phone to your car rental.

North Americans can rent a mobile before leaving home from Context Travel (www.contexttravel.com). The company will ship the phone to you in the U.S. 10 days before your departure (you'll then ship it back to them in Philadelphia). You can also have a phone shipped to you in Italy. Incoming calls are free.

Other useful resources are InTouch USA (☎ **800/872-7626;** www.intouchglobal. com) or RoadPost (☎ **905/272-5665;** www.roadpost.com). InTouch will also, for free, advise you on whether your existing phone will work overseas; simply call ☎ **703/222-7161** between 9am and 4pm EST, or go to http://intouchglobal.com/travel.htm.

Money & Costs The currency conversions quoted below were correct at presstime. However, rates fluctuate, so before departing consult a currency exchange website such as **www.oanda.com/convert/classic** to check up-to-the-minute rates.

THE VALUE OF THE EURO VERSUS OTHER POPULAR CURRENCIES

EURO	US$	CAN$	UK£	AUS$	NZ$
1.00	1.40	1.56	0.70	1.72	2.11

You'll be glad to hear that Campania is still an affordable destination in Italy: The cost of living and traveling is lower then Tuscany or Milan, and quite a bit lower than some northern Europe destinations, such as London, Copenhagen, and Amsterdam.

WHAT THINGS COST IN NAPLES

Item	Euro €
A metro or city bus ride	1.10
Can of soda	2.00
Pay-phone call	0.20
Movie ticket	8.00
Caffè lungo (American-style espresso)	1.00
Ticket to the Museo Nazionale Capodimonte (including reservation)	9.00
Taxi from the airport	19.00
Moderate three-course dinner for one without alcohol	25.00
Moderate hotel room (double)	185.00
Liter of house wine in a restaurant	10.00
First-class letter to the United States (or any overseas country)	1.60

ATMs (automated teller machines), or cashpoints, are common and present in all but the most remote localities in the region. The **Cirrus** (☎ **800/424-7787;** www. mastercard.com) and **PLUS** (www.visa.com) networks are the most common. Go to your bank card's website to find ATM locations at your destination. Be sure you know your daily withdrawal limit before you depart. **Note:** Many banks impose a fee every time you use a card at another bank's ATM, and that fee can be higher for international transactions (up to $5 or more). In addition, the bank from which you withdraw cash may charge its own fee. For international withdrawal fees, ask your bank. Deutsche Bank and BNL (Banca Nazionale del Lavoro) are those that do not charge transaction fees at other Alliance member ATMs (these include Bank of America, Scotiabank, and Barclays).

Most ATMs accept **four-** and **five-digit codes** (six digits may not work), so if you have a six-digit code you'll want to go into your bank and get a new PIN for your trip.

Credit and debit cards in Italy have chips instead of a swiping magnetic band, but "swipe" cards are widely accepted and you should not have a problem with this. Do keep cash on hand, though, as many shops have a higher minimum than in the U.S. for credit card use (most often they will not accept credit or debit cards for amounts below 15€).

Newspapers & Magazines You'll find a large variety of magazines and newspapers in Italian at local newsstands and some bookstores. Those in cities and in tourist destinations also carry some international press. For instance you'll find the *International Herald Tribune* and sometimes *USA Today, Time,* and *Newsweek.*

Passports You'll need a **valid passport** to enter Italy and Campania (the passport should be valid for at least 3 months beyond the period of stay). The length of your stay is determined by your **visa** (see "Visas and Other Entry Requirements," below). American, Canadian, Australian, New Zealand citizens, and those from a few other countries (check the list at www.esteri.it/visti) can stay up to 90 days without a visa; citizens from a country belonging to the Schengen area can enter with a simple identification card; other E.U. citizens, including Irish and British citizens, will need a passport.

See www.frommers.com/tips for information on how to obtain a passport. See "Embassies & Consulates," above, for whom to contact if you lose yours while traveling.

Police Dial ℂ **113** or 112 for emergencies.

Safety Campania is generally safe, though one of the biggest risks in the area is road accidents (see "By Car" under "Getting Around," p. 348). Always be vigilant, particularly as a pedestrian, when crossing the street or walking in a narrow street with no sidewalk.

The crime rate in Campania is generally low, and most crimes occur in certain areas, such as near Naples's Stazione Centrale and in the poverty-stricken neighborhoods of the city's suburbs. Stay away from the narrow streets of Naples's historic district and from poor neighborhoods after dark.

The most common menace for the average tourist, especially in Naples, is the plague of pickpockets and car thieves. Pickpockets are active in all crowded places, particularly tourist areas. Note that they are sometimes dressed in elegant attire, and often work in pairs or groups, using various techniques, from distraction routines to razor blades to cut the bottom of your bag. Even savvy travelers must be vigilant.

The city center is also where most car thefts occur, although vehicles are always at risk, except in the most remote rural areas. Never leave valuables inside your car, never travel with your doors unlocked, and always park in a garage with an attendant. Be careful when traveling on highways at night, as robbery scams involve fake breakdowns being staged. Instead of stopping, call the police from your mobile; they'll send a car.

A good idea is to make photocopies of your important documents: tickets, passport, credit cards, and IDs. Make sure you keep them in a different pocket or bag than the originals. Also, if you rent a car, make sure there is no rental sticker on the car that could make you a target (tourists often have expensive gear, such as cameras and electronic devices). Also, make sure no luggage or other items are visible inside the car, such as in the back seat. Do not open your trunk and display the contents in the parking spot where you're planning to leave your car unguarded: Get what you need from your luggage ahead of time.

We have heard a few reports from other areas in Italy of robberies performed by individuals who befriend travelers at stations, airports, and bars, and then take advantage of their lower level of vigilance: Choose your friends carefully.

One further concern is ATM skimming. Attached to legitimate bank ATMs usually located in tourist areas, electronic devices can capture your credit card information and record your PIN through a pin-hole camera. Always make sure the ATM you are planning to use does not look as if it has been tampered with, and cover the keypad with one hand as you enter your PIN.

Italian law is generally fair; but if you commit a crime, the law will be enforced. Do not drink and drive, do not traffic or carry illegal drugs, do not engage in illicit sexual activities, do not litter, and do not exhibit loud and drunken behavior. If you are driving, respect the rules of the road (p. 352). Also note that if you make any kind of purchase, from a cafe, to a meal in a restaurant, to a handbag, the vendor is required by law to give you an official receipt and you are required to keep it with you for a few hundred yards after coming out of the shop.

Smoking Smoking is still very common in the region, but is forbidden in enclosed public spaces, except those with separate ventilated smoking areas.

Taxes Taxes in Italy are usually included in the prices quoted, but some luxury hotels will show it separately on their bills. **VAT,** Value-Added Tax (called IVA in Italy) is imposed on most goods and services; the rate depends on the item and goes from 4% for basic food items to 20% for accessories and clothing. VAT is used in Italy for social purposes and, as a foreigner, you can ask for a refund: Non-E.U. (European Union) citizens are entitled to a refund of the IVA for purchases over 154.94€ before tax at any one store, on those goods you will take out of the country. To claim your refund, request an invoice from the cashier at the store and take it to the Customs office *(dogana)* at the airport to have it stamped before you leave. ***Note:*** If you're going to another E.U. country before flying home, you can have it stamped at the airport Customs office of the last E.U. country you'll be in (for example, if you're flying home via Britain, have your Italian invoices stamped in London). Once you're back home, mail the stamped invoice (keep a photocopy for your records) back to the original vendor within 90 days of the purchase. The vendor will send you a refund of the tax that you paid at the time of your original purchase. Reputable stores view this as a matter of ordinary paperwork and are businesslike about it. Less-honorable stores might "lose" your file. It pays to deal with established vendors on large purchases. You can also request that the refund be credited to the card with which you made the purchase; this is usually a faster procedure.

Many shops are now part of the "Tax Free for Tourists" network (look for the sticker in the window). Stores participating in this network issue a check along with your invoice at the time of purchase. After you have the invoice stamped at Customs, you can redeem the check for cash directly at the Tax Free booth in the airport (in Rome, it's past Customs; in Milan's airports, the booth is inside the duty-free shop) or mail it back in the envelope provided within 60 days. Check Global Refunds (www.globalrefund.com) for more information.

Telephones Local pay phones in Italy require prepaid telephone cards, called a *carta* or *scheda telefonica,* which you can buy at a tobacconist (*tabacchi,* marked by a sign with a white т on a black background), bar, or newsstand. The local Telecom card is available for 3€ and 5€: the duration depends on the place you are calling (within Italy or abroad), but they only last sufficient time for relatively brief calls and are valid for 1 month from the first time you use them. The card has a perforated corner that you need to tear off before inserting it into the phone slot.

To make international calls you need to purchase an international prepaid card, which varies depending on which country you will be calling the most. The cards are sold at tobacconists and some bars and newsstands. They usually allow from 200 to 700 minutes call time for 5€. You need to scratch the back to reveal the secret code and dial it after the access code indicated on the card; then dial the number you want to call.

More convenient but not necessarily cheaper is to have: (1) your own calling card linked to your home phone, or (2) a prepaid calling card that you pay monthly by credit card; both are good options. Some calling cards offer a toll-free access number in Italy, while others do not; the first kind is obviously more convenient. When calling from a public phone booth, you sometimes need to put in money or a *carta telefonica* just to obtain the dial tone, even if you are using a prepaid card; you may be charged only for a local call or not at all. Check with your calling-card provider before leaving on your trip.

You can also make collect calls directly by calling the operator (see below) or through a telephone provider in your country. For AT&T, dial ℂ **800-1724444;** for MCI, dial ℂ **800-905825;** and for Sprint, dial ℂ **800-172405** or 800-172406.

Remember that calling from a hotel is convenient but usually very expensive.

To call Italy:

1. Dial the international access code: 011 from the U.S.; 00 from the U.K., Ireland, and New Zealand; or 0011 from Australia.

2. Dial the country code for Italy: 39.

3. Dial the local area code and then the number. Telephone numbers in Italy can have any number of digits depending on the location and the type of telephone line, which can be very confusing to foreigners. The amount of numbers can range from five (for special switchboards of hospitals and other public services, such as the railroad info line of Trenitalia, ℂ **892021** for example) to a maximum of 10 (for some land lines and all cellular lines). Telephone numbers always include the area code, which can have two or three digits. Area codes begin with 0, for land lines, or 3, for cellular lines; and you always need to dial the 0.

To make international calls: To make international calls from Italy, first dial 00 and then the country code (U.S. or Canada 1, U.K. 44, Ireland 353, Australia 61, New Zealand 64). Next, dial the area code and number. For example, if you wanted to call the British Embassy in Washington, D.C., you would dial 00-1-202-588-7800.

For directory assistance: Dial ℂ **1240.**

For operator assistance: Dial ℂ **170;** the service is available only from 7am to midnight.

Toll-free numbers: Numbers beginning with 800 or 888 within Italy are toll-free, but calling a 1-800 number in the States from Italy is not toll-free: It costs the same as an overseas call.

Time Italy and Campania are 6 hours ahead of Eastern Standard Time in the United States and 1 hour ahead of Greenwich Mean Time in the U.K. (GMT+1). Daylight saving time in Italy is from the last Sunday in March to the last Sunday in October.

Tipping Tipping is not required in Italy as service charges are usually included in your bills. It is customary, though to leave a small tip if you are satisfied with the service: Give your hotel maid .50€ to 2€ per day, the doorman (for calling a cab) .50€, and the bellhop or porter 1€ to 5€ for carrying your bags to your room. A concierge might get up to 10% of his or her bill. In cafes you usually leave a small tip, such as .10€ if you had a coffee. In restaurants, your menu or your bill should say if the service charge is included; if you're not sure whether it is, ask, "È incluso il servizio?" (ay een-*cloo*-soh eel sair-*vee*-tsoh). If it is not included, add 10% to 15% to your bill. An additional tip isn't required, but it's customary to leave the equivalent of an extra couple of euros, if you've been pleased with the service. Checkroom attendants expect .50€ to 1€, and washroom attendants should get at least .50€. Taxi drivers can be tipped 10% of the fare.

Toilets Airports, train stations, museums, and major archaeological areas and attractions all have restrooms, often with attendants who expect to be tipped. Bars, nightclubs, restaurants, cafes, gas stations, and hotels should have facilities as well, but they are open only to customers. Public toilets are found near many of the major sights. Usually they're designated WC (water closet) and bear international symbols or the signs DONNE (women) and UOMINI (men). The most confusing designation is SIGNORI (gentlemen) and SIGNORE (ladies), so watch that final i and e! Many public toilets charge a small fee or employ an attendant who expects a tip. It's a good idea to carry some tissues in your pocket or purse—they often come in handy.

Visas & Other Entry Requirements European Union citizens, including U.K. and Ireland, do not need a visa.

Citizens from the United States, Canada, Australia, New Zealand, and from a few other countries, don't need a visa to enter Italy or Campania if they don't expect to stay more than 90 days and don't expect to work or study there. *Note:* The 90 days refer to your **total** stay in the Schengen area, so if you are coming to Campania as part of a longer trip in Europe, make sure you do not exceed the time limit, or you'll need to obtain a visa before entering.

Citizens from all other countries need a visa for stays of any length. *Note:* At the border you may be asked to produce the documents you presented to obtain your visa. Remember to carry them with you and have them handy at the border check.

Visit the website of the Italian Foreign Affairs Ministry at www.esteri.it/visti to find out if you need a visa.

Other Requirements: Foreigners entering Italy from a country outside the Schengen area and planning to stay more than 8 days also need to file a *permesso di soggiorno* (permit of stay). If you have already filed a permit of stay in another country in the Schengen area for this trip, you'll need to file a *dichiarazione di soggiorno* (declaration of stay) within 3 days of your entry in Italy. If you are flying from a country outside the Schengen area, the stamp you obtain on your passport at the airport is the equivalent of a permit of stay, but if you are entering Italy from a country within the Schengen area, you will need to file with the local police (you can also present the form at the local post office). *Note:* If you are staying in a hotel, the declaration of stay is automatically done for you by the hotel. But if you are staying in a private house, you'll need to handle the procedure yourself. Note also that failure to file is punished with expulsion from Italy. For the permit and declaration, you'll need a photocopy of your passport, two photographs, proof of medical insurance, proof of adequate means of financial support, and a photocopy of your return ticket. It is a simple routine check, and you should be able to breeze through this formality; just remember to bring all your documentation, including the documents you presented to obtain your **visa,** if you needed one.

To enter Italy and Campania you need to prove that you have **adequate means of subsistence.** That includes a place to stay, enough money to live during your stay and to return to your country, and **medical insurance.** At the border, you may be asked to show your return ticket as well as a hotel voucher or equivalent, and cash, traveler's checks, and credit or debit cards (or a bank account in Italy), with resources proportionate to the length of your stay.

Visitor Information The **Italian National Tourist Board** (www.italiantourism.com) is a good source of information before you go.

We also recommend writing directly (in English or Italian) to the local tourist boards for a variety of brochures as well as maps. The **Campania tourist board** covers the whole region; its address is Centro Direzionale Isola C/5, Napoli 80143 (✆ **081-7966111;** fax 081-7958576; www.regione.campania.it).

Campania is administratively divided into five provinces, each with its own **provincial tourist board** (Ente Provinciale per Il Turismo, or EPT):

EPT Napoli (covering Naples, Phlegrean Fields, Herculaneum, Pompei, Ischia, Capri, and the Sorrento peninsula): Piazza dei Martiri 58, 80121 Napoli (✆ **081-4107211;** fax 081-401961; www.eptnapoli.info).

EPT Salerno (covering Salerno, the Amalfi Coast, and the Cilento): Via Velia 15, Cap 84125 Salerno (✆ **089-230411;** fax 089-251844; www.eptsalerno.it).

EPT Caserta (covering Caserta, Caserta Vecchia, and Capua): Palazzo Reale, 81100 Caserta (✆ **0823-322233;** fax 0823-326300; www.casertaturismo.it).

EPT Avellino: Via Due Principati 5, 83100 Avellino (✆ **0825-74695;** fax 0825-74757; www.provincia.avellino.it and www.e-irpinia.it).

EPT Benevento: Via Sala 31, 82100 Benevento (✆ **0824-319911;** fax 0824-312309; www.eptbenevento.it).

In addition to the above, local tourist boards operate in all places of tourist interest; we have listed them in each individual chapter.

Water In restaurants, most locals drink mineral water with their meals; however, tap water is safe everywhere, as are public drinking fountains. Some areas of Naples have had long-term problems with the water supply, and this is why all public establishments in the city—hotels, bars, cafes, restaurants, and so on—have their own filtering devices. If you are staying in a private home, though, make sure you ask about the water supply. Unsafe sources and fountains will be marked ACQUA NON POTABILE.

Wi-Fi See "Internet & Wi-Fi," earlier in this section.

Women Travelers Naples used to be on the black list for women travelers, but conditions have improved enormously after years of refurbishment in the city's historical district. Southern Italians are also much more accustomed to seeing blond visitors.

However, women chronically attract men's attention and often have to fend off their proffered "friendship." Most often, ignoring remarks, avoiding eye contact, and proceeding on your way as if you hadn't noticed anything is the best approach.

Always dress appropriately. Especially in summer, remember that Italian women are attired more conservatively in urban surroundings than their counterparts in the United States: Reserve your strappy tanks and short shorts for the beach, ladies.

Should you ever perceive a real threat, immediately request assistance from a policeman, a storekeeper, or even a passerby (elderly women are usually perceived as particularly forbidding by young Italian males). In general, avoid seedy neighborhoods where you don't see many women strolling around, and use your common sense. Also women should not walk around alone in sketchy neighborhoods after dark.

INDEX

PHOTO CREDITS